Designing Real-World Multi-Domain Networks

Dhrumil Prajapati CCIE No. 28071, CCDE No. 20210002

Jeremy Bowman CCIE No. 51241, CCDE No. 20180016

Navin Suvarna CCIE No. 24583

Cisco Press

Hoboken, New Jersey

Designing Real-World Multi-Domain Networks

Dhrumil Prajapati, Jeremy Bowman, Navin Suvarna

Published by:
Cisco Press

2 2024

Library of Congress Control Number: 2024903903

ISBN-13: 978-0-13-803721-5

ISBN-10: 0-13-803721-3

Warning and Disclaimer

This book is designed to provide information about how multiple domains inter-work with each other. The methods and architectural designs explained here are deployed in real networks and function effectively. Every effort has been made to make this book as complete and as accurate as possible, but no warranty or fitness is implied. Just like with any large network deployments, the authors of this book highly recommend testing the integrations and its functionality in a lab environment and running all your organization-specific test cases before production deployment.

The information is provided on an "as is" basis. The authors, Cisco Press, and Cisco Systems, Inc. shall have neither liability nor responsibility to any person or entity with respect to any loss or damages arising from the information contained in this book or from the use of the discs or programs that may accompany it.

The opinions expressed in this book belong to the authors and are not necessarily those of Cisco Systems, Inc.

Trademark Acknowledgments

All terms mentioned in this book that are known to be trademarks or service marks have been appropriately capitalized. Cisco Press or Cisco Systems, Inc. cannot attest to the accuracy of this information. Use of a term in this book should not be regarded as affecting the validity of any trademark or service mark.

Special Sales

For information about buying this title in bulk quantities, or for special sales opportunities (which may include electronic versions; custom cover designs; and content particular to your business, training goals, marketing focus, or branding interests), please contact our corporate sales department at corpsales@pearsoned.com or (800) 382-3419.

For government sales inquiries, please contact governmentsales@pearsoned.com.

For questions about sales outside the U.S., please contact intlcs@pearson.com.

Feedback Information

At Cisco Press, our goal is to create in-depth technical books of the highest quality and value. Each book is crafted with care and precision, undergoing rigorous development that involves the unique expertise of members from the professional technical community.

Readers' feedback is a natural continuation of this process. If you have any comments regarding how we could improve the quality of this book, or otherwise alter it to better suit your needs, you can contact us through email at feedback@ciscopress.com. Please make sure to include the book title and ISBN in your message.

We greatly appreciate your assistance.

Please contact us with concerns about any potential bias at https://www.pearson.com/report-bias.html.

GM K12, Early Career and Professional Learning: Soo Kang

Alliances Manager, Cisco Press: Caroline Antonio

Director, ITP Product Management: Brett Bartow

Managing Editor: Sandra Schroeder

Development Editor: Ellie C. Bru

Senior Project Editor: Mandie Frank

Copy Editor: Chuck Hutchinson

Technical Editors: Arul Jagadeesan, Kyle Barnes

Editorial Assistant: Cindy Teeters

Designer: Chuti Prasertsith

Composition: codeMantra

Indexer: Ken Johnson

Proofreader: Jennifer Hinchliffe

Americas Headquarters
Cisco Systems, Inc.
San Jose, CA

Asia Pacific Headquarters
Cisco Systems (USA) Pte. Ltd.
Singapore

Europe Headquarters
Cisco Systems International BV Amsterdam,
The Netherlands

Cisco has more than 200 offices worldwide. Addresses, phone numbers, and fax numbers are listed on the Cisco Website at **www.cisco.com/go/offices.**

About the Authors

Dhrumil Prajapati: Dhrumil is a principal architect within Cisco CX's GES Architecture team. His focus lies on multi-domain networks, and he has been offering a complete lifecycle of professional services and architecture advisory for the past 13 years. His expertise extends to serving enterprise, government, and service provider entities across the globe. His services are designed to assist clients in planning, designing, deploying, managing, and interoperating all networking technology domains within their private or public infrastructure and application environments.

In his networking career, Dhrumil has designed networks for more than 150 organizations, which inspired him to write a book on the subject. He is a coauthor of *Cisco SD-Access for Industry Verticals* (https://cs.co/sda-verticals-book), and holds patents and has given multiple presentations in Cisco Live on SD-Access and multi-domain.

Dhrumil holds dual CCIEs in Enterprise Infrastructure and Service Provider, as well as a CCDE, in addition to other leading technical certificates. He also assists the Cisco Certifications team by reviewing and providing feedback for Cisco certificate exams. In addition, he leads several initiatives within Cisco CX aimed at driving delivery standardization and enhancing efficiency through automation innovation.

Currently residing in Apex, North Carolina, Dhrumil has a passion for motor racing, woodworking, and innovative electronics that enhance human life. His wife, Devanshi, and son, Ram, bring pure joy to his life, adding a touch of fun to every day.

Jeremy Bowman: Jeremy is a senior solutions architect within Cisco CX's GES Architecture team. Within the GES team, he has more than 10 years of experience focusing on designing and implementing large-scale multi-domain IBN environments that meet the client-specific requirements. Additionally, he has presented several sessions at Cisco Live. Jeremy is a CCDE and double CCIE in Enterprise Infrastructure and Security. He also has professional-level certification in three other Cisco certification tracks. Inside Cisco, Jeremy is a mentor to other architects and engineers, sits on several CX design review panels, and interacts with engineering to help further product development. When not working, he enjoys spending time with his family at home, camping, or on the lake.

Navin Suvarna: Navin possesses more than 18 years of extensive experience as a seasoned network delivery architect. With a decade-long tenure at Cisco, he has adeptly architected, designed, tested, operationalized, managed, and optimized expansive networks across service providers, global enterprises, and public sector segments. Holding the distinguished CCIE (No. 24583) in enterprise networking, Navin boasts an impressive collection of professional-level certifications.

Since the inception of software-defined networking, Navin has actively contributed to Cisco's incubation team, playing a pivotal role in incubating multiple intent-based solutions. His expertise has been instrumental in facilitating the adoption, assimilation, and rapid deployment of intricate multi-domain solutions. In the past four years, Navin has held the role of lead delivery architect for the United States Public Sector team. While specializing in multi-domain solutions, his proficiency in aligning network infrastructure with the evolving needs of the public sector has garnered affiliations with thought leaders in both the public sector and Cisco engineering. This collaboration has resulted in the development of novel features, functions, and validated practices tailored to multi-domain architectures, addressing the specific requirements of public sector clients.

While Navin's specialization remains rooted in multi-domain intent-based networks, his recent focus centers on educating clients about the value proposition of automation and guiding them on their automation journey. An active speaker, Navin has shared his insights and experiences of architecting multi-domain solutions on global platforms, including Cisco Live. He also champions hands-on demonstrations and automation show-cases, offering real-world insight into intent-based networking through automation use cases.

Beyond his professional pursuits, Navin finds joy in his 14-year marriage to his wife, Rupali. Their family includes their 12-year-old daughter, Trisha, and 6-year-old son, Vivaan. They currently reside in Research Triangle Park, North Carolina.

About the Technical Reviewers

Arul Jagadeesan (CCIE No. 9942) is a network architect in Cisco's Customer Experience Organization. As a network architect, Arul collaborates with customer IT organizations to provide a suite of professional consultative architectural and engineering solutions to achieve a high-performance network for the next generation of technology and business applications across a global infrastructure. Arul has presented at industry events such as Cisco Live on Software-Defined Networking, plus Security and Enterprise Architecture. He is PMP, CISSP, AWS, and Azure certified. Arul holds a bachelor of science degree in electronics and communication engineering and a master of science in telecommunications.

Kyle Barnes (CCIE No. 46535, CCNP DC, CCDP) is a customer delivery architect with Cisco and has more than 13 years of experience in the IT industry. He has worked in both the private and public sector alike, supporting different capacities ranging from network engineer to consultant to architect. It is with his real-world experience and aptitude for simplifying the complex that Kyle has developed a skillset of solving difficult networking scenarios. Kyle's philosophy of understanding the business requirements first has been his North Star when approaching any complex scenario. Most importantly, Kyle's humility (as he writes this in the third person) has made him an incredible relationship builder with both peers and customers alike.

Dedications

Dhrumil Prajapati:

Writing a book is a monumental task that requires a tremendous amount of personal and emotional support to reach fruition. The completion of this book would not have been possible without the unwavering support and boundless love of my beautiful wife, Devanshi. She has been my beacon, my guiding light, and the rockstar of my life. Her patience, understanding, and belief in my abilities have been the cornerstone of this journey.

My son, Ram, has shown me the true meaning of curiosity, inspiring me to explore new ideas rather than simply accepting them. He has been my source of motivation and a powerhouse of energy, propelling me to consistently strive for better.

I am deeply grateful for their sacrifices as I worked into the late hours of the night and over the weekends to bring this book to life. It's now time for us to celebrate this achievement together. This book stands as my first major accomplishment, and it was made possible because of them.

Jeremy Bowman:

Pauly, you left your family behind and came to a foreign country. You did not know what the future would hold, but you came willingly anyway. None of this would have been possible had you not been there every step of the way. There were many late-night and all-night maintenance windows, client visits, and unscheduled calls. There were lost holidays and other sacrifices so the work could get done. All of those events helped lead to the culmination of this work. You will never know how much you mean to me nor how much I appreciate all that you have done. It will always be demasiado.

Matthew, Megan, and Michael, you are my superheroes. Each of you inspire me to push harder to be a better version of me and to make you proud. I am so proud to be your dad.

Navin Suvarna:

To my esteemed parents, whose resolute support and endless encouragement have laid the foundation of my journey in the realm of technology. Your guidance and belief in my abilities have propelled me forward.

To my cherished wife, Rupali, your unwavering support, understanding, and encouragement have been my steadfast companions throughout this technical expedition. Your love has illuminated every intricate path I've traversed.

To my invaluable children, Trisha and Vivaan, your boundless energy and curiosity have inspired me to push the boundaries of knowledge. Your presence has imbued every technical endeavor with purpose and meaning.

This book is dedicated to you, my pillars of strength and inspiration, for your unrelenting support and for being the driving force behind me and for that I am forever indebted to you.

Acknowledgments

Dhrumil: I extend my heartfelt thanks to my colleagues, team, mentors, friends, and leaders. Their inspiration and collaboration have been invaluable in the creation of this book. This book is a testament to our shared journey, and I hope it will inspire others as much as they all have inspired me.

Jason Gooley, thank you for guiding me to take the first step for this book.

Jeremy: To my team, colleagues, leaders, and friends, you have all helped and contributed to this work. Thank you for your support and encouragement.

Olmedo and Abraham, you taught me more than you will ever know.

Navin: I extend my sincere gratitude to Arvind Chari and John Weston for their invaluable assistance with my ACI queries, and to Kevin Manweiler for helping me with my Meraki questions. Their expertise and insights greatly contributed to the quality of these chapters.

Additionally, I want to express my appreciation to my colleagues and friends at Cisco who patiently responded to my numerous inquiries throughout the completion of my chapters.

Reader Services

Register your copy at www.ciscopress.com/title/ISBN for convenient access to downloads, updates, and corrections as they become available. To start the registration process, go to www.ciscopress.com/register and log in or create an account*. Enter the product ISBN 9780138037215 and click Submit.

*Be sure to check the box that you would like to hear from us to receive exclusive discounts on future editions of this product.

Contents at a Glance

Contents

Icons Used in This Book

Border Node - Switch

Control Plane Node - Switch

Border Node - Router

Control Plane Node - Router

Edge Node

Extended Node

Transit Control
Plane Node (Switch)

Transit Control
Plane Node - Router

Fabric WLC

Fabric WLC HA SSO

Border Node Switch Stack

Border Node and Control
Plane Node Switch Stack

Edge Node Switch Stack

Colocated Border Node and Control
Plane Node with Layer 2 Handoff

Cisco DNA Center

Cisco Identity
Services Engine

Cisco vManage

Cisco vBond

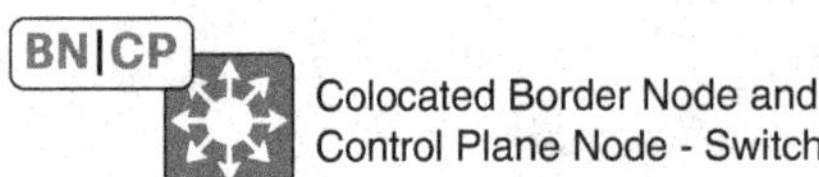
BN|CP
Colocated Border Node and
Control Plane Node - Switch

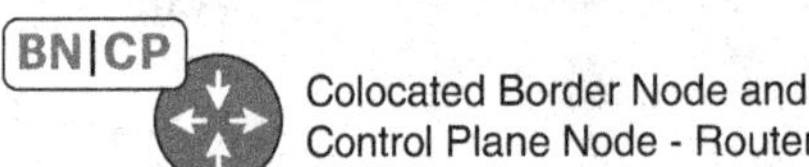
BN|CP
Colocated Border Node and
Control Plane Node - Router

EX
Policy Extended Node

BN|CP|EN
Fabric in a Box

AP
Fabric Access point

BN|CP|EN
Fabric in a Box
Switch Stack

Fabric Site

DHCP, DNS, and AD

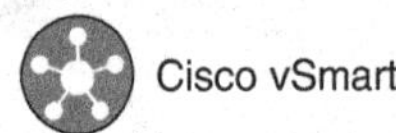
Cisco vSmart

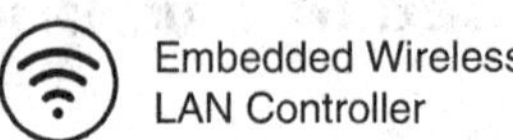
Embedded Wireless
LAN Controller

Multisite Remote Border Node

Multisite Rendezvous Point

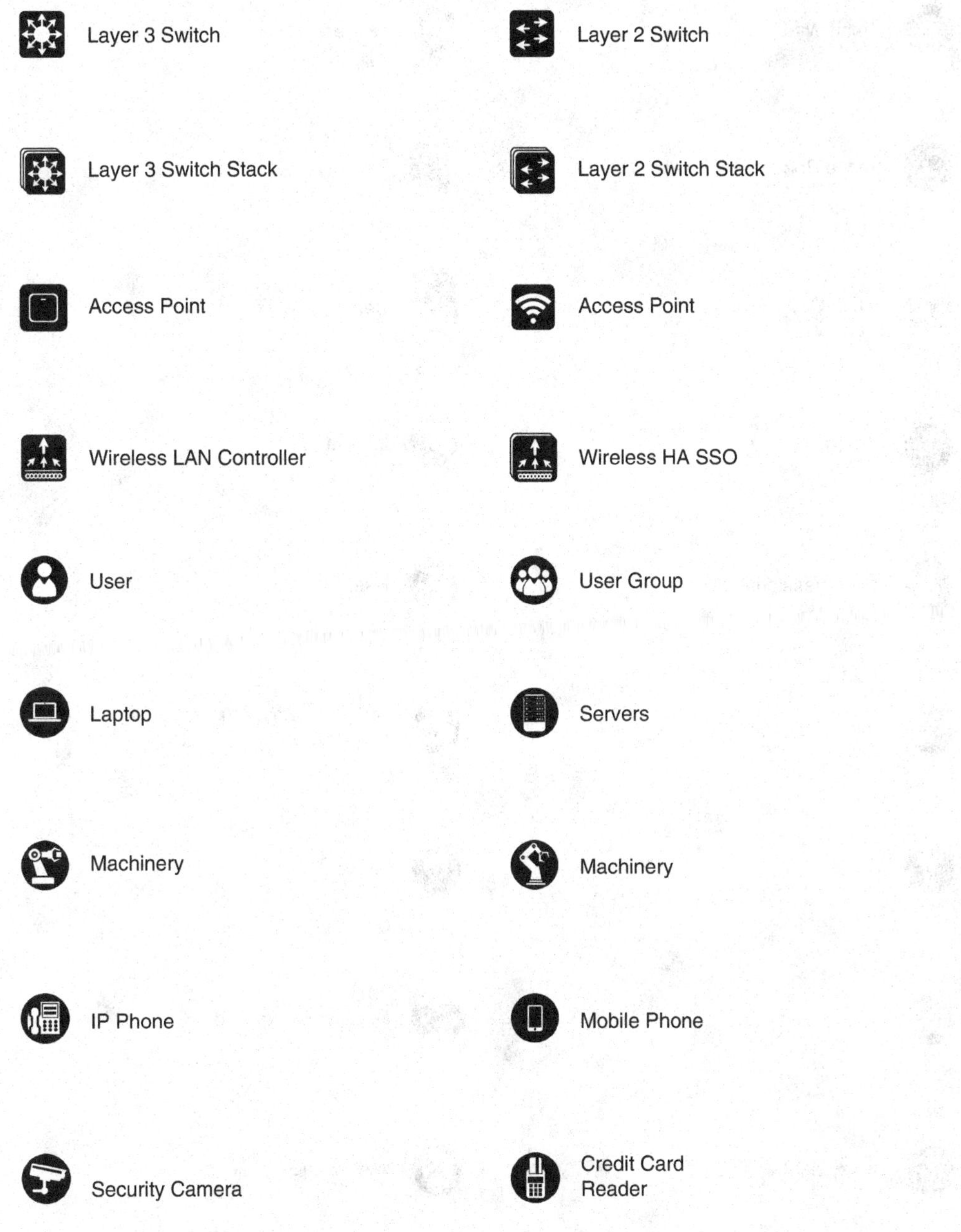
Layer 3 Switch
Layer 2 Switch
Layer 3 Switch Stack
Layer 2 Switch Stack
Access Point
Access Point
Wireless LAN Controller
Wireless HA SSO
User
User Group
Laptop
Servers
Machinery
Machinery
IP Phone
Mobile Phone
Security Camera
Credit Card
Reader

Smart Waste

Router

Badge Reader

Firewall

Smart City

Services Block Switch

IT Professional

Internet

OT Professional

User

Medical Devices

Building Management Systems

Traffic Light

Lights

Medical Devices

Security Group Tag

Street Light

WAN Edge

Command Syntax Conventions

The conventions used to present command syntax in this book are the same conventions used in the IOS Command Reference. The Command Reference describes these conventions as follows:

- **Boldface** indicates commands and keywords that are entered literally as shown. In actual configuration examples and output (not general command syntax), boldface indicates commands that are manually input by the user (such as a **show** command).
- *Italic* indicates arguments for which you supply actual values.
- Vertical bars (|) separate alternative, mutually exclusive elements.
- Square brackets ([ ]) indicate an optional element.
- Braces ({ }) indicate a required choice.
- Braces within brackets ([{ }]) indicate a required choice within an optional element.

Introduction

In most enterprise organizations, different teams of architects and engineers design, manage, and operate the various domains of the environment, the wide area network, the data center, the remote campus, or the cloud environment. With larger organizations, interaction between these groups is fundamental for a well-designed global environment. The advent of intent-based networking (IBN) has given rise to policy-driven environments. The architects create a policy designed for the single specific domain managed by a given controller. Each environment has its own controller. With each domain having its own network team, its own controller, and its own policy, a uniform end-to-end architecture becomes muddled and difficult to design, operate, and manage. This book focuses on design integration in a multi-domain environment to provide a single, consistent design across the large-scale environment.

Goals & Methods

Cisco is leading the way in defining emerging networking technologies. Over the past few years, three main technologies emerged in the software-defined world: Cisco's Software Defined Access (SD-Access), Software-Defined Wide Area Networking (SD-WAN), and Application Centric Infrastructure (ACI). These technologies have been evolving ever since and gaining huge market share in consumer networks as a replacement of traditional networks. With this new way of doing things, a lot of underlying concepts are changed, and with those changes over the past few years, we are seeing customers adopting these technologies one at a time.

Many books from Cisco Press describe these technologies as an individual entity (single-domain): SD-Access, SD-WAN, ACI, Multi-Protocol Label Switching (MPLS), and so on. These are good books to build a solid foundation when starting a journey to adopt these technologies. But when the time comes to integrate these technologies within an organization to combine and interconnect those different networks, there are no guidelines, lessons learned, or best practices available for reference. Here is where this book takes the center stage.

The authors of this book—Dhrumil, Jeremy, and Navin—have more than 35 years of combined experience in building customer networks. The objective of this book is to utilize that experience so that an engineer or architect will know how to integrate these technologies and translate the organization's business and technical intent into a fully functioning, secure, and efficient network.

The technologies described here are all new and emerging, and their adoption will only increase from here in today's world of digitization and the hybrid workspace. Although these technologies themselves will continue to evolve over time, the focus of this book is on how they interact with each other rather than a deep investigation specific to one of them. Thus, evolution or revision of any one of these technologies will not impact this book.

Part I in this book starts with a chapter on answering two big questions about multi-domain: what and why? This chapter highlights the real-world demands that are driving organizations to this inevitable networking change and how they tackle adoption of multi-domain design and technologies.

Each chapter in Part II covers a high-level overview and functionality of the technology described. They describe how this technology interacts with the other technologies and identify the key items an architect would need to keep in mind while interconnecting the other technologies.

Part III spans the last five chapters of the book, covering the real-world use cases of how these technologies will seamlessly work with each other. These chapters also give some reference architecture for individuals who would want to use these technologies in tandem with each other.

The objective of this book is to give lessons learned from actual real-world deployment of Cisco's customers that the authors have captured over several years in the industry.

Who Should Read This Book?

This book is designed for architects and engineers who want to integrate these emerging technologies within their organization. The last five use cases in this book can also act as reference materials to leaders and management who are willing to make key decisions on their organization's network transformation journey.

This book is designed to be picked up from any chapter and is not meant to be read sequentially.

How This Book Is Organized

This text is not designed to be an introduction to the various Cisco intent-based networking architectures nor a detailed discussion of all of the features and functionality available in any one specific architecture. Other publications adequately handle the presentation of that material. The authors are industry experts in designing and deploying the various IBN and cloud architectures and technologies together in various permutations. This text presents valuable insights and lessons learned from previous large-scale deployments to help with planning and design.

Although you may read the entire book from cover to cover, the text was designed to be flexible, with each chapter focusing on how one specific architecture integrates with the other architectures and technologies. This allows you to combine sections from a single chapter or multiple chapters based on your solution requirements. The final five chapters of the book focus on actual industry use cases.

Book Structure

The book is organized into three parts.

Part I: Introduction

Chapter 1, "Multi-Domain Networks," introduces the concepts of multi-domain networking. It describes how the networks have evolved to require support for multi-tenancy and reduced fault domains.

Part II: Multi-Domain Design

Chapter 2, "SD-Access and Campus Fabric," focuses on the design and deployment of Cisco's Software Defined Access solution while integrating it with other architectures, such as Application Centric Infrastructure.

Chapter 3, "SD-WAN and DMVPN," illustrates the design and deployment of the various architectures with either Cisco's Catalyst SD-WAN solution or with DMVPN.

Chapter 4, "Application Centric Infrastructure (ACI)—Integration and Multi-Domain Capabilities", provides an in-depth discussion of the Cisco Application Centric Infrastructure integrated with various WAN, cloud, and campus technologies.

Chapter 5, "Enterprise MPLS," focuses on the design and deployment of the enterprise MPLS environment while integrating with support for the multi-domain network.

Chapter 6, "Carrier Neutral Facilities," describes what a Carrier Neutral Facility is, why it is critical in today's networks, and how it integrates with other domains in the network.

Chapter 7, "Cloud," focuses on integrating multi-domain networks with the cloud.

Chapter 8, "Security," discusses some of the relevant security concerns and considerations when designing and deploying multi-domain environments.

Chapter 9, "Automation," provides a discussion on extending automation and CI/CD pipelines to automate required changes in multiple domains based on the evolution of the enterprise environment.

Part III: Real-World Use Cases

Chapter 10, "Manufacturing Use Case with SDA, SD-WAN, and CNF," illustrates a real-world deployment of SDA, SD-WAN, and CNFs integrated together.

Chapter 11, "Financial Use Case," discusses the design requirements, caveats, and end-to-end design and deployment of a multi-domain financial sector deployment incorporating SDA, SD-WAN, and security together.

Chapter 12, "Retail Use Case Using CNF, SD-WAN, and ACI," relies on an actual retail deployment to describe the design and deployment of SDA and SD-WAN with a cloud environment.

Chapter 13, "Public Sector Use Case," uses a real-world scenario to illustrate SDA and ACI integration with an enterprise MPLS environment.

Chapter 14, "Transportation Use Case," illustrates the end-to-end design and integration of SDA, SD-WAN, and ACI to address multi-tenancy in transportation.

Figure Credit

Figure 4.1a: renjithkrishna/Shutterstock

Chapter 1

Multi-Domain Networks

Overview

The evolution of the computer network has been one of the most impressive advancements in today's digital age. We have come a long way from sending "Hello World" over a wire between two computers to transmitting data at terabits per second over fiber optics. Computer networks have evolved from a single flat network with few devices to a complex mesh of interconnectivity with billions of devices connected today. In the current work environment, sharing information among devices is critical. Connectivity and communication are the foundation of the next era. How we do our daily tasks has changed dramatically over the last decade, and the last few years have accelerated that change exponentially. Being on "the grid" is almost inevitable in today's world.

This evolution from a single flat network to complex interconnectivity has fought through multiple nonstandard communication protocols such as AppleTalk, IP, IPX, SNA, DECnet, and a clear winner has risen. Internet Protocol (IP) became the protocol of choice and an industry standard. Once the standards were established, purpose-built networks began to develop—each focusing on a specific business function, an industry vertical, or both. As more and more devices were rapidly connected to the Internet mesh, these connections resulted in suboptimal designs, which led to poor performance, scalability issues, and inflexible and vulnerable networks. The evolution of compliance and industry standards came into place for highly critical networks such as financial, manufacturing, and healthcare. More and more purpose-built network domains began to develop within an organization, which raised one big question: How do we connect these multiple network domains with different needs to access resources within the organization and across the Internet?

Welcome to the era of multi-domain networks!

What Are Multi-Domain Networks?

Purpose-built network domains are crucial for an organization's success today. Each network is designed with a specific task or a business need, and they all have one most fundamental characteristic: client/server communication. These networks also have one most important need: accessing the data locally within the same premises or in a location that could be thousands of miles away. These individual network domains are like little islands of networks that share information constantly, but they need to communicate with each other somehow and over some media. After this communication is established, we have essentially built a multi-domain network!

Individual purpose-built network domains are called multi-domain networks when they are stitched together to share all required information necessary to achieve business objectives.

Although saying this may sound simple, a lot of work goes into building successful multi-domain networks. Many components need to be considered at a macro level, as well as a micro level, to design these types of networks. They need to function seamlessly and also be able to withstand any events or changes in the network infrastructure without losing connectivity or hindering business operations. Designing these networks could seem straightforward theoretically; however, for them to be successful in real-world applications, testing these network designs is vital in ensuring the networks achieve their business and technical requirements. Figure 1-1 shows individual domains that are connected directly with each other or indirectly via other domains. Regardless of size or the number of domains in an organization, all of them fall under one single management domain for better governance.

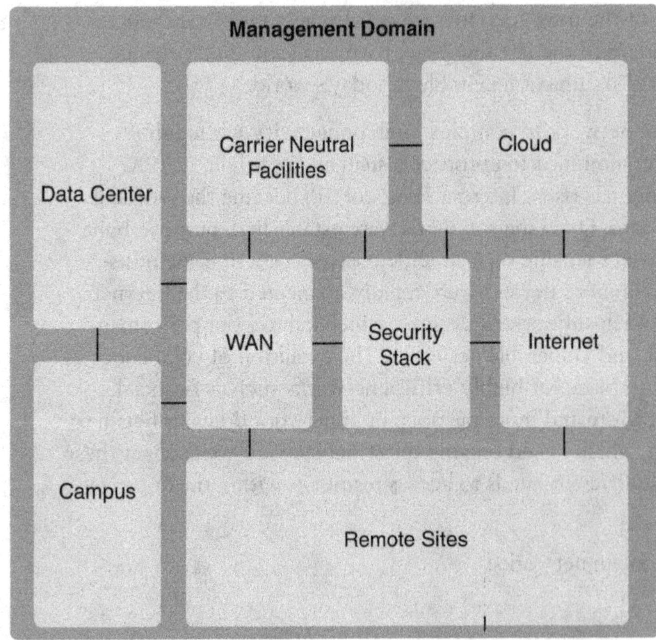

Figure 1-1 *Multi-Domain Networks*

Components of Multi-Domain Networks

Let's look at what is involved in building practical multi-domain networks. These components are essential to building a solid foundation for multi-domain networks and any networks out there.

Redundancy

Any network architect designing a network always needs to consider network redundancy. Redundancy means if the primary path—whether it is a device, link, or single component of a larger chassis-based system—for the network fails, it should switch over to a secondary path without impacting user experience. Every mission-critical computer network in the world is redundant in some shape or form. Thousands of network outages occur worldwide every day for various reasons, but when someone is browsing on the Internet, the connection seems seamless. When someone mentions the Internet being down, usually an application or a resource that the user is accessing is down or unreachable. That situation is very localized. However, in the grand scheme of things, the overall transport of the traffic, the interconnections between service providers, is designed to be highly redundant to avoid an impact to all users.

Redundancy comes in many forms, and all forms need to be thoroughly thought out. The more components added to the redundancy of a network, the more expensive it will be. There is a balance between availability (how many *9s* you want), criticality of that infrastructure, and the likelihood of failure of that infrastructure. More 9s added to 99.9 percent will result in a reduction of the network's downtime. However, it also will add to the capital and operational expenses of the network, making it expensive. Table 1-1 shows the expected downtime of the network in terms of availability.

Table 1-1 *Availability Percentages Compared to Downtime in the Network*

Availability %	Downtime per Year	Downtime per Quarter	Downtime per Month
99%	3.65 days	21.9 hours	7.31 hours
99.9%	8.77 hours	2.19 hours	43.83 minutes
99.99%	52.60 minutes	13.15 minutes	4.38 minutes
99.999%	5.26 minutes	1.32 minutes	26.30 seconds
99.9999%	31.56 seconds	7.89 seconds	2.63 seconds

Table 1-1 clearly describes how adding additional 9s to increase the redundancy and availability will reduce the impact on the network, but this comes at a cost because the entire end-to-end infrastructure needs to be highly redundant. Some systems might require an investment in this level of redundancy as it pertains to their business function. But not all of them would justify the expense. For example, Internet access for a large campus needs to be highly redundant because there might be hundreds of employees working, whereas if there is a small branch office of just five to ten people, having that high level of Internet access might not be required. In the event of an outage, the people in the small branch office might choose to work from home or a nearby coffee shop. As a rule of thumb, if the site, the purpose of the network, or the number of users or applications it serves is critical, that network would need the highest level of redundancy.

Now let's look at the types of redundancies that are available to achieve as many 9s as needed (see Figure 1-2).

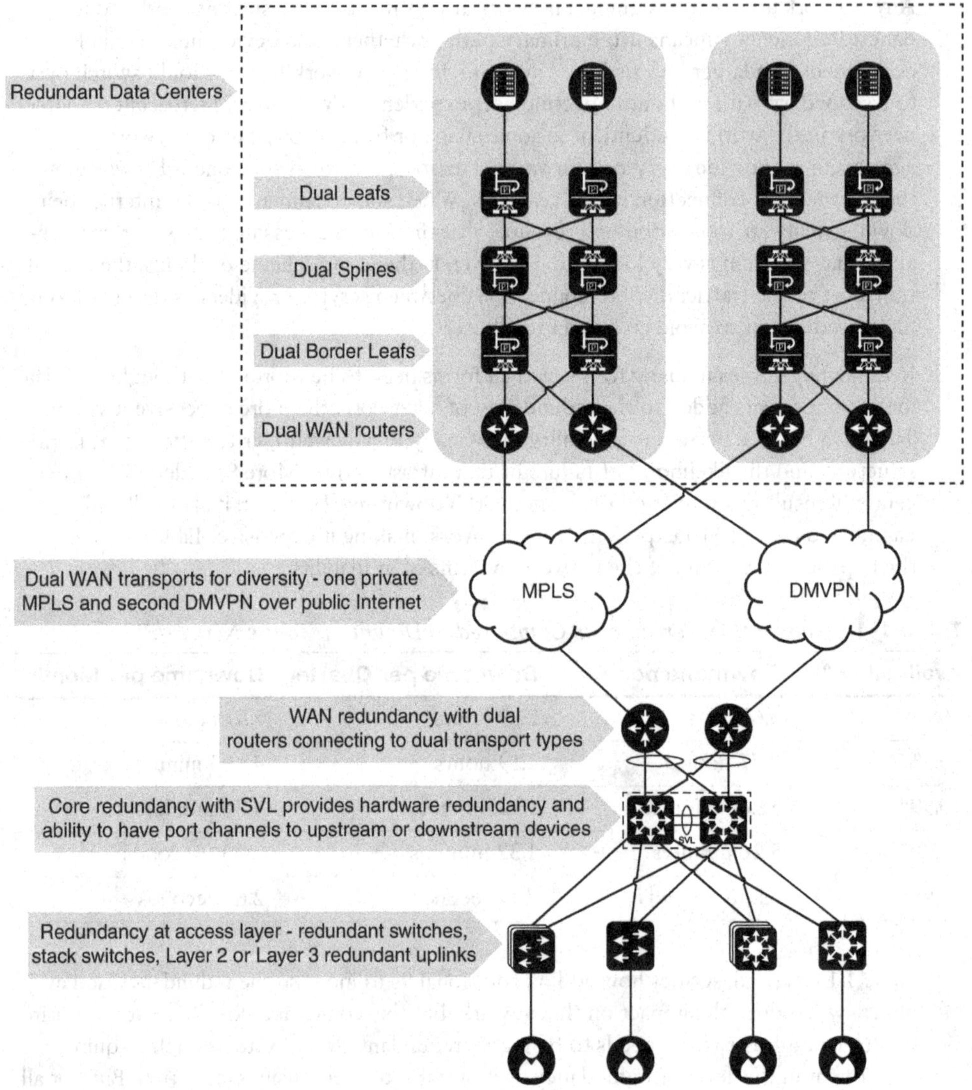

Figure 1-2 *Types of Redundancies*

Power

Power is crucial to any infrastructure involving electronics. In terms of network design, power redundancy comes in two main types: two different power feeds and backup power in the form of an uninterrupted power supply (UPS). Most critical infrastructure usually has both for the highest availability. As a best practice, it is always recommended to have dual power supplies for all critical network components. Because without power, there is no equipment function, the underlying problem with any power-outage scenario is the device bootup time and the ability to resume any applications running on that device. If a database server went offline due to power failure, there is a high chance of the database being corrupted and causing further complications.

Almost all of the gear—routers, switches, servers, storage—has redundant power supplies in an environment like data centers. These power supplies are connected to the power feeds from separate UPSs, and those UPSs get their power from different power feeds from the building, which is usually also routed via diverse areas of the building. The purpose of this is to ensure that at no point, a single fault domain is created and if one of the feeds, paths, or power supplies is down, an alternate source is there to take over the load and provide continuous service to users and other applications.

Power redundancy also implies that redundant power supplies are installed on the equipment. A redundant power supply not only helps during a failure scenario but also helps to share the load. Most modern pieces of equipment have hot-swappable power supplies that can be replaced while the equipment is running to reduce downtime further.

Device

Going one level up from power redundancy within a device, let's now discuss device-level redundancy. In this design, two devices function in the same role, backing each other up in the event of a device or hardware equipment failure. This redundancy is almost always deployed in critical environments across the network, computing, and storage infrastructure. *Network*, *compute*, and *storage* are mentioned separately here because they have their own individual requirements.

In a network infrastructure, all devices are usually in pairs. There is a rare chance that three or more devices are deployed to back up the same part of the network. Because the goal of the network is to pass traffic from one end to the other, having two devices is usually sufficient to provide backups of each other. If part of the network has a very high bandwidth requirement, high-performance routers or switches can be deployed to address that bandwidth. Having two devices gives the most flexibility with the least capital and operational expenditure. All modern routing protocols in use today are equipped to detect the failure and converge the network within a subsecond if needed.

Purpose-built First Hop Redundancy Protocols (FHRPs) are configured closer to the edge of the network to provide gateway redundancy for endpoints. These protocols are Hot Standby Router Protocol (HSRP), Virtual Router Redundancy Protocol (VRRP), or Gateway Load Balancing Protocol (GLBP). Because endpoints can have only a single default gateway for a network that they are connected to, having two devices for redundancy creates a problem on which device should respond to Address Resolution Protocol

(ARP) requests from endpoints. Hence, these FHRPs use the concept of a virtual gateway IP address to share between the two physical devices. These traditional network protocols are typically configured at the Layer 2 and Layer 3 boundary—such as distribution switches or collapsed core switches. In some networks, they could also be configured on the redundant WAN routers of a small site, where access layer switches are directly connected to the routers. HSRP and GLBP are Cisco proprietary protocols, whereas VRRP is an IETF standards-based protocol. Modern solutions such as Cisco Software Defined Access (SDA), Cisco Application Centric Infrastructure (ACI), VXLAN, and Fabric Path use anycast gateways to provide first hop redundancy. The concept of anycast gateways is that the same gateway IP address is configured on all edge switches for a specific VLAN, and an overlay fabric is used to route between different endpoints across different switches using a Layer 3 underlay network. This configuration eliminates the need for Spanning Tree Protocol (STP) and any downsides that come with it. An added benefit of the fabric-based architecture is that network convergence time is significantly reduced with the use of Layer 3 underlay routing protocols. For more details on the fabric-based solutions, see Chapter 2, "SD-Access and Campus Fabric," Chapter 3, "SD-WAN and DMVPN," and Chapter 4, "ACI and Data Center Fabric."

By default, each network device has its own management plane, control plane, and data plane. Having two devices side by side in a similar role can provide high availability, but in some instances having separate devices might not be ideal. These are situations in which Layer 2 and Layer 3 boundaries occur. In many cases, the FHRP protocols discussed earlier can take care of routing, but to utilize the Multi-Chassis EtherChannel (MEC) feature, combining two physically separate switches with separate management, control, and data planes to act as a single logical switch is more advantageous. In Catalyst switches, this feature is called a Virtual Switching System (VSS) or StackWise Virtual Link (SVL). In Catalyst access layer switches, there is also a feature called a switch stack; it essentially uses a special stack cable in the back of the switch to connect them in a ring topology and make a stack of up to eight individual switches into a single logical switch. In Cisco Nexus switches, the concept called Virtual Port-Channel (VPC) utilizes similar concepts of VSS and provides the MEC capability. However, logically and physically, both switches are separate from the management, control, and data plane. We discuss the benefits and usage of MCE in the next section.

Chassis-based systems provide another set of hardware and device redundancy, where a chassis has two supervisor engines and multiple line cards of various types of ports, density, and speed. This self-contained redundant system, at a higher level, provides a device-level redundancy. This device-level redundancy can be achieved by combining multiple chassis-based systems with the protocols like VSS and SVL to provide ultimate redundancy and resiliency. Service providers use their larger Carrier Routing Systems (CRSs) in a similar setup to serve a wide range of core and backbone traffic and services.

Compute and storage infrastructure redundancy are a little different. Because these devices—servers or storage arrays—are endpoints and serve multiple clients, they are typically deployed in more than two sets. They can be deployed in a physical form factor, virtually, or even in the cloud for more elasticity. The quantity of computing and storage required is determined by the number of applications being served, the number of transactions being performed, or the size of data being handled.

Because servers serve many clients and to avoid overutilization of one single server for a high number of requests, load balancers are used in front of the compute environment to distribute application requests across multiple servers. This is another critical aspect of redundancy. Load balancers monitor the number of requests coming in for a destination server and try to load-share traffic dynamically between multiple servers. By doing so, they also protect against the scenario of physical device failure that can take down a server. The load balancer automatically redirects traffic over to the other servers that are available. This redirection is transparent to the end users and ensures a seamless application experience. Some of the advanced compute platforms available today, such as Cisco Unified Compute System (UCS), have redundancy built up to the blade or motherboard level.

Links

Without links, there is no network. We looked at how device redundancy in a network can provide fault-tolerant infrastructure. It is implied that device redundancy cannot be achieved without connecting devices via redundant links. Locally within a single facility, most of the connections between devices are back to back. These links can come in various media—copper with RJ-45 on either end, fiber (single-mode or multi-mode), or TwinAX with SFP (Small Form-factor Pluggable) on either end being the most common ones.

Connecting devices with links is one part of the equation, but that does not give the required redundancy. The goal of the highest availability is to eliminate a single point of failure in the network. So, if each device is connected with a single back-to-back link, there is a possible risk of a split-brain scenario if that link itself fails. You can always add more links for resiliency, but then it comes down to the cost of the infrastructure. Recall the important question of availability and how many 9s we want to achieve. Adding one fiber cable is easy because it does not cost that much. However, it will consume the port on the router or a switch, which can be expensive. Typically, routers have higher per-port costs than switches because they are built for performance and advanced routing capabilities. Hence, routers have very few ports on them as compared to switches. Adding additional links to connect two switches is more cost-effective than connecting two routers with dual links. This is where architectural decisions come into play, keeping capital expenditure (CapEx) and operational expenditure (OpEx) in mind. Link redundancy on routers can be solved in other fashions as well, with the most common method being allowing backup traffic to traverse other sets of routers or switches until the primary link is restored. This way, cost and availability are both balanced. In this setup, however, we need to consider accurate capacity planning to not oversubscribe the link that can lead to more congestion or failures in the network.

The second form of link redundancy is toward the WAN side of the network. Because this design is crucial, it deserves a section of its own. Details on transport types and WAN redundancy are covered later in the chapter.

Sites and Data Centers

Previously, we looked at the micro-level components of redundancy, so now let's look at macro-level components. To ensure uninterrupted business productivity, enterprises need to think about the redundancy at a larger level—such as redundant data centers and, in some cases, sites with critical functions such as contact centers. Having a separate physical location with duplicate workloads provides two significant advantages: one is to have a backup plan if one of the locations is down due to an outage or unavailable during regular maintenance; second, in peak business workload times, both data centers can work in an active-active state to load-share resources.

Many organizations have their regional data centers or backup sites in separate cities and, if possible, even in separate time zones to cater to a more comprehensive range of users and their customers across various time zones.

In specific scenarios, organizations that do not have an extensive nationwide footprint or are limited to a city or state might also opt in for a disaster recovery (DR) site. These DR sites are not full-blown replicas of primary data centers; they host critical business functions only in a limited capacity—enough to keep the business going until the primary site is recovered and restored. The advantage of this setup is a significant reduction in CapEx and OpEx, and all significant attention to redundancy and resiliency is focused on the primary site with the highest SLAs.

Geo-Redundancy

Geo-redundancy is the most extensive form of redundancy that could span the nation and multiple countries or continents. Many global customers typically have three major regions—Americas (AMER), Europe, Middle East, and Africa (EMEA), and Asia Pacific, Japan, and China (APJC). Because each country could have its own regulations regarding data sharing and operations, there might be more subregions within these main classifications. Having redundancy for applications for all enterprise users and customers across the globe is critical. So, enterprises usually deploy multiple data centers—usually a pair of data centers in each region—and connect them using some form of backbone links. This network design typically follows a hierarchical structure where all local traffic within the region prefers local data centers and is usually in a full mesh, and if the traffic needs to flow from one region to another, it will traverse across the backbone links. In this type of setup, Internet exit points exist locally as well as across the regions.

WAN links are costly, so traffic engineering ensures all local traffic remains local, and only the most critical and necessary traffic traverses the backbone to other regions. Technologies such as Cisco SD-WAN are proving to be very effective in designing these global networks. Details are discussed further in Chapter 3.

As we move up layers of redundancy, it is imperative to understand how single points of failure can be eliminated and to what extent organizations would like to architect, design, and spend to avoid those single points of failure.

Resiliency

There is a common misconception about *redundancy* and *resiliency*. In many cases, these two terms are used interchangeably. However, they are both different and have different purposes. Redundancy, which we discussed in the earlier section, is having duplicate systems. It is a physical construct with equipment that you can see. When it comes to resiliency, it is more of a logical construct. Resiliency focuses on the ability to adapt and recover when the network is degraded, or in other words, when redundancy is unavailable or broken. A resilient network is measured by how effectively a business continues to function during a network failure or degradation. Having all the possible redundancy in the network is not great when critical business applications do not function during an outage.

The resiliency of the network needs to be addressed at all levels and all parts of the network. Network traffic engineering and application workload balancing are critical components in a highly resilient network; users will not experience any degradation of the service or application performance in the event of an outage.

WAN Redundancy and Multi-Connectivity

Wide area network (WAN) redundancy is not so different from LAN redundancy. It follows the same basic principles. However, the most significant difference is the options available in terms of media, services, and associated costs. Designing an optimal WAN is fundamental to the success of a business. WAN design warrants a careful balance between redundancy, transport types, media, SLAs from the service provider, and the type of traffic being transported across the WAN to an intended destination.

Two devices across the sites could be connected via more than one medium and multiple Layer 1 (physical) hops. Even though it might seem that two devices are directly connected, once the traffic leaves the WAN link on the router, it might have multiple different means of transport and media types along the service provider path to achieve connection to the remote site. The most common Layer 3 transports in use today are Multi-Protocol Label Switching (MPLS) or the Internet. It is highly advisable to use one link from each of the WAN routers out to different providers for the highest resiliency. Planning what services to use depends on the criticality of the site by determining the impact to business and revenue if the site is completely inaccessible. Just connecting two WAN circuits to two different routers does not achieve desired redundancy. Remember, the goal is to remove any single point of failure. In the real world, the following points are considered while designing highly redundant WAN infrastructure.

- Each WAN transport should be connected to a different WAN router.
- Diverse paths should be considered for WAN circuits leaving the building to prevent accidents, such as digging ground around the building.
- Different providers should be used for different WAN circuits in the event that one provider has an outage; this way, traffic still traverses via the redundant provider.

- A separate CWDM/DWDM should be used for each of the circuits to avoid any passive or active equipment failure.
- Separate services should be used, such as MPLS on one and the Internet on the other. This design is most common in today's networks with SD-WAN in play. This type of design achieves diversity in service, transport type, and cost.
- Different media types—a combination of fiber, copper, cable, wireless, LTE/5G, and so on—are especially good for providing redundancy at smaller critical sites. High-capacity fiber is usually not needed or is too expensive to be delivered to certain remote locations.

Figure 1-3 shows different WAN transports typically used in today's networks.

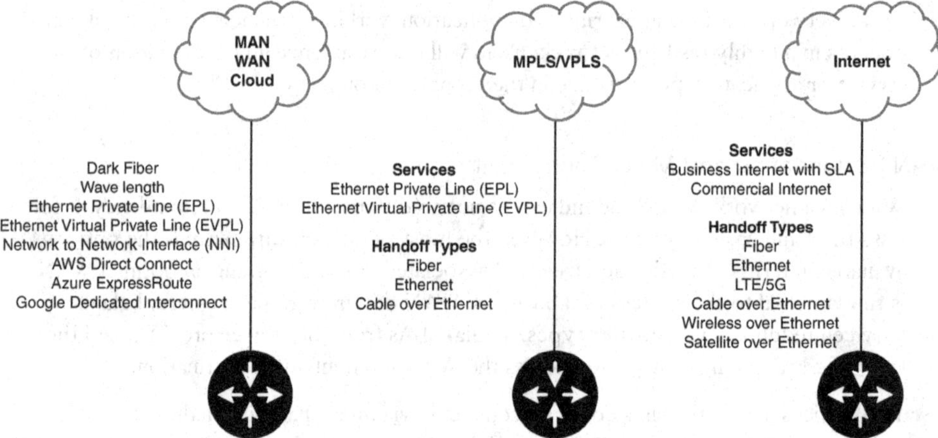

Figure 1-3 *Different WAN Transport and Service Types*

The rule of thumb is that the more critical the site, the more high-capacity links with high service-level agreements (SLAs) will be deployed. This configuration achieves predictability in the network during outage scenarios and required throughput. You will see that most of the links to data centers or Data Center Interconnects (DCIs) are dark fibers or more than 10G capacity with very low Mean Time to Repair (MTTR).

Shared Services

In the multi-domain world, shared services play an essential role within a network infrastructure. As the name suggests, shared services are "shared" across multiple domains, virtual functions, or networks. Service providers have used this concept for years by providing their clients with shared services such as the Internet and IP telephony. Using advanced routing features and virtualization stacks, they can quickly spin up a new service instance or provide access to required resources to their customers. In today's modern network, these shared services have trickled down into enterprise networks as they have started to embrace their own virtualization stacks and share physical infrastructure.

Some of the most common elements of shared services include Domain Name Service (DNS), Dynamic Host Configuration Protocol (DHCP), Internet access, cloud connectivity, Network Access Control (NAC) systems such as Identity Services Engine (ISE), Security Stack, Voice and Telephony, and Management or Out of Band (OOB) networks. Because these services serve multiple large domains, they are built as highly redundant and resilient systems. These services are usually located at data centers and colocation facilities. Some of the application services, such as DNS and DHCP, can also be located in the cloud.

Multiple Technologies

Multi-domain networks cannot be built without multiple technologies involved. Domains could be physical or logical. Physical domains have clear boundaries regarding what areas they serve, and they usually have purpose-built hardware. Some domains are more logical and span multiple domains or are almost all virtual. During the 2000s, when multi-domain networks were designed, they were created by using one or more technologies within that domain. For example, Layer 2 and Layer 3 networks with STP and simple OSPF routing dictated campus networks; MPLS or DMVPN was mainly used for WAN; and simple firewalls represented security. Even data center switching mainly used Catalyst 6500 series switches for most of the connectivity. As the demands of each domain evolved, so did the technologies supporting them. One of the biggest drivers was the virtualization in the infrastructure. This change paved the way for more solution-driven multi-domain networks. Today's multi-domain networks are composed of purpose-built hardware with multiple technologies working together seamlessly. Most domains have both—traditional network design or more software-driven controller-based design. These solutions leverage virtualization capabilities heavily, and the purpose-built hardware supports that domain's demands.

Multi-domain networks are formed by combining all the components mentioned here. It is not just one piece of technology; it is a solution built of multiple technologies, which is flexible and agile, addressing today's business demands.

Characteristics of Multi-Domain Networks

Now that we understand what multi-domain networks comprise, let's examine some key characteristics they possess. All of the modern solution-based multi-domain networks follow the same principles. Just the application of their solution is different because they are more purpose-built. Most of these networks have some form of fabric-based architecture. This architecture is flexible and elastic, which is its major advantage. It takes care of two main problems that any IT team faces: network uptime and on-demand addition of services. Let's discuss that in a little bit more detail.

Single-routing plane traditional networks are the least complex to build and easiest to manage. These were the most common types of networks for many decades. For example, service providers built ATM, cable, and broadband networks; in many cases, most were isolated. As business demands increased, organizations needed to become more flexible in adding services in a more agile fashion, and these simple networks started becoming bottlenecks. The most significant disadvantage of these networks was that a network-wide change was needed when a new service needed to be deployed. This was even more complicated if the service needed to be extended as Layer 2. The network team had to meet their SLAs of 99.9 percent or more uptime for their customers (internal or external). Therefore, any addition of new services as part of the scheduled change window might only happen once a month to maintain that uptime. This meant that new services provided could not be agile and on demand.

This situation gave birth to overlay technologies. Using the power of virtualization, the network is split into underlay and overlay. This approach does build a complex network design, but the benefits of this architecture outweigh the complexity it provides. The underlay part of the network consists of fast-converging routed infrastructure. All the nodes that are part of the physical topology are connected with Layer 3 links and usually with Bidirectional Forwarding Detection (BFD) configured on point-to-point links. This configuration achieves the fastest convergence possible, and with the use of Equal-Cost Multiple Paths (ECMP), traffic is load-shared as well. This is where IT and network teams are happy because they can meet their SLAs of 99.99 percent or higher and also have the flexibility of performing network maintenance at more predictable intervals. The overlay is built on top of the underlay. The overlay is a single virtual routing plane that can extend to any part of the network as desired. Because this routing plane is virtual, more than one can be deployed, giving that flexibility of on-demand provisioning. This feature makes businesses happy because they can sell and deploy these services or instances on the fly without worrying about the underlying infrastructure.

Managing this complexity would definitely require additional operational overhead because new ways of troubleshooting problems need to be derived. To manage the underlay and overlay networks, controller-based architecture, along with automation, plays a critical role in configuring, deploying, and troubleshooting problems. Service providers were the first ones to take one of the most commonly used overlay technologies used today to scale: MPLS. With the underlay built of Provider (P) and Provider Edge (PE) routers, deploying customer VPNs with their own dedicated routing plane was much simpler and, in today's case, mostly automated. Some modern solutions to use this underlay/overlay technology are Cisco SDA for Campus and LAN, Cisco SD-WAN for WAN, and Cisco ACI or VXLAN-EVPN with NDFC for data centers. All these solutions come with their own set of controllers—Cisco Catalyst Center, Cisco Catalyst SD-WAN Manager, and Cisco APIC—to take over the complexity of deploying these solutions; driving more template and intent-based network deployment.

Next, let's look at some of the common characteristics of multi-domain networks. These characteristics apply to any underlay/overlay technology architecture used by any business for any part of their network.

Entry and Exit Points

Fabric-based architecture provides a major advantage in the predictability of the traffic flow. This is achieved by having very specific entry and exit points in the fabric. This architecture allows us to steer traffic to specific egress points per network policy, or even send all traffic out of the fabric to a centralized security stack for inspection and firewalling. The possibilities are immense. Each overlay technology or solution has its own way to handle these entry-exit points so that the right type of traffic can be sent to the right place with high efficiency. One of the most common mistakes architects make while designing these underlay/overlay types of architecture is how traffic flows through the network. Since all overlay traffic is encapsulated in some form, underlay does not care how it is routed because it looks at the outermost IP header and forwards the packet. Poor design may result in suboptimal routing with traffic tromboning the same set of physical devices but with different overlay and underlay IP headers. The most common misconception is made when the same set of underlay links are used for primary as well as backup traffic, which creates an unwanted single point of failure. Here, the overlay seems resilient until that underlay fails, and the entire overlay fails.

Trust Boundaries

With defined entry and exit points, we can create a trust boundary. This boundary is similar to land borders between countries, and only select places allow traffic from one country to another through a checkpoint. These trust boundaries in the network create a specific trust domain for the users, endpoints, and applications residing in the network. In modern networks, these trust boundaries are almost all virtual. These virtual boundaries allow efficient use of the physical network architecture for various purposes without the concern of traffic bleeding from one trust domain to another. Solutions like Cisco SDA are truly intent-driven. You can use the same physical architecture to host trusted corporate endpoints and users, Internet of Things (IoT) devices such as badge readers and Building Management Systems (BMS), and guest users whose endpoints are entirely untrusted. Almost all of the virtual overlay technologies can be designed in a way that can have purpose-built trust boundaries. And because they are all virtual, they can be deployed on demand and with almost no capital expense.

Different Areas

Taking the analogy from the previous section, dedicated entry-exit points and boundaries create a country with a set of rules and policies governing people residing in that country. Having defined entry and exit points and trust boundaries essentially creates a network area with a specific policy for the users, endpoints, and applications residing in that network area. In Cisco SDA terms, this is known as a virtual network (VN); in SD-WAN and MPLS, it is known as VPN; and in ACI, it is a tenant. They are all similar in logical construct, but their application is different. The collection of these different areas is essentially known as a *domain*. When all these domains come together to build a unified network with various interconnections, we build an actual multi-domain network.

Fault Domains

These highly redundant and resilient multi-domain networks are not exempt from their fault domains. Newer solutions have a built-in fault containment system that prevents a major network convergence in the event one of the components in the solution fails. However, when designing integrated multi-domain architecture, we must ensure all the precautions are in place to contain faults to a specific domain and not spread throughout the network. Later in the chapter, we discuss in detail how to integrate all these technologies and explain some of the best practices that have been developed to prevent faults from traversing from one domain to another.

Why Do We Need Multi-Domain Networks?

Now we understand what multi-domain networks are and how they are built. We also know the critical components of these networks. Now the big question: Why do we need multi-domain networks? The answer is simple: In today's demanding environment, the network needs to be flexible and be deployed on demand with high resiliency. These multi-domain networks are the only ones that address today's emerging network needs.

To be competitive, any organization needs an edge on its competition and how they do business. The more user-friendly the experience is, the more customers will come to them. Similarly, the networks also need to cater to an organization's workforce. They need to be transparent and highly secure simultaneously to provide a seamless experience to their employees who work hard and be productive. With the significant global events in the year 2020 onward, demand for networks and their use changed in an instant. All the industry verticals and service providers were made to respond quickly to address the sudden shift in network utilization. The businesses that had already started their transformation ahead of time, forecasting the needs of an emerging network and digitization, became successful overnight. This sudden pivoting and changing the way businesses run overnight provided a true test of these integrated multi-domain networks. One of the most prominent successors was the adoption of cloud and cloud-based platforms and software. Businesses needed real-time telemetry and data on what was happening within their network and how they were performing with the shift in traffic patterns. Today's software-driven networks provided an answer for just that.

Now, companies have realized the benefits of the flexibility these networks offer, and they will not hold back on how they can be deployed in their organizations. Architects and engineers are asked to enhance their skill set to design, deploy, and maintain these networks. This is where we, as authors, can help and guide because we have been involved in deploying these networks since day one.

Next, let's look at some key uses of what made businesses change their mind to adapt multi-domain networks.

Information Technology as a Business (ITaaB)

Historically, IT has always been seen as a cost center from a business perspective. Before the digitization wave began in the 2010s, IT and networking were simply a cost of running a business. Innovation and automation in IT were not given that high importance, and with strict budgets, most of the equipment deployed in IT was either coming to end of life or at capacity. A significant revolution occurred when smartphones took over in the first decade of the 21st century. These phones changed how we use computers and the possibility of directly having email, web access, and messaging services on smartphones. Businesses took advantage of this capability and could give their consumers relevant information in the palm of their hands as fast as possible. In the back end, computer networks, from providers to enterprises, needed to evolve to accommodate this additional capacity and need for data with the highest level of security in mind. IT organizations began to grow with complex networks, and the cost of doing business also increased. Today, we can order food, groceries, services, and information—everything by using a smartphone in our hand.

This is not to say that smartphones brought in the digitization and Internet revolution we have today. They were one of the major contributors, and many other little things comprised IoT devices and the fundamental requirement of having information at hand as soon as possible. While the way of life was increasing, so did the network behind the scenes.

Businesses also evolved their IT as a cost center model to IT as a Business (ITaaB)—a way to utilize the network to pay for itself so that its upkeep, upgrades, and evolution can be sustained. The ITaaB model is similar to the service provider model. Just as service providers isolate their customer networks and have specific SLAs and catalogs of services, ITaaB has its own set of customers; in this case, they could be different business units, departments, or even different affiliations. This model scales well with the ability to grow horizontally or vertically. The goal of the ITaaB model is simple: leverage today's highly virtualized network and computing gear for flexible services and earn revenue from it.

Let's look at some of the ways large enterprises use this model to provide some context and how today's multi-domain networks play a massive role in this model.

Business Units

Business unit (BU) level segregation is a widely deployed network in the ITaaB model. In this design, custom purpose-built networks are created for different organizational BUs. The word *business unit* means different things to different organizations. If the enterprise is a large conglomerate, its BUs are different subsidiaries. For most organizations, their BUs are different divisions of the company, such as engineering, marketing, sales, IT, or physical security. Regardless of the interpretation, the primary objective of building this type of network is to provide isolation of the network, custom attributes, and security policies. With overlay networks in place, they can also provide different handoff points, which can be flexible in directing traffic to a specific part of the network. For example, if we create a dedicated virtual network (VN) in SDA for physical security or Building Management Systems (BMS), we can backhaul that entire VN into a border node in the data center, where we can offload all that traffic to a dedicated tenant in ACI where all physical security and BMS servers reside. This way, the traffic is completely isolated from end to end and secure. Having network segmentation via different BUs is also beneficial to employ a cross-charge mechanism for the services they are using, which is the foundation of the ITaaB model.

Another use case that we have seen grow rapidly is by local counties and cities. Counties, depending on their size, typically run their own fibers across their area and also provide critical emergency services and school infrastructure. With the evolution of the ITaaB model, it has become more cost-effective to provide segregated services to police, fire, ambulance, and school services. They all can be in their own segmented network and use a common high-speed backbone to communicate with each other. These departments could also subscribe to common Internet transit for better efficiency and centralized security.

The R&D department is another big contributor to network segmentation. This division is typically the largest consumer of bandwidth and the latest and greatest features. Giving R&D a separate overlay to connect within the campus, across the campus, and to the cloud is most important. This is where true multi-domain segmentation comes into play. The R&D department predominantly consists of intellectual property, test applications and equipment, third-party equipment to be onboarded, new solutions, and testing. Test and development networks are also part of these environments. Historically, these networks were physically separate from the production environment and connected via a firewall. The main reason was to prevent any security breaches in the production environment with test applications. Because these networks are like giant labs, the last thing any organization wants is to have any security holes or test malfunctions that can impact the production environment and cause an outage. This separate physical network saw a rise in CapEx and OpEx and was not efficient to maintain, especially when it was a non-revenue-generating lab network. With the adoption of the cloud and multi-domain overlay technologies, organizations moved away from using separate physical gear. They employed virtualization in the network and computing to drive their R&D department. They can still be virtually separate from production but maximize the utilization of their physical hardware to accommodate their test environment. Most importantly, with virtualization in place, now the test gear is not confined to a single place but can be located anywhere in the campus, cloud, or even a remote home office.

IT Boundary

The larger an organization gets, the more complex the network becomes; multiple teams are needed to manage and operate that network. With global enterprise organizations, multiple teams manage different parts of the network, compute, and server infrastructure. Sometimes each business unit has its own IT team to manage its infrastructure, and the BUs take services from the corporate IT team to provide global connectivity. This is a classic use case for multi-domain networks, with each business unit and IT team having their domain to manage and own boundary to support. IT boundaries are critical in these large networks because they transfer ownership of the network devices, their support, and maintenance. This way, each IT team can effectively serve their customers without encroaching on each other's networks.

Defining clear IT boundaries is also critical in the case of company mergers and acquisitions. Anytime a merger or acquisition is announced, the business wants to start running as "one entity," but this is much easier said than done. A lot of planning is required during the merging of the networks. Some of the biggest hurdles to overcome are addressing duplicate IPs, directing ownership of the network infrastructure, ensuring both companies' employees can work from either company's facilities, and so on. During this phase, the business wants immediate action and access to each other's networks and a plan to cut down duplicate IT costs. This is where virtualized multi-domain networks and infrastructure come in handy to spin up vital services for business continuity. This paves the foundation for not only business mergers but also network mergers.

Multi-Tenancy

Having multi-domain networks implies that multi-tenancy is in place as well. Isolating networks to serve their specific purpose is one of the most important objectives of multi-domain networks. Multi-tenancy in this context not only means isolating different business units but also isolating like traffic. This is where intent-based networking (IBN) comes into play. Let's look at different aspects of multi-tenancy with an example.

Traffic Isolation

If we were to look at the typical hospital architecture, we would want to isolate different device types into different routing planes or Virtual Routing and Forwarding (VRF). This is known as macrosegmentation. We would separate local hospital staff such as doctors, nurses, and administrative staff into one VRF; critical medical equipment into a second VRF; patients and visiting doctors into a Guest VRF, and last but not least, all critical BMS and physical security devices such as cameras, badge readers, and sensors into their own VRF. This VRF-based isolation gives complete routing plane isolation on the LAN side and also on the WAN and data center side. This isolation of trusted and untrusted traffic is key to fault isolation and providing exceptional network services to end users. Each VRF with its traffic can be offloaded to different parts of the network. Here, corporate trusted traffic can be offloaded directly into the global routing table, which can now reach applications in the data center. Medical equipment traffic can be offloaded to a firewall, which can restrict who can access those devices. Guest traffic can be offloaded directly to the Internet firewall for Internet access because they are not needed to access any corporate resources. Lastly, BMS and physical security traffic can be offloaded to a site where centralized monitoring servers, applications, and users are located. When it comes to networks like this, sites typically have local Internet exit points so that they don't have to carry a large amount of guest Internet traffic over their WAN backbone to a centralized location. This setup saves cost on expensive WAN circuits and provides a better user experience for their patients and guests.

For the WAN traffic, traffic isolation becomes crucial because we would not want to route traffic suboptimally to an exit point. For WAN networks like SD-WAN or DMVPN, where the WAN headends or hub routers are placed becomes critical. Traffic routing through DMVPN networks is straightforward, but with any SD-WAN solution, the traffic policies can get very complex. If not thought through properly, traffic can trombone and take unexpected paths, especially in a failure scenario. For MPLS-VPN networks, the problems are not too different. MPLS networks are full mesh by default, like SD-WAN or DMVPN, but without clever routing and traffic engineering, they too can get complex.

Sometimes, complex designs are needed to solve a specific business requirement. For example, if there is a centralized traffic scrubbing device stack then the business requirement would be to have all traffic coming to the data center or even between any sites go through that scrubbing facility before being sent to its destination. These types of requirements are not uncommon in large networks. Another scenario would be to have a network that functions like a hub-and-spoke, and the WAN policies are developed to mimic that design but run into issues with voice traffic. This situation happens as voice traffic now hairpins through the hub even for site-to-site communication, adding that extra bit of latency that might not be tolerated by the application. So, that issue needs to be mitigated. When we looked into the example of hospital networks, with different VRF needing to be handed off to different parts of the network, sometimes multiple overlays and complex policies are required to achieve the objective of business requirements. Hence, balance between network complexity and network manageability is crucial.

Data center and cloud networks are subject to no different treatment than LAN or WAN. While LAN and WAN networks have their challenges, data centers and the public/private cloud face their own challenges when it comes to multi-tenancy and ensuring that communication between different applications within and across VRFs is maintained. These networks tend to be high-speed low-latency type traffic, and to keep that, we need to account for as few hops as possible with the desired intent in mind. Solving connectivity of isolated multi-domain traffic is like a puzzle where we need to ensure we do not try to fit a square peg into a round hole.

Network Segmentation

Once the traffic is isolated, proper segmentation is also needed. In the world of SDA and ACI, traffic can be segmented by using Security Group Tags (SGTs) or EndPoint Group (EPG) tags, respectively. In these mechanisms a specific endpoint or a user device is tagged in the network, and microsegmentation can be enabled to enforce communication between these devices within the same VRF. The benefit of this approach is that the devices are part of the same trust zone, but we still want to prevent unwanted communication between them. Consider an example of BMS or physical security VRF. Here, BMS devices, badge readers, or surveillance cameras typically do not talk to each other. Still, they usually talk to a server within the same VRF/VLAN or at a central location. So, there is no point in having a wide open network where someone with malicious intent can access a device and start snooping around, exploiting other devices. Having microsegmentation in place helps prevent unwanted communication between these devices and enables communication only to the servers that they are supposed to talk to. This concept is similar to private VLANs in traditional networking, where we used to deploy isolated, community, or promiscuous VLANs to segment traffic within the VLANs. Intent-based networking (IBN) is the key driving factor behind this segmentation strategy, how a device is onboarded into the network, and what it is authorized to access while it is on the network.

Segmentation within the LAN can be easily defined and enforced. The more significant challenge is end-to-end segmentation. We are talking about carrying either SGTs or EPGs across the WAN. In an ideal world, every site would be connected by dark fiber, and we can carry these tags across. However, we are not in that ideal world. We are dealing with various transport types and also what WAN technology is deployed across the WAN—such as SD-WAN, DMVPN, or MPLS. Each of them has its pros and cons to deal with.

At the time we were writing this book, SD-WAN had support for natively carrying these tags. It requires integration with SDA, however. ACI is a bit different, but it could work with some tweaks. In the real world, these tweaks have more cons than pros. In later chapters, we discuss how to integrate SD-WAN. For DMVPN, carrying tags across the tunnels is straightforward. It supports inline tagging and can be enabled with a simple command. There is no support for MPLS, so we have to develop creative solutions, discussed in later chapters. The biggest roadblock to end-to-end microsegmentation is the Maximum Transmission Unit (MTU). The solutions discussed in later chapters overcome those roadblocks and achieve desired goals.

Automation and Orchestration

Thus far, we have learned that multi-domain networks are large and complex. They come with lots of moving parts, and with that, they are highly human-error-prone. Hence, all newer emerging technologies are coming up with automation and orchestration tools that can simplify the deployment. This simplification can significantly reduce the time to market and adoption of these solutions, bringing in faster returns on investment and getting that competitive edge.

When we talk about automation, it is not only about configuring routers and switches in the network, but to a much broader extent, we are talking about building processes and simplifying day-0, day-1, and day-2 operations. Automation is one piece of the puzzle, but with orchestration, we can create workflows that can automate several tasks together in a specific order or group. This is the place where we can gain that scale and accuracy in deployment. Computer networks lag behind when it comes to automation. We still use a command-line interface (CLI) to finish small, repeatable tasks. We have a long way to go, and we will help you get there. We discuss automation and orchestration in much more detail in Chapter 9, "Automation."

Summary

In this chapter, we answered two big questions: What are the components of multi-domain networks, and why do we need multi-domain networks in the first place? With the multi-domain components, we looked at how redundancy, resiliency, WAN transports, shared services, and multiple technologies play an essential role in building a multi-domain network. We also looked at the characteristics of multi-domain networks. We discussed how entry and exit points, trust boundaries, different areas, and fault domains could be used to build the most effective multi-domain networks. For the second question, we looked at why enterprises today need these multi-domain networks and how they can transform their technology and business model into a more effective and competitive market. With an ITaaB strategy, they can start building a network that can pay for itself and proliferate in today's world with the highest amount of flexibility. We also discussed the benefits of multi-tenancy and how it can provide end-to-end segmentation, which is becoming the new standard for today's emerging networks. At a very high level, we discussed how automation could help build these complex networks quickly and accurately.

Chapter 2

SD-Access and Campus Fabric

In this chapter, we discuss the following:

- How SD-Access and Campus fabrics interconnect with other domains of the network
- How minimum requirements make these interconnections work
- The limitations of these integrations
- Proven best practices that go a long way in establishing multi-domain connectivity

Overview

In this chapter, we focus on campus networks. These networks essentially contain small offices, large multi-story or multi-building campuses, manufacturing facilities, and so on. Basically, they are sites or locations where endpoints or end users are connected to the network. Humans need a place to work, manufacture products, or sell products or services. These campuses are the production houses where the majority, if not all, of the revenue is generated for an organization. Campus networks are complex in design because they require all the supporting equipment, technologies, and solutions to ensure the organization's workforce is highly productive and efficient. With the digitization of the network today and the advancement of the Internet of Things (IoT), campus networks have many connected devices other than laptops, phones, and printers. IoT brings in smart buildings that have hundreds of sensors to control lights, temperature, building access, and most importantly, surveillance. All of these IoT devices need to be connected to the network and communicate to some application that is located on a server within the campus, data center, or in a cloud. An organization's ability to ensure and maintain correct segmentation in a legacy network is challenging and, in some cases, ineffective because legacy networks do not provide the macro- or microsegmentation needed to maintain required security. Suppose an attack occurs in a legacy system that is not correctly segmented. In that case, the attacker might get access to sensitive information or restricted devices that could compromise the security or safety of the organization and its users.

This is why today's campus networks are evolving into a more fabric-based architecture, because it provides more flexibility and all the required security and segmentation to function effectively.

In today's campus networks, fabric-based architecture can be deployed by the most prominent solutions: Cisco's Software Defined Access (SD-Access), which leverages Cisco Catalyst Center as an automated orchestrator, or a manually deployed Campus Fabric using various control plane protocols. Both architectures are well supported and work following these principles:

- **Data Plane:** This plane utilizes routed underlay and virtualized overlay technology to segment traffic and increase the availability of the fabric. This data plane also ensures Virtual Routing and Forwarding (VRF)-based traffic isolation, which ensures macrosegmentation in the network.
- **Control Plane:** This centralized control plane architecture routes traffic effectively between different destinations.
- **Policy Plane:** This plane utilizes network access control (NAC) for microsegmentation and secure onboarding of the devices.
- **Management Plane:** Ideally, some form of automated management plane ensures management of devices and avoids configuration drifts.

Let's now take a deep dive into how these two types of fabrics interconnect with other domains.

Note Cisco SD-Access and Campus Fabric are vast solutions that contain multiple technologies. Understanding all the bits and pieces of these solutions is beyond the scope of this book because we mainly focus on integration of these solutions. Several good Cisco Press publications on Cisco SD-Access and Campus Fabric can be leveraged for in-depth knowledge and working of the solution itself. For the rest of this chapter, we assume you have some basic understanding of these solutions.

The functionality of Cisco SD-Access and Campus Fabric work is almost identical. In subsequent sections, we discuss all the integrations with a primary focus on SD-Access and then variations needed for the campus fabric to operate in a similar fashion.

Interaction with the Outside World

We first discuss how fabric-based campus networks interact with external connections. When it comes to fabric-based networks for the campus location, two main types exist: controller-based Cisco's SD-Access and manual or automation-driven BGP-EVPN-based VXLAN Campus Fabric.

Cisco Software Defined Access (SDA)

Cisco SD-Access is a revolutionary fabric-based campus architecture. This solution comprises various technologies that collectively define how a modern secure campus should look. This entire architecture is deployed using an orchestrater known as Cisco Catalyst Center. Because the detailed inner workings of this solution are outside the scope of this book, in this chapter, we focus on how this fabric connects with different domains. We focus on the SD-Access's border node device and connectivity options with the peer device.

Figure 2-1 shows SD-Access components at a high level. The SD-Access fabric site's border nodes (BNs) are the only gateways where traffic can enter or leave the outside world. All the endpoints and users are always connected to fabric edge (FE) nodes, but to access all the required resources outside of the fabric, the traffic has to pass through border nodes. Today, some features allow Layer 2 fabric, and in that case, there is an exemption of traffic not passing through the border nodes; the fabric acts as a giant Layer 2 switch. With border nodes being the gateway, there has to be a peer device (formerly known as a fusion router) that can collect all traffic coming in from various virtual networks (VNs), apply any applicable security policies, and then forward it out to upstream devices.

These peer devices can be of various platforms and functions. They can also be one or more peer devices connected to border nodes for different traffic routing policies. Remember, SD-Access fabric already has multiple virtual networks that must be macrosegmented. If we merge all of that traffic without any control, then there is no point in having that macrosegmentation in the first place. Hence, a peer device's role is critical in ensuring critical connectivity to all virtual networks. Some of the most commonly deployed peer devices consist of

- A Catalyst 9K or Nexus 9K Layer 3 switch with Virtual Routing and Forwarding Lite (VRF-Lite), with route-leaking between VRFs to provide inter-VN communication.
- An ASR 1000 or Catalyst 8000 series router, which would keep macrosegmented traffic in respective VRFs and send it toward WAN in another form of encapsulation or back-to-back VRF handoffs.
- Cisco SD-WAN router with dedicated service-side virtual private networks (VPNs) for each virtual network on the SD-Access side.
- Cisco FTD or similar firewalls that merge all virtual networks into one global routing table. In this scenario, each terminated VRF is in its own security zone and has access rules between different security zones (VRFs).

Regardless of the connectivity, SD-Access border nodes will hand off each virtual network individually, as shown in Figure 2-2. These virtual networks can either be handed off on a single interface using dot1q trunk, or each virtual LAN (VLAN) can be handed off via a dedicated interface to different devices (a combination of routers and/or firewalls). It is crucial to remember that the packets coming out of the SD-Access fabric will be native IP and will not have any Virtual Extensible LAN (VXLAN) tags by default. If microsegmentation needs to be preserved, additional commands must be added to retain tags. This issue is discussed in subsequent sections.

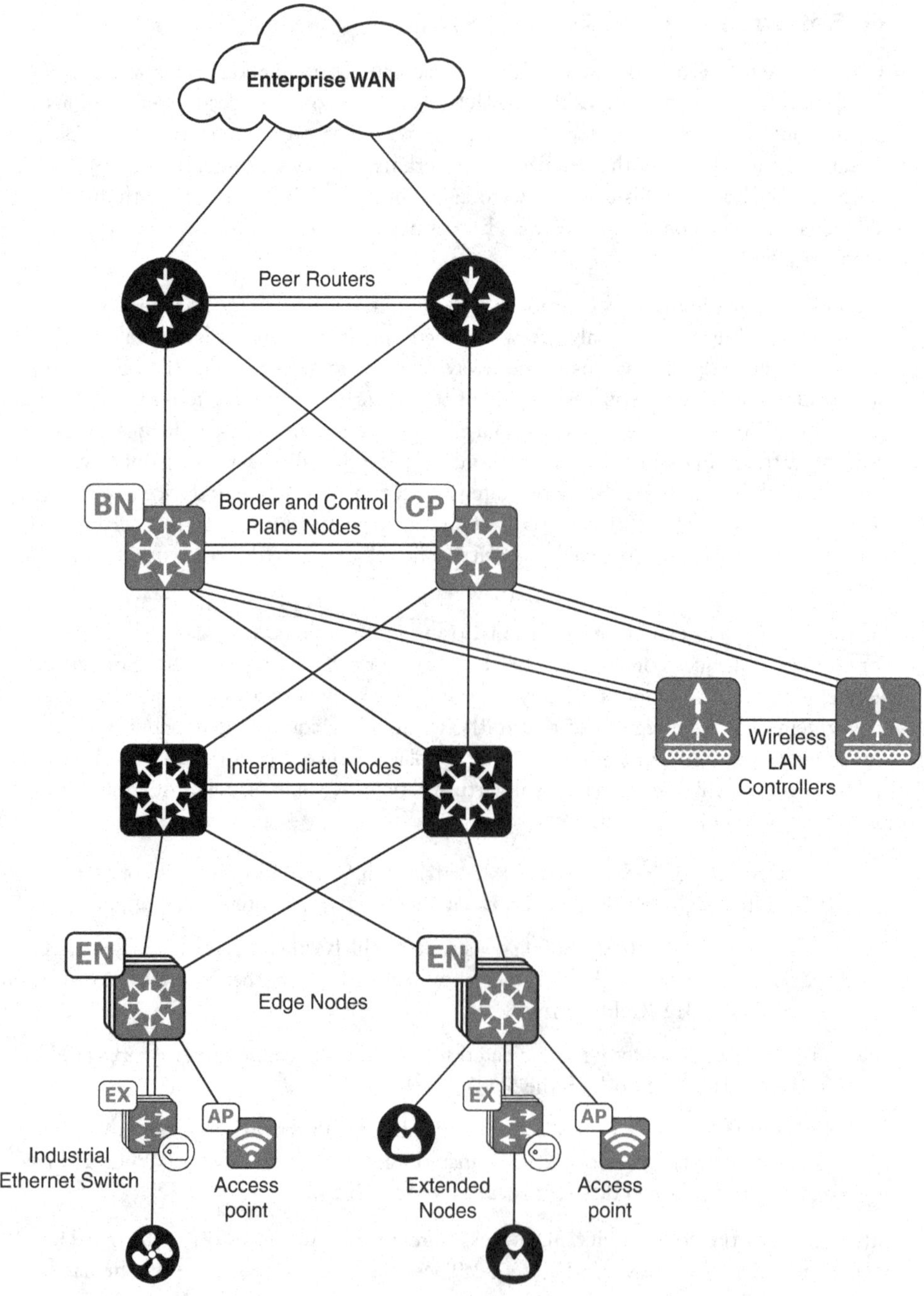

Figure 2-1 *SD-Access Components at a High Level*

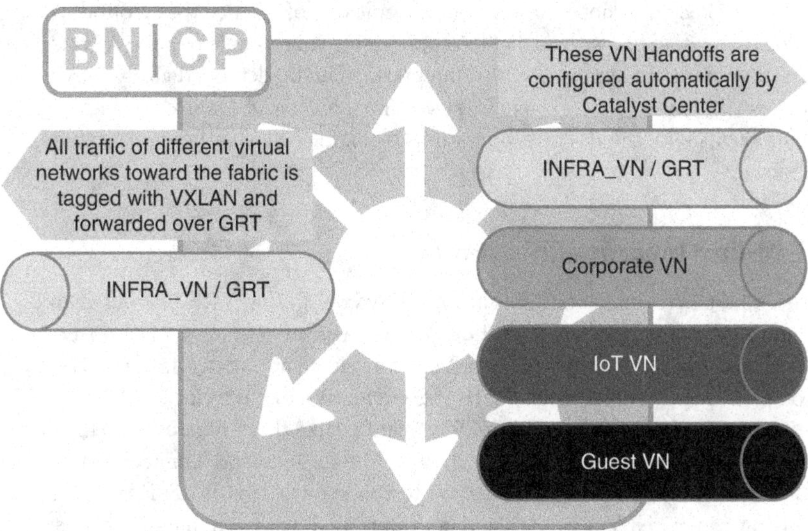
BN|CP
These VN Handoffs are configured automatically by Catalyst Center
All traffic of different virtual networks toward the fabric is tagged with VXLAN and forwarded over GRT
INFRA_VN / GRT
INFRA_VN / GRT
Corporate VN
IoT VN
Guest VN

Figure 2-2 *Basics of Virtual Network Handoff on SD-Access Border Nodes*

Campus Fabric

The Campus Fabric operates similarly to SD-Access, with the major difference being the absence of a controller and/or the routing protocols and overlay technology being used to build the fabric. This has the same components, such as the control plane, data plane, and policy plane; however, without the orchestrator, the management plane is decentralized. Detailed Cisco Validated Design guides on how to build the Campus Fabric are available on cisco.com, so we focus on how these fabrics are integrated with other domains and any variations from the SD-Access fabric.

Inter-working with SD-WAN

Cisco SD-Access and SD-WAN are among the most widely used fabric-based integrations today. With enterprises having multiple campuses and branches, it would definitely require some form of WAN connectivity to establish communication between those sites and the outside world. That's where SD-WAN comes into play. Cisco SD-WAN itself has the built-in capability of building optimal network design with macrosegmentation (VRFs) in place. These VRFs tie directly with SD-Access's virtual networks on a one-to-one basis and can route traffic effectively. This level of integration is straightforward and out of the box by default. The complexity arises when end-to-end micro-segmentation between SD-Access fabrics is desired by an organization over SD-WAN. This is where we have to design the solution so that it can carry Secure Group Tags (SGTs) across from one SD-Access fabric site to another.

Enterprises have to keep a balance between the complexity of the network from day one of the deployment and how their day two operations team is able to support this solution. Based on our field experience, this integration can be deployed easily; however, we would categorize end-to-end segmentation as a more advanced feature set with high training requirements with the day two operations team. Let's discuss how this segmentation can be done.

Default End-to-End Macrosegmentation

Default end-to-end macrosegmentation is achieved by configuring VRF-Lite between the SD-Access border node and SD-WAN Edge router. As shown in Figure 2-3, Cisco Catalyst Center will configure virtual network handoffs in an automated fashion. This orchestration process will configure handoff of Switched Virtual Interfaces (SVIs) with point-to-point /30 IP addressing toward the WAN and enable these IP addresses to run the Border Gateway Protocol (BGP) toward SD-WAN Edge. To ensure connectivity is established, you must create an interface feature template on the SD-WAN Edge with a variable field that can match VN to VRF and configure BGP with matching parameters. Once this template is pushed to SD-WAN Edge with the correct variables, BGP will be established, and the traffic will start flowing. This is the simplest form of integration that achieves end-to-end macrosegmentation without any SGT propagation. Most enterprises that we have worked with have adopted this method because it achieves two main objectives for them:

1. Get the network up and running for all virtual networks and establish desired connectivity. This will ensure that business continuity is maintained.
2. Observe the need for microsegmentation and plan the second phase with end-to-end microsegmentation with SGT propagation and enforcement.

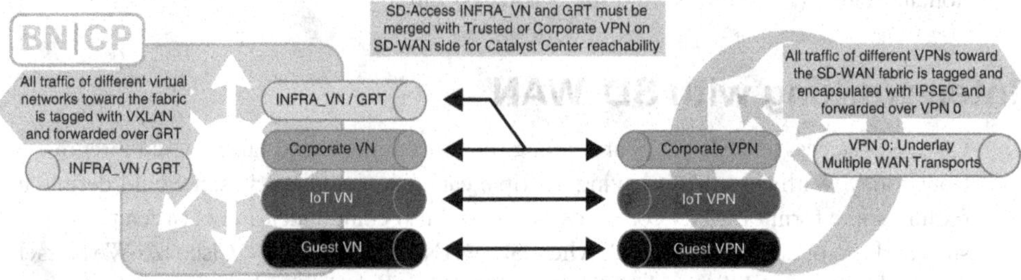
BN|CP
All traffic of different virtual networks toward the fabric is tagged with VXLAN and forwarded over GRT
INFRA_VN / GRT
SD-Access INFRA_VN and GRT must be merged with Trusted or Corporate VPN on SD-WAN side for Catalyst Center reachability
INFRA_VN / GRT
Corporate VN
IoT VN
Guest VN
Corporate VPN
IoT VPN
Guest VPN
All traffic of different VPNs toward the SD-WAN fabric is tagged and encapsulated with IPSEC and forwarded over VPN 0
VPN 0: Underlay Multiple WAN Transports

Figure 2-3 *SD-Access and SD-WAN Macrosegmentation Integration*

The major advantage of employing this design is that an organization can leverage key features of SD-WAN like Application-Aware Routing (AAR) directly from day one of the deployment because the packets coming from the SD-Access fabric are native IP packets.

With Campus Fabric, the configuration and architecture for SD-WAN integration do not change. Because the configuration of VRF-Lite and BGP is technically outside of the fabric and native IP, the integration process is identical. One of the most important points to be mindful of in Campus Fabric is the absence of an orchestrator to configure these SVI handoffs from the border node side. A custom home-grown tool or script can create these handoffs facing SD-WAN Edge.

Integrated and Nonintegrated SD-WAN Solutions

Currently, two main supported inter-workings of SD-Access and SD-WAN are integrated (one-box) and nonintegrated (two-box) solutions. A key point to be mindful of here is not to confuse the terminology—*integrated* and *nonintegrated*—with the actual integration of these two domains. Both are fully supported integration methods that give one critical advantage over the default end-to-end macrosegmentation. Both of these solutions provide end-to-end microsegmentation between SD-Access sites. For the rest of the chapter, we use the terms *one-box solution* and *two-box solution* for clarity.

A one-box solution is deployed when you have an all-in-one role for a fabric-enabled device. In this solution, the fabric-enabled device has a border, a control plane, and an SD-WAN Edge role configured. Due to a single device having multiple roles and, most importantly, an SD-WAN Edge role for SD-WAN, the implication is that this device cannot be a Cisco Catalyst 9000 series switch. Also, this device needs to have a supported SD-WAN image on which this functionality is deployed. This solution is mainly designed for small to medium branches with one or two WAN routers and a few access layer switches supporting their users. This solution reduces the need for a dedicated border and control plane node, reducing the hardware footprint at these sites and increasing ROI. Understanding the hardware and software compatibility matrix for this solution and testing your use cases before implementing it in production is highly recommended. Based on our experience, this solution is not widely deployed in the field for three reasons:

1. Many large organizations with multiple sites and branches usually have dedicated WAN and LAN teams. Because this solution combines LAN and WAN functions on a single device, who owns and maintains the solution becomes a big question for teams. Hence, they prefer not to have a single device with multiple roles.

2. With the introduction of the Fabric-in-a-Box (FiaB) feature in SD-Access, the most-desired choice is to have Catalyst 9000 series switches at a site function as FiaB with any WAN router.

3. Not having a one-box solution gives an added advantage to the adoption of SD-Access and SD-WAN solutions. An organization can adopt and deploy both of these solutions at different paces. SD-WAN is usually faster to deploy than SD-Access due to the limited number of devices, and enables an organization to start getting benefits from the solution much earlier. SD-Access can come after and would only require minor changes on the SD-WAN side to facilitate the integration.

As its name suggests, the two-box solution is deployed with a dedicated SD-WAN router and a dedicated SD-Access border and control plane nodes. Here, SD-WAN Edge could be any supported router from the compatibility matrix. Similarly, there is the freedom to choose border and control plane nodes on the SD-Access side. This is the most commonly deployed integration method because it addresses the limitations of the one-box solution. The technical inter-working is exactly the same when it comes to one-box and two-box solutions. However, in a two-box solution, you have to add some additional commands on the SVIs of the border nodes to send the packets as VXLAN tagged instead of native IP. This point is key because the SD-WAN Edge router will look for those packets to send them end-to-end microsegmented. If packets received are native IP, normal routing policies will be used to route packets out to the WAN.

We discussed how this integration works at a high level. Now let's look deeper to see how it works internally. Here, we use a reference from a Cisco Live presentation. Figure 2-4 shows how a two-box solution works under the hood. There are two levels of mappings: one at the SD-Access B/CP node and the second at the SD-WAN Edge. On the SD-Access side, B/CP nodes will ensure VN-to-VRF mapping is completed, and packets are sent through the trunk link to SD-WAN Edge with VXLAN encapsulation with the help of a CMD header. On the SD-WAN Edge side, this VRF-to-VPN mapping ensures the packet is decapsulated and then encapsulated in the IPsec layer and sent across the WAN. Return packets are handled in reverse order: IPsec layers are decapsulated and VPN-to-VRF mapping is built, and then packets are sent over the dot1q trunk interface in VXLAN encapsulation to SD-Access B/CP node. When SD-Access B/CP node receives the packet, it will forward it within the fabric based on adjacency lookup and ensure VRF is mapped to the correct virtual network and right SGTs.

Figure 2-5 shows how routing architecture works under the hood.

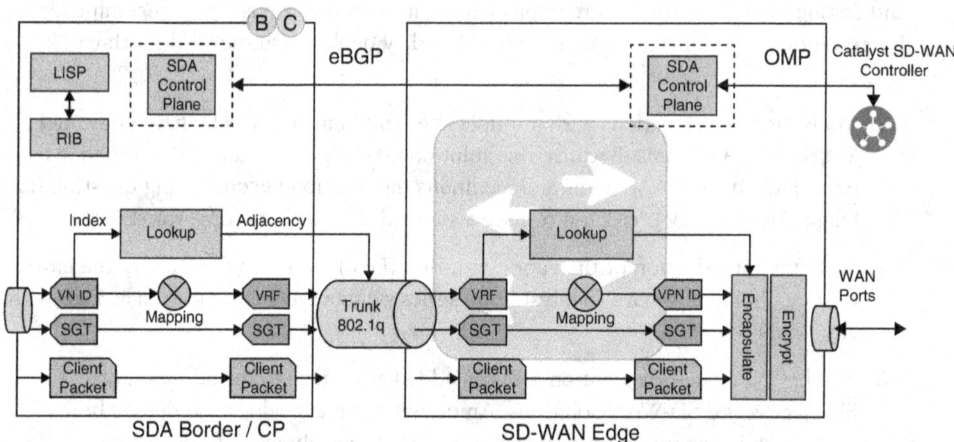

Figure 2-4 *Border Node to SD-WAN Edge Data Plane*

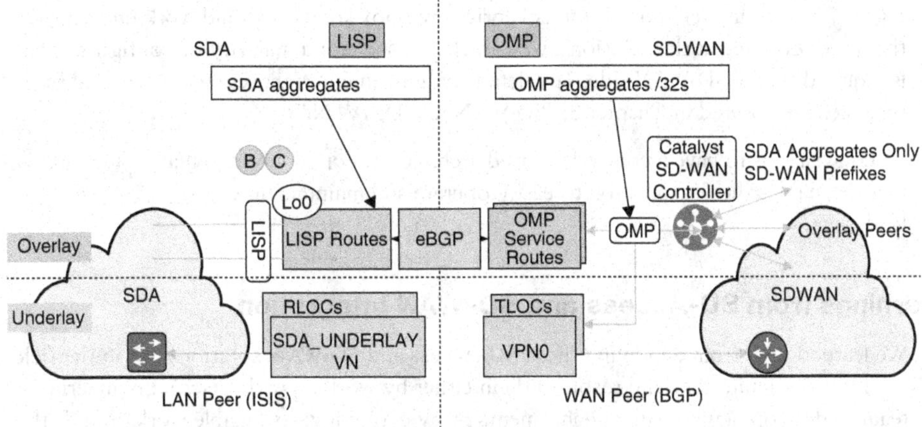

Figure 2-5 *SD-Access—SD-WAN Routing Architecture and Peering*

This setup has four quadrants. The top-left quadrant handles all the Location Identity Separation Protocol (LISP) routes from the SD-Access overlay networks, and then it redistributes them into the per-VRF BGP VPNv4 address family. All of the /32 prefixes that are learned from the SD-Access overlay are aggregated by the control plane and then advertised out to SD-WAN Edge via eBGP peering. Moving to the top-right quadrant, the routes that were received from the overlay are then injected into respective service VPNs on the SD-WAN side. These routes then are redistributed into the Overlay Management Protocol (OMP) and sent to the Catalyst SD-WAN Controller. The Catalyst SD-WAN Controller then forwards all these prefixes to all other SD-WAN Edges in the network to build the SD-WAN fabric.

The lower quadrant is the underlay of SD-Access and SD-WAN. The bottom-left quadrant shows the SD-Access underlay built using the IS-IS routing protocol. As per Figure 2-3, this underlay VN, known as INFRA_VN, is then merged with the trusted service-side VPN using the simple IPv4 BGP address family. On the SD-WAN side, the bottom-right quadrant shows VPN0 connectivity, which is essentially a collection of all the transports from where SD-WAN can build its WAN tunnels. These interface IP addresses, known as Transport Locators (TLOCs), are being used by OMP to build optimal routing topology.

Note Underlay networks for SD-Access (INFRA_VN or Global Routing Table [GRT]) and SD-WAN (VPN 0) are never merged together. They are completely isolated and need to be isolated to function.

Regarding the Campus Fabric, the one-box solution is not supported because it requires integration between Cisco Catalyst Center and Catalyst SD-WAN Manager. Because Catalyst Center does not manage Campus Fabrics, this solution will not work. A two-box solution, however, can be configured if needed. This solution would require similar commands as in SD-Access to send packets with a VXLAN header instead of native IP.

Figure 2-4 also answers how Campus Fabric's two-box solution would work underneath the hood. Looking at the solutions, we can clearly see that a majority of configuration is required on the SD-WAN side. The details on implementation, segmentation, and best practices are covered in Chapter 3, "SD-WAN and DMVPN."

Cisco's vision is to have a controller-based architecture for all fabric domains. This architecture enables the organization to easily operate and maintain an ever-changing network landscape.

Learnings from SD-Access and SD-WAN Integration

We learned a lot from deploying these SD-Access and SD-WAN solutions out in the field. We hit many limitations and resolved them either by working with Cisco's Engineering team to develop new feature enhancements or by deploying sustainable workarounds that are easy for an organization's operations team to understand and maintain the network. Some highlights of our learnings are as follows:

- The order in which these solutions are deployed is the key. Due to the nature of underlay and overlay technologies, a Catch-22 scenario occurs when SD-WAN cannot build its service-side VPNs because Catalyst Center has not configured the fabric and SVI handoffs. In contrast, Catalyst Center cannot configure underlay/overlay until it can reach all of the devices behind the SD-WAN. So a temporary SVI with static routes needs to be configured for Catalyst Center to reach the fabric devices and configure relevant SVIs with handoffs. Once handoffs are created, an SD-WAN template needs to be updated so that it can match the parameters on the SD-Access side and establish the connectivity. After connectivity is established, those temporary SVIs and static routes can be removed.
- If your organization is using or plans on using SD-Access-Transit in conjunction with these solutions, SD-Access site-to-site packets that are VXLAN encapsulated between the border nodes of two sites will *not* be intercepted by SD-WAN routers. SD-WAN routers will only decapsulate VXLAN packets that are destined to them and not the ones that are transiting through them. This is an important consideration to take into account because transiting packets will still have that additional 50 bytes of VXLAN overhead when going through the IPsec tunnel of SD-WAN. So if the WAN does not support more than 1500 bytes of standard MTU, it is highly recommended to use the SD-Access feature to reduce TCP MSS on all fabric SVIs. This approach will prevent packets from going over 1500 bytes, and any additional overhead across the path is accounted for.
- As shown in Figure 2-3, the underlay and trusted virtual network of SD-Access need to be bridged to a single trusted service-side VPN on the SD-WAN side. Although an SD-Access underlay can get its own dedicated VPN, that would result in an overly complex SD-WAN design because a majority of shared services such as DNS, DHCP, and ISE all reside in trusted VPN.

- Data center or Carrier Neutral Facility (CNF) headends should be built first so that all shared services are accessible for the SD-Access fabric to function.
- If an organization has decided to go with SD-Access and SD-WAN solutions, it is highly recommended to start first with SD-WAN at the sites so that macrosegmentation is built, ready, and tested for SD-Access to send its data.
- There are not enough words to emphasize how important solution testing is. Ensuring your use cases are tested and validated before deploying the solution in production will lead you to trouble-free success. These technologies seem complicated initially, but if deployed with proper planning and testing, they can catapult your organization ahead of the competition on the digitization journey.

Inter-working with ACI and Data Center Fabric

Cisco SD-Access and Campus Fabric data planes are identical to Application Centric Infrastructure (ACI) and Data Center Fabric. Their control and management planes, however, are entirely different. The overall objective is simple: attach macro- and microsegmentation metadata to the VXLAN header and carry that information across the underlay to build a flexible fabric. This brings a significant advantage when it comes to integrating these two domains. Regardless of the fabric combination on the other side, integration logic is the same. Even though configuration commands for SD-Access and Campus Fabric are identical, the designs shown in this section are not always scalable for the Campus Fabric deployment. Similarly, on the data center side, ACI is the go-to solution for granular macro- and microsegmentation-based architecture. Hence, Data Center Fabrics do not solve all the required scale and integration issues with other solutions like ISE. For the rest of this section, we focus entirely on SD-Access and ACI integration because they are a more scalable way to deploy fabric in respective campus and data center domains.

At the time of writing this book, no fully automated integration is available to configure SD-Access border nodes and ACI border leafs. Only some organizations that have SD-Access and ACI are adopting integration. One of the biggest holdbacks is migration to the cloud. Organizations are embracing cloud-based applications, which is driving many of their applications to use zero trust.

SD-Access and ACI integration today is relatively straightforward. To ensure end-to-end microsegmentation is preserved across both fabrics, the controller has no direct automation capability to configure any of the border nodes or border leafs. All the configuration is manual between integration points. This SD-Access and ACI integration is known as "Phase 2" integration. There are plans for more seamless "Phase 3" integration methods in the road map; however, they are in their infancy and hence not documented in this book.

Let's walk through Figure 2-6 to understand what is required in this integration. One of the key components of the integration is Cisco Identity Services Engine (ISE). Both the fabric controllers—Catalyst Center and Application Policy Infrastructure Controller (APIC)—must be integrated with ISE. This integration is essential because ISE acts as a mediator between the two controllers and shares information about Secure Group Tags (SGTs) with each other. This is what ensures end-to-end microsegmentation data is preserved between both fabrics. Both SD-Access and ACI use VXLAN-based encapsulation in their data plane, and the 16-bit value of SGT in SD-Access is used for endpoint groups (EPGs) in ACI. With ISE sharing the same bit-value information across both controllers, it essentially becomes an SGT-EPG translation engine.

Planning and designing SD-Access and ACI fabrics is very important. Because the same SGT/EPG values are used on each side of the domain, an organization should be careful to prevent overlap or wrong values. In ISE, there is an option of propagating all the new SGTs created in the SD-Access environment to ACI. This option dramatically reduces the complexity of not having the right information on the ACI side. When the integration is established and traffic is flowing, both sides will receive VXLAN-encapsulated traffic. As mentioned earlier, because there is no direct communication between Catalyst Center or APIC controllers, policy enforcement contracts need to be created on each controller so that they can be pushed to all the nodes in the respective fabric. For example, if User A is not allowed to access Application A, a contract must be created on the SD-Access side, which matches the SGT of User A and the SGT of Application A to deny it. Similarly, on the ACI side, an access contract must be created to match EPG of User A and Application A, then deny it. This way, end-to-end microsegmentation and enforcement can be achieved.

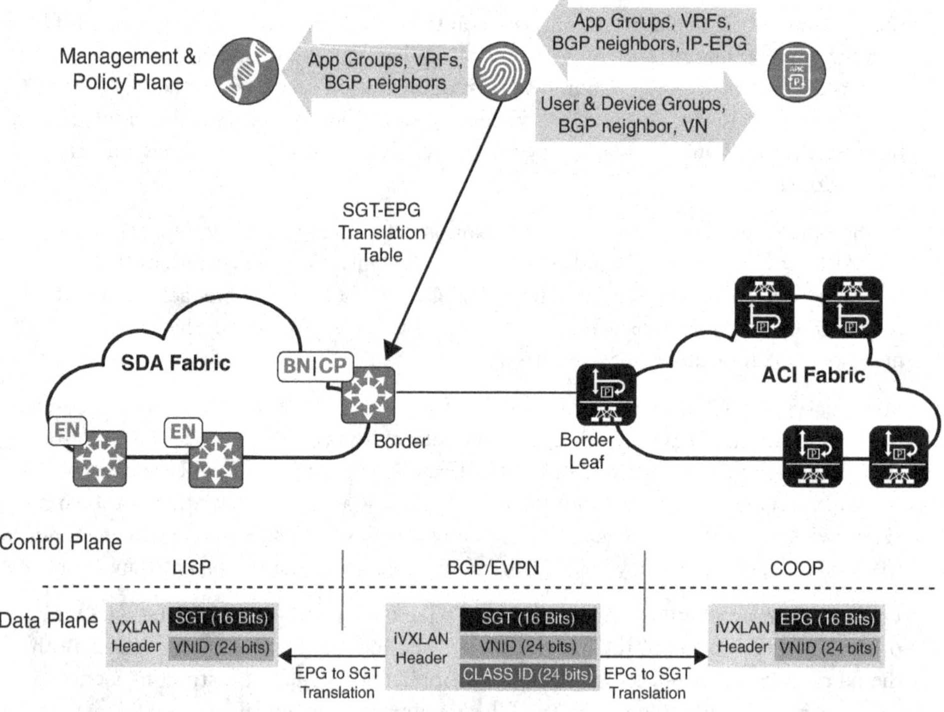

Figure 2-6 *SD-Access and ACI Phase-2 Integration*

To tie all the integration pieces together, we need to understand where we place the SD-Access border node and ACI border leaf node. Figure 2-7 shows an architecture best suited for this integrated deployment. For clarity of the drawing, only a single-homed design is shown. If the data center is located in the same campus where SD-Access fabric is deployed, then they can be directly connected via back-to-back links. Here, the SD-Access border node is placed in the data center and treated as its own site in the site hierarchy. Leveraging SDA-Transit, all fabric-site-to-fabric-site communication occurs with VXLAN headers. The SD-Access border node at the data center will then establish a BGP-EVPN connection to ACI's border leaf and start exchanging all the data with the same preserved VXLAN headers. With the BGP-EVPN address family, all the macro- and microsegmentation information is preserved and honored on the other side of the fabric. The last piece of this deployment is to leverage Cisco Metadata (CMD) between SD-Access border nodes and ACI border leafs so that the VXLAN tag is honored and transported across the link.

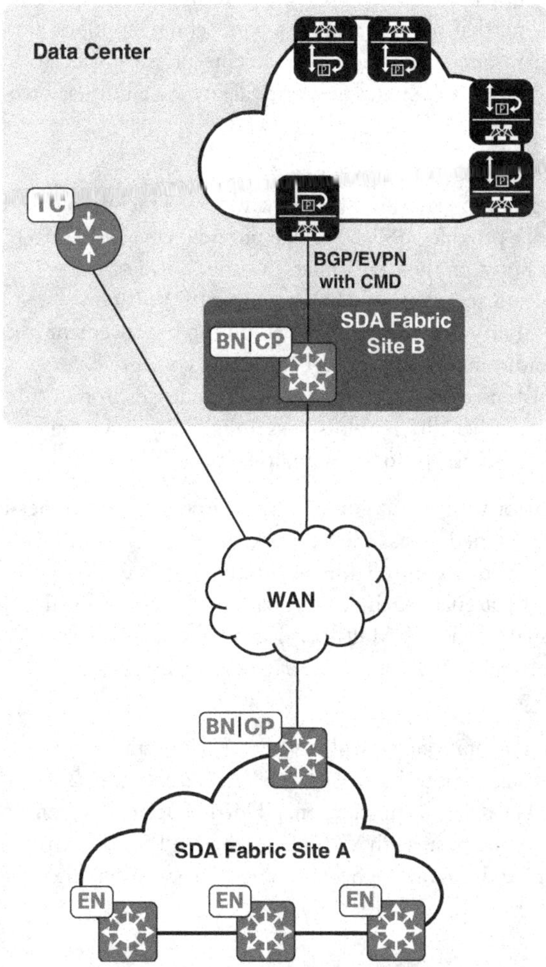

Figure 2-7 *SD-Access and ACI Integrated Design*

To summarize, for exchanging all SGT and EPG information, ISE is needed. The control planes of both fabrics are different; however, their data planes are identical. BGP-EVPN is needed to establish routing adjacency between the SD-Access border node and ACI border leaf. And at last, for enforcement of policies on both fabrics, access contracts need to be created in Catalyst Center and ACI, which are then deployed in respective fabrics.

Inter-working with MPLS

Over the past decade, large enterprises have moved toward enabling Multi-Protocol Label Switching (MPLS) in their core. This was the first stage of using overlay technologies in the network's core to carry macrosegmentation across their network without using any controllers or software-driven architecture. We have used many overlay technologies to connect the sites, such as Dynamic Multi-point Virtual Private Network (DMVPN), MPLS from the service providers, and point-to-point IPsec tunnels. But after the traffic reached the core of the network or campus, there was no easy way to maintain that macrosegmentation within the core and send that traffic to either a data center, cloud, or any large offices. As leased circuits became more cost-effective, large enterprises started to use them to connect large and medium sites and sometimes critical sites to run their own enterprise MPLS.

Enterprise MPLS solved the immediate problem of site connectivity by preserving macrosegmentation. MPLS is a proven and decades-old trusted and tested technology that was predominantly used by service providers (SPs). Service providers use MPLS to maintain clear network segmentation between their customers. With the use of the technology, they also injected specialized services such as Voice over IP (VoIP) or Internet access. With this level of flexibility provided by MPLS and the improvement in the code of the enterprise switches and routers, MPLS was enabled on enterprise networks. While service providers' customers were enterprises and businesses, for an enterprise network, their customers are either different business units (BUs) or a type of traffic such as production, development, guest, or IoT. Possibilities were endless.

Deploying enterprise MPLS is straightforward, but it comes with an operational overhead whenever a new VPN needs to be provisioned across the network. This configuration is done manually by default due to the lack of a controller. However, many organizations have homegrown scripts and tools that automate such deployments at the operational level. Today, many controllers are available, such as Multi-Services Orchestrator (MSO) or Cisco Network Services Orchestrator (NSO), to automate such deployments and operations.

With MPLS supporting only macrosegmentation, we will have default integration with SD-Access and Campus Fabric using back-to-back VRFs or VRF-Lite. Figure 2-8 shows how this integration will look. For macrosegmentation, all virtual networks from SD-Access will be mapped on a one-to-one basis with VPNs from the MPLS side. After Cisco Catalyst Center configures SVI handoffs on the border nodes, information related to VLAN, interface, and BGP Autonomous System Number (ASN) can be captured from the Catalyst Center UI shown in Figure 2-9. This information allows relevant interfaces and BGP to be configured on the MPLS VPN side to establish connectivity.

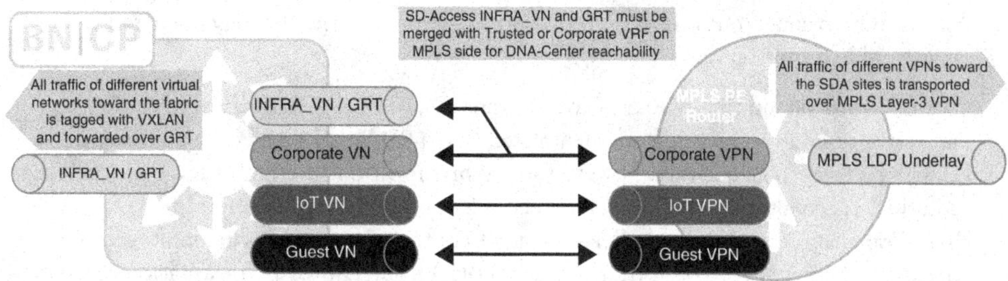
BN|CP
SD-Access INFRA_VN and GRT must be merged with Trusted or Corporate VRF on MPLS side for DNA-Center reachability
All traffic of different virtual networks toward the fabric is tagged with VXLAN and forwarded over GRT
INFRA_VN / GRT
INFRA_VN / GRT
Corporate VN
IoT VN
Guest VN
MPLS PE Router
All traffic of different VPNs toward the SDA sites is transported over MPLS Layer-3 VPN
Corporate VPN
IoT VPN
Guest VPN
MPLS LDP Underlay

Figure 2-8 *SD-Access and Campus Fabric Integration with MPLS*

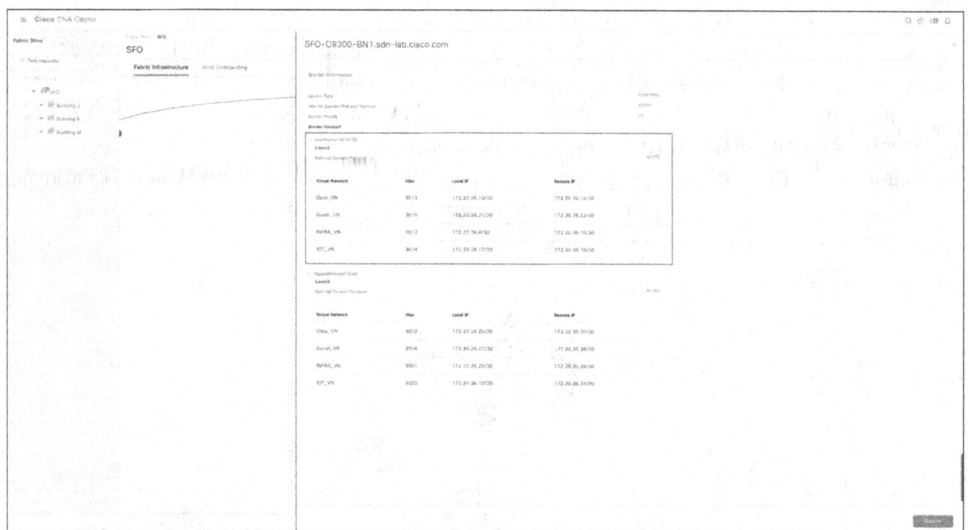
SFO
SFO-C9300-BN1.sdn-lab.cisco.com

Figure 2-9 *Cisco Catalyst Center Screen Showing Critical Information Required to Configure MPLS Parameters*

One important point to be mindful of is to bridge both SD-Access and Campus Fabric's underlay network with the trusted general-purpose corporate VRF on the MPLS side. This is required to ensure all shared services like DNS, DHCP, ISE, and Catalyst Center are easily accessible via a corporate WAN because they are needed for the SD-Access and Campus Fabrics operations and management. This method is widely used in the field today. Another option is if the organization needs to keep the underlay network separate from the corporate network, they can configure a dedicated VPN on the MPLS side to connect to this network by using inter-VRF route-leaking. This design allows desired shared services routes to be injected into a dedicated underlay VPN. This way, all required connectivity is maintained without the need to merge any networks for better security. One downside of this design is the operational overhead because route injection needs to be planned out properly so that no single point of failure may make fabric inaccessible during an outage.

We now understand that MPLS networks cannot carry SGTs natively across the network for end-to-end microsegmentation. Cisco SD-WAN is the only solution that can carry these tags natively; however, many organizations might not have adopted that solution. As an alternative, Cisco SD-Access has a WAN transit option known as SDA-Transit. In this design, dedicated transit control plane routers are strategically placed in the network. These transit control plane routers provide destination reachability information to all the border nodes of all SD-Access sites. With this information, each border node at each of the sites can directly send VXLAN-tagged packets containing virtual network and SGT information to a remote SD-Access site and preserve end-to-end microsegmentation. This capability is revolutionary because this feature of SD-Access would work over any WAN transport as long as there is underlay connectivity between the two border nodes. This feature, by default, provides all inter-SDA-site connectivity for sites that are managed by a single Catalyst Center cluster. The enhancements available today allow the same transit control plane routers to be used cross Catalyst-Center cluster, providing additional flexibility to send microsegmentation end-to-end globally. Figure 2-10 illustrates the higher-level working of transit control planes and end-to-end macro- and microsegmentation.

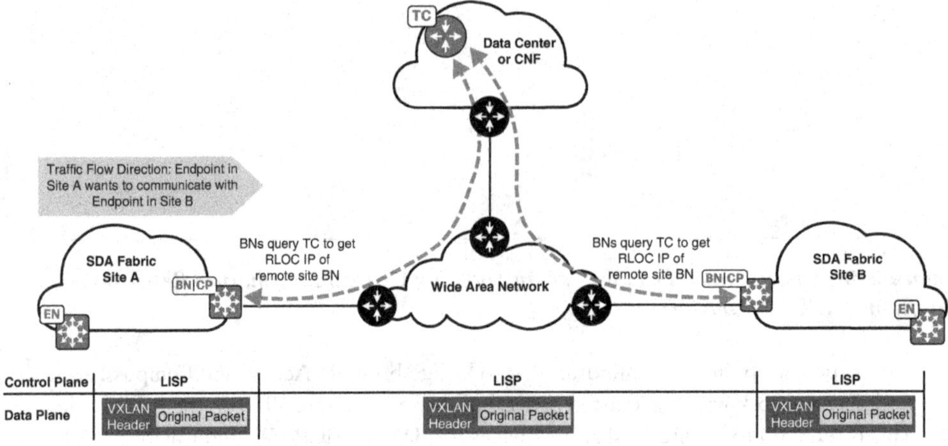

Figure 2-10 *High-Level Working of SDA-Transit*

Today, we can use SDA-Transit over MPLS with certain considerations. Figure 2-11 illustrates how SDA-Transit works over MPLS. With border nodes building direct VXLAN tunnels with another border node at a remote site, this operation occurs before even the traffic reaches the MPLS router. This implies that an additional overhead of 50 bytes will be added to all the packets traversing through the MPLS network. For this design to work, the MPLS network needs to accommodate an additional 50 bytes end-to-end with this overhead because fragmented VXLAN-tagged packets will break the traffic flow. If an additional 50 bytes of overhead cannot be accommodated in the MPLS network, an SD-Access feature can lower the TCP MSS value to 1250 bytes of all SVIs within the fabric. This will ensure any additional overhead passes through the network end-to-end without fragmentation. A TCP MSS adjustment can take care of all TCP traffic. When it comes to UDP traffic, 95 percent of the traffic out there does not exceed 500 bytes. There may be certain applications that could send a full 1500 bytes of UDP data. In that scenario, that UDP stream will not work. If your organization decides to use this TCP MSS adjustment feature, it is highly recommended that you conduct application assessments to ensure traffic flows are not disrupted.

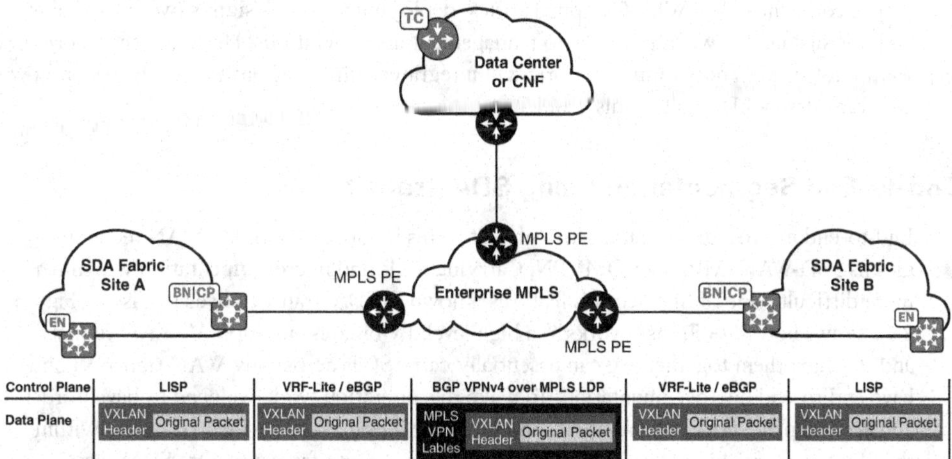

Figure 2-11 *SDA Transit over MPLS*

Inter-working with CNF

Campus and branch networks are usually stubs in nature. Today's modern networks for campuses and branches employ a hub-and-spoke model where data centers and Carrier Neutral Facilities (CNFs) are usually hubs, and remote sites are spokes. This type of design has the major advantage of backhauling traffic to a centralized location, because the majority of today's applications are cloud-based and require more north-south communication. There is some east-west traffic between the sites but not to the extent where we would need dedicated east-west designs. With solutions like SD-WAN in place, this north-south and east-west communication can be easily achieved on a granular level.

CNFs are becoming an essential component of today's networks for large enterprises. With a minimal hardware footprint, an organization can have high-capacity, cost-effective circuits delivered to them, connecting almost any providers out there. With more organizations moving toward the cloud, this design is an easy sell to centralize and aggregate all traffic for better serviceability. The details of how CNFs function is covered in Chapter 6, "Carrier Neutral Facilities." This chapter focuses on how campuses are integrated with CNF.

With the stub nature of campuses and remote locations, there is usually no direct link to CNF unless a large campus has a data center that requires direct point-to-point connectivity. There is always some WAN in the middle of connecting campuses and branches. We already discussed how SD-Access and Campus Fabric integrate with WAN solutions. What if customers want a little more flexibility in expanding that macro- and microsegmentation out in CNF? This is where leveraging some of the latest features of SD-Access would come into play. With Campus Fabrics, deploying such a design is overly complex and not sustainable when it comes to management and operations. Hence, in this section, we do not discuss how Campus Fabric will integrate with CNFs but instead focus on how software-driven SDA solves this problem.

End-to-End Segmentation Using SDA-Transit

End-to-end macrosegmentation is possible at CNFs by utilizing overlay WAN technologies like SD-WAN, MPLS, or DMVPN. Carrying SGTs and microsegmentation was much more difficult. One of SD-Access's features, known as SDA-Transit, solves this issue. Figure 2-12 shows how SDA-Transit works at a high level. By building multiple VXLAN tunnels and stitching them together, we can essentially carry SGTs across any WAN transport and have end-to-end microsegmentation. To make this operation work, we need to have border and control plane nodes at the CNFs, and those devices need to be their own sites within the SD-Access site hierarchy. This allows traffic to come out from a remote SD-Access site, leverage SDA-Transit, and send all CNF-bound traffic to border nodes in CNF using VXLAN tunneling. Figure 2-12 shows how the packet flow works with this design.

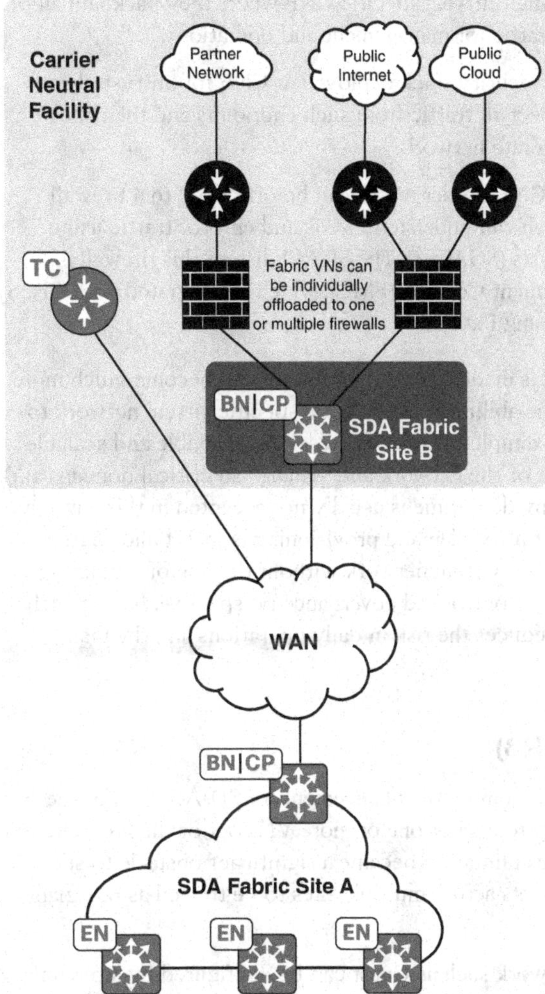

Figure 2-12 *Packet Flow Using SDA-Transit and Border Nodes in CNF*

With this architecture in place, you can bring any virtual network to the CNF using SDA-Transit and then hand it off to the respective device for further connectivity. Some of the use cases of this design are as follows:

- Guest traffic from all the sites can be backhauled to CNF so they can access the centralized Internet.
- Different business units need to prefer different CNFs for cloud or Internet connectivity. Those specific VNs can be configured on selective CNFs to backhaul traffic from all corporate sites.
- Building Management Systems (BMSs) need to pin to a specific CNF for monitoring and management.

- Physical and building security might have a specific CNF where they backhaul all of their surveillance and security traffic for management and operations.
- Organizations might have a full security stack deployed at CNF for untrusted endpoints. Here, they centrally inspect all traffic from such endpoints and then allow them back into the trusted corporate network.
- Virtual network handoffs from CNF border nodes can be offloaded to a firewall like Cisco FirePower series, which can understand SGTs and enforce traffic using Secure Group Access Control Lists (SGACLs). The SGACL list on this firewall is pushed from Firepower Management Console (FMC), which is integrated with Cisco Identity Services Engine (ISE) using PxGrid.

When we observe these use cases, it is evident that this solution can become much more flexible when CNFs are deployed. The ability to hand-pick a specific virtual network to offload it to another site is a prime example of why SD-Access is a flexible and scalable solution. CNF is the core component of the network and, usually, all critical domains and backbones are connected to CNF. Any downtime is usually not accepted in this environment. Another significant benefit of this on-demand provisioning is that it allows for adding, removing, or changing an individual virtual network without the risk of impacting traffic on other VNs. From the change control and governance perspective, having such flexibility and control significantly reduces the risk in daily operations and the maintenance of the network.

Multi-Site Remote Border (MSRB)

Multi-Site Remote Border (MSRB) was a massive enhancement for SD-Access. For the longest time, we lacked the capability to anchor one or more VNs out of the local site to a particular data center or a CNF. This limitation became a significant obstacle to specific networks that required stretched subnets across multiple sites to be treated as one giant virtual network across the fabric.

In MSRB's architecture, a virtual network such as Guest can be configured by stretching on all the sites. This is possible by having a single IP address pool across multiple fabric sites. This IP address pool, which is configured at all the fabric sites, can be anchored to a specific border and control plane node. Preserving the subnet across multiple sites provides a scalable strategy for conserving address space. MSRB dictates that a specific site or a location can be the ingress and egress point for all traffic despite the virtual network spanning across many sites. This has the added benefit of backhauling a specific type of traffic, such as a Guest, to a centralized facility for either inspection, data access, or Internet access. Figure 2-13 shows how Multi-Site Remote Border design operates. In the figure, you can see that VN1 and VN2 are spanned across all sites with local site border and control planes as their exit point out of the fabric. VN3 needs to be stretched, and it is spanned across all the sites using one giant IP subnet, and its exit point out of the fabric is the Multi-Site Remote Border located in CNF. This scenario simulates a typical guest network that needs a centralized Internet exit point. VN4 is only needed at certain sites; hence, it is only configured at site A, but its exit point is still the Multi-Site Remote Border located in CNF. This simulates an example of a development network that needs direct access to cloud and nothing else. In this drawing, one key point to notice is that Site A and Site B border nodes will not have any VN3 and VN4 configuration at all. The edge nodes will establish a direct VXLAN tunnel to the Multi-Site Remote Border. Hence, it is crucial that your WAN supports that additional 50 bytes of VXLAN overhead.

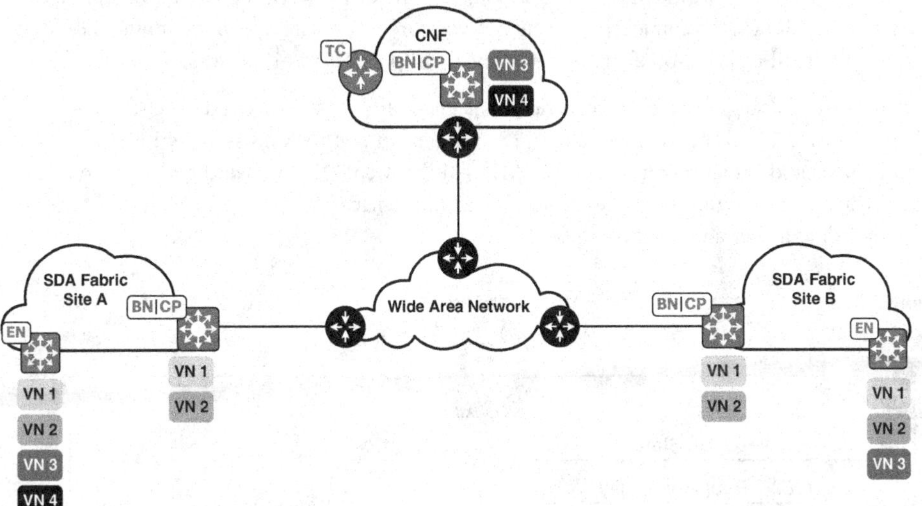

Figure 2-13 *Multi-Site Remote Border Operation in the CNF Environment*

Inter-working with Security Stack

Computer networks have evolved at a drastic pace since the beginning of the year 2020. The need to shift an organization's operations strategy and accommodating workforce from all across the world really drove many innovations. With all the innovations in remote and hybrid work strategies, the most crucial distinction was how security would play a role in the future. Securing the external perimeter of the network is crucial, but securing the internal network and who is allowed to access this network as a trusted user or an endpoint is also equally essential.

With SD-Access and Campus Fabric, security needs to be addressed in two major components:

1. **Network Access Control (NAC):** Determines which user and endpoint are allowed to onboard and access corporate resources.
2. **Perimeter Access:** Secures Internet, partner, or any external connectivity to untrusted domains.

Network Access Control (NAC)

Network access control is a fundamental first line of security to determine who is allowed to connect to the corporate network and access resources. Historically, network access control was not a major concern for most organizations. As technologies evolved and security attacks increased, regulatory compliances were made to specific industries so that some of the country's critical infrastructure was not exposed to such attacks. Industries like manufacturing, finance, healthcare, and the public sector have to adhere to some of the strictest guidelines when it comes to security. With the overall objective of zero trust, all devices connecting to the network are not trusted by default and should go through profiling and posturing before they are allowed network access.

For network access control to be enabled successfully, we would need NAC-capable switches and NAC appliances such as ISE. All current supported Cisco switches support NAC and can communicate with ISE to authenticate the user and endpoint to allow network access. Figure 2-14 illustrates typical authentication message exchanges for onboarding a user and an endpoint.

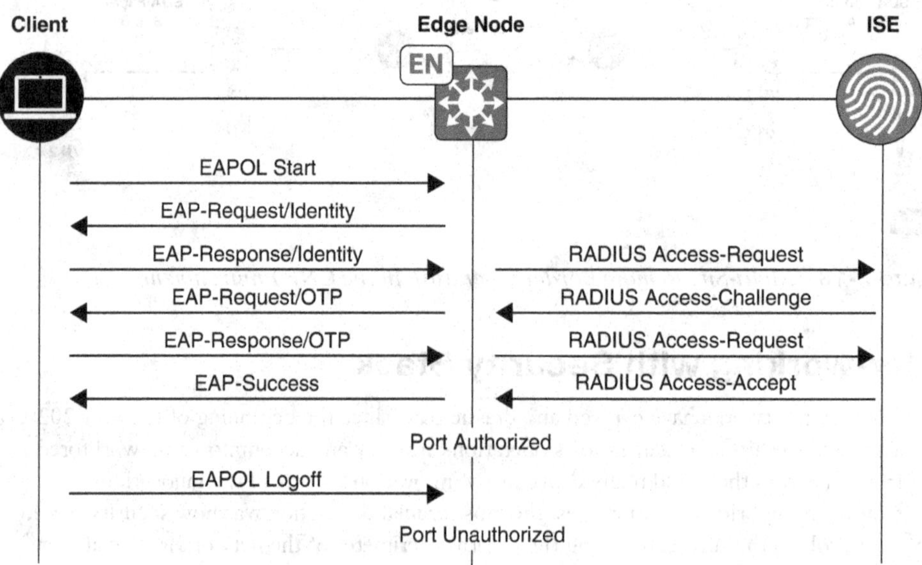

Figure 2-14 *Typical dot1x (RADIUS) Message Exchange*

Usually, not all devices support dot1x authentication. For them, MAC Authentication Bypass (MAB) is usually the fallback method. Figure 2-15 shows MAB message flows. With MAB, depending on the device profile or allowed list configured in ISE, once the MAC address of the endpoint being authenticated is received, ISE allows them similar access to the user to access the network. With dot1x authentication, the methods of authentication could be different. Some standard methods are username and password, device, or user certificate. These parameters, along with other metadata, are sent to the authentication server, which checks its data or any external integrations such as Microsoft Active Directory for the access level. Once verified, this information is sent to the switch, which would configure the correct parameters to allow that endpoint in the right VLAN and with the right level of access.

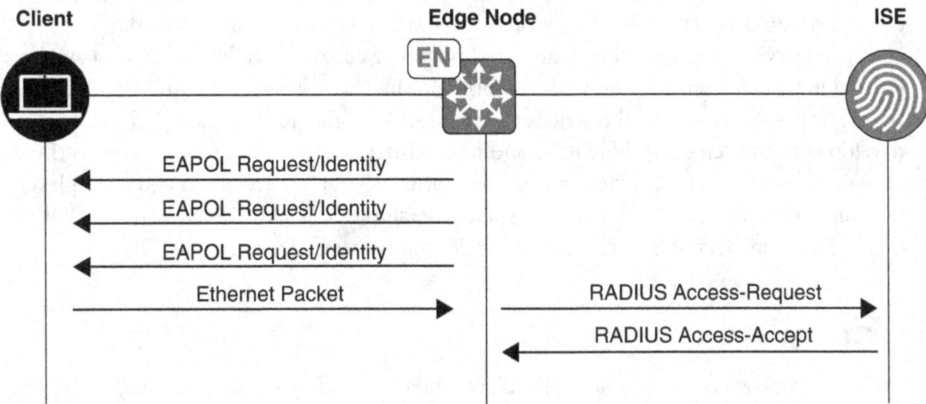

Figure 2-15 *Typical MAC Authentication Bypass Message Exchange*

With SD-Access, all of the configuration related to dot1x on the switch is configured automatically by Catalyst Center. With Catalyst Center being the orchestrator of the fabric network, its integration with ISE allows for automatically onboarding the switches. Catalyst Center also allows a user interface to configure SGACLs, closed, low-impact, or open authentication by default, or even new SGTs. Configuring the number of switches in the network with these authentication policies could become very difficult. Hence, a controller like Catalyst Center becomes essential in deploying such configurations at scale. Regarding Campus Fabric, the lack of a controller has this deployment challenge. However, simple Python scripts and API calls can configure the same configuration and settings. The switch port configuration is identical regardless of the fabric type.

Perimeter Access

With network access control taking care of the onboarding of users and endpoints, perimeter access will act as a shield for any outside connectivity. SD-Access is typically not exposed to the outside world directly because it is at a site level, and there is usually WAN connectivity to a centralized Internet egress point or a CNF. With SD-Access and SD-WAN in place, there are some use cases where SD-WAN can provide Direct Internet Access (DIA) from a local site if they have Internet-based transport. In most cases, Internet access from the site is backhauled to the CNF or a centralized Internet facility due to more advanced security stack to inspect Internet-bound traffic. Overall, when it comes to perimeter security, the fundamental rule is to prevent unauthorized access from outside the network and prevent malware from opening a secure connection from inside the network to outside.

Networks or domains typically connected to the perimeter are Internet, partner, development, cloud, and remote-access VPNs. These networks or connections terminate to dedicated perimeter firewalls. This gives Layer 3 IP firewalling capability and also intrusion prevention system (IPS) functionality to inspect all the packets coming and going through these firewalls. These firewalls and circuits are usually located in data centers or CNFs, which provide centralized points of access. Recalling what we have learned in this chapter thus far, with technologies like SDA-Transit or Multi-Site Remote Border, it is easy to backhaul traffic for networks like Guest for Internet, partner, or development to such central facilities and have a direct handoff from the border to these perimeter firewalls. This provides a clear separation of traffic at a macro and micro level by maintaining security. Figure 2-12 is such an example of backhauling traffic to CNF so that it can be inspected by perimeter firewalls and forwarded across.

Summary

In this chapter, we discussed how SD-Access interacts with other domains and the types of benefits it provides. We looked at the most common integration method used today with SD-WAN. We discussed how Cisco ACI integrates with SD-Access and Campus Fabric. Enterprise MPLS is an ever-growing deployment and, with its macrosegmentation capabilities, easily fits with SD-Access and Campus Fabric. With more organizations adopting the route of CNFs, some of the latest features of SDA-Access, like SDA-Transit and Multi-Site Remote Border, provide the additional flexibility needed to connect branches to data and external connectivity hubs. Last, we looked at how security is critical to the campus domain to ensure the right users are able to connect to the network and also prevent unauthorized network access from the outside. Overall, SD-Access and Campus Fabric are addressing today's need for macro- and microsegmentation for organizations around the globe. With multi-connectivity options, they can be easily integrated with other network domains.

Chapter 3

SD-WAN and DMVPN

In this chapter, we discuss the following:

- Common design strategies in SD-WAN and DMVPN deployments
- How to design and deploy SD-WAN to integrate with other IBN domains
- How to design and deploy DMVPN to integrate with other IBN domains

Overview

Both Cisco Software-Defined WAN (SD-WAN) and Dynamic Multi-point Virtual Private Network (DMVPN) provide the ability to abstract the WAN service provider transports from the enterprise routing environment. Additionally, both provide a means to create and extend macro- and microsegmentation, including support for Cisco TrustSec. This support allows either architecture to be utilized as part of an end-to-end security policy. Cisco SD-WAN has many advantages as an architecture over DMVPN, such as application-aware routing and built-in automation and provisioning; however, DMVPN does have its use cases. Both of these technologies fundamentally provide an efficient way of routing between the sites by providing direct site-to-site communication without the need for going through a centralized hub or a data center.

SD-WAN

Cisco SD-WAN as a technology is discussed in detail in various other Cisco Press texts. The sections in this chapter assume that you are familiar with Cisco SD-WAN. The following sections discuss designing and integrating Cisco SD-WAN with the various other domains as part of a single multi-domain strategy.

SD-WAN and SDA

Cisco's Software Defined Access, or SDA, allows the enterprise to introduce macro- and microsegmentation with automation and assurance at the local campus environment. Hosts may be dynamically or statically classified into virtual networks (macrosegmentation) and security groups (microsegmentation). When discussing SDA, it is important to remember that the control plane is based on LISP, whereas the data plane uses VXLAN.

In a multi-site SDA deployment without integration into other domains, the architect must plan for policy enforcement and ensure that the virtual network identifier (VNID) and security group tag (SGT) information is correctly propagated across either an IP transit environment or via SDA-Transit. SD-WAN allows the enterprise to extend the macro- and microsegmentation end to end in a fully integrated fashion. This way, the SGT information can be propagated across the network without additional resource utilization or reclassification as the data re-enters the SDA environment at the remote location. Even if the remote site has not been migrated to SDA, SD-WAN may be utilized to provide Cisco TrustSec policy enforcement at the remote site without the originating site being aware of the destination SGTs.

Cisco product engineering has supported two methods for integrating SDA and SD-WAN: the one-box and the two-box solutions. One of the most essential points to remember is that inline tagging for SD-WAN is only supported on routers based on Cisco platforms such as the ISR 4000 series, ASR 1000 series, and Catalyst 8000 series. Viptela-based routing platforms, such as vEdge 100 and vEdge 1000, are *not* supported for inline tagging.

One-Box SDA and SD-WAN

One-box SDA and SD-WAN is also known as an *integrated solution*. In this scenario, the SD-WAN Edge router serves as an SDA control plane and also a border node. For this to occur, the Cisco DNA Center must be integrated with the Catalyst SD-WAN Manager via API integration. The SD-WAN Edge will be a part of the Catalyst SD-WAN Manager inventory and be provisioned as a normal SD-WAN device. When the SDA fabric is created, the Cisco DNA Center will update the Catalyst SD-WAN Manager via the API integration to reprovision the SD-WAN Edge with the appropriate SDA configuration. Figure 3-1 shows how a packet changes as it traverses the one-box solution across SD-WAN from one SDA site to another. Notice that the VNID and SGT information is propagated across the network with the data packet itself.

There are distinct pros and cons to the one-box approach that must be considered as part of the overall enterprise design. As will be discussed with the two-box approach, the one-box approach removes support for modularity. This is important to consider because most enterprises are divided into multiple organizational units even when considering who manages which part of the network. For instance, one group may manage the WAN while another manages the LAN campus. The one-box approach will make it difficult for the two groups to manage their respective environments.

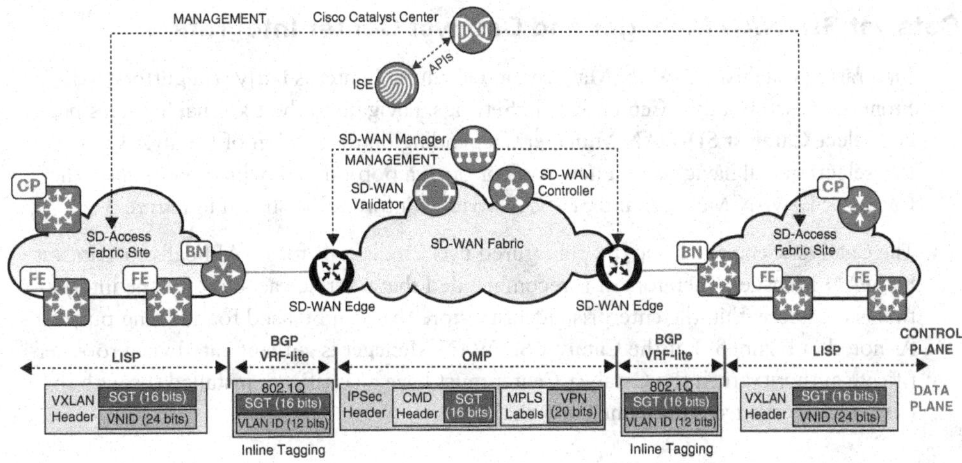

Figure 3-1 *SD-WAN-SDA One-Box Topology*

From a design consideration, it should be noted that the one-box solution requires a router to perform the border node and control plane functionality in the SDA campus. With physical redundancy included, two routers now perform those roles. While this solution works well for the control plane, because the routers have greater routing capabilities, in the data plane, the routers could inadvertently become the logical core of the local area network. In larger locations, additional functional blocks may exist outside of the SDA domain. For instance, where Nexus switches perform a local services aggregation block, an additional pair of switches performing the internal border node functionality at the intended core will better facilitate the required high-speed switching without the traffic traversing the edge routers. Figure 3-2 illustrates how the connectivity between the additional non-SDA fabric at the local site could connect directly to the core of the network while still utilizing the one-box solution. Notice that the core now performs SDA border node functionality. SDA VXLAN traffic that is egressing the location will still utilize the SD-WAN Edges, whereas traffic to these additional services will utilize the core border nodes as their VXLAN termination point.

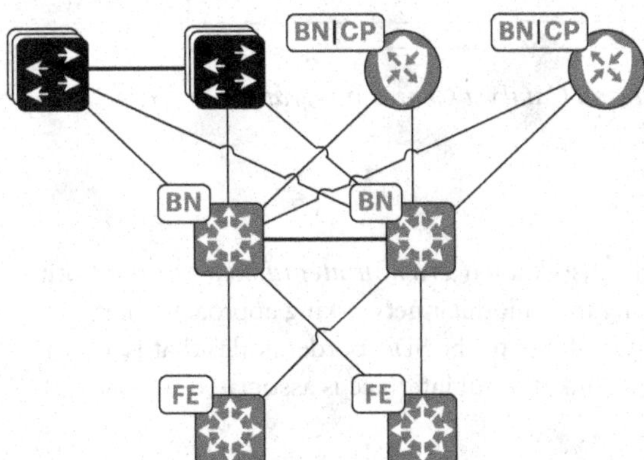

Figure 3-2 *One-Box Topology with Additional Service Domains*

Catalyst SD-WAN Manager and Catalyst Center Integration

Integrating Catalyst SD-WAN Manager and Catalyst Center is fairly straightforward. From the Cisco Catalyst Center System Settings, navigate to the External Services page and select **Catalyst SD-WAN Manager.** Depending on the version of Catalyst Center, this selection will navigate to a new page or open a pop-out, allowing you to enter the Catalyst SD-WAN Manager and SD-WAN overlay information shown in Figure 3-3.

The Catalyst Center will use the configured user credentials for its API calls to Catalyst SD-WAN Manager. Therefore, it is recommended that a service account for the integration is created within the enterprise identity store that can be used for auditing purposes. As noted in Figure 3-3, if the Catalyst SD-WAN Manager is authenticated via a root certificate authority, then the Catalyst Center must have a certificate installed through the Certificates page from the same trust chain.

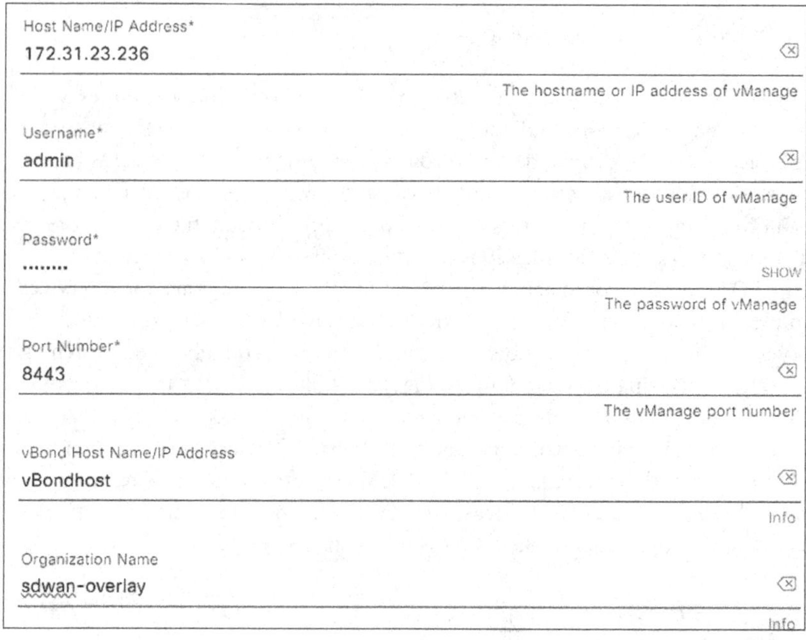

Figure 3-3 *Catalyst SD-WAN Manager and Catalyst Center Integration Process*

Two-Box SDA and SD-WAN

In the two-box SDA–SD-WAN scenario, also known as a *nonintegrated solution*, both architectures are kept separate, providing for a modular networking approach. The SD-WAN Edge devices each have a physical link to the SDA border nodes that is a dot1Q trunk. On the SD-WAN Edge side of the link, the subinterface is associated with a specific service VPN. On the border node side of the link, the SVI provisioned from Catalyst Center is associated with the corresponding SDA virtual network. In this manner, the VLAN becomes the mapping between the SDA virtual network and the SD-WAN service VPN. By enabling Cisco TrustSec (CTS) inline tagging on both sides of the interface, the SGT value may be propagated as well, maintaining both the macro- and microsegmentation of the environment.

From a design perspective, the two-box scenario allows for both a modular design and phased rollouts at the expense of potentially more hardware to install and manage. Figure 3-4 demonstrates how a data packet traverses the two-box solution while maintaining the VNID and the SGT information with the packet itself.

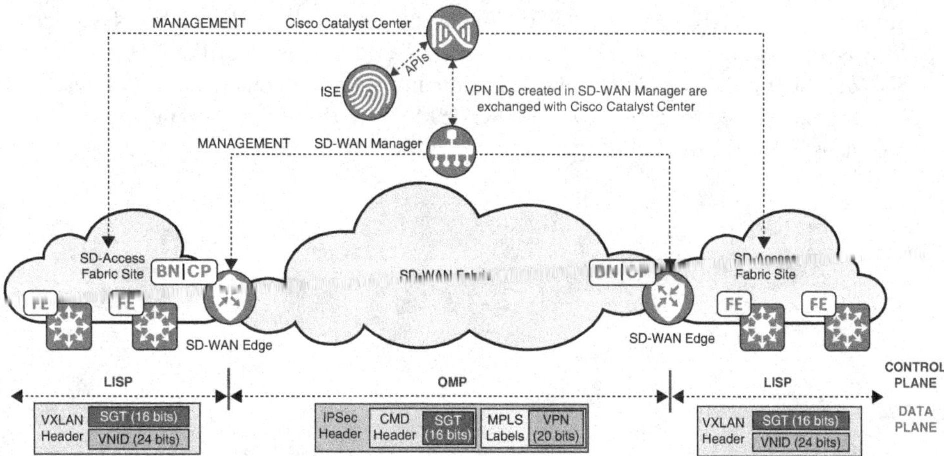

Figure 3-4 *SD-WAN-SDA Two-Box Topology*

SDA and SD-WAN Segmentation

In SDA, the VNID is a 24-bit value used to identify which virtual network a packet traversing the underlay is associated with. When a new virtual network is created in the Catalyst Center UI, Catalyst Center creates a new VNID for it that is constant across all locations. Whenever that virtual network is provisioned at an SDA site, Catalyst Center uses the VNID as the LISP instance ID, which is mapped to the VRF on the switch with the correct virtual network name. The VNID is carried across the underlay as part of the VXLAN header. Additionally, the VXLAN header carries the SGT value. The SGT is a 16-bit value that indicates to which security group the source of the packet belongs.

For data egressing the SDA environment, it is forwarded as a VXLAN packet to the correct border node. After the packet arrives at the border node, it is decapsulated and forwarded based on the VRF instance associated with the VNID. If the destination security group is known by the border node, it will enforce applicable policy. This is not always the case because it would depend on the configuration of the border node.

With SD-WAN, the service VPN ID is inside the IPsec header prior to forwarding on the transport layer. Additionally, the CMD header commonly associated with Layer 2 frames has been added to the IPsec header on an SD-WAN packet to allow the SGT information to be propagated also.

The last piece of the discussion pertains to connecting the SDA environment and the SD-WAN environment together. Whether the one-box or two-box solution is utilized, there must be a consistent mapping between the two architectures. In the one-box solution, mapping is done via Cisco Catalyst Center. After the Catalyst SD-WAN Manager to Catalyst Center integration has been performed as described previously, the individual SDA virtual networks are mapped to specific SD-WAN service VPNs in the Catalyst Center UI. When an SD-WAN Edge is provisioned at an SDA location, the mapping of Service VPN to VNID configured in the Catalyst Center is used. The SD-WAN Service VPN is used as the name of the VRF on the SD-WAN Edge for all of the SDA and SD-WAN appropriate configurations. When the integration is complete, the Catalyst Center page utilized to tie the SD-WAN Service VPN to the SDA virtual network is shown, as in Figure 3-5.

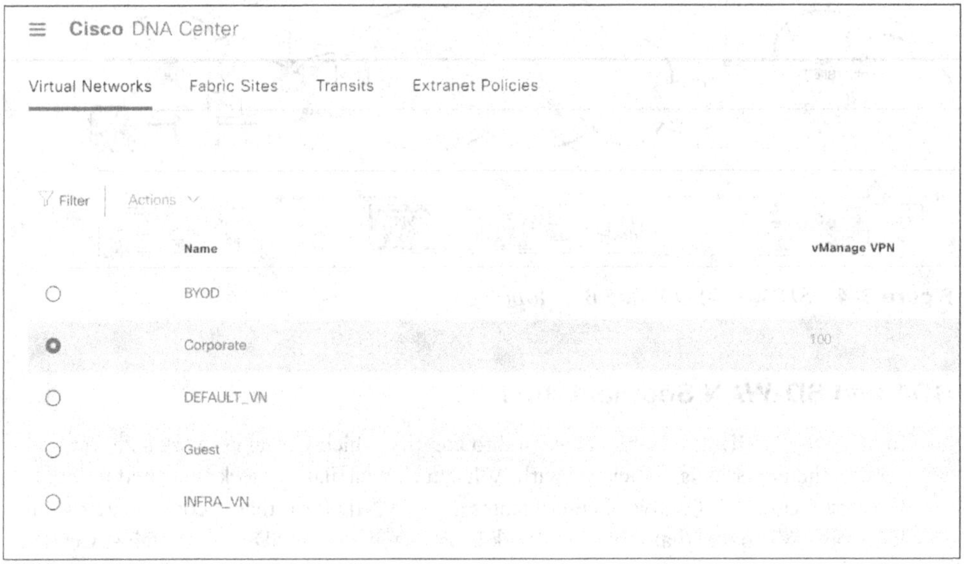

Figure 3-5 *One-Box VNID to Service VPN Mapping*

In the two-box solution, the mapping between VNID and service VPN is achieved through the use of the VLAN carrying the traffic between the two devices. It is critical to standardize the VLAN mapping across the environment. Doing so facilitates easier operation and troubleshooting of a multi-site environment when operations engineers know that a specific VLAN is used to connect SD-WAN Edge to the border node in the SDA Corporate VN and SD-WAN service VPN 500 at all locations. The VLAN mapping ensures that macrosegmentation is maintained; however, support for the microsegmentation propagation must be intentionally added. This is achieved by configuring inline tagging on both sides of the link, allowing the SGT information to be propagated via the CMD header in the frame. Care should be taken to ensure that the device SGT also is trusted on both sides. In Example 3-1, the inline tagging is configured on both the physical interface and the subinterface carrying the traffic. The SGT with ID number 2 is the All Cisco TrustSec Devices SGT.

Example 3-1 *Inline Tagging Configuration*

```
! LAN Interfaces
interface GigabitEthernet0/0/0
 cts manual
 policy static sgt 2 trusted
!
interface GigabitEthernet0/0/0.100
 cts manual
 policy static sgt 2 trusted
!
```

SDA and SD-WAN Best Practices

As is seen throughout this book, standardization across the environment is critical. When creating any standardized mapping, ensure that future proofing is considered. Is there a potential for additional network devices for horizontal scaling at the location? Will additional macrosegmentation be added to the environment that may need to be considered?

The SDA INFRA_VN, or SDA underlay, should be contiguous with a service VPN in SD-WAN. The SDA underlay may be mapped to a unique SD-WAN service VPN or utilize one used by the general corporate VPN. The former allows the underlay management to be reachable from the local environment without traffic leaving the site, and the latter maintains the macrosegmentation requiring traffic to egress the site, possibly fusing the two routing domains together at a centralized firewall environment.

When the SDA and SD-WAN multi-domain environment is built out, it is recommended to build the centralized data center environment first—the services and SD-WAN Edge headend devices. At the remote sites, the process of building and validating the SD-WAN environment first facilitates a smoother transition to deploying SDA.

When Cisco TrustSec is enabled at a site, care should be taken to ensure one device does not become inaccessible. In a location where physical redundancy exists, the engineer should ensure that the SDA devices are accessible across both pathways prior to enabling CTS. Additionally, it is important to remember that CTS must be enabled on the physical and subinterfaces on the link.

In the event that it is a small site with minimal hardware and connectivity—for instance, a single SD-WAN Edge cabled to a single Fabric-in-a-Box (FiaB) switch—redundant pathways may not exist. In this instance, it is recommended to have the CTS configuration as a simple text file on the flash of the switch. The file may be copied into the running configuration on the switch. At this point, the reachability to the switch will be lost; however, all of the configuration in the text file will be applied. The SD-WAN device may then be reprovisioned to include the CTS, restoring the connectivity.

SD-WAN and ACI

Cisco's Application Centric Infrastructure (ACI) allows the enterprise to introduce macro- and microsegmentation with automation and assurance within the data center. ACI uses a structured hierarchy including tenants, contexts, and endpoint groups (EPGs) to create macrosegmentation and microsegmentation. The EPG is similar to the SGT in the SDA and SD-WAN environments. It allows for policy enforcement based on logical group membership.

When SD-WAN and ACI are deployed, the individual macrosegmentation that is created within the DC ACI environment is extended to the remote site location. For instance, the enterprise may provide managed services to their end customers, internal or external, and want to ensure segmentation from the DC to the site. Having an SD-WAN service VPN for each ACI tenant will maintain that segmentation. While the current APIC and Catalyst SD-WAN Manager allow for integration via REST APIs, that integration only supports a dynamic application-aware routing policy signaling from ACI to SD-WAN. Therefore, all of the routing interconnectivity must be performed individually in both environments. For this reason, standardization again becomes important.

Imagine an enterprise environment without SD-WAN or ACI consisting of two data centers and multiple remote locations. This enterprise currently has all of its clients in a single global routing table without any segmentation. Now, they would like to migrate to full segmentation with both ACI and SD-WAN deployed. It will take some time to build the ACI environment and migrate the relevant services into each tenant. It will also take time to migrate each of the individual sites to SD-WAN. How is this performed without issues?

First, we must consider all of the possible traffic patterns. There is traffic from the nonmigrated data center environment to the nonmigrated remote locations through the service provider environment using the current CE equipment. This traffic will exist throughout all the migrations until both the SD-WAN and the ACI migrations are fully completed, although the amount of traffic will decrease with each migration window. As the migrations proceed, there will be traffic from the ACI environment through the SD-WAN environment to the remote locations. At first, this traffic will not exist at all and will increase as migrations occur. There will also be traffic between the nonmigrated data center environment and the new SD-WAN remote locations, as well as nonmigrated remote sites with the newly migrated ACI environment. Additionally, traffic will exist between migrated and nonmigrated sites, and an existing data center with the ACI environment.

All of these traffic patterns will exist in some amount from the beginning of the project until the end. Therefore, from a routing and switching perspective, there are four domains: the SD-WAN environment, the ACI environment, the existing data center, and the existing WAN environment. It is recommended to create an additional routing and switching layer within the data center that performs aggregation and routing between the domains. In Figure 3-6 notice a new aggregation layer has been inserted between the legacy WAN environment, the new SD-WAN devices, the legacy data center services infrastructure, and the new ACI environment. This new layer will allow the routing to drive traffic to the correct blocks based on the destination location—whether already migrated to the new environment or not.

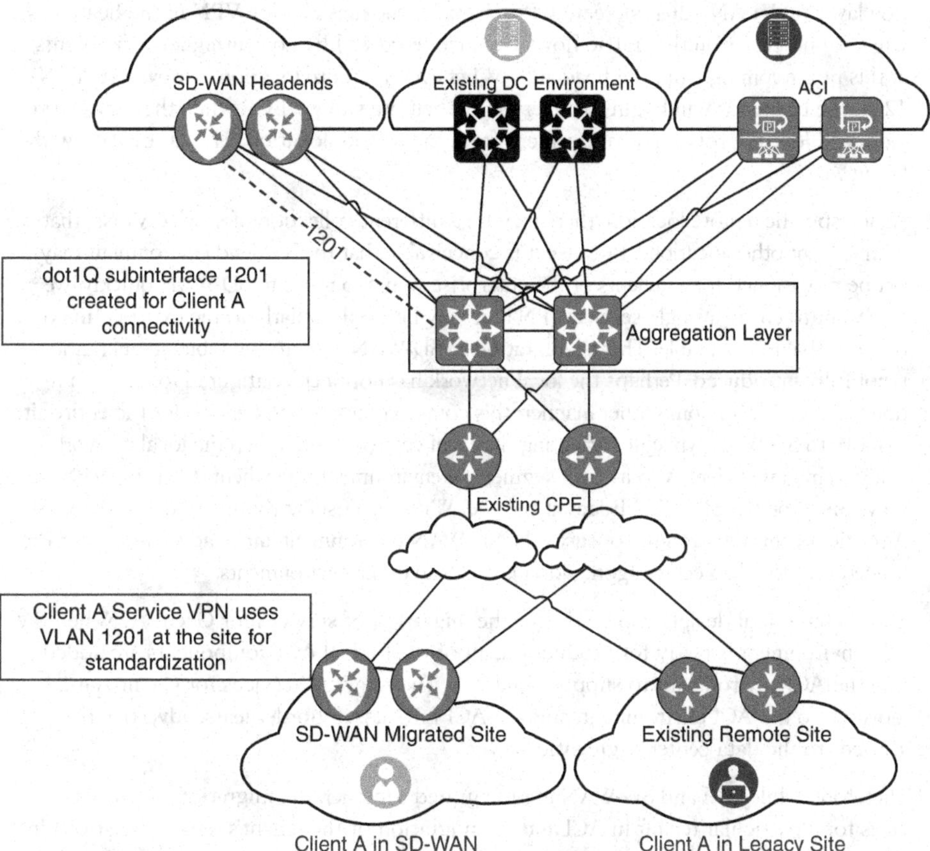

Figure 3-6 *SD-WAN–ACI Topology*

When the environment is designed and implemented, the use of standardized VLANs will facilitate an easier migration per client. After an aggregation layer is created within the data center to facilitate interactions between the environments, the SD-WAN headend devices may be stood up appropriately. When this has happened, the ACI and SD-WAN environments are migrated at their own individual rates. This approach allows the WAN team to focus on just the remote location migrations while the data center team is able to focus on client services.

Consider the migration of Client A. At first, the services for the client exist in the existing data center environment, and the remote locations that service this client all use the global routing table with the service provider. When the aggregation layer and the SD-WAN headends are in place, the migration of the client is transparent to the client, with the exception of the required routing updates during maintenance windows. Perhaps the ACI environment is not built out while the SD-WAN environment is ready for production. The service VPN for this client is provisioned on the headends—for example, VPN 1201. As part of the provisioning, BGP peering between the headends and the aggregation layer on VLAN 1201 is created. Provisioning the new service VPN in the headends will have no effect on the traffic flows because there will be no routing advertisements at this point coming from the headends. Whenever a remote location is moved to VPN 1201, the headends will begin to advertise the remote site via BGP while the service provider will lose the routing advertisement from the remote location. This is the case with Client A.

At any specific remote location, there may be a different collection of service VPNs, that is, clients, from other locations. Because it is conceivable that the headend environment may not be provisioned for all clients or the enterprise wants to move to SD-WAN quickly, we may want to create a single-service VPN that may be used similarly to the existing function of the global routing table. That is, migration to SD-WAN is performed, but segmentation is not fully introduced. Perhaps the local network has not been configured for segmentation via VRF Lite or some other manner; this common service VPN allows for the entire site to move to SD-WAN while not affecting the local environment. When the local network is ready to migrate Client A to its own segmented environment, the Client A service VPN is provisioned on the SD-WAN Edges at the site. With the ensuing routing updates, the Client A traffic for this remote site now uses the SD-WAN environment and is advertised from the headends to the data center aggregation layer to all other environments.

This architectural design also works for the migration of services for Client A. When the ACI environment is ready for production, all of the logical ACI components are added into the ACI environment to support Client A. The required services for Client A are moved into the ACI environment, and the ACI L3Outs, or border leafs, advertise the services to the data center aggregation layer.

Therefore, while ACI and SD-WAN are integrated together, the migration of the services for a particular tenant in ACI and the migration of the tenant's remote locations in SD-WAN may proceed at their own individual pace. The aggregation layer handles the routing between the various environments. As shown in Figure 3-7, the aggregation layer allows a remote site that has been migrated to SD-WAN already to interact with a remote site that has not. The reason is that the SD-WAN headends are advertising to the aggregation layer the SD-WAN remote site prefixes to the legacy WAN environment, and vice versa. With an L3 MPLS offering from the service provider, it is conceivable that these sites are able to send traffic directly to each other across the service provider. However, because the SD-WAN traffic is encrypted while the legacy traffic across the service provider is not, during this hybrid state of migrated and nonmigrated sites, the headends and the aggregation layer must be utilized to interconnect the domains.

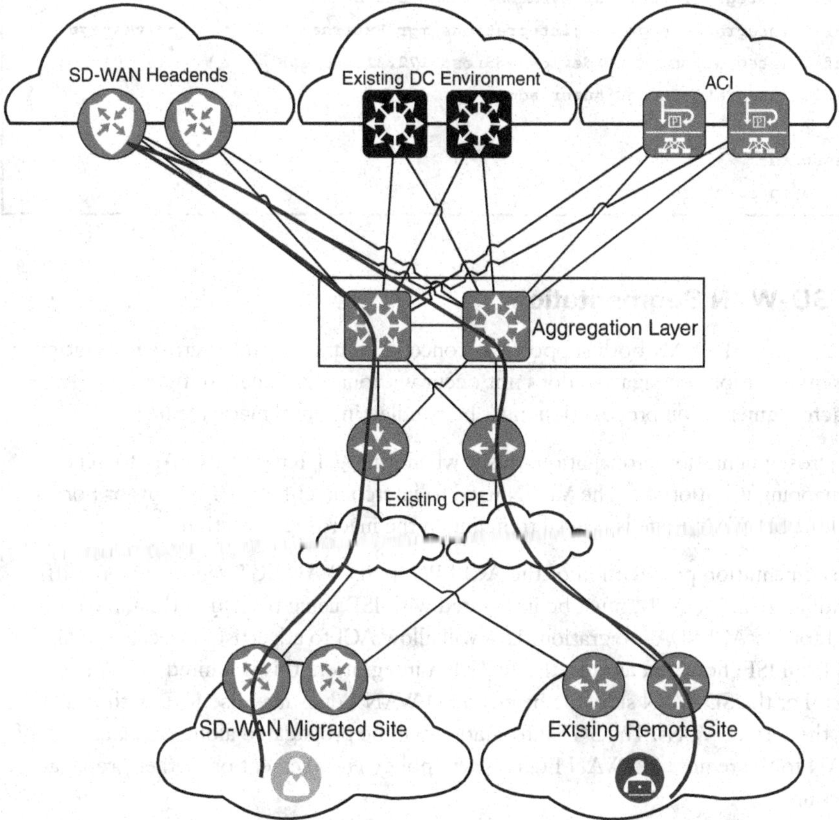

Figure 3-7 *SD-WAN–ACI Traffic Flows During Migration*

Catalyst SD-WAN Manager and APIC Integration

Integration of the Catalyst SD-WAN Manager with the ACI APIC is performed on the APIC itself. A static user on the Catalyst SD-WAN Manager is required for the APIC to communicate with the Catalyst SD-WAN Manager. For security, auditing, and best-practice purposes, it is recommended to use a service account for the integration, as well as authentication via an external identity store. Doing so will facilitate proper user auditing, as well as the ability to manage the account via the appropriate operations processes.

Example 3-2 illustrates the configuration process required to integrate the APIC and the Catalyst SD-WAN Manager together.

Example 3-2 *Catalyst SD-WAN Manager and APIC Integration Process*

```
apic1#conf t
apic1(config)#integrations-group MyExtDevGroupClassic
apic1(config-integrations-group)#integrations-mgr External_Device Cisco/vManage
apic1(config-integrations-mgr)#device-address 172.31.209.198
apic1(config-integrations-mgr)#user admin
Password:
Retype password:
apic1(config-integrations-mgr)#
```

ACI and SD-WAN Segmentation

While ACI and SD-WAN both support the concepts of macro- and microsegmentation, microsegmentation propagation does not occur without additional configuration. Also, the macrosegmentation propagation must be handled in a systematic manner.

For macrosegmentation propagation, this is where the ACI Tenant to VLAN to Service VPN mapping is important. The VLAN used to interconnect the ACI L3Out, or border leaf, to the SD-WAN Edge is crucial to maintain the macrosegmentation.

Microsegmentation propagation of the ACI EPG to SD-WAN SGT values is more difficult and limited. The APIC must be integrated with ISE using pxGrid in the same manner as used for the ACI-SDA integration. This will allow ACI to advertise or receive EPGs to and from ISE; however, as with the ACI-SDA integration, this is limited to a single context. For the SD-WAN side, the headend SD-WAN Edges may use SXP with ISE in any of the service VPNs. The SGT information will be propagated along the data path of SD-WAN to the remote SD-WAN Edge, where policy enforcement or further propagation may occur.

ACI and SD-WAN Best Practices

For ACI and SD-WAN integration together, the two most important aspects are standardization of the handoff between them and the support for migrated and nonmigrated traffic flows. For the former, it is recommended to use a planned VLAN to Service VPN numbering. This approach prevents confusion later when some clients have migrated to ACI while others have not, or when some sites or clients have been migrated to SD-WAN while others have not. For the latter, the use of the aggregation layer with BGP allows the enterprise to connect the legacy and new environments together while using BGP to affect policy routing, if necessary.

SD-WAN with MPLS

Because SD-WAN is designed to utilize multiple independent transports from various service providers, integrating SD-WAN with an MPLS deployment is rather straightforward.

There are numerous reasons why the enterprise may want an SD-WAN deployment while still utilizing an L2VPN or L3VPN MPLS deployment.

The first scenario is quite obvious: migration from MPLS to SD-WAN. In this scenario, the enterprise already maintains a WAN topology facilitated by their MPLS provider and plan to move to SD-WAN, perhaps to take advantage of less expensive broadband circuits. However, there are other scenarios where both the MPLS environment and the SD-WAN environment will coexist by design. For instance, the interconnection between data centers may be through an L2VPN offering that should be maintained even after the remaining WAN has migrated or deployed SD-WAN.

In most scenarios, the primary concern for design and implementation will be on proper route filtering. Depending on the routing protocols utilized within the environment, it is possible to inadvertently cause a routing loop through redistribution, as well as create suboptimal routing. For this reason, it is recommended that all best practices around route redistribution are strictly followed, including marking all prefixes that are redistributed from one protocol to another. This may be via OSPF and OMP tags, BGP communities, and so on.

SD-WAN has various built-in mechanisms to prevent route looping. For instance, when the OMP overlay AS has been configured, this ASN is added to the BGP as-path attribute when the SD-WAN Edge advertised the prefix into BGP. Additionally, when the SD-WAN Edge advertises an OMP prefix into OSPF, the down bit is set. The SD-WAN Edge works in a similar fashion to an MPLS PE node. However, without proper care, the mechanism used by SD-WAN to prevent route looping could be bypassed.

SD-WAN and the Cloud

Over the past several years, enterprises have started to move heavily into the cloud. This is true with many of the largest enterprises that had been traditionally cloud averse. The strong push to a hybrid work environment, as well as the availability of integrating with Secure Access Service Edge (SASE) architectures, has helped facilitate the migration to the cloud. Additionally, SD-WAN itself not only participates in SASE but also offers various solutions via Cloud OnRamp to assist in deploying into the cloud.

Cisco's SD-WAN offers three virtual platforms for extending the SD-WAN environment into the cloud: the CSR1000V, the vEdge-cloud, and the Catalyst 8000v. The first two here are approaching the end of life, so the virtual platform of choice moving forward should be the Catalyst 8000v. Both Amazon Web Services (AWS) and Azure offer the Cat8kv with multiple compute options in various zones and regions. As with any cloud virtual deployment, the compute requirements should be carefully considered based on throughput requirements, as well as overall cost. For instance, there are scenarios where doubling the compute for a virtual SD-WAN Edge in AWS doubles the cost of the VM; however, the throughput of the SD-WAN Edge itself is not doubled. In this scenario, it is more cost-effective to double the number of virtual SD-WAN Edges deployed in AWS. Doing so not only doubles the cost and the compute resources but also the total amount of throughput in the virtual environment. Therefore, horizontal scaling in the cloud is not just a useful practice for applications but also for the virtual network functions.

Discussing the cloud deployment is not dissimilar from any other network deployment. Does the environment constitute a greenfield deployment or brownfield? In SD-WAN, that question is even more important than usual because the current Catalyst SD-WAN Manager versions support only greenfield integration for certain Cloud OnRamp features. Therefore, if, for instance, the deployment already has VPCs in AWS that the enterprise wants to deploy SD-WAN virtual routers into, the Catalyst SD-WAN Manager Cloud OnRamp workflows will not work in that scenario. However, whether it is brownfield or greenfield, the overall design will be the same with the differences coming from how the virtual routers are deployed and maintained.

Either way, the virtual cloud SD-WAN Edge is configured from Catalyst SD-WAN Manager via templates just like any other SD-WAN router. The cloud environment itself may be considered to be another site in the SD-WAN environment. As with all routers, there is a finite number of tunnels and throughput the virtual router may support, so the control policy should be defined to ensure those thresholds are not exceeded.

SIG

One of the fundamental pieces of SASE is Secure Internet Gateway (SIG). As applications have moved to the cloud, such as Microsoft Office 365, the traditional paradigm of Internet direct from the data center or centralized location has created bottlenecks in network throughput because the Internet circuits in the centralized location were not deployed for all of the application traffic. As such, enterprises look to offload the Internet application traffic at the remote site. However, this opens new concerns from a security perspective, especially because the data center environment is normally built with security inspection and defense in depth in mind.

How then do we secure the remote site Internet edge, ensuring that application traffic is inspected without additional hardware? The first part of the answer is SIG. With SIG, the SD-WAN Edge will use API calls to the cloud service, commonly Cisco Umbrella or other third-party vendor solutions. The API calls to the cloud service are used by the SD-WAN Edge to create a direct point-to-point encrypted tunnel to the service provider. With the addition of a SIG service route to steer Internet-destined traffic or specific traffic applications across the SIG tunnel, the remote-site application traffic specified by the policy is sent encrypted to the provider. Depending on the policy and service offering, the provider then performs the required inspection on the application traffic. The provider uses NAT Translation of the application traffic so that return traffic for the application is returned to the cloud prior to sending to the remote site over the encrypted tunnel.

As with almost all technologies in networking, SIG supports redundancy. We may configure active/standby tunnel pairs where one tunnel terminates in one zone or region, and the other tunnel in the pair terminates in another zone or region of the provider. Also, the SD-WAN solution probes across the tunnel to monitor state, so the application traffic may be steered through the data center in the event that the SIG pathway is not viable. Up to four active/standby tunnel pairs may be configured on a single SD-WAN Edge to achieve maximum throughput performance for the SIG tunnels as a single tunnel throughput is capped based on the software version.

In Figure 3-8, traffic destined to the enterprise uses the SD-WAN fabric across the various service providers following the various SD-WAN policies; however, traffic that is destined for the Internet follows the encrypted SIG tunnel to the SIG service provider.

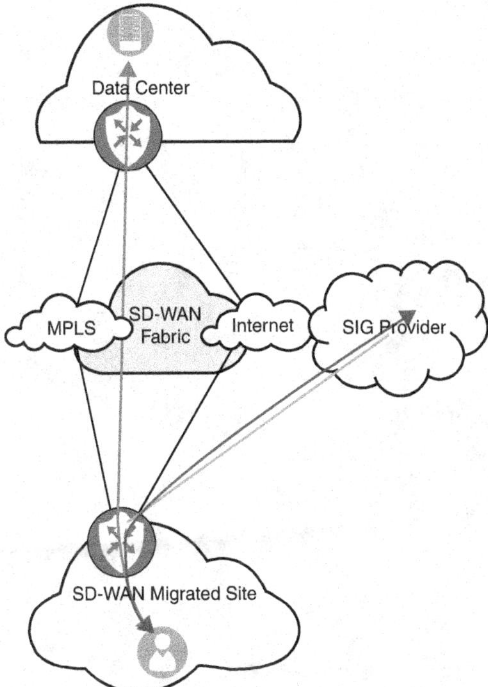

Figure 3-8 *SD-WAN SIG Traffic*

Cloud OnRamp

The Cisco SD-WAN solution offers several enhancements as part of the Cloud OnRamp (CoR) features that facilitate SD-WAN cloud connectivity. Cloud OnRamp for SaaS allows the SD-WAN solution to integrate and properly steer application traffic for select applications that are cloud hosted, such as Office 365, Dropbox, and others. With CoR SaaS, the solution probes the pathway through the DIA circuit from the site, as well as the pathway through the data center via the normal SD-WAN tunnels. Based on the probe performance and configured policy, the SaaS application traffic is steered appropriately between the options. Cloud OnRamp for IaaS handles the provisioning of virtual SD-WAN Edge devices within the cloud provider, AWS, or Azure. As part of the provisioning of the environment, the appropriate VPCs or VNets are configured based on the workflow. Additionally, Software-Defined Cloud Interconnect (SDCI), which evolved from the Cloud OnRamp for Multicloud workflow, allows for the creation of middle-mile topologies. In these workflows, the SD-WAN Edges at remote sites create SD-WAN tunnels to one of the two supported providers, Equinix or Megaport. The provider then provides SD-WAN tunnels direct to the cloud provider over the provider's infrastructure, reducing the requirement on Internet traversal. All of these Cloud OnRamp options may be used separately or together. This scenario is illustrated in Figure 3-9.

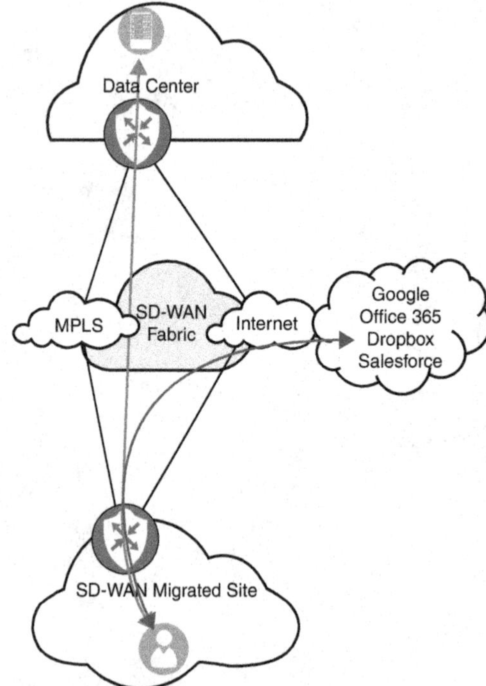

Figure 3-9 *SD-WAN Cloud OnRamp for SaaS*

In this figure, user application traffic destined for one of the SaaS providers uses the direct Internet access at the SD-WAN site directly. All other traffic follows the SD-WAN fabric pathways. Configuring CoR SaaS within Catalyst SD-WAN Manager is fairly straightforward. From the Administration Settings page within Catalyst SD-WAN Manager, enable Cloud OnRamp for SaaS. Additionally, Cloud Services and Catalyst SD-WAN Analytics must be enabled from the same page. This will require entry of a one-time password and cloud gateway URL that are provided at the time of system setup. After the feature is enabled, you can use the Cloud OnRamp for SaaS configuration pages to view and manage how the SaaS applications should be monitored. Additionally, support for SaaS can be systematically deployed across the environment on a per-site basis as required.

Setting up Cloud OnRamp for IaaS or Cloud OnRamp for Multicloud requires associating the cloud service provider account. As of the 20.9 Catalyst SD-WAN Manager UI, the CoR IaaS functionality is moved into the Cloud OnRamp Multicloud page. Because these are enterprise accounts, it is again recommended to follow best practices and security operations requirements around creating a service account for this part. After the appropriate account has been configured within Catalyst SD-WAN Manager using the Associate Cloud Account workflow, the UI allows the user to associate and tag the VPCs that will then be used within the Intent Management. The Intent Management piece is where the branch-to-cloud connectivity is defined within the workflow.

The same workflows allow the user to create middle-mile connectivity through either Megaport or Equinix via the Software-Defined Cloud Interconnect controls. Just as following the workflows allows cloud SD-WAN Edges to be provisioned in AWS or Azure, these workflows allow the circuits between middle-mile locations to be allocated as required. Figure 3-10 shows the various cloud and on-premises environments that may be interconnected via SDCI.

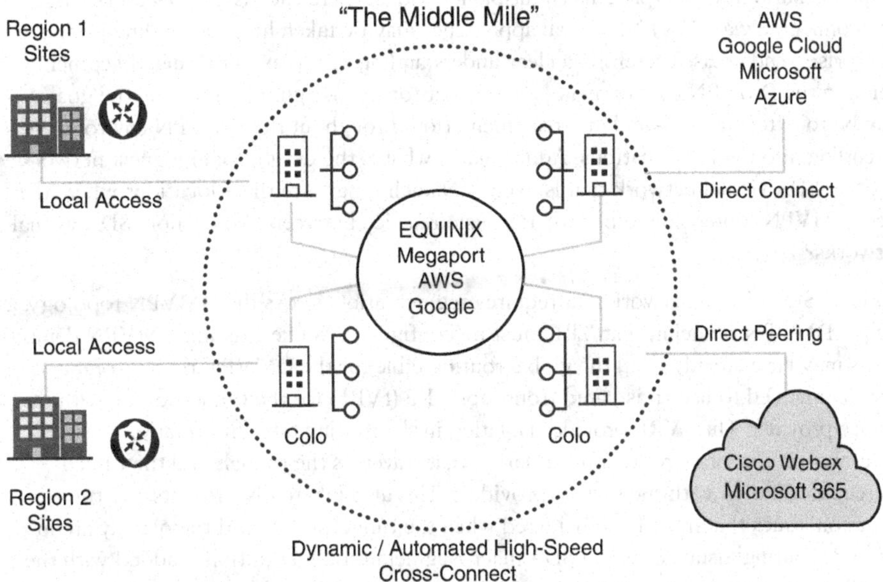

Figure 3-10 *SD-WAN Software Defined Cloud Interconnect*

As shown in the figure, with the SDCI working in the middle of the architecture, SD-WAN is capable of creating dynamic tunnels between sites and the nearest colocation facilities. The facilities themselves then provide direct peering to application providers, direct connection to other cloud services, or global connectivity to other regions and colocation facilities.

DMVPN

Dynamic Multi-point Virtual Private Network (DMVPN) is an older tunneling technology for WAN utilization that allows for simplified configuration of a hub-and-spoke topology while offering support for dynamic spoke-to-spoke tunnels. The technology also includes support for IPsec encryption across the tunnels, allowing for secure communications between all of the enterprise locations.

Similar to SD-WAN, DMVPN is capable of carrying the SGT information across the encrypted tunnel architecture. While there are numerous advantages and benefits when using SD-WAN as compared to DMVPN, numerous DMVPN deployments exist in production today.

The details of how DMVPN itself works are discussed in various Cisco Press texts. For questions on configuring DMVPN, please review those works.

DMVPN and SDA

One of the more common DMVPN multi-domain strategies is the integration with SDA. In this scenario, the enterprise has multiple locations where each is an SDA fabric site interconnected via DMVPN. Several approaches may be taken here, depending on the enterprise's end goals. Therefore, a clear understanding of the extent of macrosegmentation in the DMVPN environment is important for the design. For instance, the goal may be to extend macro- and microsegmentation throughout the DMVPN environment extending into the hub locations. Additionally, what is the design for any guest network or other SDA virtual network that is using VN anchoring? Are there locations where the local DMVPN router should behave as a fusion device between two or more SDA virtual networks?

For each SDA virtual network that requires segmentation across the DMVPN topology, a unique DMVPN tunnel in that VRF must be configured. While existing DMVPN deployments may have already used the global routing table for the DMVPN tunnel source, it is recommended to use an isolated frontdoor VRF (fVRF) for the tunnel source with the service provider. This fVRF provides isolation in the routing table information between the global or corporate routing information that traverses the tunnels and the tunnel source information with the service providers. This also inherently prevents any tunnel recursion issues that must be considered when the tunnel source and the overlay are in the same routing instance. When SDA macrosegmentation integration is added with the DMVPN environment, this will further reduce the overall complexity by having a single VRF used as the fVRF for all of the tunnels across all VRFs.

Note that the various DMVPN tunnels at the spoke sites may not be required at all locations. The tunnel requirement would be based on what SDA virtual networks are configured at a specific location. In Figure 3-11, the red virtual network is extended from one SDA location to one remote location while the blue virtual network exists at both SDA locations and the other remote location. The extension of the SDA virtual network with the DMVPN tunnel topology depends on the placement of the virtual networks, as well as the individual enterprise requirements. From the DMVPN topology to the SDA border node is a dot1Q trunk mapping VLANs to SDA virtual networks. As mentioned in other chapters throughout this book, using standardized VLAN mapping will facilitate smoother and simpler operations in production.

After a DMVPN tunnel has been configured for the respective SDA virtual network, adding SGT inline tagging to the tunnel and the interface between the SDA BN and the DMVPN router will allow for microsegmentation propagation.

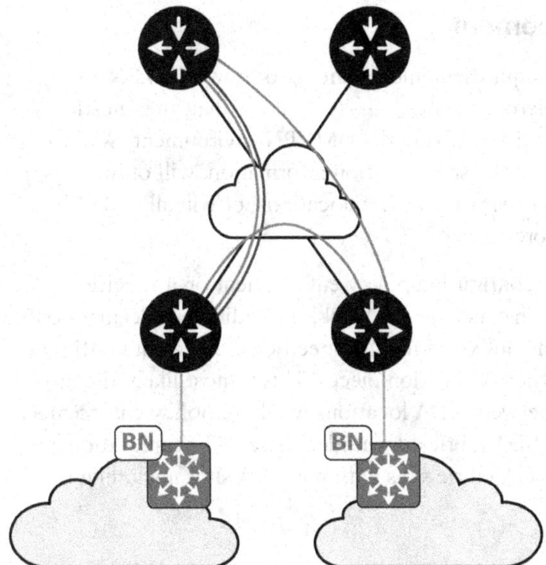

Figure 3-11 *DMVPN-SDA Topology*

Example 3-3 illustrates the use of the frontdoor VRF configuration to isolate the transport while the tunnel interface itself is in the corporate VRF with the SGT value propagated. This sample configuration would be for the headend while the remote site would have the relevant NHRP configuration changes.

Example 3-3 *DMVPN-SDA Configuration*

```
! Per-VN Tunnel Interface
interface Tunnel0
 vrf forwarding Corporate
 ip address 10.0.0.1 255.255.255.0
 tunnel vrf Underlay
 no ip redirects
 ip mtu 1400
 ip nhrp authentication test
 ip nhrp map multicast dynamic
 ip nhrp network-id 100000
 ip nhrp shortcut
 ip nhrp redirect
 ip tcp adjust-mss 1360
 tunnel source GigabitEthernet0/0/0
 tunnel mode gre multipoint
 tunnel key 100000
 tunnel protection ipsec profile profile-dmvpn shared
 cts manual
 propagate sgt
!
```

DMVPN and SDA Policy Enforcement

As mentioned previously, the design requires an understanding of how DMVPN will be utilized to maintain macro- and microsegmentation. As a part of that, the question of policy enforcement should be considered within the DMVPN environment. Will the DMVPN environment simply propagate the segmentation information, will only the headends enforce policy for traffic egressing to the hub locations, or will all DMVPN devices be responsible for policy enforcement?

Based on the answer to this question, configuring policy enforcement on a specific DMVPN device may be required. For instance, if DMVPN is providing enforcement only at the headend locations, then only the hubs will require specific enforcement configuration while the spokes will need only the propagation pieces. This is most likely the most common scenario, as traffic passing between SDA locations will have policy enforcement at the fabric egress point, such as the SDA fabric edge node. There will be migration scenarios where DMVPN is connecting SDA fabric sites with non-SDA sites, including the hub locations.

SDA and DMVPN Best Practices

For migrations to SDA with DMVPN, it would be expected that the DMVPN topology for a single network already exists in the enterprise, and the remote locations are transitioning to SDA. For this scenario, it is recommended to stand up the additional tunnel or tunnels in DMVPN at the hub and required spoke sites first. Routing and connectivity should be validated first prior to the SDA conversion. Here, standardizing tunnel numbers with SDA virtual networks is a good practice to facilitate easier management, operations, and troubleshooting.

Additionally, utilize the existing DMVPN tunnel for the SDA underlay topology. This will ensure that during migration, when devices are being configured in SDA, there will always be connectivity from the SDA underlay management interface with the Catalyst Center in the event that routing or connectivity issues occur in the newly deployed DMVPN tunnels. The overlay traffic will move into the new tunnel topology, leaving just the SDA underlay traffic in the original tunnel system.

DMVPN and ACI

DMVPN with ACI is similar to SD-WAN with ACI with the exception that there is no integration of the APIC with another controller. Just as with the SD-WAN–ACI integration, it is normally expected that macrosegmentation will be maintained between DMVPN and ACI, whereas microsegmentation propagation may not be a requirement. However, just as with the former, microsegmentation propagation may be configured, but again, with the limitation that the EPG mapping is limited to a single ACI context.

As seen in the DMVPN-SDA discussion, multiple DMVPN tunnels will be required on each DMVPN speaker with one tunnel per VRF required for macrosegmentation. It is recommended to use a fVRF for the tunnel source to reduce the complexity associated with ensuring tunnel route recursion does not occur.

Additionally, as discussed in the "SD-WAN and ACI" section earlier, the use of an aggregation layer between the ACI, DMVPN, and legacy environments will facilitate smoother migrations to either ACI, multi-tenant DMVPN, or both.

ACI and DMVPN Segmentation

It is possible with DMVPN to extend both the macrosegmentation and the microsegmentation created in ACI across the WAN topology; however, both are more complicated to configure and manage via the CLI as compared to the Cisco SD-WAN solution.

For macrosegmentation, the DMVPN environment may be made VRF aware by creating multiple DMVPN tunnels on each router for each required VRF. For each tunnel system, a unique NHRP ID and tunnel key should be utilized to ensure the various tunnels remain isolated. The use of CLI templates will greatly reduce the management overhead.

Extending microsegmentation from the ACI environment to the DMVPN environment is much more complicated and requires more manual configuration. In the preceding chapter discussing SDA, the SDA integration with ACI was shown using ISE pxGrid. Via ISE, the ACI EPG information is translated to the Cisco TrustSec SGT information. Using SDA, the Cisco DNA Center facilitates the management of the ISE deployment. With DMVPN, the Cisco TrustSec SGTs would have to be manually administered on ISE and connected to the appropriate ACI EPGs. Additionally, all of the Cisco TrustSec configuration must be manually configured. This would include adding SGT propagation on the DMVPN tunnels themselves, as shown previously, and including SXP peerings to the ISE for each VRF managed.

ACI and DMVPN Best Practices

It is best practice to standardize the DMVPN tunnel numbering for each ACI context with the VLAN used to interconnect the two at the hub locations. If an ACI tenant does not need to be extended to a specific remote site, do not configure that tenant's tunnel at that site. This will limit the number of IPsec SAs required on each router, as well as the number of NHRP registrations.

If macrosegmentation is to be extended to the remote locations, then the macrosegmentation is inherently maintained via the various VRF tunnels. Microsegmentation propagation must be configured, if desired, using inline tagging on the tunnel configuration. For the remote endpoints in DMVPN to support Cisco TrustSec, they will need to support SXP communication with ISE. The scaling of the latter should be carefully considered because one pair of ISE nodes supports only 200 SXP peerings, which are counted as per VRF per device. Therefore, 20 devices with 10 VRFs each can reach the maximum limitation easily. ISE can scale to support 800 total SXP peerings with eight ISE nodes; however, a better scaling mechanism would be to utilize an SXP reflector—a dedicated router capable of handling a higher quantity of SXP peerings. As shown in Figure 3-12, the user creates an IP-to-SGT mapping on the ISE Policy Administration Node (PAN). This also could have been created dynamically by ISE. The IP-SGT mapping is forwarded to the policy node with the SXP support enabled. The SXP Policy Service Node (PSN) will forward the update to the configured peer SXP Reflectors. The SXP Reflector could be an ASR1002HX or a Catalyst 8500 to facilitate the scaling. On the SXP Reflector side, the SXP peerings are per-VRF; therefore, the SXP Reflector updates only the DMVPN remote endpoints that have the specific VRF. Updates are not sent to other locations. When the SXP Reflector system is used, the load is reduced on the ISE environment while increasing the scale limitations. This does increase the count of devices to manage; however, these additional routers may be considered as server functionality similar to BGP route reflectors because they do not need to participate in the data path.

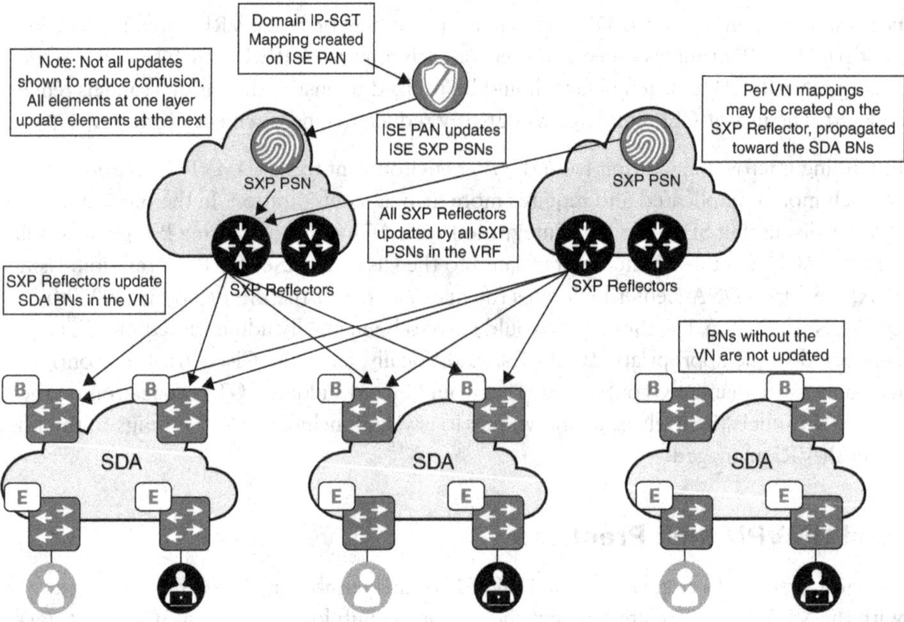

Figure 3-12 *SXP Reflector System*

Summary

Both Cisco SD-WAN and DMVPN solutions integrate well with the other domains, allowing the enterprise to extend the business intent and segmentation across the WAN environment between domains. While both solutions provide macrosegmentation via VRFs and microsegmentation by propagating the SGT value from one side of the WAN to the other, the management and configuration of the segmentation are quite different. For SD-WAN, the Catalyst SD-WAN Manager facilitates management of the SD-WAN Edge routers, whereas DMVPN requires manual configuration or use of another automation tool to manage the configurations. Additionally, DMVPN requires a unique tunnel system for each macrosegmented VRF, whereas the SD-WAN solution uses a single tunnel system with the ability to create logical topologies per VRF. In both solutions, having a single standard, such as VLAN-to-VRF mapping, used at all of the remote locations improves management and operational efficiencies.

Chapter 4

Application Centric Infrastructure (ACI)—Integration and Multi-Domain Capabilities

In this chapter, we discuss the following:

- Cisco ACI overview—ACI Fabric overview, policy model, and forwarding within the ACI fabric
- Cisco ACI multi-domain integration use cases and implementation details:
  - ACI and SD-Access pairwise integration
  - ACI and SD-WAN pairwise integration
  - ACI and MPLS/SR-MPLS pairwise integration
  - Hybrid cloud ACI integration
- General practices, guidelines, and limitations around ACI integration with multi-domain networks

Overview

Cisco ACI is a solution that utilizes a software-defined networking (SDN) fabric to cater specifically to data centers and cloud provider environments. It offers a comprehensive solution for network virtualization at both Layer 2 and Layer 3 levels, making it suitable for organizations seeking a scalable, agile, and multi-tenant network. Before we delve into the technical details of ACI, let's first establish a clear understanding of what an SDN network entails.

Originally defined by the Open Networking Foundation, SDN is a solution that separates the control plane and data plane, allowing direct programming of the control plane. In a typical SDN setup, there is a central control point known as the controller, which handles network management and control plane functions. This controller can be programmed through a graphical user interface (GUI) or a northbound interface using REST APIs (commonly referred to as northbound APIs). To communicate with the network devices, these controllers utilize southbound interfaces (APIs) based on protocols such as OpenFlow, RESTCONF, or OpFlex.

The level and nature of control carried out by an SDN controller can vary. Generally, SDN controllers employ two approaches to interact with networking devices: imperative control (see Figure 4-1) and declarative control (see Figure 4-2). In the imperative approach, controllers handle all control plane functions and explicitly instruct networking devices on how to handle network traffic. This is achieved by sending instructions to program the forwarding tables of networking devices. OpenFlow utilizes the imperative approach. On the other hand, the declarative approach does not completely remove intelligence from the network devices. ACI utilizes a declarative approach, where configuration policies are sent from the ACI controllers (known as Application Policy Infrastructure Controller (APIC)) to the networking devices (such as leafs and Top of Rack [ToR] switches). The responsibility of implementing the policies and setting up the fabric control and forwarding lies with the networking devices.

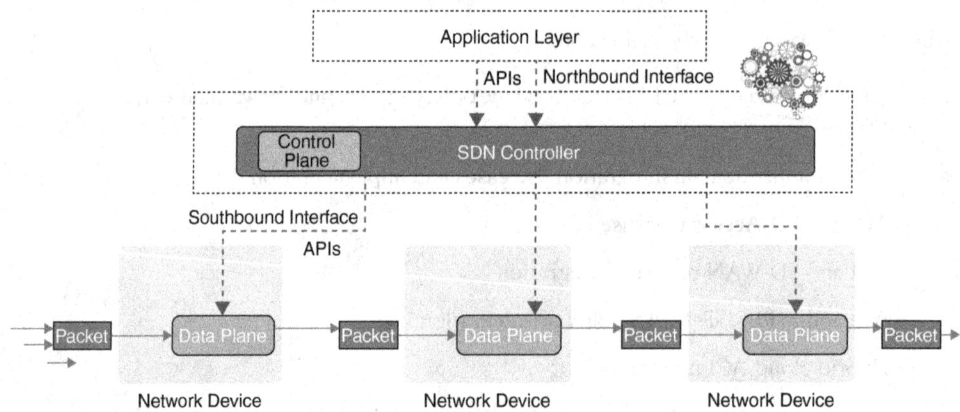

Figure 4-1 *SDN Approach—Imperative Control*

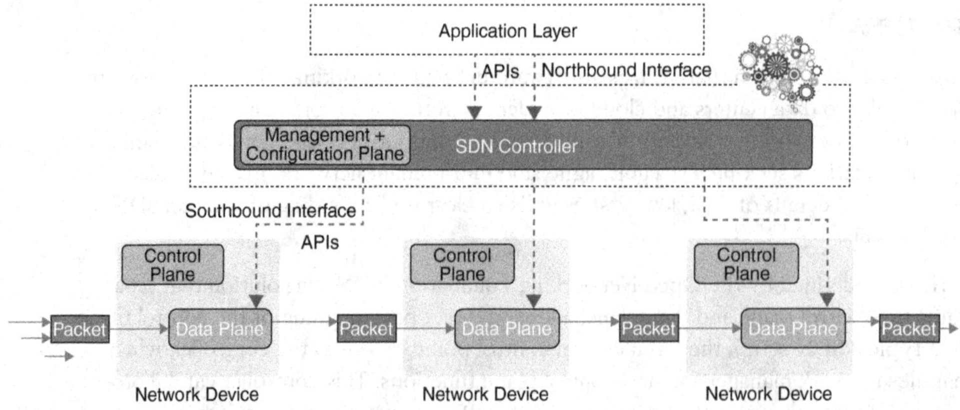

Figure 4-2 *SDN Approach—Declarative Control*

In today's highly competitive business landscape, the success of any organization hinges on the effectiveness of its applications. It is crucial for businesses to swiftly deploy and manage new applications within their networks, while also staying agile in response to the evolving needs of their users and customers. However, there has traditionally been a disconnection between infrastructure and applications, resulting in significant delays between application arrival and user availability. This delay primarily stems from the time-consuming process of provisioning infrastructure resources, such as network, compute, and storage, which can take days or even weeks. Additionally, modern applications are increasingly deployed as microservices, leading to significant east-west traffic between compute nodes hosting these microservices. The dynamic nature of microservices, which are spun up and dismantled within and across domains, necessitates a network capable of supporting compute mobility. Moreover, this network should enable consistent enforcement of security policies within and across domains, while also accommodating compute mobility.

In traditional networks, provisioning infrastructure for applications has always been a manual process involving multiple touchpoints on various infrastructure devices. This method is not only time-consuming and repetitive but also prone to human errors. Moreover, the agile network demands of modern applications, which require support for compute mobility within and across domains, necessitate intricate infrastructure designs and additional network protocol overhead. The increasing need to simplify network operations while expediting the deployment of modern applications is the primary driving force behind the inception of SDN networks in data centers.

The reimagination of data center infrastructure led to the development of ACI, a software-defined networking solution designed specifically for the needs of modern applications in data centers. As a result, the core principles of Application Centric Infrastructure (ACI) were constructed based on cloud-native concepts to effectively support application architecture.

ACI operates on a policy model that separates the network design from the physical infrastructure. Its primary focus is on addressing the requirements of applications in terms of networking, security, and services. This approach enables application needs to be expressed as policies, thereby decoupling the network configuration from the underlying infrastructure. In ACI, every aspect of the network configuration is defined by policies that specify the desired behavior of the network to effectively support a particular application.

For example, in contrast to traditional network practices that involve designing intricate details of routing and bridging using VLAN/VXLAN, VRFs, Layer 2 and Layer 3 protocols, route leak, and route handoff, ACI takes a different approach. In an ACI architecture, an application architect can simply define the application intent using an application profile and create endpoint groups for each component (web, backend, and database). Additionally, security policies, known as contracts, can be defined to govern communication between these groups.

Rather than dealing with the complexities of configuring specific network constructs like VLANs, VRFs, VNIs, IP subnets, and IP ACLs, the ACI controller takes charge. It consumes the defined intent and distributes it to the network devices. These devices then map the intent to the appropriate traditional constructs, effectively abstracting the complexity from the architect responsible for defining the policies.

At its core, an ACI domain is constructed using Cisco Nexus switches arranged in a CLOS fabric (see Figure 4-3), specifically a spine-leaf architecture. This architecture is designed to efficiently support the east-west traffic demands of applications, as discussed earlier. In this setup, the source and destination switches for endpoints involved in east-west traffic are always two hops away from each other.

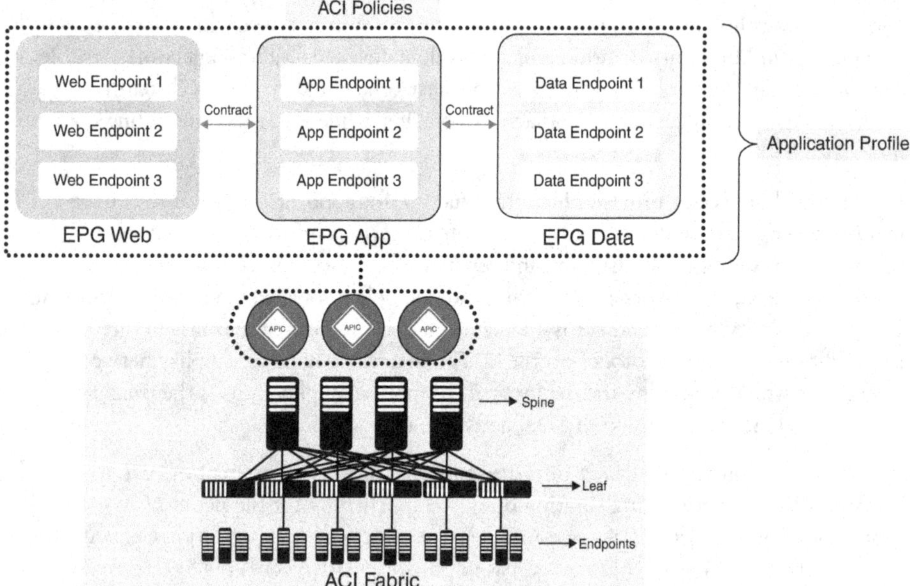

Figure 4-3 *ACI Overview*

Additionally, the ACI controller, known as the APIC, plays a crucial role in the domain. It provides centralized management and handles configuration plane functions for the set of leafs and spines that fall under the control of the APIC domain.

Key Components

Now that we have provided an overview of SDN and ACI, let's dig into some of the key components that constitute the ACI architecture.

OpFlex Control Protocol

ACI employs a southbound protocol called OpFlex to facilitate communication between the APIC and the Nexus Switches within the ACI fabric. OpFlex operates using a declarative control approach, as discussed earlier when comparing imperative and declarative control.

In an imperative control system, the controller explicitly instructs the switches on how they should be configured, providing them with precise instructions and configurations to handle network traffic. However, with the declarative control approach used by OpFlex (see Figure 4-4), the APIC controller asks the Nexus switches to achieve a desired state without specifying exactly how to do so. Instead, the controllers communicate generic policies and intent to the Nexus switches, relying on the switches' intelligence to interpret and translate the intent and policies into locally significant protocols and configurations to reach the desired state. The controller does not have knowledge of the specific steps taken by each device to achieve the desired state; its role is primarily to ensure proper distribution of policies without being in the forwarding path.

Referring back to our previous example of a three-tier application, once the ACI administrator configures the APIC controllers with endpoint groups for each tier of the application and defines the policies that allow communication between these tiers, the controller will render these policies on the Nexus switches. The Nexus switches, in turn, will translate the policies into locally significant VLANs, VRFs, and stateless access-control lists. This translation process enables the switches to effectively implement the intent defined by the policies set by the ACI administrator.

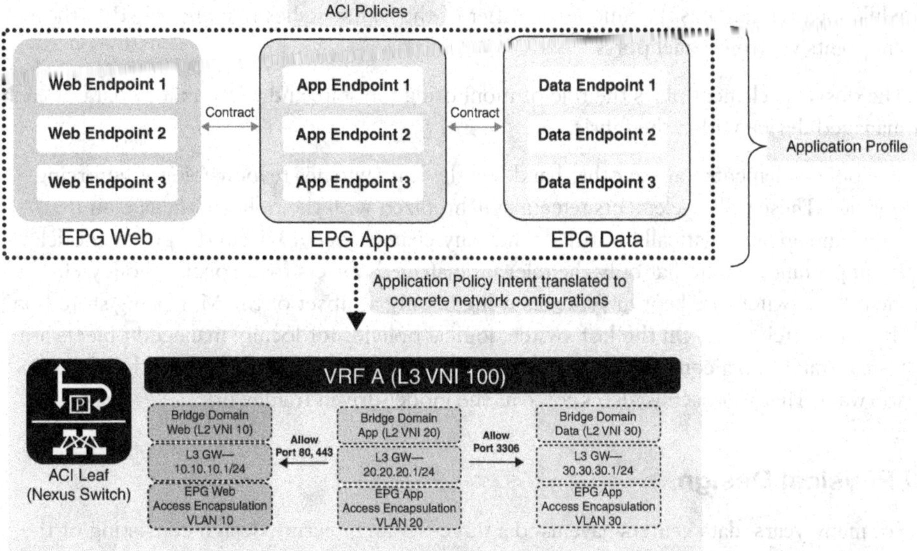

Figure 4-4 *ACI–Declarative Control Approach*

In summary, imperative control emphasizes the specific steps and instructions on "how" to configure networking devices, while declarative control centers around defining the desired outcomes or "what" should be achieved.

In essence, OpFlex operates as a policy-driven system designed to efficiently manage a vast array of networking devices. It achieves this by abstracting policies and relying on intelligent networking devices to interpret and implement them. This reliance on devices to understand and act on the defined policies exemplifies the declarative approach of OpFlex.

The fundamental components of an OpFlex system (see Figure 4-5) consist of

- Policy Database
- Endpoint Database (Mapping Database)
- Observer
- Policy Elements

The policy database serves as a centralized repository that contains all policy definitions established by an APIC administrator. These policies are stored in a structured manner known as the Management Information Tree (MIT), which is discussed further in the "ACI Policy Model" section.

The endpoint database, also referred to as the mapping database, is another centralized database hosted on designated networking devices called Spine switches. It stores crucial information about endpoint identity and location. Endpoint identity includes details such as the IP and MAC addresses associated with endpoints connected to the leaf switches, while location denotes the unique identifier of the leaf switches that are linked to these endpoints via front panel ports.

The observer element plays the role of monitoring the state and performance data of each managed device within the fabric.

The policy elements, on the other hand, are the leaf switches responsible for enforcing policies. These policy elements remain synchronized with the policy database on the APIC and are automatically notified when any changes occur within the policy model. It's important to note that only the relevant managed objects for a specific policy element (leaf switch) are kept in sync, resulting in only a subset of the MIT being stored on the leaf switch itself. On the leaf switch, logical policies for locally managed objects are transformed into a concrete model that can be executed in hardware by the local NXOS software. This approach is also known as the model-driven framework.

ACI Physical Design

For many years, data centers have used a three-tier architecture design consisting of the core, distribution, and access nodes. This design had some inherent limitations, outlined in the "Spines and Leaf Fabric Design" subsection, particularly in addressing the needs of modern-day applications, and the very requirements of these modern-day applications have paved the way to reconsider the three-tier design and have resulted in the inception of a leaf-spine design.

The section provides an overview of the leaf-spine design for an ACI fabric and discusses the benefits of transitioning to leaf-spine fabric-based infrastructure for modern-day data centers.

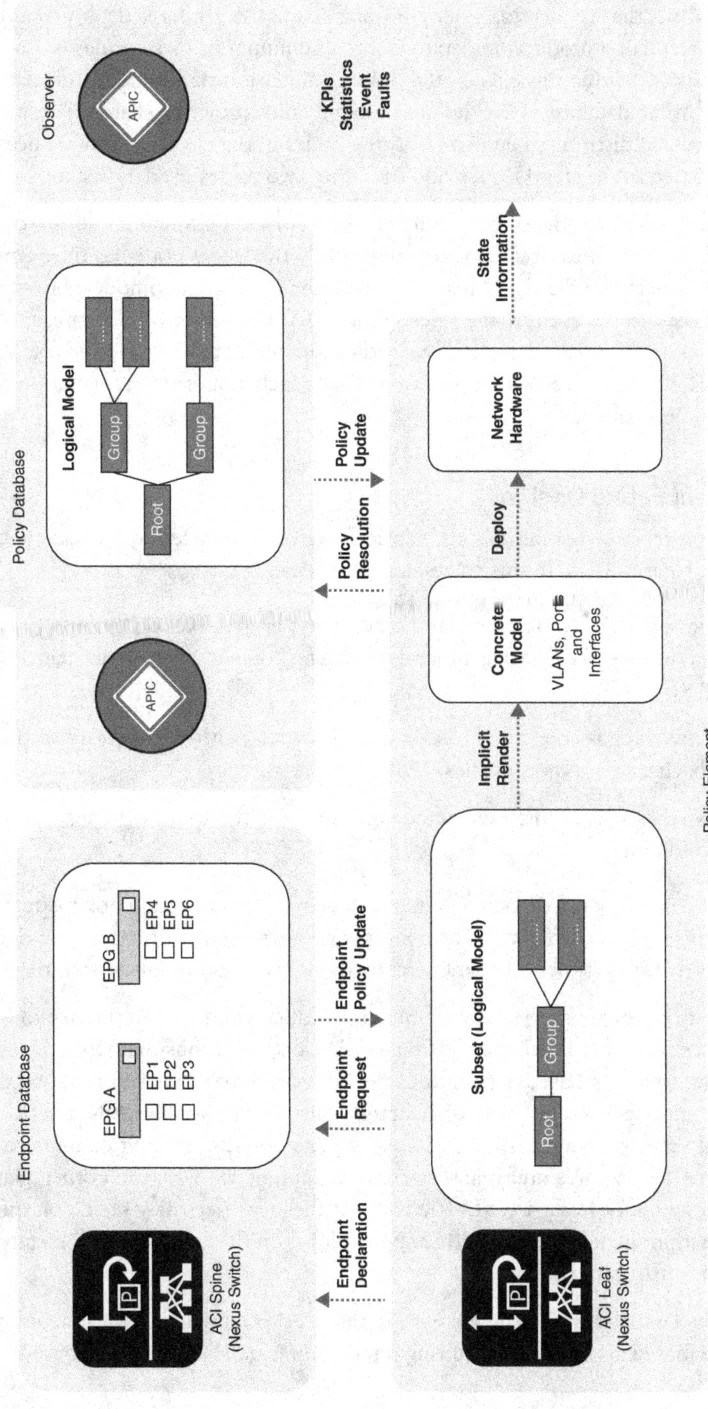

Figure 4-5 *ACI–OpFlex Logical Model*

Application Policy Infrastructure Controller

In an ACI fabric, the Application Policy Infrastructure Controller is deployed as a clustered controller. For a production deployment, a minimum of three nodes is required for the APIC cluster. Within this cluster, the policy database is distributed, and each managed object in the database is divided into atomic units known as shards. These shards are replicated and distributed among the three nodes in the cluster, with one node of the three designated as the shard leader, and the other two nodes used as backup.

When a change is made to a policy for a managed object, a minimum quorum of two shards must be present to execute the change. Only the leader node has the authority to write the change to the shard and distribute it to the other backup nodes, provided that a quorum exists. In the event that the leader node (APIC controller) becomes unavailable, the two other nodes in the cluster will negotiate among themselves for the role of a new leader. As long as there are two shards available to reach a quorum, write actions or policy changes will be permitted.

Spines and Leaf Fabric Design

The ACI infrastructure's spine and leaf fabric design is influenced by the clos network, named after Charles Clos. In this spine-leaf fabric design:

- Endpoints, which can be bare-metal servers, hypervisor-based computes, or networking devices like firewalls or load balancers, connect to the front panel ports of the leaf switch.
- Each leaf switch is connected to every spine switch, with the majority of deployments having two spine switches.
- Leaf switches are not interconnected, and similarly, the spine switches are not interconnected either.

There are two primary traffic patterns in a data center: east-west and north-south traffic flows. North-south traffic flows involve ingress and egress of traffic from the data center, while east-west traffic flows refer to lateral flows between endpoints within the fabric.

East-west traffic flows have become dominant in data centers due to the rise of microservices-based applications. Unlike monolithic applications that rely on single systems, microservices-based applications are built on distributed multi-system capabilities. Each component within these distributed multi-system applications functions as an independent service. As a result, a single query to an application built on a microservices architecture often requires multiple services to communicate with each other, generating a significant amount of east-west traffic flows as these services may reside on different endpoints within the fabric. Monolithic applications, on the other hand, typically exhibit north-south traffic patterns.

Other factors contributing to the increase in east-west requirements within data centers include distributed applications requiring replication (e.g., Hadoop), distributed compute (e.g., Docker and containers), and east-west VM migration for applications deployed on hypervisor platforms.

Unlike traditional three-tier architectures, a spine-leaf fabric reduces the number of hops required for east-west traffic flows. At any given time, an east-west traffic flow in a spine-leaf fabric will transit through a maximum of three hops: the source leaf, the spine, and the destination leaf. This is possible because each leaf is connected to a spine, resulting in a full mesh topology. Consequently, the number of hops and latency for east-west traffic flows in a spine-leaf fabric are predictable, unlike in a three-tier architecture where an east-west traffic flow could potentially transit through only a distribution node or both the distribution and core nodes, depending on the location of the endpoints. This indeterministic traffic pattern in a three-tier architecture can impact latency and time-sensitive applications.

Additionally, the spine-leaf architecture enables horizontal scaling and incremental expansion. It allows for the fabric to be expanded horizontally to accommodate increased scale by adding new leaf switches and connecting them to the existing spines in the fabric. Alternatively, additional links can be added from the existing leaf switches to the spines, providing oversubscription on the spines to support bandwidth-intensive traffic flows and applications. Importantly, these expansion and modification processes can be carried out without impacting live production traffic.

Nexus Dashboard Orchestrator

In certain deployments, it is necessary to have separate ACI fabrics with independent APIC clusters to meet specific requirements related to fault isolation, availability, and change management. In such multi-site deployments with active-active requirements, it becomes crucial to support Layer 3 and Layer 2 extension between the sites, which, in turn, entails extending control plane exchange (MP-BGP Ethernet VPN) between the sites, implementing a common overlay (VXLAN for end-to-end encapsulation), and ensuring end-to-end security policy definition and enforcement.

The ACI Nexus Dashboard Orchestrator (NDO), previously known as Multi-Site Orchestrator (MSO), serves as the conduit for extending network and identity information across multiple fabrics or ACI sites through a unified management interface (see Figure 4-6). ACI NDO facilitates namespace normalization between the different sites. Each site utilizes a local namespace, where a local pool of identifiers (IDs) is used to identify VRFs and endpoint groups (EPGs) within that specific site. However, when there is a need to extend network and identity semantics across multiple sites, namespace normalization becomes necessary. The role of ACI NDO is to instruct the local APICs at each site to program translation tables on their spines, allowing for ID translation to enable inter-site policies and inter-site communication. In summary, ACI NDO provides a single touchpoint or "manager of managers" to configure and interconnect separate ACI sites, including Cloud ACI sites that are managed by their respective controllers (APIC cluster, Cloud APIC [Cloud Network Controller] instances in public cloud).

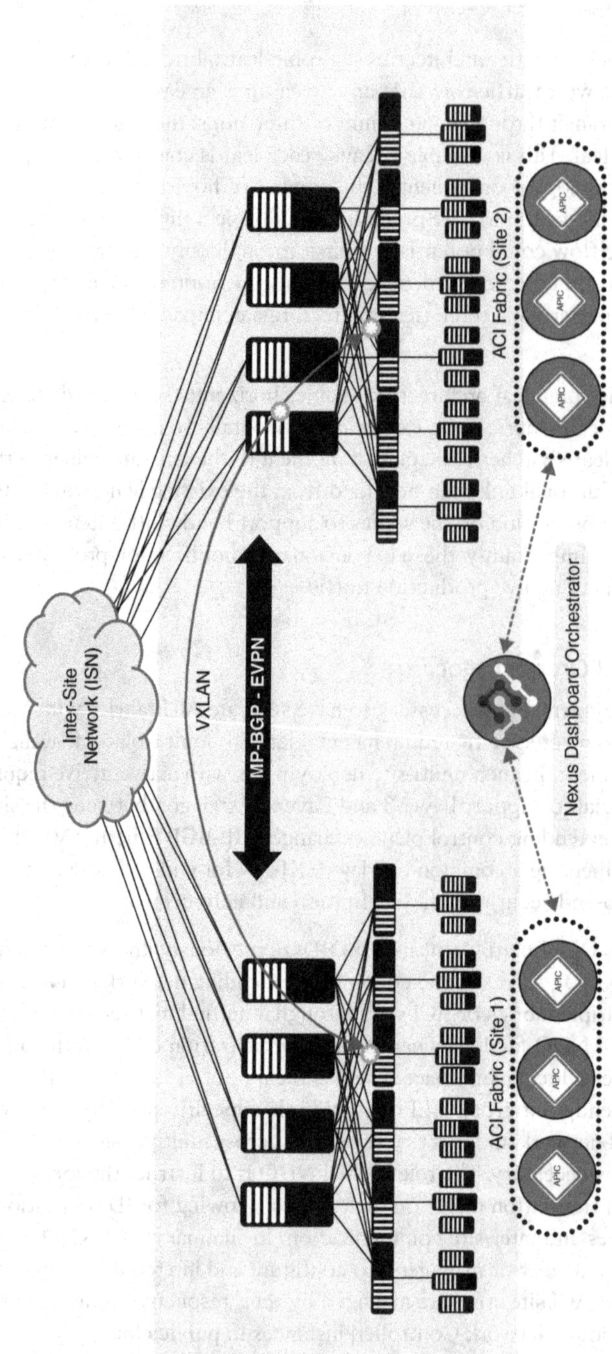

Figure 4-6 *ACI–NDO + Multi-Site Architecture*

ACI Policy Model

The ACI fabric consists of both physical and logical components, such as physical switches and logical configurations like tenants, bridge domains, endpoint groups, and contracts. These components are managed by policies and stored in the Management Information Tree within the policy database on the APICs.

Each physical and logical component is identified as a managed object (MO) within the MIT and is organized in an object-oriented data structure in the policy database. Each MO is assigned a distinguished name (DN) and contains properties that describe its relationship to other objects in the hierarchy, including parent–child relationships (1:1 or 1:N mapping), object attributes, and the relative and absolute path of the object within the hierarchy. For example, all policies configured under the tenant object, such as VRFs, bridge domains, and endpoint groups, will be direct or indirect children of the parent tenant object. Similarly, all objects defined for access policies, such as VLAN encapsulation for front-panel ports and interface types (access ports, port channels), will be direct or indirect children of the infra tenant object.

Tenant Policies

Tenants serve as logical containers where application requirements are defined, including application profiles, application endpoint groups, and contracts. Figure 4-7 illustrates the hierarchy of the tenant object and its relationships with other objects in the hierarchy. Direct lines represent direct parent–child relationships (1:1 or 1:N), while dotted lines indicate indirect relationships (1:1 or 1:N) between objects in the hierarchy.

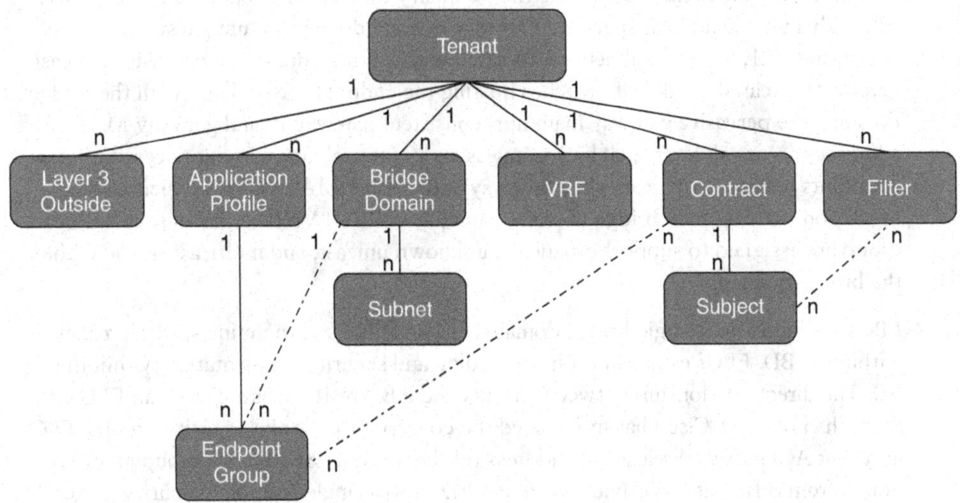

Figure 4-7 *ACI Tenant-Managed Object Hierarchy*

From a policy perspective, a tenant acts as a logical isolated unit that can represent different suborganizations or business units within an organization, or different lifecycles associated with applications within an organization (e.g., production, development, user-acceptance testing). However, there is also an option to relax the logical isolation by defining a common tenant, where managed objects and policies are not isolated and can be shared with other tenants in the policy database.

Layer 3 network segmentation within tenants is facilitated by VRF-managed objects. With VRFs, multiple logical routing units can coexist within a network device, allowing for the existence of several Layer 3 (L3) services, even with duplicate IP address spaces. Communication between VRFs can occur through a Layer 3 fusion device external to the fabric or through route leaking within the fabric. Each VRF is assigned a VXLAN virtual network identifier (VNID), which is covered further in the routing and forwarding subsection.

An application profile serves as a logical container to group endpoint groups for an application. For our previous example on a three-tier application, each tier of the application can correspond to a group of endpoints grouped together in an endpoint group within an application profile, that is, an individual endpoint group for each web, backend, and database endpoints placed together in one application profile representing the three-tier application.

An endpoint group is a logical grouping of endpoints that share similar functions and have similar security and network policy requirements. Endpoints, such as VMs, containers, or bare-metal servers, can be grouped into EPGs based on factors like their Layer 2 encapsulation, IP and MAC addresses, or any other unique identifier learned by ACI through federation with other virtual domain managers.

In ACI, bridge domains (BDs) define the boundary for Layer 2 broadcasts. While VRFs establish a unique address space, each bridge domain defines the unique subnet space within the VRF. When a subnet is associated with a bridge domain, a pervasive/anycast gateway is created on all leaf switches hosting the endpoints associated with the bridge domain. The pervasive gateway maintains consistent gateway IP and gateway MAC addresses across all leafs, enabling seamless endpoint mobility without necessitating endpoints to repeatedly learn their gateway address and MAC via ARP when relocating. Upon creating each bridge domain, a unique VXLAN VNID and a unique multicast group are assigned to support broadcast, unknown unicast, and multicast traffic within the bridge-domain.

EPGs are linked to a single bridge domain (BD) and are used to define security zones within the BD. EPGs establish both forwarding and security segmentation within the BD. The direct relationship between an EPG and a BD restricts associating an EPG with more than one BD. Cisco has introduced the concept of endpoint security groups (ESGs) in recent ACI software releases to address this limitation. ESGs enable grouping of endpoints from different EPGs under different BDs into a single endpoint security group, but further details on this enhancement are beyond the scope of this book.

EPGs can also be utilized to reference endpoints and prefixes for endpoints external to the fabric by employing *external EPGs*. These external EPGs are associated with the Layer-3 Out (L3Out) construct, which consists of external routing configuration policies governing forwarding and security segmentation for traffic flows external to the fabric. More information on this is covered in the "ACI and SD-Access Pairwise Integration" section.

ACI follows a white-list model, meaning that any inter-EPG communication between two EPGs is not allowed unless there is an explicit contract (policy) in place. This contract defines the ports and protocols permitted for communication between the two EPGs. Within the EPG–Contract relationship, an EPG can function as either a consumer or a provider of a contract. When an EPG provides a contract, other EPGs can initiate communication with it based on the rules defined in the contract, including specific ports and protocols. Likewise, when an EPG consumes a contract, the endpoints within that EPG are allowed to communicate with endpoints in the EPG that provides the contract, following the rules outlined in the contract.

Access Policies

Access policies in ACI determine how endpoints, such as VMs, containers, and bare-metal servers, are connected to the ACI fabric. These policies need to be defined before tenant policies can be established. Figure 4-8 illustrates the hierarchy of the access policies in ACI.

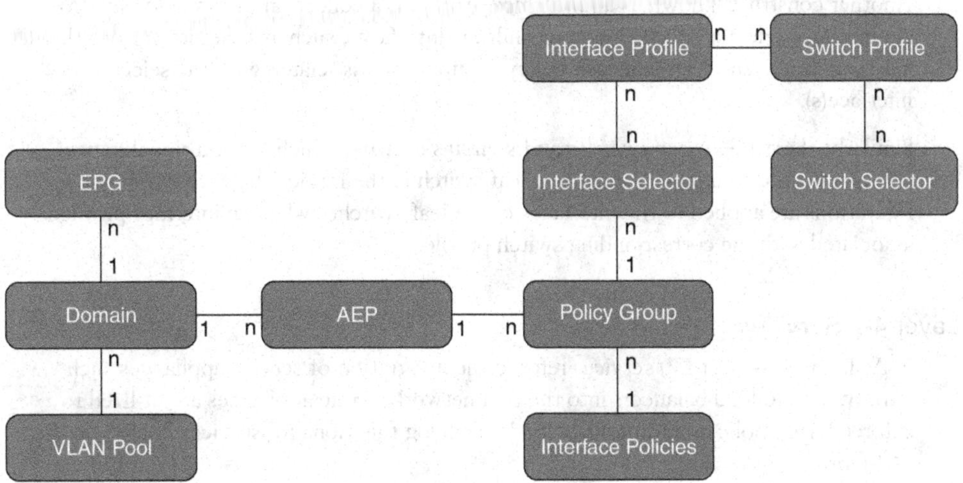

Figure 4-8 *ACI Access Policy Objects*

All endpoint groups within an ACI fabric are associated with a domain. A domain specifies the VLAN pools that can be linked to an EPG. VLANs in ACI are used to identify the mapping between endpoints and EPGs when traffic is received on the front panel ports. When traffic arrives on a front panel port, it can be either untagged or tagged. In the case of tagged traffic, if there are multiple encapsulations associated with a trunk port, the encapsulation is used to determine the specific EPG to which the endpoint belongs. In situations where ACI controller integration with Virtual Machine Managers

(VMMs) like vCenter or OpenShift is not available or other means of endpoint-to-EPG mapping identification are not present, the VLAN encapsulation on the front panel port helps identify the associated EPG. Organizations often designate specific VLAN groups for different purposes, such as shared services (e.g., DNS, NTP, AD services) or for distinguishing between production and development workloads. The combination of VLAN pools and domains in ACI allows for the desired level of segmentation, controlling which endpoints can use certain VLANs and which VLANs can be associated with specific EPGs.

Attachable Access Entity Profile (AAEP or AEP for short) is another logical construct that governs the association of VLAN pools with leaf switch interfaces, rather than with EPGs. AEPs define the binding of VLAN pools from a domain to leaf switch interfaces. This provides an additional level of enforcement, ensuring that only specific leaf interfaces or switches designated for specific endpoints and EPGs can be associated if the AEP allows the relationship between the switch interface and domain.

ACI utilizes several logical constructs to define and apply link layer policies to front panel ports (switch interfaces). Individual link layer policies, such as LLDP, CDP, Link Speed, and Link Aggregation Type, are defined using *interface policies*. These interface policies are then grouped together using an *interface policy group*, allowing for the collective application of these policies to interfaces.

Another construct, known as an *interface profile*, is a collection of *interface selectors*. An interface selector specifies one or multiple interfaces, such as Ethernet 1/1 or Ethernet 1/1-10, and references an interface policy group to be associated with the selected interface(s).

Similarly, there are *switch profiles* and *switch selectors*, which are additional logical constructs used to uniquely identify a leaf switch in the fabric. The access policy configurations are applied to the interfaces of the leaf switches when an interface profile is associated with the corresponding switch profile.

Layer 4-7 Services

In ACI, Layer 4-7 (L4-L7) services refer to the integration of service appliances such as firewalls and load balancers into the ACI network. These appliances are utilized to enforce L4-L7 policies and perform load-balancing functions for services hosted on the ACI fabric.

The L4-L7 appliances, which can be physical or virtual network functions, are connected to the front panel ports on the leaf switches. ACI provides various policy objects, such as service graphs and Layer-3 Outs, to facilitate the integration of these appliances. These policy objects enable routing of traffic to the service appliances either by using routes in the VRF routing table or through policy-based routing (PBR) to redirect traffic.

Service graphs consist of function nodes that reference the L4-L7 device, as well as terminal nodes (provider and consumer EPGs). By using service graphs, it is possible to chain multiple L4-L7 functions together in a single policy. For example, all external traffic received on the ACI fabric can be filtered and inspected through an L4-L7 firewall and then subjected to load balancing using a load balancer.

While routing traffic to an L4-L7 appliance can be achieved through routing tables, PBR provides an alternative method of routing traffic using policies. With PBR, specific traffic, destined for an endpoint group, can be redirected to an interface on the L4-L7 device, initiating the chain of function nodes before reaching the EPG.

Routing and Forwarding in ACI Fabric

Routing and forwarding semantics within the ACI Fabric are covered in this section.

VXLAN Overlay

Traditional networks have relied on VLANs (dot1q) to achieve segmentation in multi-tenant networks. The VLAN ID field in the Ethernet header is limited to 12 bits, allowing for a maximum of 4096 network segments. While this may seem like a substantial number, it falls short of the segmentation requirements for modern enterprises and service providers who may need to support hundreds of users or customers. Additionally, VLANs require the use of protocols like Spanning Tree Protocol (STP) to establish a loop-free topology for each network segment or group of segments. However, STP has a known vulnerability where a failure in one part of the network can bring down the entire data center or campus network, more so, STP also results in the shutdown or blocking of half of the network bandwidth to maintain a loop-free topology. To address these limitations, Equal Cost Multipath (ECMP) networks and Virtual Extensible LAN (VXLAN) were introduced.

VXLAN is a tunneling protocol and overlay scheme that enables the extension of a Layer 2 network over a Layer 3 underlay network. Each VXLAN segment is identified by a 24-bit VXLAN Network Identifier (VNI), which allows for over 16 million segments compared to the 4096 segments supported by VLAN IDs.

In ACI, the functioning of VXLAN is straightforward. As traffic enters the ACI fabric, it is encapsulated in VXLAN (using a UDP datagram and MAC-IN-UDP encapsulation) on the source leaf switch. The encapsulated traffic is then forwarded across the fabric through the spines, and upon reaching the destination leaf switch, it is de-encapsulated, policies are applied, and if the policies permit communication for the traffic flow, the traffic exits the fabric. The leaf switches and certain spine switches responsible for encapsulation and de-encapsulation are referred to as VXLAN Tunnel Endpoints (VTEPs).

Please refer to Figure 4-9. The outer IP header's source IP address is the address of the source leaf switch, also known as the source VTEP. On the other hand, the destination IP address of the outer IP header is the address of the destination leaf switch, known as the destination VTEP. If the destination endpoint's IP/MAC address is unknown, the destination IP address of the outer IP header will be the Anycast VTEP address on the spine switches. It's important to note that the spine switches host the endpoint database for all endpoints connected to the ACI fabric. In cases where the source switch is unaware of the destination endpoint's location, it will forward the traffic to the spines for destination lookup. This process is commonly referred to as Spine Proxy.

Figure 4-9 also includes the VNI field. The VNI is populated either with the VRF VNI or the BD VNI, depending on whether the traffic is being routed or bridged. If the traffic received on the source leaf switch has a destination MAC address that matches the pervasive gateway (GW) configured for the subnet associated with the bridge domain (BD), it indicates that the traffic needs to be routed. In this case, the VNI used will be the L3 VNI associated with the Virtual Routing and Forwarding instance. On the other hand, if the destination MAC address does not match the pervasive gateway MAC, it implies that the traffic needs to be bridged. In such cases, the VNI used will be the L2 VNI associated with the bridge domain that is associated with the endpoint group on which the source traffic was received.

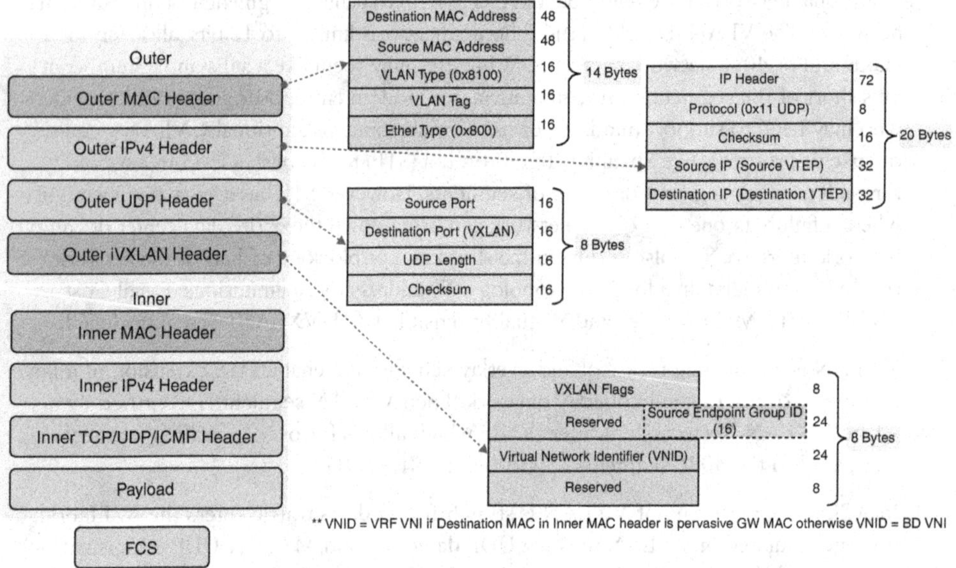

Figure 4-9 *ACI–iVXLAN Encapsulation*

The ACI VXLAN deployment, also known as intelligent VXLAN (iVXLAN), utilizes the reserved field in the VXLAN header to carry the identifier for the source EPG. This identifier is used on the destination VTEP to perform the lookup for security policies. Security policies, which are configured through contracts, are enforced on the destination VTEP. Similar to traditional access control lists (ACLs), contract policies are programmed in hardware using a source and destination identifier. In traditional ACLs, we use source IP and destination IP addresses to identify the source and destination endpoints. However, with contracts in ACI, we use the source EPG identifier and destination EPG identifier to identify all the source and destination endpoints belonging to those respective groups.

Endpoint Learning and Council of Oracles Protocol (COOP)

In ACI, each leaf switch maintains a forwarding table that includes entries for both local and remote learned endpoints, referred to as the endpoint table, as well as entries for local and remote IP prefixes, known as the longest prefix match (LPM) table (see Figure 4-10).

For Layer 3 traffic, when a leaf switch receives a packet, it first looks up the endpoint table for the destination IP (/32). If a matching /32 entry is found, it forwards the traffic accordingly. However, if no /32 entry is found, the leaf switch then looks up the LPM table for non-/32 IP route information to determine the appropriate forwarding path.

For Layer 2 traffic, the leaf switch performs a lookup in the endpoint table using the destination MAC address. If the MAC address is known, the traffic is forwarded accordingly. In cases where the destination MAC address is not known, the leaf switch either floods the traffic within the local bridge domain associated with the endpoint group for the endpoint or forwards it to one of the spine switches for further processing.

When a leaf switch receives a packet with a specific source MAC address (MAC A) on a front panel port, it learns and registers MAC A as a local learned endpoint entry in the endpoint table. Similarly, when a packet with a specific source IP address (IP A) or an ARP request with a sender IP A is received on a front panel port, the leaf switch learns and registers IP A (/32) as a local learned endpoint entry in the endpoint table. Additionally, the leaf switch learns MAC A as a remote entry in the endpoint table when it receives Layer 2 traffic with MAC A as the source from the spine switches. Similarly, IP A is learned as a remote entry when Layer 3 traffic with IP A as the source is received from the spines.

The longest prefix match table in ACI primarily contains entries for pervasive subnet routes (non-/32s) for local bridge domain subnets on the switch. Additionally, if there is a contract relationship between the source leaf switch and the destination leaf switch, the LPM table will also include pervasive BD subnet routes for remote BD subnets. The LPM routes for remote BD subnets are programmed with the next-hop set as the anycast VXLAN Tunnel Endpoint address on the spine switches to facilitate Spine Proxy.

The LPM table also incorporates external routes obtained from sources outside the ACI fabric. These routes are learned on a specific set of leaf switches known as *border leafs* and are then redistributed into the Multi-Protocol BGP (MP-BGP) route table on the fabric, on a per-VRF basis. The other leaf switches in the fabric download these external routes, using MP-BGP, into their local routing tables based on the locally configured VRF instances. By programming pervasive routes in the LPM table, the fabric can identify the local subnet routes. If there are no matching pervasive routes (non-/32 routes) and a default route is learned from an external routing source, the leaf switch will forward the traffic to the border leafs for external routing. On the other hand, if there is a matching pervasive route, the traffic will be encapsulated in VXLAN and sent to the anycast address on the spines.

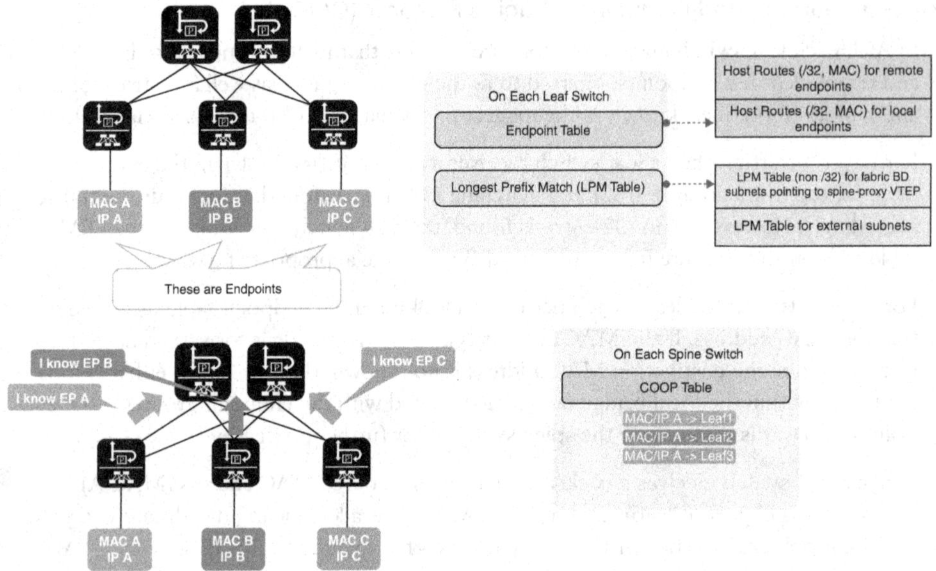

Figure 4-10 *ACI–Endpoint Learning*

Endpoint learning in ACI is based on the concept of endpoint identity and endpoint location. *Endpoint identity* refers to the IP address (/32) and MAC address associated with the endpoints, while *endpoint location* refers to the VTEP associated with the leaf switch where the endpoint is learned.

When a local endpoint is learned by a leaf switch, it adds the identity of the endpoint (IP address with a /32 subnet and MAC address) to its local endpoint table. Subsequently, the leaf switch reports this information, along with the location of the endpoint (the local switch's VXLAN Tunnel Endpoint, or VTEP), to one of the spine switches using the Council of Oracles Protocol (COOP). The spine switch maintains an endpoint database that includes entries learned through COOP from all leaf switches. It ensures that this database is synchronized with other spine switches in the fabric using the same COOP protocol. As a result, each spine switch possesses a comprehensive record of every endpoint in the system, often referred to as the *mapping database* or *endpoint database*.

Because this database is accessible to every leaf switch, a leaf switch does not need to broadcast traffic for unknown Layer 3 destinations. If a leaf switch does not have information about a specific remote endpoint (with a /32 subnet) in its local endpoint table, it can look up the LPM table for the pervasive subnet route associated with the remote endpoint. Based on the results of the lookup, the leaf switch forwards the packet either to the spine switches (for fabric subnets) or to the border leaf switches (for external subnets). If the traffic is directed to the spines for a fabric subnet, the spine switch will examine the endpoint database for the endpoint's IP address (/32) and send the traffic directly to the destination leaf switch (commonly known as Spine Proxy) (see Figure 4-11). However, if the spine switch is not aware of the remote endpoint's IP address (/32), assuming it might be a silent host, the spine switch will perform an ARP glean to request the address (if ARP flooding is enabled for the bridge domain subnet) or simply drop the traffic (if ARP flooding is not enabled).

In the ACI fabric, any Layer 2 broadcast traffic, including multi-destination traffic, Layer 3 unknown multicast traffic, within a bridge domain, is flooded throughout the fabric within the corresponding BD. This flooding is achieved by utilizing a designated multicast group specifically assigned to that BD. When the BD is initially created, these multicast groups are automatically assigned, and all participating leaf switches in the BD join the multicast tree associated with that group. Forwarding tags (FTAGs) are used to load-balance multi-destination traffic as it traverses the multicast tree. This FTAG is embedded in the packet's destination multicast address. Spine switches and intermediate leaf switches then forward the multi-destination traffic based on the FTAG IDs. At any given time, only one link forwards traffic per FTAG between any two nodes in the fabric. Each spine switch has the potential to act as the root for one of the FTAG trees. The ACI fabric can support a maximum of 12 FTAGs. If a leaf switch has a direct connection to a spine switch designated as a FTAG root, it will use the direct path to connect to the FTAG tree. If there is no direct link, the leaf switch will utilize one of the transit nodes that is connected to the FTAG tree. Having a larger number of FTAG trees improves load balancing within the fabric.

Figure 4-12 illustrates the forwarding for multi-destination traffic broadcast/multicast traffic using the FTAG tree.

When a leaf switch receives traffic for unknown Layer 2 destinations or ARP requests and does not have a local or remote entry for the destination MAC address, it has two options. First, it can flood the traffic within the local bridge domain associated with the source endpoint group, causing it to be flooded to all leaf switches participating in the BD. Alternatively, it can proxy the traffic to the spine switches for endpoint database lookup. The decision to flood or proxy the traffic to the spines for unknown Layer 2 destinations and ARP is a configurable setting within the BD configuration.

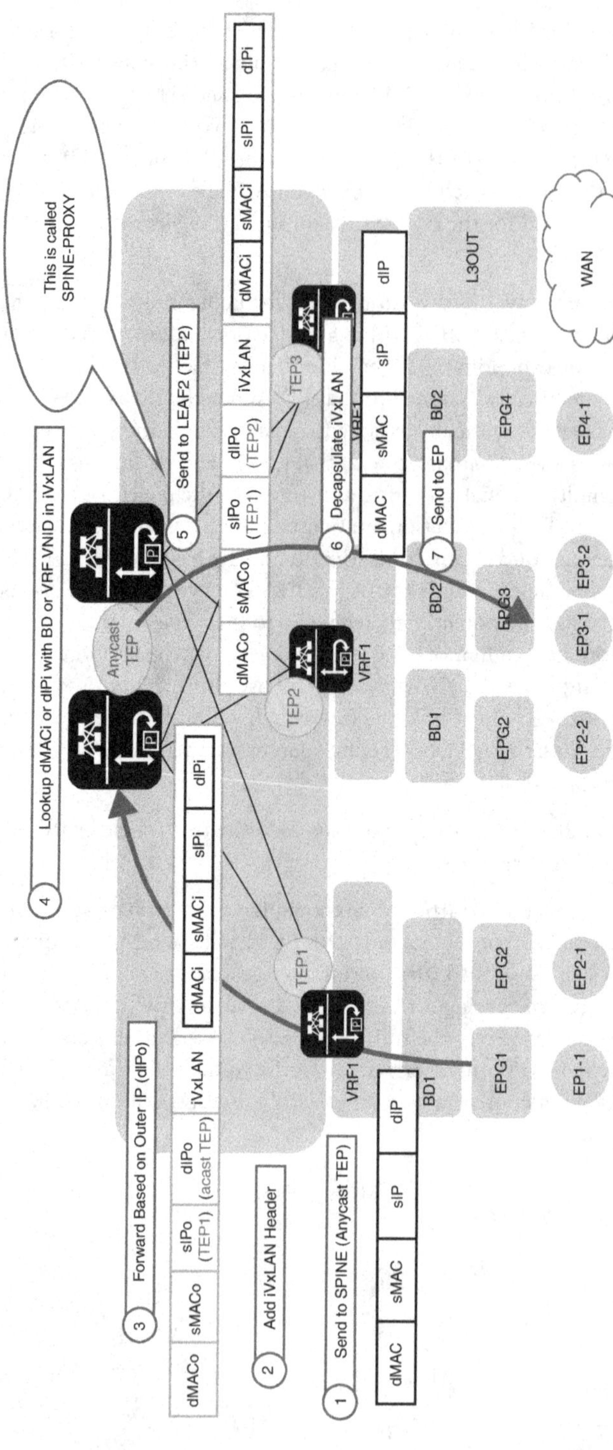

Figure 4-11 *ACI–Spine Proxy*

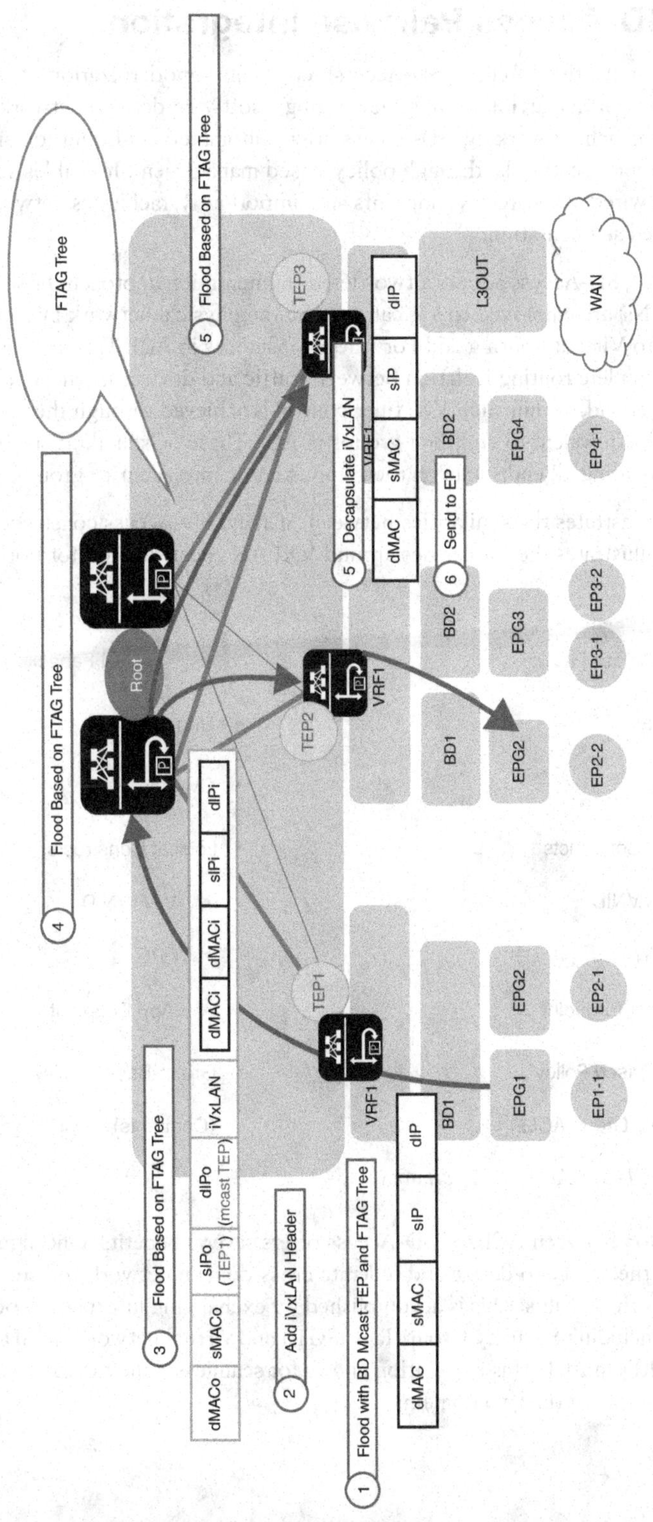

Figure 4-12 *ACI–Flood with FTAG tree*

ACI and SD-Access Pairwise Integration

Cisco Software Defined Access (SD-Access) represents a modernization of traditional enterprise networking architecture by leveraging a software-defined networking approach for campus/branch networking. SD-Access offers automated configuration and deployment of enterprise networks through policy-based management. It enables seamless mobility for wired and wireless endpoints and, importantly, facilitates network and identity-based segmentation.

Similar to ACI, SD-Access adopts a two-tiered segmentation approach. First, virtual networks (VNs) are employed to logically divide the physical network into distinct segments, akin to Virtual Routing and Forwarding instances in ACI. This macrosegmentation allows for complete routing isolation between traffic and devices in one VN compared to another. Second, within each VN, finer control is achieved through the use of scalable groups (SGs), equivalent to endpoint groups in ACI. These SGs facilitate microsegmentation by segmenting all endpoints on the campus fabric into security groups.

Figure 4-13 illustrates the similarities between ACI and SD-Access constructs, and Figure 4-14 illustrates the similarities around VXLAN encapsulation for both ACI and SD-Access.

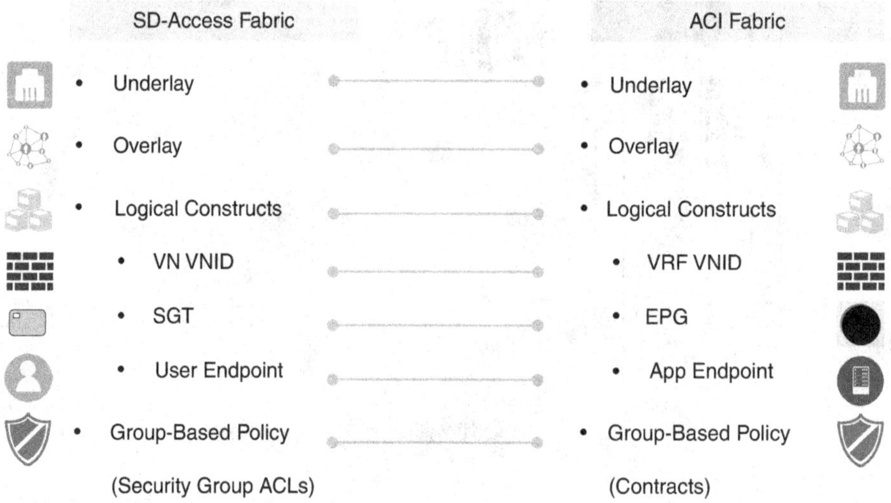

Figure 4-13 *ACI–SD-Access Constructs*

The integration between ACI and SD-Access offers several benefits. One significant advantage is the ability to define and federate cross-domain network and security policies across both domains. This is accomplished by exchanging information between the controllers, including Security Group Tags (SGTs) and virtual networks in SD-Access, and EPGs and VRFs in ACI. This integration allows for seamless policy enforcement and consistency between the two domains.

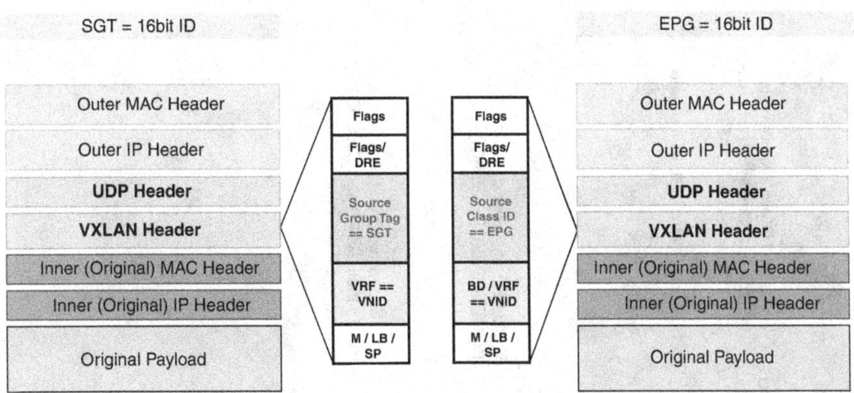

Figure 4-14 *ACI–SD-Access VXLAN Encapsulation*

SD-Access–ACI: Group/Identity Automated Mapping Federation (Microsegmentation Use Case)

This integration of SD-Access and ACI allows for the seamless sharing and coordination of identity information between the two systems. Both ACI and SD-Access utilize similar principles for implementing microsegmentation, such as security policies (contracts in ACI and SGACLs in SD-Access) and endpoint groups (EPGs in ACI and SGTs in SD-Access). This exchange of identity information empowers administrators to enforce consistent policies within the ACI system by utilizing group information from SD-Access. Similarly, it enables policy enforcement within the SD-Access system by utilizing group information from ACI. As a result, end-to-end segmentation is possible, allowing a specific group of users in the campus network to access only a designated set of application workloads in the data center.

To enable this integration, Cisco Identity Services Engine (ISE) serves as the policy element that facilitates the federation and normalization of group and group-membership (group-to-IP mappings) between the two domains. To establish the integration, the following requirements must be met:

- The SD-Access Controller (Catalyst Center) needs to subscribe as a client to obtain SGTs from ISE through their Public Exchange Grid (pxGrid) client/server relationship.
- SSL communication is required to support REST APIs between the ACI APIC and ISE. ISE acts as an API initiator and registers for ACI attach/detach events (IP/EPG bindings) for internal ACI endpoints. Similarly, ISE also initiates APIs to notify APIC of new IP/SGT bindings for endpoints sourced from SD-Access.
- Scalable Group Exchange Protocol (SXP) should be enabled on ISE to learn and share IP to group mappings to and from ISE. While the communication between ISE and APIC is handled by REST APIs rather than SXP, ISE's SXP feature must be enabled and configured for ISE to register IP to EPG mappings learned from APIC.

Figure 4-15 illustrates the federation between ACI and SD-Access controllers to automate sharing of identity and group mapping information using ISE.

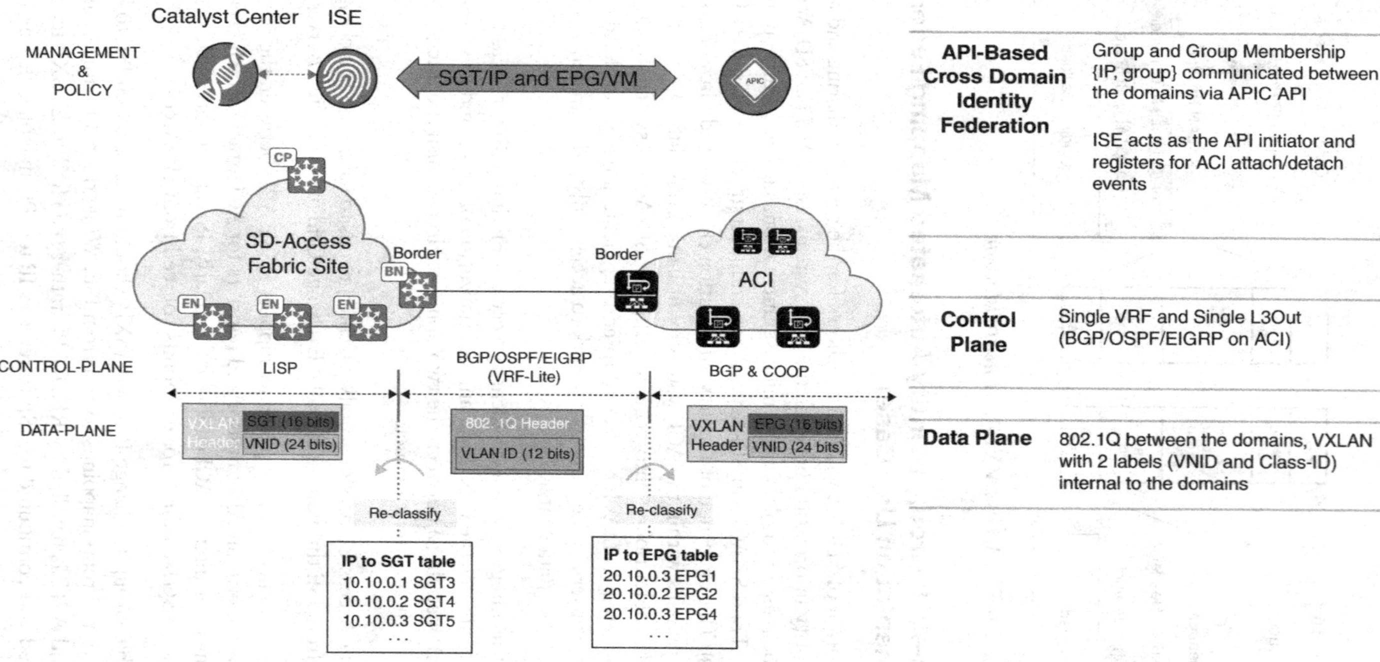

Figure 4-15 *ACI–SD-Access Group/Identity Automated Mapping*

In the initial phase of integration, the exchange of group and group-to-IP information is limited to a single ACI Tenant (single VRF) within the ACI fabric. The APIC can only send EPG and EPG-to-IP mappings for a single VRF/Tenant to SD-Access. Similarly, ISE can send SGT and SGT-to-IP mappings to the APIC to only one L3Out on a single VRF/Tenant. However, ongoing development in Cisco's cross-domain integration aims to enhance ISE to APIC group/identity mapping to support multi-fabric and multi-tenancy capabilities. This will enable the exchange of group and IP mappings for multiple VRFs and tenants within the same or across multiple ACI fabrics.

After communication is established between the two domains, and the exchange of group (SGTs/EPGs) and group-to-IP information occurs, administrators can leverage the IP/Group binding information to enforce policies. These policies can be enforced on the ACI border leafs, SD-Access border/fusion nodes, or even on a transit firewall (FW) located between the two domains.

When it comes to policy enforcement on the ACI side, the propagated SGTs from ISE are translated into external EPGs (see Figure 4-16). After completing the exchange of group and group-to-IP information, the ACI administrator can enforce policies using contracts. These contracts include the necessary port-protocol information to enable communication between the external EPGs associated with SD-Access endpoints and the internal EPGs for endpoints within the ACI fabric in the data center.

Due to the involvement of normal IP routing and forwarding between the domains, ACI needs to classify traffic from SD-Access into the correct external EPG. This explains why IP addresses are sent along with the group information. The same process is applicable to SD-Access as well.

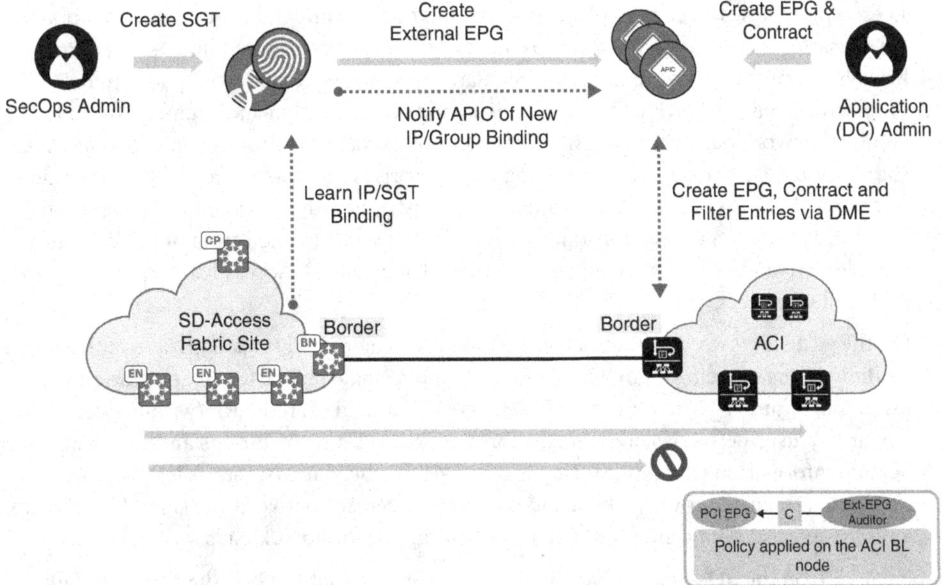

Figure 4-16 *Policy Applied on ACI Border*

Similarly, on ISE, the propagated EPGs are transformed into SGTs (see Figure 4-17). The ISE administrator can create SGACLs to enforce policies for the propagated EPGs and their corresponding SGTs obtained from ACI. To implement and program these SGACL policies, protocols like SXP/pxGrid can be utilized on a transit firewall or an SD-Access border node.

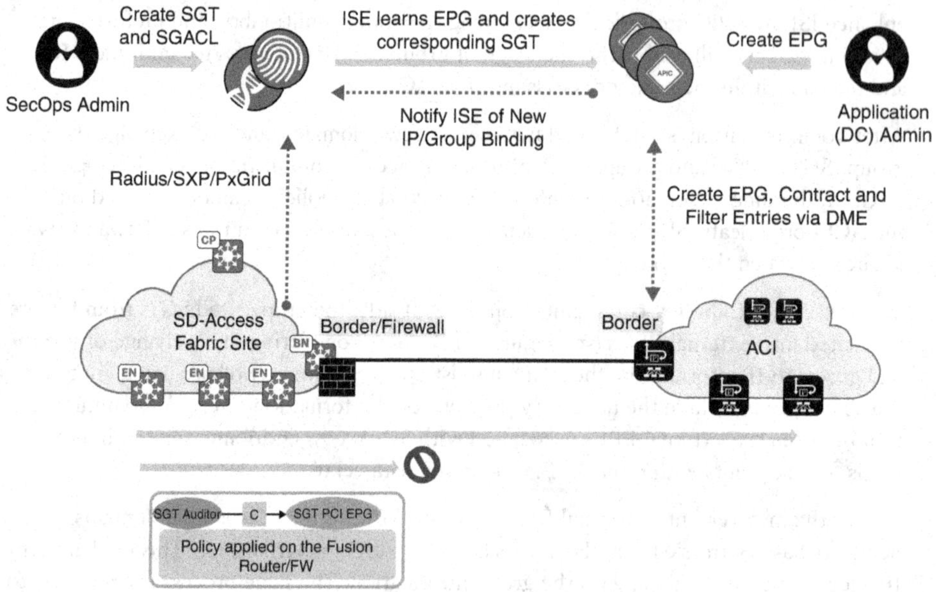

Figure 4-17 *Policy Applied on Fusion Router/Firewall*

Let's explore how the control plane inter-working of this integration operates in a practical scenario. In most enterprise setups, multiple VNs are configured in SD-Access to achieve segmentation for user access. Similarly, in the data center, workloads are distributed across multiple VRF instances to ensure logical separation and segmentation of application workloads However, when it comes to exchanging groups and group membership information between the two domains, enterprises must work around the constraint of a single VRF. To overcome this limitation, many organizations deploy a fusion router/firewall. This fusion device consolidates the VN networks learned from SD-Access into a single VRF and utilizes that single VRF to exchange all SD-Access-learned routes with ACI, and vice versa.

On the ACI side, two approaches can be followed. The first approach involves adhering to the limitations of a single L3Out, single VRF, and a single tenant for all application workloads (see Figure 4-18). Alternatively, a shared L3Out and shared VRF (within a common tenant or a user-defined shared tenant) can be used to learn the groups and group membership information through ISE (see Figure 4-19). Subsequently, inter-VRF contracts can be utilized to enable route leaking and policy enforcement between the shared VRF and multiple internal data center VRFs that host the application workloads.

Each SGT on the SD-Access domain can map to an external EPG on the shared L3Out. The administrator can define finer granular policies to allow for communication between the external EPGs and the internal EPGs belonging to the internal application VRFs.

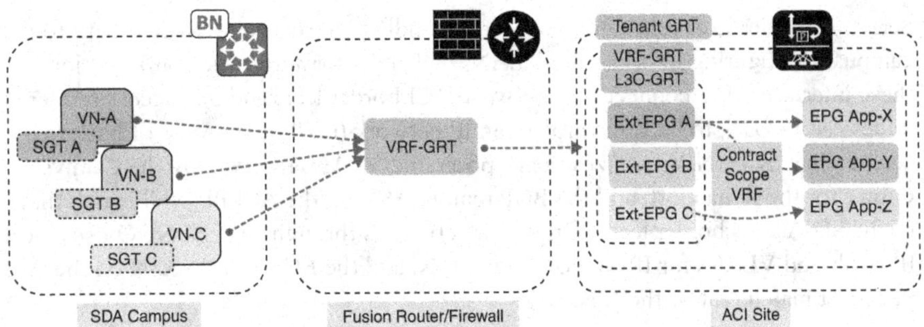

Figure 4-18 *Single L3Out, Single VRF, and Single Tenant on ACI*

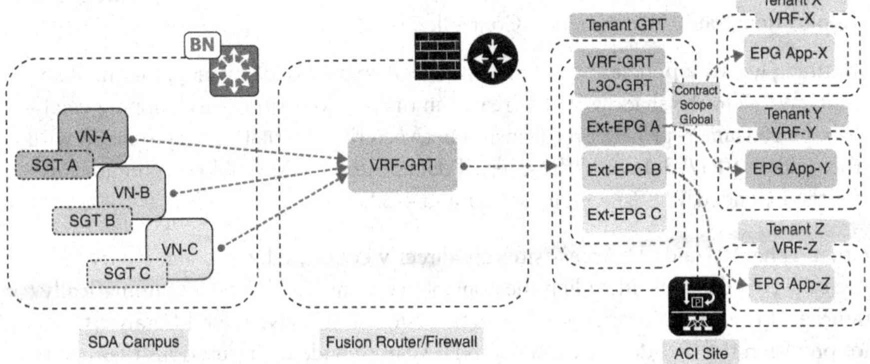

Figure 4-19 *Shared L3Out, Shared VRF, and Shared Tenant on ACI*

SD-Access–ACI: VN-to-VRF Automated Mapping Federation (Macrosegmentation Use Case)

The Cisco Nexus Dashboard Orchestrator (NDO) offers a feature called Automated VN-to-VRF mapping for SD-Access ACI integration. This functionality enables the automatic linking of campus virtual networks to single or multi-data center VRFs using IP handoff. This integration allows for macrosegmentation across campus and data center domains, and also provides cross-domain visibility for extended networks. It allows you to validate cross-domain peering status and verify the reachability of campus networks from the data center.

To facilitate this automated VN-to-VRF exchange, REST communication is required between the Cisco Catalyst Center Controller for the SD-Access domain in need of extension, and the Nexus Dashboard Orchestrator (see Figure 4-20). The integration involves several steps:

1. Onboarding Cisco Catalyst Center to NDO by providing the Catalyst Center device IP and a user account with read-only privileges. NDO will then use REST APIs to retrieve the configuration of VNs and BN devices within the SD-Access domain controlled by Catalyst Center.

2. Selecting border leafs (BLs) and their corresponding interfaces for connectivity to the campus. Configuring IP pools and VLANs will allow for automatic configuration of these interfaces. The connectivity between ACI border leafs and SD-Access border nodes can be back to back or through an IP network (IPN). In the case of back-to-back connectivity, NDO utilizes the IP pools and VLANs reserved by the Catalyst Center for the IP handoff, and the BGP remote ASN on the ACI BLs will match that of the SD-Access border leafs. If the connectivity is through an IPN, NDO uses local IP pools and VLANs for IP handoff to the IPN, and the BGP remote ASN on the ACI BLs must match that of the IPN.

3. Selecting the VNs that need to be extended to the data center. NDO will create a shadow VRF and shadow L3Out (with an external EPG) in ACI's Common Tenant for each VN that needs extension. The NDO will then push this configuration to the Application Policy Infrastructure Controller.

4. Defining network policies to control inter-VRF connectivity by mapping the data center VRFs to the shadow VRFs created in the previous step. This mapping establishes a consumer–provider relationship between the external EPG associated with the shadow VRF/L3Out and the internal data center VRFs, enabling communication for the extended VNs (see Figures 4-21 and 4-22).

Note that if the ACI and SD-Access sites are directly connected, the connectivity between the two domains, including the control plane and data plane, is automatically configured. However, if the sites are connected using an IPN, NDO and Catalyst Center do not provision the IPN devices. Instead, NDO can provide configurations that can be applied to the IPN nodes connected to the ACI BLs and SD-Access BNs. It is also important to ensure that the IPN devices support VRF-Lite for IPN connected sites.

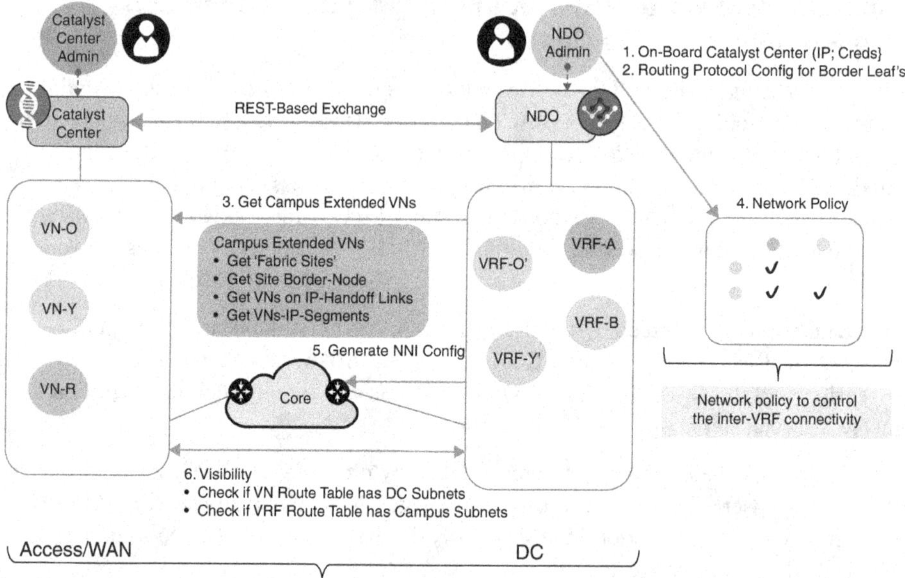

Figure 4-20 *ACI–SD-Access VN-to-VRF Automated Mapping Workflow*

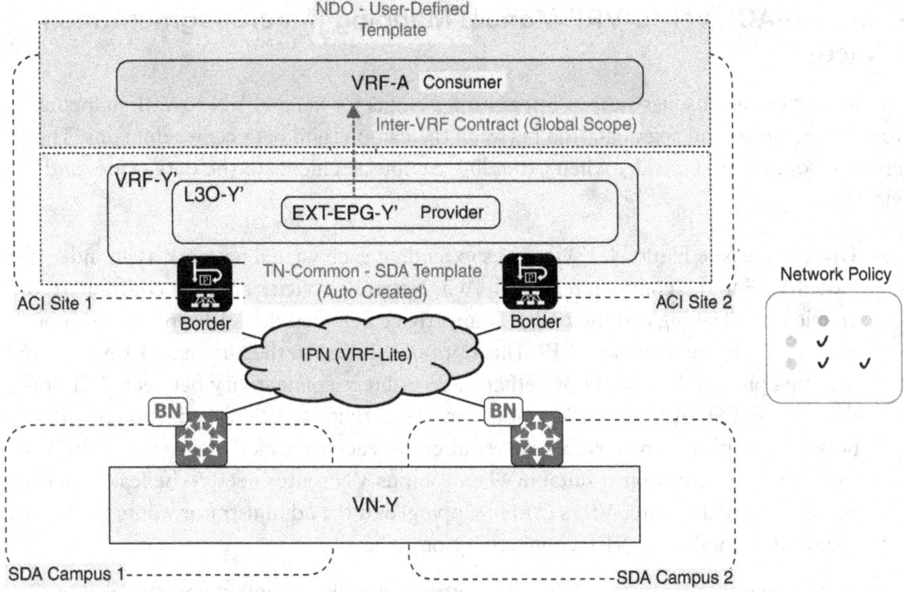

Figure 4-21 *Policy: VN-to-DC Internal VRF (M:N mapping)*

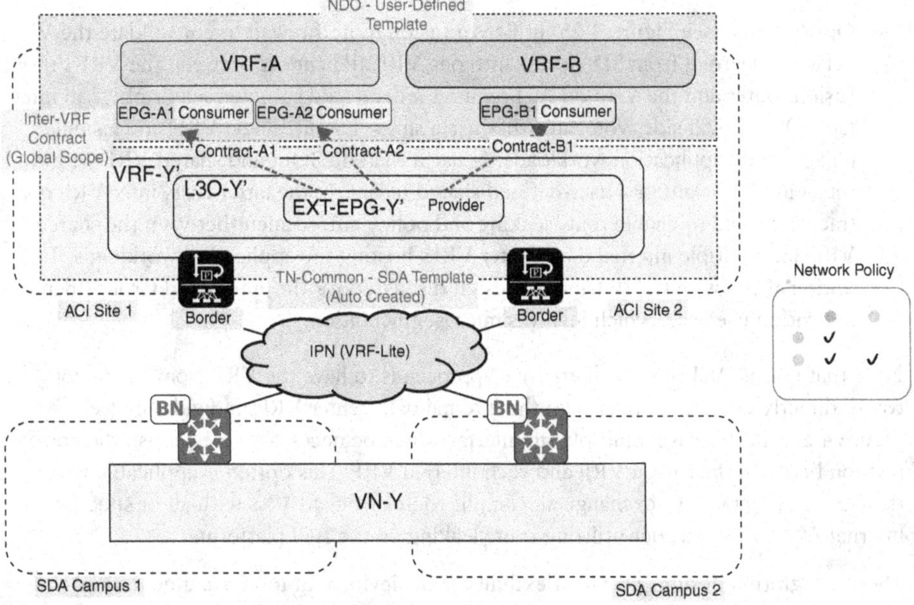

Figure 4-22 *Policy: VN-to-DC Internal VRF (Granular Policies)*

SD-Access–ACI: VN-to-VRF Manual Mapping (Macrosegmentation Use Case)

In this section, we discuss various integration designs for manual VN-to-VRF mapping to achieve end-to-end segmentation between the campus and data center domains. There are three options to consider when extending campus segments to the data center and vice versa:

- Option one (see Figure 4-23) involves extending each virtual network as an individual VRF in the common tenant on ACI. Network policies are then configured to enable route leaking and inter-VRF connectivity between the VRFs in the common tenant and the data center VRFs. This option is similar to the automated VN-to-VRF mapping provided by NDO. Whether there is direct connectivity between ACI border leafs and SD-Access border nodes, or connectivity is established through an IP network, multiple subinterfaces are required for each extended VN to stitch the VN to the VRF. This option is suitable when campus VN routes need to be leaked across one or more data center VRFs (M:N mapping) and the administrator wants to control route leaking and inter-VRF connectivity on ACI.
- Option two (see Figure 4-24) involves extending each VN and connecting it directly to the data center VRF. Similar to option one, multiple subinterfaces are required for VN-to-VRF stitching. This option provides a one-to-one mapping of VN to VRFs and eliminates the need for route leaking and inter-VRF connectivity on ACI.
- Option three (see Figure 4-25) utilizes a fusion route/firewall to consolidate the VN networks learned from SD-Access into one VRF. IP handoff between the VRF on the fusion router and the VRF on ACI requires a dedicated subinterface or physical interface. On the ACI side, you can either use a single L3Out, single VRF, and a single tenant for all application workloads, or use a shared L3Out and shared VRF within the common tenant or a user-defined shared tenant. In the latter case, inter-VRF contracts are used to enable route leaking and policy enforcement between the shared VRF and multiple internal data center VRFs hosting the application workloads. This option aligns with the IP handoff design discussed for the automated Group/Identity federation use case, which involves microsegmentation.

Note that on the ACI side, an alternative approach is to have the VRF from the fusion router directly connect or peer with the internal data center VRFs individually (see Figure 4-26). In this case, multiple subinterfaces will be necessary to establish the connection between the fusion VRF and each internal VRF. This option is applicable when there is a requirement to exchange all campus routes from all VNs with all or specific internal ACI VRFs, without utilizing route leaking on the ACI platform.

These integration designs provide flexibility in achieving end-to-end segmentation between the campus and data center domains, allowing you to choose the most suitable option based on your specific requirements.

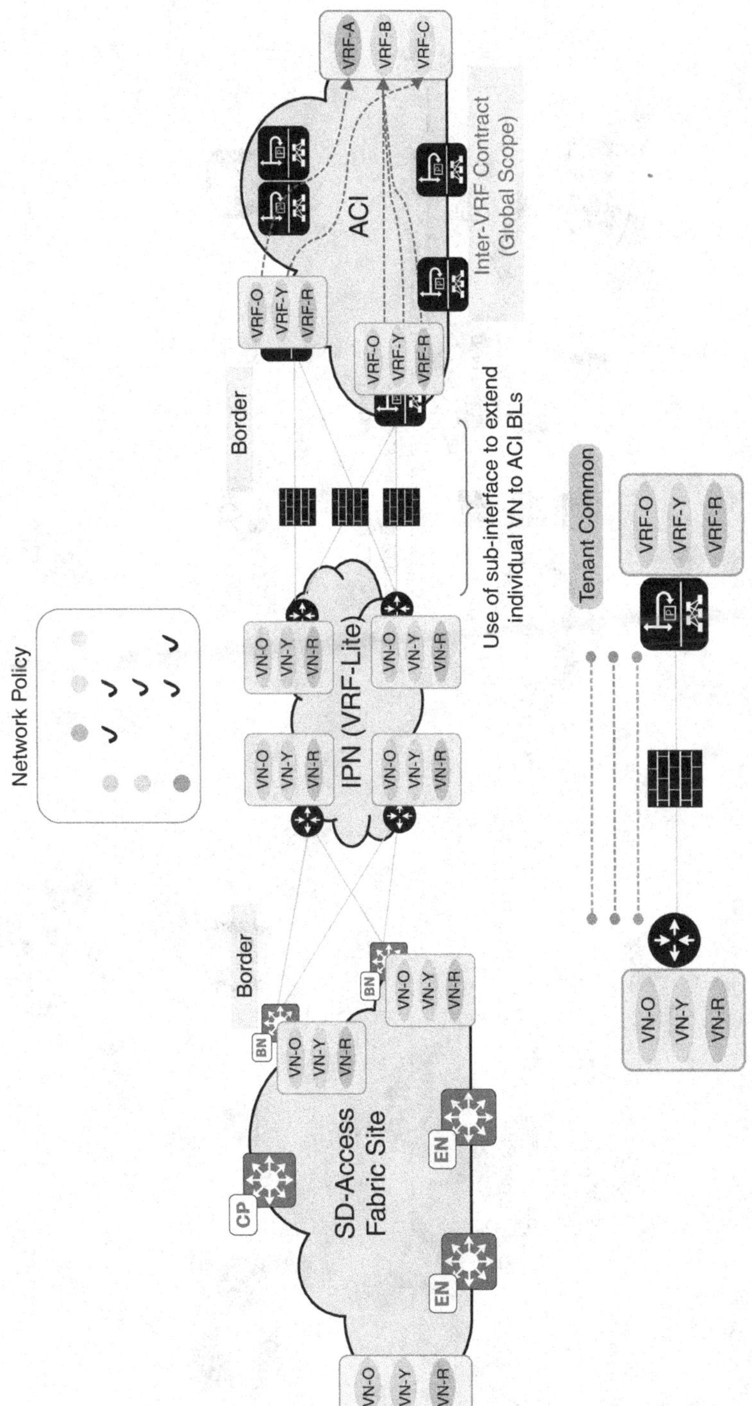

Figure 4-23 *ACI–SD-Access VN-to-VRF Manual Mapping (Option1)*

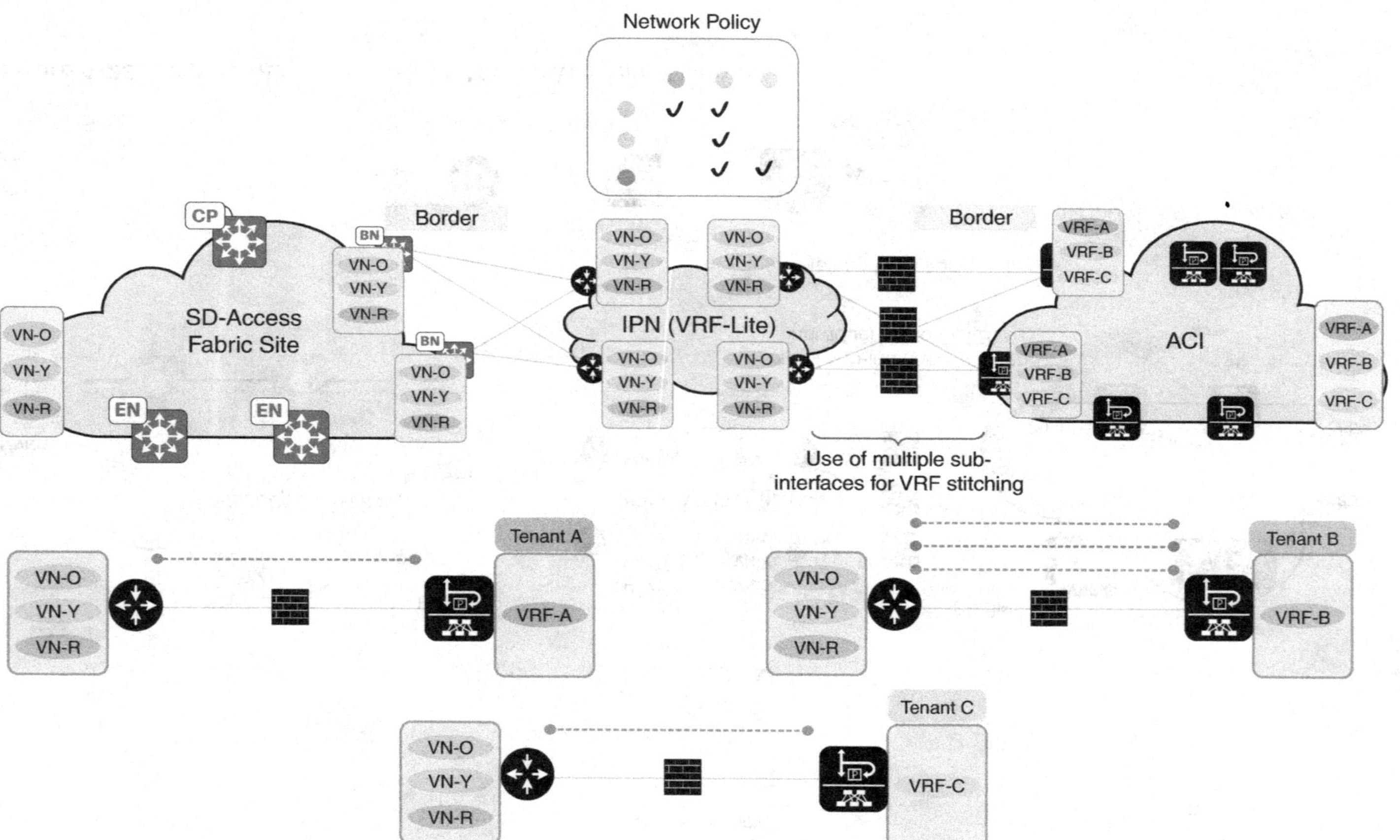

Figure 4-24 *ACI–SD-Access VN-to-VRF Manual Mapping (Option2)*

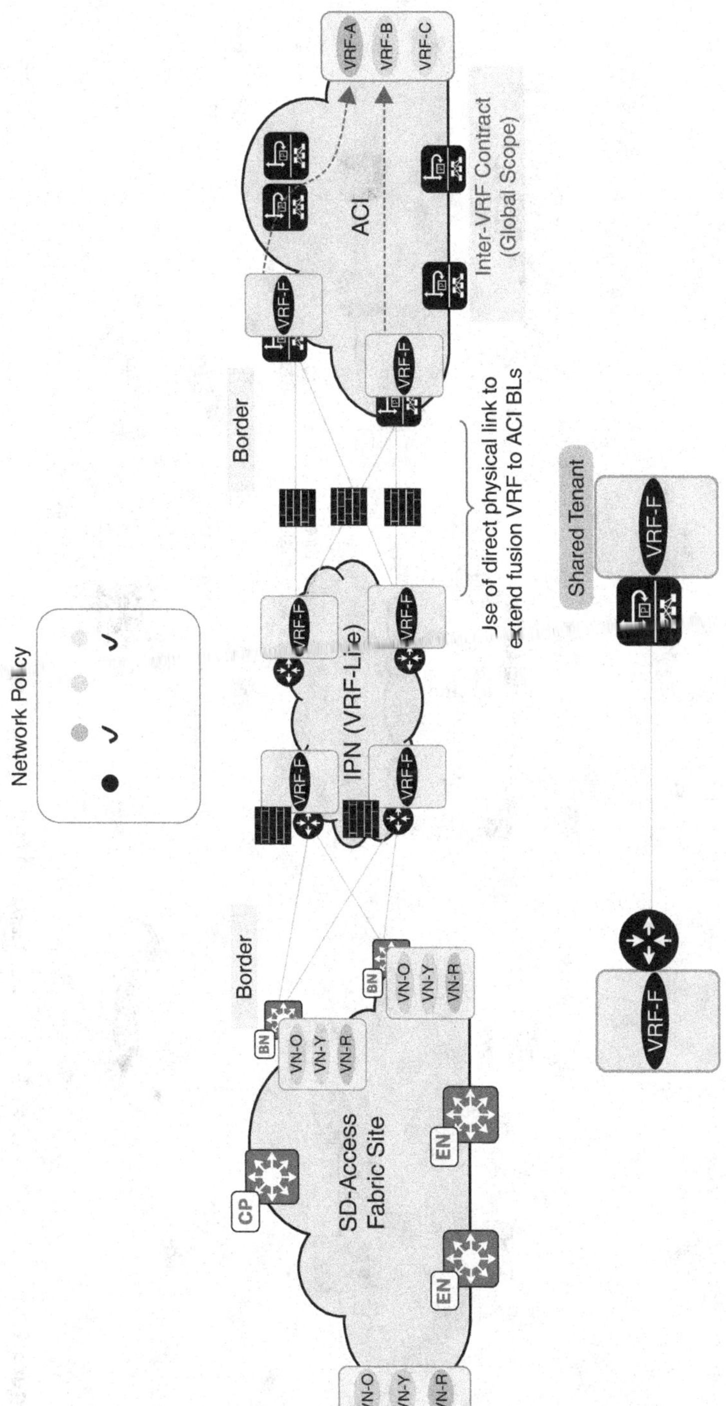

Figure 4-25 *ACI–SD-Access VN-to-VRF Manual Mapping (Option3.1)*

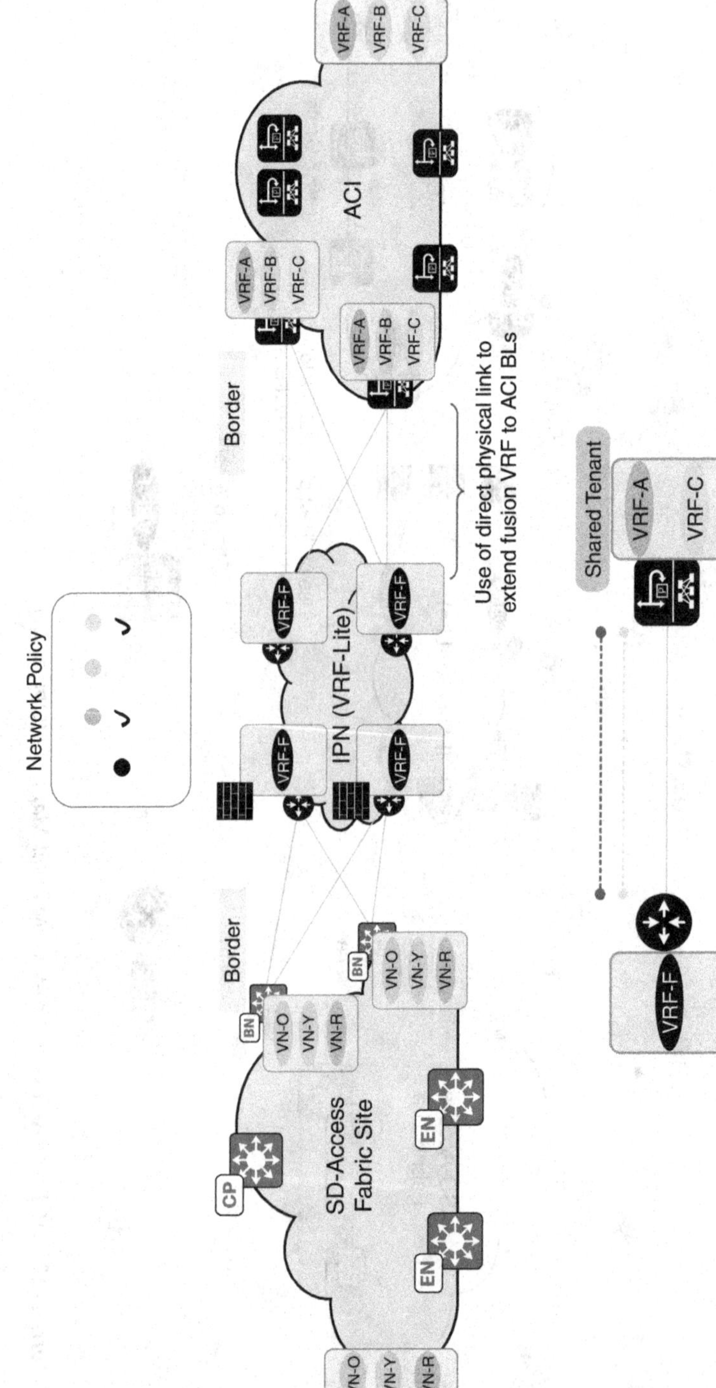

Figure 4-26 *ACI–SD-Access VN-to-VRF Manual Mapping (Option3.2)*

Guidelines and Limitations Around ACI–SD-Access Integration

While Cisco provides detailed documentation on guidelines and limitations for ACI SD-Access integration, it is important to be aware of common considerations and common pitfalls that may arise during implementation.

- It is important to note that using a shared VRF and shared L3Out for VN-to-VRF mapping has multicast limitations. Layer 3 multicast routing is not supported through a shared L3Out. Therefore, if there is a need for Layer 3 multicast routing for data center VRFs, associating them with the shared L3Out will not work for multicast traffic.
- Inter-VRF route leaking in the case of shared L3Outs requires the following configuration:
  - The BD subnet scope for the internal VRFs (VRFs hosting the application workloads) should be set with "Shared between VRFs."
  - The shared L3Out EPG subnet scope must be set with "Shared Route Control Subnet" and "Shared Security Import Subnet."
  - The contract scope for inter-VRF contract between the shared L3Out EPG and the internal VRFs/EPGs should be set to a global scope.
- When implementing automated federation for an identity/group, it is crucial to refer to the ACI scalability guide to ensure that the number of external EPGs (translated SGTs) supported per L3Out and the number of /32 host mappings supported per translated SGT are within the validated limits.
- Similarly, for automated federation of VN to VRF, it is important to consult the ACI scalability guide to verify the maximum number of Catalyst Center devices/clusters that can be onboarded onto NDO, the number of VNs that can be extended to the data center, and the maximum number of VRFs each extended VN can be mapped to.
- In enterprise deployments, it is common to position the fusion router/firewall in the data center near the ACI border leafs. This approach allows for maintaining VN segmentation across WANs and other branch/campus networks. The fusion router/firewall can then collapse the segments in the data center using explicit policies to enforce north-south policy enforcement for all campus-to-data center traffic and vice versa.

ACI and SD-WAN Pairwise Integration

Cisco Software-Defined WAN (SD-WAN) represents an evolution of traditional intelligent WAN architecture by utilizing a software-defined networking (SDN) approach for WAN overlay networking. This approach involves decoupling control plane elements from data plane forwarding, along with enabling centralized intelligence, network overlay automation, simplified operations, and centralized provisioning, management, and troubleshooting.

Cisco SD-WAN's automated overlay is transport-independent, allowing for the utilization of various transports in an active-active fashion to extend WAN connectivity to data centers, branches, and the cloud. Throughout this extension, it maintains application awareness, enforces strict service-level agreements (SLAs), ensures end-to-end network segmentation, and encrypts enterprise transport data with strong security measures.

The integration of ACI and SD-WAN involves an API-driven federation between the ACI controllers and SD-WAN controllers. This integration enables the sharing of contextual data to identify application traffic and endpoints within the data center. When these identifiers are utilized, application-aware policies with stringent SLAs can be implemented in the WAN environment.

Figure 4-27 illustrates the policy exchange between ACI controller (APIC) and SD-WAN controller (Catalyst SD-WAN Manager). First, the APIC makes several API calls to Catalyst SD-WAN Manager to get VPN and SLA classes from the WAN, and subsequently, the APIC will push DSCP to SLA mapping and endpoint IP addresses for endpoints within the ACI fabric to Catalyst SD-WAN Manager.

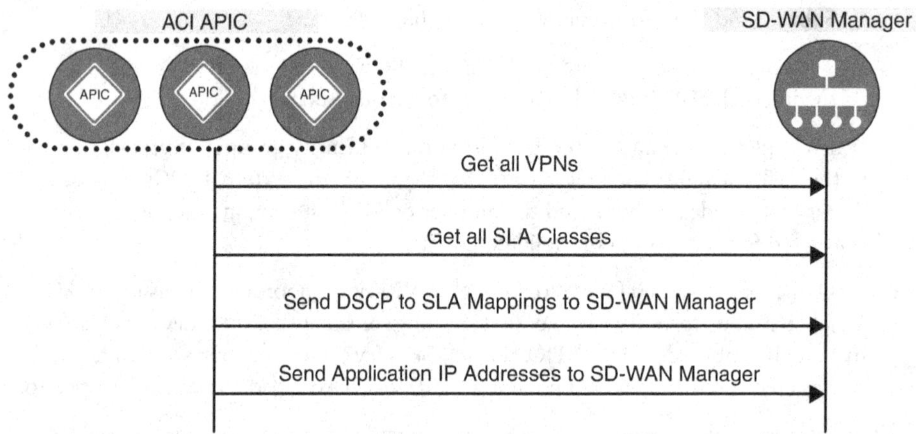

Figure 4-27 *APIC–Catalyst SD-WAN Manager Policy Exchange*

Currently, two types of ACI SD-WAN integration are available (see Figure 4-28). The first type involves connecting the data center (ACI) to the branch using SD-WAN, and vice versa. This integration allows for seamless communication and policy enforcement between the data center and branch locations. The second type of integration is multisite connectivity between data centers (ACI-to-ACI) using SD-WAN. This type of integration facilitates the establishment of secure and efficient communication between multiple data center locations that are utilizing ACI.

By leveraging the integration between ACI and SD-WAN, organizations can achieve enhanced application visibility, dynamic policy enforcement, and optimized performance across their WAN infrastructure.

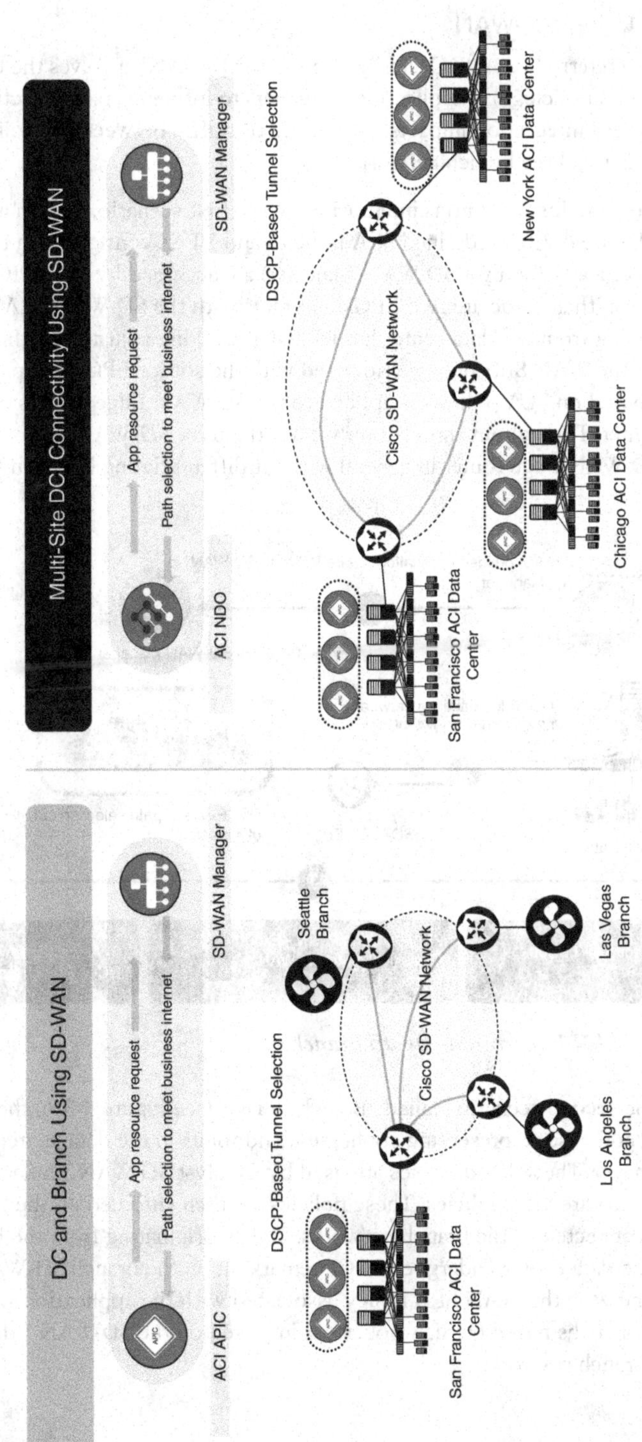

Figure 4-28 *SD-WAN Integration Options–Branch and Multi-Site*

DC and Branch Using SD-WAN

The integration referred to as "DC and Branch Using SD-WAN" involves the utilization of application-aware policies and application identifiers to influence path selection within the SD-WAN. This integration impacts the routing of traffic between endpoints located in the data center and the branch network.

There are two scenarios within this integration. In the first scenario, known as "DC to Branch" (see Figure 4-29), predefined SLA policies and VPNs configured in the SD-WAN controller (specifically Catalyst SD-WAN Manager) are accessed by the APIC. The ACI administrator can then associate ACI EPGs/contracts with the SD-WAN SLA policy. Traffic originating from the data center has its DSCP marking adjusted on the ACI border leafs based on the WAN SLA policy associated with the source EPG. This path selection enforcement based on SLA policies is applied to the SD-WAN Edge routers connected to the data center. Throughout this chapter we use the term *SD-WAN Edge routers* to denote any SD-WAN Edge router in general without differentiating between Viptela-OS/IOS-XE routers.

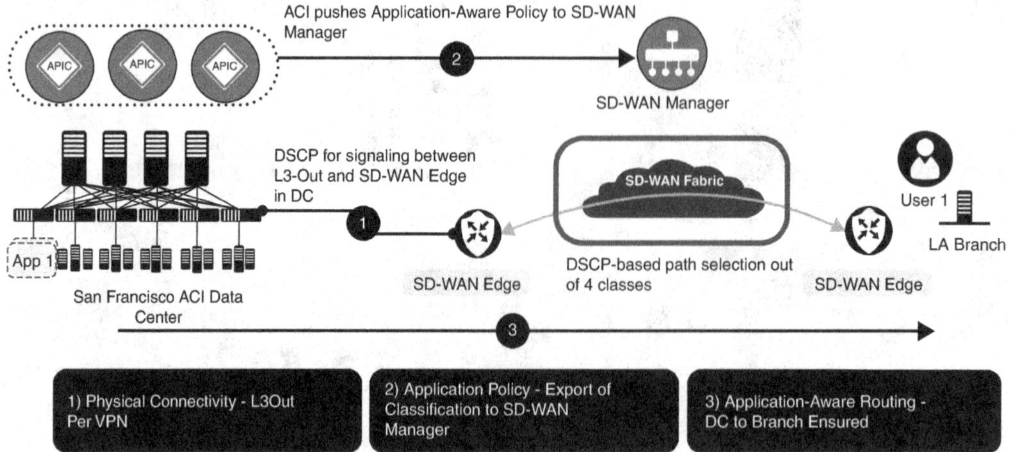

Figure 4-29 *SD-WAN Integration–DC to Branch*

Similarly, in the second scenario, called "Branch to DC" (see Figure 4-30), the APIC sends application IP addresses representing application endpoints in the data center to Catalyst SD-WAN Manager. These IP addresses are used by Catalyst SD-WAN Manager to populate application-aware SLA policies. These policies are then enforced on the SD-WAN Edge routers connected to the branch networks. Traffic originating from the branch and destined for the data center undergoes DSCP remarking on the branch SD-WAN Edge routers, aligning with the WAN SLA policy associated with the application IP addresses. The selection of paths based on SLA policies is imposed on the SD-WAN Edge routers linked to the branch network.

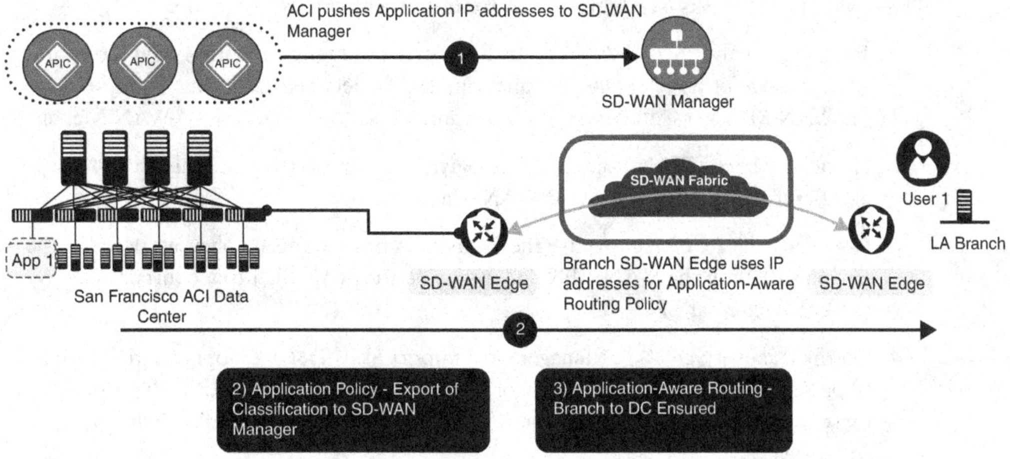

Figure 4-30 *SD-WAN Integration–Branch to DC*

Figure 4-31 illustrates the configuration touchpoints on both APIC and Catalyst SD-WAN Manager to facilitate the integration.

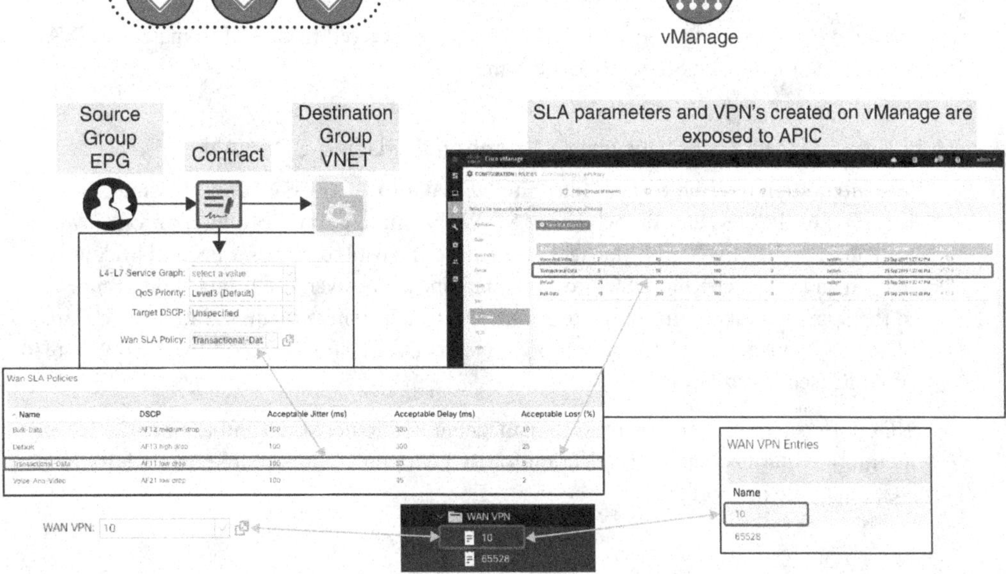

Figure 4-31 *SD-WAN Integration–DC and Branch–Configuration*

The configuration tasks (see Figure 4-32) for both scenarios are as follows:

1. Integrate Catalyst SD-WAN Manager as a partner integration within APIC to enable the exchange of policy plane information via API between APIC and Catalyst SD-WAN Manager. APIC retrieves SLAs and VPNs from Catalyst SD-WAN Manager.
2. Associate the SD-WAN Edge with the partner integration, specifically the DC Edge and Branch Edge, in Catalyst SD-WAN Manager.
3. Configure the ACI tenant to use the WAN SLA policy. This involves associating the tenant VRF with the WAN VPN and assigning the WAN SLA to a contract used by the WAN external EPG.
4. On the Catalyst SD-WAN Manager side, import SLA–DSCP mapping and SLA–EPG IP prefix mapping for application workloads hosted on the ACI fabric. Incorporate these into the application-aware policy and allocate VPNs and SLAs to the branch and DC sites.
5. Activate the policy in Catalyst SD-WAN Manager, which is then pushed to both Catalyst SD-WAN Controller and SD-WAN Edge routers in the network to finalize the process.

By following these configuration steps, organizations can effectively implement the "DC and Branch Using SD-WAN" integration, enabling application-aware path selection and SLA enforcement between the data center and branch networks.

Figure 4-33 illustrates the use of IP prefixes (/32) received from ACI to match SD-WAN policies on the branch SD-WAN Edge routers.

Multi-Site DC (ACI-to-ACI Intersite) Connectivity Using SD-WAN

The integration referred to as "Multi-Site DC (ACI-to-ACI) Connectivity Using SD-WAN" is similar to the "DC and Branch Using SD-WAN" integration. Both integrations involve utilizing Catalyst SD-WAN Manager as a partnering tool to gather VPN and SLA information and implementing DSCP-to-SLA mappings. However, the primary difference lies in the approach taken for multi-site DC-to-DC traffic, where the integration with Catalyst SD-WAN Manager is established through Nexus Dashboard Orchestrator (NDO) instead of APIC (see Figure 4-34).

NDO offers a centralized method to manage multi-site networks and is essential for any integration that impacts path selection for ACI endpoints' site-to-site connectivity in an ACI multi-site network.

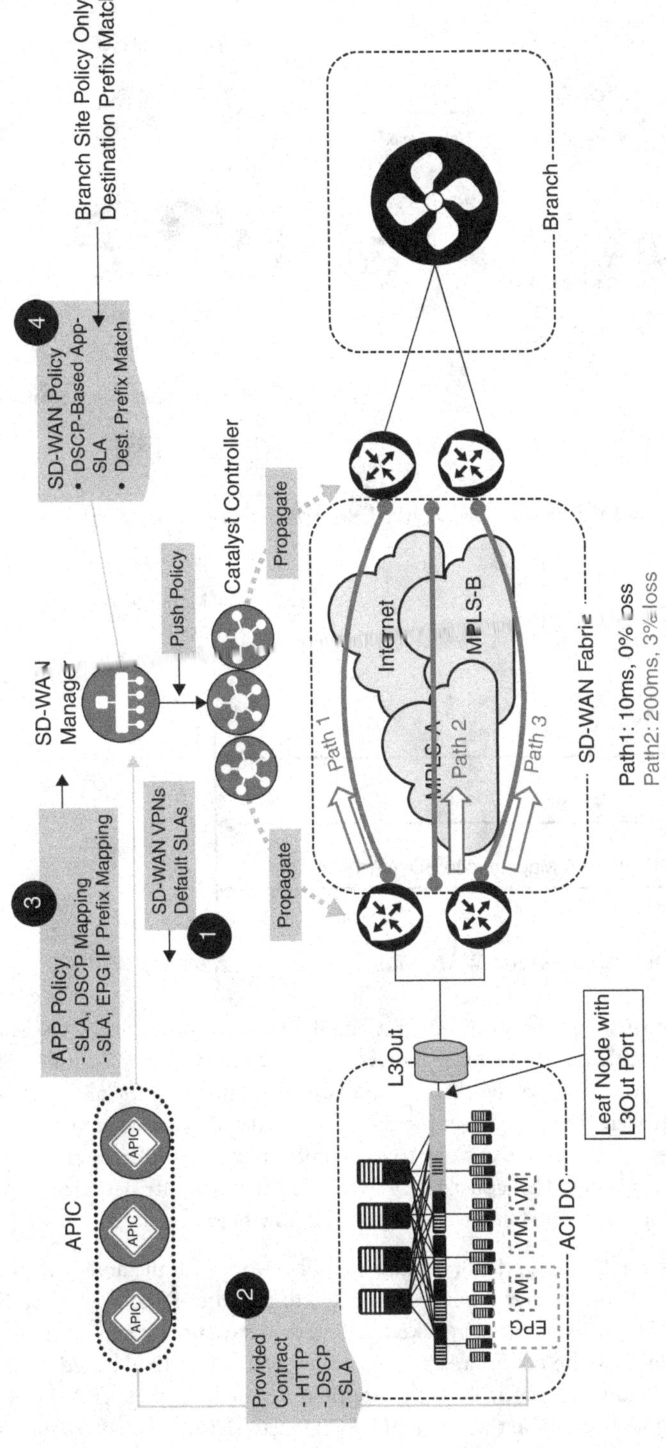

Figure 4-32 *SD-WAN Integration–DC and Branch–Workflow*

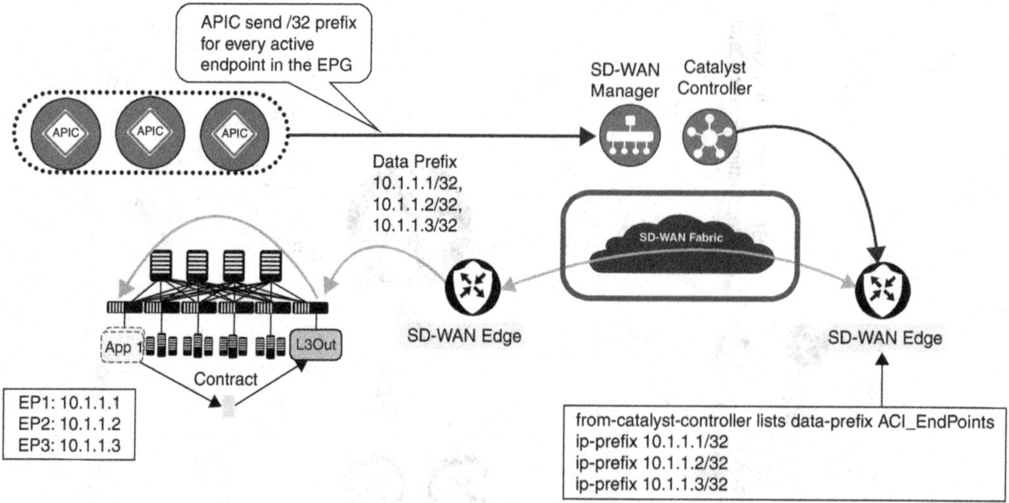

Figure 4-33 *SD-WAN Integration–DC and Branch–Destination Prefix Match*

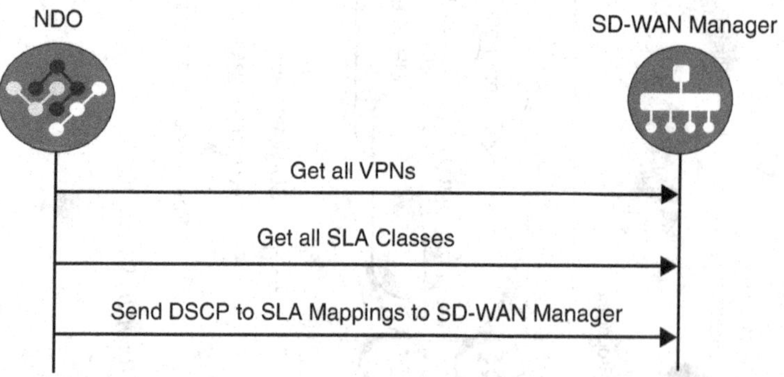

Figure 4-34 *NDO–Catalyst SD-WAN Manager Policy Exchange*

Before we discuss the specifics of integrating NDO with Catalyst SD-WAN Manager, it is important to understand the inter-site QoS dynamics within an ACI multi-site network. In a traditional ACI site, QoS levels for user and control plane traffic are configured on the APIC controller. However, when the data plane and policy plane are extended to additional ACI sites, it becomes necessary to have uniform per-hop QoS marking and queuing behavior across all sites. This consistency extends to the inter-site network responsible for transit connectivity, enabling east-west traffic flow between sites.

To achieve this consistency, NDO provides administrators with the ability to set up DSCP-to-COS mappings on the spines connected to the Inter-Site Network (ISN) (see Figure 4-35). This ensures that cross-site traffic receives treatment similar to internal site traffic. The spines can be configured to adjust the outer DSCP field based on the internal VXLAN COS field when traffic exits the site/fabric. Similarly, the VXLAN COS field can be set on the spines based on the external DSCP received as traffic enters the site/fabric.

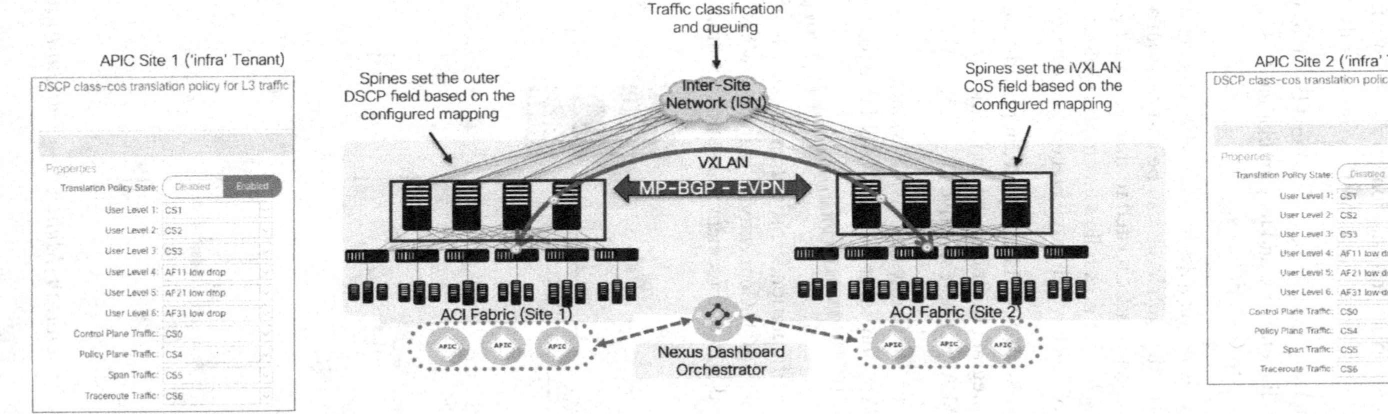

Figure 4-35 *ACI Multi-Site–Intersite QoS Behavior*

The configuration tasks for this integration are as follows (see Figure 4-36):

1. Integrate Catalyst SD-WAN Manager as a partner within NDO to enable the exchange of policy plane information via API between NDO and Catalyst SD-WAN Manager. NDO retrieves SLAs and VPNs from Catalyst SD-WAN Manager.
2. Configure NDO with comprehensive Global DSCP to COS policies. Here, the NDO administrator will configure and map individual DSCP values to the QoS levels for the Global DSCP to COS policies.
3. On the NDO, you will also assign the QoS levels defined in the previous step to the inter-site EPG traffic. QoS levels can be chosen from a contract or at the EPG level, covering all inter-site traffic related to that specific EPG. The prioritization sequence for QoS Level selection is as follows: contract QoS level takes precedence over source EPG QoS level, which takes precedence over default QoS level.
4. On the Catalyst SD-WAN Manager side, import the SLA–DSCP mapping provided by NDO and integrate them into the application-aware policy. Assign the appropriate VPNs and SLAs to the respective DC sites.
5. Activate the policy in Catalyst SD-WAN Manager, which will be propagated to both Catalyst SD-WAN Controller and SD-WAN Edge routers within the network to finalize the process.

By following these configuration steps, organizations can effectively implement the "Multi-Site DC (ACI-to-ACI) Connectivity Using SD-WAN" integration, ensuring consistent QoS policies and SLA enforcement across an ACI multi-site network.

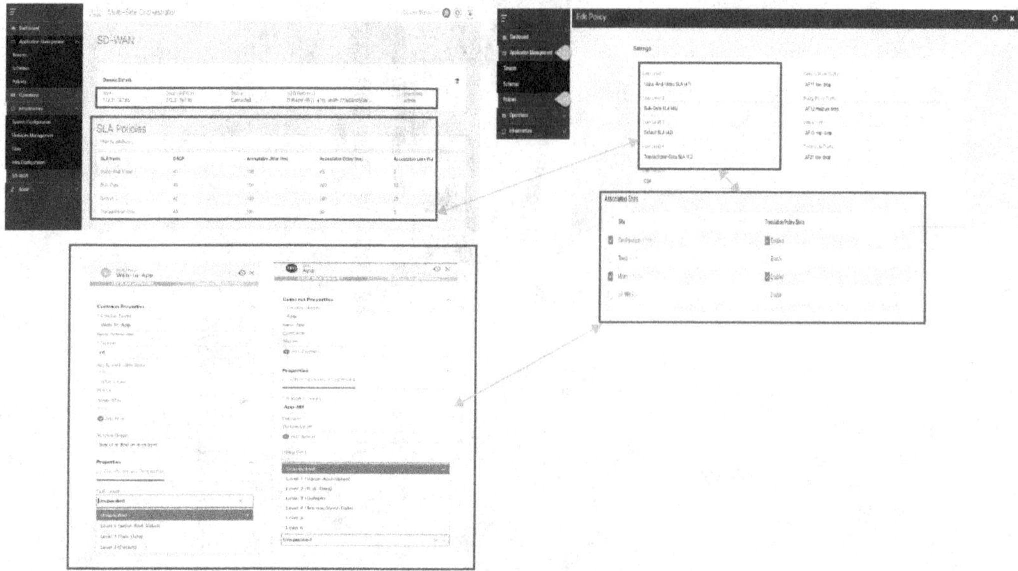

Figure 4-36 *SD-WAN Integration–Multi-Site–Configuration*

Guidelines and Limitations Around ACI SD-WAN Integration

While Cisco offers comprehensive documentation with guidelines and limitations for ACI SD-WAN integration, it is important to be aware of common consideration and common pitfalls that may arise during implementation.

- In the DC and Branch use case, for DC-to-WAN traffic, SLA matching is based solely on DSCP values. For Branch-to-WAN traffic, SLA matching is done using destination IP prefixes.
- When associating the WAN SLA policy to the EPG–L3Out contract on APIC in the DC and Branch use case, ensure that the QoS priority for the contract is set to a value other than Unspecified. The WAN SLA policies will not function correctly if the QoS Priority is set to Unspecified.
- In the DC-to-DC (inter-site using ISN) use case, SLA matching is only performed based on DSCP values.
- SLA class names are predefined and cannot be modified.
- DSCP-to-SLA mappings are automatically configured and cannot be modified.
- Jitter, Delay, and Loss values can be adjusted through Catalyst SD-WAN Manager. However, when accessed via APIC or NDO, these values are read-only.
- Currently, the ACI–SD-WAN integration supports a maximum of four SLA classes.
- Each SD-WAN Edge router can only be linked to a single partner integration.
- Policy implementation always occurs from the service VPN to the WAN direction.

ACI and MPLS/SR-MPLS Pairwise Integration

Unlike other ACI integrations mentioned in the book, the MPLS/SR-MPLS (Segment Routing—MPLS) pairwise integration with ACI offers the ability to use the same transport for all L3Outs as the MPLS-based WAN.

This integration extends the transport to ACI, providing several advantages:

1. It allows an enterprise or service provider to extend label distribution from the MPLS Core to the ACI border leafs using a single control and data plane session, instead of separate sessions per VRF. This unified MPLS/SR-MPLS transport from ACI to the SP Core addresses scalability challenges typically associated with VRF-Lite solutions.
2. It enables traffic engineering capabilities to steer traffic to and from ACI based on parameters such as color, latency, link congestion, IGP metric, and so on, using features like Segment Routing Traffic Engineering (SR-TE) in the SP Core.

Figure 4-37 illustrates connectivity using VRF-Lite handoff between ACI BL and DC-PE. In this case, per-VRF interfaces and routing protocol sessions are established between the BLs and DC-PE. Automation and scalability of VRF-Lite are the main challenges in this setup.

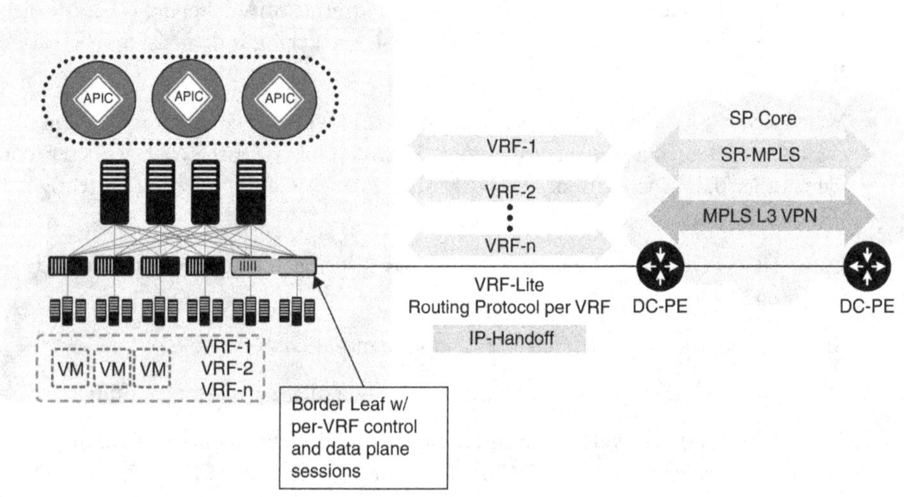

Figure 4-37 *ACI-to-DC-PE Handoff Using VRF-Lite*

In contrast, Figure 4-38 demonstrates the same connectivity using SR-MPLS handoff and unified MPLS/SR transport between the BLs and DC-PE. In this scenario, BGP Label Unicast (BGP-LU) is used for underlay label (transport-label) exchange between the two domains, along with BGP EVPN peering to carry prefixes per VRF, MPLS labels per VRF, and color community. With a single control plane and data plane session instead of per-VRF sessions, automation and scalability challenges faced in the VRF-Lite solution are eliminated.

By leveraging the MPLS/SR-MPLS pairwise integration with ACI, organizations can benefit from a unified transport approach and utilize traffic engineering capabilities for efficient and scalable connectivity between ACI and the MPLS-based WAN.

Traditional MPLS networks group packets with similar characteristics using forward equivalence class (FEC), forwarding them with MPLS labels and the Label Distribution Protocol (LDP). In contrast, MPLS-SR simplifies MPLS by allowing the source to choose a path through source-based routing. Segment identifiers (SIDs) from a centralized path computation element (PCE) are added to the packet header as an ordered list of segments, guiding the path to the destination. Each node in the path follows the encoded instructions in the header.

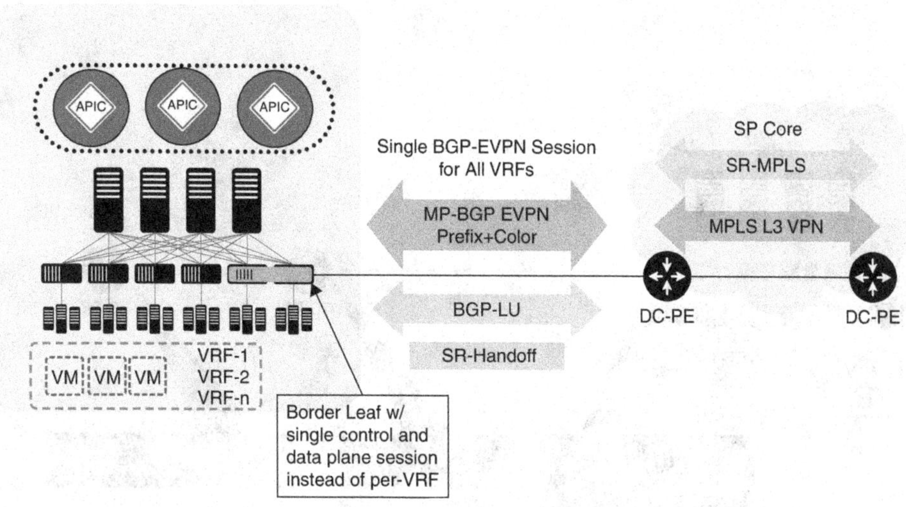

Figure 4-38 *ACI-to-DC-PE Handoff Using MPLS/SR-MPLS*

With MPLS-SR, each node is assigned a node segment ID (SID) from the global Segment Routing Global Block (SRGB). The IGP (OSPF/ISIS) or BGP signals the assigned SIDs within the SR domain, enabling each node to have a shortest path to every other node in its MPLS table. The PCE computes the shortest path for the destination prefix and translates it into a list of segments (SIDs) added to the ingress packet. As the packet traverses the network, each node pops the resulting label from the stack until it reaches the destination.

MPLS-SR can be enhanced further with the Flexible Algorithm (Flex Algo), which allows the inclusion of additional segments with different properties, such as low latency or dual plane, in the end-to-end path computation. Each router maintains additional properties like latency for its links and floods this information into the IGP. A new SID tied to the latency TE property is configured on each router. These properties enable the provisioning of dynamic constrained paths considering link latency or application constraints, offering flexibility to automatically steer application traffic based on operator-defined logic.

When ACI is integrated with MPLS/MPLS-SR, two options are available. The first option (see Figure 4-39) is to use BGP color communities to advertise ACI fabric prefixes and define SR-TE/Flex Algo paths in the transport network based on these color communities. The second option (see Figure 4-40) is to use prefixes advertised from the ACI fabric on the DC-PE to define SR paths in the transport. It is generally recommended to utilize color communities where supported to simplify configuration by reducing the need to match prefixes on the DC-PEs.

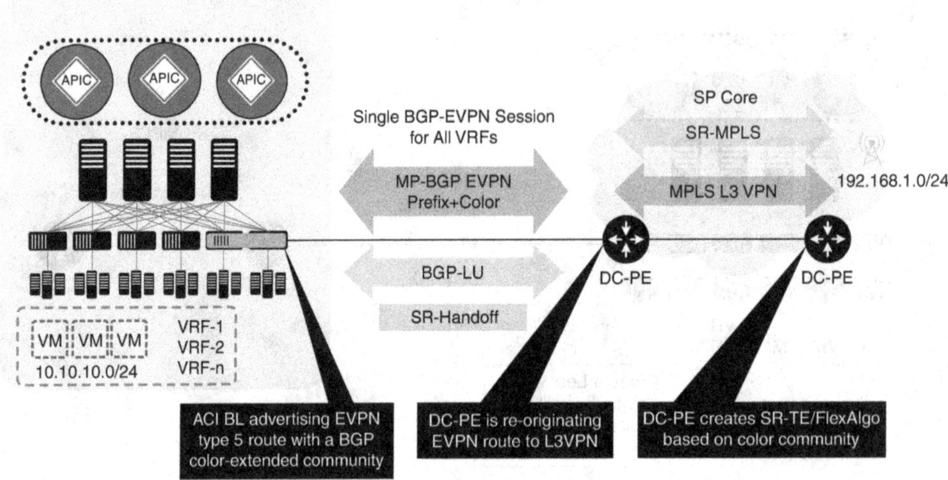

Figure 4-39 *SR-TE in Transport Using Color Communities*

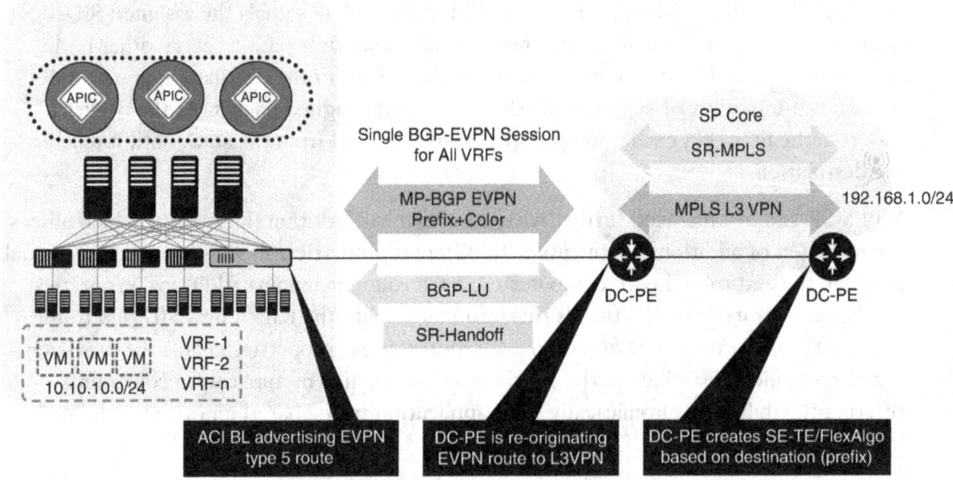

Figure 4-40 *SR-TE in Transport Using Destination Prefixes*

In addition to color communities and destination prefixes, packets sourced from the ACI fabric can be marked with DSCP values using EPG, contract, and L3Out QoS policies (see Figures 4-41 and 4-42). These DSCP values can be re-marked on the egress, specifically the ACI border leafs, with EXP values based on the original DSCP markings in the packet header. The transport network can perform QoS based on the DSCP/EXP markings from the data center (DC), or the DC-PE can use the DSCP/EXP markings from the DC to define SR-TE/Flex Algo paths in the transport.

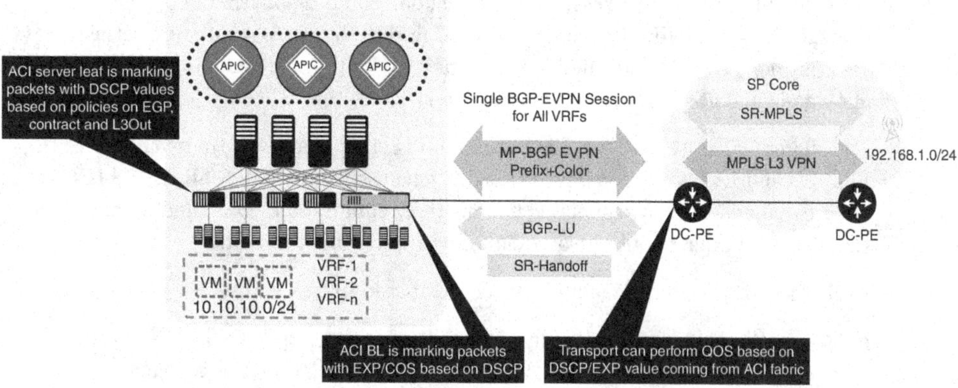

Figure 4-41 *DC and Transport QoS Using MPLS/SR-MPLS*

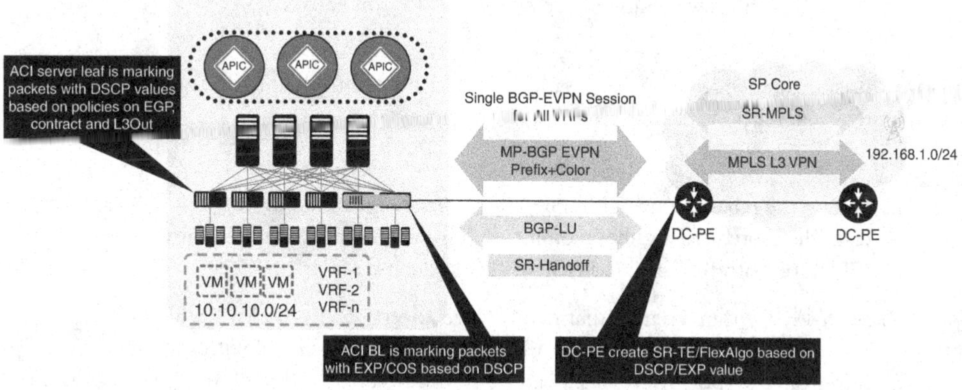

Figure 4-42 *SR-TE in Transport Using QoS*

Here is a list of important considerations for the control plane integration between ACI border leafs and MPLS/SR-MPLS DC-PEs:

1. The MPLS/SR-MPLS handoff is achieved using BGP Label Unicast (BGP-LU) sessions between the front panel port of ACI BLs and the first-hop router. These sessions enable the exchange of transport loopback prefixes and the corresponding transport labels. No additional IGP configuration is required for transport label exchange when using BGP-LU.

2. Alongside BGP-LU sessions, a BGP EVPN session is established between the loopback addresses of ACI BLs and DC-PE routers. These EVPN sessions facilitate the exchange of VPN prefixes, labels, and BGP communities.

3. Both BGP-LU and EVPN sessions must be configured as external BGP (eBGP) sessions. Internal BGP (iBGP) is not supported in the current ACI software releases. If sessions need to be established between peers with the same AS number, the BGPs' **allowas-in** and **as-override** features can be utilized.

4. The shared underlay MPLS/SR-MPLS L3Out is created in the infra tenant for both BGP-LU and EVPN sessions. Additionally, tenant-specific MPLS/SR-MPLS L3Outs are created within their respective tenants that require the L3Out functionality. The shared Infra L3Out should be associated with the Tenant L3Outs.

5. MPLS/SR-MPLS handoff requires three distinct loopback addresses:

    a. Router ID: This is automatically assigned and corresponds to the RID in the overlay-1 VRF. Changing this RID can cause route flapping or outages.

    b. BGP EVPN Loopback: This is used for establishing the eBGP single-hop/multi-hop session with the DC-PE router.

    c. MPLS Transport Loopback: This serves as the next hop for the bridge domain (BD) prefixes when advertised to the DC-PE router.

Note It is recommended to use the same loopbacks for both BGP EVPN and MPLS transport whenever possible.

6. Due to the reliance on BGP, minimizing convergence time during link failures is crucial. Therefore, it is highly recommended to use Bidirectional Forwarding Detection (BFD) for both BGP-LU and BGP-EVPN sessions.

7. Each VRF within a tenant that needs to be advertised to the MPLS/SR-MPLS transport requires its respective VRF L3Out to be associated with the Infra L3Out. Import and Export route maps can be configured on the VRF L3Out to apply route policies based on prefixes and/or BGP communities, advertise prefixes into the MPLS/SR-MPLS network, and filter prefixes from the MPLS/SR-MPLS network. For prefixes learned from the MPLS/SR-MPLS transport, external EPGs with configured subnets should be created under the VRF L3Out. The external EPG can then be associated with internal EPGs using contracts to enable communication with endpoints within the ACI fabric and, in some cases, allow the leakage of externally learned subnets between ACI VRFs (see Figures 4-43 and 4-44).

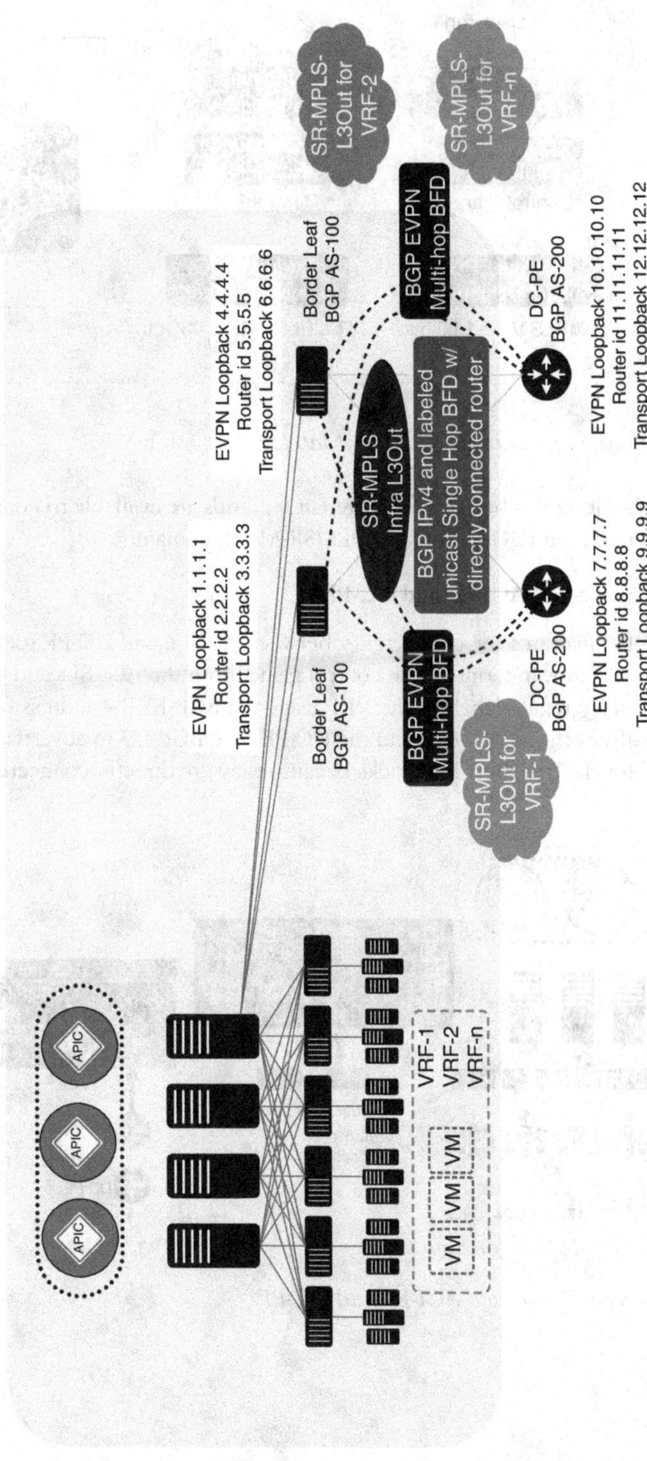

Figure 4-43 *Control Plane for MPLS/SR-MPLS*

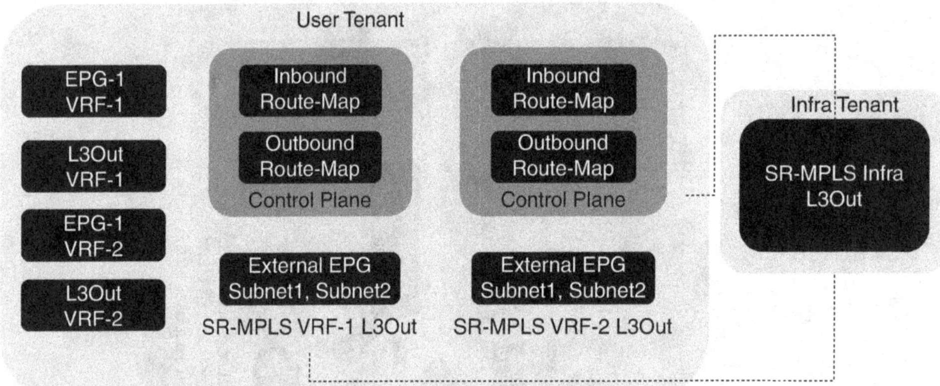

Figure 4-44 *Inbound and Outbound Route Map for User L3Out*

At the time of writing this book, three different methods are available to connect ACI MPLS/SR-MPLS-based L3Outs to the MPLS/SR-MPLS domain:

- **Directly connected ACI-BL and DC-PE**

  Figure 4-45 illustrates the connectivity between ACI-BL and DC-PE for MPLS/SR-MPLS handoff. In terms of the control plane, both the ACI-BLs and the DC-PEs advertise an aggregate label for the VRF using the BGP-EVPN address family. Additionally, both the ACI-BLs and the DC-PEs use BGP-LU to advertise an implicit-null label for the transport loopbacks because they are directly connected.

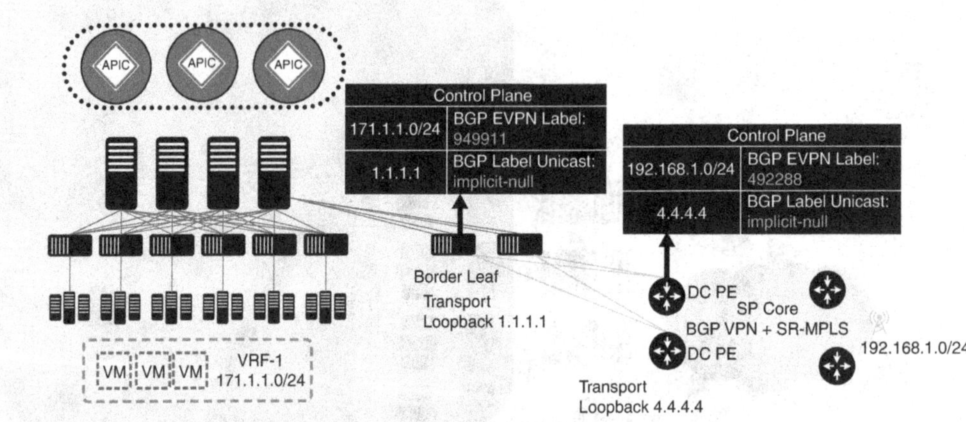

Figure 4-45 *Directly Connected ACI-BL and DC-PE*

Figures 4-46 and 4-47 illustrate the data plane communication between ACI-BL and DC-PE for MPLS/SR-MPLS handoff.

In the data plane, the process is as follows:

1. The source leaf encapsulates the packet from the source ACI endpoint into a VXLAN header and forwards it to the ACI BLs.
2. The ACI-BLs de-encapsulate the VXLAN header and encapsulate the packet toward MPLS/SR-MPLS with the inner (aggregate) VRF label (BGP EVPN label). The outer label is not used due to the implicit null label exchange between the directly connected ACI BLs and DC-PEs.
3. The DC-PEs de-encapsulate the packets coming from the ACI-BLs and further encapsulate them with a VPNv4 inner label and MPLS transport outer label based on prefix/color for the destination.

In the reverse direction:

1. The DC-PEs receive MPLS/SR-MPLS packets with the MPLS transport label (outer label) and a VPNv4 (inner label) from the SP core network.
2. The DC-PEs send the SR-MPLS packet to the ACI-BLs with the inner aggregate VRF label (BGP EVPN label). Once again, no outer label is used because the DC-PEs and ACI-BLs are directly connected and utilize the implicit null label.
3. The ACI-BLs de-encapsulate the MPLS/SR-MPLS packet and encapsulate it into the VXLAN header within the ACI fabric.

- **MPLS LDP network between ACI-BL and DC-PE**

  Figure 4-48 illustrates the connectivity between ACI-BLs and DC-PEs for MPLS/SR-MPLS handoff when the two domains are interconnected through a transit MPLS LDP network. From a control plane perspective, both the ACI-BLs and DC-PEs advertise an aggregate label for the VRF prefix using the BGP-EVPN address-family. For the transport label, BGP-LU advertises an implicit-null label for the transport loopbacks of the ACI-BLs toward the first-hop DC-P routers. The DC-P routers are configured to use LDP for label exchange with the DC-PEs. Consequently, the DC-P routers generate an LDP label for the ACI transport loopbacks and exchange it with the DC-PEs. To facilitate label exchange for ACI transport loopbacks, the next-hop DC-P redistributes the ACI transport loopback prefixes (/32s) from BGP-LU to the IGP protocol running toward the DC-PE.

  In the reverse direction, the same principles apply (see Figure 4-49). The DC-PEs advertise a transport label for the transport loopback to their next-hop routers (DC-Ps) using LDP. The DC-Ps, in turn, use BGP-LU to generate a BGP-LU label and advertise the DC-PEs' transport label further down to the ACI-BLs. The DC-Ps also redistribute the DC-PE transport loopback prefixes (/32s) from IGP to BGP-LU.

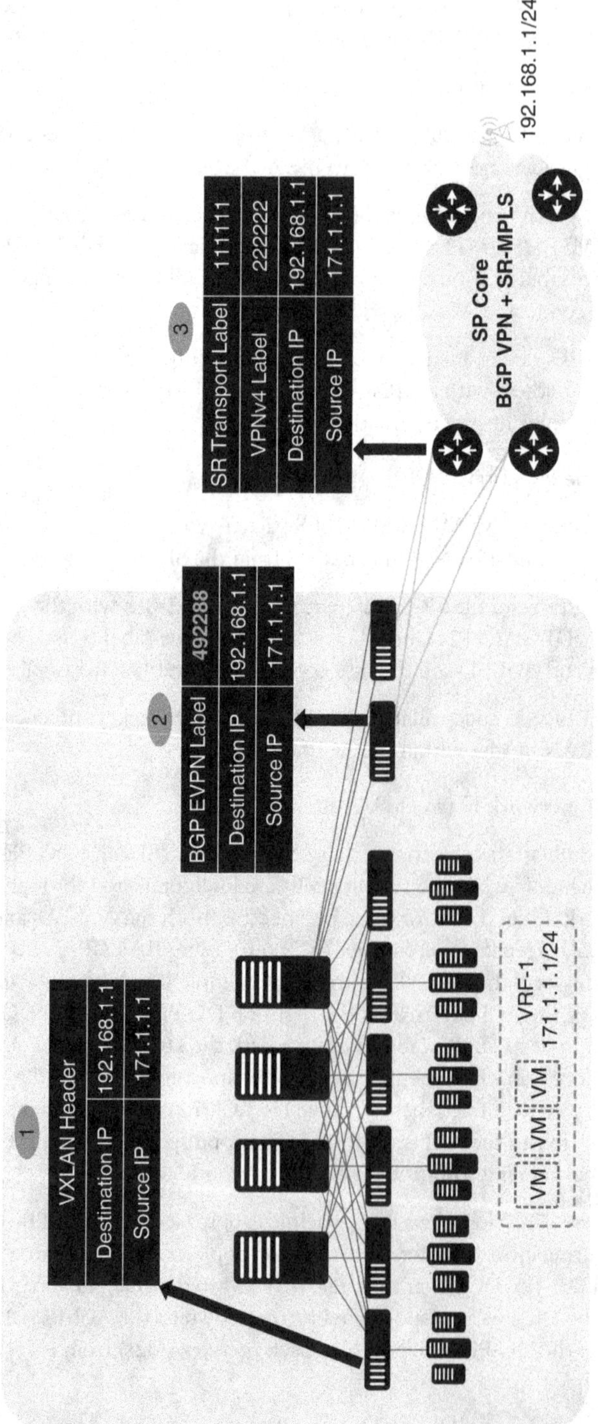

Figure 4-46 *Packet Walk for Data Plane Connectivity from BL to PE*

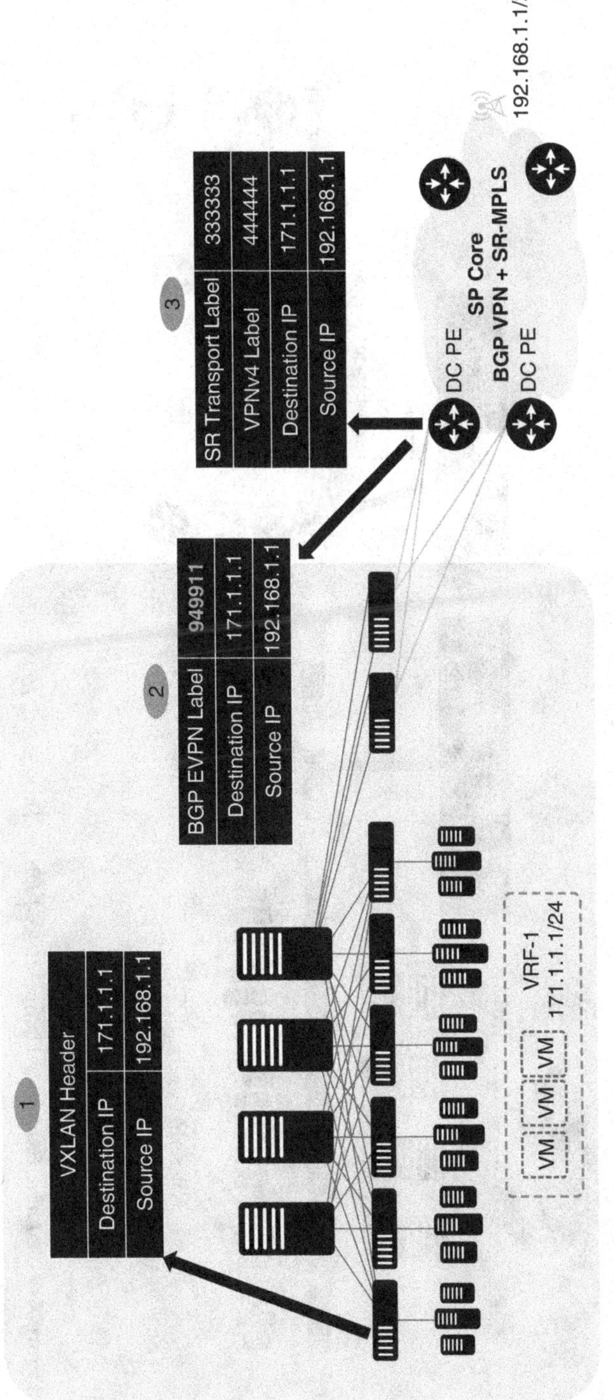

Figure 4-47 *Packet Walk for Data Plane Connectivity from PE to BL*

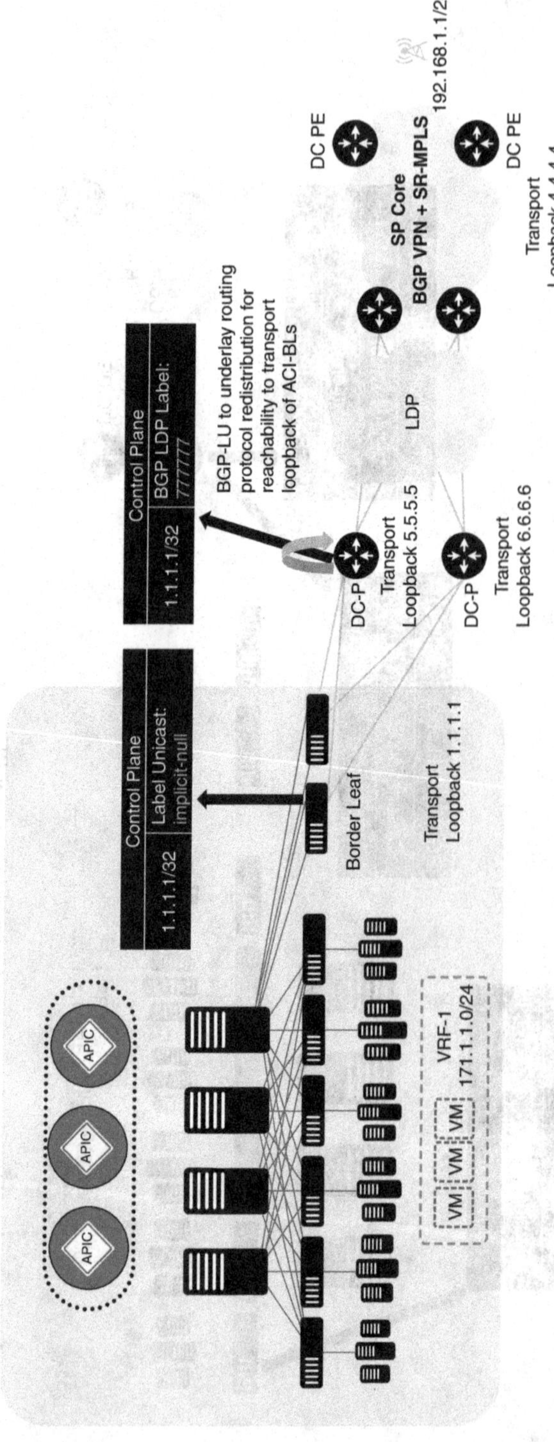

Figure 4-48 *Label Exchange Using MPLS-LDP as Transit (BL to PE)*

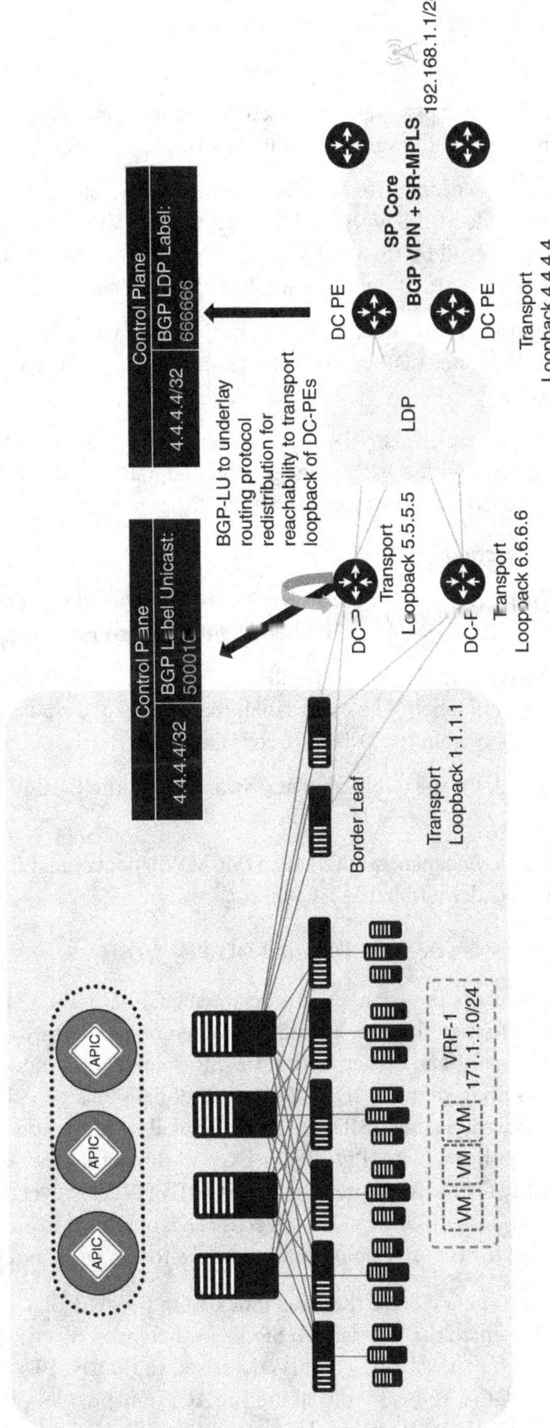

Figure 4-49 *Label Exchange Using MPLS-LDP as Transit (PE to BL)*

Figures 4-50 and 4-51 illustrate the data plane communication between ACI-BLs and DC-PEs through a transit MPLS LDP network.

In the data plane, the process is as follows:

1. The source leaf encapsulates the packet from the source ACI endpoint into a VXLAN header and forwards it to the ACI-BLs.
2. The ACI-BLs de-encapsulate the VXLAN header and encapsulate the packet toward MPLS/SR-MPLS with the inner (aggregate) VRF label (EVPN label). The outer label used will be the transport label learned for the DC-PEs, which is obtained from the DC-P routers using BGP-LU.
3. The DC-Ps look up the outer label and swap it with the LDP-learned label for the DC-PE (the outer LDP label can be an implicit null if the DC-PE is directly attached to the DC-P).
4. The DC-PEs de-encapsulate the packets coming from the DC-Ps and further encapsulate them with a VPNv4 inner label and MPLS transport outer label based on prefix/color for the destination.

In the reverse direction:

1. The DC-PEs receive the MPLS/SR-MPLS packets with the MPLS transport label (outer label) and a VPNv4 (inner label) from the SP core network.
2. The DC-PEs send the SR-MPLS packet to the DC-Ps with the inner aggregate VRF label (EVPN label). The outer label used will be the transport label for the ACI-BLs, learned from the DC-Ps' router using LDP.
3. The DC-Ps look up the outer label and swap it with the BGP-LU learned label for the ACI-BLs.
4. The ACI-BLs de-encapsulate the MPLS/SR-MPLS packet and encapsulate it into the VXLAN header within the ACI fabric.

- **MPLS SR network between ACI-BL and DC-PE**

  Figure 4-52 showcases the connectivity between ACI-BL and DC-PE for MPLS/SR-MPLS handoff when the two domains are interconnected through a transit MPLS SR network. As mentioned earlier, within the SR domain, each node is assigned a label known as a node segment ID (SID) from a global block called SR Global Block (SRGB). These assigned labels (SID) are then signaled to other nodes within the SR domain through either IGP (OSPF/ISIS) or BGP. In this setup, the ACI-BLs advertise an aggregate label for the VRF prefix using BGP-EVPN. However, for the transport label, BGP-LU from the ACI-BLs also advertises a label index in addition to the implicit-null label for the ACI transport loopbacks to the DC-P nodes.

  When the DC-P routers receive the label index from the ACI-BLs, they use it to generate a new label where the new label = SRGB + label index received. This new label becomes the SID for the ACI-BLs and is advertised to the DC-PEs using IGP-SR. Additionally, the DC-P routers redistribute the ACI transport loopback prefix (/32) from BGP-LU to the IGP-SR protocol running toward the DC-PEs.

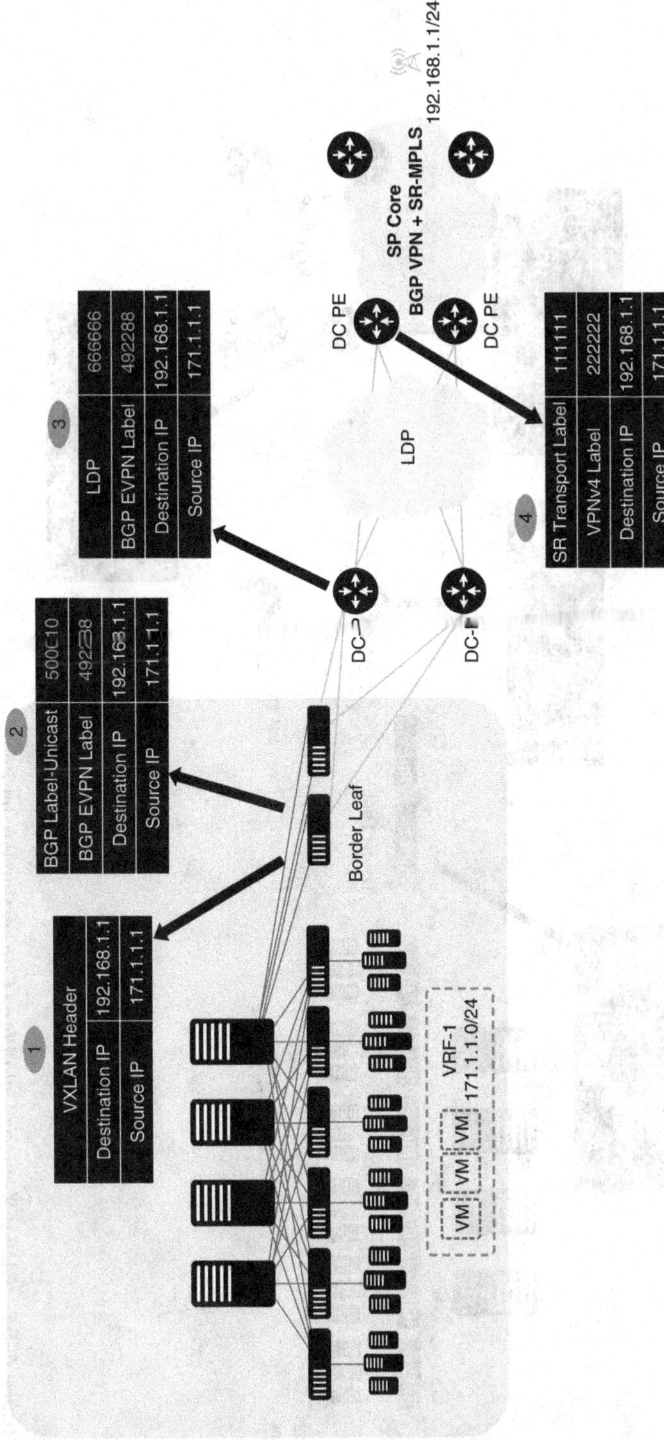

Figure 4-50 *Packet Walk for Data Plane Connectivity from BL to PE*

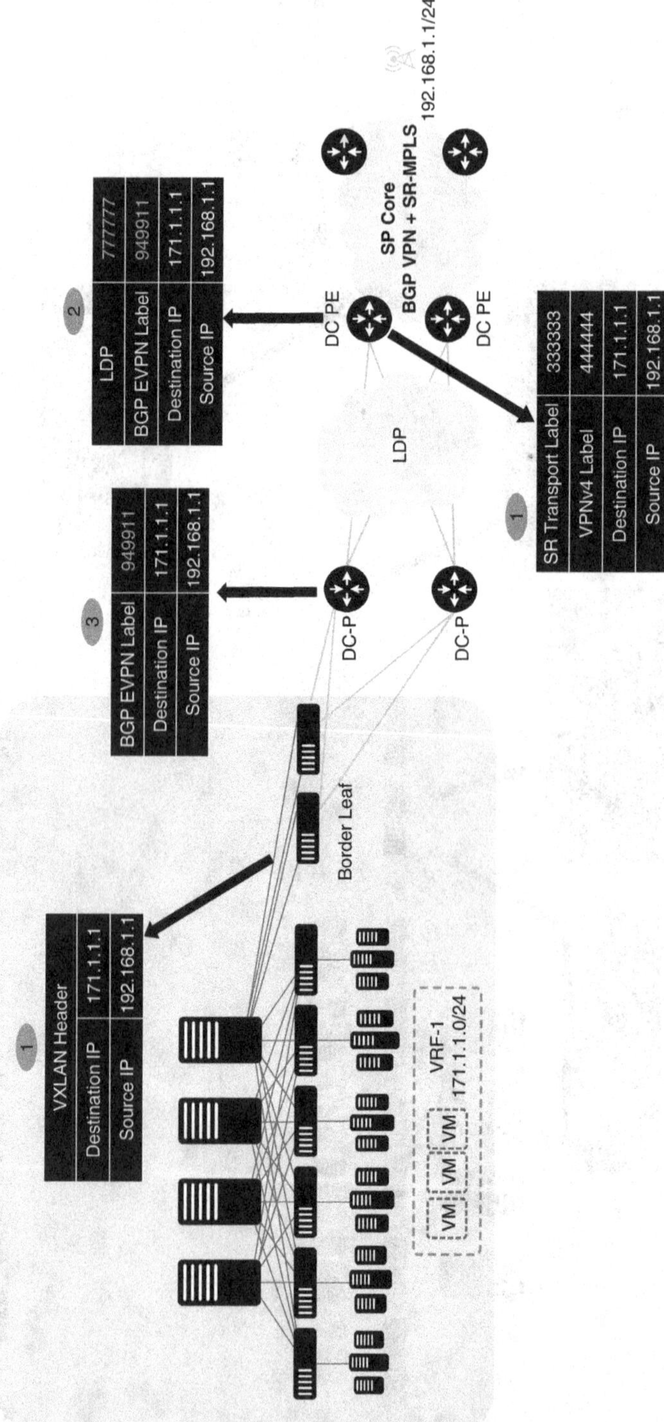

Figure 4-51 *Packet Walk for Data Plane Connectivity from PE to BL*

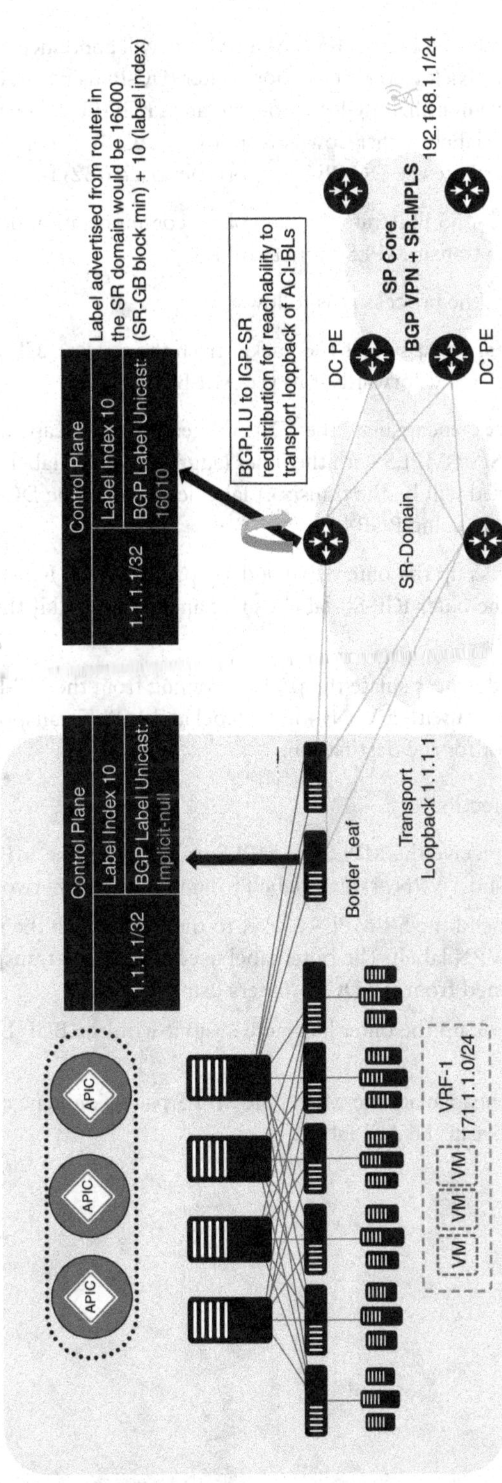

Figure 4-52 *Label Exchange Using MPLS-SR as Transit (BL to PE)*

In the reverse path (see Figure 4-53), the DC-PEs will announce a transport label for the transport loopback to their next-hop router (DC-P) using SR-IGP. Subsequently, the DC-P router will utilize BGP-LU to generate a BGP-LU label and advertise the DC-PE transport label further downstream to the ACI BLs. Furthermore, the DC-P router will redistribute the DC-PE transport loopback (/32) from IGP-SR to BGP-LU.

Figures 4-54 and 4-55 illustrate the data plane communication between ACI-BL and DC-PE through a transit MPLS SR network.

In the data plane, the process is as follows:

1. The source leaf encapsulates the packet from the source ACI endpoint into a VXLAN header and forwards it to the ACI-BLs.
2. The ACI-BLs de-encapsulate the VXLAN header and encapsulate the packet toward MPLS/SR-MPLS with the inner (aggregate) VRF label (EVPN label). The outer label used will be the transport label learned for the DC-PEs, obtained from the DC-P router using BGP-LU.
3. The DC-P looks up the outer label and swaps it with the IGP-SR learned label for the DC-PE (the outer IGP-SR label can be an implicit null if the DC-PE is directly attached to the DC-P).
4. The DC-PEs de-encapsulate the packets coming from the DC-P and further encapsulate them with a VPNv4 inner label and MPLS transport outer label based on prefix/color for the destination.

In the reverse direction:

1. The DC-PEs receive the MPLS/SR-MPLS packets with the MPLS transport label (outer label) and a VPNv4 (inner label) from the SP core network.
2. The DC-PEs send the SR-MPLS packet to the DC-Ps with the inner aggregate VRF label (EVPN label). The outer label used will be the transport label for the ACI BLs, learned from the DC-P routers using IGP-SR.
3. The DC-Ps look up the outer label and swap it with the BGP-LU learned label for the ACI BLs.
4. ACI-BLs de-encapsulate the MPLS/SR-MPLS packet and encapsulate it to the VXLAN header in the ACI fabric.

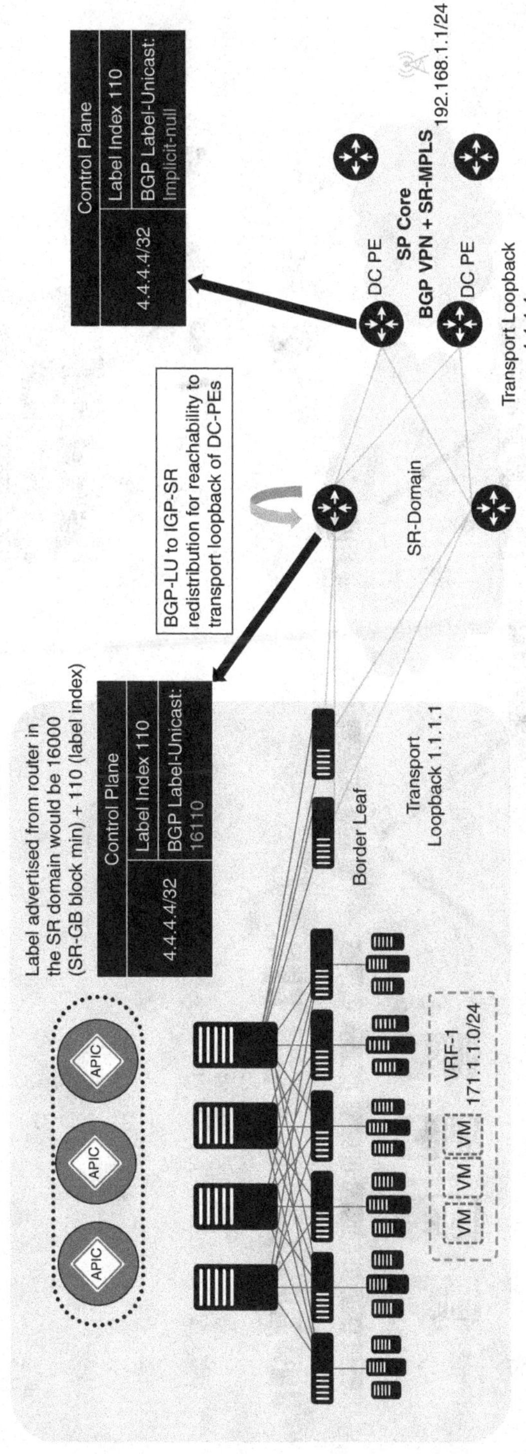

Figure 4-53 *Label Exchange Using MPLS-SR as Transit (PE to BL)*

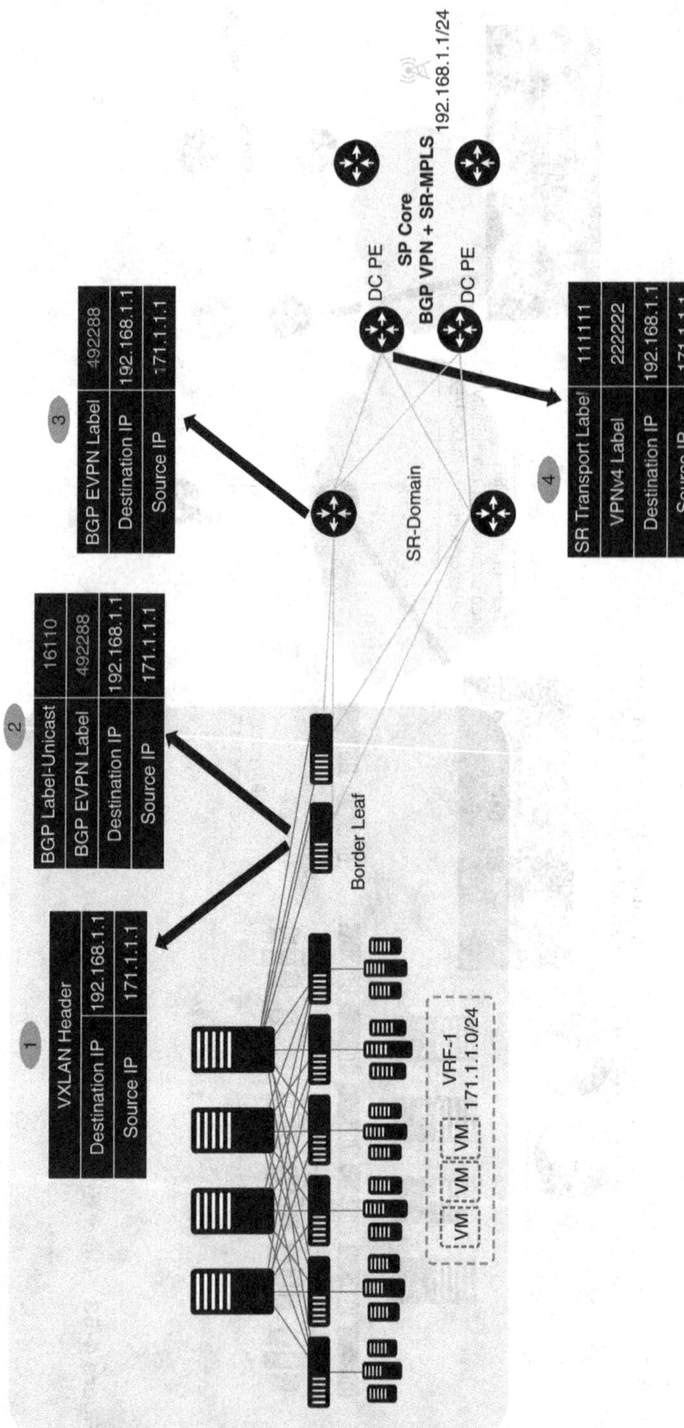

Figure 4-54 *Packet Walk for Data Plane Connectivity from BL to PE*

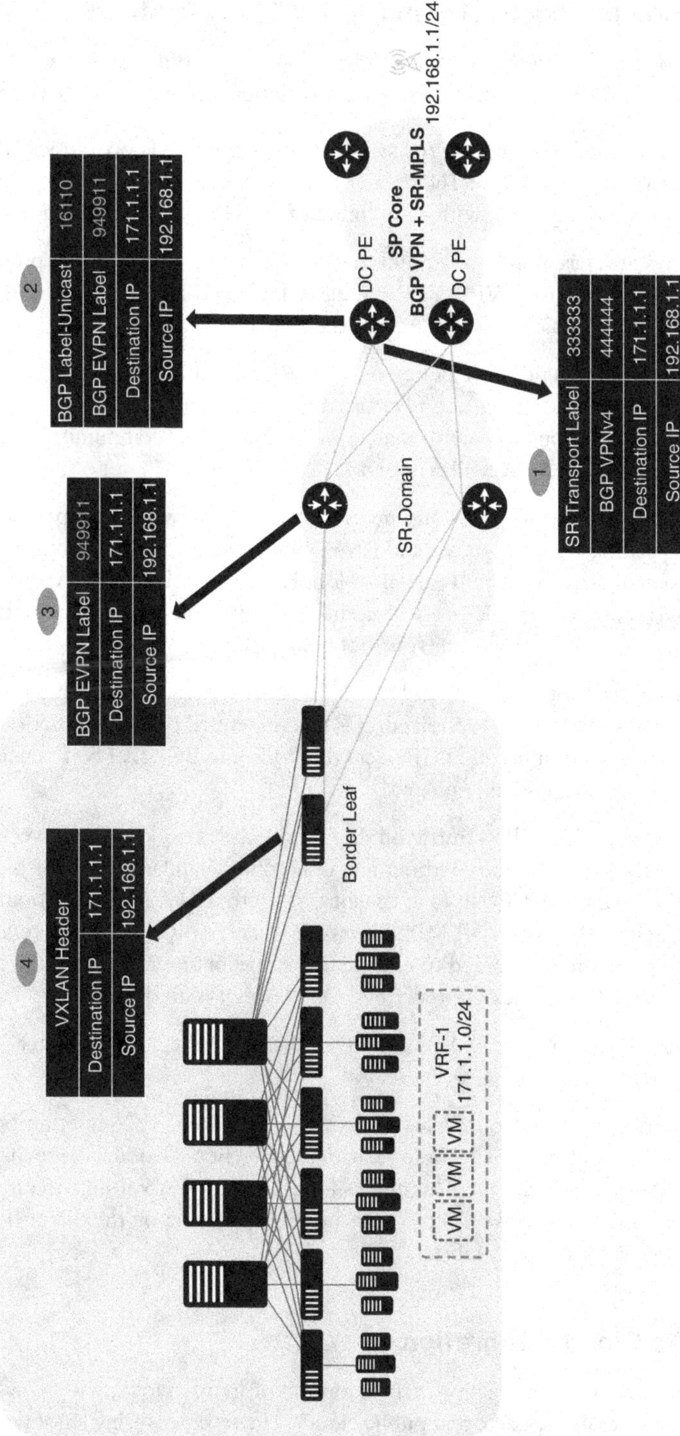

Figure 4-55 *Packet Walk for Data Plane Connectivity from PE to BL*

Guidelines and Limitations Around ACI MPLS/SR-MPLS Integration

While Cisco provides comprehensive documentation that outlines guidelines and limitations for ACI SR-MPLS integration, here are some important points to consider:

- It is recommended to configure the same Segment Routing Global Block for all nodes within the SR domain. The default SRGB range in ACI is 16,000 to 23,999, but it can be user-configurable with a minimum of 16,000 and a maximum of 471,804.
- ACI always advertises an implicit null for underlay transport loopback prefixes (/32s). However, for the EVPN VRF aggregate label, a different range of 948576 to 1068576 is used, which is separate from the SRGB range.
- By default, the inbound route policy on the VRF L3Out accepts all prefixes, but the outbound route policy does not advertise any prefixes. It is crucial to configure an explicit outbound route policy to match prefixes and BGP communities for advertisement to the MPLS/SR-MPLS network.
- The base Infra L3Out in ACI is automatically configured with route policies to allow inbound prefixes of IPv4 unicast and IPv4 labeled unicast address families to learn EVPN control plane plane and transport loopbacks from the MPLS/MPLS-SR network. Outbound route policies are also automatically configured to advertise EVPN control plane loopbacks and transport loopbacks for the ACI BLs.
- BGP sessions for both BGP-LU and EVPN must be external BGP (eBGP) sessions. Internal BGP (iBGP) is not supported. It is recommended to use Bidirectional Forwarding Detection for all eBGP peers (BGP-LU and BGP EVPN) to ensure fast failure detection during link outages.
- By default, incoming MPLS traffic on ACI-BLs is classified into QoS level 3, retaining the original DSCP values without any re-marking. Similarly, the ACI-BLs do not change the original DSCP values of tenant traffic from ACI source endpoints when forwarding it to the MPLS/SR-MPLS network. Custom SR-MPLS QoS policies and/or contracts can be configured to change this behavior and map incoming MPLS EXP to COS/DSCP values or predefined QoS levels within the fabric.
- Redundant paths between ACI-BLs and DC-PEs should be used for faster convergence.
- In ACI multi-site, multi-pod deployments with MPLS/SR-MPLS integration, it is recommended to configure each site/pod with a different VRF and a different MPLS/SR-MPLS Infra (base) L3Out. This allows for SR-MPLS WAN utilization for east-west communication between sites/pods instead of relying on the direct IP network between the spines in each fabric.

ACI and Public Cloud Integration

The reality for most enterprises now is the adoption of hybrid cloud, with workloads spread across on-premises, edge, and public clouds. However, ensuring smooth operations of hybrid cloud applications across these distributed environments comes with challenges in meeting location-dependent requirements such as low latency, regional data compliance, and resiliency. Additionally, maintaining consistent communication and security policies across different platforms adds complexity to the equation. Without proper support from interconnecting software, achieving availability and compliance becomes a difficult task.

To address these challenges, Cisco Nexus Dashboard Orchestrator (NDO) and Cisco Cloud Network Controller (CNC) come into play. They provide the necessary interconnection, as well as abstraction and normalization, enabling enterprises to maintain a consistent security and policy posture across all cloud environments. This helps reduce the learning curve associated with public cloud environments.

Figure 4-56 provides a high-level mapping of the Cisco CNC policy model to native constructs found in public clouds.

Azure Cloud		Cisco ACI		AWS Cloud
Organization	←	Security Domain	→	OU
Region	←	Site/Pod	→	Region
Subscription	←	Tenant	→	Account
Virtual Network	←	VRF/Context	→	VPC
Subnet	←	VRFCIDRs	→	Subnet
App Security Group	←	EPG	→	Security Group
Network Security Group	←	Contract, Filters	→	Security Group Rule
Inbound Rule	←	Consumed Contracts	→	Inbound Rule
Outbound Rule	←	Provided Contracts	→	Outbound Rule

Figure 4-56 *Mapping of ACI Policy Model to Cloud Native Constructs*

When extending the Cisco ACI fabric to the public cloud, Cisco NDO plays a crucial role as the centralized policy distribution component. It allows you to define the network and security policies for your hybrid-cloud applications in a programmatic manner. These defined requirements are then transmitted to the on-premises controller (Cisco APIC) and the Cloud APIC controller (Cisco CNC). The Cisco APIC controllers running on-premises receive the policies from NDO, render them, and enforce them locally.

However, there is a slight difference with Cisco CNC due to the fact that public cloud vendors do not natively speak ACI. Therefore, NDO policies need to be translated into cloud-native policy constructs based on the mapping defined in the previous diagram. These translated policies are then applied to the respective public cloud instances. In this case, Cisco CNC plays a crucial role because it provides the policy translation and programming functionalities for the cloud environment. It ensures automated connectivity for workloads in the public cloud by translating all policies received from NDO and programming them into cloud-native constructs/resources such as virtual private cloud (VPC), security groups, security group rules, and more using the cloud-native policy APIs.

Figure 4-57 illustrates the Cisco Cloud ACI operational model using NDO and CNC.

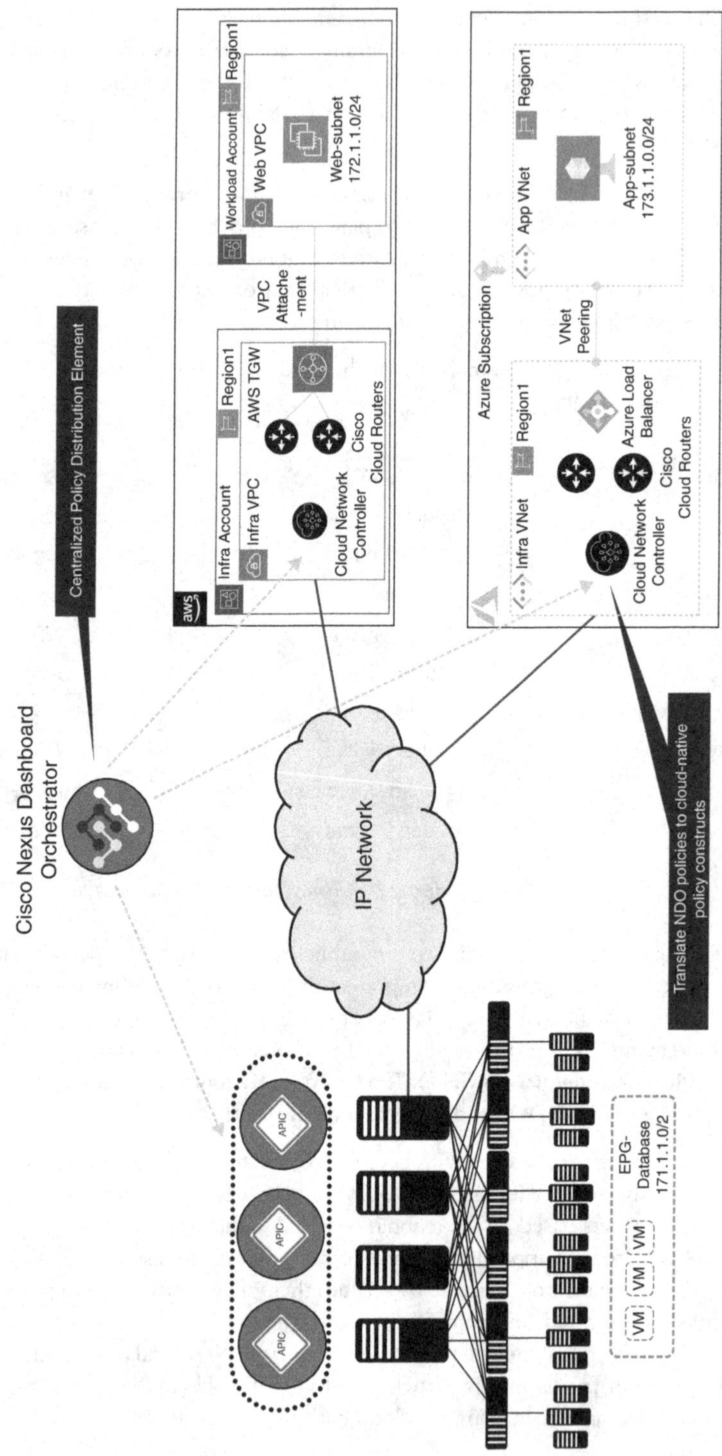

Figure 4-57 *Cisco Cloud ACI Operational Model*

Cisco NDO serves as the centralized policy distribution element responsible for site registration of both on-premises Cisco ACI data center sites and cloud sites. It automates the creation of overlay connectivity between all sites, including on-premises and cloud, while acting as the unified console for inter-site policies. When defining inter-site policies for private and public cloud, NDO has the ability to selectively distribute policies based on application requirements. For example, if a hybrid cloud application requires the web tier to be deployed in the public cloud while keeping the app and database tier on-premises, NDO can distribute policies only to the relevant sites.

Cisco NDO can be deployed either on-premises (running on a K8S Service Engine Platform) or on the public cloud. On the other hand, Cisco CNC is a micro-services-based software deployment that runs natively on supported public cloud platforms.

It's worth noting that while the most common approach is to use NDO to define network and security policies and distribute them to CNC, you also have the option to define these policies directly on the CNC for the cloud site.

Both NDO and CNC automate the configuration of various network-related elements across different cloud platforms to establish underlay and overlay connectivity between sites in a hybrid cloud environment. Examples of these elements include VPCs, CIDRs, subnets, transit gateway (TGWs), TGW peering, security groups, security group rules, Application Load Balancers (ALBs), route tables in Amazon Web Services (AWS), as well as virtual networks (VNets), CIDRs, subnets, VNet peering, network security groups, application security groups, Azure Application Gateway, network load balancers, and route tables in Azure. Additionally, Cisco Cloud Routers (CCRs) are also supported in the configuration automation process.

Underlay and Overlay Intersite Connectivity

The on-premises Cisco ACI sites and the ACI cloud site in the public cloud are connected through an underlay IP network. This underlay IP network can utilize either the public Internet or private connections such as AWS Direct Connect (DX) for AWS or Azure Express Route (ER) for Microsoft Azure. The main purpose of the underlay IP network is to provide the necessary IP reachability for the communication of the overlay control plane and data plane between these sites.

Figures 4-58 and 4-59 illustrate the connection setup between the on-premises site and the ACI cloud site for AWS and Azure respectively.

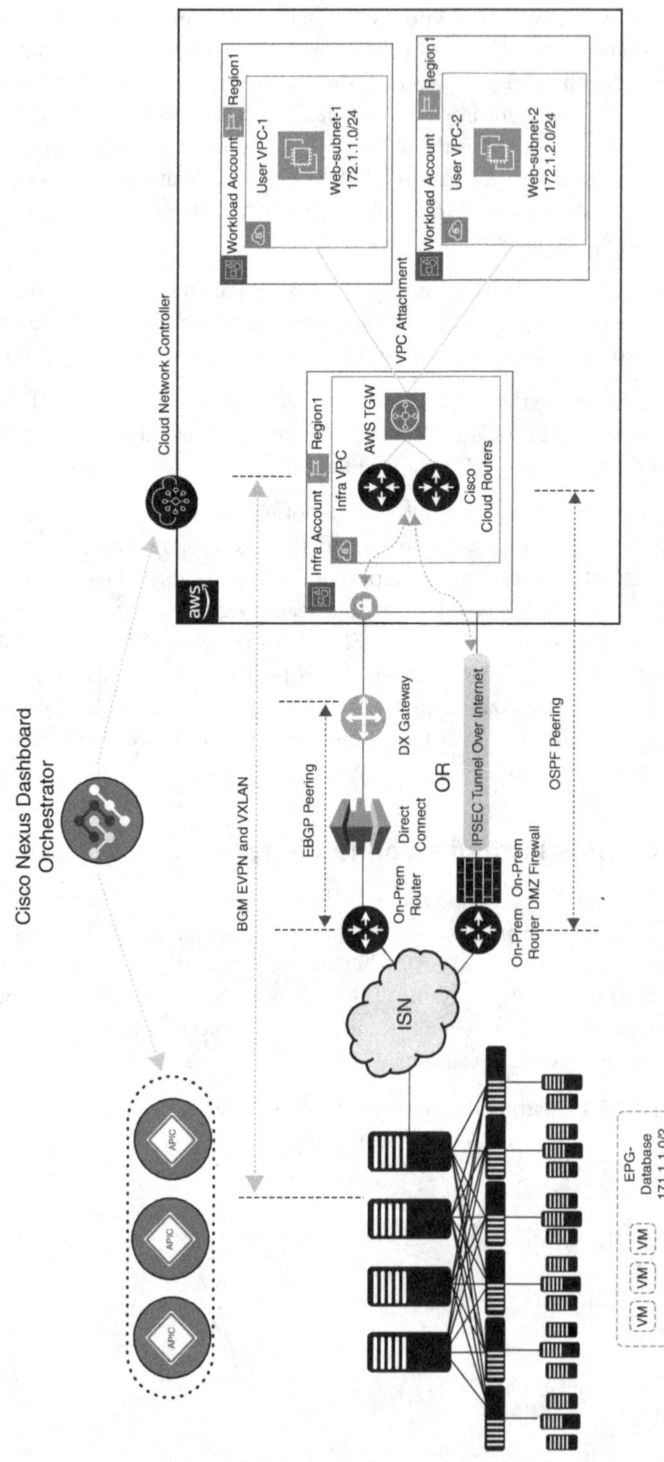

Figure 4-58 *Underlay, Overlay Connectivity Between On-Premises and Cloud Site–AWS*

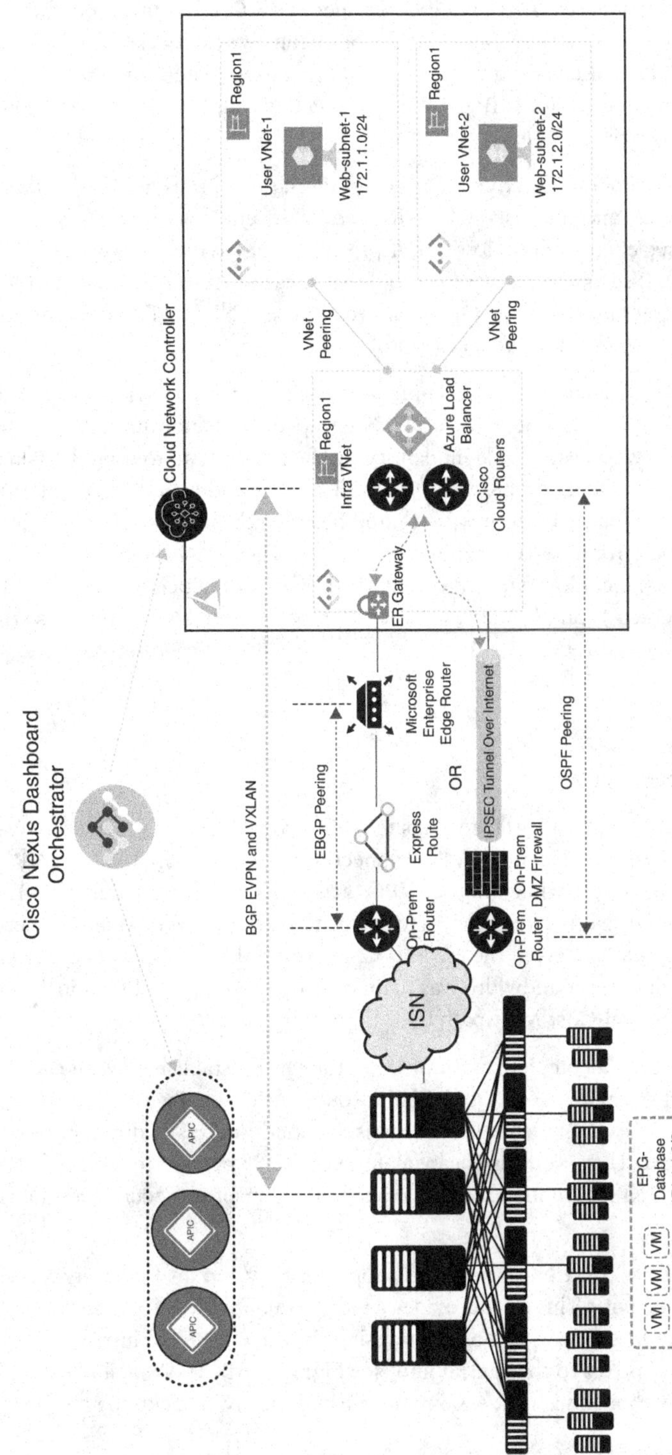

Figure 4-59 *Underlay, Overlay Connectivity Between On-Premises and Cloud Site–Azure*

For the foundational network's IP underlay connectivity, OSPF is utilized. OSPF is used between the on-premises ACI Spines and the on-premises routers via the ACI inter-site network. Similarly, OSPF is used between the on-premises routers and the Cisco Cloud Routers through the underlying IP network. This underlying IP network can be either the public Internet or private pathways.

In cases where Internet connectivity is used, an IPsec tunnel is established between the on-premises routers and the Cisco Cloud Routers. This tunnel allows for OSPF peering through the IPsec connections. However, if private connectivity like AWS DX or Azure ER is employed, IPsec may not be required. In such cases, AWS DX or Azure ER will establish eBGP peering with the on-premises routers, and NDO will configure static routes on the Cisco Cloud Routers instead of OSPF.

The overlay network connecting the on-premises ACI sites and the cloud sites utilizes BGP EVPN as its control plane, with VXLAN encapsulation and tunneling for the data plane. VXLAN plays a critical role in identifying the appropriate routing domain when extending a VRF across an on-premises Cisco ACI fabric and various cloud platforms. Tenant host routes and prefix routes are shared between these sites using BGP EVPN route types: type-2 for hosts and type-5 for prefixes. The establishment of overlay network connectivity, including Multi-Protocol (MP-BGP) EVPN peering between the ACI Spines and the Cisco Cloud Routers, whether with or without IPsec tunnels, is streamlined and automated through NDO.

Traffic Flows

From an AWS perspective:

Before ACI release 5.0, CNC utilized transit virtual private clouds (VPC) with a VPN overlay approach to establish multi-VPC connectivity. In this setup, the infra VPC served as the central transit hub, while the user VPCs acted as spokes (see Figure 4-60). VPN tunnels were established between the virtual private gateways (VGWs) in the user VPCs and the Cisco Cloud Routers in the infra VPC. However, this design had complexities and performance limitations. Bandwidth was limited to 1.25 Gbps per VPC tunnel, and VGW did not support Equal-Cost Multipath (ECMP) routing.

In this configuration, a complete mesh of IPsec tunnels is established, with each VGW forming connections with every Cisco Cloud Router. Additionally, each Cisco Cloud Router establishes IPsec tunnels with other Cisco Cloud Routers in different regions over the public Internet. These tunnels encapsulate BGP EVPN peering for control plane communication and VXLAN tunnels for data plane transit, ensuring secure communication between sites.

Starting from release 5.0, CNC introduced support for AWS transit gateway to simplify multi-VPC connectivity. This shift provides a more straightforward setup with enhanced bandwidth capabilities. TGW acts as the transit hub, while both the infra VPC and user VPCs connect as spokes to the central hub (see Figure 4-61). TGW facilitates routing between VPCs within and across AWS regions using the AWS backbone.

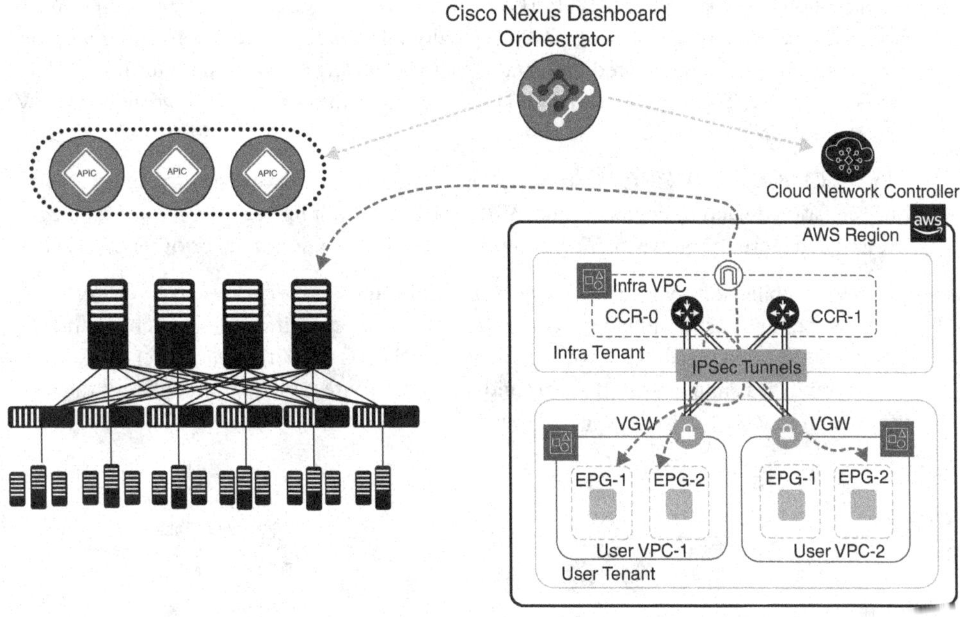

Figure 4-60 *IPsec Tunnels with VGW*

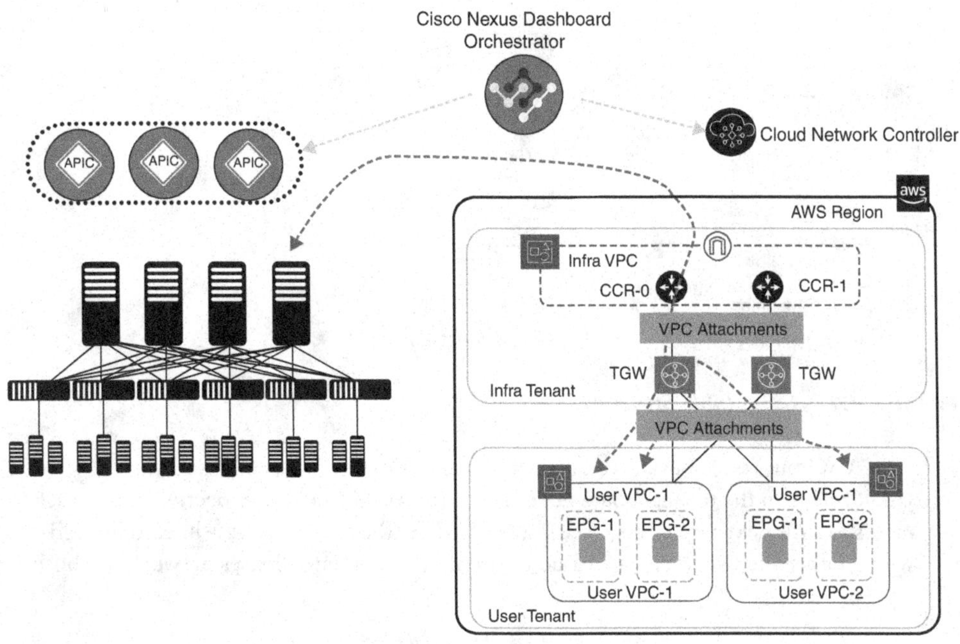

Figure 4-61 *AWS Transit Gateway (TGW)*

Unlike VGW peering that uses BGP, TGW forwards packets based on static routes. When both TGW and VGW are present, TGW typically takes precedence due to lower administrative distance (AD) associated with static routing. During initial setup, multiple TGWs are not required. The same TGW can be used by the infrastructure to serve all other AWS tenants in the same region.

Cloud ACI leverages AWS TGW to provision cloud-native network infrastructure for various scenarios, including regional multi-VPC connectivity, inter-region network connectivity, and connectivity between AWS cloud sites and on-premises sites or other cloud sites.

The responsibility of configuring route tables and routes lies with the CNC for both the transit gateway and individual virtual private clouds. Specifically, for each tenant, the CNC creates a dedicated TGW route table within the TGW. Within each user VPC, the CNC establishes an ingress route table and an egress route table that includes all the subnets within that particular VPC (see Figure 4-62).

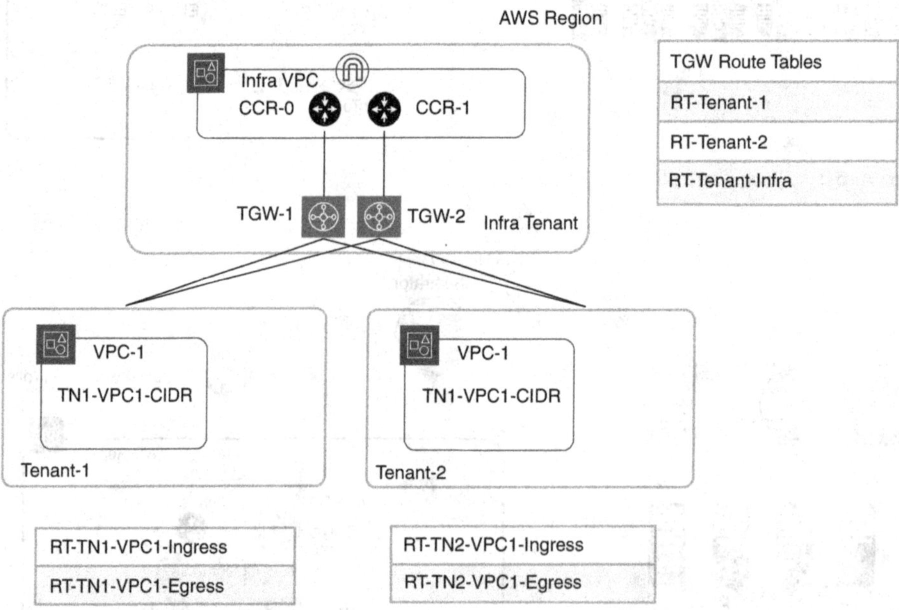

Figure 4-62 *Route Table Structure*

The TGW route table designated for a user's tenant disseminates all associated VPC CIDR routes to the tenant's route table. These routes include the respective VPC attachments as their next-hop targets (see Figure 4-63). If the user's tenant is interconnected with another site, whether it's a cloud environment or an on-premises network, via both

TGW and locally deployed Cisco Cloud Routers, a 0.0.0.0/0 route is included in the tenant's table. This route is configured with the infra VPC TGW attachment as the next-hop target.

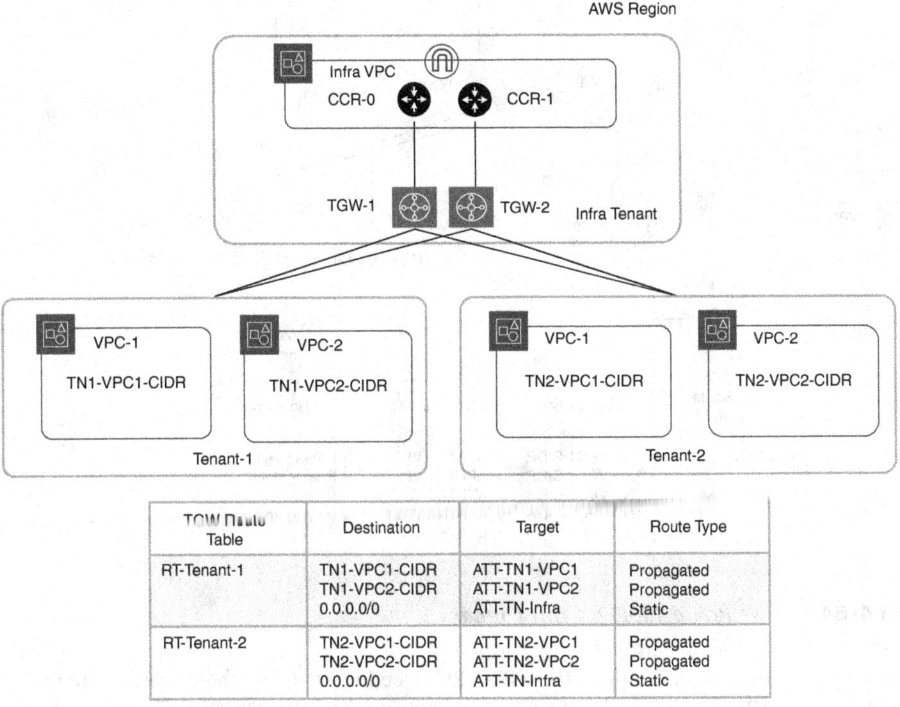

TGW Route Table	Destination	Target	Route Type
RT-Tenant-1	TN1-VPC1-CIDR TN1-VPC2-CIDR 0.0.0.0/0	ATT-TN1-VPC1 ATT-TN1-VPC2 ATT-TN-Infra	Propagated Propagated Static
RT-Tenant-2	TN2-VPC1-CIDR TN2-VPC2-CIDR 0.0.0.0/0	ATT-TN2-VPC1 ATT-TN2-VPC2 ATT-TN-Infra	Propagated Propagated Static

Figure 4-63 *TGW Route Table for User Tenants*

Additionally, the TGW programs all VPC CIDR routes of user tenants into its route table for the infra tenant. These routes are configured with the respective VPC attachments as their next-hop targets (see Figure 4-64). Traffic originating from other sites, whether in the cloud or on-premises, utilizes this route table to reach their intended destinations within the user VPCs. If the region is interconnected with another site, whether in the cloud or on-premises, via TGW and locally deployed Cisco Cloud Routers, a static 0.0.0.0/0 route is added to the infra tenant's route table. This route is configured with the Elastic Network Interface (ENI) of the Cisco Cloud Routers in the infra VPC as the designated next-hop target.

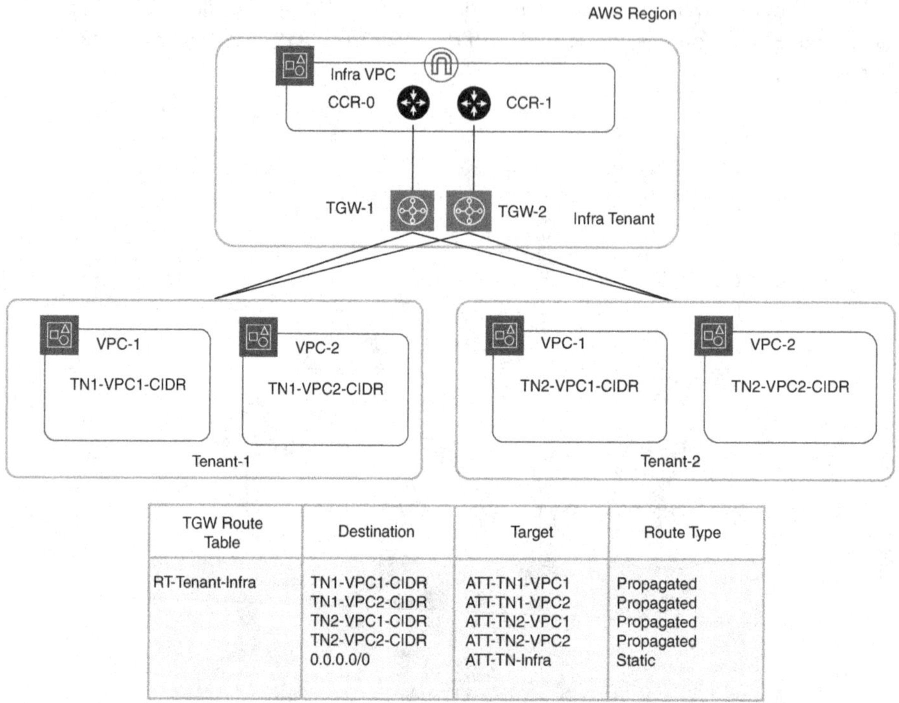

TGW Route Table	Destination	Target	Route Type
RT-Tenant-Infra	TN1-VPC1-CIDR TN1-VPC2-CIDR TN2-VPC1-CIDR TN2-VPC2-CIDR 0.0.0.0/0	ATT-TN1-VPC1 ATT-TN1-VPC2 ATT-TN2-VPC1 ATT-TN2-VPC2 ATT-TN-Infra	Propagated Propagated Propagated Propagated Static

Figure 4-64 *TGW Route Table for Infra Tenant*

Regarding route programming in the user VPCs (see Figure 4-65), the ingress route table within a user VPC includes a local route entry for its own VPC CIDR. However, in the egress route table of the user VPC, in addition to the local route for its own VPC CIDR, the following routes are configured:

- If the VPC needs to communicate with other VPCs, remote VPC CIDR routes are established with one of the TGWs designated as the next-hop target.
- If the VPC needs to communicate with VPCs located on other sites, whether in the cloud or on-premises, remote site prefix routes are set up with one of the TGWs as the next-hop target.
- If the applications within the VPC utilize the Internet gateway (IGW) for Internet access, implying that one or more application network profiles within the VPC have external EPGs configured for Internet connectivity, a 0.0.0.0/0 route is programmed with the VPC's IGW as the designated next-hop target.

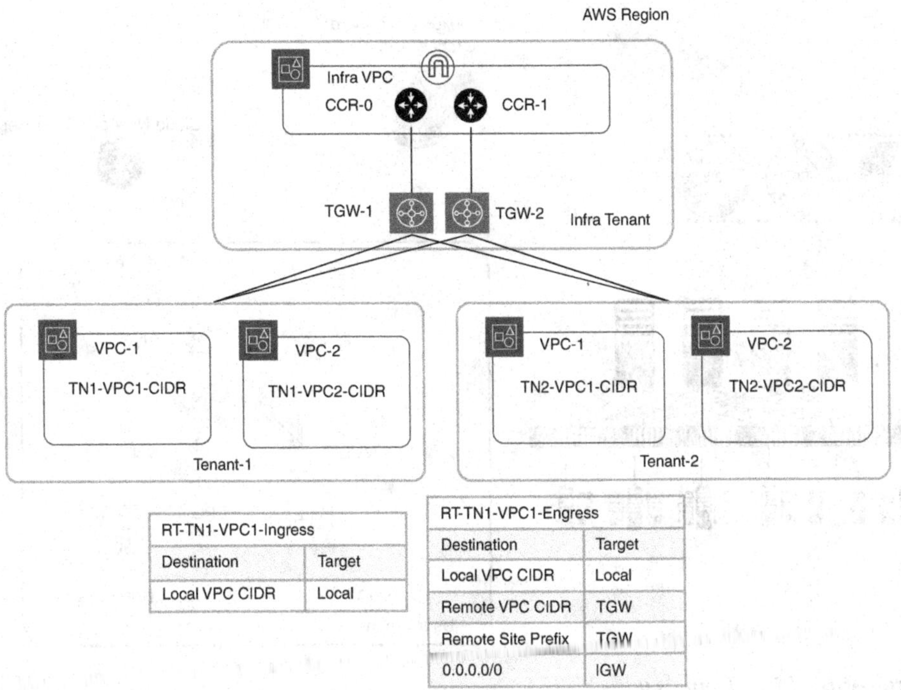

Figure 4-65 *Route Programming in User VPCs*

From an Azure perspective:

Before the release of ACI version 5.0, CNC utilized the infra virtual network (VN) using a VPN overlay approach to establish multi-VNet connectivity; like AWS, in this setup, the infra VNet operated as the central transit hub, while the user VNets functioned as the spokes. VPN tunnels were established between the virtual network gateways (VNGs) within the user VNets and the Cisco Cloud Routers situated in the infra VN. However, it's important to emphasize that the VNGs offered limited bandwidth, making them suitable primarily for situations requiring encryption, but where bandwidth and latency restrictions were acceptable.

Additionally, like AWS, a comprehensive network of IPsec tunnels was set up, with each virtual network gateway establishing connections to every Cisco Cloud Router (see Figure 4-66). Moreover, each Cisco Cloud Router initiated IPSec tunnels with the Cisco Cloud Routers situated in other regions over the public Internet. Within these tunnels, the BGP EVPN peering for control plane communication and the VXLAN tunnels for data plane transit were encapsulated, thereby ensuring secure communication between these different sites.

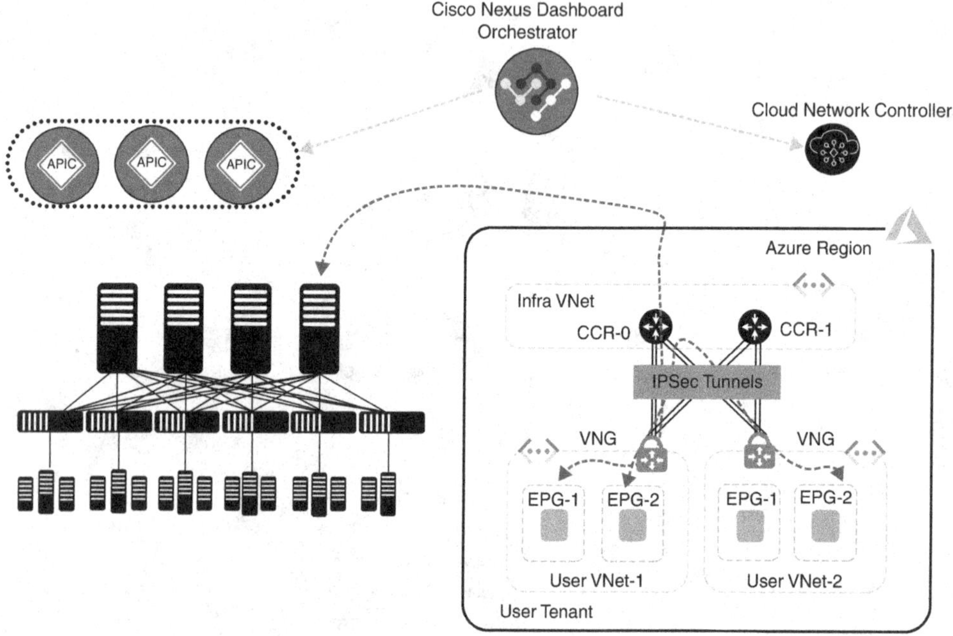

Figure 4-66 *IPsec Tunnels with VNG*

Starting from the release of 5.0, the solution introduced VN peering to enable multi-VN connectivity. VN peering offers a high-performance and low-latency connection, which is especially valuable for scenarios like cross-region data replication and database failover. Organizations with strict data policies prefer VN peering because it keeps all traffic within the Microsoft backbone, ensuring private and secure connections without relying on public Internet gateways. This results in minimal latency.

In VN peering (see Figure 4-67), the CNC still utilizes the Infra VN as the central transit hub and the user VNs as spokes. However, this approach allows seamless connection of Azure VNs without needing a full mesh of VPN tunnels. Once peered, the VNs appear as a single entity for connectivity purposes. Traffic between endpoints in the peered VNs is routed through the Microsoft infrastructure, similar to traffic within the same VN. Importantly, this communication occurs through private addresses, avoiding any routing through the public Internet. VN peering can take two forms: local peering within the same region or global peering across different regions. When a prefix is reachable via both local and global VN peering, the local VN takes precedence due to its lower cost.

CNC also automatically provisions the Azure Load Balancer (ALB) in the infra VN, alongside the Cisco Cloud Routers. It also configures user-defined routes (UDRs) within User VNs to establish network connectivity within the cloud sites. Communication between user VNs and between a user VN and an on-premises site is facilitated through the Cisco Cloud Routers via the Azure Load Balancer located in the Infra VN, guided by the UDRs configured within the user VN.

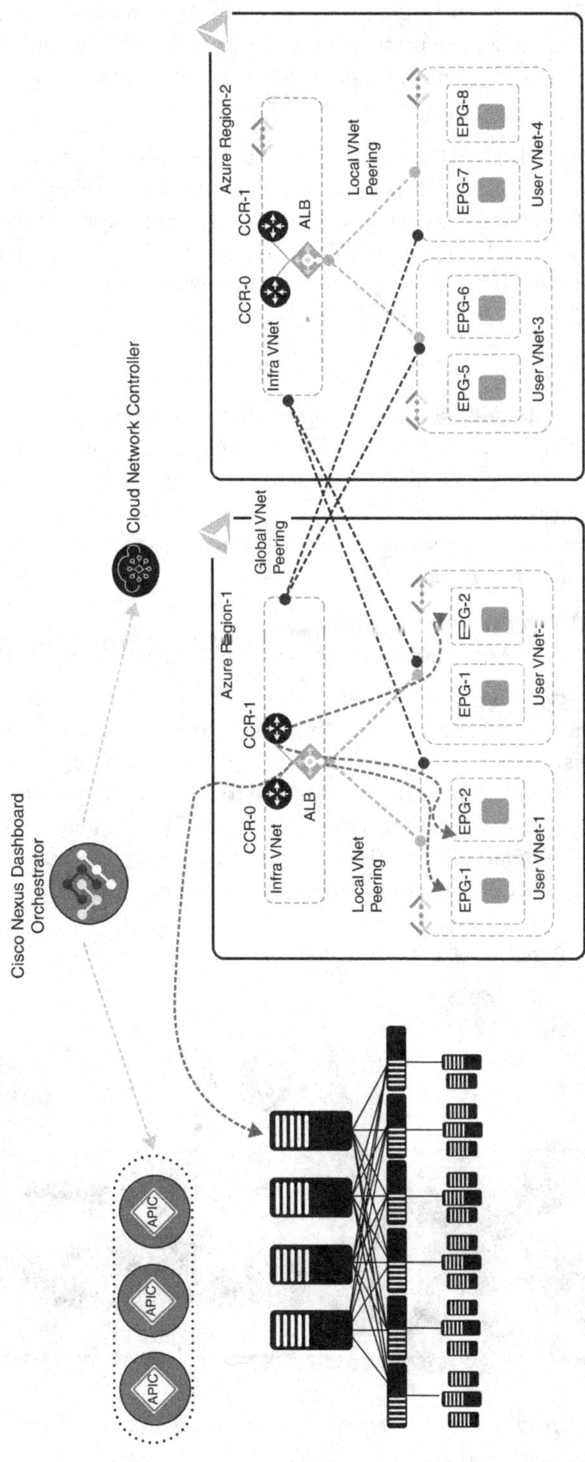

Figure 4-67 *VN Peering*

The Azure Load Balancer plays a crucial role in balancing connections to the Cisco Cloud Routers. Intra-region connections utilize local VN peering with the infra VN within the same region, while inter-region connections use global VN peering with the infra VN in another region.

It's important to note that VN peering relies on static routes, unlike the use of BGP with virtual gateways. Additionally, VN peerings are non-transitive, meaning that if VN A is peered with VN B, and VN B is peered with VN C, it doesn't automatically imply that VN A can communicate with VN C through VN B as a transit VN. This is why Cisco employs a hub-and-spoke model for VN peering, avoiding complex and meshed configurations.

Design Option

This section delves into multiple design choices that are commonly used to integrate Cisco ACI with multi-cloud environments. What remains consistent across all of these choices is the ability of ACI's multi-cloud integration to normalize the intricacies involved in hybrid cloud deployments. This normalization is achieved by ensuring uniformity in network and security policy framework across on-premises infrastructure and various public cloud environments.

Applications Stretched Across Sites (Intra-Tenant/Intra-VRF)

In this particular scenario (see Figure 4-68), the VRF instance is extended across three distinct environments: on-premises ACI, Amazon Web Services (AWS), and Microsoft Azure. This extension is implemented to enable Layer 3 connectivity between these environments. Within ACI, this VRF is connected to a virtual private cloud in AWS and a virtual network in Microsoft Azure. Within this VRF, a hybrid cloud e-commerce application is defined with multiple tiers. The "web-frontend" tier spans across AWS, Azure, while the "inventory-backend" tier resides within the on-prem ACI fabric.

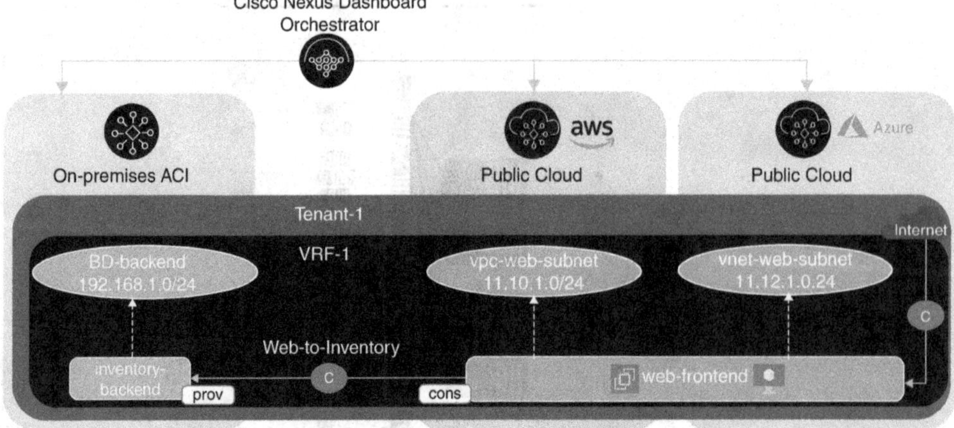

Figure 4-68 *Application Stretched Across Sites (Intra-Tenant, Intra-VRF)*

Figure 4-69 illustrates the schema and template definition on NDO for the "stretched intra-tenant" use case.

Schema	Template	Sites	Policies*
hybrid-cloud-stretched-app	stretched	AWS, Azure	VRF-1 (web CIDRs)
			web EPG & BD
	stretched	AWS, Azure, DC1	web-to-inventory contract & filter
	azure-only	Azure	internet EPG
			internet-access contract & filter
	dc1-only	DC1	inventory backend EPG & BD
			web-to-inventory contract association

Figure 4-69 *Schema and Template Definition*

It's worth noting that communication within an endpoint group does not require the use of a contract, even if the endpoints are located in different environments. For example, an AWS instance within the "web-frontend" EPG can communicate with an Azure virtual machine in the same "web-frontend" EPG without the need for a contract. When an EPG is stretched across multiple environments, Cisco NDO normalizes and automatically deploys the required routing and security policies in each environment, even if the public cloud environments have different methods of implementing these configurations.

The responsibilities of an administrator include creating VRFs, EPGs, and contracts between EPGs using NDO. NDO, in collaboration with Cisco APIC and the Cloud Network Controller, handles the deployment and normalization of these configurations across the various environments.

It's essential to note that due to the "web-frontend" EPG extension across both Azure and AWS cloud environments, the provisioning of the "web-frontend" EPG should be included within an NDO template associated with both cloud sites for AWS and Azure. Any changes made to the stretched template will be consistently applied to all sites. Therefore, it is crucial to incorporate configuration elements in the stretched template that are compatible with both public cloud sites.

When the "web-frontend" EPG is extended across multiple sites, the subnet associated with the "web-frontend" EPG within each public cloud platform is announced to the corresponding Cisco Cloud Routers. These routers then exchange routes between themselves, enabling inter-cloud connectivity. Moreover, the contract relationship established between the "inventory-backend" EPG and the "web-frontend" EPG leads to a route exchange for the "inventory-backend" EPG subnet with the Cisco Cloud Routers. Similarly, the subnet linked to the "web-frontend" EPG on the cloud sites is advertised from the Cisco Cloud Routers to the on-premises site.

Applications Stretched Across Sites (Inter-Tenant/Inter-VRF)

We will utilize this scenario to illustrate a use case where a shared-services resource from an on-premises provider is shared with consumer resources in the cloud. Examples of shared-services provider resources include commonly used databases, DNS, and Active Directory (AD) services that are utilized by applications and users both on-premises and in the cloud.

From a network policy perspective, enabling communication between different Virtual Routing and Forwarding instances will require the exchange of routes between the consumer and provider VRFs. From a security policy perspective, the contract relationship between the VRFs must be configured with the appropriate scope.

If the consumer and provider VRFs are located in different tenants, the contract relationship should be set to a global scope. Conversely, if the consumer and provider VRFs reside in different VRFs within the same tenant, the contract relationship should be set to a VRF scope.

In the case of an inter-tenant contract spanning across multiple sites, both sites must be associated with both tenants in the NDO "Tenants" configuration. This ensures that NDO has the necessary credentials to manage the cloud environments. However, the tenants do not need to be deployed to both sites through the "Schema" configuration. Refer to Figure 4-70:

- The EPG "database" is located in VRF1 within the on-premises ACI site under tenant1.
- The EPGs "web-frontend," "web-catalog," and "web-payment" are situated in VRF2 within the cloud sites under tenant2.
- Both the on-premises ACI site and the cloud sites are associated with tenant1 and tenant2 in the NDO "Tenants" configuration.
- Schema template1 for tenant1 is deployed exclusively on the on-premises ACI site, while template2 for tenant2 is deployed solely on the cloud sites.

Figure 4-71 illustrates the schema and template definition on NDO for the "stretched inter-tenant" use case.

It is important to note that the behavior of route leakage between different VRF instances or tenants in a hybrid solution differs slightly from that within an on-premises ACI fabric. In an on-premises fabric, selective subnets are leaked to the other VRF based on the contract relationship between EPGs. However, in a multi-cloud hybrid solution, all CIDRs and routes are leaked with the other VRF if there is an inter-VRF contract in place.

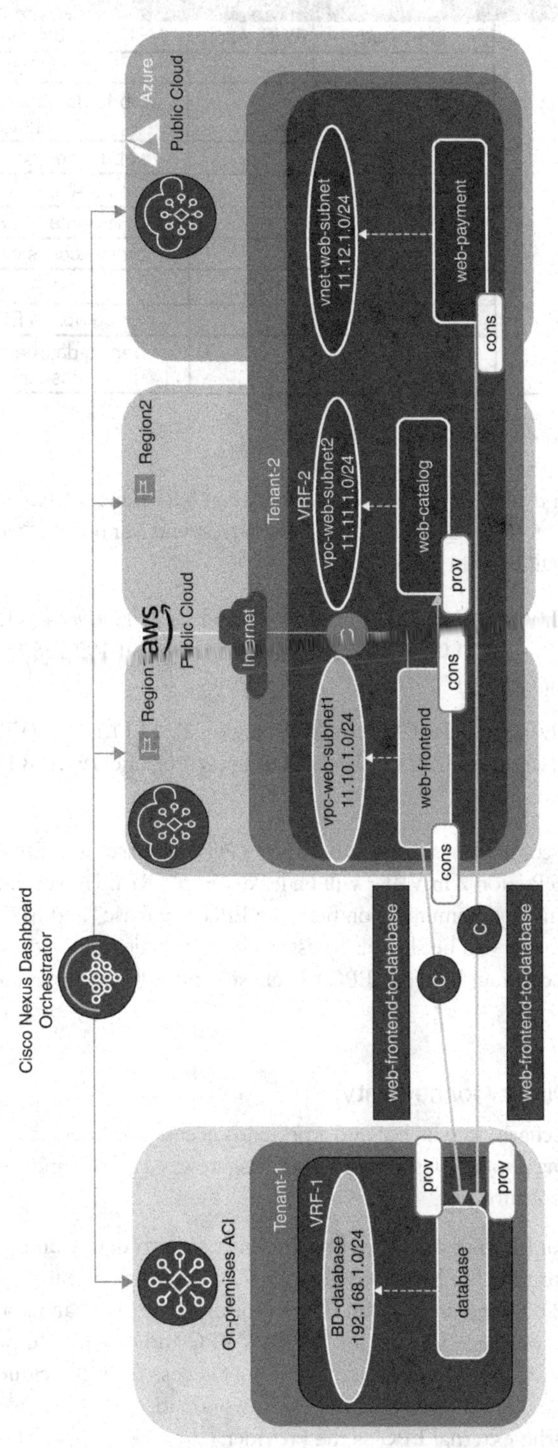

Figure 4-70 *Application Stretched Across Sites (Inter-Tenant, Inter-VRF)*

Schema	Template	Sites	Policies*
hybrid-cloud-shared-app	stretched	AWS, Azure	VRF-2 (web CIDRs & Regions)
			web EPGs & BDs
			web-to-database contracts & filters
			web-to-web contracts & filters
			web-to-web contracts association
	aws-only	AWS	internet EPG
			internet-access contract & filter
	dc1-only	DC1	VRF-1
			database EPG & BD
			web-to-database contract association

Figure 4-71 *Schema and Template Definition*

For example, even if the inter-VRF contract between VRF1 and VRF2 allows communication only between EPG "database," EPG "web-frontend," and EPG "web-catalog," the following routes will exist in each VRF:

- **VRF1:** 11.10.1.0/24 (VRF2 CIDR in AWS Region 1), 11.11.1.0/24 (VRF2 CIDR in AWS Region 2), 11.12.1.0/24 (VRF2 CIDR in Azure), and 192.168.1.0/24 (On-prem Bridge Domain subnet)
- **VRF2:** 11.10.1.0/24 (VRF2 CIDR in AWS Region 1), 11.11.1.0/24 (VRF2 CIDR in Azure Region 2), 11.12.1.0/24 (VRF2 CIDR in Azure), and 192.168.1.0/24 (On-prem Bridge Domain subnet)

Even if there is no contract relationship between EPG "database" and EPG "web-payment," the CIDR for AWS Region 2 in VRF2 will be leaked into VRF1. However, this does not imply that there will be communication between EPG "database" and EPG "web-payment." Instead, only the routes will be shared. To establish communication between the two, an additional explicit contract between EPG "database" and EPG "web-payment" needs to be configured.

Cloud to Internet (Direct Connectivity)

This is a typical scenario in which cloud workloads access the Internet directly, utilizing cloud-native routing capabilities like the Internet gateway in AWS and the default system route in Microsoft Azure.

To support external Internet connectivity, you don't have to define an L3Out but just an external EPG for the cloud site (see Figure 4-72). Creating an external EPG (Internet EPG) under the NDO template with an IP selector of 0.0.0.0/0 (meaning all prefix) will instantiate an IGW on the AWS side for the AWS VPC and/or will also program a default system route in the Azure VNet. To permit Internet access from the cloud workloads, you will need to apply a contract between the cloud workload EPG (EPG "web-frontend") as the consumer and the external EPG as the provider.

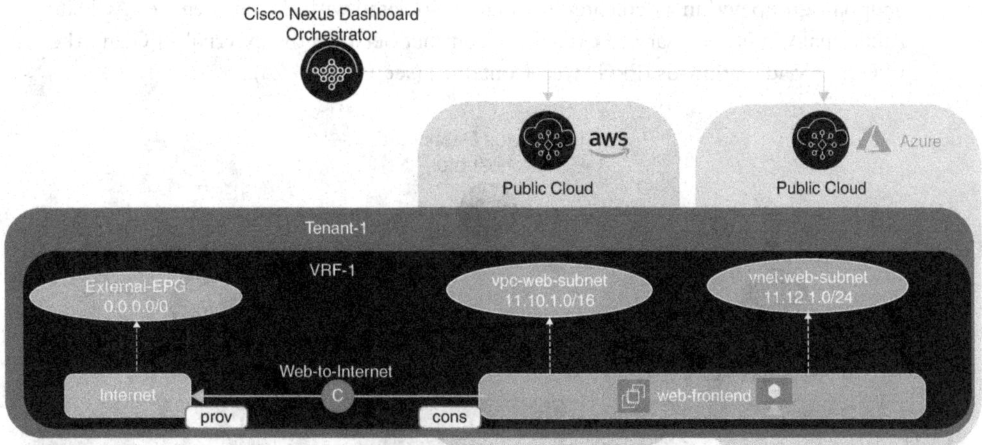

Figure 4-72 *Cloud to Internet Using Cloud Native Routing*

In this scenario, traffic originating from endpoints on the Internet and destined for the cloud endpoints in the cloud workload EPG (the consumer, EPG "web-frontend") is not initially allowed because a contract for a cloud site establishes a permit rule only for traffic from the consumer to the provider. However, the return traffic from the provider to the consumer is automatically permitted (even without an explicit permit rule) because the previous traffic from the consumer to the provider has been observed. Therefore, if there is a possibility that Internet-based endpoints may initiate communication with cloud endpoints in the cloud workload EPG (EPG "web-frontend"), it is essential to configure the external EPG (Internet EPG) as the consumer and the cloud workload EPG (EPG "web-frontend") as the provider for the contract.

Figure 4-73 illustrates the schema and template definition on NDO for the "Cloud to Internet" use case.

Schema	Template	Sites	Policies*
hybrid-cloud--l3out	stretched	AWS, Azure	VRF-1 (web CIDRs & Regions)
			web EPGs & BDs
			Internet EPG
			Internet-access contract & filter

Figure 4-73 *Schema and Template Definition*

Cloud to Internet/External Destinations Using On-Prem L3Out Connectivity

This use case becomes relevant when there is a requirement to establish connectivity between an external network (such as a wide area network, branch network, or the Internet) and public cloud workloads through an on-premises ACI fabric. To implement this use case, you will need to utilize a Layer 3 Out (L3Out) and define an external endpoint group within a dedicated template associated with the on-premises ACI site. Additionally, it is necessary to establish a contract between the external EPG and the EPG for cloud workloads (EPG "web-frontend") (see Figure 4-74).

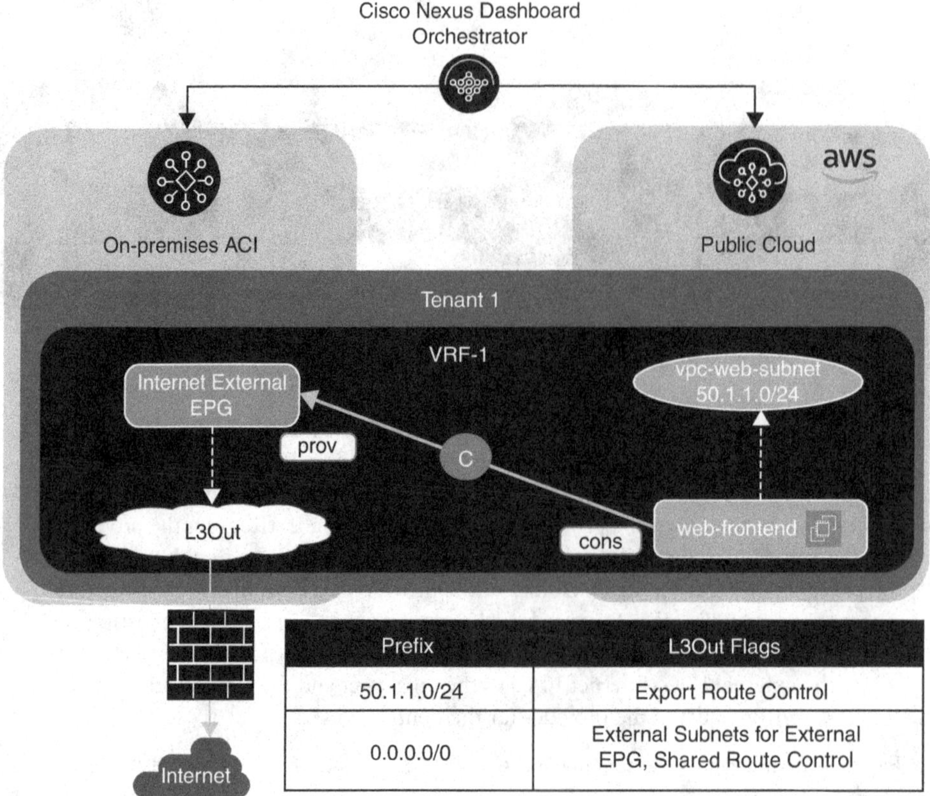

Prefix	L3Out Flags
50.1.1.0/24	Export Route Control
0.0.0.0/0	External Subnets for External EPG, Shared Route Control

Figure 4-74 *Cloud to Internet/External Networks Using On-Prem L3Out*

To advertise the CIDR prefixes associated with EPG "web-frontend" in the public cloud, you must configure the CIDR prefix within the external EPG connected to the on-premises L3Out. It is crucial to set the flag to "Export Route Control" for proper functioning. Furthermore, to propagate the externally learned prefixes from the on-premises ACI to the cloud site through the on-premises L3Out, you need to associate the externally learned prefixes with the external EPG and set the flags to "Shared Route Control" and "External Subnet for the External EPG."

If desired, an on-premises firewall can be utilized to enforce specific L4-L7 security policies for traffic entering and exiting a cloud site. This can be achieved by connecting a north-south firewall to the on-premises L3Out.

Figure 4-75 illustrates the schema and template definition on NDO for the "on-prem L3Out" use case.

Schema	Template	Sites	Policies
hybrid-cloud-native-l3out	stretched	AWS & DC1	VRF-1
			Web-to-l3out contract & filter
	aws-only	AWS	Web EPG + backdoor access
	dc1-only	DC1	L3Out*
			External EPG

Figure 4-75 *Schema and Template Definition*

In scenarios where multiple VRFs/tenants are defined on the public cloud network and connectivity needs to be established for workloads in these VRFs/tenants with the on-premises L3Out, it is recommended to use a dedicated VRF (dedicated L3Out) in the on-premises fabric (see Figure 4-76). This approach ensures external connectivity for all cloud workloads.

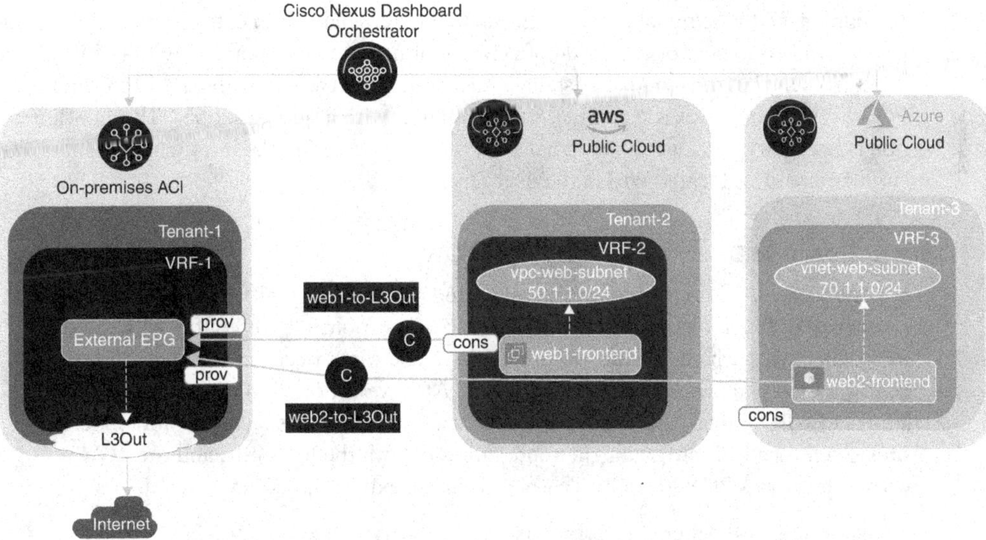

Figure 4-76 *Cloud to Internet/External Networks Using Shared On-Prem L3Out*

While it is possible to use two separate L3Outs in the on-premises fabric, each with their corresponding distinct external EPGs for VRF2 and VRF3, this design may result in overlapping subnets if a contract relationship exists between the two VRFs. It is important to remember that in a hybrid cloud deployment, when route leaking is enabled between VRFs, all CIDR/prefixes, including externally learned prefixes, will be leaked between the VRFs. This can potentially lead to overlapping subnets being learned for the external networks in the routing table of the two VRFs and may result in traffic blackholing.

Cloud to External Enterprise Sites

This use case is relevant when there is a need to establish direct connectivity between external private IP networks, such as branch networks, and public cloud workloads, without routing traffic through on-premises ACI fabrics. In this scenario, the termination point for external connectivity can be cloud native gateways, such as the AWS transit gateway or the Azure VPN or Express Route gateway. Alternatively, Cisco Cloud Routers can also be used as the termination point, with the advantage of supporting higher route scale compared to cloud native gateways.

In all cases, Border Gateway Protocol (BGP) is used as the dynamic protocol for communication between the external devices and the termination points located in the infra tenant. IPsec is utilized as the underlying tunneling technology to establish secure connections. Security policies are enforced independently at each cloud site, with AWS employing security group (SG) rules and Microsoft Azure implementing network security group (NSG) rules.

Cloud to Enterprise Destinations Using Azure VPN/ER GW

In Figure 4-77, the external endpoint group plays a crucial role in categorizing all external prefixes linked to networks outside of Azure that need to communicate with the EPG "web-frontend" in the cloud. To establish the contract between the external EPG and EPG "web-frontend," it is important to configure it with a "global scope." This configuration is necessary because the external EPG is deployed within the infra tenant, while EPG "web-frontend" is located within the user tenant.

Cloud to Enterprise Destinations Using AWS TGW

For AWS, the AWS transit gateways are created as part of the initial Cloud Network Controller (CNC) setup. The CNC administrator is responsible for configuring the external connectivity, which includes setting up BGP and IPsec peering with the appropriate configuration parameters for the peer device. Afterwards, the CNC automates the creation of BGP sessions and IPsec tunnels to establish connections with remote external sites. Additionally, it programs the route tables in both the user VPC and the TGWs within the infra VPC with routes learned from the external peer devices.

Similar to the external connectivity with Azure native gateways, AWS also utilizes the external endpoint group to classify all external prefixes associated with networks external to AWS that require communication with the EPG "web-frontend" in the cloud (see Figure 4-78). To establish the contract between the external EPG and EPG "web-frontend," it is necessary to configure it with a "global scope." This configuration allows for an inter-tenant relationship between the external EPG deployed in the infra tenant and the EPG "web-frontend" deployed in the user tenant.

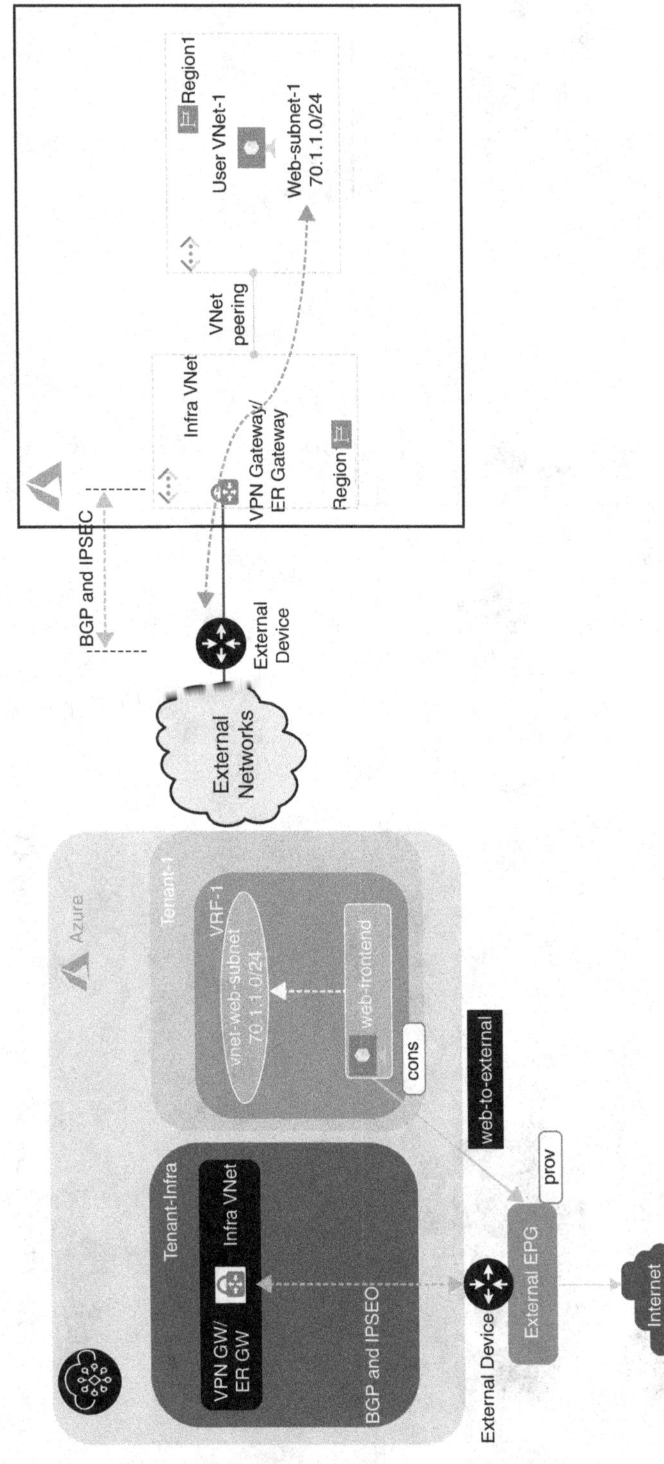

Figure 4-77 *Cloud Access to External Sites Using Azure GW*

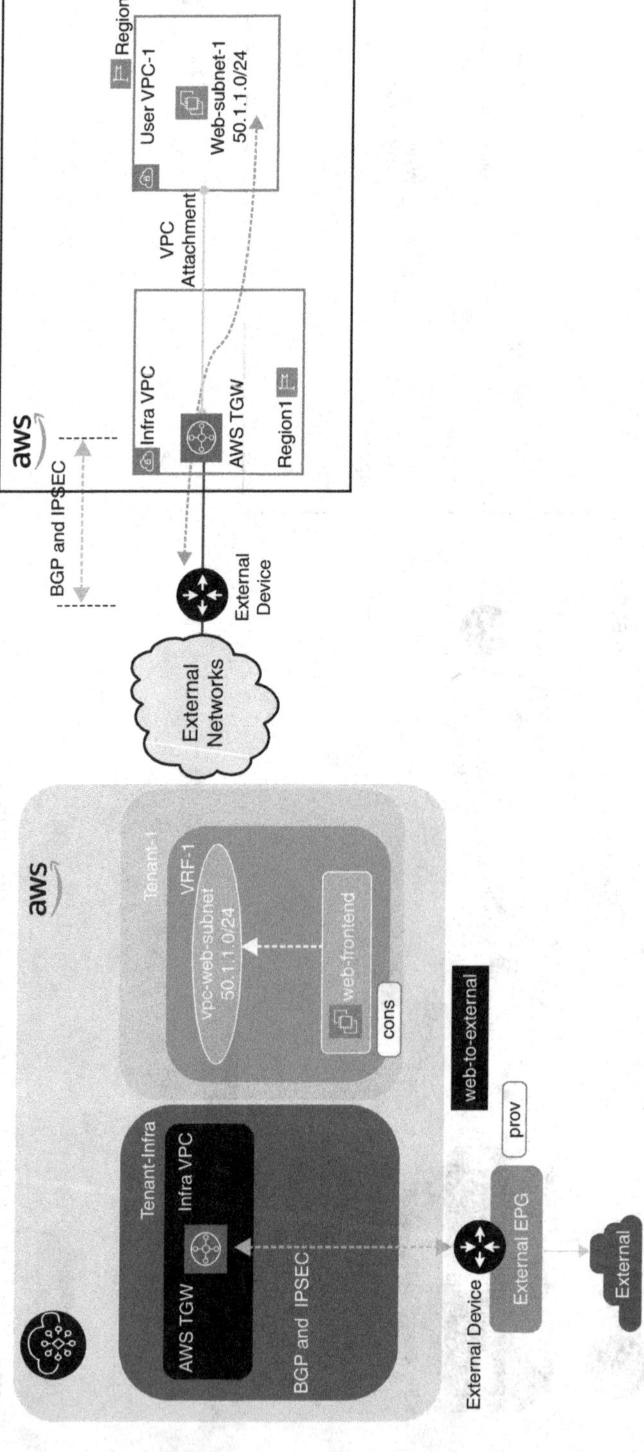

Figure 4-78 *Cloud Access to External Sites Using AWS TGW*

Cloud to Enterprise Destinations Using Cisco Cloud Routers

Just like AWS transit gateways, the Cisco Cloud Routers are provisioned during the initial setup of the Cloud Network Controller (CNC). The Network Deployment Orchestrator (NDO) communicates with the CNCs to configure these cloud routers for establishing connections with external remote devices using BGP and IPsec (see Figure 4-79).

It is important to note that Cisco Cloud Routers are primarily designed to provide direct connectivity, rather than acting as transit points. This means that the cloud routers in AWS cannot be used as a pathway for traffic from a remote external network to reach a destination in Azure, and vice versa. Additionally, the cloud routers cannot be utilized as a transit mechanism to enable connectivity between an external network and the on-premises ACI fabric.

Be aware that for the external connectivity options mentioned earlier, whether using AWS TGW or Cisco Cloud Routers, the CNCs are capable of generating configuration templates for external peers. However, it remains the responsibility of the network administrator to manually configure these external peers. This process involves downloading the configuration files from the CNC and subsequently enabling and validating the external connectivity.

Cloud to External Enterprise Sites Using SD-WAN

This deployment of Cisco SD-WAN Edge routers allows for external peering with termination points located within the public cloud infra tenant. This means that SD-WAN Edge routers can be deployed anywhere, including within a public cloud environment, to establish BGP and IPsec peering connections with various components such as Cisco Cloud Routers, Azure VPN/Express Route gateways, and AWS transit gateways. These connections, between the SD-WAN Edge routers and the termination points on the cloud, can be established over the public Internet or utilize private connections such as AWS Direct Connect (DX) for AWS or Azure Express Route (ER) for Microsoft Azure. This integration (see Figures 4-80 to 4-83) enables end-to-end connectivity and segmentation, connecting SD-WAN branch networks to public cloud workloads.

In terms of ACI configuration, each branch network has the option to be associated with an individual external endpoint group, which allows for the potential configuration of different external EPGs for each branch network. For example, you can classify and associate the network for branch-A with external EPG-A, and similarly, branch-B can be classified and associated with external EPG-B (see Figure 4-84). Alternatively, multiple external branch networks can be grouped within a single external EPG.

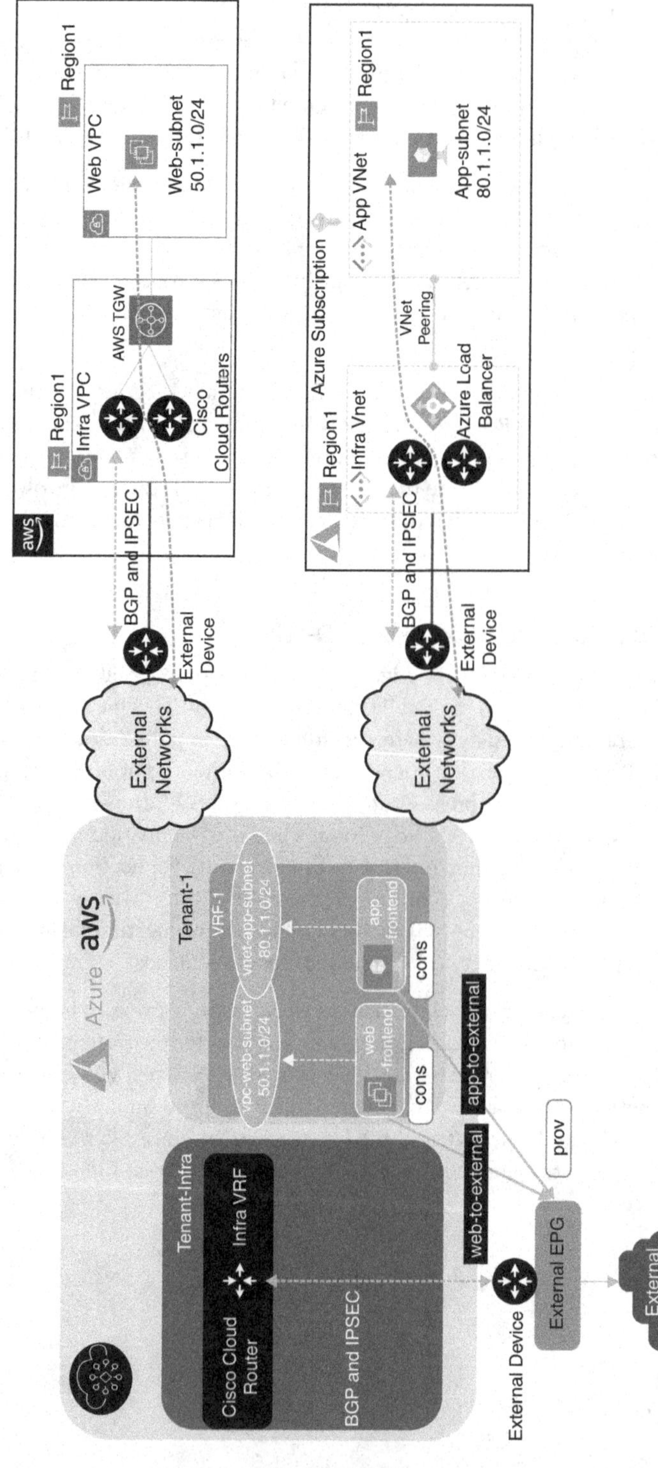

Figure 4-79 *Cloud Access to External Sites Using Cisco Cloud Routers*

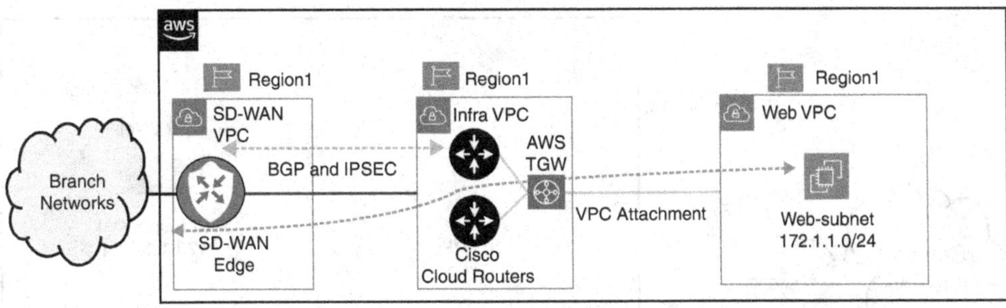

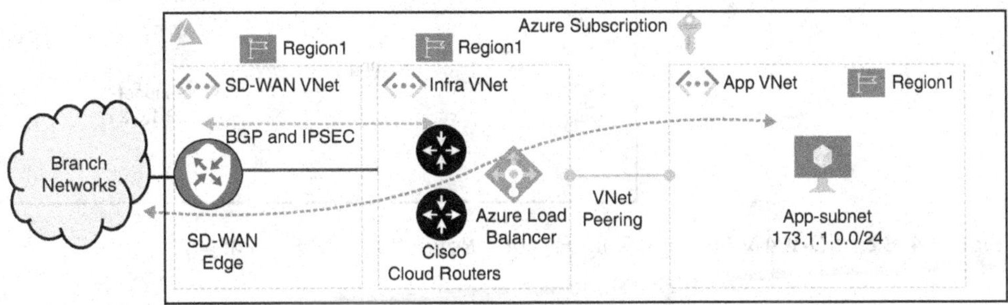

Figure 4-80 *SD-WAN Interop Using Cisco Cloud Routers*

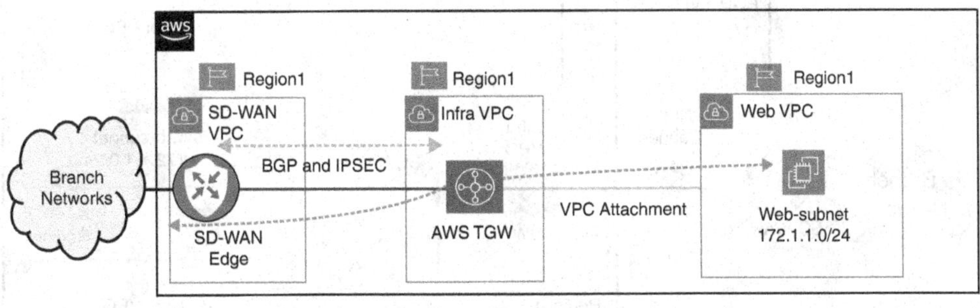

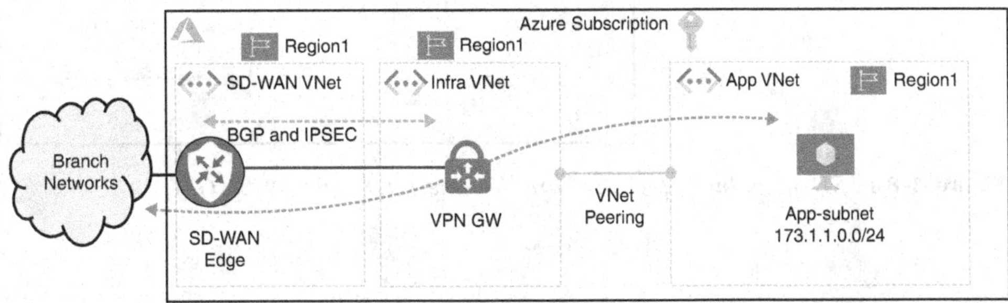

Figure 4-81 *SD-WAN Interop Using AWS TGW and Azure VPN GW*

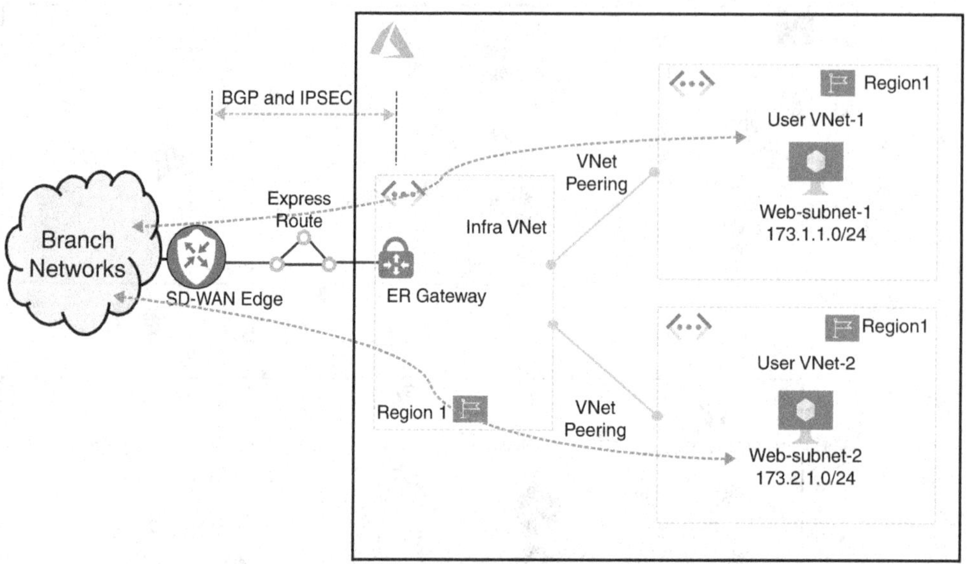

Figure 4-82 *SD-WAN Interop Using Express Route (ER) and ER GW*

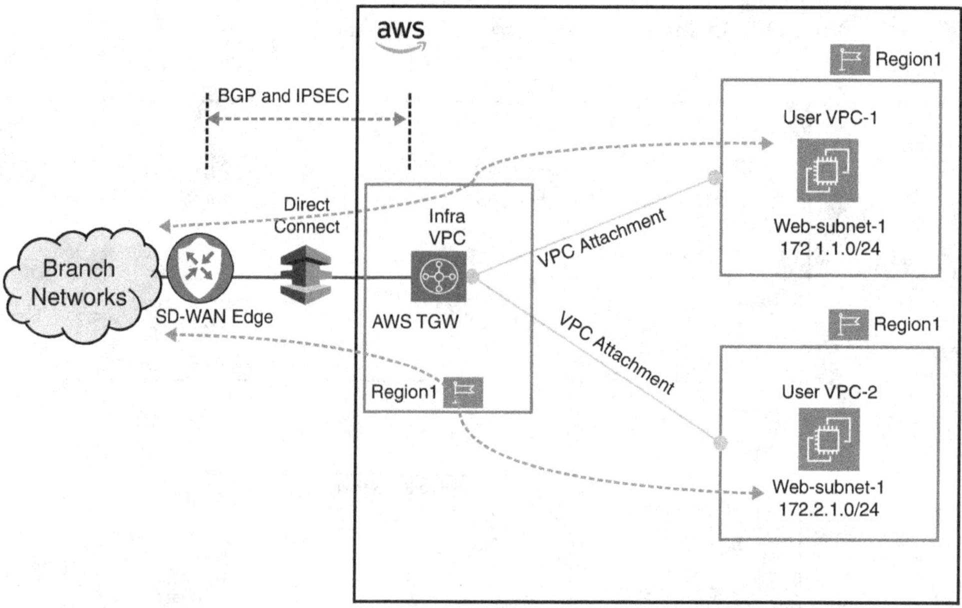

Figure 4-83 *SD-WAN Interop Using Direct Connect (DX) and AWS TGW*

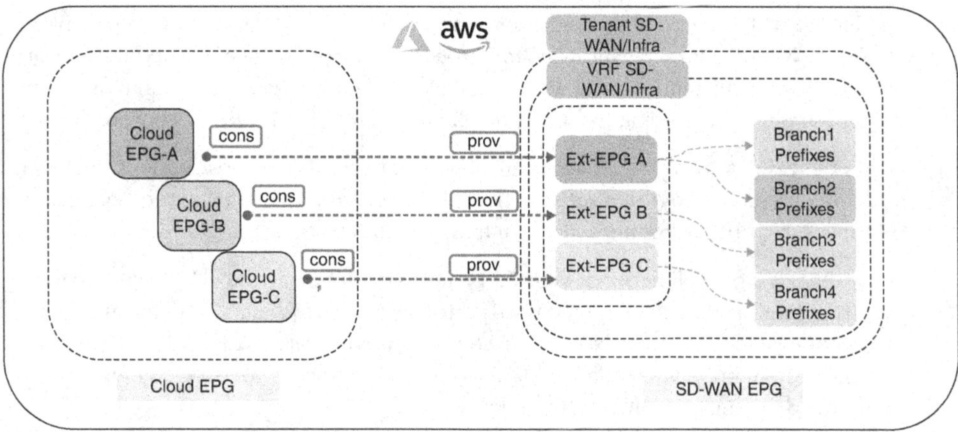

Figure 4-84 *SD-WAN Interop–External EPG Classification*

When utilizing separate external EPGs, you gain the advantage of defining explicit security policies (contracts) for each external branch network individually. These policies can be implemented as security group rules on AWS or network security group rules on Azure. This approach provides administrators with precise control to enforce specific policies governing communication between external branch networks and cloud workloads.

It is important to note that while the Network Deployment Orchestrator can generate configuration templates for BGP and IPsec connectivity for termination devices within the infra VPC, as well as configuration templates for external SD-WAN peer devices, it is the responsibility of WAN administrators to utilize these templates to configure the corresponding SD-WAN Edge routers to establish BGP and IPsec connections.

Guidelines and Limitations Around ACI and Public-Cloud Integration

While Cisco offers comprehensive documentation that outlines guidelines and limitations for multi-cloud ACI integration, it is important to be aware of common pitfalls and considerations that may occur during the implementation process.

Here are some key points to consider:

- For ACI and AWS integration, each ACI tenant, including the ACI infra tenant, requires a separate AWS account. If you have one ACI infra tenant and two ACI user tenants, you will need a total of three AWS accounts.
- Creating new ACI user tenants in AWS can be done through two methods: associating an AWS account with an ACI user tenant using the AWS access key ID and secret (untrusted user tenant), or associating an AWS account with an ACI user tenant using the CloudFormation template (trusted user tenant). It is recommended to use trusted user tenant for production deployments because the AWS access key ID and secret can expire.

- Ensure that you have full administrator access for the AWS IAM user when deploying CNC in the infra tenant using the CloudFormation template. If you do not have a user with full administrator access, make sure the user meets the minimum permissions required according to Cisco guidelines for AWS IAM roles and permissions.
- In the case of Azure, ACI tenants are associated with Azure subscriptions. You can either use the same Azure subscription to create multiple ACI tenants or use multiple subscriptions for multiple tenants within an Azure account.
- If there is a firewall between your on-premises deployment and cloud deployment, make sure to allow the required port/protocols for control, data, and management communication for the CNC and Cisco Cloud Routers as per Cisco documentation. The firewall may also require NAT/PAT translations to allow outside communication to the on-premises APIC, NDO, and routers.
- For AWS deployments, if a region does not have Cisco Cloud Routers, VPCs in that region will need to use Cisco Cloud Routers in another region for inter-site connectivity (cloud to on-premises, cloud to cloud). In this case, VPCs without cloud routers will need a virtual private gateway deployed in each VPC to peer with the Cisco Cloud Routers in the other region. Alternatively, VPCs in the region without cloud routers can utilize inter-region transit gateway peering to route traffic to the region with Cisco Cloud Routers.
- For Azure deployments, if a region does not have Cisco Cloud Routers, virtual networks in that region will need to use Cisco Cloud Routers in another region for inter-site connectivity (cloud to on-premises, cloud to cloud). Virtual networks in the region without cloud routers will use global VN peering to route traffic to an Application Load Balancer (ALB) in another region with Cisco Cloud Routers.
- When implementing public cloud integration with ACI, it is essential to refer to the CNC scalability guide to verify the scalability numbers.

Summary

In this chapter, we explored the various integration methods available to integrate ACI with other domain architectures. We discussed the basics of an SDN network and delved into the detailed aspects of ACI architecture, including the ACI policy model, data plane, and control plane learning.

We covered different integration options such as group identity and VN federation between ACI and SD-Access; SLA and VPN federation between ACI and SD-WAN; and MPLS/SR-MPLS integration with ACI. Additionally, we discussed the design choices for integrating ACI with multiple clouds.

Overall, this chapter provided an overview of the integration possibilities and considerations when connecting ACI with other domain architectures.

Chapter 5

Enterprise MPLS

In this chapter, we discuss the following:

- What enterprise MPLS is and why it is becoming more and more common in modern networks
- The key components of enterprise MPLS
- How well enterprise MPLS integrates with other domains
- Lessons learned and best practices on deploying enterprise MPLS

Overview

Today's multi-domain networks have one theme in common: they are all based on using flexible overlay fabrics for their traffic by utilizing a highly available underlay infrastructure. Multi-Protocol Label Switching (MPLS) is no different. MPLS is one of the oldest overlay technologies to be used and has a proven track record of being very dependable. Believe it or not, if you are trying to access any application or resource out on the vast Internet, the chances that your traffic will traverse through an MPLS network are 99 percent. Today's networks rely on MPLS to function because this technology is used not only by service providers but also by large enterprises as they move toward an IT-as-a-Business (ITaaB) model.

The need to segment traffic at a macro level is increasing. Each business unit in the large enterprise environment has its own application and traffic requirements. To overcome this complex requirement, the ITaaB model was developed. Historically, an IT organization in an enterprise has always been a cost center and not a revenue generator. With the rapid evolution of digitization in the past two decades, it was evident that an organization's IT infrastructure had to be evolved, which came with a cost that most organizations were unwilling to spend. An organization cannot just upgrade a part or portion of the IT infrastructure; everything needs to evolve proportionally. The network, computing systems, applications, and security—all are critical systems of an organization. When the focus of an upgrade is made only on one piece and not all, catastrophic failures could occur, and we have seen that happen over and over when the largest of organizations fail and all of their business comes to a halt when such failures happen. And that comes with a big revenue loss.

ITaaB takes such complexities away and provides a means of stable and consistent upgrades in the IT infrastructure as we move more and more toward a digitized world. With ITaaB, an IT organization within an enterprise essentially becomes a "service provider" for the company's different business units. Instead of each business unit purchasing and maintaining its own set of equipment with nonintegrated and incompatible systems, the IT organization takes full ownership of all the network, system, application, and security components and, in turn, cross-charges a "subscription" or "management fee" to the business units. Let's discuss the benefits to different organizations:

- **IT organization**
  - The architecture of all the infrastructure is consistent across the globe.
  - The organization gets standardization in the procurement of hardware and software.
  - With ownership of all IT infrastructure, the IT organization also benefits from bulk pricing and discounts from vendors.
  - The IT organization generates revenue by cross-charging to the department that pays for the procured equipment. This changes IT from being a cost center to a revenue center.
  - The IT organization can provide a catalog of services ranging from the highest service-level agreements (SLAs) for some critical revenue-generating business units to lower SLAs for some backend offices and administrative units.
  - The IT organization provides macro- and microsegmentation capabilities for the entire organization.
  - The IT organization gets better high-capacity WAN circuits and transport types for aggregated throughput and delivers different SLAs.
  - There is a centralized point of infrastructure maintenance, triage, and issue resolution.
  - Security governance is centralized.
- **Business units**
  - No additional staff is required to maintain IT equipment.
  - The benefit of bulk pricing on the gear will take away their capital expenses (CapEx) and reduce operational expenses (OpEx).
  - Each business unit can subscribe to different SLA levels based on the need of that business unit.

- There is on-demand connectivity to different departments or the cloud through a central organization.
- The business units can leverage state-of-the-art security infrastructure.

As you can see, ITaaB provides excellent benefits to large enterprises and provides them with a structure that can scale horizontally and vertically. From a network infrastructure perspective, an enterprise MPLS provides flexibility that can fit into this ITaaB model effectively and provide the connectivity a business needs.

In any sized network, IT management is faced with two important requirements. From the business side, the services and applications should never go down. From the services side, they should have the flexibility to add or remove any services or applications they need without interfering with the network. In a traditional monolithic network architecture, where everything is in one big global routing table, it is hard to achieve that design because any network changes could bring down the services momentarily. This is why, decades ago, service providers embraced MPLS. MPLS, with its Layer 3 or Layer 2 VPNs, is essentially an overlay technology running on top of a highly resilient and scalable Label Distribution Protocol (LDP)-based routed underlay. With this design, they can maintain their underlying routed infrastructure without worrying about overlaying customer VPNs. Similarly, they can add any new customers to their MPLS networks without impacting any other customer who is sharing the same infrastructure or service provider features. Today, after years of evolution, this process is so automated that if a customer wants to deploy a new site, that customer logs in to the service provider's web portal to submit the request, and all the backend configuration is provisioned via automation.

In the MPLS world, there are two main types of routers: provider (P) and provider-edge (PE) routers. Provider routers are a mesh of routers that connect with all the P and PE routers. They only hold the network information of the underlying core infrastructure and are completely oblivious to the customer networks or prefixes. In P routers, no customer VRFs are configured, which is a most significant benefit because it conserves the Ternary Content Addressable Memory (TCAM) space on the routers. This implies that they do not have to be as memory intensive as PE routers because their function is primarily to transport traffic from one interface to the other. P routers typically run only IGP, like IS-IS or OSPF and LDP routing protocols. PE routers, on the other hand, do all the hard work of managing different VRFs for different customers and also managing each customer's routing table. They need more TCAM space and are usually among the most potent routers available in the market. PE routers run many routing protocols, depending on what the customer is running. Sometimes multiple instances of the same protocols are also run to connect to different customers. Today, there is a huge standardization on using BGP or a static route as a connectivity protocol with customers to simplify the design and provide the best SLAs to their customers. The tunneling of these VRFs over the core is an important concept that is discussed in later sections of this chapter.

Figure 5-1 shows a high-level overview of an MPLS network.

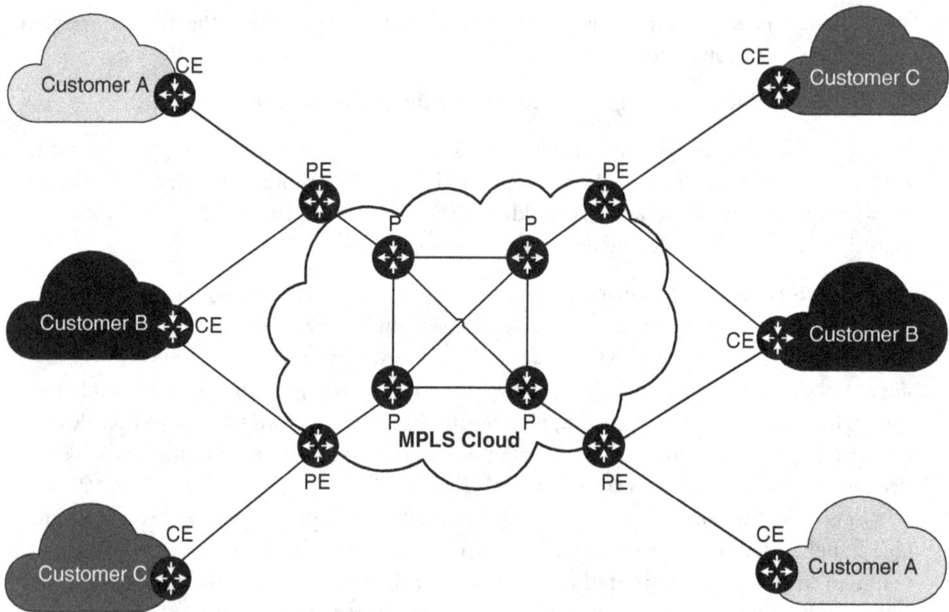

Figure 5-1 *High-Level Overview of the MPLS Network*

> **Note** The detailed innerworkings on how MPLS is configured and operated are beyond the scope of this book. Great Cisco Press publications on designing effective MPLS architectures can be used as a reference.

Interaction with the Other Domains

We discussed how the IT-as-a-Business model has evolved, and MPLS is one of the key components in connecting different networks. In this book, MPLS deserves its own chapter. From a high level, MPLS would seem like any other WAN transport, such as using SD-WAN or Dynamic Multi-point Virtual Private Network (DMVPN), but there is a significant difference. While SD-WAN or DMVPN helps connect remote sites with data centers or CNFs, MPLS achieves similar connectivity but also acts as a super core for large enterprises that have a global presence. In the remaining sections of the chapter, we discuss how similar and different such connectivity types are and how MPLS helps bridge the gaps.

Inter-working with SD-Access

Cisco Software Defined Access (SD-Access) is a fully automated controller-based fabric solution deployed at large campuses to the smallest of sites. This solution aims to eliminate manual maintenance and operations of the devices deployed at all the sites.

With the controller known as Cisco Catalyst Center, all the devices at the sites are discovered, managed, and configured with correct variables by Catalyst Center. This solution is revolutionary because it builds the network with both macro- and microsegmentation in place.

Macrosegmentation in SD-Access is defined as a routing-plane separation. Here, all the traffic with a similar purpose or trust level is put into a single routing plane. These routing planes are virtual in nature—known as Virtual Routing and Forwarding (VRF)—and share the same physical infrastructure of routers and switches with other VRFs. This creates complete isolation of the network in that routing plane, and to provide end-to-end connectivity, any routing protocol supporting multi-VRF capability can be used. Microsegmentation in SD-Access is achieved by assigning Security Group Tags (SGTs) to all the endpoints and classifying their identity within a VRF. For example, in a trusted corporate VRF, we can create separate SGTs for devices like laptops or computers, phones, and printers. In building-management VRF, separate SGTs for badge readers, fire sensors, smart lighting, and surveillance cameras might be needed. Similarly, even though not required, separate SGTs can be used for guests and contractors in the guest network.

With access contracts defined globally within Catalyst Center's TrustSec matrix, security group access control lists (SGACLs) can be configured, limiting communication between various SGTs within the VRF. This concept is similar to private VLANs, where we could create isolated, community, or promiscuous VLANs within a VLAN. Cisco Identity Services Engine (ISE) is used with SD-Access to deploy and enforce this microsegmentation.

With MPLS and SD-Access integration, only macrosegmentation integration is supported. MPLS does not have any capability to carry SGTs within its labels; hence, the source identity of the packet is lost the moment it enters into the MPLS world. However, we discuss the alternatives to achieve macro- and microsegmentation in the network where MPLS is used as a WAN protocol.

MPLS and SD-Access Default Integration

By default, SD-Access and MPLS integrate with back-to-back VRF-level macrosegmentation. From the SD-Access side, IP-transit needs to be configured. To create SVI handoffs in Catalyst Center, border automation workflow is used. This workflow will create individual SVIs per VRF per Layer 2 connection it has with one or more MPLS PE routers. This Layer 2 connection is a trunk link that also needs to be configured on the MPLS PE router. The dot1q-supported interface on the MPLS PE router needs to be put on the respective VRF in order for all the traffic from the SD-Access fabric to be transported to other sites. Figure 5-2 shows how VRFs are merged and transported to other sites where they are needed.

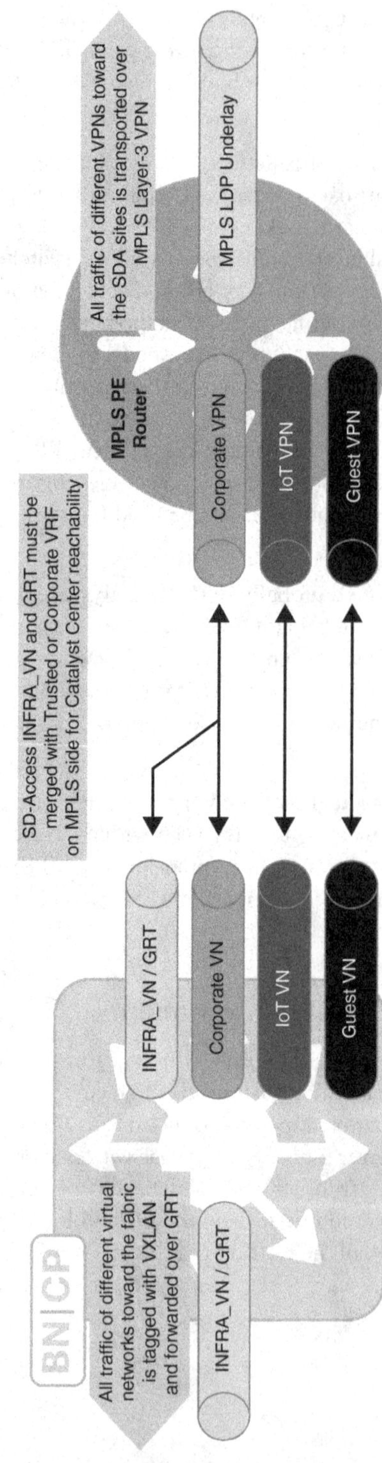
BN|CP
All traffic of different virtual networks toward the fabric is tagged with VXLAN and forwarded over GRT
INFRA_VN / GRT
INFRA_VN / GRT
Corporate VN
IoT VN
Guest VN
SD-Access INFRA_VN and GRT must be merged with Trusted or Corporate VRF on MPLS side for Catalyst Center reachability
Corporate VPN
IoT VPN
Guest VPN
MPLS PE Router
All traffic of different VPNs toward the SDA sites is transported over MPLS Layer-3 VPN
MPLS LDP Underlay

Figure 5-2 *MPLS to SD-Access Default Integration*

Using SXP to Distribute SGTs

With the limitation of MPLS not being able to carry SGTs across the network, an alternative solution can be used. Although not as effective as carrying SGTs natively and inline with the data plane, this solution does allow microsegmentation at all sites. As its name suggests, the Security Group Tag Exchange Protocol (SXP) allows a mechanism to exchange SGT information to the sites where WAN transports, like MPLS, cannot carry tags within the data packet. The protocol allows IP-to-SGT mappings or bindings to be exchanged between network devices. The device sending IP-SGT bindings is known as the *speaker*, and the device taking this information and installing it in its memory is known as the *listener*. Because Cisco ISE has all the data about IP-SGT bindings, it becomes the topology speaker. At the time of writing this book, ISE supports only SXP version 4 (SXPv4). One critical point to be mindful of is that SXP is not VRF-aware. Hence, for each VRF, multiple SXP peerings are needed.

SXP sessions can be made directly with ISE in a network with a few sites. This design, however, does not scale when hundreds of sites are spanned out globally. Also, when more virtual networks are in the fabric, more memory and CPU resources are required on the border nodes to maintain that IP-SGT binding table for each virtual network. To improve this limitation of scale, SXPv5 was created; it reduces this configuration and operational complexity. SXPv5 establishes only a single SXP peering with a network device for all virtual networks instead of one per virtual network. At the time of writing this book, SXPv5 is supported only on network devices. Hence, with the limitation of ISE only supporting SXPv4, an SXP reflector is required in the design. Figure 5-3 shows what this architecture looks like.

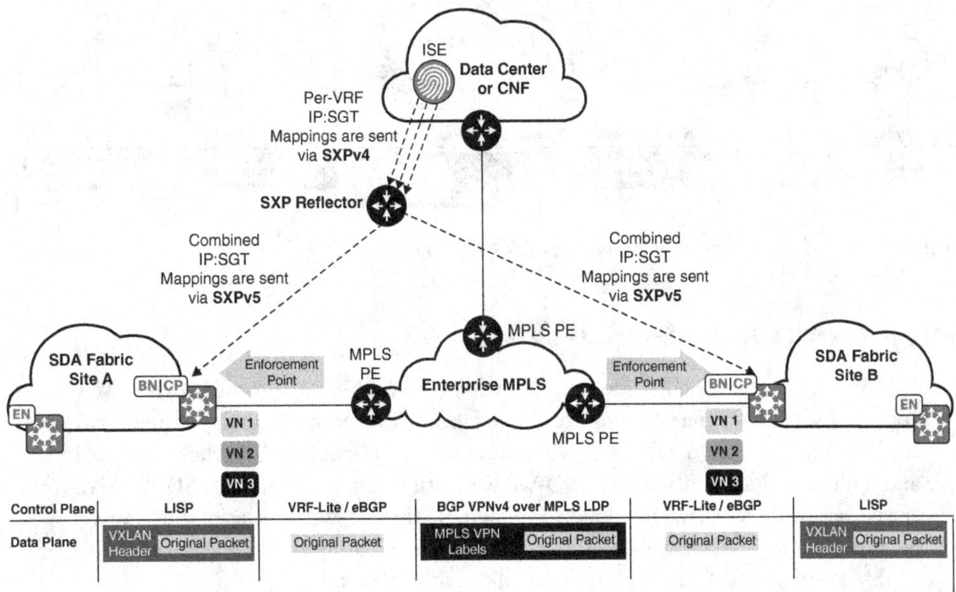

Figure 5-3 *Leveraging SXPv5 to Propagate IP-SGT Bindings Across the SD-Access Fabric Sites*

SXP is a viable alternative for networks that do not support the propagation of SGTs in the data plane. However, our experience says using inline tagging as much as possible is always recommended. The additional configuration and operational overhead required for SXP must be planned out properly so that security is not compromised in case of any issues. With inline tagging, resources on routers and switches are also conserved, which implies you will not need high-performance devices at all sites.

With the limitation of MPLS not being able to carry inline tagging natively from one fabric site to the other, SD-Access Transit is an alternative. With SD-Access Transit, we are able to leverage a centralized transit control plane (TCP) router, which has information about remote site prefixes. Here, the SD-Access border node queries the transit control plane about the RLOC of the remote-site border node, and after the response is received, the local border node builds a VXLAN tunnel directly with the remote-site border node. This preserves the packet's virtual network and SGT information and transits through the MPLS network. The caveat with this design is that the MPLS network needs to support an additional 50 bytes of VXLAN overhead. Figure 5-4 shows how the SD-Access Transit network operates with the MPLS network.

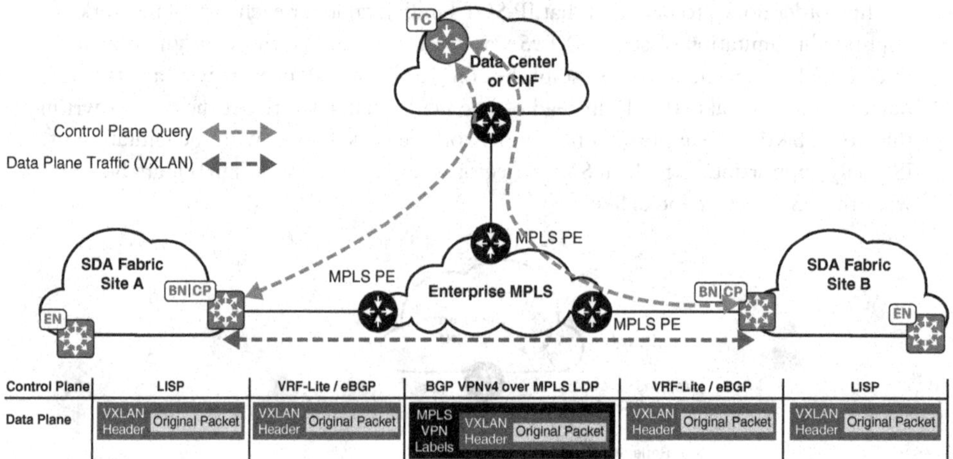

Figure 5-4 *SD-Access Transit over MPLS Network*

Inter-working with SD-WAN

Cisco's Software-Defined Wide Area Network (SD-WAN) is a controller-driven WAN solution. SD-WAN offers a complete WAN fabric with centralized management and security, creating a secure overlay WAN architecture across campus, branches, data centers, and multi-cloud applications. The SD-WAN solution runs on a range of SD-WAN routers across hardware, virtual, and cloud form factors. This SD-WAN solution builds on the Secure Access Service Edge (SASE) architecture, integrating some of the latest Cisco Umbrella and other cloud security portfolios and vendors.

At a high level, SD-WAN uses cloud-based controllers known as Catalyst SD-WAN Manager, Catalyst SD-WAN Validator, and Catalyst SD-WAN Controller. With Catalyst

SD-WAN Manager being the management plane of the SD-WAN infrastructure, it manages all the other controllers and SD-WAN Edge routers, giving it a single point of interface. Right out of the box, SD-WAN provides macro-level segmentation, which is a routing plane separation. Additional features, when enabled, can interact with the Cisco SD-Access solution and provide transit capabilities for SGTs and extend microsegmentation to the fabric.

Cisco SD-WAN interacts with MPLS in two different ways. The first one is the most common; it is as a WAN transport option. The second interaction is with enterprise MPLS deployed as a super core. Let's look at both and see what this integration would look like.

MPLS as a WAN Transport

MPLS as a WAN transport is the most common form of connectivity method for SD-WAN. This is not a true integration because MPLS is used as a transport. SD-WAN builds its VPN tunnels using this MPLS transport and connects with other sites. So, in reality, no native IP traffic passes through the MPLS after SD-WAN builds its tunnels. All traffic is encapsulated. Figure 5-5 shows how MPLS plays a role as a transport and provides connectivity for the SD-WAN underlay to build its overlay tunnels.

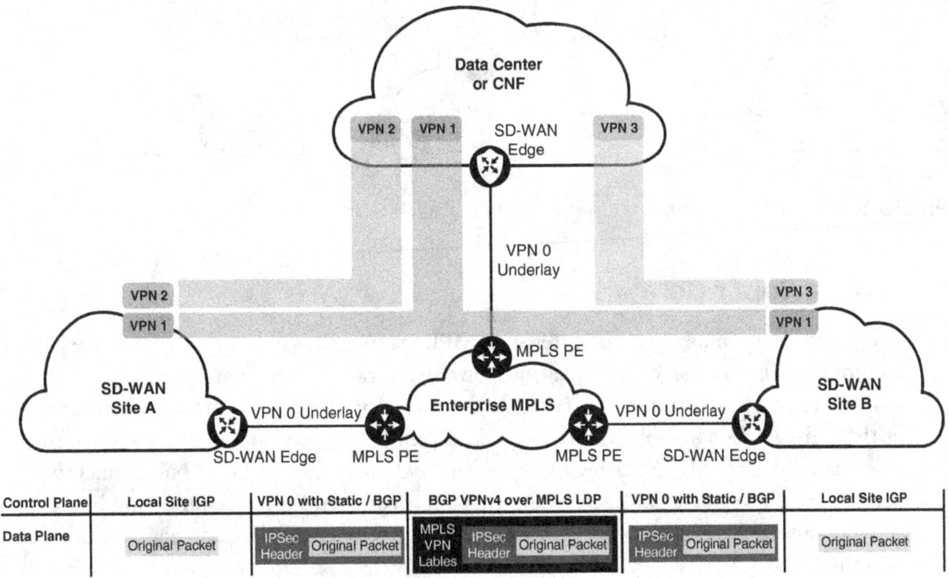

Figure 5-5 *MPLS as a WAN Transport for SD-WAN*

For an organization subscribing to MPLS services from a service provider, it is always a private VPN. In most cases, there is no Internet access from this network because organizations prefer to backhaul all the Internet traffic to a centralized location. This backhauling of traffic allows organizations to inspect the traffic through their security stack and ensure corporate security policies are enforced. For SD-WAN, it needs to ensure control connections are always maintained to its controllers like Catalyst SD-WAN Manager,

Catalyst SD-WAN Validator, and Catalyst SD-WAN Controller. These controllers are located in the cloud, so Internet connectivity for SD-WAN Transport Locators (TLOCs) connected to the MPLS network needs to be allowed to form secondary or backup connections to the controllers. This way, in the event control connections via Internet transport fail, connectivity and management are maintained. Figure 5-6 shows how the control connections through MPLS transport are configured.

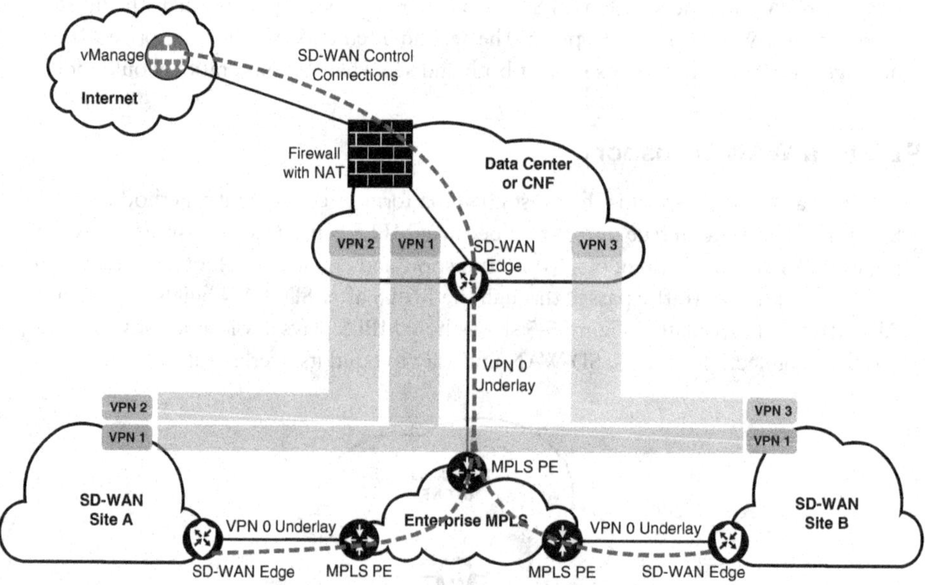

Figure 5-6 *SD-WAN Control Connections via MPLS Transport*

MPLS as a Super Core

The most common use case for enterprise MPLS is its use as a super core for large global enterprises. These massive organizations have networks so large that it is not feasible for any one team or even sometimes one solution to maintain connectivity. The sheer size of these networks sometimes reaches the scale limits of a solution. For this reason, the trusted and proven MPLS comes to the rescue and provides that backbone connectivity where one or more solutions across the globe can connect. Besides connecting branches and campuses, this super core also connects to data centers, CNFs, partner networks, and also the cloud.

For this section, our focus is on SD-WAN connectivity with the MPLS super core. Figure 5-7 illustrates how this super core connects to the SD-WAN architecture. In a typical design, the integration happens at a macro level between SD-WAN headend routers and the MPLS super core. This routing-plane separation allows the enterprise to maintain separate business functions more effectively and can be easily integrated with core devices that have limited support for the microsegmentation capability. To achieve microsegmentation, technologies like SXPv5 can be used for enforcement closer to the edge.

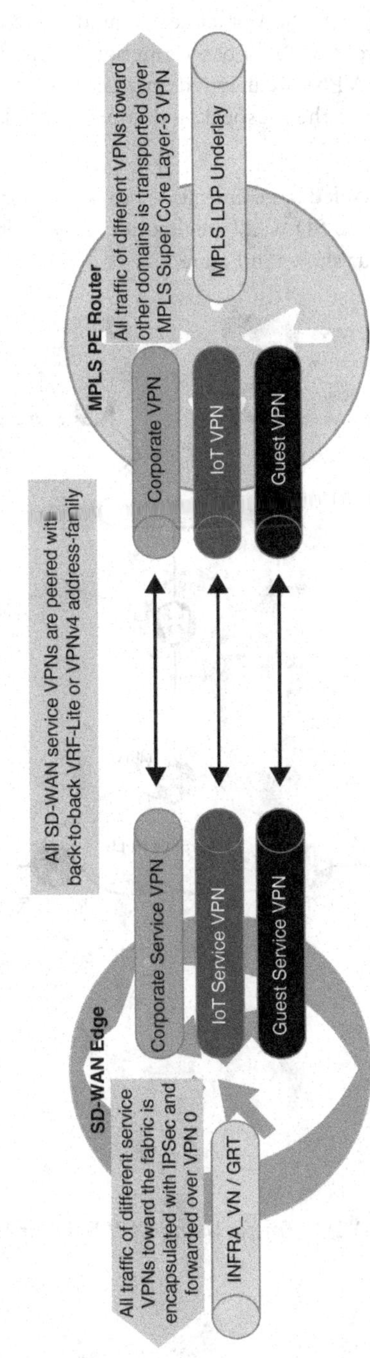

Figure 5-7 *SD-WAN Integration with MPLS as a Super Core*

The MPLS super core is optimized for one purpose: to transport packets at the highest capacity and speed. With Cisco best practices in mind, there is not a lot of deep packet inspection or access control list (ACL)-based filtering in this super core. With SD-WAN integration, all the service VPNs are mapped on a one-to-one basis to MPLS VPNs. These VPNs are then backhauled to their respective destinations to be offloaded for further connectivity.

MPLS super cores have enabled large enterprises to zone their networks into various regions and have regionalized SD-WAN architecture. Any inter-region traffic traverses through various domains, as shown in Figure 5-8.

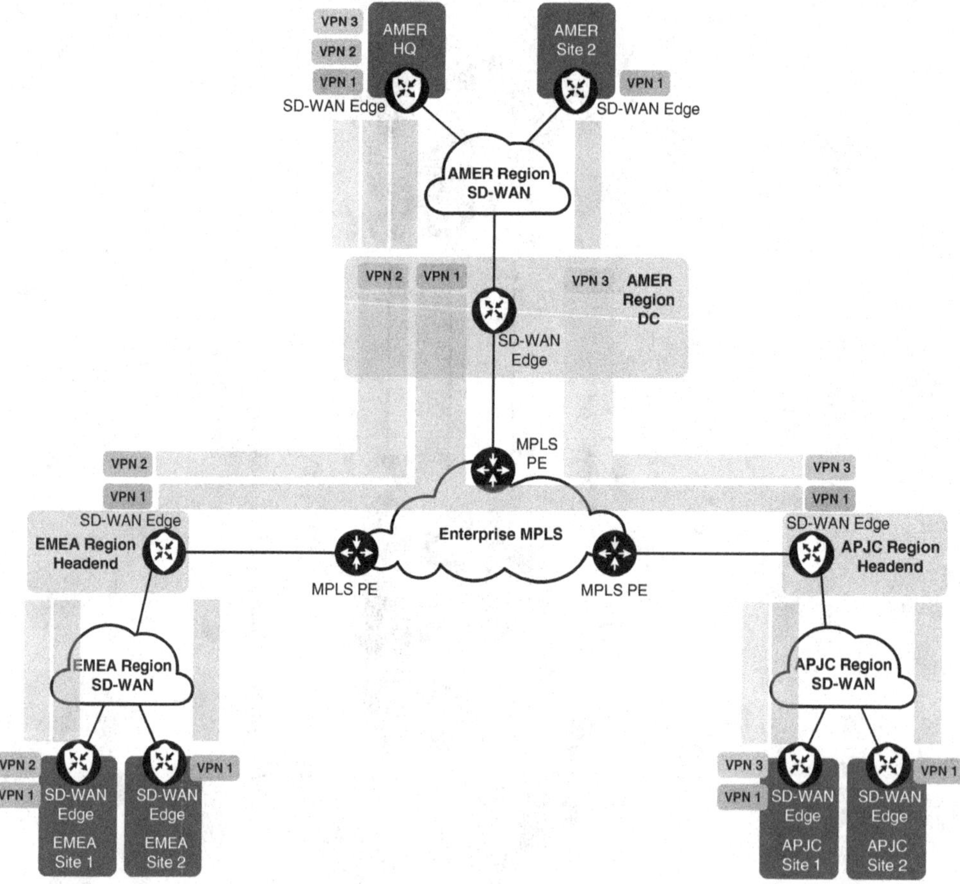

Figure 5-8 *Inter-Region SD-WAN Traffic Using MPLS Super Core*

Let's look at two examples that can be derived from this figure. The first example is site-to-site communication. This communication could be a simple file transfer or a phone call from one branch to another. In this scenario, traffic from the AMER region site will leave the local site and enter SD-WAN fabric. This SD-WAN fabric will then carry this traffic to its headend SD-WAN Edge router. When the SD-WAN Edge router receives the packet, it then will be dropped into the service VPN, where it is destined to be based on the configured SD-WAN policies. This packet will be native IP and will be transported to the MPLS PE router using back-to-back VRFs or VRF-Lite. In a typical design, this peering between SD-WAN and the MPLS PE router is configured using the BGP routing protocol. Now the packet will be received by the MPLS PE router, which will be forwarded to the EMEA PE router based on the route lookup for that specific MPLS VPN. This packet will then be label-switched all the way to the destination PE and then be handed off to the EMEA region's SD-WAN headend. Now the reverse process starts. This EMEA region's SD-WAN headend router will transport the packet to the destination site using the SD-WAN fabric, and then it will be sent to the destination endpoint.

There are some key topics to be mindful of when looking at architecture like this. Quality of Service (QoS) tagging is maintained throughout the transport. In each of the domains, when a packet is handed off from one domain to another, all these solutions have a default behavior of honoring the QoS tags and forwarding the packet. If the domains like MPLS and SD-WAN have their own QoS policies defined, these packets will go through those policies based on their markings. For example, with site-to-site communications, different QoS policies and traffic priorities will be configured for a file transfer and a phone call.

The second example for this inter-region super core is access to the Internet. For this architecture, it does not make sense to backhaul the local Internet traffic to a centralized location for the entire globe. Doing so creates a bad experience for the user because the latency is greatly increased and, depending on the region, certain applications or resources might not be accessible. Hence, a solution is required to offload regional Internet traffic to a regional Internet provider and get a better user experience. To explain this scenario, let's refer to Figure 5-9.

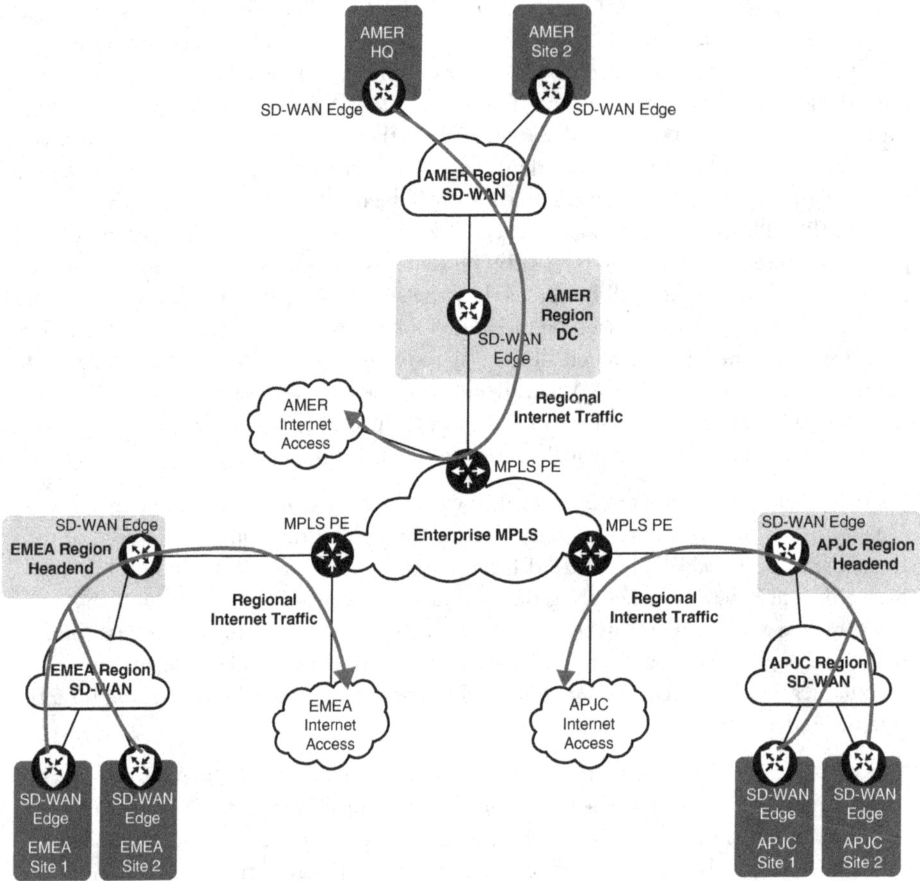

Figure 5-9 *Internet-Bound Traffic Using MPLS Super Core*

Here, when a packet destined for the Internet leaves a local site, it enters into the SD-WAN fabric. This Internet traffic could be in different VPNs like corporate or guest. When this traffic reaches the SD-WAN router, it is carried toward the regional SD-WAN headend in the respective VPNs. The SD-WAN headend then sends this traffic as native IP to MPLS PE in their respective VRFs. Here, the MPLS network is configured to steer Internet-based traffic to a local regional exit point for all of the VRFs. Hence, this Internet-bound traffic will then traverse to a local Internet exit point—again by maintaining routing-plane separation. When this traffic reaches the PE router located in the regional Internet exit point, it is then connected to a local security stack for inspection before being sent out to the Internet service provider (ISP). Referring to Figure 5-10, if the traffic is coming from a trusted VRF like corporate, the MPLS PE can offload that traffic to a security stack, which ensures no malicious or compromised traffic goes in or out of the network. Similarly, if the traffic is coming from the guest network, it might have stricter rules in accessing certain sites or resources, but a high level of inspection might not be required. The flexibility that is offered in this type of design can scale horizontally as well as vertically.

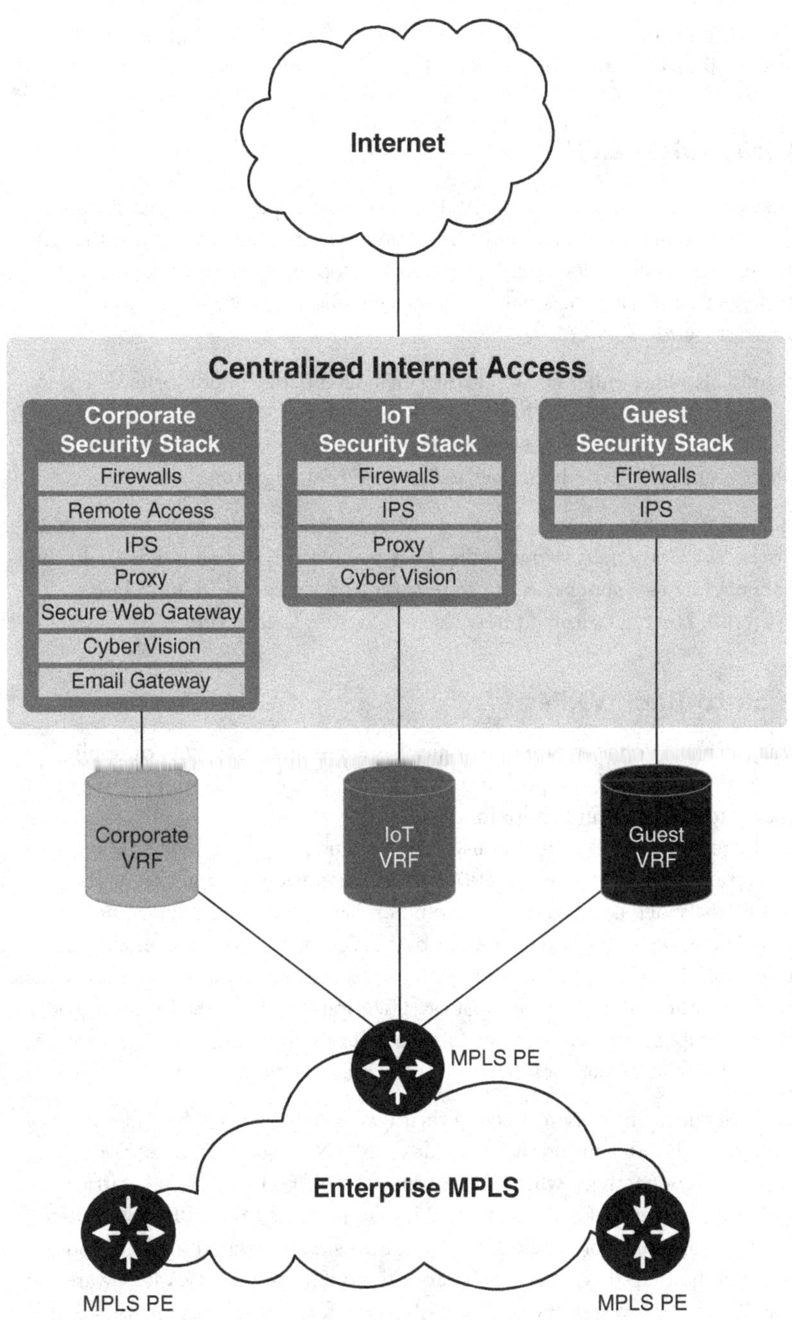

Figure 5-10 *Internet Traffic Handoff from MPLS PE Router*

We discuss this MPLS super core concept a little more in subsequent sections of this chapter because it ties to all of the domains for different purposes. Stay tuned!

Inter-working with ACI

Cisco's Application Centric Infrastructure (ACI) is a controller-based data center fabric solution. It is part of an intent-based networking framework to enable agility in the data center. It captures high-level business and user intent in the form of a policy and translates this into the network constructs necessary to dynamically provision network, security, and infrastructure services.

Data centers could also have other non-controller-managed data center fabrics. Some examples are Fabric Path or BGP-EVPN-based VXLAN fabric. When they communicate outside of the data center with other domains, their integration is identical to ACI, and hence throughout this section, we focus on ACI and MPLS integration.

Because MPLS is a WAN transport connecting different domains, it integrates with ACI in two main ways. The first one is by providing back-to-back VRF connectivity, and the second is by connecting as a super core. In some large enterprises, there could be a combination of both. Next, let's look at how this integration is achieved.

MPLS with Back-to-Back VRFs

Data centers, as the name suggests, are essentially large aggregation points of applications, file storage, and powerful computing to run critical business functions and provide all required access to the users and endpoints in the network. At certain times, these facilities are so large that they may also house other tenants, partners, or multiple business units' applications. Due to the automation and orchestration capabilities of the ACI solution, it is vastly deployed to manage complex data center architecture needs. However, equally along those lines, BGP-EVPN-based VXLAN fabrics are an alternative option. Because of ACI's multi-tenant, macro-, and microsegmented network capabilities, it is becoming the solution of choice for most organizations. ACI also has a multi-pod capability, where multiple pods with similar functionality are built either in the same or different facilities to scale the network for better redundancy and resiliency.

With all these applications and data residing in their own segments, MPLS can be used to connect the right VRF or tenant on the ACI side to a VPN on the MPLS network side. Figure 5-11 shows the connectivity when MPLS is used to offload data center traffic as back-to-back VRF. In this setup, between the ACI border leaf and MPLS PE router, there is a simple VRF-Lite configuration. Each VRF on the ACI side is mapped to a VRF on the MPLS PE side using the BGP routing protocol. For this configuration, any VRF-aware routing protocol can be used. However, the protocol of choice for most deployments is BGP.

This design is used primarily when we want to connect all the applications, data, and computing environments with the users. In the event that we need to connect multiple PODs over an IP network or have dedicated links between data centers for replication of traffic, this solution might not scale.

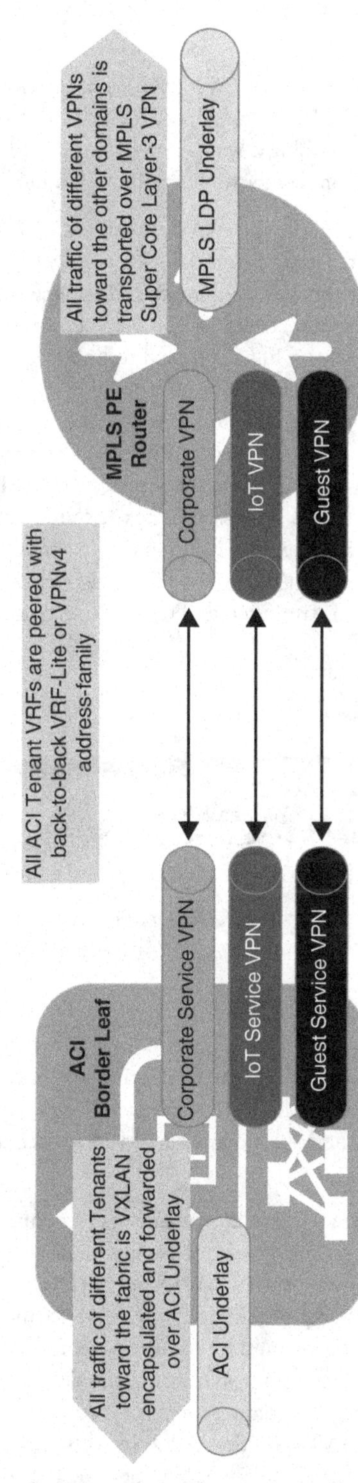

Figure 5-11 *ACI and MPLS Connectivity with Back-to-Back VRFs*

MPLS as a Super Core

The MPLS super core concept is radical. With the data center integration, it can definitely support the back-to-back VRF-Lite approach, as we discussed earlier. However, with the benefits of MPLS technology, we can also configure Layer 2 pseudowires or dedicated Layer 3 VPNs for data center replication traffic. Let's discuss both options.

Most organizations need to connect the two data centers with some form of direct dark fiber or wavelength transport. This is a pure Layer 2 connectivity need that is mainly used for stretching a VLAN across the data centers due to application requirements. This Layer 2 stretch also provides stretch subnets across the data centers for application failover. In some cases, these point-to-point links are used to link external services like the Internet for failover. So instead of procuring additional circuits, which may have a high cost if the distance between the data centers is very large, the MPLS core can help simulate a point-to-point connection between the two data centers by the configuration of Layer 2 pseudowires. These Layer 2 pseudowires can extend between any MPLS PE routers in the network. Figure 5-12 shows how these pseudowires can be used to either simulate Layer 2 trunk links between the data centers or stretch specific networks like the Internet across the data centers or CNFs. This figure also shows an extension of the cloud connection from the CNF to the research and development facility of an organization.

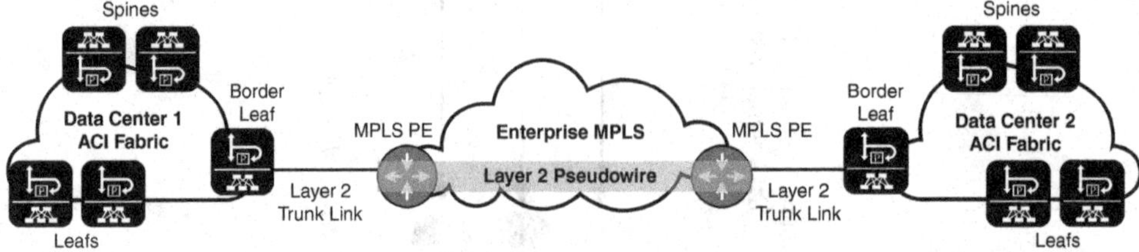

Figure 5-12 *Using MPLS Layer 2 Pseudowires as Point-to-Point Extensions Between Different Sites*

Some organizations might have more than one data center facility in a region. Stretching multiple point-to-point connections for a Layer 2 VLAN extension might lead to suboptimal routing because spanning-tree at the destination switches might block one of the links. To avoid such complexities, the Layer 2 Virtual Private LAN Service (VPLS) can be configured. VPLS simulates the MPLS core as a virtual switch as compared to multiple point-to-point links.

Solutions like ACI use their own internal mechanisms to connect their multi-pods over an IP backbone network. To connect multiple pods spanned across different locations, a dedicated VPN can be configured on the MPLS network. The sole purpose of this VPN would be to provide the required underlay transport capability to ACI's inter-pod network. Another major use case would be to have a dedicated VPN for data center replication traffic. With massive storage systems in the data center, databases and files have to be replicated between redundant data centers to provide high availability and resiliency. Having a dedicated VPN on the MPLS for this type of traffic provides the benefit of configuring custom MPLS Traffic Engineering (MPLS-TE), such as Fast

Reroute (FRR). FRR achieves subsecond failover in the event a node or a link fails in the MPLS network. With FRR, a critical replication does not get impacted and can still be given a higher priority than other traffic. Another benefit of a dedicated VPN is that not all PE routers will need to have it configured. This VPN is configured only on the data center PE routers. Figure 5-13 illustrates the uses of a dedicated VPN.

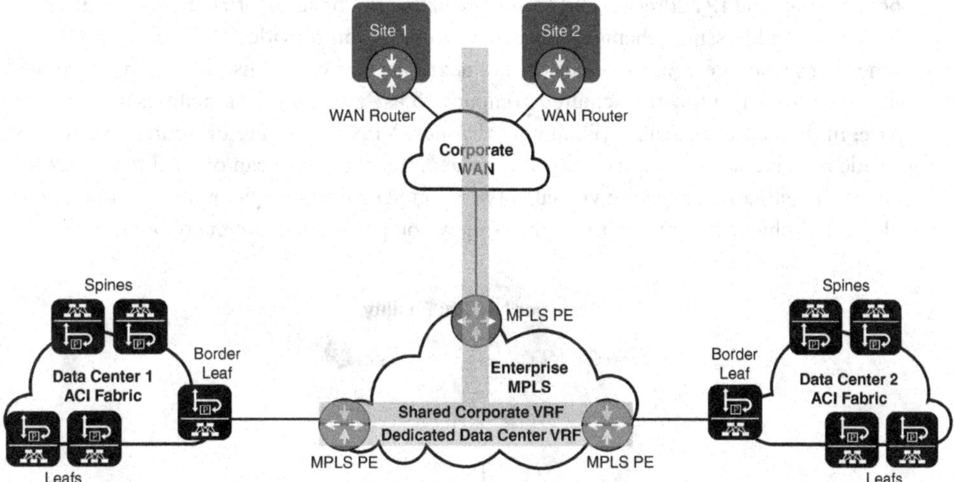

Figure 5-13 *Dedicated VPN Use Case Between Data Centers in MPLS Super Core*

Inter-working with CNF

A Carrier Neutral Facility (CNF) is a large congregation of various circuits, providers, and networks. The primary objective of having a CNF in an enterprise is to organize the traffic flow and connectivity requirements across the network. If not built correctly, the networks for large enterprises can easily get out of control with multiple ingress and egress points. This is where the CNF can bring in the structure and control points in the network so that the ingress and egress traffic can be predictable and secure.

MPLS and CNFs go hand in hand because they both complement each other. With CNF providing a good aggregation point, MPLS can connect to that aggregation point and effectively distribute the traffic where needed. MPLS is versatile when it comes to leveraging all of the features it offers. In this section we discuss some of the main use cases on how MPLS helps with this traffic distribution.

MPLS to Offload Selective VRFs

The MPLS network's most commonly used feature is spinning VRFs only where needed. This feature of selective VRF offloading greatly reduces network complexity. Figure 5-14 shows the scenario. Let's look at an example of an enterprise acquiring a small company. Here, an enterprise offers the newly acquired company the ability to function as a separate entity, but to save costs, the enterprise spins up a dedicated VRF in a data center for this new company to migrate and house all of their applications instead of maintaining a separate infrastructure. To provide this isolated routing plane, the acquiring enterprise spins a VPN on MPLS PE on the data center and another on CNF PE. CNF PE has a WAN connection to the acquired company to provide application access. Although these two networks are not fully merged and integrated into a single routing plane, this design is a quick and easy way to integrate two companies' networks without the worry about overlapping IP addresses and to start realizing the benefits of cost consolidation. While the IP addressing schema is corrected, firewalls can provide NAT and access to each other's resources. As an extension and next phase of cost consolidation, the acquiring enterprise may allow the acquired company to use their physical facilities and office space. In this scenario, again, spinning up that new VPN on the site PE router can quickly provide required access connectivity. From there, the enterprise can offload that VPN by connecting either to a separate virtual network on SD-Access fabric or a separate link on a dedicated physical infrastructure for that new company. There are many possibilities.

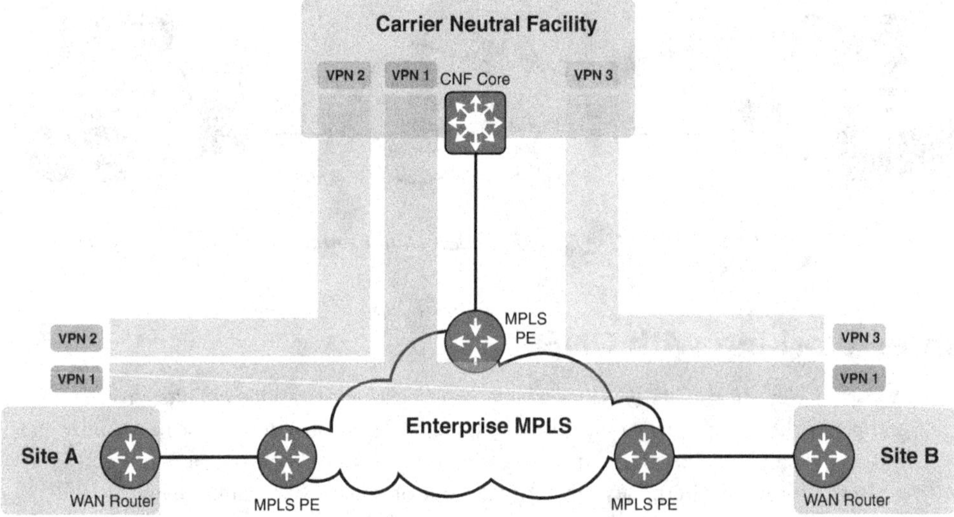

Figure 5-14 *Selective VRF Offloading Using MPLS*

MPLS for Inter-VRF Routing and Merging Services

In a traditional network of an organization, there might be a need to have separate networks like development and production. They need to be kept separate and most likely connected via firewalls to create an isolated fault domain and keep development testing away from production. However, now a lot of computing and testing happens in the cloud due to its benefit of offering a pay-as-you-go model, which can be scaled on demand. And with virtualization in the campus, most development and production traffic is now virtualized in different VRFs over the same physical routing and switching infrastructure. With this new design concept, traditional networks need to evolve and leverage other means of segregating traffic and providing access to services.

One example is using inter-VRF routing capability of the MPLS network. When the prefixes are received on MPLS PE routers, a BGP policy can be implemented to set specific route-targets for the prefixes that are received from the remote router. These route-targets can be matched and allowed to be leaked into another VRF using route-target import functionality. Figure 5-15 shows how this feature works. The use case we are trying to achieve is one in which certain development and production prefixes need to access the Microsoft Azure public cloud for cloud-based Active Directory (AD) infrastructure and applications. With the route-leaking capability, selective prefixes can be leaked and provided access to certain resources. Another use case would be the centralized Internet access or shared IP Telephony Services.

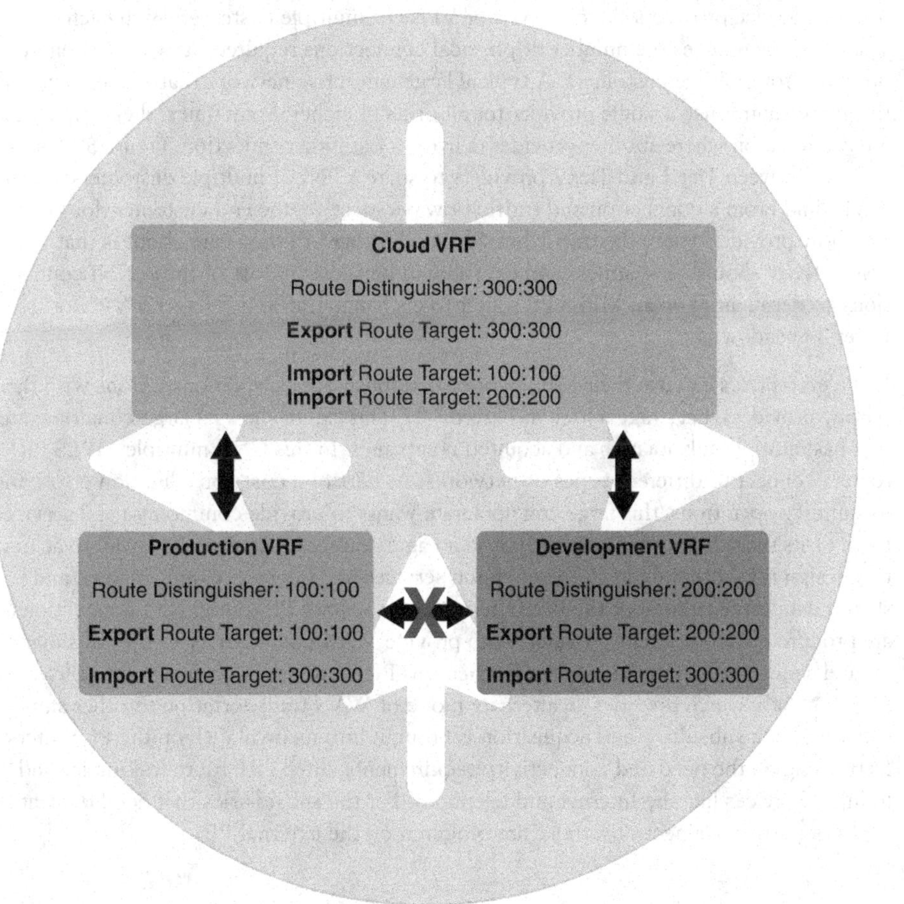

Figure 5-15 *MPLS VPN Route-Leaking*

Inter-VRF route-leaking is not an MPLS VPN-specific feature. It can also be configured and deployed on any VRF-enabled router. However, MPLS VPN provides that framework to transport packets from one PE to another by maintaining these route-targets and not using VRF-Lite.

Using MPLS to Connect NNI

The majority of the connections we see are client-to-network interfaces (CNIs). These connections are typically leased from service providers where only one client or customer is connected to it—for example, an Internet connection from an ISP or an MPLS connection from an MPLS provider. From the provider's perspective, on that single link, only one customer is connected.

A network-to-network interface (NNI) is between two service providers. Over this connection, service providers share VLANs or VPNs of multiple customers with each other. This interface reduces the number of physical connections required between two large providers for multiple customers. A typical large enterprise network that is spread across the globe cannot use a single provider for all of its branches. Sometimes, these branches are in a location where another provider delivers a last-mile connection. Figure 5-16 shows an NNI between Tier 1 and Tier 2 providers to share VPNs of multiple customers over a single link. From a connection and traffic flow perspective, the end customer does not care how providers route the traffic between each other. All they care about is that the connectivity should be seamless and data should be secure. Most of these NNI connections are terminated on an MPLS PE router to exchange traffic in a Layer 3 VPN or Layer 2 pseudowires.

Large enterprises can use their MPLS core to establish direct NNI connections with their service providers. Let's take a look at Figure 5-17. This figure shows a large conglomerate that has multiple subsidiaries and acquired companies. In this CNF, multiple MPLS PE routers connect to different types of networks. As part of a cost consolidation effort and to simplify operations, this large conglomerate wants to provide commonly used services to all of its subsidiaries and acquisitions in an aggregated design. The best way to achieve this design is by bringing in all the common services like Internet, cloud, partner, and shared data center to one of the PE routers. On the second PE router, NNI connections are procured from different providers who provide WAN connectivity to the subsidiaries and acquisitions. To take it a step further, this PE router is also connected to the DMVPN hub, which provides an alternate mode of WAN transportation to other subsidiaries. Each subsidiary and acquisition is brought into its own VRF on the PE routers. Depending on the need and connectivity requirements, inter-VRF route-leaking is used to inject services like the Internet and telephony. For the subsidiaries that need dedicated cloud or partner connections, those are procured on the external PE.

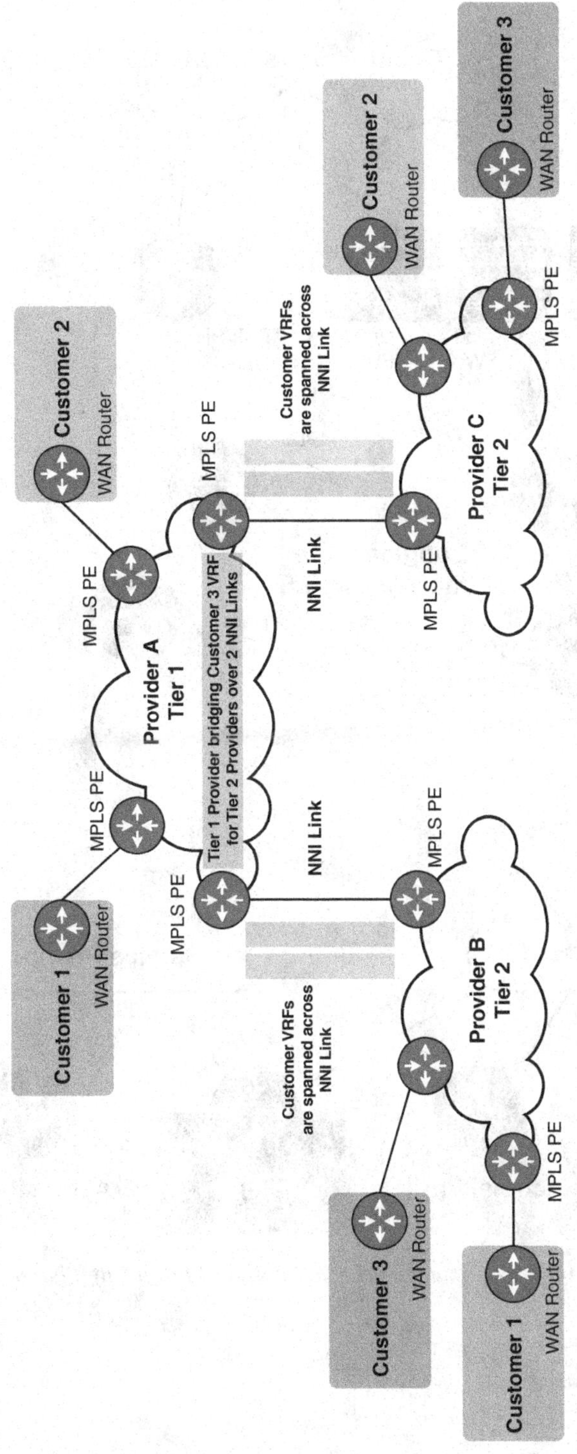

Figure 5-16 *A Typical NNI Connection Between Two Service Providers Servicing Multiple Customers*

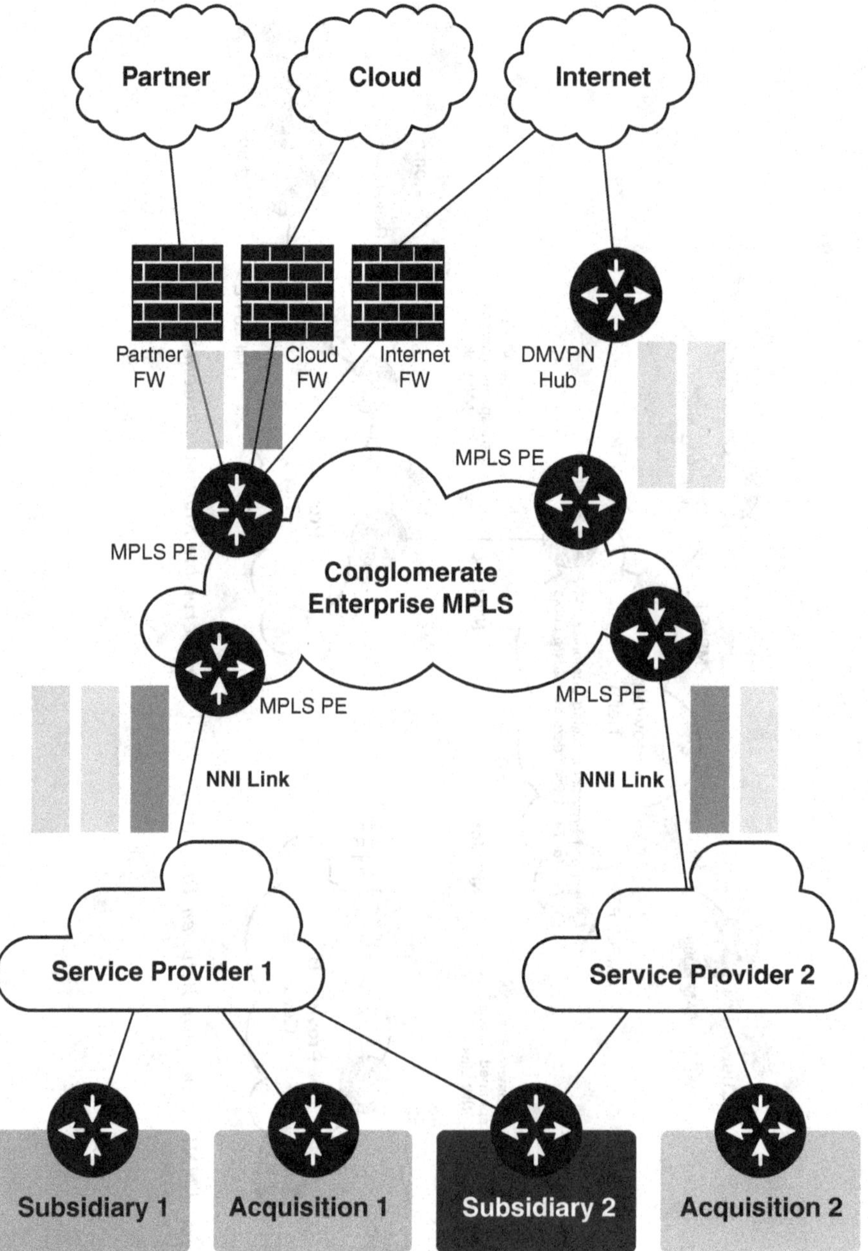

Figure 5-17 *Conglomerate Example of Using NNI and Providing Shared Services*

This architecture simplifies the operations and management of a large organization. The organization can easily replicate this design across multiple regions or CNFs for added redundancy and resiliency. The use of this design is not uncommon. This architecture is robust and scalable and enables a large enterprise to adopt an IT-as-a-Business (ITaaB) model. This is the most effective way to run a large business and gives granular control of the traffic flow and access to services and resources. Another major advantage of this design is that when a conglomerate acquires a new company or dissolves one, changes to the network can be handled quickly by adding or removing VRFs on the PE routers or modifying inter-VRF route-leaking rules to allow or deny access to shared services.

Inter-working with Security Stack

Because MPLS is a WAN transport technology, there is no direct connection to any endpoint in the edge. The traffic it passes does maintain end-to-end macrosegmentation across the MPLS fabric. Some of the primary forms of security are the BGP peering or any other form of routing protocol adjacency between MPLS PE routers and directly connected edge routers or other provider routers. Secure passwords should protect these routing adjacencies as per Cisco's best practices.

MPLS VPNs can also be leveraged to steer traffic to a central security stack. A security stack is a group of devices that are used to inspect the traffic, apply any security policies, and then transmit out to the other end. Some of the components are proxy servers, intrusion prevention systems (IPSs) or intrusion detection systems (IDSs), firewalls, secure web gateways, VPN and remote access, email gateways, distributed denial of service (DDoS) protection, cyber vision, and so on. A combination of one or all of these components becomes a security stack that ensures an organization's network remains secure.

Having an entire security stack deployed on all the sites may not be scalable, both operationally and financially. Hence, these stacks are usually deployed at a centralized location like a CNF. Depending on the organization's security governing policy, some of the applications in the trusted VRF can be sent out to access resources in the data center, cloud, or Internet directly. However, some networks, such as a partner or development network, cannot be given direct unrestricted access. All the traffic in that type of network needs to be run through the entire security stack to ensure no malicious or compromised traffic enters through a trusted production network.

To achieve this result, MPLS has a built-in feature that can backhaul all the untrusted traffic to a centralized facility and then offload it to the security stack. After the traffic passes through the security stack, it is then sent and merged with the trusted production traffic. Figure 5-18 shows such a design. Here, by manipulating route-distinguisher and route-target attributes of VRF and leveraging the MPLS fabric, we can easily redirect all the traffic to a centralized facility or inspection. This is a known way to create honeypots in Internet service providers to protect many of their customers from external attacks. Only then is inspected and trusted traffic allowed to send to ISP's customers.

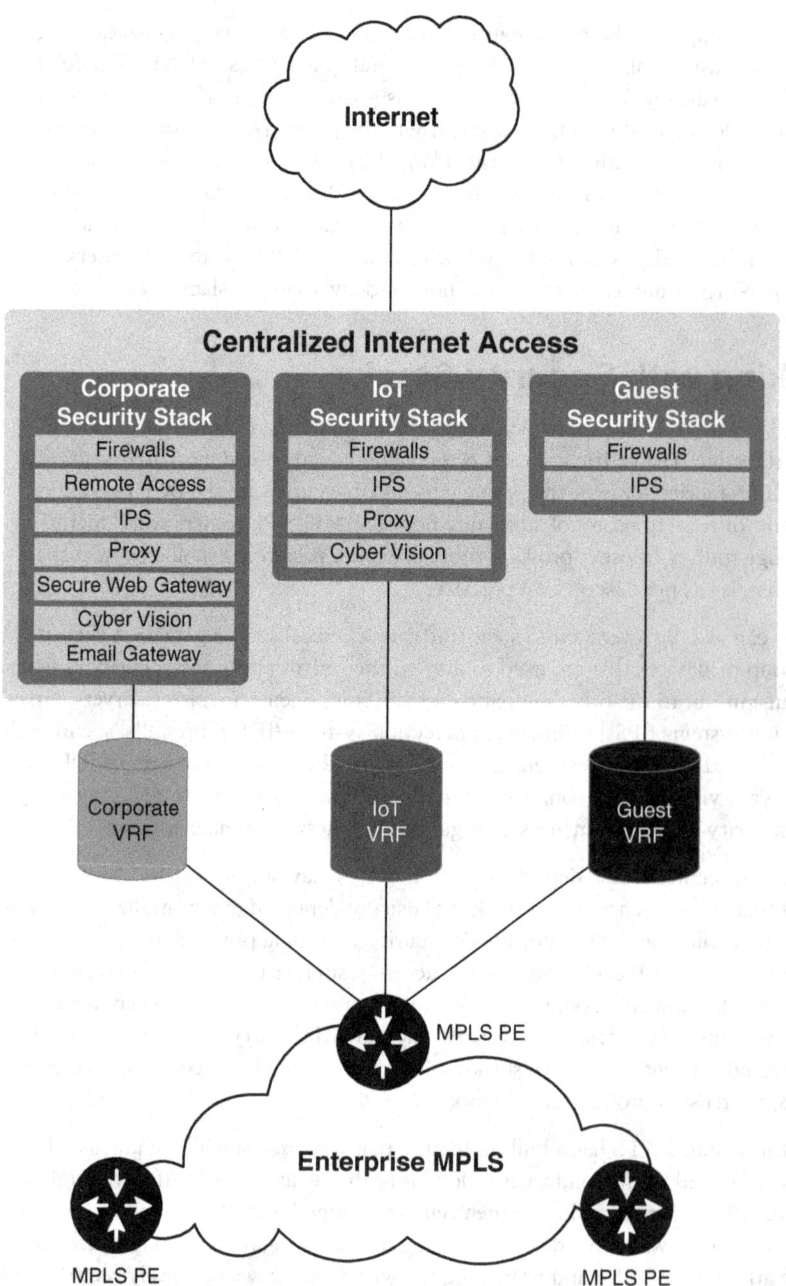

Figure 5-18 *Using MPLS to Backhaul Traffic to the Security Stack*

Summary

In this chapter, we learned how flexible enterprise MPLS can be. We discussed how it interacts with SD-Access and campus networks by keeping macrosegmentation and leveraging SXPv5 to scale microsegmentation. We discussed how MPLS could be a super backbone connecting different WAN solutions and providing connectivity to data centers and CNFs. We looked at different integration points with CNFs and how traffic can be routed by manipulating route targets. Overall, this versatile and scalable technology is vendor-agnostic and can scale horizontally and vertically for large enterprises.

Chapter 6

Carrier Neutral Facilities

In this chapter, we discuss the following:

- What Carrier Neutral Facilities are and why they are becoming critical components in today's networks
- What makes a Carrier Neutral Facility
- How well a Carrier Neutral Facility integrates with other domains
- Lessons learned and best practices for designing Carrier Neutral Facilities

Overview

Since the inception of the Internet in the early 1960s, its evolution has been staggering. From connecting the first two computers to connecting modern Internet of Things (IoT) devices, the Internet has expanded in terms of connectivity and the amount of data being transferred between devices. The Internet has become a commodity. Today, it is available to most remote parts of the world through the use of satellites. With ever-growing devices connecting worldwide and outer space from our space stations, interconnectivity between different providers and organizations is critical. Since the 1990s, Internet service providers (ISPs) have provided Internet connectivity to various government and commercial networks. Because their customers needed to talk with each other and also with other customers, network access points (NAPs) came into existence. These NAPs were strategically located facilities that acted as carrier hotels where all the ISPs worldwide had their presence. In these NAPs, all ISPs are interconnected among themselves, essentially building the Internet's backbone.

With high-speed residential Internet now accessible to everyone in most countries, whenever a user is accessing any resource from the web within the same country or in another, they might have to exit out of the ISP's network and into another and, in some cases, move across several ISPs to access the desired resource. Depending on the users' ISP and footprint, they would have predefined exit points in most NAPs where they can exit out of their network. With the evolution of e-commerce, large organizations, over the past two decades, have needed much faster communication with their users and data. This has meant that some of their critical applications conducting the business required being physically much closer to the NAPs. Latency is proportional to the physical distance of the devices. Because we cannot change the speed of light, which is the main form of transmission over fiber connections, a user residing in New York will have higher latency accessing an application located in Los Angeles than in Washington, DC. Accessing a small amount of data will almost have no difference, but this latency adds up when we talk about large file transmissions or multiple streams of back-and-forth data during an e-commerce transaction. All this ties to user experience and how a buyer is influenced to buy products from a vendor. If the speed of data such as a product catalog or transaction is not fast enough, they would lose interest and move on to the next vendor. So, having critical data closer to the user in a predictable manner is a crucial design parameter in today's networks.

Carrier Neutral Facilities (CNFs) are evolutions of NAPs. Today, as their name suggests, they are *carrier neutral*. Historically, only large service providers were part of NAPs. Today, some NAPs are built that way, but as data came closer to the user, these facilities needed to expand. Consequently, many new small providers came into existence not only by providing interconnectivity between different providers but also by providing a space for other medium to large organizations to have a rack or two of space to host their critical application servers and infrastructure, which requires direct access to the ISPs. These CNFs are usually located within or close to NAPs, providing latency-sensitive connections between applications and users.

Today, CNFs not only house e-commerce applications and latency-sensitive data but are also critical components in aggregating traffic from all remote sites of an organization. In a hierarchical design, connecting CNFs of a multi-national organization provides structure to the traffic flow as well as predictability in the performance of their network. Let's see how CNFs inter-operate between different domains.

Interaction with Other Domains

Carrier Neutral Facilities are usually treated as backbone components of the network infrastructure. With CNFs' proximity to critical resources, data centers, and aggregated connectivity to all the remote sites, they are at the center of and are critical for a network. They can also connect to CNFs in the same region to provide redundancy and to other regions to provide inter-region backbone connectivity. Figure 6-1 shows a high-level connectivity layout for a CNF. In subsequent sections, we discuss its interaction with each of the network domains.

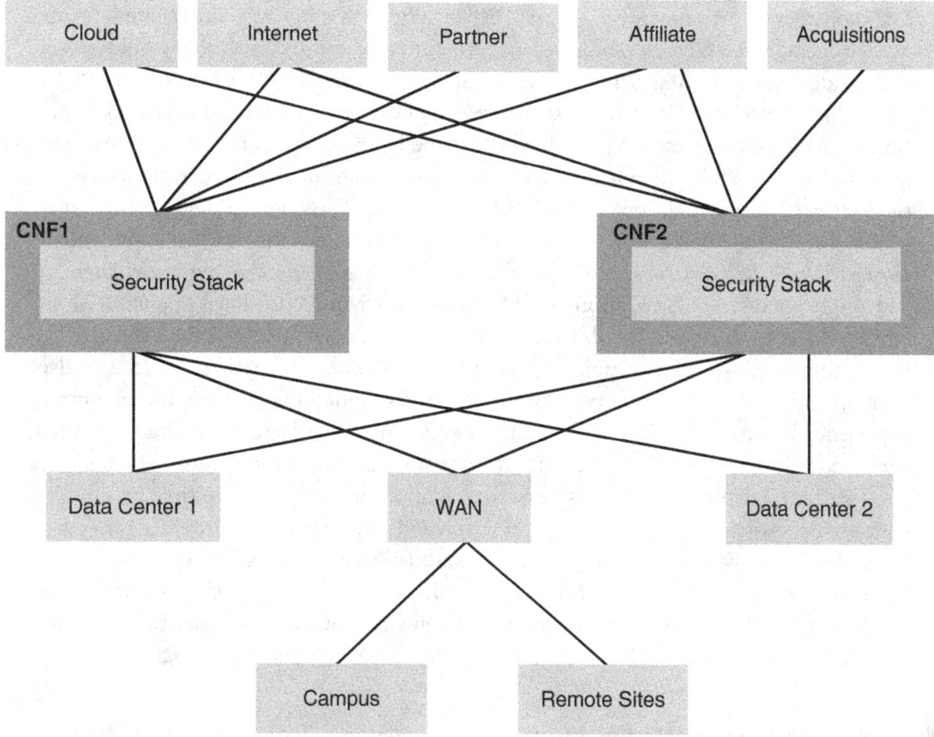

Figure 6-1 *High-Level CNF Overview*

Inter-working with SD-Access and Campus Fabric

Cisco's Software Defined Access (SD-Access) or Campus Fabric onboards an organization's users and endpoints and allows them to access digital resources located across the organization. In a large enterprise network, these campus networks come in various sizes, from a few hundred people to a few thousand. Usually, the largest of the campus networks are corporate headquarters or regional headquarters for an organization. Having the most efficient network connectivity for these large facilities is paramount because the need to access resources quickly and the bandwidth required are directly proportional to the number of users and endpoints at the site. Therefore, historically, corporate headquarters were also home to corporate data centers where users would have direct access to the data without the involvement of any WAN connections.

As time passed and the adoption to the cloud and data increased, data needed to be relocated close to users and away from the corporate offices. With the increased latency and involvement of WAN and, in some business verticals, an increase in e-commerce, as data was moved closer to users, there was a need to shift data centers out of the corporate offices and to more centralized locations.

Let's consider an e-commerce business. Historically, with corporate data centers located at their headquarters, an e-commerce business operated out of California would be able to provide fast and reliable service to customers based out of California or in nearby states due to proximity to data centers where applications are located. This configuration is fine if the business is local. However, if the business wants to expand across the nation or even globally, the farther its customers are from the data center, the worse the user experience might be, confined by latency and WAN connectivity at the data center. So, it would make more sense for that business to move its critical applications closer to the NAPs or CNFs, providing direct access to multiple ISPs with low latency and ample bandwidth. Now, another problem arises: when the business applications are moved closer to the users, the development teams who constantly maintain the applications and patch them have to upload a great deal of data every day over WAN and also back up and restore business-critical applications. Although the problem of customer experience is solved, the experience of the development and IT teams degrades as their workload response times increase. And the situation becomes even more complex with the distributed deployment of business-critical applications across multiple geographical regions. To resolve this complexity, production and development environments needed to be closer for faster and efficient patching and deployment. This is one of the reasons large enterprises are moving their data centers away from their corporate headquarters to CNFs, because with development and production workloads being closer to each other, now the users maintaining these applications only have to transact minimally to modify that data.

Coming back to the point of how today's campus networks interact with the CNFs, depending on the type and number of users located at a site, a direct connection to the CNF might be required to achieve ideal low latency connectivity that can maintain macro- and microsegmentation. Monolithic networks—the networks that are built with a single routing plane or just with a global routing table (GRT)—do not require any form of macro- and microsegmentation to carry over to different segments of the network. In that scenario, connectivity to the CNF will be straightforward Layer 3 with a routing protocol like BGP.

In terms of SD-Access and Campus Fabrics, the logic is different. With macro- and microsegmentation deployed, a detailed plan needs to be in place for extending the segmentation strategy from campus to the CNF. In this scenario, all Virtual Routing and Forwarding (VRF) instances must be carried through. Let's discuss how that can be achieved. The two scenarios discussed next assume there is only a dark fiber, point-to-point wavelength, or some form of Ethernet private line (EPL) connectivity between the CNF and the site with the SD-Access or Campus Fabric deployed.

Approach with VRF-Lite

When the campus network's macrosegmentation needs to be carried to the CNFs, the Virtual Routing and Forwarding-Lite (VRF-Lite) approach seems to be the quickest and easiest way to achieve the desired outcome. With this approach, the primary objective is to establish macrosegmentation connectivity across the WAN from a local site with SD-Access or Campus Fabric enabled.

In a typical fabric environment at a campus site, there are two VRFs: corporate and guest. The corporate VRF is considered a trusted network where all the endpoints and traffic from all of the endpoints do not go through any kind of inspection or firewalls for internal traffic. This traffic is inspected and firewalled at a central location, such as a CNF, where it exits out of the corporate environment to access the Internet or a partner network as needed. Depending on the organization's adoption of cloud and Software-as-a-Service (SaaS) model, the traffic pattern of a trusted corporate network would vary. With low adoption of cloud- and SaaS-based applications, the traffic pattern is predominantly east-west within the site as well as site to site. Some examples of these applications would be Voice over IP (VoIP) or local file sharing or emails. With a majority of the applications residing in the centralized facility, such as data centers, a CNF would become a transit hub to collect all traffic from WAN connections and then, using a high-capacity backhaul, send the traffic to data centers. With the organizations that have already started on their cloud or SaaS journey, the traffic pattern is highly different. In this scenario, the traffic is predominantly north-south. There is little communication east-west because most of the data is being downloaded or uploaded to the cloud. In either of the scenarios, CNFs become aggregation points of all the traffic, and when the trusted traffic flow hits the CNF core, depending on the destination, it would take the path outside of the corporate network through the security stack or within the corporate network by using other WAN connections to connect to different sites or the data center.

Guest networks in the corporate environment have a different type of traffic pattern. Because all the traffic is untrusted, it is generally backhauled to the CNF, where the security stack is, and then directly exits out to the Internet. Depending on the organization's security and traffic engineering policy, there might be a requirement to inspect and police guest traffic for any malicious activities and to throttle the bandwidth if that traffic shares the same Internet circuit as the corporate network. Higher priority and bandwidth availability are always given to corporate Internet traffic.

This VRF-Lite approach is good for spanning a small number of VRFs across a campus site and a CNF. However, the biggest limitation with this strategy is to support microsegmentation. Because the traffic carried across the link is not VXLAN encapsulated, SGTs cannot be carried forward easily. There are mechanisms such as using CMD inline tagging or SXP peering with ISE, but these methods do not scale well. There is also the added complexity of running multiple VRF-aware routing processes for each of the logical links between the campus site and CNFs. This VRF-aware routing will need to be carried across the CNF core and terminated to the respective exit points in the network.

In summary, even though VRF-Lite is a viable option to quickly turn up macrosegmentation between a campus site and CNFs, due to scale limitations and the complexity involved with the design, this is not a widely deployed solution.

Dedicated Borders at the Data Center

Extending macro- and microsegmentation in the CNF is much easier with solutions like SD-Access or Campus Fabric. Because both of these technologies use the data plane to send macro- and microsegmentation information, analyzing the packets becomes a lot easier and also scalable. This design can be scaled to transmit many virtual networks to the CNFs with minimal configuration. Let's discuss how this can be achieved with the design. Because SD-Access and Campus Fabrics work in an identical fashion, we use SD-Access as a reference example.

As shown in Figure 6-2, the CNF is considered another site in the network infrastructure. Here, this site has dedicated border nodes (BNs) that have required virtual networks that need to be extended from the campus site. Data from campus sites, or any other SD-Access-enabled sites, is transmitted across the WAN with VXLAN encapsulation. The control plane mechanism relies on transit control plane nodes that are located at the CNFs. The role of the border nodes at the CNF is to provide encapsulation and decapsulation of the VXLAN-based data plane traffic.

The traffic flow for an endpoint that needs to access a partner network will look like the following:

1. An endpoint from a campus needs to access data from an application residing in a partner network. For this, the packet is sent to the local border node because it is the gateway to reach networks outside of the fabric after initial lookups are done.

2. After the packet reaches a local border node, it will query the transit control plane node to find the location of the site that has access to the partner's network.

3. The transit control plane responds with the IP address of the CNF border node.

4. The campus border node then re-encapsulates the data packet with VXLAN with macro- and microsegmentation information and sends the packet over the WAN to the CNF border node.

5. The CNF border node then decapsulates the traffic, and then, based on the route lookup, it will forward the packet as a native IP packet to the partner firewall.

In this scenario, regardless of the destination network, the previously described flow remains similar. The same concept can also be extended to other sites with SD-Access fabric enabled because the underlying infrastructure of transit control planes will be reused across all of those sites.

Another feature that is available in the SD-Access architecture is called Multi-Site Remote Border (MSRB). This feature is similar to the architecture we described earlier, but MSRB removes the additional step of encapsulation and decapsulation at the local border because they don't exist for the virtual network in question. With MSRB, the VNs are directly anchored at the border nodes in the CNF. So, for the networks whose VNs are anchored at the CNF, the edge node directly builds that VXLAN-encapsulated packet, which directly exits out of the border nodes at the CNF.

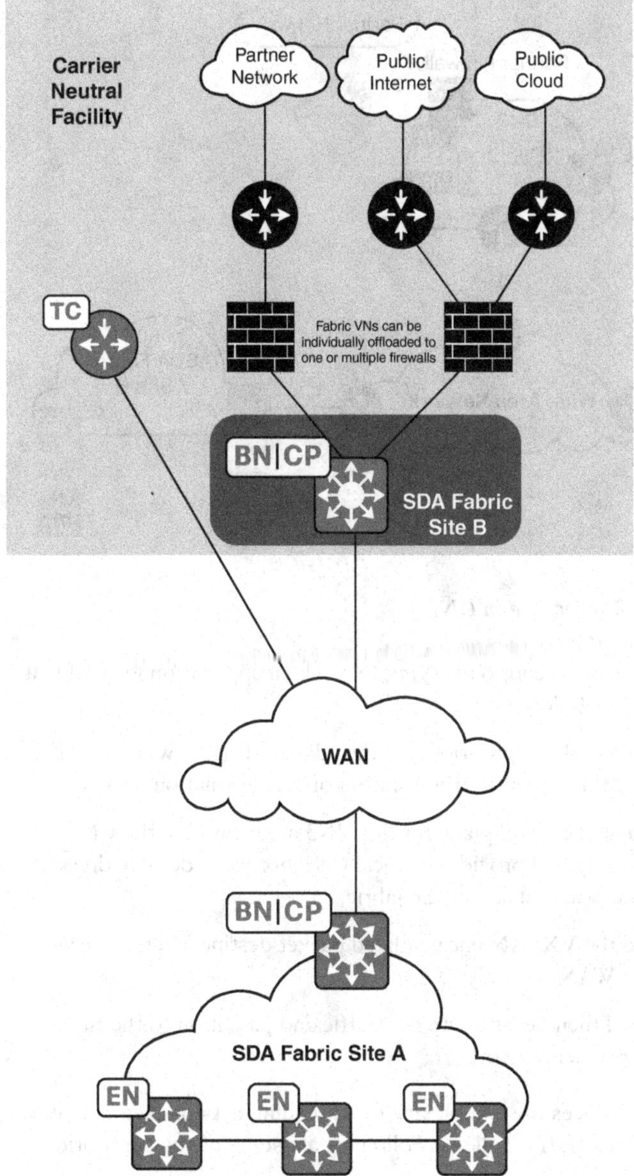

Figure 6-2 *Extending Macro- and Microsegmentation Using Dedicated Borders in CNF*

Let's look at how this traffic flow works in Figure 6-3.

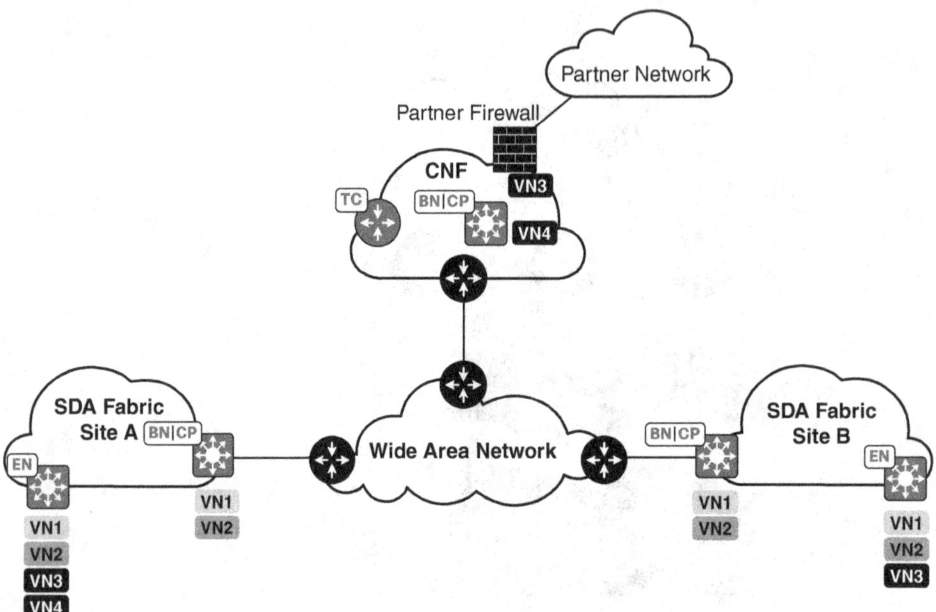

Figure 6-3 *Multi-Site Remote Border Use in CNF*

Here, taking the same example of an endpoint trying to reach an application located in a partner network, the steps are as follows:

1. An endpoint needs to access the application and the edge node (EN) will query control plane (CP) node for VN3 to identify the location of the destination network.
2. Because the border node and control plane for this VN3 are located in the CNF using the MSRB feature, they will provide the local CNF border node IP address as access to networks for gateway outside of the fabric.
3. The edge node will build the VXLAN-encapsulated packet destined to that border node traveling across the WAN.
4. The CNF border node will then decapsulate the traffic and pass it on to the firewall that is connected to the partner network.

MSRB is a great feature that reduces the complexity for extending network segmentation to facilities that need centralized traffic policies. Following are some of the applications of these features:

- Guest network for multiple sites that exit out of CNFs or centralized security stacks
- Physical security networks that send all access and surveillance data to a centralized location

- Extension of a partner network to remote sites
- Building Management Systems (BMSs) and IoT sensors, where various sensors and devices send data to central servers for data processing

In any of these approaches, scaling of virtual networks becomes highly simplified. However, some considerations need to be taken into account to make this work. The WAN maximum transmission unit (MTU) is critical. In an ideal scenario, these connections between campus sites and CNFs are usually dark fiber connections that provide great flexibility to increase MTU to accommodate an additional 50 bytes of VXLAN encapsulation. However, for the sites that are connected via some other form of WAN like MPLS or SD-WAN, traffic flow might not work due to VXLAN fragmentation. In this scenario, TCP-MSS can be adjusted to 1250 bytes to account for any kind of overhead.

Using the transit control plane (TCP) or Multi-Site Remote Border (MSRB) correctly can also have an impact on how overall fabric traffic flows across the organization's network. TCP provides flexibility with inline tagging over SD-WAN but adds additional lookups in between, whereas MSRB does not provide inline tagging but will provide an ability to use one single IP address pool across multiple sites, which is an ideal use case for guest networks.

In either scenario, having border nodes at the CNF greatly reduces the complexity across the WAN and can easily carry the macro- and microsegmentation attributes of the network.

Inter-working with SD-WAN, MPLS, and DMVPN

Carrier Neutral Facilities play an important role when it comes to SD-WAN or DMVPN architecture. For any organization, designing their WAN infrastructure in the most optimal manner is crucial. When it comes to any technology that is being used as the WAN technology, the CNF positions itself as a hub for the region it is serving or, in some cases, the centralized or only exit point for any external connectivity in the organization. Understanding the nature of the CNF, it provides connectivity to various parts of the network—networks such as campuses, remote sites, data centers, partner connections, cloud, and the security stack. Just like an airline pulling all of their passengers from different destinations in one of their hubs to provide one-stop connectivity to other destinations, the CNF becomes that hub for all the data. With its simple network architecture, it can also provide various options on maintaining macrosegmentation. Because SD-WAN, provider MPLS, enterprise MPLS, and DMVPN are all WAN technologies providing similar macrosegmentation capabilities, we discuss all of them in this section.

Regardless of the technology used for an organization's WAN—SD-WAN, DMVPN, provider MPLS (P-MPLS) or enterprise MPLS (E-MPLS)—carrying that macrosegmentation in a core is necessary. Most of the time, macrosegmentation is all that is required because it provides a routing plane separation. All four technologies are able to maintain macrosegmentation of the traffic natively. Some do it in a single tunnel, whereas others do it in multiple tunnels. Overall, the goal is to send traffic from one site to the other for one or more networks. Because Carrier Neutral Facilities are a hub for all the network traffic, maintaining macrosegmentation is critical. When it comes to microsegmentation, it is always nice to have but is not required at the CNF level because most of the microsegmentation enforcement is done at the end domains, such as SD-Access, ACI, and the security stack, that are all connected to CNFs.

Next, we discuss how each of the WAN technologies connected to CNF headends maintain the macrosegmentation.

Software-Defined Wide Area Network (SD-WAN)

SD-WAN is an emerging technology with very high potential. With a software-driven controller-based architecture, it is flexible enough not only to keep end-to-end macrosegmentation like traditional WAN but also to maintain microsegmentation capabilities. In an SD-WAN architecture, tunnels are built once across sites with multiple VRFs that are carried within a single tunnel using MPLS labels as tags to differentiate them. This way, end-to-end segmentation is carried across the entire infrastructure regardless of what VRF the traffic is in. When the traffic reaches the headend, each of the VRFs can be offloaded to any domain as desired.

The network shown in Figure 6-4 is one of the most common designs for a large organization. This SD-WAN takes care of macrosegmentation by separating the routing plane of each security zone. Here, security profile traffic, such as corporate, guest, development, and partner/affiliate traffic, is kept in separate VPNs on the SD-WAN side. These VPNs are then mapped to individual VRFs on the CNF side as well as on the remote sites, including campus. When the segmented traffic reaches the CNF, with the use of back-to-back VRFs or VRF-Lite, this traffic can be offloaded into the respective domain. In most cases, these VRFs terminate on a firewall for security so that the traffic can be inspected. In this scenario, all site-to-site traffic is carried in respective domains and zones across SD-WAN. There is no expectation of traffic bleeding into another VRF or VPN; hence, macrosegmentation is maintained end to end. Whenever traffic is expected to leave one routing plane for another, it has to traverse the firewall or some form of a control point to control and monitor what traffic flows through.

The following traffic flows are shown in Figure 6-4:

- **Traffic pattern 1:** This general corporate traffic is trusted and always allowed to access applications related to the organization's day-to-day business function. This type of traffic has direct access to all users and applications because they are in a trusted zone. The only time the traffic will be subject to a firewall inspection is when the traffic is leaving for the Internet and/or another partner/affiliate.
- **Traffic pattern 2:** This development traffic is isolated from production for security reasons. For this organization, development traffic leverages public cloud infrastructure to scale and test their applications and products on demand. Hence, they are put into their own VRF to keep the traffic isolated. When the applications are production-ready, they are transferred to the production environment via the data center firewall.

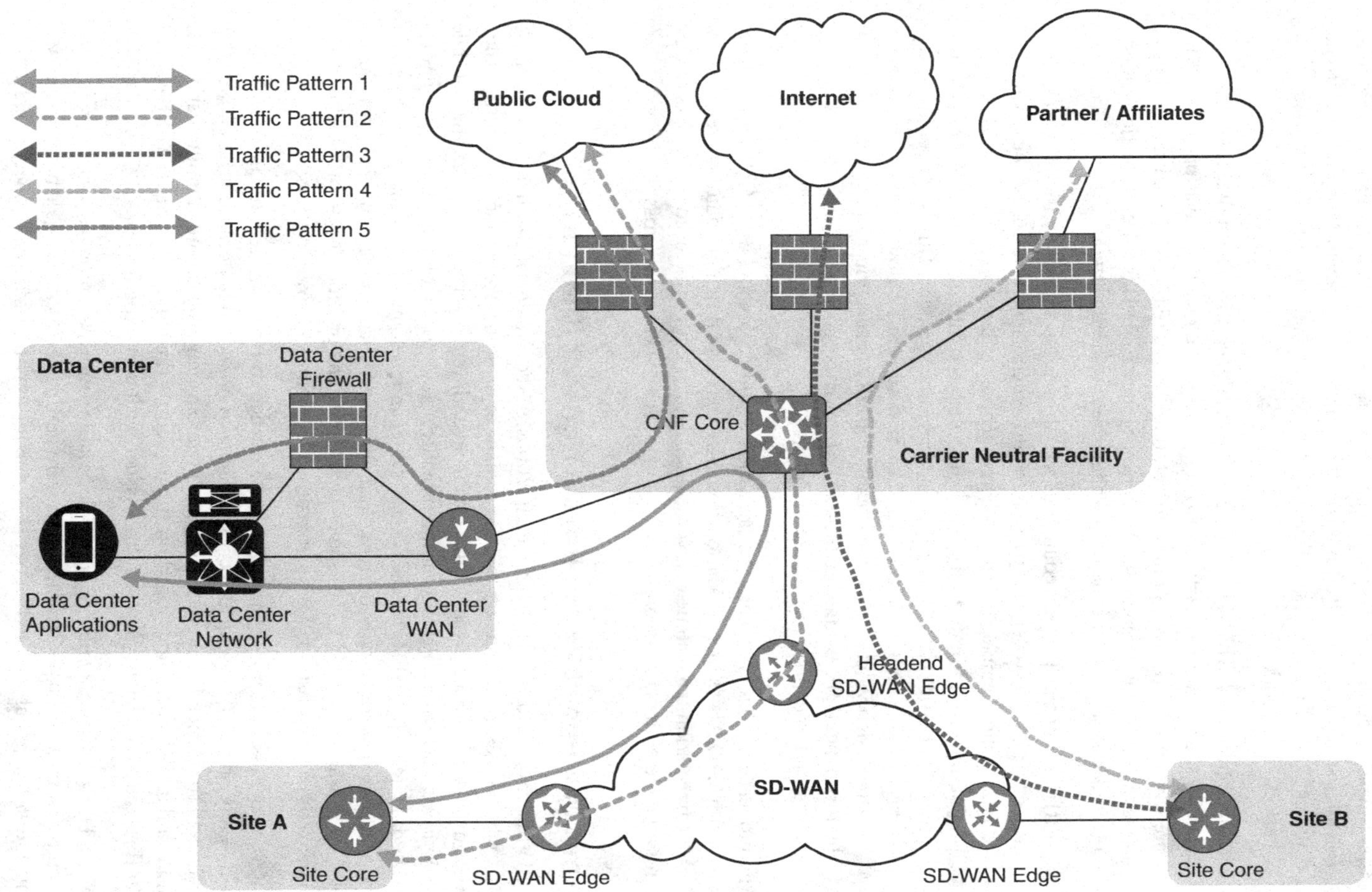

Figure 6-4 *VRF Offloading at CNF with SD-WAN*

- **Traffic pattern 3:** This type of traffic is for guest Internet access. Guests have no business accessing corporate application data. That traffic is completely isolated and in almost all cases directly dropped off to the Internet transit. Many organizations subject guest traffic to inspection and security policies to control what goes in and out of the network.
- **Traffic pattern 4:** This type of traffic does not need to access any local organization's resources as a primary function. This may be a recent acquisition or an affiliate whose networks are not merged yet, but they share physical real estate or office space with a large organization for business functions. This type of traffic is directly offloaded to a partner/affiliate firewall and out to their network.
- **Traffic pattern 5:** The preceding four traffic patterns are mainly focused on isolation of traffic. However, this pattern requires access to traffic across those routing planes. In the example, a pattern where traffic from development is ported over to production or corporate traffic needs to access the Internet; to do so, it has to go through a firewall-like device for control and management. This is where domains are bridged in a controlled fashion. In some cases, traffic flow would be suboptimal, but this design will benefit from greater control because this type of traffic is not in high volume. If the volume increases, more of these shared exchange points can be configured to offload and distribute traffic.

This model shows one way that an organization would deploy and use a CNF and its flexibility with SD-WAN as their WAN solution. SD-WAN also provides additional features with microsegmentation that can be coupled with SD-Access. It can be used to transport SGTs across the WAN to maintain both macro- and microsegmentation across the network.

Dynamic Multi-point Virtual Private Network (DMVPN)

DMVPN has been around since the early 2000s. Cisco Systems introduced this technology, which was a game changer for many small- to medium-size businesses. Historically, when a private WAN solution was needed from an Internet service provider, the last-mile options were heavily dependent on the provider's reach to the region where the site was located. Frame-relay, ATM, business DSL, cable, and in some cases plain old telephone service (POTS) were the only options. And with many local and regional providers in play, there was not a good direct connectivity from one provider to the other. This also increased the high cost for WAN connections to maintain private circuits.

Internet circuits were not secure, so if a site needed to be connected, organizations had to rely on point-to-point IPsec VPN. This was not scalable because it had inherent issues: all traffic needed to route through the hub for any site-to-site communication. As more and more technologies relied on IP protocols—the biggest one being Voice over IP (VoIP)—the added latency caused more issues with user experience.

When DMVPN was introduced, it was designed to provide a more cost-effective solution to private WAN links. Internet links were getting cheaper due to demand, and it was much easier to get at remote locations—sometimes with residential connections. Having a router behind a NAT device limited the use of IPsec VPN because it needed static IPs on both sides to form a tunnel. When DMVPN was introduced, it solved some of the fundamental issues and brought a lot of small- to medium-size businesses together and also provided an alternative approach for large organizations that would back up their primary private WAN links with DMVPN on cheaper Internet connections.

DMVPN was able to solve the following issues:

- Dual-hub routers can be used at a single location, or a single-hub router can be used at two different locations.
- Multi-point Generic Routing Encapsulation (GRE) over IPsec is used to establish VPN tunnels.
- Remote end tunnels do not need static IP, so they can be behind a NAT or DHCP-based IP.
- With the use of DMVPN phase 3, only the first few packets route through the hub until a site-to-site dynamic tunnel has formed. This capability was great for VoIP services because VoIP and any other site-to-site traffic had no need to go through the hub site.
- Using dynamic routing protocols over DMVPN enabled better convergence in the network.
- The multi-VRF capability of DMVPN also enabled multiple DMVPN clouds for multiple VRFs.

With SD-WAN, all VRFs are tagged with a label and traverse over the same tunnel, whereas with DMVPN, all the VRFs have their own dedicated tunnel interfaces. This design has its own advantages and disadvantages, but at a very high level, they both function similarly.

The design in Figure 6-5 is common among small- to medium-size organizations; with large organizations, there is usually a primary provider-managed MPLS (P-MPLS) WAN cloud. Macrosegmentation with DMVPN is achieved by logically isolating all routing planes into different DMVPN clouds. The hub devices of these clouds may be the same or different, depending on the organization's requirements. Regardless of WAN technology, the traffic patterns are the same. The figure illustrates macrosegmentation for corporate, guest, development, and partner/affiliate traffic. These DMVPN clouds are then mapped to individual VRFs on both CNF and remote locations. When the segmented traffic reaches the CNF, with the use of different hub routers, they can be directly connected to each security zone for application and data access. In most cases, these connections terminate on a firewall for security purposes so that the traffic can be inspected. In this scenario, all site-to-site traffic is carried in respective domains and zones across DMVPN without traversing the hub. There is no expectation of traffic bleeding into another VRF or VPN; hence, macrosegmentation is maintained end to end. Whenever traffic is expected to leave one routing plane for another, it has to traverse the firewall or some form of a control point to control and monitor traffic that flows through.

The following traffic flows are shown in Figure 6-5:

- **Traffic pattern 1:** This general corporate traffic is trusted and always allowed to access applications related to the organization's day-to-day business functions. This type of traffic has direct access to all users and applications because they are in a trusted zone. The only time the traffic will be subject to a firewall inspection is when the traffic is leaving for the Internet and/or another partner/affiliate.
- **Traffic pattern 2:** This development traffic is isolated from production for security reasons. For this organization, development traffic leverages the public cloud infrastructure to scale and test their applications and products on demand. Hence, they are put into their own VRF to keep the traffic isolated. When the applications are production-ready, they are transferred to the production environment via the data center firewall. With DMVPN, because this is partially trusted traffic, this traffic can share the same physical infrastructure as the production traffic.
- **Traffic pattern 3:** This type of traffic is for guest Internet access. Guests have no business accessing corporate application data. That traffic is completely isolated and in almost all cases directly dropped off to the Internet transit. Many organizations subject guest traffic to inspection and security policies to control what goes in and out of the network.
- **Traffic pattern 4:** This type of traffic does not need to access any local organization's resources as a primary function. This may be a recent acquisition or an affiliate whose networks are not merged yet, but they share physical real estate or office space with a large organization for business functions. This type of traffic is directly offloaded to a partner/affiliate DMVPN hub and then to the firewall that connects to the affiliate's network.
- **Traffic pattern 5:** The preceding four traffic patterns are mainly focused on isolation of traffic. However, this pattern requires access to traffic across those routing planes. In the example, a pattern where traffic from development is ported over to production or corporate traffic needs to access the Internet; to do so, it has to go through a firewall-like device for control and management. This is where domains are bridged in a controlled fashion. In some cases, traffic flow would be suboptimal, but this design will benefit from greater control because this type of traffic is not in high volume. If the volume increases, more of these shared exchange points can be configured to offload and distribute traffic.

This model is a classic example of how DMVPN is used in most organizations. The advantage is in keeping the traffic isolated and the ability to offload where it is needed. The disadvantage is that this is still a major CLI-based technology. There are no central controllers that dynamically manage the tunnels and traffic flows and conduct traffic engineering. However, all the configurations of the DMVPN hubs and spokes can be automated using simple Python scripts or Ansible playbooks.

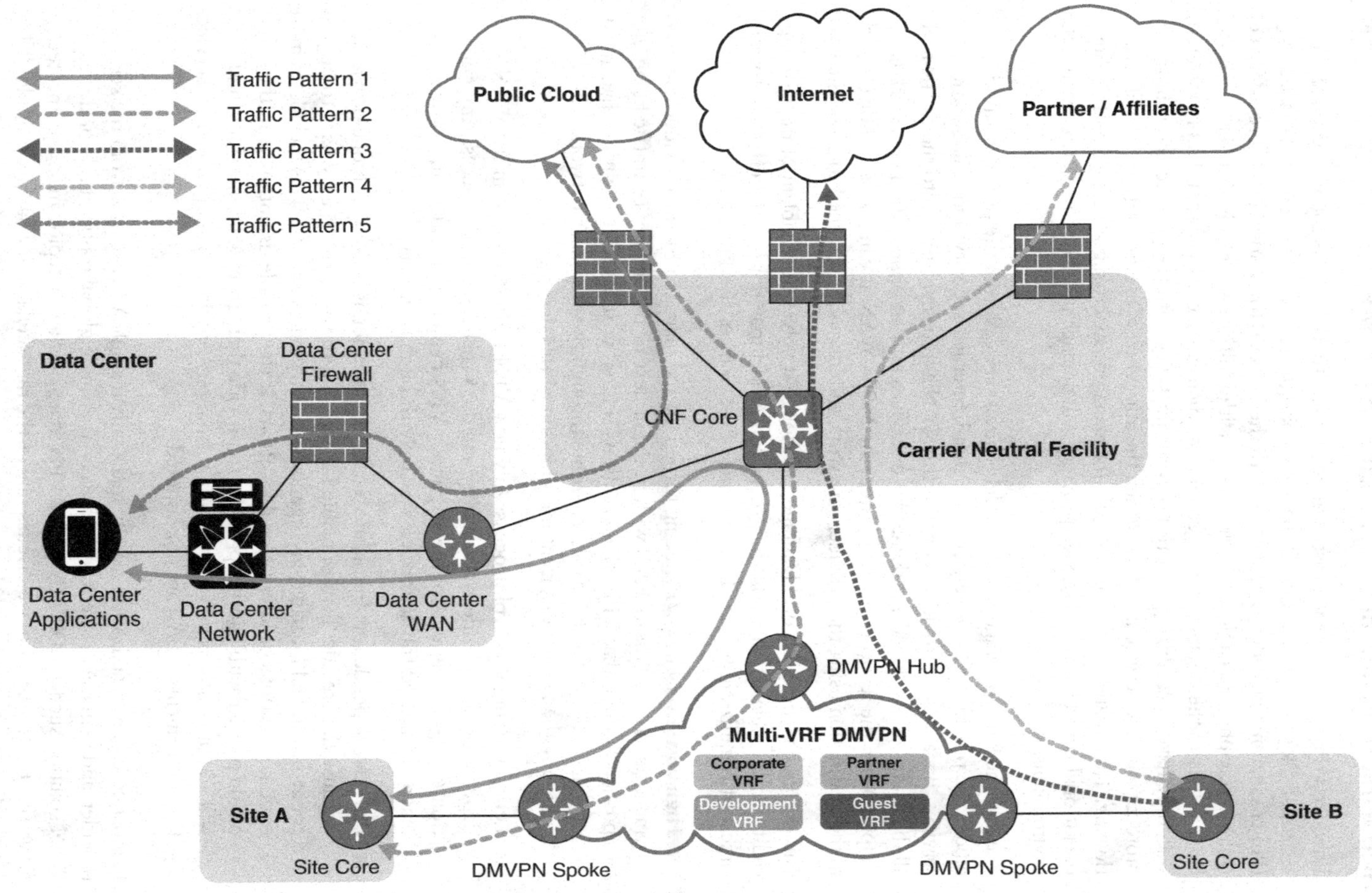

Figure 6-5 *VRF Offloading at CNF with DMVPN*

Provider-Multi-Protocol Label Switching (P-MPLS)

Provider MPLS is one of the most common connectivity options for an organization. Essentially, a provider manages all the VPN configuration on their routers: provider edge (PE) or customer provider edge (CPE). With the VPN configuration in the provider's control, a single physical cable or Layer 2 trunk with multiple VLANs in different VRFs is handed over to the organization to connect to their environment. From the organization's side, they have to establish point-to-point connectivity with the pre-decided routing protocol with the service provider. When the adjacency is established, traffic will start flowing. The organization is responsible for managing macrosegmentation within their operational control, and the service provider will manage macrosegmentation within their environment.

There is one key advantage of this model: shared services from the provider. In this model, the provider can natively provide cloud, Internet, security, and collaboration services. Because the provider is part of the WAN and has visibility into the traffic and all the routes of the network, adding these services into an organization's network is simple. When the respective traffic enters the MPLS WAN, it can take the shortest path to the destination using the provider's network and may not even need to go to the CNF.

This design has three key disadvantages. Although it solves the problem of maintaining end-to-end segmentation across the WAN, this model may not even be effective for the largest of organizations. Let's look at some of the cons of this model:

- **High cost:** Every new VPN being turned up and managed by the provider will have management costs associated with it. Regardless of the amount of traffic being pushed through that VPN, there is always a fixed cost associated with management of that VPN and having it natively route through the provider's network. This factor is usually the biggest deterrent for adoption of this design.
- **Lengthy change control process:** Any new VPN turn-up process in the WAN depends on the provider's availability and their change control process. Any migration, changes, or issues for the respective VPN need the provider's involvement as macrosegmented traffic traverses natively through their network.
- **Provider dependency:** In this model, an organization is locked with one provider. Because the provider is responsible for carrying traffic natively, they have to be present at any and all locations an organization is trying to expand. This includes remote regional locations or international locations. If the provider is not present, they would partner with another provider to provide that last-mile connectivity, and costs will add up. There is no easy transition from one provider to another if their service-level agreements (SLAs) are not honored.

In most cases, an organization usually takes only a single VPN service from the service provider, and then they either use it natively as a single global routing table or deploy a WAN solution such as SD-WAN or DMVPN as an overlay to deploy macrosegmented networks. For this section, we discuss one of the rare scenarios of having multiple different VPNs from a service provider for different functions.

The network illustrated in Figure 6-6 showcases multiple provider VPNs for an organization that carries macrosegmentation across all of their sites and to the CNF. When the traffic reaches the CNF, it usually gets handed off via individual links to different domains or a trunk port from the CPE device. A majority of the WAN routing is controlled by the provider. In this scenario, the same provider can also provide Internet transit, and routing can be directly offloaded to the Internet from the sites or the guest networks using the provider's services. Similar to SD-WAN and DMVPN scenarios, all traffic in the VRF and VPN will remain in its respective routing plane. Any inter-VRF routing will have to be done via a firewall or a centralized control device.

The following traffic flows are shown in Figure 6-6:

- **Traffic pattern 1:** This general corporate traffic is trusted and always allowed to access applications related to the organization's day-to-day business function. This type of traffic has direct access to all users and applications because they are in a trusted zone. For this scenario, if the traffic needs to access the Internet, the MPLS provider can directly route traffic to the Internet using their own backbone and cloud-based security stack with centralized security policies. This traffic does not need to come to the CNF and can take the shortest path out of the provider's network. This could be a viable solution for the organization if they use Internet for cloud connectivity and do not have direct connections.

- **Traffic pattern 2:** This development traffic is isolated from production for security reasons. For this organization, development traffic leverages public cloud infrastructure to scale and tests their applications and products on demand. Hence, they are put into their own VRF to keep the traffic isolated. When the applications are production-ready, they are transferred to the production environment via the data center firewall. Similar to Internet access, if the organization is using a specific cloud provider for their development workloads, the provider can also provide that "as-a-service" model and have that traffic offload via their network directly. Any workload transfers from development to production will be backhauled to the CNF, which in turn will be terminated on the firewall before entering the corporate network.

- **Traffic pattern 3:** This type of traffic is for guest Internet access. Guests have no business accessing corporate application data. With Internet as a service from the provider, this traffic is directly offloaded to the nearest Internet exit point from the provider. If inspection of traffic is required, an organization can try to leverage the provider's cloud-based inspection service or other cloud-based security products to offload local traffic inspection from their own network.

- **Traffic pattern 4:** This type of traffic does not need to access any local organization's resources as a primary function. This may be a recent acquisition or an affiliate whose networks are not merged yet, but they share physical real estate or office space with a large organization for business functions. This type of traffic is directly offloaded to a partner/affiliate firewall and out to their network. An added advantage would be if an affiliate has their own MPLS network with the same provider; in that case, they can either merge the VPNs or have VRF-Leaking to natively access networks without traversing all the traffic through CNFs. This can provide immediate scale and flexibility in connections.

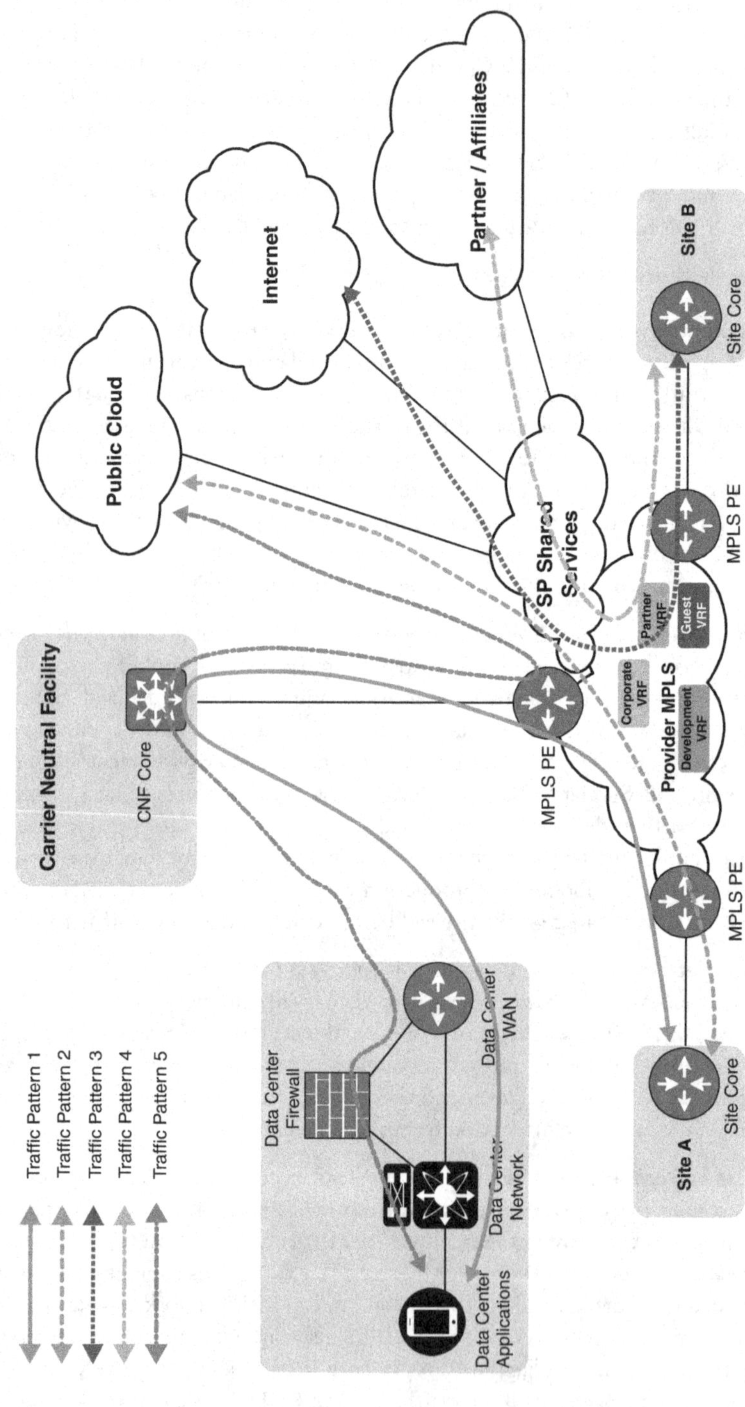

Figure 6-6 *VRF Offloading at CNF with Provider MPLS (P-MPLS)*

- **Traffic pattern 5:** The preceding four traffic patterns are mainly focused on isolation of traffic. However, this pattern requires access to traffic across those routing planes. In the example, a pattern where traffic from development is ported over to production or corporate traffic needs to access the Internet; to do so, it has to go through a firewall-like device for control and management. This is where domains are bridged in a controlled fashion. In some cases, traffic flow would be suboptimal, but this design will benefit from greater control because this type of traffic is not in high volume. If the volume increases, more of these shared exchange points can be configured to offload and distribute traffic. This type of inter-domain traffic must be routed to the CNF, where it can be controlled and monitored.

Despite some of the major disadvantages of this model, some organizations might opt in for some flexibility, depending on workloads and types of applications they use. For organizations that are not subjected to strict compliances and have already embarked on cloud-native applications and Internet-based solutions, this model will scale the most because the provider MPLS will do most of the heavy lifting. The costs of having dedicated cloud connections and Internet connections will be offset by having those services natively from the service provider. This also reduces management and complexity because most of the security policies can be handled via the service provider's software-driven deployment and management plane.

Enterprise Multi-Protocol Label Switching (E-MPLS)

Enterprise MPLS, from the technology and design perspective, is no different from MPLS that is used by the provider. In E-MPLS, the organization typically manages the entire MPLS network and in most cases has their own dedicated team managing that infrastructure. For extremely large organizations or conglomerates whose networks span across the globe, have multiple data centers, and also have branches, campuses, and many affiliates, they tend to have their own WAN where they can manage and control the traffic in-house. From a security perspective, having their own WAN gives them better control to take any immediate action if some part of their network is compromised. For these large organizations, their brand reputation is paramount, and the data flowing in their network is in petabytes. Secure and efficient transport is key. These are the organizations that run IT as a Business (ITaaB). Because they control the WAN and MPLS, they are the provider for their customers, who are different business units in an organization.

For these customers, CNFs play a key role. These are the hubs that bring in all the traffic across the regions or globe and provide high-speed backbone connections to different domains and resources. Figure 6-7 shows how CNFs became part of the global backbone and built that critical MPLS network that could scale and evolve. Organizations providing P-MPLS-like capabilities can even take it further to add more features to the network. With a large network, each domain would have their own connection point and enterprise-managed PE device that is capable of offloading as many VRFs as they would like for that domain. This flexibility helps scale macrosegmentation capabilities to a whole new level.

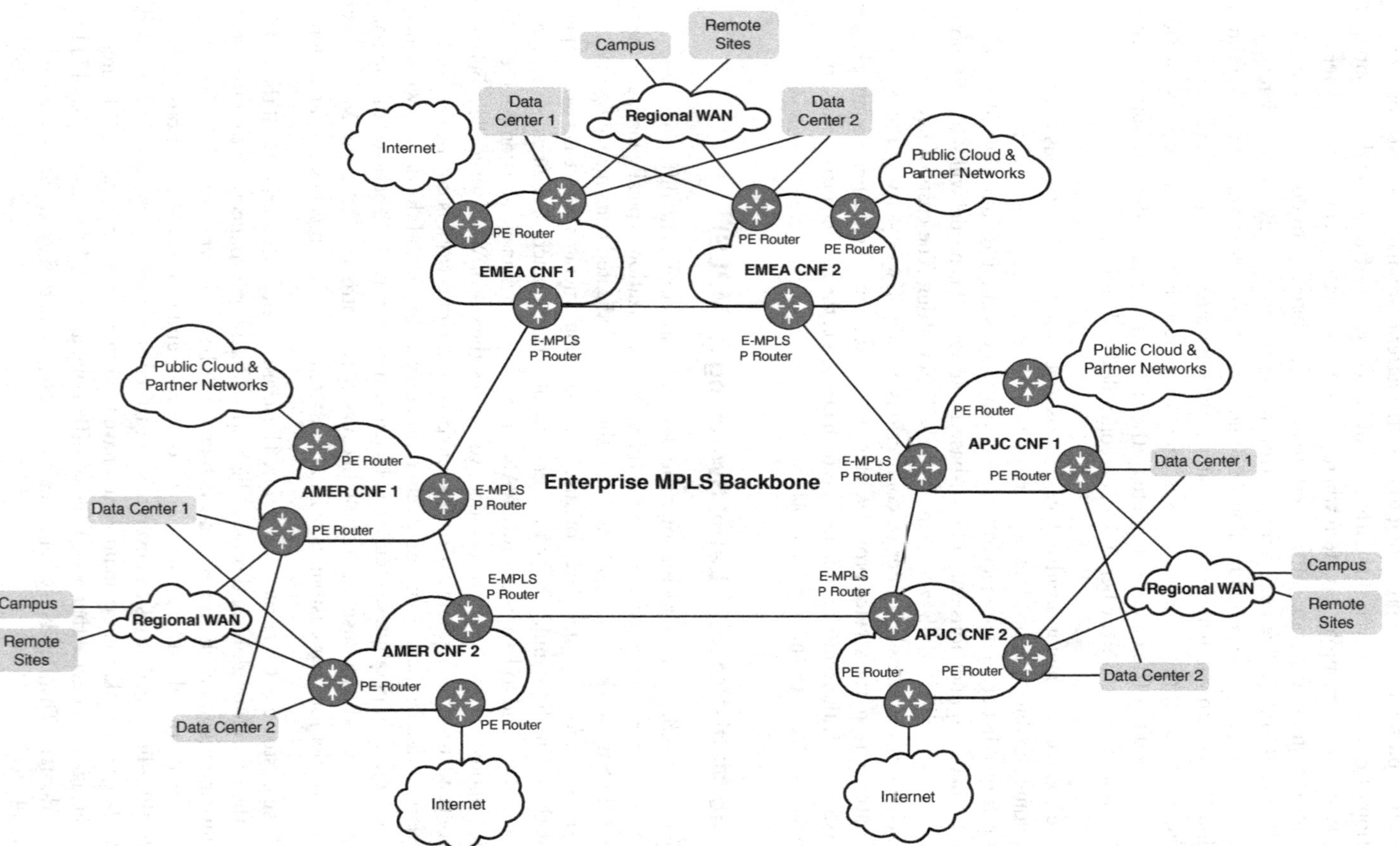

Figure 6-7 *CNFs as Part the Global MPLS Backbone*

The following are some of the key capabilities that can be achieved with E-MPLS and CNFs:

- CNFs can house all enterprise PE devices that can directly connect to critical services such as Internet transit, cloud, large campuses, and enterprise data centers using dark fiber.
- Using E-MPLS, point-to-point pseudowires can also be created for any applications or services needing a direct connection across the WAN. For example, backup and replication traffic might need a direct point-to-point Layer 1 or Layer 2 connection to another data center. Using E-MPLS, this can be achieved by creating a point-to-point pseudowire.
- Link aggregation can be used between CNFs across multiple dark fiber providers. Because all the traffic will be encapsulated using MPLS labels and highly resilient Layer 3 routing protocols, aggregating links will assist in better convergence and high uptime of the network.
- MPLS-VPN Option A (back-to-back VRFs) can be run with other service providers from the CNFs to quickly onboard an acquisition into the organization's network and share critical resources.

Overall, on top of providing multi-domain connectivity that we discussed with SD-WAN, DMVPN, and P-MPLS-based design, this E-MPLS model changes the CNF's purpose a little to be more focused on what kind of specialty connection it can provide and then integrates to the global backbone of an organization. The traffic flows are similar to other WAN options, but with the nature of specialized CNFs, these flows may enter one CNF and exit out of another CNF for end-to-end connectivity.

Let's discuss the flows shown in Figure 6-8. With five different traffic patterns, these traffic flows are similar in nature; the biggest difference is the entry and exit points of the CNFs. The overall end goal is the same: keep the end-to-end macrosegmentation and ensure any inter-VRF traffic passes through a control point where the intent of the traffic can be inspected and firewalled.

- **Traffic pattern 1:** This general corporate traffic is trusted and always allowed to access applications related to the organization's day-to-day business function. This type of traffic has direct access to all users and applications because they are in a trusted zone. The only time the traffic will be subject to a firewall inspection is when the traffic is leaving for the Internet and/or another partner/affiliate. In this figure, this traffic is aggregated to AMER CNF 2, where all WAN connections in the form of MPLS, SD-WAN, or DMVPN are converged and mapped to respective VPNs. Then, using the E-MPLS backbone, the respective VRFs are backhauled and mapped to the data centers where those applications are housed. In this figure, the data centers are connected to AMER CNF 1 and 2.

- **Traffic pattern 2:** This development traffic is isolated from production for security reasons. For this organization, development traffic leverages public cloud infrastructure to scale and test their applications and products on demand. Hence, they are put into their own VRF to keep the traffic isolated. When the applications are production-ready, they are transferred to the production environment via the data center firewall. Here, client traffic is coming in from AMER CNF 1. This CNF has direct connectivity to the cloud. When the applications are ready to be brought into the production environment, this inter-domain transfer happens at AMER CNF 1 via a firewall, and then data is offloaded into the corporate VRF and synced to AMER data centers 1 and 2.

- **Traffic pattern 3:** This type of traffic is for guest Internet access. Guests have no business accessing corporate application data. That traffic is completely isolated and in almost all cases directly dropped off to the Internet transit. Many organizations subject guest traffic to inspection and security policies to control what goes in and out of the network. All guest traffic coming in APJC CNF 2 is directly mapped to the guest VPN on MPLS and offloaded for direct Internet access and security inspection.

- **Traffic pattern 4:** This type of traffic does not need to access any local organization's resources as a primary function. This may be a recent acquisition or an affiliate whose networks are not merged yet but share physical real estate or office space with a large organization for business functions. This type of traffic is directly offloaded to a partner/affiliate VPN concentrator and then to the firewall that connects to the affiliate's network. All affiliate and partner networks terminate in APJC CNF 1. The traffic from all the sites is backhauled via MPLS to APJC CNF 1 to egress to the respective affiliate traversing the firewall.

- **Traffic pattern 5:** The preceding four traffic patterns are mainly focused on isolation of traffic. However, this pattern requires access to traffic across those routing planes. In the example, a pattern where traffic from development is ported over to production or corporate traffic needs to access the Internet; to do so, it has to go through a firewall-like device for control and management. This is where domains are bridged in controlled fashion. EMEA CNF 1 is one of the locations to provide Internet access for the entire organization in that region. By utilizing shared service capabilities of the MPLS and VRF-Leaking, any Internet-bound traffic from any CNF is directly routed to EMEA CNF 1 for inspection and egress. All remote user VPNs are also terminated in EMEA CNF 1.

As Figure 6-8 shows, CNFs can be versatile in the E-MPLS model. Some of the largest organizations are deploying such networks with the scale and flexibility they need. In some cases, technologies like segment routing may also be used. The goal is to ensure macrosegmentation is maintained end to end and the same physical infrastructure can be leveraged for multiple business functions.

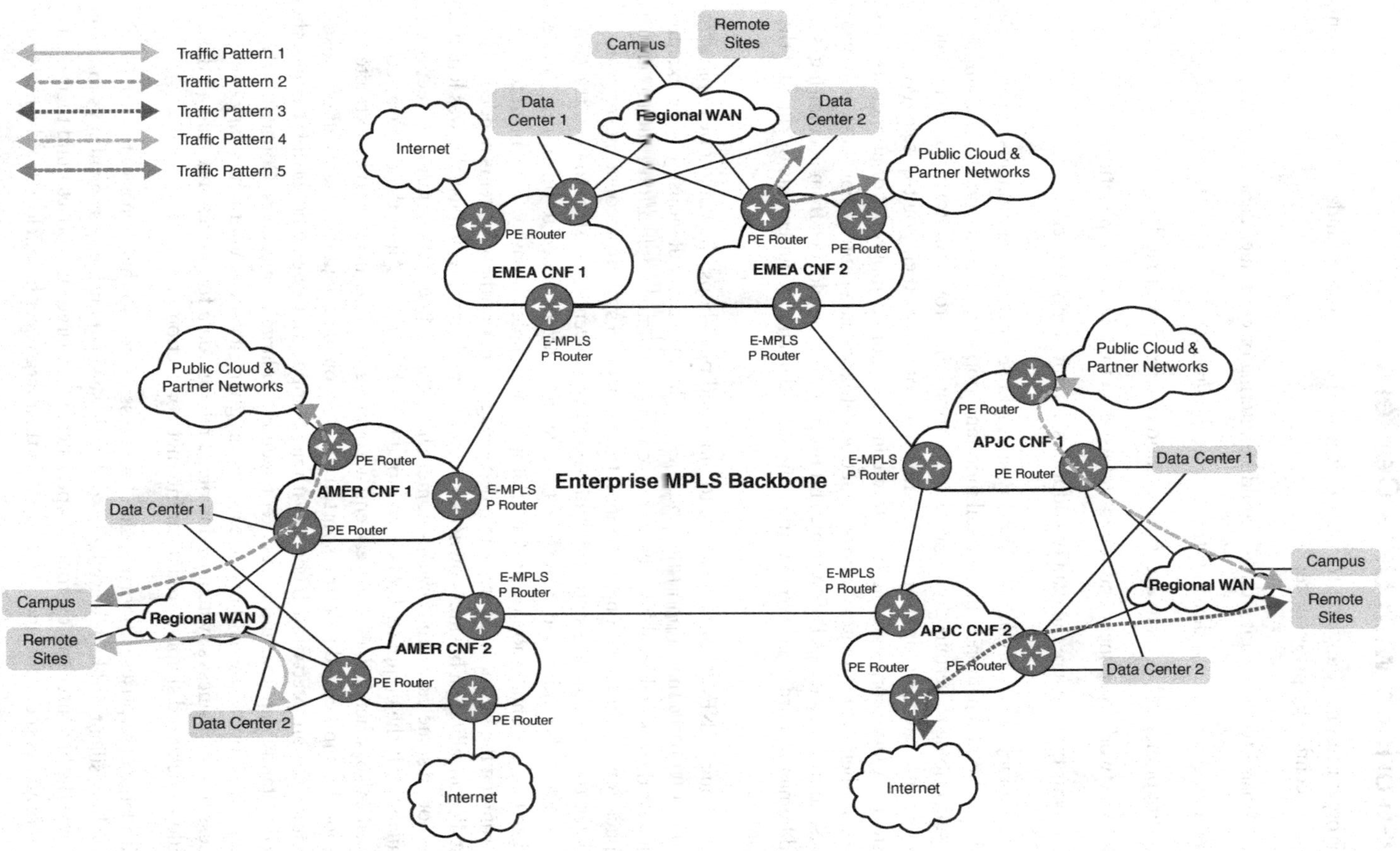

Figure 6-8 *VRF Offloading at CNFs with E-MPLS*

Inter-working with Data Centers

For organizations of any size to function today, they need five fundamental components from a technology perspective:

- A place to store digital data—could be internal or consumer data
- A place to host applications that run the business
- Endpoints and users to access, add, modify, or remove that data
- A network to connect endpoints and users to that data or applications
- Security to ensure the data or endpoints are not compromised

Now, looking at any organization of any size, all five of these components are applicable to them. Some small ones, like a retail mom-and-pop shop, would operate in a simple way by subscribing to certain cloud-based applications that store inventory, transact a sale, and execute payments at a small fee, with endpoints being their point-of-sale (PoS) systems. A large corporate big-box store can use a more complex set of applications to store all their data, inventory, and transactions at large data centers. For these organizations, endpoints such as PoS sytems, and users such as employees from accounting, sales and human resources have to live up to these fundamental requirements of running the business.

Even though CNFs are not applicable to mom-and-pop shops, they might be applicable to the enterprises that support their businesses. Taking the retail industry as an example, many of these small local businesses rely on some common applications, such as an application conducting monetary transactions via a PoS system, accounting software to keep track of business expenses and payroll, and inventory system to keep track of stock. From the end-user perspective, these systems are designed to be intuitive and easy to use because small shop owners are not usually technically savvy. They need to focus on running the business. More than a decade ago, most of these systems needed to be installed locally on a business owner's computer or a laptop, which usually was left at the shop or, in some cases, the owner's home. That posed a huge risk in terms of security and availability if the computer broke down or a theft happened. All of the data was compromised. Also, when it comes to year-end accounting, the data needed to be extracted from the local computer and then transported to an accountant digitally. Today, all of those complexities are pretty much gone. With most applications being enabled for cloud, they are constantly patched, and data is kept securely in large data centers. Consequently, year-end accounting would become as easy as giving an accountant temporary user access to the business's system to download relevant data for processing. And all this could be achieved simply through an Internet connection.

With large enterprises supporting small business owners in this scenario, their networks must be resilient and highly available so that these small businesses can always function. To give the best user and customer experience, these large enterprises build their data centers across the globe and, depending on their large user base, closer to the region or country for a low-latency experience. With the number of data centers across the region and globe, having full-mesh connectivity between them for data synchronization and resiliency is not scalable. The formula for the number of links needed for full-mesh connectivity between sites is as follows:

$$Links = \frac{N \times (N-1)}{2}$$

Here, N is the number of sites. With an enterprise having eight smaller data centers across North America regionally located to larger cities, the number of connections needed for full-mesh connectivity would be as follows:

$$Links = \frac{8 \times (8-1)}{2} = \frac{56}{2} = 28 \text{ links}$$

The cost associated with operating these low-latency links is very high, and on top of that, the complexity of running routing protocols and convergence adds up. Figure 6-9 shows the complexity of this design.

This is the point where CNFs come in. CNFs can be located at key locations and provide a hub-and-spoke model to connect all these data centers at low latency. This model is scalable because any time a large enterprise wants to grow, they can simply provision redundant links to one CNF or one each to different CNFs for resiliency. This will allow them to scale and provide similar SLAs as full-mesh connectivity. In Figure 6-10, the number of links that are needed is significantly reduced, with a further reduction in the complexity of routing protocols and network management. For these large enterprises, these CNFs don't need to be large in terms of equipment footprint. They can have smaller CNFs at key network access points (NAPs), where they can have direct access to multiple Internet service providers to provide transit connectivity to some of the largest carriers of the country or globally. This way, every consumer who is using those major Internet providers can have direct access to the enterprise's commercial applications. This connectivity essentially gives one-hop access for these small businesses, thus increasing their overall user experience.

The third major pillar for these large enterprises is connectivity for their own employees. Developing and maintaining these commercial applications takes resources, and they are mostly located in regional offices. These offices are connected by the enterprise's private WAN to the CNF, where they can access data centers, the cloud, and the Internet. These enterprises have two different sets of applications: one for internal use and another for their customers. Both need their own development environment and easier ways to transfer those tested development workloads to the production environment. In many cases, some of these applications would have a cloud-based deployment model, where all the patches to the software are deployed via cloud for maximum scale.

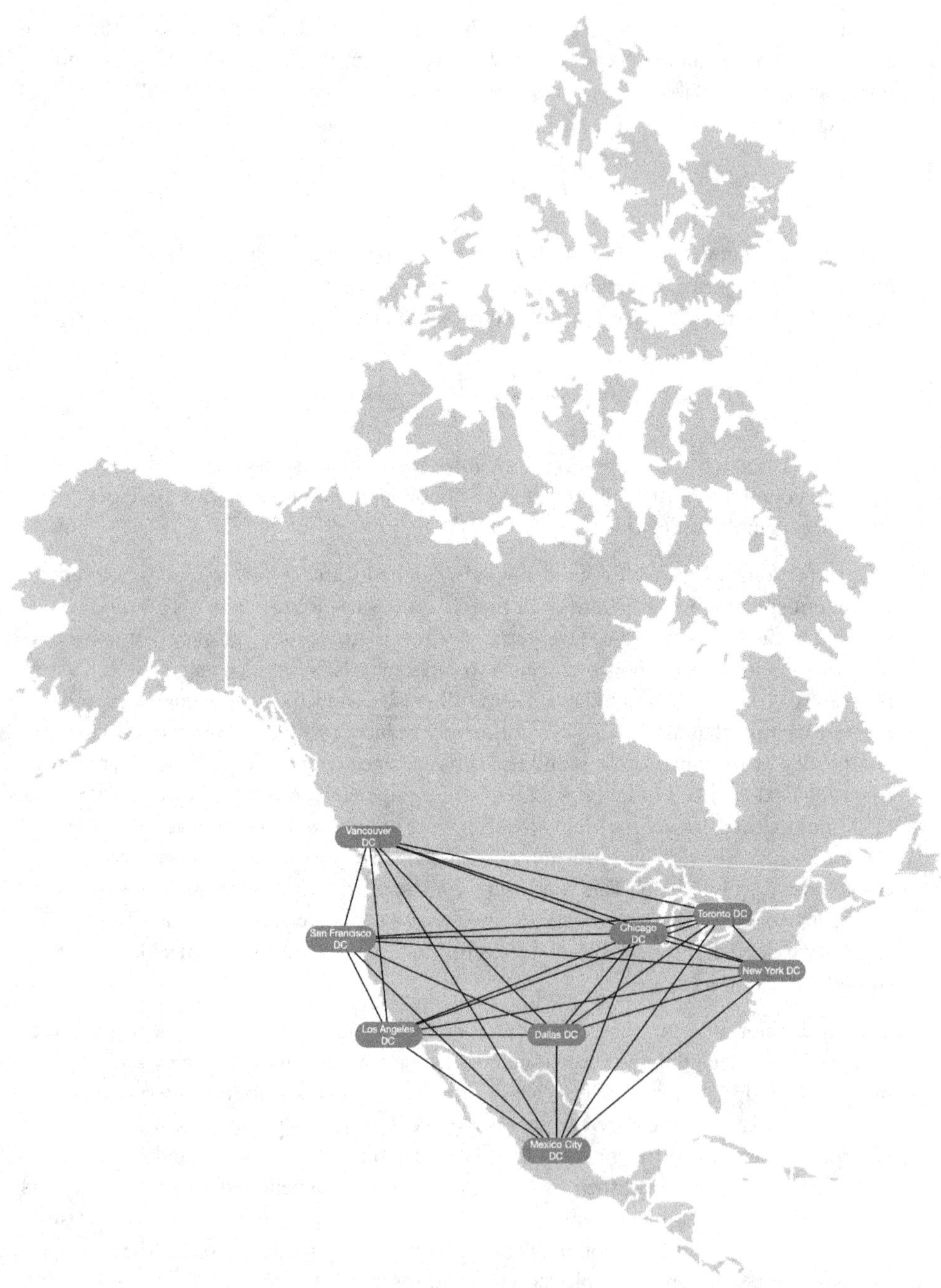

Figure 6-9 *Full-Mesh Connectivity with Data Centers*

To summarize, data center and CNF integration goes a long way. Its primary function is helping large organizations to scale and provide an extension to the data centers where they can reach the organization's consumers or employees at scale. On top of all this connectivity, one of the other dimensions is ensuring traffic separation. Recall that enterprise and commercial applications need to be separated because one is critical for an organization to function, whereas other applications generate revenue for the organization. Revenue generation always takes precedence; therefore, securing those applications so that there is no data breach and having them always accessible helps to maintain the SLAs with the end customer. This, in turn, builds trust and brand reputation.

Modern data centers use fabric-based architecture. Solutions like ACI and BGP-EVPN fabrics are scalable and provide the flexibility of maintaining macrosegmentation while keeping CAPEX and OPEX low by sharing the same high-performance physical hardware. These data centers are connected to CNFs in two ways.

- Direct dark fiber connectivity
- Utilizing solutions

Connecting Data Centers and CNFs with Dark Fiber

The scenario discussed in the preceding section, where a large enterprise provides commercial applications to a small business, is a good example of how data centers are most likely to be connected via dark fiber. Commercial cloud-based (public or private cloud) applications are designed to be as close to the end users as possible. So, in most cases, large enterprises have dedicated data centers that house those applications and usually don't mix internal and external applications in one place. The data centers that house internal applications are usually located close to the large campuses where the end users are expected to access them more frequently. Here, macrosegmentation is conducted at a physical separation level. Because networks are physically separated, running virtualization or dedicated WAN solutions for interconnectivity is not required. In most cases, these data centers are part of the E-MPLS backbone because they need to be connected to each other and provide additional features such as point-to-point pseudowires for replication and backup traffic.

This form of connectivity is the simplest, and it is purpose-driven due to the demanding functions. The idea is to ensure a business keeps generating revenue regardless of what internal change controls are conducted. This traffic is usually not touched unless a compliance or a vulnerability issue occurs, as in the old saying of "if it ain't broke, don't fix it."

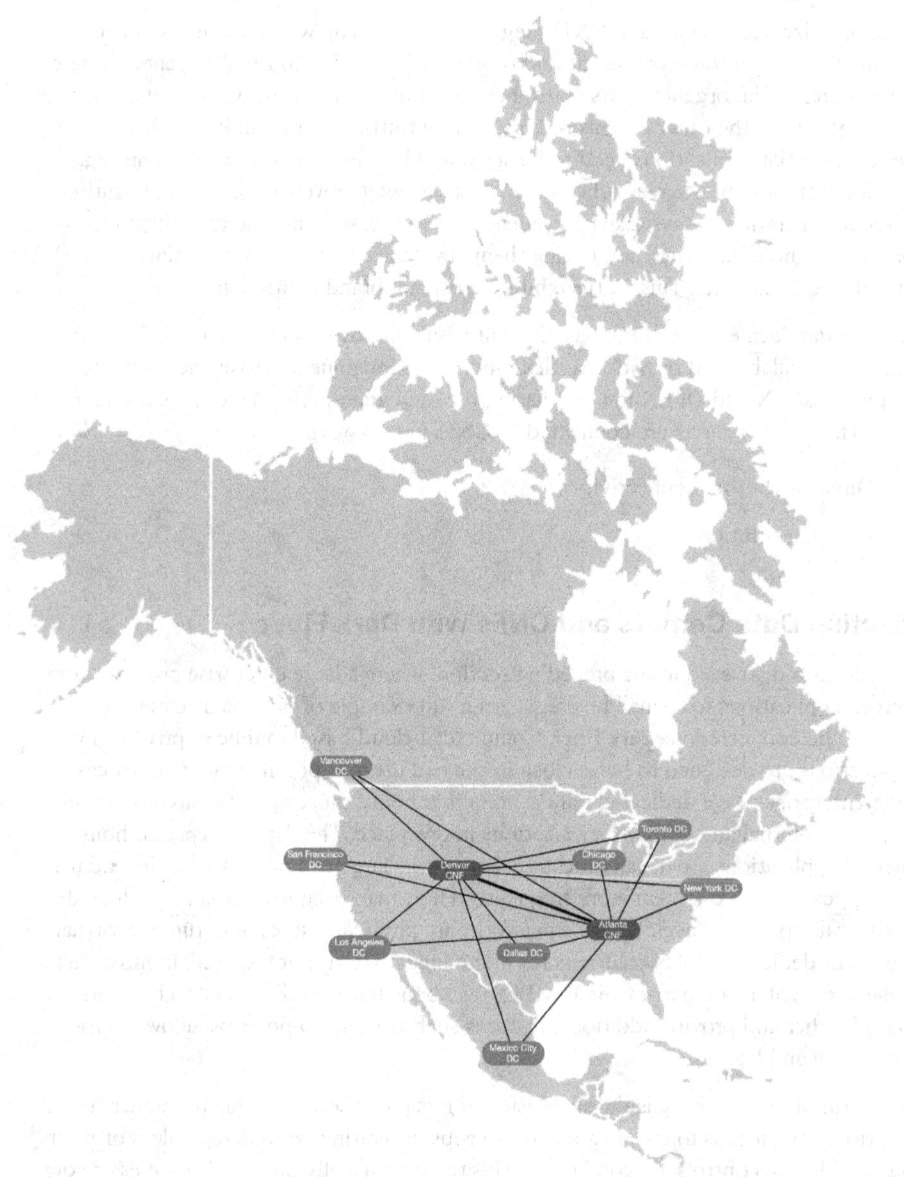

Figure 6-10 *Data Center Connectivity with CNFs*

Another example with a similar setup is with large manufacturing customers. Similar to large enterprises having commercial applications for their paid customers, large product manufacturers have factories that produce revenue-generating products. These products include heavy machinery, pharmaceuticals, consumer goods, or vehicles. These manufacturing facilities are considered revenue generating, and they usually are 24/7/365-day operations. They work in shifts, and they are accustomed to having product-specific custom applications that are highly critical to the environment. If any outage occurs in the application environment, production is impacted, and for some of the largest of manufacturers, the cost of such outages could be millions of dollars per hour. For this specific reason, many manufacturers traditionally have mini data centers locally in factories. These are basically some of the servers that connect and communicate with the programmable logic controllers (PLCs) and that have to be low-latency traffic. However, many of the applications that collect production output data and other critical pieces need to be stored at a centralized location where users can access that data for generating reports and running forecasts. This is where the dedicated data centers come into play, and they are usually kept physically separate from the regular enterprise application data center.

Figure 6-11 shows how, in critical environments, data centers helping with the revenue-generating function of a business are kept separate from the non-revenue-generating functions. These revenue-generating data centers are usually connected via dark fibers to CNFs for the highest availability and low-latency connectivity. These links also have different SLAs with the dark fiber service providers that help with maintaining up to five nines in the network.

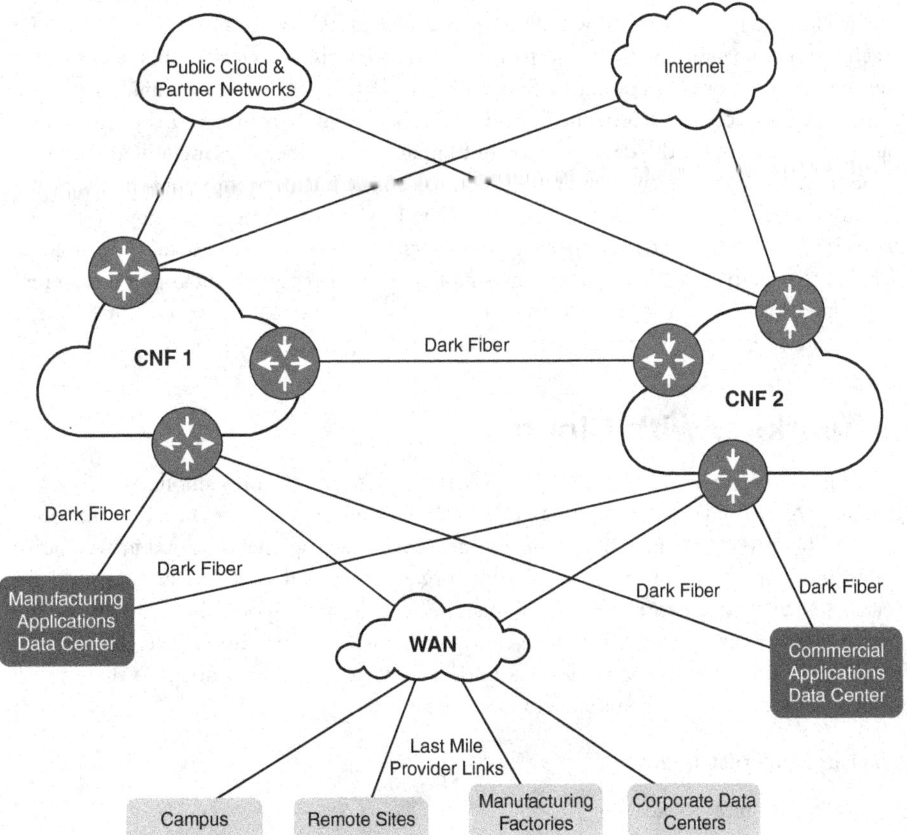

Figure 6-11 *Separation of Revenue-Generating Data Centers with Dark Fiber-Based Connectivity to CNFs*

Connecting Data Centers and CNFs with a WAN Solution

Most organizations do not have a high number of data centers for applications that are not revenue-generating. With the adoption of the cloud, it is not uncommon that organizations tend to leverage both the cloud and on-premises servers to host their applications and run their day-to-day business. To save costs, they would tend to leverage a fabric-based architecture in the data center, such as ACI. With the adoption of hybrid work, cloud, and CNFs, these data centers are now being decoupled from the local campus locations and moved to a specialized facility that can maintain the required infrastructure. The recovered data center space in the campus is then repurposed for office space and a better work environment. As shown in Figure 6-12, these data centers are treated just like any other remote sites but with higher bandwidth and SLA requirements. These data centers use some form of a WAN solution, such as SD-WAN, P-MPLS; E-MPLS, or if the organization is small, low-cost DMVPN is usually the choice.

These data centers have macrosegmentation because they separate multiple business functions using VRFs. Hence, a separate routing plane is critical. Here, if ACI is used, the border leafs from the ACI are directly connected to the WAN router using back-to-back VRF, and all the traffic is offloaded into the WAN. Depending on the destination, if the traffic is to the remote sites, it will directly cut through the WAN and bypass the CNF to reach the remote site. The CNF will receive traffic from the data center that is destined to Internet, partner, or cloud domains. Separating the data center from the campus and other critical facilities creates a separate fault domain that is highly resilient. If there is a major outage in the campus, the data center is not impacted, all other sites are still able to continue to access applications that are required to run the business, and only the users at the campus are impacted. Even campus links can be downsized because they do not need to account for all the traffic coming in from other remote sites to the data center that is local to the campus. If the organization is global or cross-regional, backup and data replication can also be scheduled at different times, because depending on the time zone of the remote site, backups can start early while spreading the load on the links.

Inter-working with Cloud

Cloud integration with the CNFs is one of the simplest integrations among all other domains. At the time of writing this book, many organizations are still trying to adopt the cloud journey, and since 2020, this journey has picked up speed. Cloud infrastructure is designed for all sizes of businesses. Some organizations subscribe to simple cloud services such as Microsoft Office 365; in some cases, entire e-commerce businesses run on the cloud. There are three types of cloud infrastructure—private, public, and hybrid. Regardless of an organization's cloud adoption journey, it all comes down to three basic connectivity options to the public cloud infrastructure:

- Direct Internet access
- VPN over Internet access
- Direct private connections to the cloud

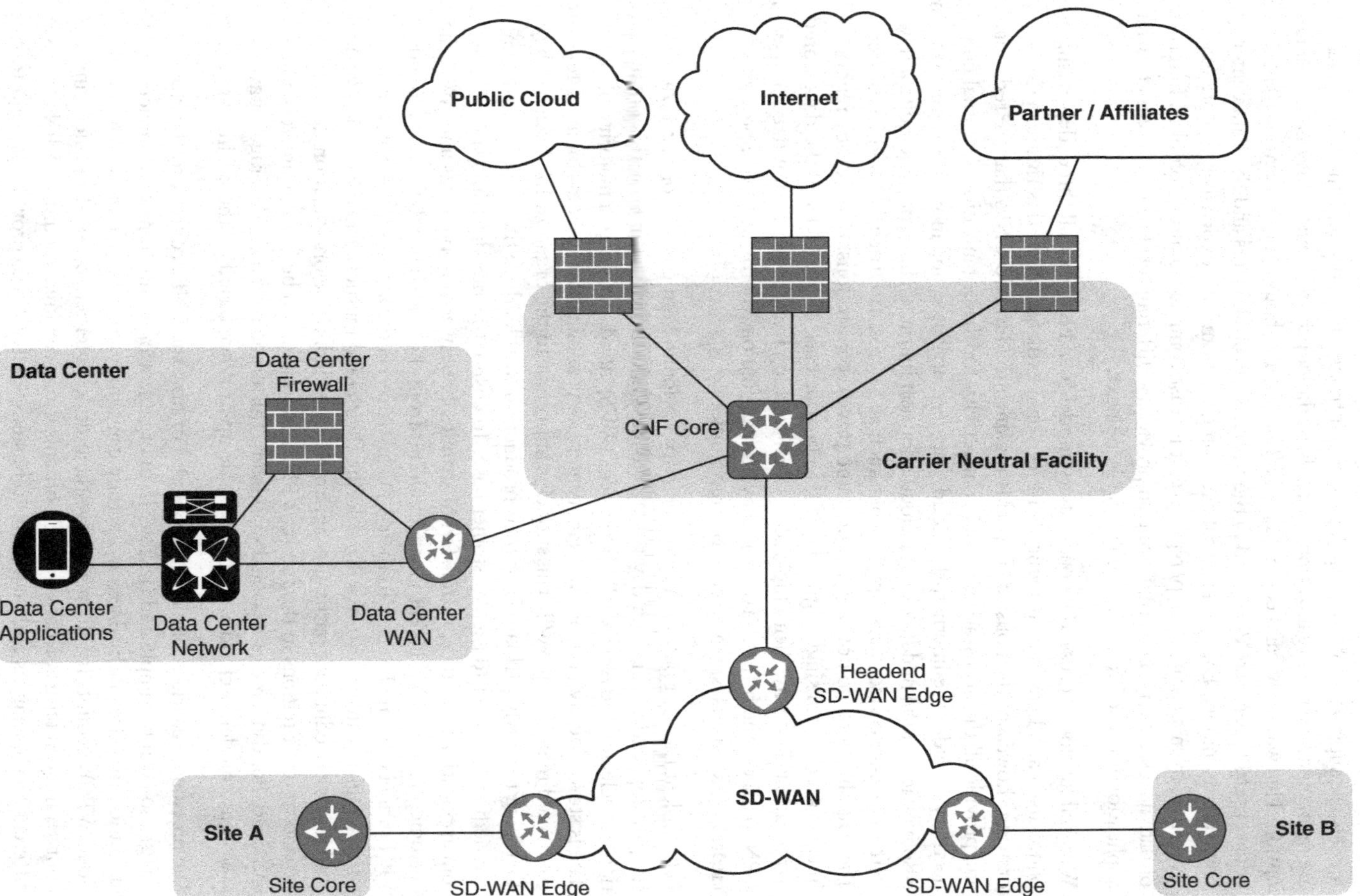

Figure 6-12 *Data Center Connectivity with CNF Using a WAN Solution*

When it comes to organizations adopting CNF-based architecture, all three connectivity models are supported. With the private cloud infrastructure, because the data centers are maintained by the organization themselves, direct private connectivity is the default option. This way, they can keep access to all the data in-house and in-network. These connectivity types were discussed in the earlier section on CNFs and the data center connectivity model. Each connectivity option goes from least expensive to more expensive. Also, from a complexity perspective, it is least complex to more complex. In terms of data access, each connectivity option provides a different level of data access to what application it is used for. We discuss that issue next.

With public cloud access, the connectivity models can be one or all three, depending on the use case. Let's look at Figure 6-13 for some explanation. In this figure, a simple drawing showcases the holistic view. This organization has two CNFs that are redundant and provide all the necessary external connectivity for the organization. External connectivity includes the Internet, the cloud, partners, affiliates, and more. This organization is somewhere in the middle of their cloud adoption journey. They consume quite a few Software-as-a-Service (SaaS) applications such as Microsoft Office 365 and Salesforce. These applications do not require dedicated private connections. Hence, they rely on Internet access with single sign-on (SSO) to provide ease of access to all the data stored in the cloud. This way, their employees, when working from home, do not need to use VPN to access the office network if they are working on Microsoft Office products creating documents, spreadsheets, or presentations.

Let's look at the next part of the connectivity option in Figure 6-13. For organization-specific applications that run day-to-day business and their e-commerce, this organization has selected the Amazon Web Services (AWS) cloud. Although a majority of the data is stored locally in their own data centers, new application and development tests are conducted regularly in AWS. This model is important to the organization because they are trying to slowly offload all of their production workloads to the cloud so that they can be housed closer to their customer base. To ensure this raw data, in terms of custom applications and files, is transferred seamlessly between on-premises and AWS, the customer has one AWS Direct Connect circuit from their primary CNF and a redundant VPN tunnel over the Internet to their VPC instance via the second CNF. This ensures cost savings because they are still exploring their cloud journey. The data access is highly available with redundant paths and can grow as needed. If the organization decides to expand to other regions in the future, VPN connections can be brought up very quickly and used. For dynamic or seasonal workloads, this organization can leverage a pay-as-you-use model of cloud and quickly scale up or down based on the business need.

The previous scenario is one of the examples of how the CNFs connect to the cloud. Integration can be simple and flexible. If an organization wants to maintain macrosegmentation for different business units, they can simply create different virtual private cloud (VPC) accounts for them and give them direct Internet access. If business units want security in terms of data transfer, organizations can create multiple VPN tunnels to different VPC instances and map them to business unit VRFs to provide that end-to-end segmentation.

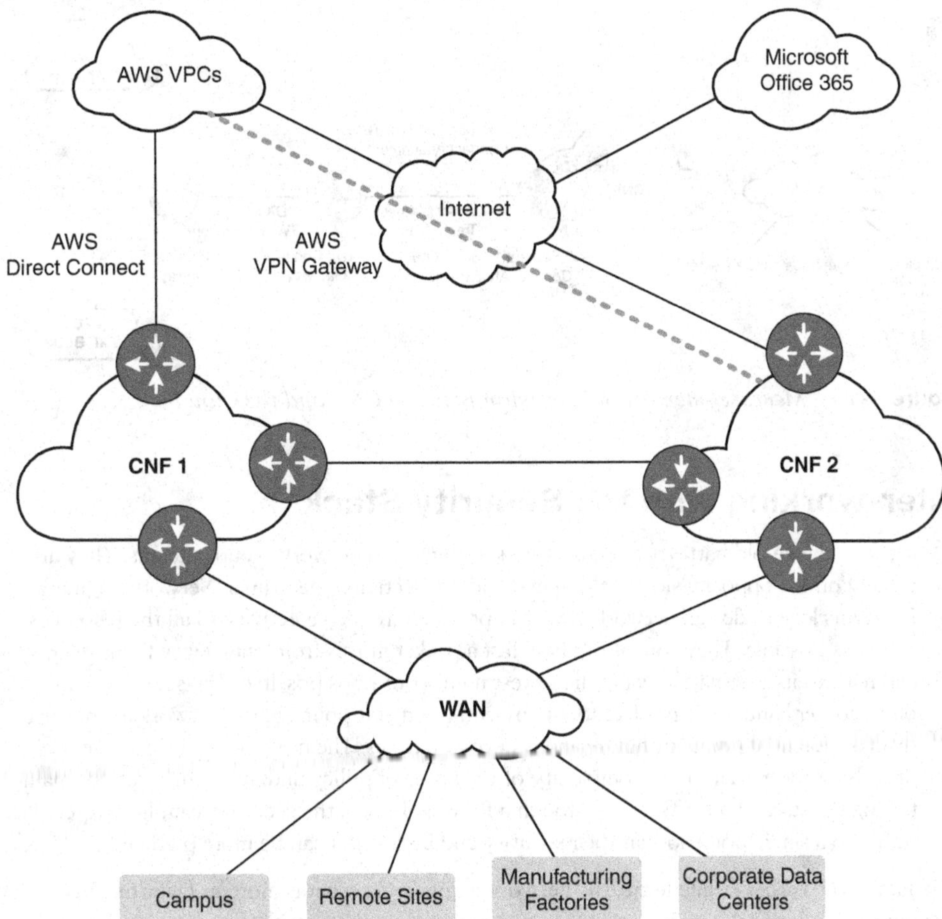

Figure 6-13 *Cloud Integrations with the CNF*

Figure 6-14 shows another alternative when macrosegmentation is involved. In this scenario, different business units can still utilize macrosegmentation by extending their Virtual Routing and Forwarding (VRF) over Direct Connect and connecting to their own VPC instance with complete traffic isolation. As a backup, they can have another Direct Connect circuit at a secondary CNF or utilize VPNs as a backup. The biggest advantage of this level of extension is to ensure all business units follow strict enterprise security and compliance guidelines while achieving true isolation of traffic and not impacting each other.

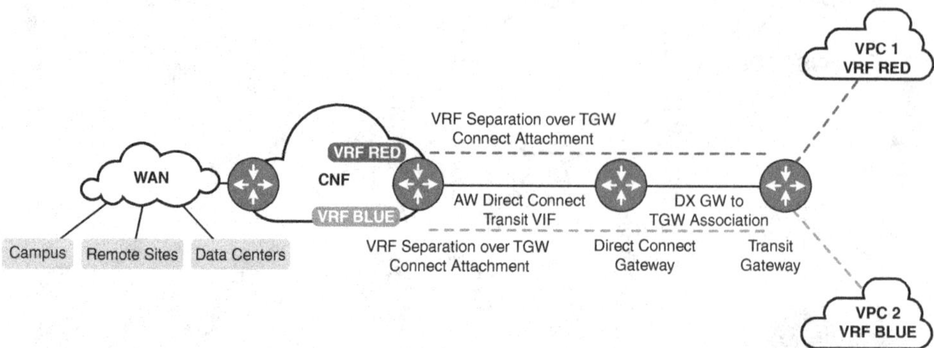

Figure 6-14 *Macrosegmentation Extension Between CNF and the Cloud*

Inter-working with the Security Stack

There is an age-old battle between network systems and network security teams. They are usually on the opposite side of the speed and connectivity spectrums. Network engineering teams love to design networks that can provide direct connectivity to all the resources as fast as possible. They care about how fast a packet moves from one device to another and reaches its destination using the lowest number of hops possible. The security team, on the other hand, does not like too many entry and exit points in the network as they see them as potential points of failure and security breaches. The more points to manage is directly proportional to the complexity of the security policy and, most importantly, maintaining the state of a traffic flow through a firewall. Hence, the security team likes to choke traffic to a single point so that their security and inspection can be more predictable.

Taking the earlier airline logic, the network engineering team is more in favor of direct point-to-point flights between source and destination, whereas the security team likes a more hub-and-spoke centralized model. In reality, both models can be achieved together if planned properly. Just like any country, they would not let all the international air traffic enter every city in the country because that would increase their security risks and customs checkpoints. So, countries designate some of their large cities to be the "connectivity hubs" to the outside world. All international travel will have to enter or exit via those major city airports—for example, New York–JFK, Los Angeles–LAX, Chicago O'Hare–ORD. This tactic greatly reduces stress on border security, and also countries can concentrate a lot of resources at fewer locations for higher resiliency. Within a country, however, airlines can have any point-to-point network they like based on the traffic demand and can roam freely. This is similar to how computer networks are built too. Let's take a look in terms of networking terminology in Figure 6-15.

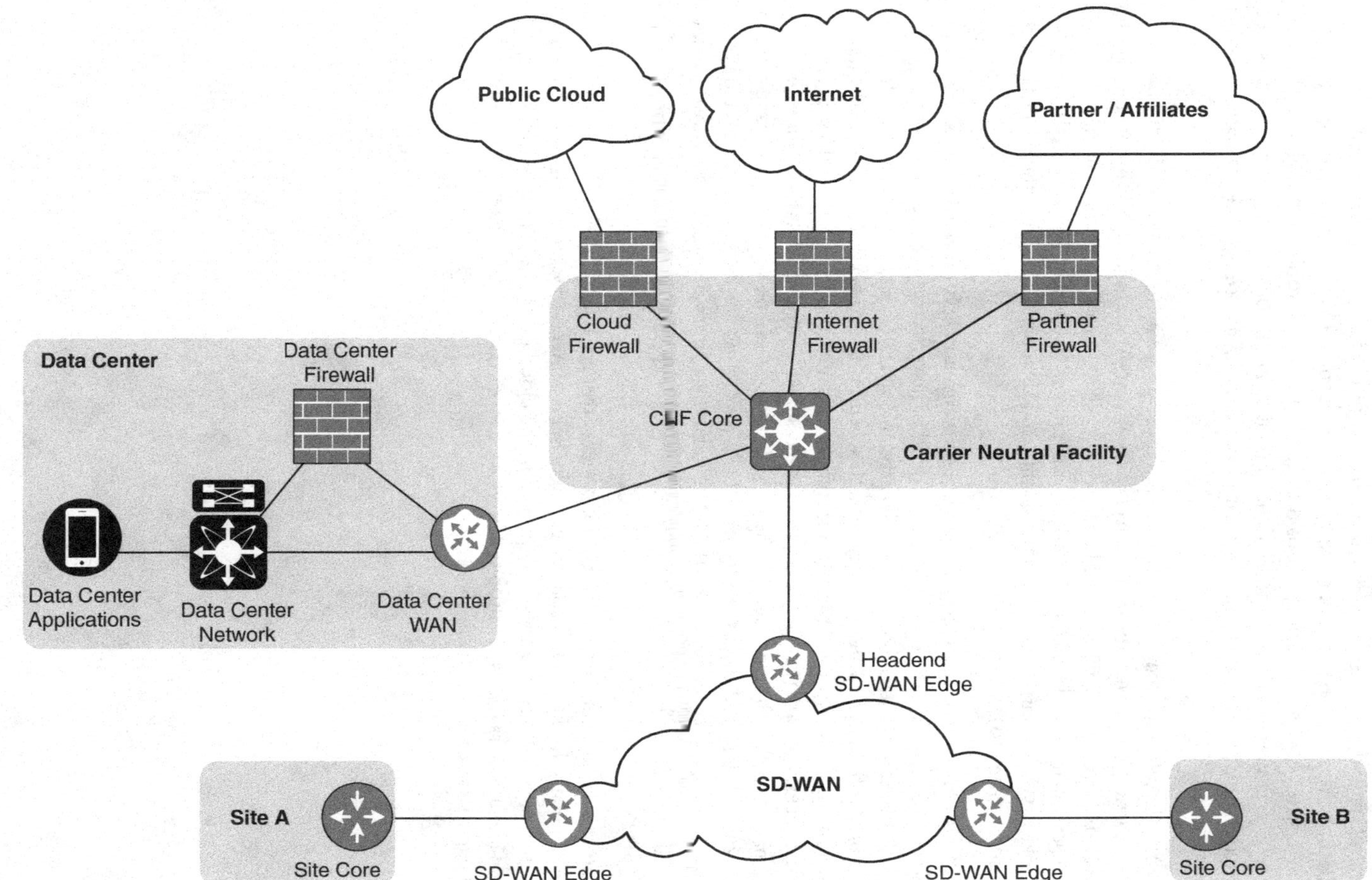

Figure 6-15 *High-Level Traffic Domains and Perimeter Security*

In the figure, CNFs are like the major city airports. They are the hubs where all the traffic transiting within the network and also in or out of the network is aggregated. This is an ideal point where the network security team can deploy their security stack and ensure any traffic coming in or going out of the organization's network is thoroughly inspected. The goal is simple: do not trust anything coming from the outside, and if anything is leaving the organization's network, ensure it is not carrying any sensitive information that can be misused.

Network traffic can vary in type. Although most traffic is transactional, the type of data carried is what is important. In today's world, most external applications use Secure Sockets Layer (SSL) or Transport Layer Security (TLS) as a data encryption model. Legacy unencrypted transport protocols are rarely in use today. With the CNF being the choke point, all traffic aggregates the facility and then passes through the security stack before exiting to the Internet.

In the past, many of the security components were actual physical appliances or applications housed within the organization's network. The term *stack* in security referred to layers of security devices connected linearly, and all traffic had to pass through those layers similar to impure water passing through several filters to get purified. With the adoption of the cloud, many of these stack components may reside in the cloud itself, and in most cases, they are part of the package when subscribing to SaaS applications. In some scenarios, such as Internet access, the ISPs also provide some security services like a honeypot or distributed-denial-of-service (DDoS) protection so that traffic can be blocked much earlier, even before hitting the CNF. Regardless, firewalls are still the most critical component of perimeter security, and they will always be present in some shape or form to guard the network.

Figure 6-16 shows typical security components that are located in the CNF as critical components. In this figure, components like Remote Access, Secure Web Gateway, Email Gateway, and Proxy can also be deployed in the cloud or by the ISPs and application service providers (ASPs) to drop traffic close to the source or as far away from the organization's network as possible.

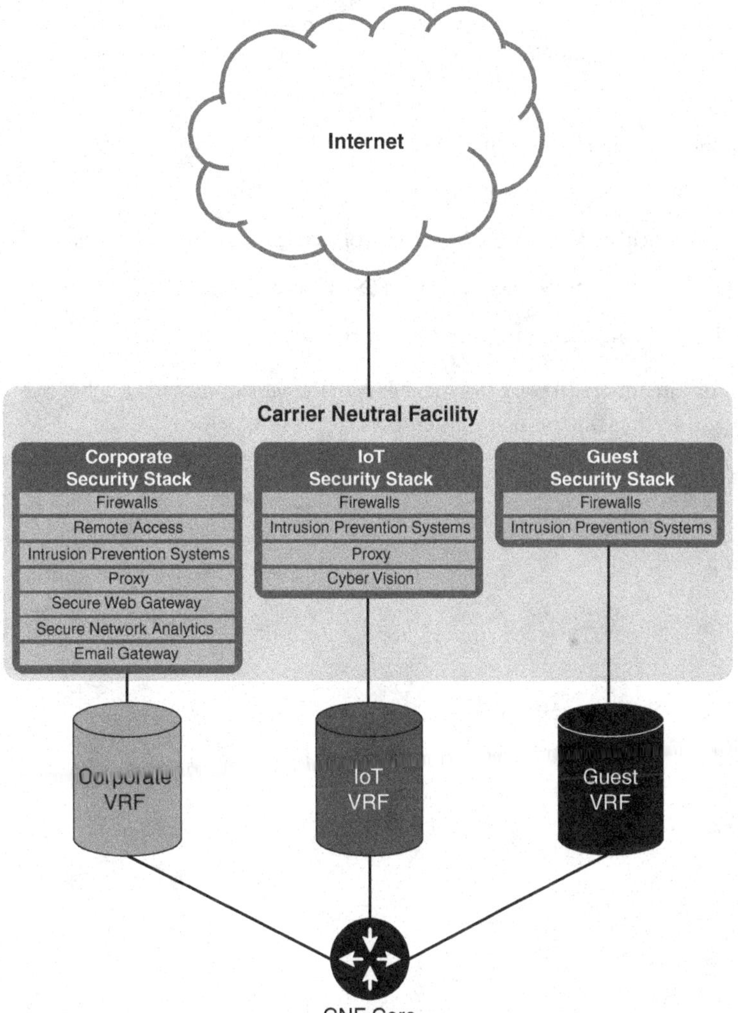

Figure 6-16 *Typical Security Components in the CNF*

Summary

Carrier Neutral Facilities are versatile in nature. More and more organizations are trying to adopt this model so that they can be flexible and have versatile connectivity to various network domains. With connectivity options to the campus, data center, WAN, cloud, and security, a fundamental component of macrosegmentation can be maintained end to end. The goal of the CNF is to aggregate traffic and provide hub-like connectivity to different domains. CNF adoption is fairly new, and its golden architecture is not clearly defined yet. When we keep the simplicity and purpose in mind, the fundamentals of the CNF include

- No more than one or two racks' worth of equipment
- Predominantly network and security components
- Compute only for critical applications such as network controllers or NAC appliances
- As close proximity to the network access points (NAP) as possible
- Direct connections to other CNFs to form a network backbone ring

Following these simple architectural principles will ensure the versatility of the CNF by providing low cost and greater functionality in terms of network connectivity.

Chapter 7

Cloud

In this chapter, we discuss the following:

- Evolution and types of cloud networks
- Integration of different domains with the cloud infrastructure

Overview

Technology has a way of going in circles throughout its development lifecycle. It all comes down to the development pace of two different aspects: the processing speed of compute resources and the transmission speed of networks connecting those compute resources. The advancement of any technology is highly dependent on these two factors. Today, the largest tech giants are working on building the fastest supercomputer, but that computer is only as good as the data it can extract through its network connectivity. Supercomputers cannot do any better if the information they are trying to process is only accessible via a 1-gigabit link—even though, about 10 years ago, 1-gigabit speed seemed to be very high.

Returning to the circles of the development lifecycle, the first generation of computers was massive and occupied a room. They had a large footprint, but by comparison, data processing then was minuscule. At that time, transferring data from one computer to another was not considered, and much of the data was added in manually. When large universities and organizations started to develop their own version of the computer, all of them were unique and solved some unique purpose. This is the point when transfer of data from one computer to another was needed, and they relied on a basic form of taking the output from one computer onto some form of media such as magnetic tape and physically transporting it to another location and inserting into another computer. These operations could take days. Those storage drives took many forms, from magnetic tapes to floppy drives. In 1969, when the first packet-switched computer network was built, the world started to change. Transmitting data was faster (obviously), but due to lack of standardization of transmission protocols, it was still in evolution. Then major companies started shifting their focus to centralized data storage, resulting in mainframe design. At this point, dumb terminals with minimal required hardware were accessing data that was stored at a central location—kind of a smaller version of the cloud.

As size of the data grew, we jumped into a second version of the cycle. Computer hardware was progressing at a rapid pace, and while the industry was standardizing the transmission protocols, the adoption of computers skyrocketed so that all the data started to be hosted locally on the computers again. This locally stored data was quickly accessible with custom applications, but the need to transfer data was still there. With the birth of the Internet Protocol-based transmission protocol, the World Wide Web was developed and changed the way people and businesses around the world conducted business and shared information. This was a crucial turning point in the history of the network. With standardization of Internet protocols, a client/server-based model evolved. Personal computing became more accessible and started to come into every home. Now computer applications and networks were evolving at a rapid pace. With the birth of e-commerce, e-learning, and email, every computer needed some form of network connectivity. Telecommunication technologies were also evolving in parallel. Phones were becoming smarter. The ability to not only send Multimedia Messaging Services (MMS) but also access the web over the phone led to a boom in the amount of data that needed to be transferred over a service provider's network. Service providers started converting their DSL and cable-based networks to IP-MPLS-based backbones that could route any traffic over their core—data or voice, residential or business.

As access to information became more and more prevalent over public infrastructure, data centers started to develop. Each organization would have some form of data center in their infrastructure where they started to store all applications and data centrally. For e-commerce, these data centers were placed closer to the network access points (NAPs) for faster access. At this point, a cloud-based infrastructure started to develop. With the rising cost of procurement and operation of physical hardware and software, pay-as-you-go models to scale applications were becoming the norm. Cloud architecture was evolving and getting more and more accessible. Many of you may remember holiday seasons when you were trying to purchase products online only to wait for the overloaded servers to respond and complete the transactions. Completing a transaction seemed like winning the lottery. With on-demand flexibility of the cloud-based infrastructure, this is not the case anymore. Large organizations can easily and automatically scale their e-commerce infrastructure based on demand and ensure customer experience is not impacted. This improvement goes a long way in retaining customers and brand reputation.

The evolution of technology is never-ending—periods of storing data locally, then centrally, and back to locally and then centrally. This evolution comes with major breakthroughs in technology and the way we do our work today. Now, with the help of the cloud, you can snap a picture on your phone, which immediately synchronizes to the cloud, and then can access it from your computer in seconds. No need to transfer those pics to the computer via a cable or a storage drive. Having data in the cloud also makes it accessible to any platform without barriers. No need for custom software. In most cases, all you need is a web browser, which is available on all computers and phones today.

There are three main types of cloud deployments for organizations: private, public, and hybrid.

Private Cloud

In the late 1900s, organizations mainly had on-premises data centers. Most of the servers in the data centers were run as individual appliances, commonly known as "pizza boxes." There was a dedicated physical server for the application. This system worked when data access was less frequent and the Internet was still growing. After the dot-com bubble and rapid access to the Internet, more and more computers began to connect to the network. Access to more data and greater speed to access that data was required, and more servers needed to be deployed to address that demand. With the retail example described earlier, seasonality changes resulted in suboptimal usage of hardware because an organization simply could not procure more physical hardware for the demand that must be met for only two to three weeks of the year. A better form of hardware utilization was needed.

In the 1960s, IBM invented the hypervisor, so virtualization was somewhat possible. In the early 2000s, VMware introduced a virtualization product that revolutionized how servers were deployed. To get the best return on investment (ROI) on physical appliances, a hypervisor was used. A hypervisor basically acts as a mediator between physical resources of an appliance and allows more than one different operating system to run by logically carving out the physical resources of an appliance. Running more than one virtual server on a single physical box allowed organizations to oversubscribe the resources and be efficient in how these servers were run.

With the advancement in these technologies, server clustering was developed; it grouped multiple physical servers into a large pool of resources and ran virtualization on top of it. This technique gave better resiliency and redundancy. Also, this clustering allowed virtual servers to be moved from one physical server to another, so any maintenance could be carried out without taking down actual servers. This clustering of servers eventually evolved into clusters of data centers and formed a private cloud in which an organization could scale their applications for employees or customers as needed. To make true cloud-like capability within a data center, on-demand provisioning capability with end-to-end automation of application and services deployment was added to existing data centers.

The major disadvantage of the private cloud is the ownership of the gear. In a private cloud, the physical space, power, cooling, equipment, cabling, and support staff are owned and/or operated by the organization. This has a massive impact on CapEx and OpEx because this ownership includes maintenance and upgrades. Proper planning still needs to be carried out regarding when to maintain and patch servers, upgrade hardware, and even forecast future growth. Despite the cost, there might be some compliance requirements in which organizations have to use their own private cloud for the nature of business they are in.

Although many public cloud providers provide dedicated compute, memory, and storage resources just as if an organization has their own data center, that could be determined as a private cloud of its own. However, it is not truly a private cloud because physical resources and the network are not in the organization's control. This model is termed Infrastructure as a Service (IaaS). For clarity, in this chapter, we refer to a private cloud as an organization's own data center that is highly virtualized to provide cloud-like services to its business units. Also, this infrastructure provides the scale, flexibility, and on-demand service capability, with the only difference being who owns the operations and the cost of procuring and maintaining underlying infrastructure costs.

Public Cloud

A public cloud is essentially the opposite of a private cloud. The biggest disadvantage of the private cloud—ownership of the physical infrastructure—is taken over by a third party. Organizations can simply "rent" physical resources such as compute and storage, including network bandwidth on demand. The billing is usually done by the second or by the minute, depending on how much they use these resources. The name *public* implies this physical infrastructure is open for the public to use at a price. Even though the physical resources are shared, the provider maintains data isolation and ensures that data from one organization is not shared with another. The power of virtualization is at its maximum here. Today, the majority of the applications and all of the Software as a Service (SaaS) offerings are delivered via a public cloud infrastructure.

The public cloud is an OpEx for an organization. With its pay-as-you-go model, an organization can scale up or down as needed. No capital expenditure required. The only disadvantage of the public cloud is that due to its shared nature, some organizations are not able to utilize it and still have to build their own private cloud infrastructure.

Hybrid Cloud

A hybrid cloud is the best of both worlds. It provides a compromise and addresses the limitations of both the private and public cloud infrastructure. In a hybrid cloud, essentially, an organization uses their physical data center and public cloud infrastructure simultaneously. The data that is critical and cannot leave the corporate infrastructure is kept locally in the private cloud, and much of e-commerce or public-facing data is pushed to the public cloud for better efficiency. The overall goal of this infrastructure setup is to maximize the cost and data control. Many legacy or custom applications might be used internally, and pushing them to the public cloud may not be viable due to their heavy footprint. To expand on the earlier retail use case, in the times of high demand and holiday seasons, an organization might leverage a public cloud for added scale and then decommission it after the season is over while maintaining their primary physical data centers for daily normal traffic.

The cloud networks in themselves are fully automated and self-contained networks. They provide simple external connectivity for organizations or business units to connect to run their business functions. The detailed inner workings of the cloud infrastructure are covered in several Cisco Press books. This book covers integration of the cloud to other domains, so the rest of this chapter focuses specifically on how different domains of an organization will connect with the cloud infrastructure.

Integration with Campus Networks

The data flowing in the network consists of a client trying to access a piece of information from a server located somewhere. This fundamental exchange of information between clients and servers takes many forms. Clients might retrieve data from the server or upload the data. A client might be a mobile device, a laptop, or even an IoT device, whereas the server can be physical or virtual, on-premises, or in the cloud. Campus networks and the cloud are on the extremes of this client/server communication. Campus networks are essentially a large collection of clients. They have users, laptops, mobile devices, IoT devices, sensors, and so on. They also come in various sizes—from large headquarters with thousands of users to small branch offices with as few as five users. Regardless of the size, data being accessed is mostly similar; the major difference is the bandwidth and availability requirements. The applications that are being accessed by the clients are usually located in the organization's private cloud or public cloud.

Campus Integration with Private Cloud

A private cloud is usually a highly virtualized data center. This space is essentially a cluster of physical compute boxes, storage arrays, and high-performance network gear providing ultra-low latency connectivity between these components. With virtualization on top leveraging shared physical resources, it becomes easy to scale servers and applications among different clusters and provide the highest resiliency for the data center. Due to the high cost of gear ownership and the operational costs, in today's world, more and more organizations are moving away from a private cloud and adopting a hybrid cloud model. In most cases, unless there is a compliance requirement, most of the applications and servers are moved to the cloud. Today, many of the day-to-day general applications are cloud-based and offered as Software as a Service. With this approach, application administration becomes much easier and scalable as the business grows. A private cloud is used only to host applications that are critical to the business or that need to meet certain security compliance requirements.

With campus networks, in a typical enterprise, most users would need access to applications such as Microsoft Office, file storage such as SharePoint, calling and meeting software such as Webex, and certain CRM, HRM, or catalog services as per their business role. These services are usually offered as SaaS. If there is custom software or a database where critical client and customer data has been stored, it is usually located in the on-premises private cloud infrastructure. In most cases, this type of highly restricted data or personally identifiable information (PII) falls under compliance of certain industry verticals, and adherence is a must. Audits are performed periodically to ensure these compliance requirements are met and applicable security policies are in place. Figure 7-1 shows a typical application location in a private or hybrid cloud scenario.

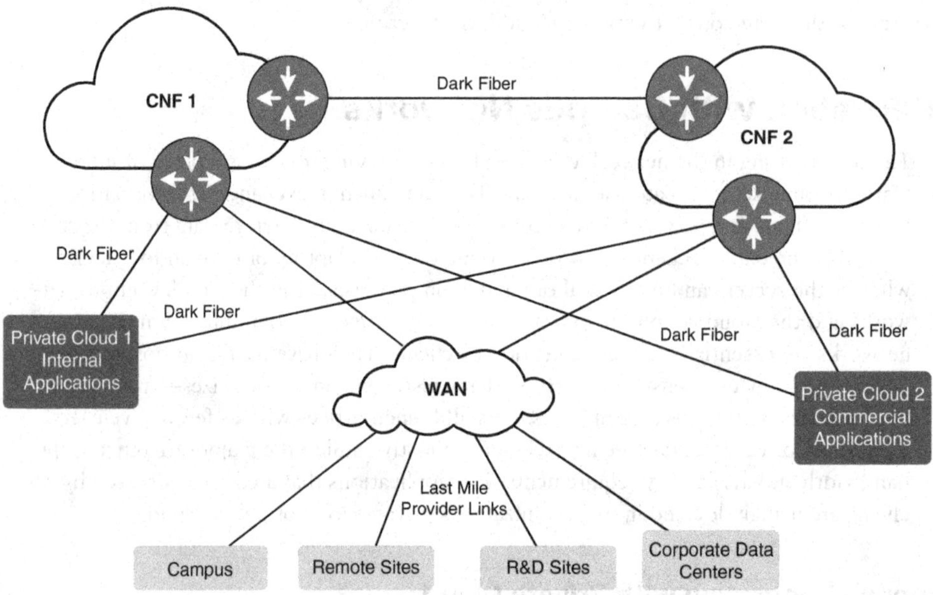

Figure 7-1 *Application Access Across a Private Cloud*

When it comes to the architecture for integration, campus networks are not usually directly connected to the cloud infrastructure. On rare occasions, a private cloud is built on a large campus HQ and is connected to the shared services segment of the infrastructure. Figure 7-2 shows the architecture of an SD-Access campus fabric endpoint accessing data from private cloud infrastructure. In scenario 1 of this diagram, endpoints and users accessing applications in the private cloud will exit out of the local campus border nodes and will traverse through the campus core routers to the local data center. This access is local and does not leave the site for any data access. If an organization has only a single on-premises private cloud, remote sites will traverse through the WAN and will access the data in this main campus HQ. For scenario 2, if an organization has a dedicated data center spread across a large region, the local user traffic will utilize a private WAN to access the applications residing in the data centers. This traffic flow is similar for any and all sites because the data center is located outside of the campus space.

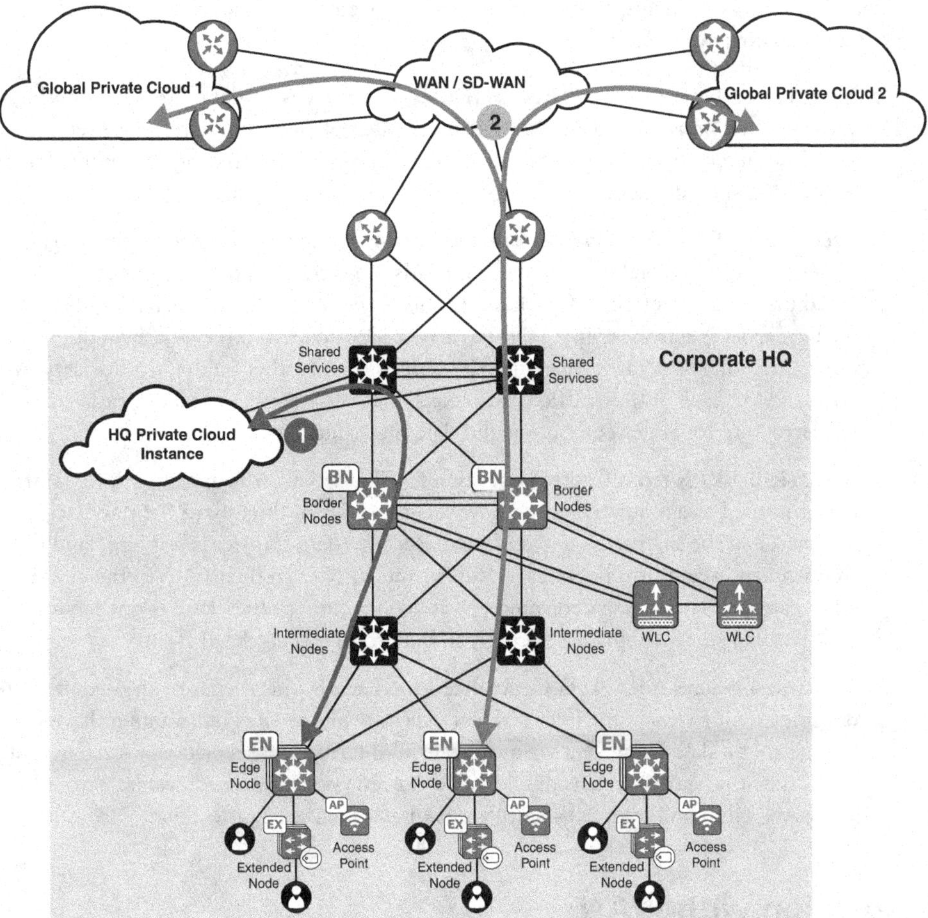

Figure 7-2 *SD-Access and Private Cloud Infrastructure*

Campus Integration with Public Cloud

Public clouds are located in a shared space and are typically accessed via the Internet or via direct connections from cloud providers. Depending on the use case, security policies, and the amount of data being transferred from users to the cloud, an organization might choose to leverage pure Internet-based access, virtual private network (VPN) over the Internet, or a direct private connection from the cloud provider. SaaS applications also fall under a similar category. In most conditions, SaaS applications could be accessed in two different ways: the back end with all the bulk data being accessed via private cloud connections or VPN to transfer bulk data securely, and the front end facing the users via pure Internet with TLS or SSL security and multi-factor authentication. This allows users to access their part of the data securely over the public Internet. More applications are going with a cloud-based model so that they can provide access to user data across one or more platform form factors securely and offer consistent and real-time data access.

Figure 7-3 shows how a user from campus can access data from the public cloud. There are four scenarios in place.

- **Scenario 1—Direct Internet Access (DIA):** A user accesses data directly from the local Internet breakout via SD-WAN's Direct Internet Access feature. This scenario could be suitable for a majority of cloud-based applications that support multi-factor user-based authentication.
- **Scenario 2—Cloud Provider's Dedicated Link:** Per a corporate policy, any and all data to the cloud is highly sensitive and needs to go through the corporate's dedicated private connection to the cloud. In this scenario, all the data is backhauled to the Carrier Neutral Facility (CNF), where it is offloaded to the cloud via direct connection. In some cases, there may be a firewall to further tighten the security. A common use case of this traffic type is R&D data that uses the scalable public cloud infrastructure for larger computing and data modeling.
- **Scenario 3—VPN from Central Location to Cloud:** Similar to scenario 2, this traffic pattern type has a requirement to allow secure backhaul directly to the public cloud instance, and the Internet is not preferred. Because data transfer is not large and less frequent, an organization opts in for site-to-site VPN from their CNF to the cloud VPN gateway. This way, a dedicated private connection to the cloud is not required, and data can still be uploaded securely in bulk from a centralized facility.
- **Scenario 4—SaaS Access via Centralized Internet:** In this scenario, an organization does not want to leverage direct Internet access at all the sites but wants to have better control on data being sent via a centralized Internet and security stack. Hence, all cloud traffic—SaaS as well as public cloud-hosted applications—traverses through the WAN, CNF, and regional security stack before accessing the cloud.

Integration with WAN

In an organization, a wide area network (WAN) is usually a self-contained domain that connects all of the sites and facilities via some form of transport. This connection is private so that all the data communication between the sites is not compromised, and most importantly, the use of public IP addressing is not required. This private connection comes in many forms—with the most expensive being dark fiber between the sites to provide 100 percent physical isolation of traffic and transport ownership to having physically shared and logically isolated MPLS-VPN like private networks. The least expensive transport type is pure business Internet. Today, an organization can get more Internet bandwidth at a fraction of the cost of private MPLS connections. So, to optimize the transports, organizations would use an overlay of VPN tunnels on top of the Internet connections to ensure the data is sent across the site securely.

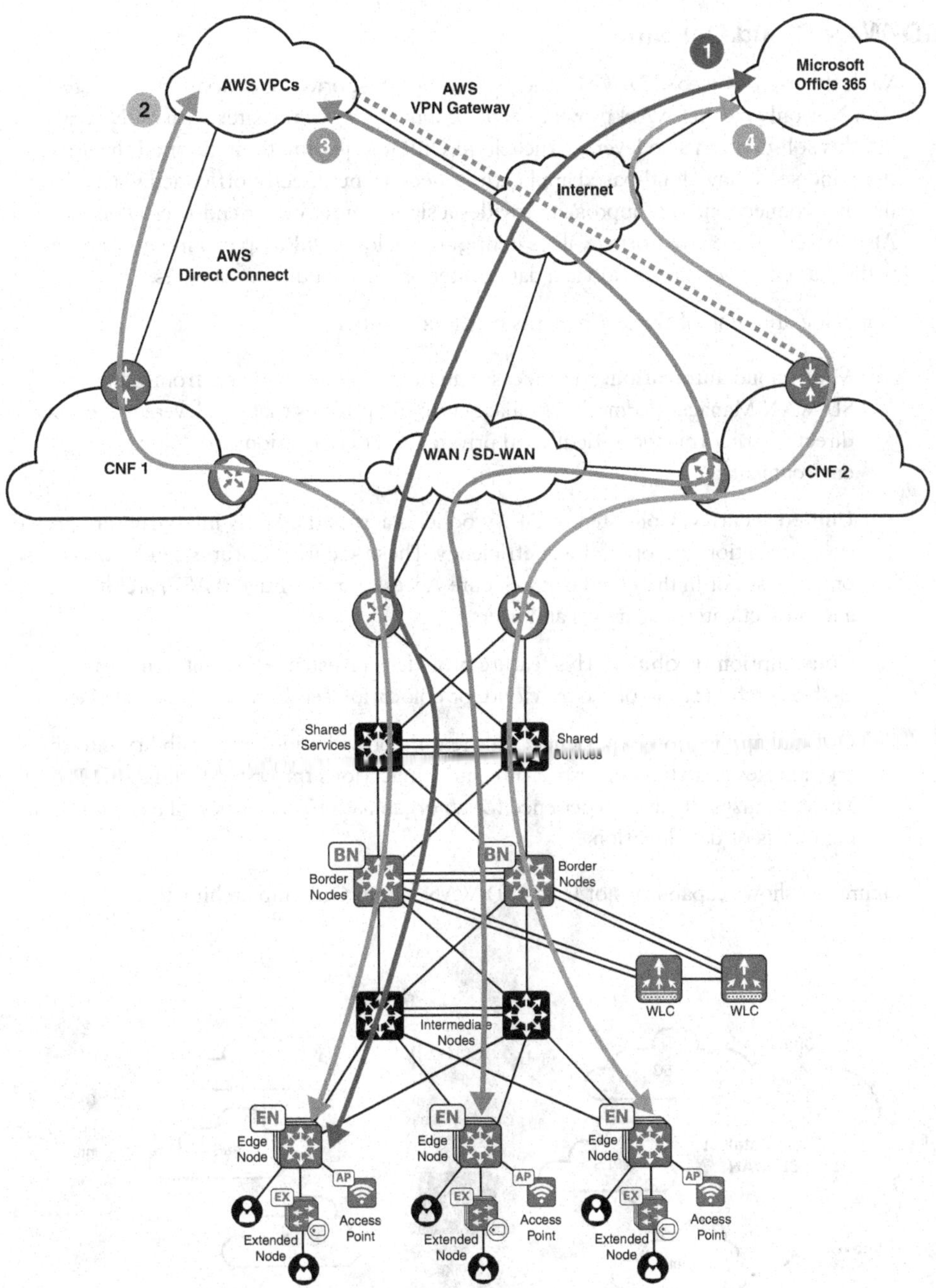

Figure 7-3 *Public Cloud Access from Campus Networks*

SD-WAN Cloud OnRamp

With the use of Cisco's SD-WAN, these Internet transport connections can go a step further. Not only can SD-WAN provide secure connectivity to the sites with VPN tunnels, but this solution can also leverage the Cloud OnRamp feature to monitor all the applications and see if any cloud-based applications need to be directly offloaded via a local Internet connection. This approach provides a significantly better end-user experience. Also, based on the monitoring values configured, Cloud OnRamp can monitor alternative paths that can reach the cloud via a data center or even via direct connects.

Following are some of the key benefits of Cloud OnRamp:

- **Multi-cloud automation:** SaaS access can be configured directly from Catalyst SD-WAN Manager (formerly vManage) to build policies that can leverage a branch's direct Internet transport, dedicated private direct connections, or colocation environments.
- **Unified security:** Consistent security policies across the WAN infrastructure provide standardization and operational efficiency. These security features can be deployed on-premises or in the cloud using Secure Access Service Edge (SASE) architecture and protect enterprise assets and users.
- **Consumption flexibility:** This feature provides consistent UI architecture that enables orchestration of Cisco, cloud, or colocation services from a single place.
- **Optimal application experience:** This feature provides in-depth visibility into the on-premises and cloud infrastructure and applications traversing through SD-WAN. This optimizes the user experience for an organization's users as well as customers, regardless of data location.

Figure 7-4 shows capabilities of Cisco SD-WAN Cloud OnRamp architecture.

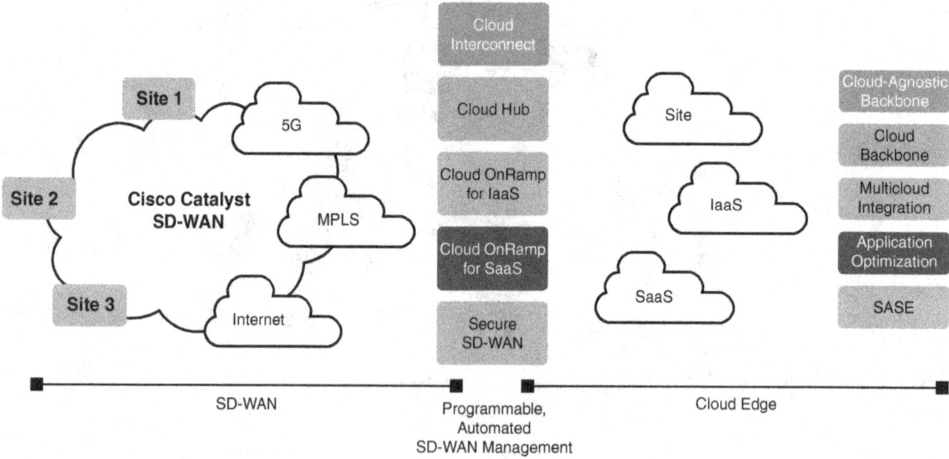

Figure 7-4 *SD-WAN Cloud OnRamp Capabilities*

Modern Transit Network Using SD-WAN Cloud OnRamp

SD-WAN architecture is versatile. It connects sites of all sizes—small, medium, and large—seamlessly and securely. On top of that, it also connects cloud infrastructure to the SD-WAN network, which works and behaves just like any other site. This is very powerful. By connecting cloud infrastructure to the WAN as another site, an organization can essentially bring an entire virtual data center to the users for data and application consumption. All the major cloud providers have some form of transit networks. These transit networks essentially connect all of the virtual cloud instances—VPCs for AWS and GCP, and VNETs for Azure—to a centralized hub. That hub, in turn, establishes secure VPN connectivity to the organization's corporate network and provides streamlined connectivity between on-premises and cloud instances and within cloud instances. Figure 7-5 shows the high-level architecture of a cloud provider's transit VPC network.

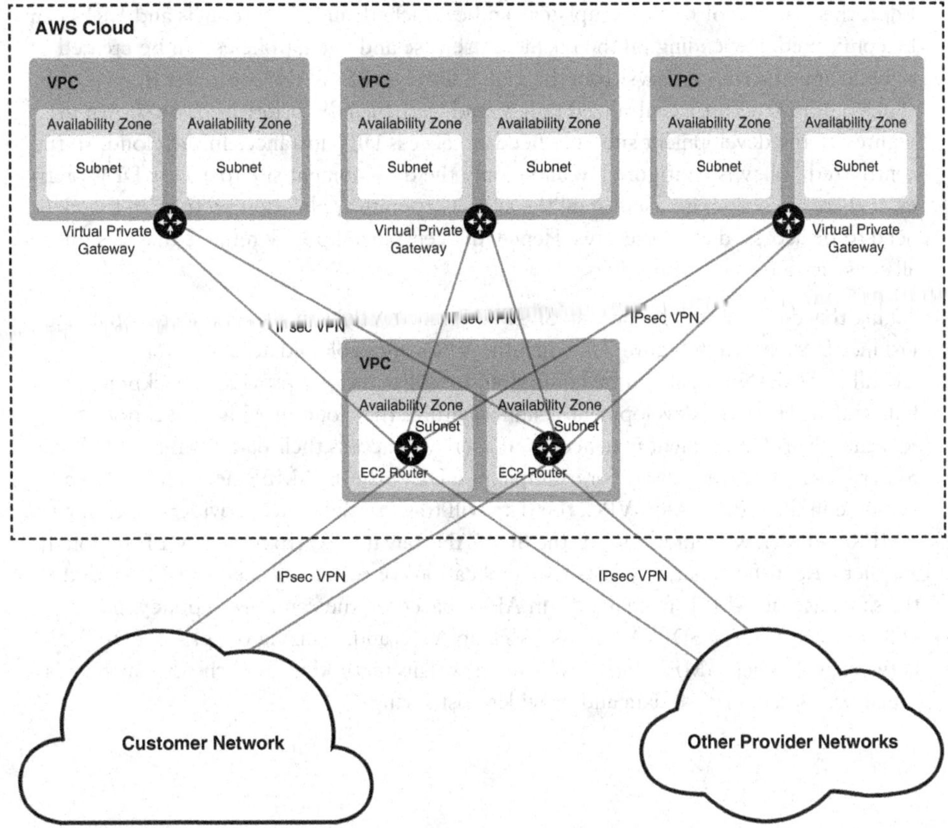

Figure 7-5 *A Cloud Provider's Typical Transit VPC Network*

A transit VPC network from the cloud provider is a default option that provides inter-VPC connectivity, to the corporate and other provider networks. Although it can be automated, it is not flexible due to the requirement of full-mesh IPsec tunnels and is not as feature rich as an SD-WAN-enabled network.

Figure 7-6 shows a transit VPC with SD-WAN routers. Visually, this reference architecture is not so different from native transit VPC, but in terms of functionality, it is a game-changer. Some considerations with the design add to the cost, such as additional bandwidth, licenses, and overhead. However, bringing the cloud as an SD-WAN site with granularity and feature sets of SD-WAN has long-term benefits. These benefits outweigh the costs and simplify the operations and WAN strategy of an organization. The SD-WAN architecture uses Catalyst 8000v virtual routers as SD-WAN Edge (formerly cEdge). These routers are onboarded in the SD-WAN network like any other physical routers. Once they are onboarded in Catalyst SD-WAN Manager and enabled as WAN Edge, the same set of device templates can be attached, and VPN tunnels and VRFs can be configured. Depending on the business use case and need, policies can be created to build specific traffic flows from the global Catalyst SD-WAN Controller (formerly vSmart) infrastructure's centralized policy, and traffic can be prioritized. As shown in Figure 7-7, the development site only needs to access DEV instances in the cloud, so the centralized policy is configured to allow only the development site to access DEV prefixes. If there are corporate users at all the sites, corporate application prefixes in the cloud need to be accessed at all the sites. Hence, the centralized policy reflects that design, and all sites can access those prefixes.

Taking this design a step further, an SD-WAN transit VPC can also connect global cloud instances. As shown in Figure 7-8, when the VPCs are deployed across various regions globally, SD-WAN transit can be configured to utilize a cloud provider's backbone for bulk traffic. Here, the development instances utilize the cloud provider's backbone to replicate their development instances, and users will access their data from the SD-WAN router closest to their region. For example, if a DEV user in AMER needs to access a resource in the APJC region VPC, the data will traverse the cloud provider's backbone to AMER and then will egress out of the SD-WAN transit VPC from the AMER region. In another case, if fewer latency-sensitive applications or resources need to be accessed via the same user in AMER from a VPC in APJC, based on the centralized policy, that traffic will egress out of the SD-WAN transit VPC in APJC and, utilizing the global SD-WAN network, will reach AMER and to the end user. This method utilizes cheaper Internet as a transport for less critical data and provides cost savings.

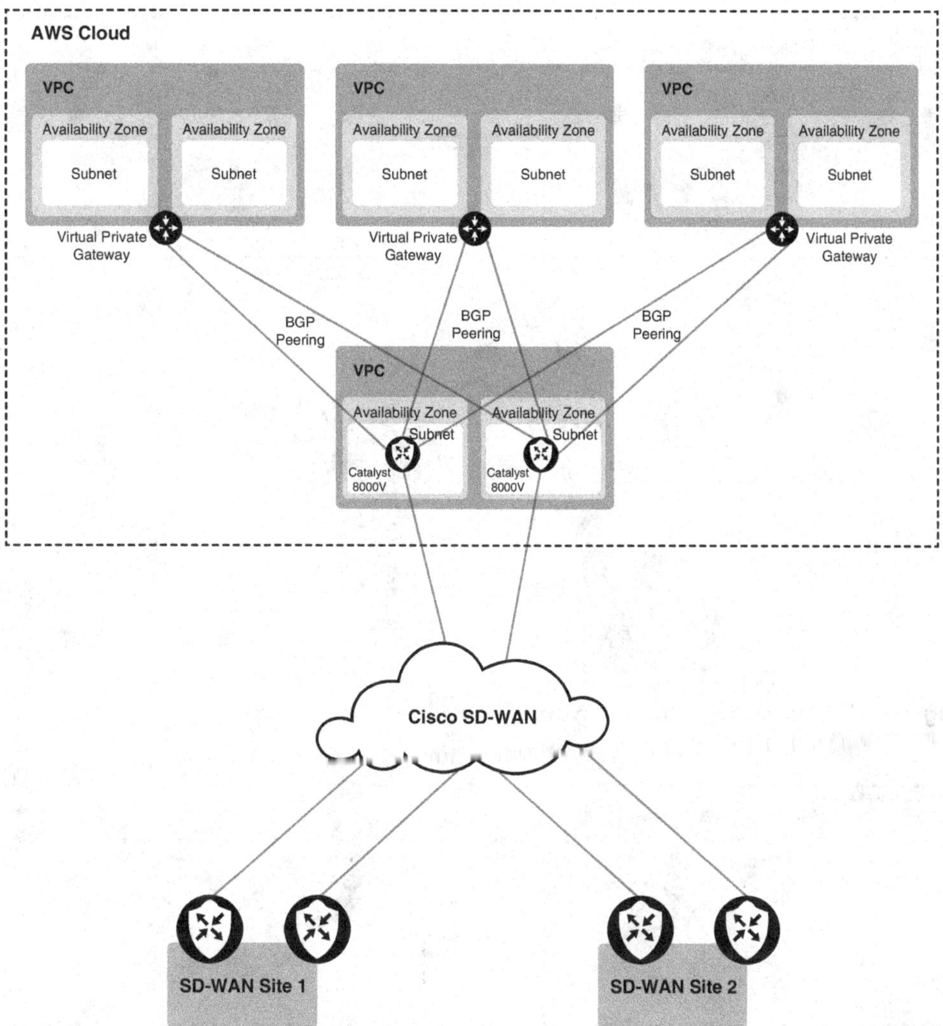

Figure 7-6 *Cloud Transit VPC Using SD-WAN Virtual Routers*

Figure 7-9 provides a summarized version of SD-WAN transit VPC architecture. This architecture addresses flexibility, serviceability, scalability, and resiliency of WAN infrastructure. All of this is achieved by leveraging centralized policy creation and automation. In the age of accessing any application anywhere, this is the go-to solution for any organization for growth and operational efficiency.

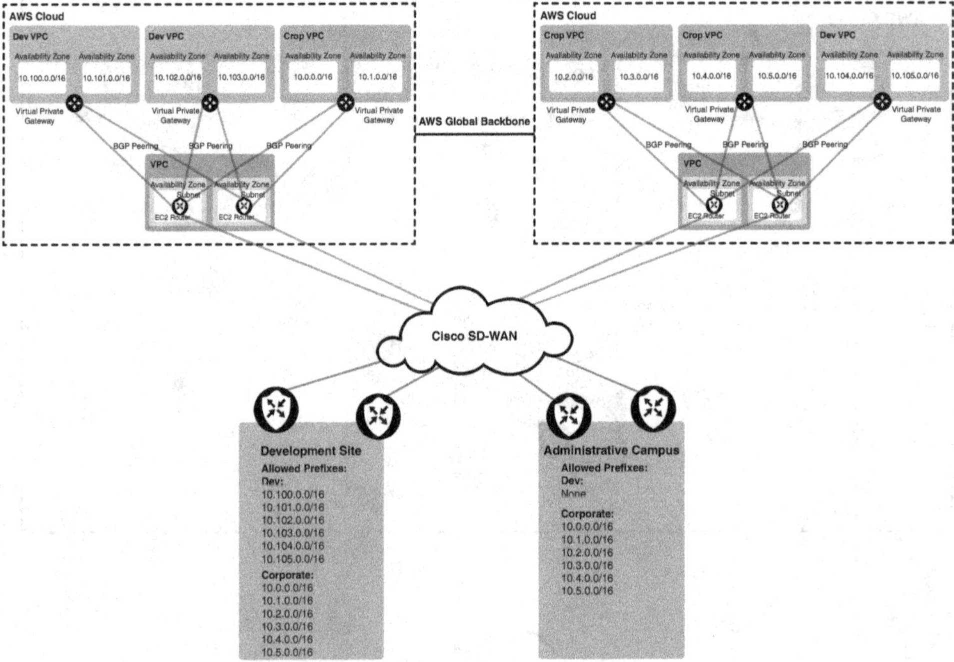

Figure 7-7 *Instance-Specific Policy Parameters on SD-WAN Transit VPC*

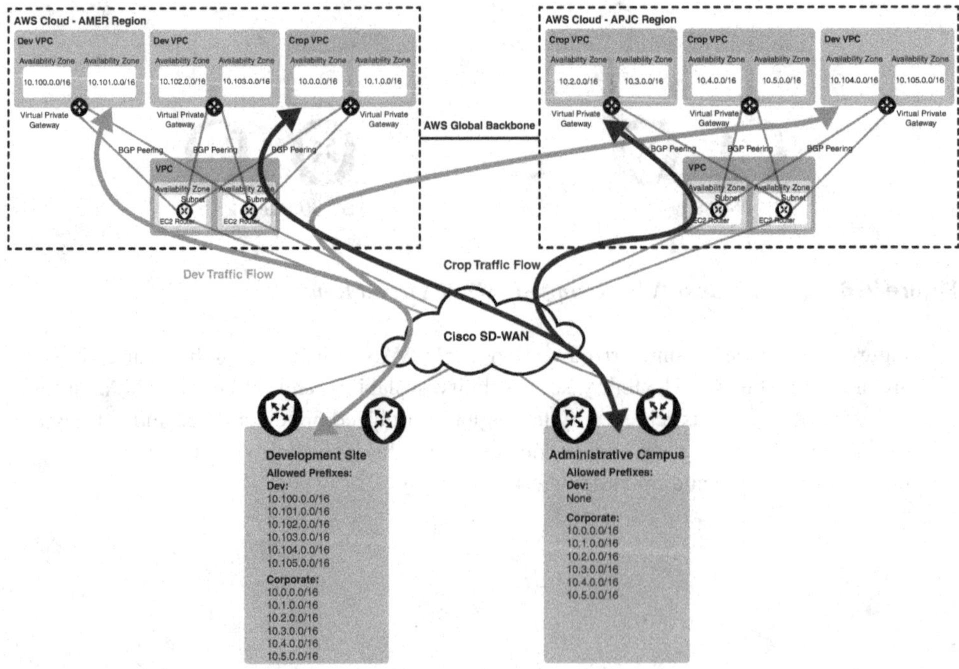

Figure 7-8 *SD-WAN Transit VPC Across Multiple Regions*

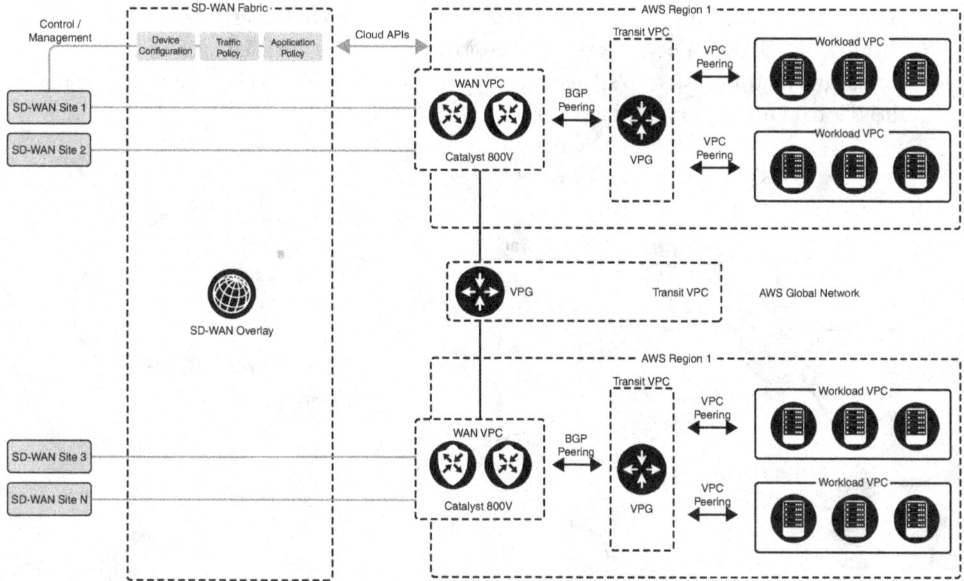

Figure 7-9 *Summarized Version of SD-WAN Transit VPC Architecture*

Integration with CNFs

Carrier Neutral Facilities (CNFs) provide essential connectivity across multiple domains. CNFs act as a hub that can span across the globe, aggregating traffic from multiple domains. Analogically, CNFs are like traffic police at a major intersection directing traffic to various avenues. For cloud connectivity, CNFs are an ideal spot when it comes to aggregating these links. Private point-to-point links from the cloud providers could become expensive, depending on the bandwidth being consumed. So, a better alternative is to have them at a centralized location where all the traffic can be aggregated.

CNFs and Private Cloud

A private cloud is essentially a highly virtualized data center. To ensure the flexibility and interconnectivity is maintained, these large facilities can be connected directly to the CNFs via dark fiber or a wavelength service from the service providers. Figure 7-10 provides insight into how CNFs can be connected to a private cloud. Because CNFs act as hubs for a network architecture, the connectivity private cloud provides simplified macro- and microsegmentation capabilities. Here, once the traffic arrives in its respective VRF, that VRF can be extended to the private cloud via VRF-Lite for end-to-end macrosegmentation. Using an IP network, two private clouds can also connect with each other for data replication and high availability.

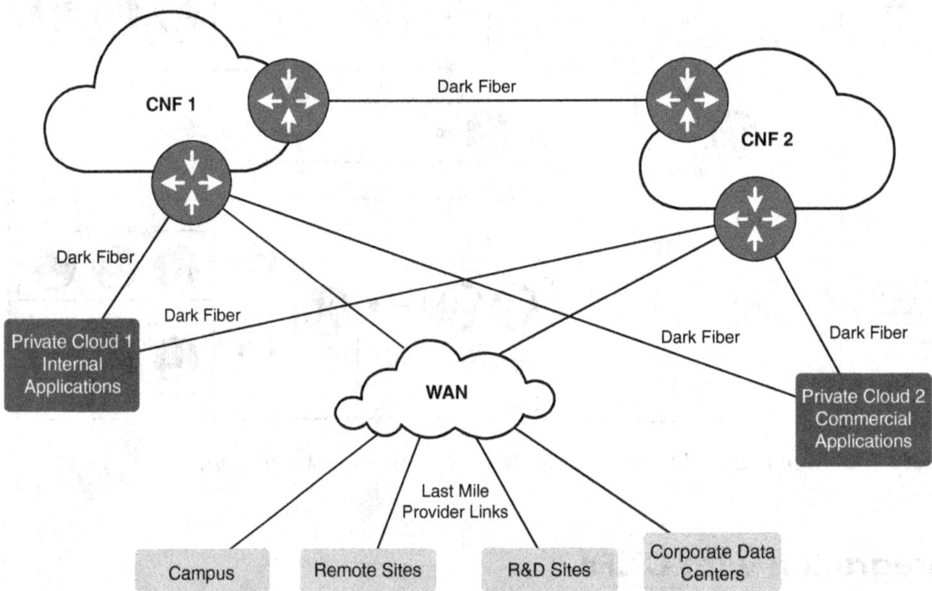

Figure 7-10 *CNF Connectivity to Private Cloud*

Another alternative is the addition of border nodes in the private cloud that can extend macro- and microsegmentation without the need of VRF-Lite. Figure 7-11 shows how that can be achieved. Traffic flow is controlled via transit control-planes as part of the SD-Access architecture. These border nodes at the private cloud act as a "site" that has BGP peering with the private cloud gateways. In this scenario, macro- and microsegmentation is transported all the way via VXLAN to the border nodes. These border nodes can offload each virtual network to a respective zone in the private cloud, or if the private cloud supports VXLAN or has ACI as part of the underlying network infrastructure, a single trunk link with the back-to-back VRFs can be configured between SD-Access border nodes and ACI border leafs. Using a CMD header tag, SGTs can be passed, and new enforcement contracts can be created on both sides of the network.

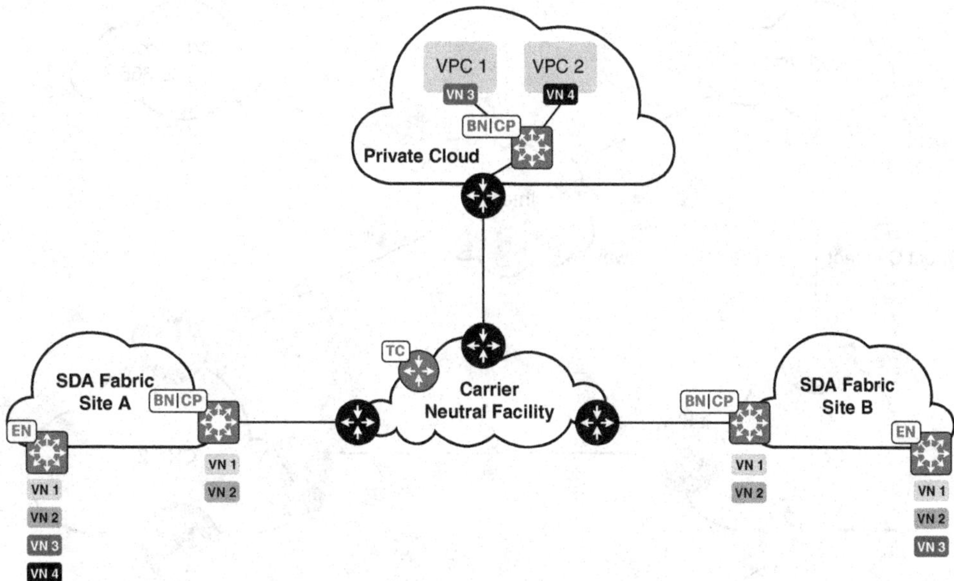

Figure 7-11 *Macro- and Microsegmentation Extension Using SD-Access Border Nodes*

CNFs and Public Cloud

Fundamentally, a public cloud can be connected via a direct private point-to-point connection or via the Internet. In both scenarios, CNFs play an important role in providing that connectivity. CNFs are located at or near network access points, which provides ideal connectivity options to the cloud. In Figure 7-12, the direct point-to-point connectivity that is provided by the cloud can be terminated directly on the external routers. The traffic from these types of connectivity is usually firewalled for inspection unless there is a direct VPN on top of the direct connection. On the other hand, if pure Internet-based access is being used, such as for SaaS applications, the applications themselves provide transport layer security to secure the traffic. For such traffic, the external firewalls perform Network Address Translation, and the cloud access can be achieved just like any other online application.

Having direct connections to the cloud can be very expensive and is usually beneficial if there is a guaranteed amount of bandwidth being utilized. To achieve redundancy, most organizations procure only a single direct connection link to the cloud per CNF, so each CNF can act as a backup of each other in the event of a failure. Due to proximity to the cloud providers in the CNF, these links are extremely stable, so overengineering is not needed. Another alternative to achieve active/standby for these direct cloud connections is to have a VPN over Internet as a backup to the direct cloud connection. This way, a majority of the traffic flows through the direct connection, and in the event of a failure, routing will divert traffic via a VPN tunnel to the cloud VPN gateways.

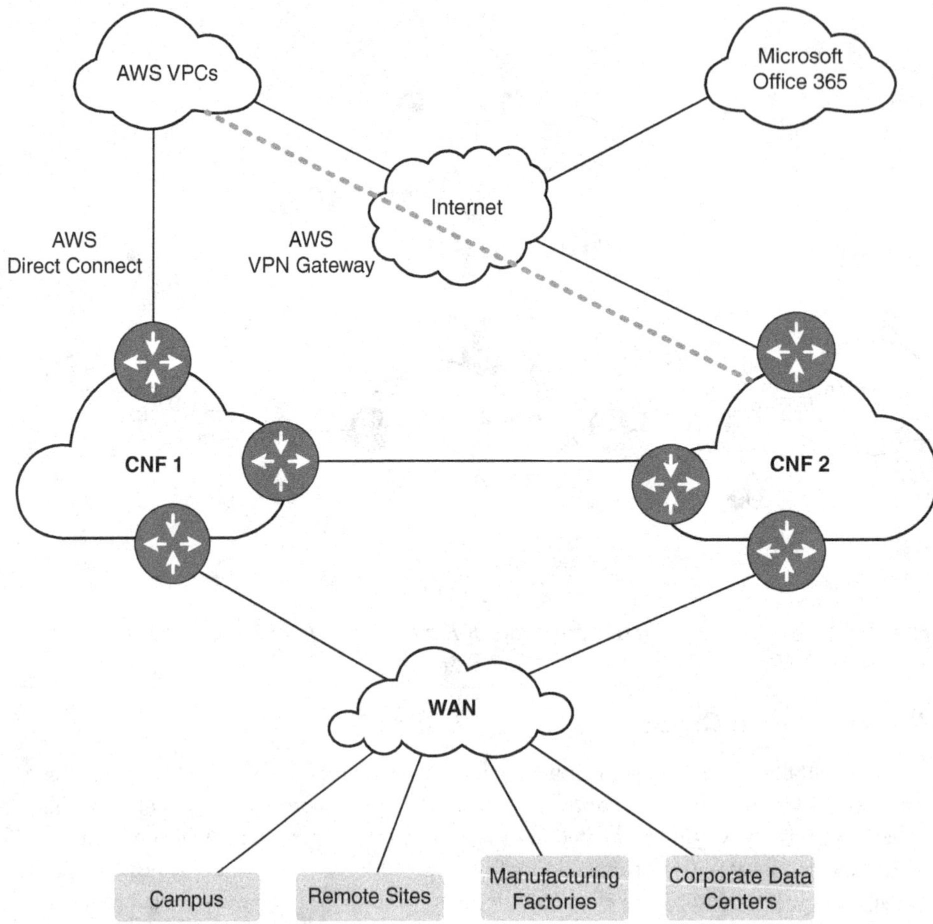

Figure 7-12 *CNF Connectivity to Public Cloud*

Integration with MPLS

Enterprise Multi-Protocol Label Switching (MPLS) is local to enterprise networks. Public cloud access is typically not possible or is avoided for security measures. However, for private cloud, it is a versatile solution. In this scenario, MPLS PE routers are configured across the enterprise network to provide a macrosegmented network. As shown in Figure 7-13, a private cloud might have virtual instances of various business units for their business function. Enterprise MPLS would fetch that traffic from local sites in to their respective VRF and then backhaul it to the private cloud instance that has all the applications and containers. This same MPLS network can also be used as a point-to-point network for data replication across the WAN for higher scalability.

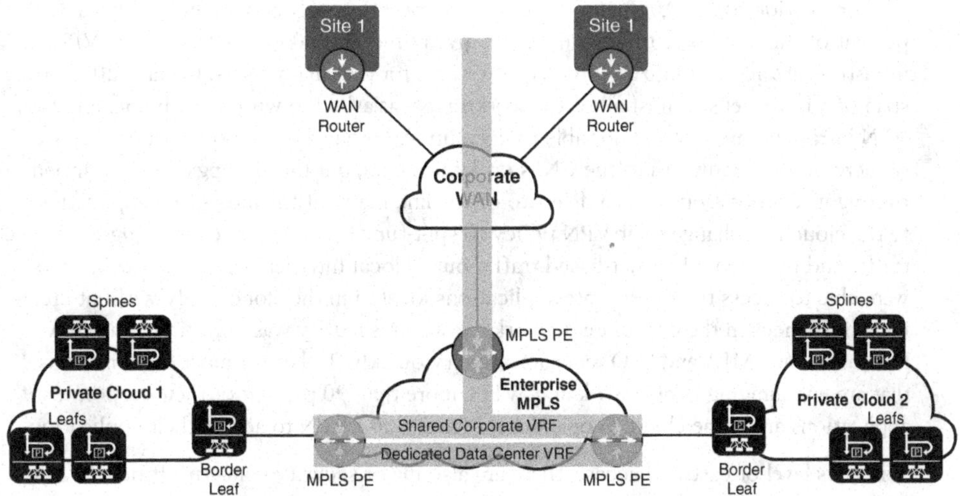

Figure 7-13 *MPLS and Private Cloud Connectivity*

Integration with Security Stack

Security is ever evolving. In today's digital networks and the model of accessing any application anywhere, security cannot be just contained on-premises. Security needs to be present on the devices, applications, and the traffic in transit in between. Security needs to be end to end. With a zero-trust security model, security needs to evolve to be everywhere, and at the same time, it needs to be transparent to the users so that it is not seen as a laborious task for them. It is a human trait to take the path of least resistance. If any task—as simple as an authentication—takes longer than 30 seconds, human patience wears thin because people do not want to be kept waiting for the data they need to access. A person will bear 30–45 seconds of commercials on a video playback, but 15 seconds on multi-factor authentication (MFA) seems like an eternity. Hence, many organizations have to enforce such measures and enable single sign-on (SSO) so that users have to authenticate only once, and they can access multiple applications.

A lot goes on in the background during the SSO process. The application that may reside in the cloud or on-premises needs to be enabled for SSO and to leverage those credentials. The user device needs to maintain the respective authentication cookies for a set number of hours or a number of times from the first authentication to ensure reauthentication when that timer or counter runs out.

Since 2020, there has been a major shift in how such authentications are performed. Previously, the first line of defense was the corporate office. If a user in the office was connected to corporate Wi-Fi or a network with simple dot1x authentication, that user would have access to all internal applications. Due to a major surge in the work-from-home (WFH) model in the 2020s—and that, too, occurred with short and immediate notice—there was a massive surge in VPN access to corporate infrastructure. Previously, if a corporation had 100,000 employees, the corporation only accounted for about 10 percent of the workforce to be remote at a given time (10,000 users). Hence, the VPN infrastructure and centralized Internet were sized for that many users. In early 2020, in a span of a few weeks, almost all of the workforce was asked to work from home, and the VPN infrastructure was just not able to keep up. An organization can buy more licenses or increase the bandwidth to the CNFs or data centers, but those things do not happen overnight. Corporations had to divert to offloading many of the most-used applications to the cloud and change their VPN policy to split-tunneling by only encrypting corporate traffic and offloading Internet-based traffic out to local Internet access. This way, users were able to access their corporate applications located in the cloud easily without creating a bottleneck in the corporate network. However, security was important, and they had to leverage MFA and SSO mechanisms very quickly. Today, for most organizations that are encouraging hybrid work and WFH, more than 90 percent of their corporate applications are in the cloud. People do not have to use VPN to access their applications.

With this level of ease and access, there are also major security concerns. If no one has to use VPN to access the corporate network, and all data from a user's corporate laptop is wide open to the Internet, how can an organization ensure assets and intellectual property and capital can remain secure from prying eyes? This is where many of the security mechanisms that were on-premises evolved to support the cloud model. Cloud-based security can be divided into the following categories:

- Domain Name System (DNS)
- Email
- Files and data storage
- Application access and authentication
- Malware and threat detection
- Overarching visibility of all applications that reside in the cloud

Let's expand on these six points. It was evident that when VPN was not being used by any corporate laptop, it basically had an opportunity to access any resource on the web. Because 99 percent of all the data access over the Internet—direct or redirect—occurs via domain names and URLs, securing the DNS was most critical. There are solutions like Cisco's Umbrella, which monitors all the safe-to-use domain names and DNS name resolutions. If an organization mandates their corporate group policy for all of their laptops to hard-code the DNS servers to a service like Cisco's Umbrella, all the URL requests and resources will go through a secure DNS system that could prevent unwanted or illegal website or URL access. This cloud-based security solution acts as a first-line defense for corporate assets that are exposed to the public Internet. An organization can also create custom DNS zones and entries for their corporate applications that can enable better security and visibility and further restrict some more URLs that are prohibited by an organization's security policy.

Email security is another big piece of cloud-based security. With a majority of organizations using Microsoft's email service, Cisco's Email Threat Defense, in conjunction with Microsoft's Outlook or Google's business mail, can be a highly secure solution for an organization. Many times, a simple email can wreak havoc in a corporate network when a user unknowingly clicks an attachment or a hyperlink that triggers malware attacking the user's device or a corporate network. Historically, corporate firewalls protected against unwanted access from inside or outside of the corporate network, but with no VPN and anywhere access, this becomes a bigger security risk. Hence, cloud-based solutions like these can provide a similar level of security because all the emails and attachments can get scanned in the cloud before being delivered to the user's inbox. Also, this provides centralized visibility on what types of threats are being circulated and dynamic filters can be placed or modified.

File and data storage is another major change in an organization's network. With cloud storage costs at an all-time low and that, too, with variable plans, storing data in the cloud that can be accessed from any device and from anywhere is a no-brainer. A majority if not all of the largest enterprises in the world rely on Microsoft Office products for their business functions. With the Office 365 model, users can create a Word document or an Excel spreadsheet that can be accessed by their peers and modified at the same time. All this is possible with cloud-based file storage. With a massive amount of file storage available that provides version control capabilities, there is no need to send files internally in an organization in an email. A user can simply put that file in Microsoft's OneDrive and share the link for that file with read or write permissions to other users. This way, everyone always has the latest copy of the file that can be downloaded locally on a machine for offline editing. Once the machine is online and connected to the Internet, the file is automatically synced to the cloud. This seamless work experience is possible with back-end application security and the application provider ensuring all the data is only accessible to the organization and permitted users. Some organizations have strict policies whereby a laptop's entire hard drive has to be backed up to the cloud, so in the event an employee's laptop is damaged or stolen, the data can be quickly restored to a new device or, in the case of a stolen device, can be erased remotely. This is individual file storage in the cloud, and other flavors are the corporate file storage applications such as Microsoft's SharePoint, Apple iCloud, Google Drive, Box, and Dropbox. All of them offer SSO and access from any device—laptop, tablet, or phone. Some of the third-party applications can also leverage such storage systems to back up their own data; for example, WhatsApp can back up a user's entire chat history to iCloud. The possibilities are endless, and so are security threats. A lot of encryption and authentication goes on in the background and it is transparent to the end user, while those large organizations ensure data integrity and sovereignty.

When it comes to cloud-based applications that are made available from SaaS providers such as Salesforce and Oracle, those applications' data remains in the application service provider's (ASP) private cloud. All the data is containerized and isolated to ensure maximum security between organizations. In many cases, these applications contain personally identifiable information (PII), so data compliance and security are paramount. With the standardization of data access, where users no longer have to create individual accounts and separate passwords for each application access, SSO has again proven to be the solution for unified and seamless access. The SSO in most cases is tied with multi-factor authentication, where the first piece is the organization's Active Directory credentials, and the second factor is an authenticating application such as Cisco's DUO. Applications like DUO ask users for a unique key or passcode that is valid only for a short period of time, and that passcode is sent to the registered device that the user always carries with them. Once that one-time password (OTP) is entered in the second phase of authentication, it is ensured that the user is actually who they claim to be, and the application allows their level of privileged access. All of these authentication transactions are in real time, and just like SSO, they are timer based. If someone enters an incorrect OTP or an attacker does not possess the device that OTP is sent to, the request is timed out and the application is locked out.

The fifth piece of cloud-based security is malware and viruses. Solutions like Cisco's Secure Endpoint provide active and passive malware and threat detection. Any and all traffic that traverses through the device is scanned with known signatures. This application resides in the endpoint and updates its signatures with a cloud-based server that constantly monitors global threats and malware signatures. Anytime a major event is detected globally, there is a push from the global cloud server to the endpoint agent, and depending on company policy, an immediate scan of the system is initiated. On a regular basis, these agents scan the entire machine periodically against known signatures regardless. Cisco Secure Endpoint, alongside Cisco DUO, provides a zero-trust model that enables users to access any of the corporate applications without the need to use VPN to get into the corporate network.

The last and final piece of security is visibility. A lot is happening when a user is accessing a piece of data from the cloud—whether that may be using a corporate secure resource or watching a video online. Visibility needs to be in place so that threats can be detected and preemptive actions can be taken. Cisco's Secure Network Analytics and Full Stack Observability is crucial in identifying what is happening in the network regardless of whether an endpoint is connected via an office network or via a home office's public Internet. Visibility plays a key role and has averted many of the major risks to large corporations. These large organizations are always targets for vulnerabilities. In any data breach, an attacker has to get the connection right only once, whereas an organization being attacked has to get it right every single time. This statement is not to be taken lightly because it can compromise brand image or data or even certain critical components of national infrastructure at an unfathomable scale. In the modern world, an organization will always be like a Big Brother watching over what their employees do and what is happening on their corporate assets. This is all in the name of securing their corporate brand, preserving intellectual property, and most importantly, protecting the faith and investment their consumers and investors put in them.

Note As an author of this book and a Cisco employee, I can proudly say that Cisco has enabled its workforce to truly work from anywhere. With previously mentioned cloud-based security models, secure DNS, emails, file storage, SaaS application access, secure endpoint, VPN-less connectivity via DUO, and overarching governance, my work experience has changed significantly. I rarely have to use VPN to get into the corporate network—sometimes once every three to four weeks. This shows the power of leveraging the cloud and security together. These types of work experiences can be achieved, and Cisco has done this. **Fun Fact:** At the time of writing this section of the chapter, this author (Prajapati) was in a remote village of my hometown in India with Internet access via my smartphone's hotspot. I know every word I typed in this document was being synced to my OneDrive without any risk of data loss. That is the power of secure cloud-based applications in 2023.

Summary

In this chapter, we discussed different ways a cloud architecture can be integrated with the existing network domains. The cloud is a massive domain on its own, but it is highly self-contained, and there are several books and articles on how it functions and how it can be automated. Hence, those details are beyond the scope of this chapter. In this chapter, we discussed what private, public, and hybrid clouds are and how these clouds integrate with the campus, WAN, as an extension to existing data centers, CNFs, MPLS, and its role in providing cloud-based security solutions. Not all organizations are ready to adopt every bit of integration today. And some simply cannot do so because of compliance reasons. However, as evolution of technology is inevitable, there will be solutions that can make a difference in how a public cloud can be made accessible to all organizations to increase their overall efficiency.

Chapter 8

Security

In this chapter, we discuss the following:

- Designing with security in focus
- Designing individual domains with security
- Designing security policies for end-to-end protection

Overview

The term *security* means many different things to different people. For some, it may be a large fence around the outside of a building. For others, it may mean checking an identification badge. Yet, still others may first think of the security associated with their financial future. There are many definitions of what security is; however, the shortest definition may be peace of mind. This chapter does not go into the intricate details of achieving security, such as inspection, encryption, and cryptography; instead, it focuses on the design and implementation of security policies in the multi-domain environment.

Whether it is defined or not, every network has a security policy. The lack of a policy is in itself a security policy, meaning that the security policy is to allow all traffic. The network architect has defined the security policy to be that all traffic is permitted. It is not uncommon for large environments to have separate network and security teams. In fact, many verticals have regulatory requirements mandating such a separation. However, even with the separation, it is vital that everyone in the organization is aware of what the overall security policy is. This includes the network engineers, the application developers, the executive assistants, and the facilities management team. The reasoning is simple: the entire system is only as good as its weakest link.

Security Policy

At its core, a security policy is a written statement indicating how a company intends to protect its physical and IT resources. The security policy should be a continuously updated, living document that adapts to the changes in the environment. The security policy should define what are the acceptable uses within the environment by the end users, partners, vendors, and clients. Typically, network engineers are not the ones writing the security policy; however, they should be aware of its existence and what it states.

Most network engineers are not in the habit of thinking about how end users and, just as importantly, how malicious users will use the network. However, the design of the network should take into account, from the beginning, the organization's security policy and ensure that it is implemented correctly. A written security policy is a good thing; however, it means little if the network left a wide hole for an attacker to drive a truck through.

Security and SDA

Cisco's Software Defined Access, or SDA, has been discussed in other chapters of this book relative to how to integrate and design it with the other networking domains. From a security perspective, SDA comes out of the box ready for serious security conversations. SDA allows the enterprise to introduce macrosegmentation and microsegmentation, along with support for Cisco TrustSec. All of the technologies used by SDA have been available in networking for quite some time; however, SDA allows the technologies to come together in an automated deployment fashion to limit mistakes and take advantage of the inherent increase in security.

Consider the traffic patterns in a traditional campus network. Traffic to the servers in the data centers from end clients, as well as traffic between end clients, only rarely traverses the security devices, such as firewalls and intrusion detection/prevention systems. Instead, only the traffic from the local campus to the Internet has been traditionally inspected and firewalled. In one client environment, a single contractor's laptop was infected with ransomware. The contractor connected via a wireless connection to the enterprise network at a single campus location, and the ransomware was able to spread within minutes to the vast majority of computers globally, both servers and workstations. The main culprit that allowed the spread was the lack of patching by the system administrators. The malware was able to take advantage of a vulnerability where a patch released more than a year in advance was not applied. This is a good example of having a written security policy yet not actually using it. However, even without patching all of the workstations and servers, the network design could have been able to help limit the exposure. This is where architectures, such as SDA, excel.

The first concept to discuss is macrosegmentation. Realistically, an SDA virtual network is a Virtual Routing and Forwarding instance, or VRF. It should be considered as a single logical network. In a hospital environment, for instance, a single SDA virtual network (VN) may consist of the doctors, nurses, attorneys, human resources, and their various workstations and servers, while a separate SDA VN might consist of guests, and a third may be made up of the various physical security gear—cameras, DVRs, badge readers, and so on. It is easy to visualize how the guest users who are not affiliated with the hospital would need to be separated from the mission-critical devices on the network in the intensive care facilities. SDA allows all of these endpoints to connect to a single physical network while creating the required logical separation of multiple networks.

Because each of these SDA VNs is separated via separate VRFs, the network controls how, if at all, users or services in one VN are capable of reaching users or services in another VN. A good example of this is with an IoT virtual network. Imagine an organization that has security cameras spread out throughout their building. The cameras should be able to send a video stream to redundant DVRs, and the DVRs should be able to be managed by certain physical security personnel. Additionally, all of the cameras and the DVRs are from a single vendor. We would not expect the cameras to suddenly have network traffic to other vendors or other personnel. In fact, the cameras should always only have traffic to and from the vendor's DVR. The administrator is able to log in to the DVR and make updates that are pushed from the DVR to the camera. The DVR only expects traffic to or from the camera, as well as administrative traffic through its own web interface from either of the various physical security personnel. Some personnel will have higher privileges than others on the portal, but it will always be web traffic in this example. One final requirement: all traffic to and from the DVRs to the physical security personnel must be inspected.

In this scenario, the flow of traffic is straightforward and relatively easy to understand. How does this become a security policy, and how is it implemented with SDA? First, for SDA, a virtual network for the security devices is created. The cameras and the DVRs will exist on the network in the security VN. As the fabric allows the virtual network to exist on all of the access layer devices in the campus, the camera can connect to the closest wiring closet just as any other endpoint in the SDA environment. Using DHCP and dynamic onboarding with dot1X or MAB, the camera is brought online in the security VN with its IP address. Based on the vendor, the DHCP server can provide the required options to allow the camera to locate its DVR. The DVRs are also in the same security virtual network; however, they are most likely located in the on-site SOC, for instance. Based on the SDA configuration for the subnet(s) the cameras and DVRs are in, the devices could potentially use Layer 2 broadcasts or even multicast among themselves with full network isolation from corporate users.

Because the physical security personnel are also company employees, they will most likely reside in the more open corporate virtual network. At first, this seems as if it makes communication with the cameras and DVRs more difficult; however, the VRF separation works favorably because the requirement exists for traffic to be inspected between the personnel and the DVRs. The Layer 3 border node handoff for the security virtual network can be the outside interface on an inspection device, such as a firewall. The firewall's inside interface then connects back to the fabric's corporate virtual network. Once the interconnection of routing between the VRFs on the firewall and border nodes is handled, then the indicated security policy starts to be addressed.

The security policy is not fully complete, however. Cameras should not talk to cameras. Cameras from vendor one should not be able to communicate with DVRs from another vendor. This is the point at which microsegmentation and Cisco TrustSec begin to shine. For this particular security policy, three Security Group Tag, or SGT, values are needed: cameras, DVRs, and security personnel. From Catalyst Center (formerly DNAC), or ISE, Cisco's Identity Services Engine, depending on how the integration was performed, the SGTs are created. Additionally, security contracts that permit the vendor-specific cameras to send and receive traffic from the vendor's DVRs are allowed in the Cisco TrustSec, or CTS, matrix. Additionally, traffic between the DVRs and the security personnel is allowed. All other traffic to or from the cameras and to or from the DVRs is blocked. Now, the macro- and microsegmentation combined with the CTS rules will only allow traffic to flow as indicated in the provided security policy.

It is important to note that understanding these types of traffic flows and their security requirements should be flushed out as part of the design discussions of the SDA environment. It is not difficult to add a virtual network or additional SGTs to a deployed SDA fabric; however, when designing from the start, understanding the flows, along with the larger picture of the organization's security policy, will provide good insight into determining what virtual networks are required, as well as the proper placement of handoffs to firewalls and other inspection devices.

Security at the SDA User Edge

Security policy is not limited to what source traffic is allowed to what destination, but also it defines how the edge should be secured. For instance, if a user connects a laptop to an SDA fabric edge node, what should the switch do? Should the user just immediately gain access to the environment, or should the user be required to authenticate, and what about the state of the user's device?

In a wide open deployment, the SDA fabric could be deployed with no authentication or open authentication with the user-facing interfaces statically configured for a specific VLAN/subnet in a specific VN. When we consider those old printers or other older hardware that normally does not play well with dot1x, for instance, this seems like a nice and easy solution. However, from a security perspective, this solution is not that good. There are several ways in which an attacker could make use of an open authentication statically configured port. It is easy to imagine a user replacing the printer's network connection with their own. Without additional defense-in-depth mechanisms in place, the user could easily spoof the printer's IP address and begin probing the enterprise environment.

But what if the printer's VLAN had a printer-specific SGT associated with it, limiting what nodes and what ports or protocols are allowed? While this does limit what traffic the attacker is able to send out, it still allows the attacker to obtain information about the environment. For instance, what devices are sending to this specific device with what information, ports, and protocols? For a printer, it may be somewhat meaningless data, but an attacker is always looking for information about the environment. The more information the attacker acquires, the more capable they are of achieving a successful attack.

So, how then do we move to a closed authentication approach at the fabric edge while still allowing these older, more temperamental devices onto the network. It is recommended to use additional onboarding strategies, such as, MAB with dot1x. One of the commonly overlooked tools in host onboarding is the robust profiling and rules that may be created in ISE. It is not uncommon to have multiple printers from the same vendor, or again, other organization devices that do not easily support dot1x made by one or two vendors. The administrator can use the OUI field of the MAC addresses on these devices to create MAB-specific rules in ISE to allow for dynamic authentication and authorization.

But dot1x takes time to time out, at which point, the device may not be able to utilize DHCP for IP addressing. If that is the case, then configuring a different authentication template instead of the closed authentication template to do closed authentication but with MAB first allows the user to assign this new authentication template to these specific ports. This configuration effectively hardens the interface, bypassing dot1x and allowing DHCP to occur earlier on the device. Yet, our attacker also could spoof the MAC address of the target device.

There is always a point in every design when we must consider if this is overengineering. If the attacker takes the MAC address of the target device and its IP address, then even DHCP snooping is not going to be able to block that traffic. The network is facing a determined and skilled attacker. In this case, the defense-in-depth strategy must be utilized. First, the CTS rules in SDA should have been written so that only the required traffic to or from the target device—a printer in this example—is allowed. This would mean only management traffic to the printer and the necessary protocols to allow printing. Also, ISE profiling or another tool's profiling capabilities should be used to monitor the endpoints on the network. Once the attacker's endpoint is discovered to not be a legitimate printer, for instance, then ISE can be used to trigger a Change of Authorization (CoA) on the port. The CoA can be used to quarantine the device, preventing its access to the rest of the environment.

Why not simply use open authentication with profiling from the start? The reason is simple: deterrent. A serious attacker does not simply state they are going to attack the system today. Instead, a serious attacker plans the attack over weeks and months while obtaining as much information about the environment as possible. For the casual user who simply does not know any better, and for the less experienced or poorly thought-out attacks, using MAB as authentication allows the real device to be authenticated correctly, while deterring the casual attack. In addition, for those real, more sophisticated attacks, utilizing MAB alone will not stop the attacker, but it will slow them down to allow the profiling tools more time to ascertain the risk and allow for quarantining the host.

Security Inside the SDA Fabric

An endpoint has been securely onboarded into the network at the SDA fabric edge node whether it is wired or wireless. How do we maintain the security policy within the fabric? This is one of the many advantages of the SDA fabric itself. The SDA fabric embeds the source's SGT into all of the data packets transmitted by the source as it traverses the fabric. This allows for security policy enforcement at the egress edge of the fabric.

For traffic between a source and destination that both exist in the same virtual network at the same location, that traffic, by default, is allowed. As described previously, the SGT of the source is embedded into the data packet as part of the VXLAN header. The data packet is forwarded across the fabric to the fabric edge node with the attached destination. The fabric edge node that is decapsulating the packet now knows both the SGT of the source and the SGT of the directly connected destination. This information, along with the Security Group Access Control List (SGACL) that is automatically downloaded by the edge node from ISE, allows the device to decide whether to forward the packet or drop the packet. Note that for data path traffic in SDA, policy enforcement is always at the egress edge of the fabric. In other domains, policy enforcement may be at ingress; however, with SDA, it is always performed at egress from the fabric.

For traffic between a source and destination in two different virtual networks, if routing between the two virtual networks has not been configured, then it will not be possible to forward traffic between the endpoints. However, imagine an environment similar to Figure 8-1 where a firewall has been directly attached to the Layer 3 border node in the SDA fabric. In this scenario, traffic egressing the fabric in virtual network A is forwarded to the firewall in the VLAN associated with VN A. The firewall may now perform the appropriate inspection of the packet before returning the traffic toward the SDA border node, but now, the packet is returned on the VLAN associated with VN B. At this point, the fabric devices now process the packet as belonging to the VN B instead of VN A. Depending on the configuration of the SDA border nodes and the firewall, the source SGT information in VN A embedded in the packet may get lost; however, because the firewall is performing inspection, this may not be relevant.

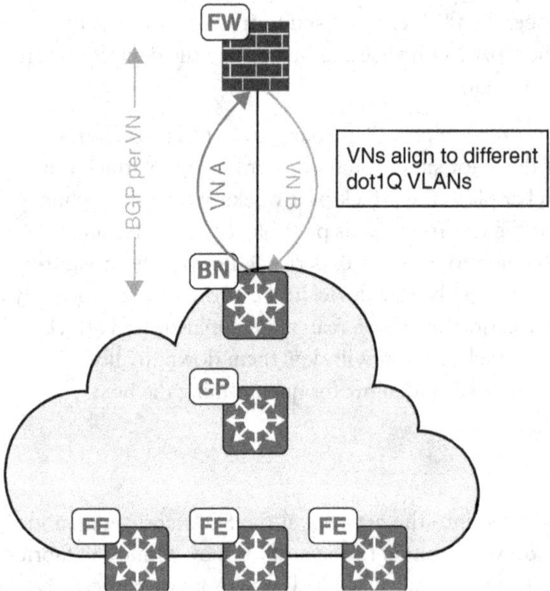

Figure 8-1 *SDA Fabric with an External Firewall*

However, if, instead of having a firewall to perform the hairpinning between the virtual networks, some other Layer 3 device is utilized, configuration is required to apply policy. By default, when the Layer 3 border node forwards a data packet toward the external router, the source SGT information is lost because the VXLAN header is removed. To retain the information with a device, SGT inline tagging may be utilized. Here, the SGT information is embedded in the Cisco Metadata (CMD) portion of the frame header. This information, along with the dot1Q VLAN identifier, maintains the macro- and microsegmentation information within the data packet itself. When this feature is enabled on both the SDA border node and the directly connected router, the source SGT information is propagated out of virtual network A in the frame header and then returned to the border node in virtual network B in the same manner. This then prevents the source SGT information from being lost in transit and allows the egress fabric edge node to perform policy enforcement on egress. Figure 8-2 illustrates how the packet and the information change as they progress in the scenario.

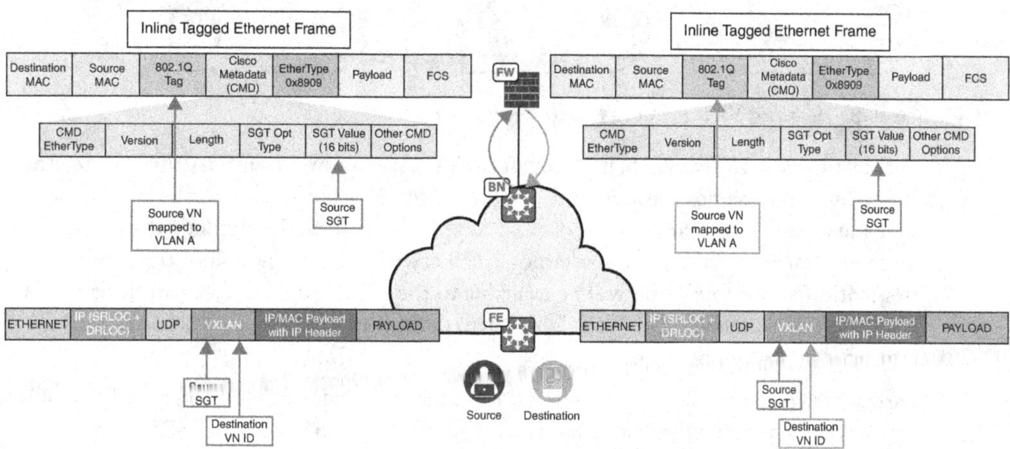

Figure 8-2 *SGT Propagation Between SDA Virtual Networks via Inline Tagging*

Not all vendors support SGT inline tagging. Therefore, there are other options to consider to preserve the source SGT and enforce policy. We could statically configure IP-to-SGT mappings on the SDA border node(s) for the IP addresses in other VNs. This is a simple solution, but clearly, it does not scale well and is not very manageable. A more dynamic solution would be to utilize an SXP peering from each VN on the SDA border node to ISE. This would allow the border node to dynamically learn the IP-to-SGT mappings in each virtual network. The concern with the SXP solution is that the ISE itself can only support 200 SXP peerings per pair of dedicated SXP policy service nodes, up to 800 on four pairs of nodes. For large-scale SDA deployments with multiple border nodes at each location supporting several virtual networks, the enterprise would surpass 200 peerings quickly. The SXP peerings can be scaled by using an intermediate-level router to peer directly with ISE and with the remote border nodes. As shown in Figure 8-3, the intermediate-level router acts as an SXP reflector forwarding the dynamically learned IP-to-SGT mappings from ISE to the SDA border nodes throughout the topology.

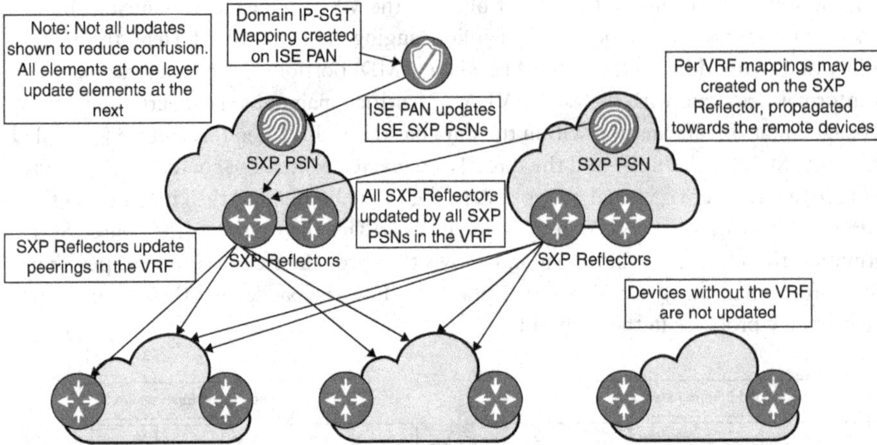

Figure 8-3 *Scaling SXP Peerings with a Reflector*

For traffic between two hosts in different SDA sites, or between an SDA site and external to the fabric, the same considerations for the source SGT must be made. Either the source SGT must be propagated with the data packet, or the IP-to-SGT mapping information must be available on the SDA border node. Otherwise, because not all of the source and destination SGT information will be available to the edge node, it will forward the policy based on the Unknown SGT. By default, then, the traffic would be forwarded as long as routing is in place appropriately.

Earlier in the chapter, we mentioned that the default behavior inside a single virtual network is to permit all traffic. This is a configurable option within the ISE TrustSec matrix configuration that can be set to deny all traffic by default. Using the default setting, when the enterprise begins to create their individual rules governing allowed and dropped traffic between user groups, those configured rules supersede the default permit behavior. For traffic flows between groups where a rule is not defined, the default configuration is used. Consider the TrustSec matrix in Figure 8-4. When traffic is sourced from the Block1 user to the Block2 user, the Block3 user, or the Block4 user, this traffic is denied due to the specific rule; however, any traffic sourced from the Block1 user toward other users where no policy is defined, such as Admin_Server, that traffic is permitted due to the default Permit IP, as shown at the bottom of the matrix.

The default Permit IP behavior in ISE is the preferred setting. For most security engineers, this would most likely not be their first thought. When changing the default permissions, as shown in Figure 8-5, the user can create a default ACL that is utilized; however, making this change should be done with the utmost care. This ACL will be applied to any traffic in the fabric where a more specific rule does not exist, including normal control plane traffic inside fabric. Incorrectly changing the default permissions could prevent the fabric itself from communicating between switches or prevent AP-to-WLC communications, for instance. Therefore, an enterprise that is changing the default permissions on the matrix should carefully plan and fully test the new default permissions prior to implementing them in production. The recommended approach is to retain the default Permit IP ACL, define policy for users in the same virtual network appropriately, and use virtual networks for macrosegmentation where appropriate.

Destination
Source
Admin_Server 25/0019
Admin_User 23/0017
Auditors 9/0009
Block1 1901/076D
Block2 1902/076E
Block3 1903/076F
Block4 1904/0770
BYOD 15/000F
Campus_Server 24/0018
Contractors 5/0005
Auditors 9/0009
Block1 1901/076D
Block2 1902/076E
Block3 1903/076F
Block4 1904/0770
BYOD 15/000F
Deny IP
Default
Enabled
SGACLs : Permit IP
Description : Default egress rule

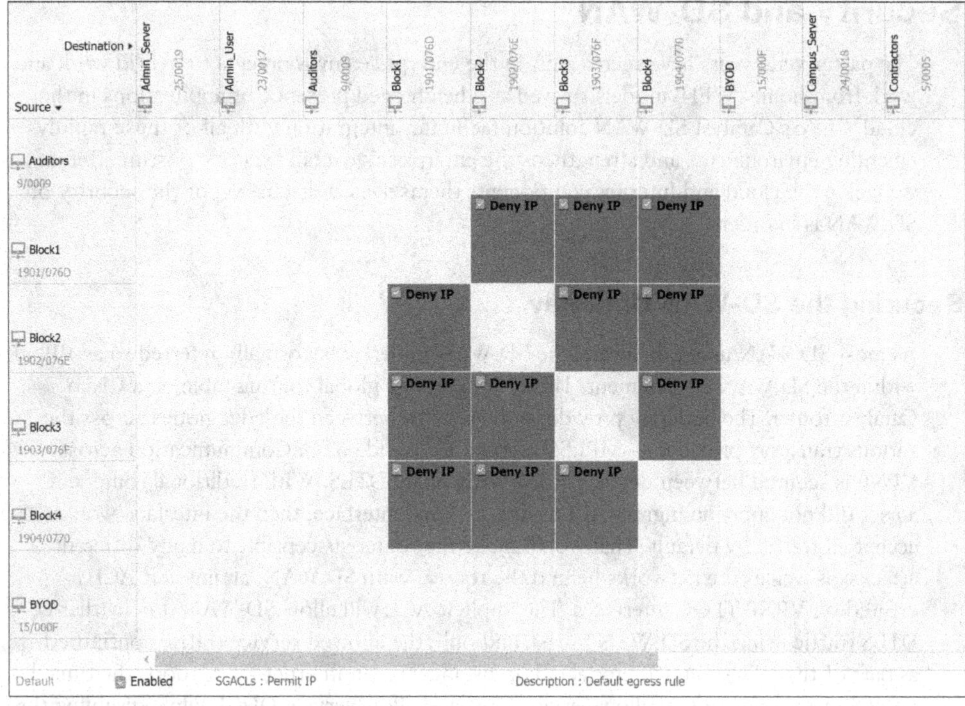

Figure 8-4 *TrustSec Matrix*

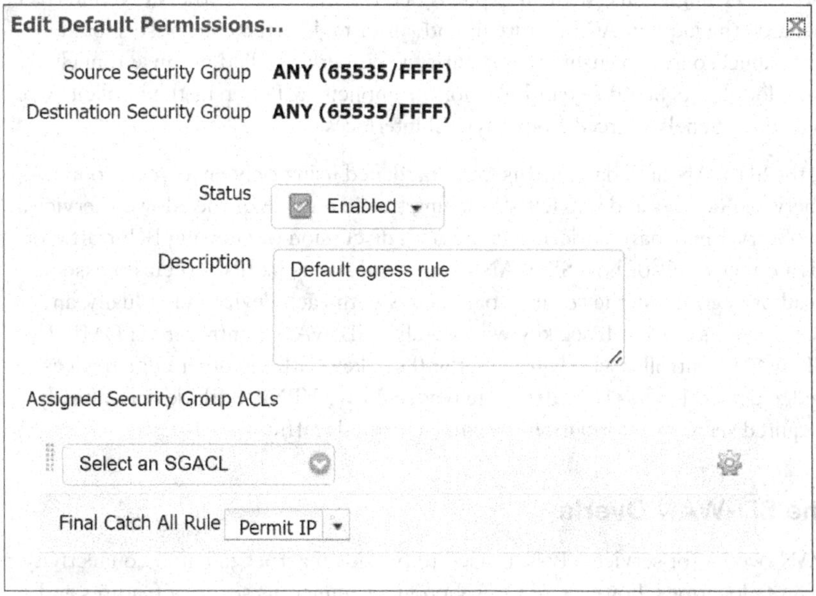

Edit Default Permissions...
Source Security Group ANY (65535/FFFF)
Destination Security Group ANY (65535/FFFF)
Status Enabled
Description Default egress rule
Assigned Security Group ACLs
Select an SGACL
Final Catch All Rule Permit IP

Figure 8-5 *Default TrustSec Permissions*

Security and SD-WAN

The past several years have seen a shift in the enterprise environments to hybrid work and work-from-home (WFH) models, as well as a heightened presence of applications in the cloud. Cisco's Catalyst SD-WAN solution facilitates integration with all of these rapidly emerging environments and strengthens the enterprise's overall security posture. Before we tackle the cloud and Internet components themselves, a discussion of the security of SD-WAN is in order.

Securing the SD-WAN Underlay

As most SD-WAN users are aware, the SD-WAN underlay is normally referred to as VPN0 within the SD-WAN environment. This is actually the global routing table on a Cisco Catalyst router. The underlay provides connectivity between the edge nodes across the various transport providers—MPLS, Internet, LTE, and so on. Communication across VPN0 is secured between devices in SD-WAN using DTLS. With traditional routers, if a user did not apply an ingress ACL to the external interface, then the interface would accept all traffic by default. That would make the router susceptible to many different attacks, as well as the networks behind the router. With SD-WAN, an implicit ACL is created on VPN0 TLOC interfaces. The implicit ACL will allow SD-WAN traffic (that is, DTLS traffic using the SD-WAN ports), and only the allowed service traffic configured as part of the VPN0 tunnel interface. For instance, on an Internet-facing port, the tunnel configuration may require allow-service DNS and allow-service DHCP while disabling the other services. In that scenario, the implicit ACL would allow the permitted services and SD-WAN traffic while blocking other traffic to the router, such as BGP. The implicit ACL feature also may be augmented with an explicitly configured ACL on the VPN0 interface. When relying on the implicit ACL feature in code prior to 17.9, the enterprise should consider the tunnel source to ensure that security is properly applied because tunnels sourced from loopbacks had different behavior for implicit ACLs versus the implicit ACL feature applied to tunnels sourced from physical interfaces.

Therefore, the SD-WAN underlay itself is fairly hardened using only encrypted communications between devices and implicitly blocking traffic outside of the allowed services. The astute observer may have noticed there was no discussion of allowing IKE traffic or ESP. This is a direct result of how SD-WAN creates and shares its IPsec security associations. Instead of negotiating the security parameters with each device individually, an edge device shares its current IPsec key with Catalyst SD-WAN Controller via OMP. The Catalyst SD-WAN Controller will then share the IPsec key with the other edge devices. So, when edge device 1 sends traffic to edge device 2 over VPN0, both devices already have the required security information to send encrypted traffic.

Securing the SD-WAN Overlay

The SD-WAN overlay, or service VPNs, is used to provide macrosegmented connectivity between remote locations; however, SD-WAN provides numerous security features and enhancements in addition to connectivity.

In a multi-domain environment, the established security policy should be applied at one location or domain and be maintained and enforced throughout the enclave, including in the SD-WAN environment. Cisco SD-WAN provides numerous security features that may be utilized to enhance the security posture. When we consider multi-domain environments, SGT classification and propagation and Cisco TrustSec enforcement are both fully supported on the Cisco SD-WAN Edge (formerly cEdge) routers. With SGT propagation, SD-WAN may be used to connect two SDA locations. This mitigates some of the concerns with SXP discussed earlier, because now, the SD-WAN environment prevents the border nodes from having to learn the IP-to-SGT mappings, either statically or dynamically. But the SD-WAN domain does not necessarily have to hand off to an SDA location. At a small branch location, the SD-WAN router may be the only Layer 3 device at the location. It is able to perform the ingress SGT classification and marking, as well as the egress policy enforcement. This is also beneficial for larger locations that may not have migrated to SDA to be able to extend the security policy from the migrated SDA environments to other non-SDA locations.

But the SD-WAN provides so many more security features than just what is made available through Cisco TrustSec. For instance, the SD-WAN Edge router itself may be configured as a stateful firewall using zones. An interface or a service VPN, as well as multiple interfaces or service VPNs, may be configured to belong to a specific zone on the router. Policy may then be created to permit or deny traffic between zones with stateful inspection. Even more, the policy rules themselves can take advantage of the SGT markings to further improve the overall policy, all while taking advantage of the classification and marking that may have been performed in a different domain in the environment.

In Figure 8-6, the location has a mini-DMZ with local services that should be Internet facing. To minimize complications of routing, this particular site has a single-service VPN. For simplicity, imagine that the DMZ servers should only be accessible via TCP port 80 from the Internet. The servers are maintained as read-only servers, so they should not be initiating traffic to the corporate environment.

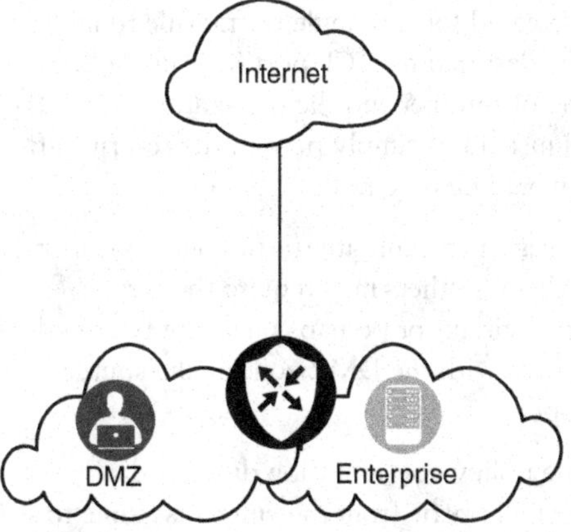

Figure 8-6 *Remote Site DMZ Services*

When zone-based policy is considered, the policy should be designed as unidirectional using inspect instead of allow where possible to allow the return traffic without complicating the policy application. There are three zones in the scenario. The enterprise zone consists of the corporate users and devices that have already been authenticated within the environment. The DMZ zone consists of these read-only servers, and the Internet zone is the untrusted world beyond the Internet-facing interface.

From a policy perspective, any traffic originating in the enterprise zone should be allowed toward the servers in the DMZ zone; however, to simplify the policy and improve the security, the traffic will be inspected instead of simply allowed. The policy could be written with tighter controls. Perhaps, the policy should only allow replication traffic, management, and monitoring traffic. If that were the case, then an SGT- or IP-based policy could be written also. To demonstrate in this scenario, all traffic from the enterprise zone will be allowed and inspected going to the DMZ zone. Because the policy inspects the traffic, then any return traffic from the DMZ zone in response to the enterprise zone-initiated traffic is allowed back through the zone-based firewall. Keep in mind that the protocol utilized may not be allowed back through the firewall without a permit in the reverse direction. For instance, inspection with SIP traffic tends to cause issues with return traffic. Therefore, as always, care should be taken when creating the final security policy to ensure traffic flows appropriately. In this scenario, the idea is to simply demonstrate the behavior.

Policy application on the zone-based firewall is from a source zone to a destination zone. Therefore, for the zone pair of enterprise zone to DMZ zone, the inspect all policy is applied. In this scenario it is not necessary to apply a policy in the reverse direction. Because the security policy states that the DMZ zone should not initiate traffic toward the enterprise zone, then by not applying a policy in that direction, only the return traffic that matches the previously created inspection entries will be allowed. All other traffic will be dropped.

This then leaves the discussion of the Internet traffic. This premise is actually the same. Here, the only traffic that should be allowed into the DMZ zone from the Internet is TCP port 80 traffic. Therefore, a security policy is created for the single traffic rule to inspect traffic from the Internet zone to the DMZ zone destined for TCP port 80. This policy is applied to the zone pair with the source zone of Internet and the destination zone of DMZ. Once again, because inspection is used instead of simply permit, the return traffic is allowed, and no other policy configuration would be required.

This now means that the DMZ servers themselves cannot initiate traffic to any location. This may be satisfactory for some use cases, whereas others may require the servers themselves to be actively monitoring the Internet circuit or perhaps querying back-end services. In that case, unidirectional policy written with the DMZ zone as the source zone may be utilized to add the additional support.

The following code snippets provide the sample policy configuration discussed previously. In Example 8-1, the policy to inspect all traffic from the enterprise zone to the DMZ zone is illustrated. Example 8-2 demonstrates inspecting only the TCP port 80 traffic from the Internet to the DMZ zone. In Example 8-3, the enterprise zone to

DMZ zone policy is refined to demonstrate only permitting (via inspection) traffic from the admin SGT, the monitoring_servers SGT, or the replication_servers SGT.

Example 8-1 *Zone-Pair Policy: Enterprise Zone to DMZ Zone*

```
! Enterprise Zone to DMZ Zone Example
! Create zones
zone security Enterprise
zone security DMZ
!
! Associate zones with interfaces
interface GigabitEthernet0/0/1
 zone-member security Enterprise
interface GigabitEthernet0/0/2
 zone-member security DMZ
!
! Create the unidirectional policy
ip access-list extended ACL-ALL
 10 permit ip any any
!
class-map type inspect match-any CM-ALL
 match access-group name ACL-ALL
!
policy-map type inspect SPI-ENT-TO-DMZ
 class type inspect CM-ALL
  inspect
 class class-default
  drop log
!
! Create the zone pair which is unidirectional
zone-pair security ZP-ENT-TO-DMZ source Enterprise destination DMZ
 service-policy type inspect SPI-ENT-TO-DMZ
!
```

Example 8-2 *Zone-Pair Policy: Internet Zone to DMZ Zone*

```
! Per-VN Tunnel Interface
! Create zones if not already created
zone security Internet
 vpn 0
zone security DMZ
!
```

```
! Per-VN Tunnel Interface
! Create zones if not already created
zone security Internet
 vpn 0
zone security DMZ
!
! Associate zones with interfaces
interface GigabitEthernet0/0/2
 zone-member security DMZ
!
! Create the unidirectional policy
ip access-list extended ACL-TCP80-ONLY
 10 permit tcp any any eq 80
!
class-map type inspect match-any CM-TCP80-ONLY
 match access-group name ACL-TCP80-ONLY
!
policy-map type inspect SPI-INET-TO-DMZ
 class type inspect CM-TCP80-ONLY
  inspect
 class class-default
  drop log
!
! Create the zone pair which is unidirectional
zone-pair security ZP-INET-TO-DMZ source Internet destination DMZ
 service-policy type inspect SPI-INET-TO-DMZ
!
```

Example 8-3 *Zone-Pair Policy: Using SGTs with Inspection*

```
! Using SGTs in Policy
! Create the unidirectional policy
class-map type inspect match-any CM-ALLOWED-USERS
 match identity user-group source Admin
 match identity user-group source MonitoringServer
 match identity user-group source ReplicationServer
!
policy-map type inspect SPI-ENT-TO-DMZ
 class type inspect CM-ALLOWED-USERS
  inspect
 class class-default
  drop log
!
!
```

Note that the identity class created in the final example could be part of a subsequent class-map definition that matches on Cisco's Network Based Application Recognition, or NBAR, applications, for instance, that further restricts the allowed permissions.

SD-WAN Security and the Cloud

In the modern world of hybrid work and cloud applications, ensuring security and secure communications is now even more critical. SD-WAN facilitates this with support for both remote access and the Secure Internet Gateway (SIG) features. For the remote access feature, remote users with Secure Client software installed can create a secure connection into the enterprise environment whether on-premises or in the cloud through an SD-WAN Edge router configured to accept the connections.

With Secure Internet Gateway, the Cisco SD-WAN Edge creates either an unencrypted tunnel using Generic Routing Encapsulation (GRE) or an encrypted tunnel using IP security (IPsec) to the cloud security service provider, for instance, Umbrella. After the tunnel has been created, then local service-side traffic destined for the Internet may be directed through the SIG tunnel instead of routing over the SD-WAN tunnels to the centralized data centers via policy. Not only does this allow for Internet traffic to be handed off directly to the Internet circuit at the local site, thus reducing the load in the data centers, but it also allows for additional layers of security and inspection from cloud-based services. For instance, normal web traffic on ports 80 and 443 may be inspected not only via a Cloud Delivered Firewall, but also proxied via the Secure Web Gateway, thereby allowing the security and inspection environment to ensure that end clients are protected from malicious files and websites.

Because each remote enterprise location is capable of creating SIG tunnels into the cloud security provider's environment globally, then security itself may be centrally managed while protecting end hosts from across the enterprise estate. It should be noted that the security provided by Umbrella does not require SIG tunnels from SD-WAN Edge devices although they provide an exceptional means to control and steer traffic. For instance, end hosts themselves may utilize client software, such as AnyConnect, to provide the same cloud security services without the SIG tunnels configured.

Security and DMVPN

Not all environments have migrated their traditional IOS-XE routers to controller mode for Cisco's Catalyst SD-WAN. There is also still a place in the multi-domain environment for DMVPN. As with every other point in the enterprise environment, security in DMVPN is of paramount importance.

Securing the DMVPN Front Door

Unlike SD-WAN, which provides the use of the implicit ACL feature to ensure that only SD-WAN encrypted packets and the specified allowed services are permitted inbound on the service provider-facing link, DMVPN will allow all traffic inbound without configuring protection. There are two fundamentally recommended best practices for DMVPN security from the start: using a front-door VRF and applying an ingress ACL to protect the router.

Using a front-door VRF facilitates an improved security posture and simplifies the overall routing design and configurations because recursive routing over the tunnel is no longer a concern. Example 8-4 illustrates the configuration concept of a front door VRF. Only the relevant configuration is shown for simplicity.

Example 8-4 *DMVPN Front Door VRF Configuration*

```
! Front Door VRF
vrf definition Underlay
 address-family ipv4
!
interface GigabitEthernet0/0/0
 vrf forwarding Underlay
 ip address 192.168.0.1 255.255.255.252
!
interface Tunnel100
 ip address 10.0.0.1 255.255.255.0
 tunnel vrf Underlay
 tunnel source GigabitEthernet0/0/0
 tunnel mode gre multipoint
!
```

In this configuration, the tunnel interface is maintained in the global routing table (GRT). The lack of a **vrf forwarding** command configures the router to place the IP address of the tunnel in the GRT. The subsequent **tunnel vrf** command configures the router to use that particular VRF for tunnel packets. The VRF used in the **tunnel vrf** command matches the VRF configured for forwarding on the physical interface that is the tunnel source. Therefore, from a route-switch perspective, traffic arriving to the router in the global routing table will be forwarded out the tunnel interface based on the information in the GRT; however, after that data has been encrypted and/or encapsulated, based on the tunnel configuration, then the configured tunnel VRF routing information will be used to route the tunnel packet to the remote end. This same method of a front door VRF is used automatically in SD-WAN itself; however, the GRT is used for the front door VRF instead of the specified VRF.

Next, the router itself must be protected on the service provider-facing circuit. This is achieved via an ingress ACL. When the ingress ACL is constructed, it is important to allow only the required inbound traffic for normal operations and no more. For the DMVPN tunnels to function normally using IPsec, it would be expected to allow in UDP ports 500 and 4500, as well as the ESP protocol. The UDP ports allow for the IKE phase one and two exchanges and NAT traversal while the ESP protocol permits the actual encrypted packets into the router. For some use cases, this may be all that is required for the ingress ACL configuration. From a security perspective, note that using source and destination IP addresses to further limit the attack surface area exposed by the ingress ACL is recommended; however, we realize that some interfaces may be Internet facing, making the use of the any keyword for the source IP address the more practical solution.

The ingress ACL may require additional ports and protocols in order to support normal router functionality. For instance, BGP with the service provider may be required for MPLS-facing circuits or DHCP for dynamic addressing on broadband circuits. For each of the scenarios faced by the user, only the ports and protocols required for that location should be utilized. While maintaining a single standardized ACL that exposes all the conceivable combinations of ports and protocols across the global environment, it unnecessarily exposes the router to potential attack vectors. Instead, the organization should create a single ingress ACL that has the components that address the possible configuration permutations; however, only the required ACEs for a particular site should be applied. In Example 8-5, a standard configuration example is shown. Notice that the ACL includes remark entries allowing for the end operations engineers to know which entries should be applied and which should not.

Example 8-5 *DMVPN Ingress ACL Sample Standard Configuration*

```
! Standard Ingress ACL
ip access-list extended ACL-INGRESS
 10 remark Security ACL Version: 1.0
 20 remark Permit Tunneled Traffic - All Locations
 30 permit udp any any eq 500
 40 permit udp any any eq 4500
 50 permit esp any any
 60 remark BGP Locations Only
 70 permit tcp any any eq bgp
 80 permit tcp any eq bgp any
 90 remark DHCP Services Required
 100 permit udp any eq bootps any eq bootpc
!
```

Security and DMVPN

As mentioned briefly in the previous section, the DMVPN environment should be configured to use IPsec profiles on the DMVPN tunnels to encrypt the traffic. GRE encapsulation for DMVPN is supported; however, the recommended approach is with the IPsec encryption on top of the multi-point GRE. As with all IPsec point-to-point communications, identity verification is fundamental to secure tunnel establishment. You should utilize the latest recommended and secure methods for IKE phase 1 and phase 2 key exchange and identity verification. Most enterprises utilize a shared secret on their routers to limit configuration. While operations and management normally dictate this behavior, realize that PKI is the preferred option although this creates additional overhead around certificate signing requests and renewals, and so on. With the shared secret approach, it is recommended to use key chains with rotating keys. In this way, routers are able to utilize the current key; however, the overall security posture is enhanced with the changing keys.

Additionally, the NHRP configuration should be further secured via NHRP authentication. While only adding a small additional layer of configuration and support, it does strengthen the overall security posture of the control plane with a security in-depth approach.

In the earlier section, the DMVPN tunnel was placed in a front door VRF. It would not be expected that data or management plane traffic would arrive to the router from that VRF. As such, the router should not allow traffic to the control or management plane from that VRF. Using some keywords, such as **vrf-also**, on the access-group configuration of the VTY line permitting SSH, for instance, should be done with care. Because the tunnel is in a VRF, the keyword would allow access to the VTY lines from that space. Therefore, in a multi-VRF environment, where management and/or control plane access is required in one VRF but not another, it is recommended to ensure proper filtering is in place to prevent the undesired behavior. An access-list denying inbound control and management traffic to all of the router's IP addresses attached on the exposed interfaces would reduce the attack surface while still allowing traffic from the corporate VRFs on other interfaces.

Security and ACI

Cisco's Application Centric Infrastructure (ACI), which is discussed in depth in other chapters of this book, provides the data center environment with intent-based networking based on policies. As with the other IBN domains, both macrosegmentation and microsegmentation are supported. While the hardware between SDA and ACI are different, the security concepts are not.

Just as SDA utilizes SGTs for microsegmentation and policy enforcement within a single virtual network as described previously, ACI uses an endpoint group (EPG) to do the same. Likewise, ACI supports macrosegmentation via tenants. This allows the enterprise to create tenants to separate end client environments or production from QA environments.

As is the recommended practice, the concept of zero trust should be applied where possible. In the ACI environment, part of this may come from an allowlist approach for the contracts. With an allowlist approach, a contract is explicitly configured to allow traffic from EPG1 to EPG2. Without the explicit contract, all traffic is dropped between the two EPG hosts.

One feature that ACI provides that should be used with care is contract inheritance. The idea of the feature is to simplify policy configuration. This is done by configuring EPG2 to inherit the contracts of EPG1. In doing so, EPG2 now has all of the contracts that are configured for EPG1, and it will obtain any new contracts that are subsequently added to EPG1. This does simplify the configuration of EPG2; however, care should be taken to ensure that reconfiguration of EPG1 does not provide EPG2 with additional unneeded privileges.

An interesting feature in ACI that provides the equivalent of a private VLAN is the intra-EPG isolation. With this feature, an EPG host is unable to send traffic to another host with the same EPG. Each host can send traffic to other EPGs if the contract is created to permit the traffic. Alternatively, an intra-EPG contract could be created to limit what communication is allowed.

As with SDA, communication between EPGs is stateless. The contract either permits the ports and protocols, or it does not. With either service graph insertion or network stitching of the L2 ACI fabric, either an NGFW or NGIPS may be added into the ACI fabric virtually or physically. This allows for security inspection between hosts. The networking stitching is meant to be more of a static solution where the service insertion allows for more dynamic management of the security posture. With the service graph approach, traffic destined to a particular EPG is forwarded first through the security environment, inspected, and then forwarded if appropriate.

Security and the Cloud

The transition to hybrid work, work from home, and cloud-based applications has made security in the cloud vital to normal business operations. Most cloud service providers, including AWS, Azure, and GCP, visualize security as a shared responsibility between the service provider and the consumer, the enterprise. The service provider is responsible for the security of the physical environment that is the cloud. For instance, the service provider will maintain the physical security of the locations where their data centers reside and ensure the segmentation between cloud environments of different users. The consumer, that is, the enterprise, is responsible for the security of the virtualized environment itself, the virtual routers and the endpoints within the environment. Depending on the service offering, the service provider may provide the security for an application all the way through to the application layer. For instance, a database offering provided by a cloud provider may include operating system, security, and application updates to the underlying application and hardware, allowing the end user to focus only on the data and secure access.

While the level of support from the service provider varies depending on the offering, the responsibility of security is shared between the consumer and the service provider in every case. Therefore, the security of the cloud, its applications and endpoints, should be part of the single enterprise security policy.

When considering security in a cloud environment, the enterprise should consider the cloud as another physical location in their environment with direct Internet access. With private cloud providers, the enterprise does have a secure link into their environment. This may make some aspects unneeded, but maintaining that mindset from a security perspective will improve the deployment and decision-making.

As with all environments, the premises of zero trust and least privilege should be followed in the cloud, as well as segmentation and firewalling where appropriate. As with a data center, the cloud environment should be designed using a two- or three-tier approach depending on the actual requirements. The outer tier, facing the Internet or provider edge, should be an isolated networking space that provides hardened security services, such as firewalling and inspection. Similar to the ingress ACL approach seen in SD-WAN and DMVPN earlier, only the allowed ports and protocols expected from the external world should be allowed in past this tier or zone. The next tier or tiers should provide the segmentation required of the cloud environment to perform the required enterprise services. The correct terminology for the subnets and services used varies between cloud service providers; however, the concepts are the same. These virtual tiers should provide the enterprise with the required segmentation, isolation, and inspection as would be seen in an on-premises location.

Security and Zero Trust

The digital world continues to evolve, making it virtually impossible for one book, much less, one chapter of a book, to fully address all of the recommended best practices and requirements for hardening an environment; however, one over-arching premise should be the guide for enterprise security moving into the future: zero trust.

The concept of zero trust is simple: no user or device can access any resource or data in the environment until their context (user, device, location) has been verified and is permitted. This is done with every access request even if that context was previously verified. The concept of context is critical here. Perhaps a corporate user should be allowed permission to access the corporate internal website from any device; however, access to sensitive corporate information should be allowed only for an authenticated user from a corporate-managed device connected to the corporate network in a secure fashion (directly in a building or via a secure VPN).

All of the discussions within this chapter on security and security policy work fully with a zero-trust policy. It would be expected that authentication and authorization access to any of the network devices or services is performed via AAA or IdP to maintain a zero-trust posture.

Summary

This chapter focused on the security aspects associated with each of the domains in the enterprise environment. It should be noted that new security threats are always emerging, as well as new security standards to address them. Normal security best practices and device-hardening mechanisms should be utilized, in addition to the topics discussed, to enhance the overall security posture of the enterprise. All of these mechanisms should be designed to follow the single governing security policy.

Chapter 9

Automation

In this chapter, we discuss the following:

- Incorporating automation for deployments
- Utilizing automation in individual domains
- Utilizing automation as orchestration across multiple domains

Overview

While working in network engineering, users will come across a wide range of definitions for the term *automation*. To some, it may mean a simple script that logs in to one or more devices and retrieves some **show** command output. For others, the term may apply to a system that orchestrates provisioning across multiple locations, devices, and architectures. In the scope of this chapter, *automation* refers to a more advanced system of utilizing a CI/CD pipeline to manage the production environment while ensuring that the production environment follows what was previously designed and validated in quality assurance testing.

As with all of the architectures discussed within this chapter, numerous other publications go into the intricate details of what a CI/CD pipeline is, as well as how to implement and deploy one. This chapter focuses on setting up a CI/CD pipeline with the various multi-domain architectures and its potential uses.

CI/CD Pipeline

The obvious first question, then, is what is a CI/CD pipeline? *CI/CD* refers to *continuous integration* and *continuous deployment*. Alternatively, many consider the *CD* to signify *continuous delivery*. We will use the first definition going forward. The goal of a CI/CD pipeline is to create a system where the design, environment, and configurations that are deployed into production are exact replicas of the environment utilized for testing. In this way, the errors that are introduced into production through human error, differing environmental constraints, and so on, are eliminated, therefore reducing the risks in production.

Many network engineers are all too familiar with keeping the configurations for devices in Excel spreadsheets. We (the authors of this book) have worked with large global enterprises that used Excel spreadsheets to create the configuration standards deployed across the global enclave. This approach is quite common and allows engineers a shared location to reference what a configuration should be. However, the spreadsheets do not always lead to viable automation use cases. Instead, they may require interpretation by an engineer and must be converted into a device specific configuration, often manually.

The next evolution of configuration management and standardization with support for automation leads to code repositories. At this point, you would imagine the discussion is based on just CLI configurations; however, the various IBN architectures discussed in this chapter all come with controllers that can utilize REST API interactions. Therefore, our code repository can be a collection of both CLI configuration text files, as well as scripts required to effect change via APIs. The single best code repository tool is Git or GitHub. With Git, design engineers can create branches to work on new configuration snippets. These snippets can then be validated in testing prior to merging into the mainline and becoming the standard. As shown in Figure 9-1, this is the very heart of the continuous integration part of the pipeline. There is a single standard configuration to start. A new feature enhancement must be configured, for instance. The network design engineer creates a branch for this new feature enhancement configuration and develops the code.

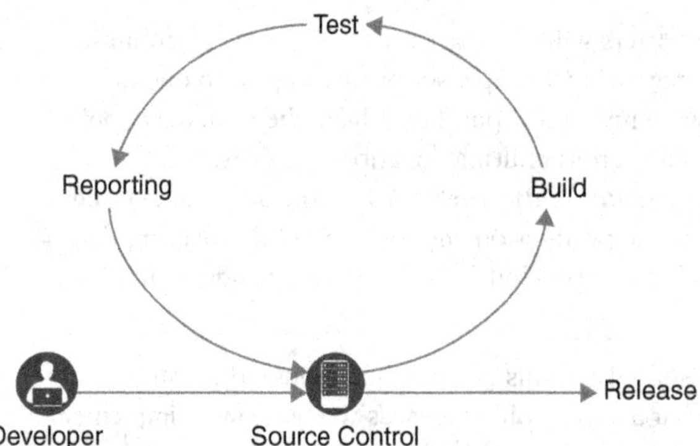

Figure 9-1 *Continuous Integration*

Because the configuration changes are isolated on the newly created branch, other engineers are able to continue to access the current standards via the main branch. In the meantime, the design engineer is free to work on the configuration and test, as appropriate. After the target configuration has been created, the design engineer can promote the intended configuration branch for testing in the next testbed. Depending on the client, the number of test environments may vary—local developer testbed, system testbed, quality assurance testbed, or other. This is part of the beauty of the CI/CD pipeline in that it may be modular to fit the requirements of the client. Regardless of the number of testbeds, the same process will occur. That is, first the code is pushed into Git for acceptance. This triggers the code to move into the next testbed for deployment and testing. As shown in Figure 9-2, after a new feature has moved completely through the pipeline, is tested, and then accepted, it is merged into the main branch, making it available for deployment into production. The same tools that are used for deployment in the testbeds are used for deployment in production. This then ensures that the production environment and configuration are exactly the same as what was tested in each of the testbeds.

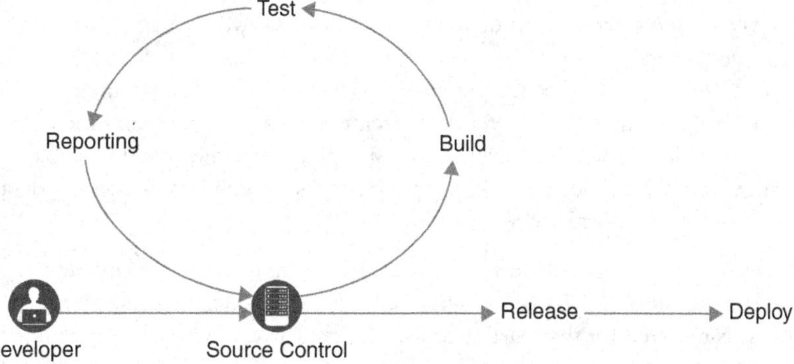

Figure 9-2 *Continuous Deployment*

For all of this to happen, multiple tools must be utilized to handle the various pieces of the puzzle. For the code repository, Git and GitHub tend to be the preferred choice. The test environment should mimic what is used in production. For smaller environments, especially for initial code development and deployment, virtualized environments provide a cost-effective way of providing virtual hardware to the designers. This is not the complete setup though. The CI/CD pipeline still needs to be able to actually automate the testing, creation, and configuration of the testing. This is done via other tools. For instance, GitLab supports integration with Git repositories. When there is a new commit, GitLab can use runners to instantiate a testbed, configure the devices with the newly updated code, perform test cases, revert the environment, and provide the test results. This allows the developers and the approvers to determine whether the code is ready to be promoted to the next level or requires additional work.

With a CI/CD pipeline, new deployments in production are always capable of taking advantage of the latest validated configurations, allowing for faster adoption of new features while also improving the production environment quality by identifying issues early on through testing and prohibiting features that are not ready for production.

The rest of this chapter examines using automation via a CI/CD pipeline with each of the various multi-domain architectures. Note that combining the automation concepts from each of the domains allows for a fully orchestrated multi-domain environment.

Automation and SDA

A critical part of Cisco's Software Defined Access, or SDA, is the Cisco Catalyst Center (formerly DNA Center). The Catalyst Center supports numerous applications that provide automation and orchestration across the managed devices in the SDA environment. The Catalyst Center allows users to provision new virtual networks (VNs) with new IP address space, as well as many other aspects to new or existing sites. This section examines how to develop and utilize a CI/CD pipeline to support the automated deployment of a new virtual network to one or more targeted SDA site locations. While creating a new VN may not be common, provisioning it to a new site for a service offering may be. Therefore, we discuss the complete picture.

Imagine the steps required to create and deploy a new virtual network to an existing SDA location for a single engineer. The engineer first would have to create the virtual network in Catalyst Center. This would require the engineer to navigate to the **Provisioning > Virtual Networks** page in Catalyst Center, select **Create Virtual Network**, and then create the name correctly. In a production scenario, even typing the name would be subject to human error. In the CI/CD pipeline, these simple mistakes are eliminated because data is validated as part of the approval processes.

Now that the new VN, called AUTO1 in Example 9-2, has been created, the engineer must identify what site the VN will be deployed to, what subnets will be utilized, whether multicast is required for that particular location and VN, as well as numerous other settings that may be required both for wired and wireless functionality. However, all of these settings are just variables that may be part of the code repository managed pipeline. Consider the sample network hierarchy shown in Figure 9-3.

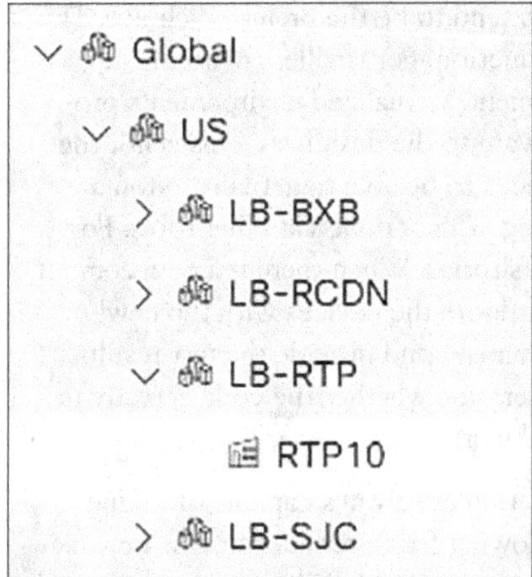

Figure 9-3 *SDA Sample Hierarchy*

In this environment, there are several areas under the US area, where the focus will be building RTP10 that is part of the LB-RTP area. The new AUTO1 VN will be deployed to this site. As part of the deployment, the site will need two new subnets: one for wired users and one for multicast support. Additionally, the Layer 3 border nodes must handle the handoff to the external environment, so the WAN subnet and target border nodes also must be addressed. These are characteristics that would occur at any potential site. How would this be managed as code? The answer is simple. The repository will host two files. The first file will handle the required order of API calls. This could be written in Python or some other language. There are numerous SDKs for Catalyst Center available that could also be leveraged. With that in mind, the API file will be shown as pseudocode, as shown in Example 9-1.

Example 9-1 *Catalyst Center Pseudocode for Site VN Creation*

```
! Load site data from YAML variables file
sitedata = Load(data_yaml_filename)
! Acquire Catalyst Center token through user authentication
token = dnac.login()
! Determine if the VN exists in the Catalyst Center deployment
VN = dnac.GetVN(sitedata['VN'])
if (not VN) then dnac.CreateVN(sitedata['VN'])
! Create required subnets in the site
site = sitedata['site']['name']
for network in sitedata['site']['subnets']:
    dnac.CreateNetwork(site, network)
!
```

In this pseudocode, the variable information is all passed in from the YAML configuration file specific for the deployment. The automation tool would then log in appropriately to Catalyst Center and determine if the VN with the provided name exists. If it does not, it is created. Then the required subnets are created for a particular location that will be used for the deployment. Example 9-2 shows what the YAML configuration file could look like at this point.

Example 9-2 *SDA YAML Parameters*

```
---
# AUTO1 YAML Parameters for Site: Global/US/LB-RTP/RTP10
VN: AUTO1
site:
  name: Global/US/LB-RTP/RTP10
  subnets:
    - RTP10-AUTO1-WiredUsers:
      type: Generic
      ipv4:
        globalpool: 10.0.0.0/8
        prefixlength: 24
```

```
        subnet: 10.0.1.0
        gateway: 10.0.1.1
        dhcp:
          - 10.127.0.1
        dns:
    - RTP10-AUTO1-Multicast:
      type: Generic
      ipv4:
        globalpool: 10.0.0.0/8
        prefixlength: 24
        subnet: 10.0.2.0
        gateway:
        dhcp:
        dns:
!
```

The YAML file now contains the required information to create the target virtual network and the subnets for the site. With the correct ordering of API calls, an automation system can now repeatedly provision the target site or multiple sites with the virtual network and the wired user subnet. It is not enough for full connectivity, but it did not take much effort just to get to this point. Additionally, remember that this data is kept inside the CI/CD pipeline code repository, so numerous individuals are able to review the data for correctness, as well as multiple test environment validations.

Imagine a CI/CD pipeline where all of the subnets at all of the individual site locations are already maintained as a collection of YAML variable files, perhaps one for each location or even one file for each VN at each location. If the enterprise wishes to add networks to a single location, the YAML file is updated appropriately, which keys the entire CI/CD pipeline and approval processes. The changes are tested in a testbed, passed and approved through the approval ticketing system, and pushed to production automatically either instantly at each step or at specific maintenance window times based on the requirements.

Automation and SD-WAN

This chapter has already shown how a working CI/CD pipeline can be utilized to facilitate automation of tested and approved changes into production. With Cisco's Catalyst SD-WAN solution, the same principles apply for the Cisco Catalyst SD-WAN Manager, formerly known as vManage. Essentially, everything that may be configured or monitored via the UI in Catalyst SD-WAN Manager is an accessible REST API that may be utilized for automated monitoring and configuring. This makes integrating the SD-WAN solution into a CI/CD pipeline for configuration and test case analysis rather straightforward.

This section looks at automation of the following use case: the enterprise has three cloud-hosted environments for SD-WAN—one for production, one for quality assurance, and one for development. The production environment should always consist only of standardized versions of templates that have been approved through prior testing in the QA environment. If a particular version of a template does not exist in the QA environment, it cannot exist in the production environment. There is one exception to this rule. Because operations may have to make real-time break-fix solutions, an operations correcting template may exist in production, but the service ticket must be prepended to the template name. In all other cases, the name of the template in production must match exactly the QA template name, which includes the version number.

How does a template get into the QA environment and approved? This is where the development environment comes into play. The architects and engineers can put whatever templates are needed for feature development, break-fix analysis, and so on, into the development environment. Whatever they may be working on, the version number of the template in development will always be one iteration higher than the currently approved version in the QA environment. The same rule exists for templates between the QA environment and the development environment: a template in the QA environment must match exactly the same version template in the development environment. Therefore, a developer creates a new version of a template in the development environment. When the developer feels the template is ready to progress to the next level, the QA testing environment, that template is promoted. If the template does not pass testing in QA for whatever reason, it is removed from the QA environment, and the developer is able to continue testing and development in the development environment.

This entire process could be performed manually; however, usage of a CI/CD pipeline improves the management and efficiency of the entire process.

An SD-WAN template may be exported from the development environment Catalyst SD-WAN Manager as a JSON file with an API call. This one file can then be added into a GitHub repository. Once the file is committed into the repository, the CI/CD pipeline tool, such as GitLab, is triggered to initiate the deployment of the template file into the QA environment. Based on the template use case, this could include provisioning of a new SD-WAN Edge with the template attached and various validation steps. Once the QA testing has been completed and the appropriate service tickets are marked as approved, that specific template is promoted to the production environment, again via API calls, making the template available for production usage.

Figure 9-4 shows the workflow for the template as it progresses through the pipeline.

Now that you understand the process, the following pseudocode examples will demonstrate the coding steps required to facilitate the workflow shown in Figure 9-4. It should be noted, as before, the pseudocode is only for illustration purposes and not written in any specific language. In Example 9-3, the developer has created a target test template in the development environment. Now the template itself must be added into the GitHub repository or updated, if appropriate.

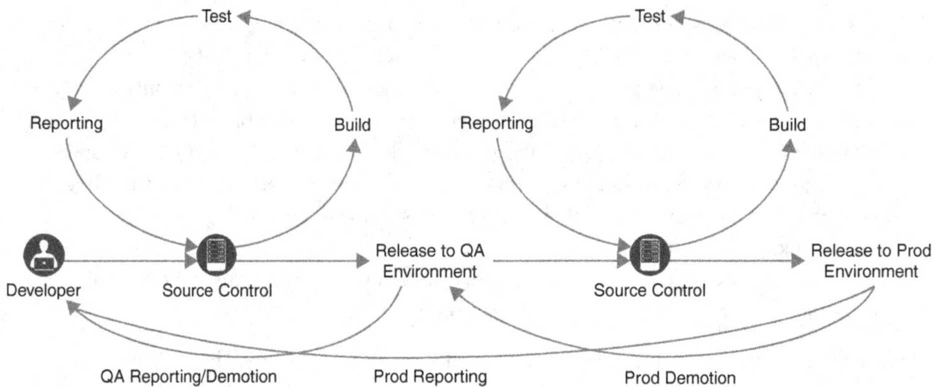

Figure 9-4 *SD-WAN Template CI/CD Pipeline Workflow*

Example 9-3 *Pseudocode for Template Addition to Repository*

```
! Template name may come from an external source
templateName = Load(externalSourceWithName)
! Create an authenticated session to development Catalyst SD-WAN Manager
session = vManage.login()
! Obtain the JSON information required of the template
data = session.DownloadAPI(templateName)
! Add/update the file in the GitHub repository
github.AddFile(data)
! Commit the change to trigger the next phase
github.Commit(message)
!
```

The preceding example shows the pseudocode that could be used to extract an SD-WAN template from the development Catalyst SD-WAN Manager and add it into the GitHub repository. Once the file has been committed, presumably on its own branch, the CI/CD pipeline tool is triggered to move to the next portion of the pipeline. In this use case, the CI/CD pipeline tool would be promoting the template from the development environment to the QA environment. The pseudocode shown in Example 9-4 demonstrates how this could be coded.

Example 9-4 *Pseudocode for Template Promotion*

```
! templateName is known from the filename information
!
! Create an authenticated session to QA Catalyst SD-WAN Manager
session = vManage.login()
! Add the file contents to the Catalyst SD-WAN Manager
session.CreateTemplate(templateName, fileData)
!
```

At this point, the template that was developed by the engineers and architects in the development environment has been added and committed into the GitHub repository, which has triggered the pipeline tool to add the template into the QA environment and has triggered any required test cases associated with the template. These test cases may be carried out via automatic tests configured in the pipeline tool or manually via the QA testers or a combination of both. Regardless of the tests that are carried out, either the template passes, or it does not. In the latter case, the template is removed in the same automated fashion from the QA Catalyst SD-WAN Manager, and the developer is informed of the results to continue development.

If the template does pass the required tests, however, then the same method used in Figure 9-4 to promote the template from development to QA is used to promote the template from QA to production. Notice that because the file is kept in a GitHub repository, only the final committed form of the template (based on the JSON data file) is allowed into the QA and production environments.

While maintaining the SD-WAN templates in a GitHub repository for a CI/CD pipeline is a good illustration of how automation may be leveraged in an SD-WAN environment, it is not the only possible use case. Maintaining the various variable information required for devices across the environment may be tedious and can lead to human errors. Having those data files as part of a CI/CD pipeline and approval process helps reduce production issues arising from copy/paste errors while also providing additional data backup to the Catalyst SD-WAN Managers themselves.

Automation and DMVPN

With the various Cisco IBN architectures, it is rather straightforward to integrate the architecture with the enterprise automation systems due to the well-developed REST API each offers through its various controllers. However, DMVPN does not require any controller for provisioning and operations. As such, the enterprise has to use either NETCONF or RESTCONF directly with the routers or add the routers to some other controller, such as the Cisco Catalyst Center, to abstract the RESTCONF/NETCONF layer with the particular controller. Other options not previously discussed in this chapter are valid, including the use of NSO, for instance. Because other sections of this chapter discuss the various Cisco IBN controllers used with each architecture, this section focuses on usage with NSO. As a future note, Catalyst SD-WAN Manager 20.15 software is expected to support monitoring of autonomous mode routers with later versions also supporting managing the devices. These enhancements will significantly improve automating all of the routers in the environment through a single controller API.

In the previous section with SD-WAN, the development environment, the QA environment, and the production environment each utilized a separate Catalyst SD-WAN Manager deployment. With NSO, a single NSO deployment may be used to manage the different environments simply by providing a different inventory file for each appropriate environment. The inventory files allow the NSO to interact with the devices in the different environments appropriately without affecting the other environments. By adding the inventory files to the repository, the enterprise is now able to utilize the same CI/CD pipeline systems created in other sections to provision a tested and standardized DMVPN solution across the environment.

When an organization is designing the data file structures to store in the repository, current and future enterprise requirements should be considered to make the files more manageable. For instance, when any new solution is implemented into production, there becomes a hybrid state where some sites or devices have been migrated, whereas others have not. Perhaps new hardware or new locations are expected to come online in the future. Or, with DMVPN and macro-segmentation, there may be multiple VRFs that should be supported, though not all VRFs exist at every location. Example 9-5 provides a sample folder structure that illustrates having individual data files within router and site-specific folders. The entire folder structure is added into the file repository; then, whenever there is an update to a file in the folder, the runner initiates the provisioning, test, and approval workflows as required.

Example 9-5 *Sample DMVPN Data Folder Structure*

```
.
├── site1
│   ├── router1.yml
│   └── router2.yml
├── site2
│   └── router3.yml
└── site3
    └── router4.yml
!
```

While the preceding figure folder structure indicates using YAML files for the data variable information, the enterprise could use any variable file format, such as CSV, based on their requirements.

Automation and ACI

The APIC APIs have been continually developed and improved over the years since the advent of ACI. This has led to significant contributions in open-source tools and SDKs for automating ACI.

One of the best systems for utilizing a CI/CD pipeline is through the Terraform ACI provider. With Terraform, the entire ACI environment—for instance, the bridge domains, contexts, tenants, and networks—is maintained in Terraform data files. Terraform initialization creates a Terraform state file on the current state of the deployed environment. When the user or system deploys a change in the environment, Terraform obtains the current actual state of the environment, compares the actual state and the desired state, and makes the necessary changes to have the desired state in production.

This system not only ensures that the intended standard is deployed, but it also corrects manual changes that may have been introduced incorrectly. Interestingly, if Terraform is unaware of a tenant or other object deployed in ACI, Terraform will not delete that object, allowing the enterprise to make some manual additions if required with overwriting them.

Imagine a multi-tenant ACI environment where each tenant is perhaps an end client of the enterprise. As clients are brought onboard and others are leaving, it is necessary to automate the creation of the environment and ensure proper deletion later, if necessary. Terraform will read every file in the folder with the correct file extensions (.tf, .tfvar). Therefore, each individual tenant may be maintained in its own Terraform data file that includes the entire ACI environment for that client. When the file is added into the file repository, the commit triggers the CI/CD pipeline to initiate the Terraform workflow to apply in the target environment. Terraform uses the ACI provider type to connect to APIC and deploy the new state. Once automated testing and validation are completed, the pipeline can move to the next phase to obtain approval prior to deploying in subsequent test environments or production. Example 9-6 illustrates how a single tenant with a single network might look in a Terraform data file, as well as the Terraform code required to deploy it.

Example 9-6 *Sample Terraform File*

```
provider "aci" {
    username     = "theuser"
    password     = "thepassword"
    url          = "https://theapic.domain.com"
    insecure     = true
}
resource "aci_tenant" "tenant1" {
    name         = "TheTenant"
    description = "ACI Tenant for Client 1"
}
resource "aci_vrf" "vrf1" {
    tenant_dn    = "${aci_tenant.tenant1.id}"
    name         = "Client1-VRF"
}
resource "aci_bridge_domain" "bd1" {
    tenant_dn            = "${aci_tenant.tenant1.id}"
    relation_fv_rs_ctx = "${aci_vrf.vrf1.name}"
    name                 = "BD1-Name"
}
resource "aci_subnet" "subnet1" {
    bridge_domain_dn     = "${aci_bridge_domain.bd1.name}"
    name                 = "BD1-Subnet"
    ip                   = "192.0.2.1/24"
}
resource "aci_application_profile" "app1" {
    tenant_dn            = "${aci_tenant.tenant1.id}"
    name                 = "App1-Profile"
}
resource "aci_application_epg" "epg1" {
    application_profile_dn = "${aci_application_profile.app1.id}"
    name                   = "web"
    relation_fv_rs_bd      = "${aci_bridge_domain.bd1.name}"
}
```

The enterprise can take this simple initial file and extend it with both variable substitution and looping, as well as additional ACI feature support to create a fully automated and CI/CD-incorporated ACI environment complete with development, test, and production environments. Obviously, it is recommended that credential information and other sensitive information not be stored in any file that is part of the repository. Therefore, the username, password, and server information would be expected to be provided via environment variables, for instance, instead of manually configured as shown here. This example is strictly for illustrative purposes only.

Automation Across Multiple Domains

As with all design questions for multi-domain architectures, it is often best considered when broken down into the constituent domains. For instance, consider an enterprise environment with ACI, SDA, and SD-WAN. The enterprise has macrosegmentation for each line of business that is extended from ACI through SD-WAN out to SDA. A new line of business is being planned, and the network must be provisioned accordingly.

For ACI, the environment will require a new tenant with new VRFs, bridge domains, networks, and so on, as shown in the previous section; perhaps this requires a new Terraform file in the repository to create the multiple objects. Meanwhile, SD-WAN will require a new Service VPN template that then must be attached to device templates at sites A, B, and C. Therefore, the SDA environments at sites A, B, and C must have the new SDA virtual network provisioned at those locations complete with end host IP subnets and multicast support.

If the individual domain automation pieces have already been set up, this becomes a simple matter of designing the CI/CD pipeline to perform additional provisioning and testing that incorporates all three domains at each phase.

With multiple systems and controllers utilized, all with their own unique API calls, keeping the automation segmented based on the domains is a viable option, keeping in mind that simplifying where possible is also recommended. For instance, data that is used by all the domains may be best to exist in a single data file instead of in unique data files for each domain to prevent accidental copy/paste errors.

Summary

Automation is a wide-open topic that improves operations, as well as standardization and validation. There are numerous directions and usages for automation across all of the domains. These may all be facilitated by the usage of a CI/CD pipeline and Infrastructure as Code. In this chapter, we discussed how scripts, and workflows for SD-Access, SD-WAN and ACI help with simplified operations for those environments. It is understood that controllers are primarily focused on specific domains, however, with CI/CD pipelines and workflows, they can all be tied together for a larger intent-based networking. The possibilities are endless; this idea is just scratching the surface of multi-domain integration with automation.

Chapter 10

Manufacturing Use Case with SDA, SD-WAN, and CNF

In this chapter, we discuss the following:

- The requirements of a typical manufacturing plant and the resources it needs to be able to function
- How multiple technologies can be integrated seamlessly and be sustainable for long periods of time
- Faster troubleshooting and operationalization
- How to deal with various product SKUs and their integration in a typical manufacturing plant

Use Case Overview

We authors got an opportunity to work on a large transformational deal for a manufacturing entity. This case study is derived from a successful deployment of such a network transformation, and it is suitable for this book because it covers the integration of multi-domain technologies such as Cisco SD-Access, Cisco SD-WAN, and Carrier Neutral Facilities (CNFs). In this chapter, we discuss the business and technical requirements, along with the solutions that satisfy these requirements, and deliver the outcome that has proven to be a great success. This case study is a real-world deployment of fully integrated technology. Using this design as a framework, such solutions can be deployed with added features and with little variances in terms of hardware, routing protocols, and technologies being used. The most important part is to understand the business function and how an organization needs to segment the traffic and let it flow within the organization. One of the biggest outcomes of this transformation was to convert a company's IT organization from a cost center to a revenue-generating organization with the IT as a Business model. This transformation has reaped rewards for the current organization, and we hope this case study will inspire new and transformed networks.

Summary of Requirements

Manufacturing industries have vastly different requirements for network architecture. Regardless of what products are being manufactured—consumer goods, electronics, industrial machines, or medicines—the overall logic is the same at a very high level. Raw material comes in from one end and gets processed by various sets of machines that assemble and produce a final product. Today, a majority of industries are very high tech in nature. Many of their machines are equipped with sensors and cameras that constantly monitor production, and with the help of that telemetry data, production pace or settings can be changed to affect final product quality or quantity.

Because machines are designed around the specific products they are manufacturing, they are highly customized and have different types of data and applications running them. These applications usually talk directly with the machines and, in most cases, reside in the same VLAN as the machines. There is a large amount of Layer 2 communication between them. These individual machines and their applications are considered operational technology (OT). Because a company's revenue is directly tied with the production of goods, this network environment becomes highly critical and needs to be secured.

The design of manufacturing networks has evolved over the years, with the major difference being physical versus logical design. Historically, to prevent security breaches and provide the highest amount of uptime in the network, manufacturing networks (OT networks) were physically isolated from corporate networks (IT networks). All OT networks were joined to the IT side via a firewall to ensure security and uptime. OT networks did not change much, and most relied on a "configure once and forget" type architecture, and proper maintenance and patching of the network equipment were not as frequent as on the IT side. With the advancement in high-performance switches and routers and organizations achieving their sustainability goals, corporations have started to leverage virtualization on the network gear that provides similar security and maximizes their hardware footprint in the intermediate distribution frames (IDFs). These solutions have become more integrated as well as controller-driven.

The following sections in this chapter identify some of the critical business and technical requirements in the manufacturing industry and how multi-domain solutions are able to solve them. Each industry vertical has its own requirements to ensure the business runs as efficiently as possible. The overall goal of the network architecture is to ensure that manufacturing uptime is as high as possible, and network maintenance should be proactive rather than reactive. This ensures better predictability, and business can pivot well ahead in time. For example, if a manufacturing plant in the region needs heavy maintenance requiring two weeks of downtime in one production line due to an issue, knowing that fact ahead of time can help the business plan to offset production goals to another region's manufacturing plant while that maintenance is carried out. This solution ensures constant production and loads can be shared. This solution would have been very difficult if that particular issue had not been diagnosed ahead of time and the machine had halted unexpectedly. Business cannot just shift production of a line to other plants without planning ahead because a lot depends on the complex logistics of raw materials and finished goods and also the workforce that is involved in producing those goods. Getting that early insight is critical now, and it is one of the foremost considerations in any manufacturing industry.

Today, the production lines producing high-tech goods have very high downtime costs. Some can go upwards of millions of dollars an hour in lost production time and personnel costs. A major outage in a production line could impact the supply of incoming raw materials to outgoing goods that are being hauled by trucks. There can never be a perfect running score for a production line, but by ensuring that all the critical components of the production lines are monitored via sensors and any digital devices, a near-perfect score could be achieved. The better the score, the better the production and more predictable outcomes and operations.

The case study in this chapter is not tied to a specific industry. However, it does focus on some of the higher-value goods that are being produced. Continuous production is critical due to demand. Fundamentally, there are two types of requirements: business and technical. These two are set by different stakeholders, and different types of solution components are mapped to them. For this scenario, we focus on how Cisco SD-Access, SD-WAN, and CNF have been integrated to provide seamless end-to-end connectivity. This use case also focuses on the use of automation to drive successful deployment of these new solution domains.

Business Requirements and Solution Mapping

Business requirements drive business outcomes. As the name suggests, they are directed and governed by the business. They are more strategic in nature and focus on growth of the business and impact the finances and reputation of the organization. For this case study, Table 10-1 showcases the business requirements of this organization and the mapped solutions for those requirements.

Table 10-1 *Business Requirements*

Requirement	Solution
Infrastructure is needed to support the business in growing to a multi-tenant model, producing goods for different business-to-business end consumers.	Deployed solutions of SD-Access, SD-WAN, and CNFs are all multi-tenant capable.
The organization needs to adopt to the industry of the future with scale and support for automated and remote-guided vehicles.	Deployed solutions target a wireless-first strategy with high-capacity fabric-enabled wireless.
A highly resilient network infrastructure is needed to provide 99.999 percent availability.	The deployed solution utilizes underlay and overlay architecture with subsecond failover. Additionally, with the use of automation, this deployment reduces human error responsible for outages.

Requirement	Solution
The addition of rogue and unmanaged devices is needed across the manufacturing plant.	Standardization of product SKUs and the utilization of dot1x across the network infrastructure will assist in restricting the addition of unmanaged and unsecured devices into the network.
Network data needs to be captured in real time to provide preemptive support and reduce reactive support.	A controller-based architecture will assist in the collection of critical data from the network and facilitate the operations team to be more proactive in issue resolution.
Device and network maintenance across IT or OT infrastructure should not impact each other's operations but should ensure highest uptime.	This solution is a highly resilient chassis-based underlay and overlay architecture. Routed underlay provides the fastest convergence, and the overlay architecture is highly serviceable and enables the organization to add additional services and networks without impacting other virtual networks.
The network needs to be sustainable in terms of its energy footprint.	The deployed solution uses chassis-based highly resilient and efficient hardware. Today's emerging technology can leverage such hardware and, using virtualization on top, can build multiple virtual networks, further reducing the requirement of dedicated equipment. Current high-performance hardware with software-defined technologies ensures macro- and microsegmentation of networks on the same physical devices.

Technical Requirements and Solution Mapping

Technical requirements deliver the outcome of business requirements. These requirements are more tactical in nature. After the business requirements are determined, they set the foundation for the technical requirements. The implementation of the technical requirements is the final outcome of the business requirements. For this case study, the requirements described in Table 10-2 are technical. There are a lot more of them because they map to many of the business and solution requirements and vice versa.

Table 10-2 *Technical Requirements*

Requirement	Solution
Highly resilient infrastructure	An overlay- and underlay-based architecture provides the highest resiliency and business continuity with low convergence time.
Highly redundant infrastructure	All critical devices are paired with similar devices for full and complete redundancy, including power supplies and redundant links.

Requirement	Solution
Highly serviceable infrastructure	Decoupling design from the underlay and overlay architecture will allow for the addition of new services without impacting the existing production environment.
Highly scalable infrastructure	Fabric-based and controller-driven architecture provides a flexible growth model without a major impact to the network.
Leverage automation for day-0 to day-N operations	Controller-based architecture provides automation capabilities for day-0 to day-N operations.
Network visibility	Controllers provide assurance data and network insights.
Securing the IT and OT network with firewalls	The deployed solution includes logically separating IT and OT networks into distinct routing planes while using the same physical infrastructure. Any traffic leaving or entering the OT routing plane must route through the firewalls, maintaining secure macrosegmentation.
Device upgrades should limit the impact on the network	The deployed solution isolates cross-device dependency. All devices are active-active in data forwarding and can converge with subsecond failover. The Spanning Tree Protocol has been removed from the equation.
Separation of IT, OT, and Guest networks	IT, OT, and Guest networks are logically separated in separate routing planes, leveraging common physical infrastructure.
Support for 40G, 100G, and 400G links for high-capacity throughput from access to backbone	The deployed solution accounts for high-capacity links using the latest available Catalyst 9000X series switches.
Connectivity to cloud and Internet should traverse via CNFs	All sites are connected via SD-WAN with headends being in CNF for most direct connectivity to cloud and Internet access.
Dot1x- and MAB-based NAC to be deployed	ISE is configured with NAC and TrustSec to leverage dot1x- and MAB-based authentication. Additionally, SGTs are imposed on the endpoints for identity-based access control.
Partner and vendor connectivity to be terminated in the DMZ of CNF	A separate DMZ domain is created in CNF to terminate all partner and vendor connections.

Deployed Solution

The business and technical requirements listed in Tables 10-1 and 10-2 show the foundation and roadmap to the solution that is being deployed. Based on those requirements, the solution deployed on the LAN, or campus, side is Cisco's SD-Access; on the WAN side, it is Cisco's SD-WAN. To ensure uniformity across all the manufacturing sites in terms of data access and retrieval, all the sites are connected via CNFs across the globe. This will completely transform the network and enable this organization to run the IT as a Business for all of its manufacturing divisions. To aid in faster deployment and consistency across the entire network from day-0 to day-N, automation has been considered across all solution domains.

Figure 10-1 shows how all the solution domains come together to form an end-to-end segmented multi-domain network. Let's briefly discuss each of the solution domains and how they were designed to address the business and technical requirements. One of the critical points to remember is that the deployed solution in this case study is highly flexible and scalable. This was one of the key requirements. Regardless of the size of the plant—100,000 sq ft to 4,000,000 sq ft—the architecture remains the same. The only change is the quantity and type of equipment being used. All of the current generation of Cisco equipment is built with unified operating systems in mind, so regardless of the product number in the family (Catalyst, Nexus, and so on), they will be able to perform identically. Just the scale numbers are different in terms of capacity and throughput.

SD-Access

For SD-Access architecture, we reference Figure 10-2. Here, the SD-Access solution has a significant advantage in terms of automation, sustainability, and highly modular architecture. With one of the significant advantages being to be able to utilize the same sets of physical devices for OT and IT parts of the network, an organization is able to maximize their return on investment (ROI) and also achieve sustainability goals by reducing the amount of physical equipment. A fabric-based architecture utilizes virtualization on the physical switches. With that, it increases serviceability and the ability to add on new virtual networks and VLANs without impacting other overlay networks. This flexibility is vital when an organization is trying to achieve 99.999 percent of uptime for its production.

Access Layer Architecture

Figure 10-2 shows a typical three-tier architecture for core, distribution, and access. Starting from the bottom, an intermediate distribution frame (IDF) architecture has been standardized. All IDFs include Catalyst 9400 series chassis-based switches. They provide flexibility in terms of line cards containing UPoE+ as well as fiber-based ports. All the endpoints directly connect to these switches. The advantage of a chassis-based architecture is the ability to expand as needed and, also, maintenance. With redundant supervisor engines, resiliency is maintained. The UPoE ports on the switches are used to connect Wi-Fi 6E access points providing mGig connectivity. This satisfies their Wi-Fi-first strategy. With the port density and adequate power supplies on Catalyst 9400 series switches, their wireless infrastructure provides ample coverage, even in brownout conditions. This solution was designed with port priority in mind, which will selectively power down the access points so that an entire section of the network is not in a blackout mode.

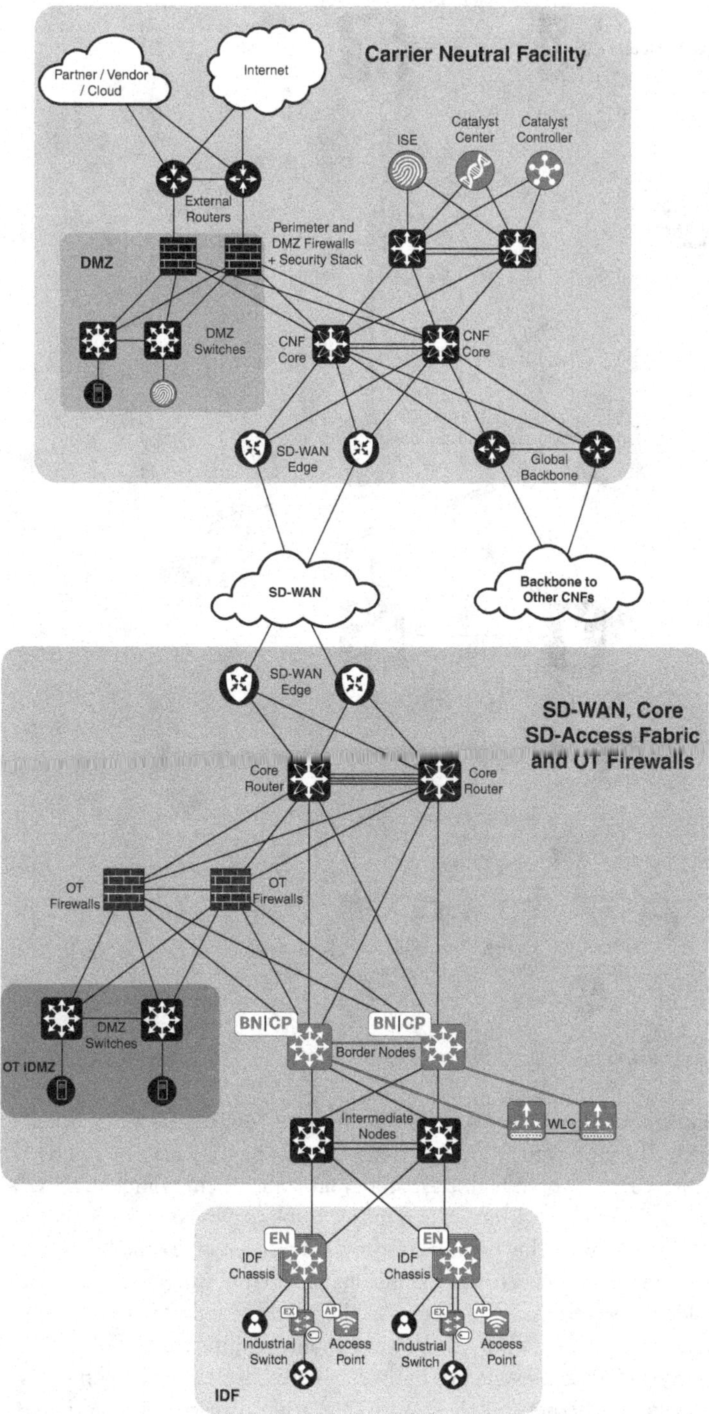

Figure 10-1 *High-Level Multi-Domain Architecture*

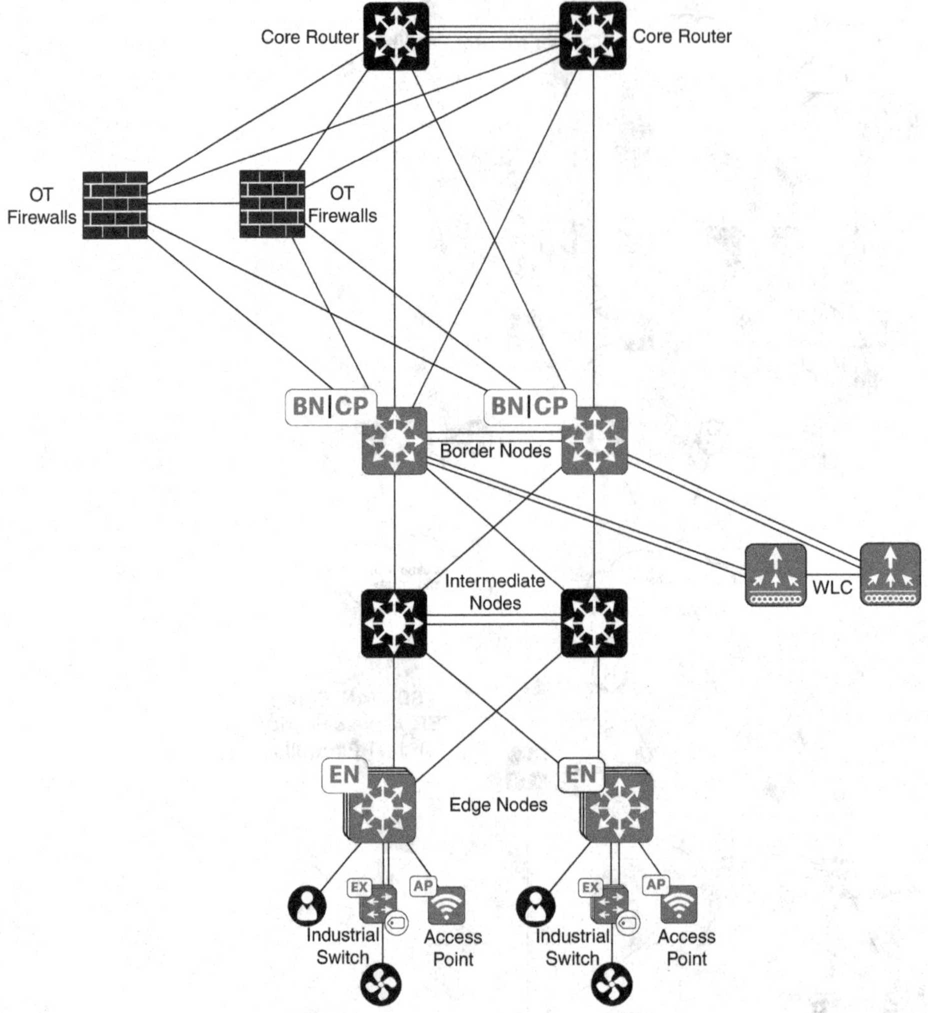

Figure 10-2 *SD-Access Architecture*

A manufacturing plant of any magnitude requires some form of ruggedized networking equipment. This is due to the environment these devices are put in; they may be exposed to high heat, cold temperatures, or even high dust and/or an abrasive environment. Cisco's Industrial Ethernet switches are state of the art and meant to be deployed in nonstandard conditions. Manufacturing plants of this organization were no different. These IE switches were deployed in the machines and acted as extensions of the IDF where a clean room for regular Catalyst 9000 series switches was not possible. All these industrial switches were PoE capable and also were able to provide power to some remote access points. The fiber ports on the Catalyst 9400 series switches in the IDFs provided backhaul connectivity to the deployed Industrial Ethernet switches. With this, a star topology was designed for the extended network.

From a security perspective, the entire network was dot1x enabled with a centralized network access control (NAC) engine. For NAC, Cisco's Identity Services Engine (ISE) was used. Dot1x provided perimeter security to all the endpoints that ended up connected via wired or wireless to the network, regardless of the network domain they were in—IT or OT. Knowing the OT and IoT side of the network, not all endpoints were dot1x capable. For such endpoints, MAC Authentication Bypass (MAB) was selected as a second option when do1x fails. The network and security team conducted an exercise ahead of time to identify all the endpoints that were not dot1x capable, and a database of known or trusted endpoint MAC addresses was created. This database was then referenced by ISE when dot1x failed, and the device went on to authenticate via MAB. Securing the network starts at the source. If the edge network is not protected, then it becomes difficult to enforce rogue traffic when it already has access to the network. This perimeter security was the foundational first line of defense. This model also provided someone connecting a rogue 8-port unmanaged switch to temporarily expand the network. This way, all network changes were controlled, and unwanted organic growth was drastically reduced.

Core and Distribution Layer Architecture

The distribution layer (also known as the intermediate layer) in SD-Access functions as an aggregation layer, where access layer switches from all IDFs and small closets are aggregated to a set of devices. Because the underlay network is all routed infrastructure, there was no need to consider any potential issues with VLANs and spanning tree. With the routed links, Equal Cost Multipath (ECMP) was used, and to ensure subsecond convergence in the event of a link failure, Bidirectional Forwarding Detection (BFD) timers of 300 milliseconds (times three) were used on the links. The only major difference with the distribution layer is the type and the quantity of the platform used to aggregate all those links and capacity. With the requirement of 40G bandwidth from access to distribution, all the access layer switches in the IDFs were provisioned with dual 40G uplinks to the distribution switches—one to each distribution switch. For large manufacturing plants, Catalyst 9600—chassis-based—switches were used to aggregate all the links from the access layers. In some plants, there were multiple buildings, so a second pair of distribution switches was needed to reduce the number of spanned fibers from one building to another. In the medium-sized plants, a 48-port Catalyst 9500 switch was used. And lastly, in small plants, sometimes there was no requirement for distribution switches because there were few access layer switches that connected directly to the border nodes. Regardless of the model of the distribution switches, careful consideration was made to ensure the uplinks from distribution to the border nodes were at the minimum of 100G per port for small and medium plants and 400G per port for large plants.

Border nodes are a gateway for all traffic coming in and going out of the fabric. The deployed solution had three virtual networks (VNs): IT, OT, and Guest. At a minimum, these three VNs were configured at all manufacturing sites. Fabric border nodes handed off these VNs to different parts of the networks. As shown in Figure 10-3, the IT VN from the border node was handed off directly to the backbone router. These routers were essentially high-performance Catalyst 9500 series switches that provided 100G or 400G connectivity to the fabric and were designed to function as a high-speed traffic aggregation point. The IT VN from the border node was dropped into the global routing table (GRT) of the backbone routers.

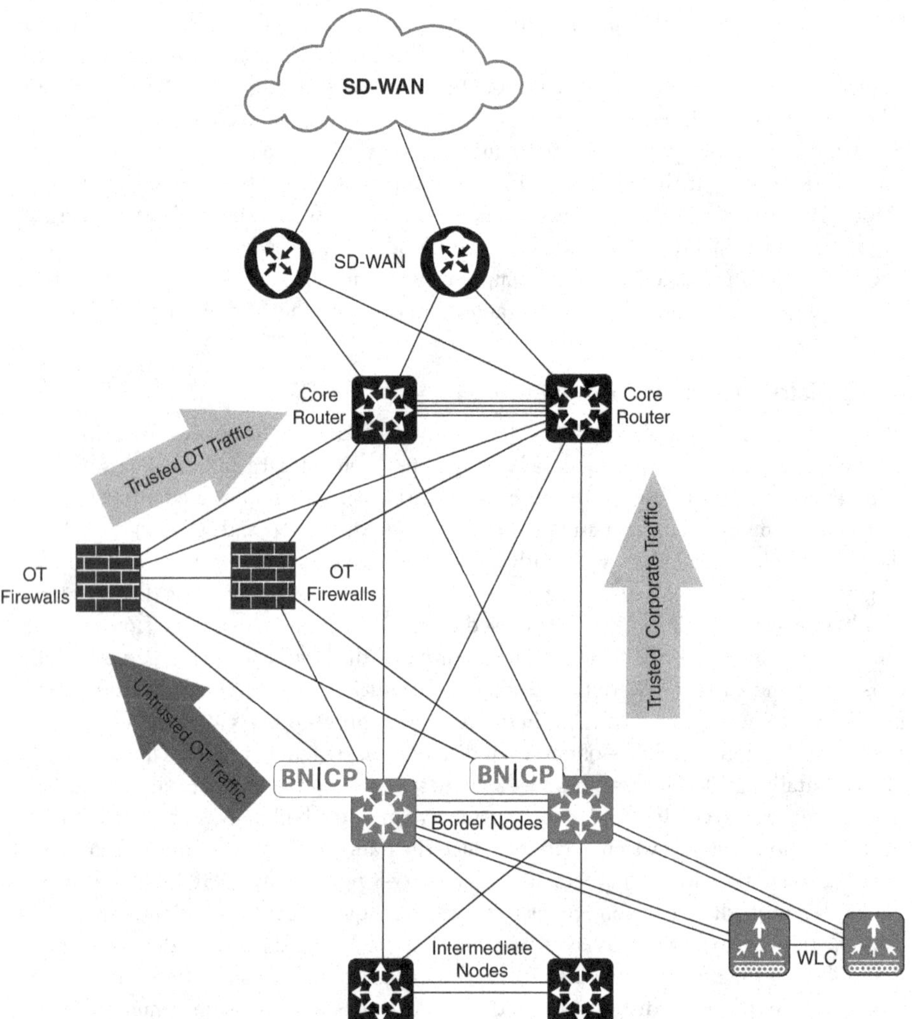

Figure 10-3 *Core and Distribution Layer*

The OT network, by compliance and security policy, has to traverse through the firewalls. These firewalls are connected to the border nodes and backbone router. The OT VN from the border nodes offloads all the OT traffic to these firewalls, where it is inspected and firewalled. The scrubbed traffic then traverses the links to the backbone router and gets merged into the global routing table. This is the only point in the entire network of the site where IT and OT traffic are traversing in the same routing plane. For Internet access, all corporate traffic—OT and IT—will be backhauled to the CNF and will pass through the security stack for inspection.

The Guest network has its own use case. There is no need for guest traffic to access any internal corporate resources. Hence, it is backhauled directly to SD-WAN Edge, where SD-WAN Edge will leverage direct Internet access (DIA) to offload guest traffic directly to the Internet. This guest traffic handoff will use a VRF-Lite approach and will have direct BGP peering between border nodes and SD-WAN Edge. In this scenario, the backbone router will act as a pure Layer 2 switch and pass the traffic between the border nodes and SD-WAN Edge. Figure 10-4 shows a block diagram of routing among different components of the core and distribution networks.

Wireless Architecture

One key business requirement for this use case was to have wireless-first architecture for all of the manufacturing plants. The three fundamental pillars of the wireless-first architecture are

- Wireless coverage and RF design
- The predominant use of Wi-Fi 6 or 5 GHz where possible
- The utilization of mGig capabilities of access points for maximum data throughput

Wireless coverage is essential because black holes could cause significant problems when it comes to manufacturing floors. Many pieces of equipment, such as automated guided vehicles (AGVs), may stop functioning if they lose their wireless signal, causing a business disruption. The transformed network is highly resilient, and this network infrastructure requires an equally robust wireless infrastructure. Additionally, with RF design, considerations have been made to utilize access points with external antennas that can be either omni or directional antennas to cover a long aisle with heavy metal racks on both sides. Consideration has also been made to account for industrial-grade ruggedized access points that are needed at high vibration, dust, or heat areas and still provide required coverage.

These state-of-the-art access points support multiple frequencies like 2.4 GHz, 5 GHz, and also 6 GHz. The deployed solution utilized 6 GHz where possible and 5 GHz as an alternative, avoiding 2.4 GHz frequency altogether. The organization set a directive to ensure that all new equipment being connected to this network must support 6 GHz or 5 GHz frequency to ensure consistency as well as reliability.

Utilizing mGig ports for access point connectivity enables wireless infrastructure to push traffic at 5G speeds on the proposed switches. With the use of mGig there is also a design consideration of how to configure wireless infrastructure. Using CAPWAP mode on the access points is not recommended because the amount of traffic being pushed from the APs will easily overpower wireless controllers that are not designed to push traffic at 100G or more.

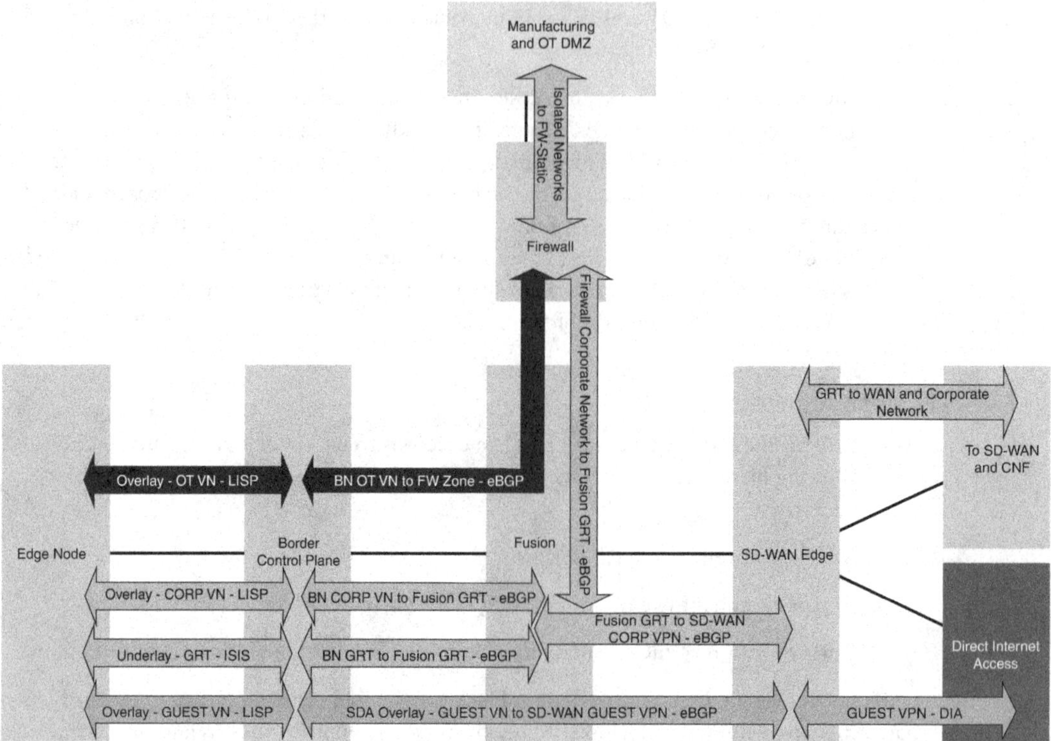

Figure 10-4 *Routing Block Diagram Between Border Nodes and SD-WAN Edge Routers*

Wireless LAN controllers (WLC) are another critical component that will be connected directly to the border node. These nodes are scaled for the number of access points rather than the capacity. With the Fabric-Enabled Wireless (FEW) architecture, there is no need to backhaul all data plane traffic to the wireless LAN controllers. All the traffic will be offloaded by access points to their respective switches in right VNs using VXLAN. All the enforcement will happen at the access layer switches. These WLCs will have a CAPWAP tunnel to all the access points for management and authentication.

As shown in Figure 10-5, the controllers will be connected directly to the border nodes of the campus fabric where they provide direct connectivity to the access points. The WLCs are in HA mode and connected to the border node, each with a port channel to a single border node for link redundancy. WLC uplinks will be dual 40G with 10G direct back-to-back connectivity between each other for HA.

For high resiliency, all access points will be connected to two different switch chassis within the same IDF. Additionally, the switch ports will be configured with the power-shed feature, which will set different priorities of the interfaces based on the location of the access points. In the event of the loss of a single power supply or a power feed, only selective APs will be shut down to prevent blackouts.

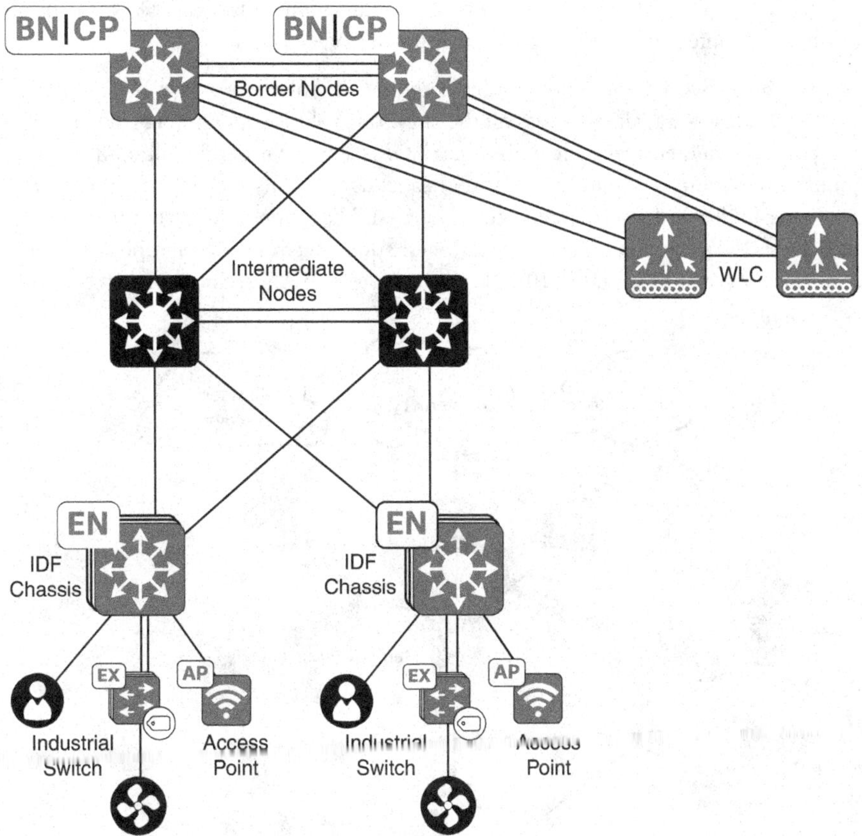

Figure 10-5 *Wireless Architecture*

SD-WAN

SD-WAN Edge is an essential component of any site because it provides connectivity to the rest of the corporate infrastructure. For the deployed solution, Cisco's SD-WAN provided macrosegmented network architecture.

As shown in Figure 10-6, the SD-WAN Edge routers are Catalyst 8000 series SD-WAN Edge routers supporting various bandwidths from 10G to 100G based on the sites where they are being deployed. These chassis are redundant and will be configured with two critical VRFs. The first VRF is the internal VRF providing connectivity to the campus core and other domains of the network. This will be a trusted zone, and all the traffic will traverse between the campus core, SD-WAN, and perimeter firewalls. The second VRF is a Guest VRF, and the purpose of that VRF is to terminate the Guest VN from the SD-Access fabric and offload that to the Internet transport using direct Internet access (DIA). This is critical because there is no requirement to backhaul guest Internet traffic to centralized Internet access. However, because the guest user authentication is provided by the ISE that is located in an Internet DMZ in the CNFs, only ISE-specific prefixes are allowed over the guest overlay to all the sites. The default route in the guest VN is generated locally and pointed to local Internet transit for that VN.

SD-WAN for this network is simplified but effective. With only two overlay VPNs—Corporate and Guest—transiting across all the sites, this solution plays a big role in simplifying operations and ensuring the highest uptime. The WAN is highly hub-and-spoke per region. Each region has a pair of SD-WAN headends that fully mesh with all regional sites. Any inter-region traffic is handed off to the CNFs' backbone router that forms a ring with other CNFs for data access. This hub-and-spoke network is then replicated to all the regions for scalability. Figure 10-7 shows the overall WAN architecture.

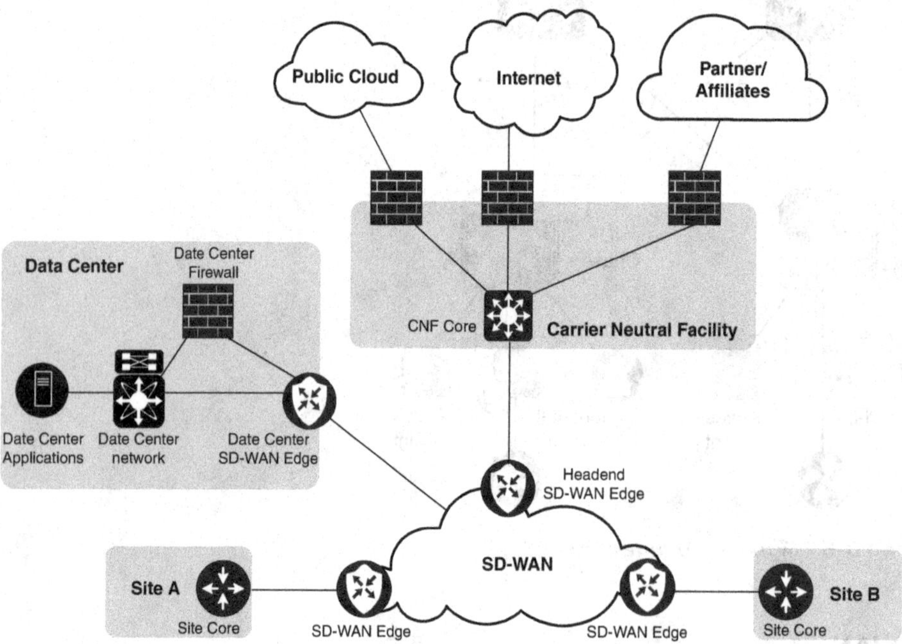

Figure 10-6 *Regional WAN Architecture*

Carrier Neutral Facilities (CNFs)

In this deployed case study, the Carrier Neutral Facilities act as regional hubs to aggregate and process all regional traffic. As shown in Figure 10-7, each region—Americas (AMER), Europe, Middle East, and Africa (EMEA), and Asia Pacific, Japan, and China (APJC)—had dual CNFs that connected in a ring format. The inter-links between CNFs did not need to be as high capacity as sites. Hence, they were provisioned with 10G bandwidth between each hub as compared to 100G or 400G at local sites. One of the major reasons for low bandwidth between the backbone routers was localization of traffic flow. To reduce cross-regional traffic throughput due to high latency and long-run fiber costs, bulk traffic (such as cloud, Internet, and VPN) was offloaded via local CNFs. Predominant cross-CNF traffic consisted of local application sync and cross-regional backups. Hence, there was no need to have more than 10G of backbone connectivity between CNFs.

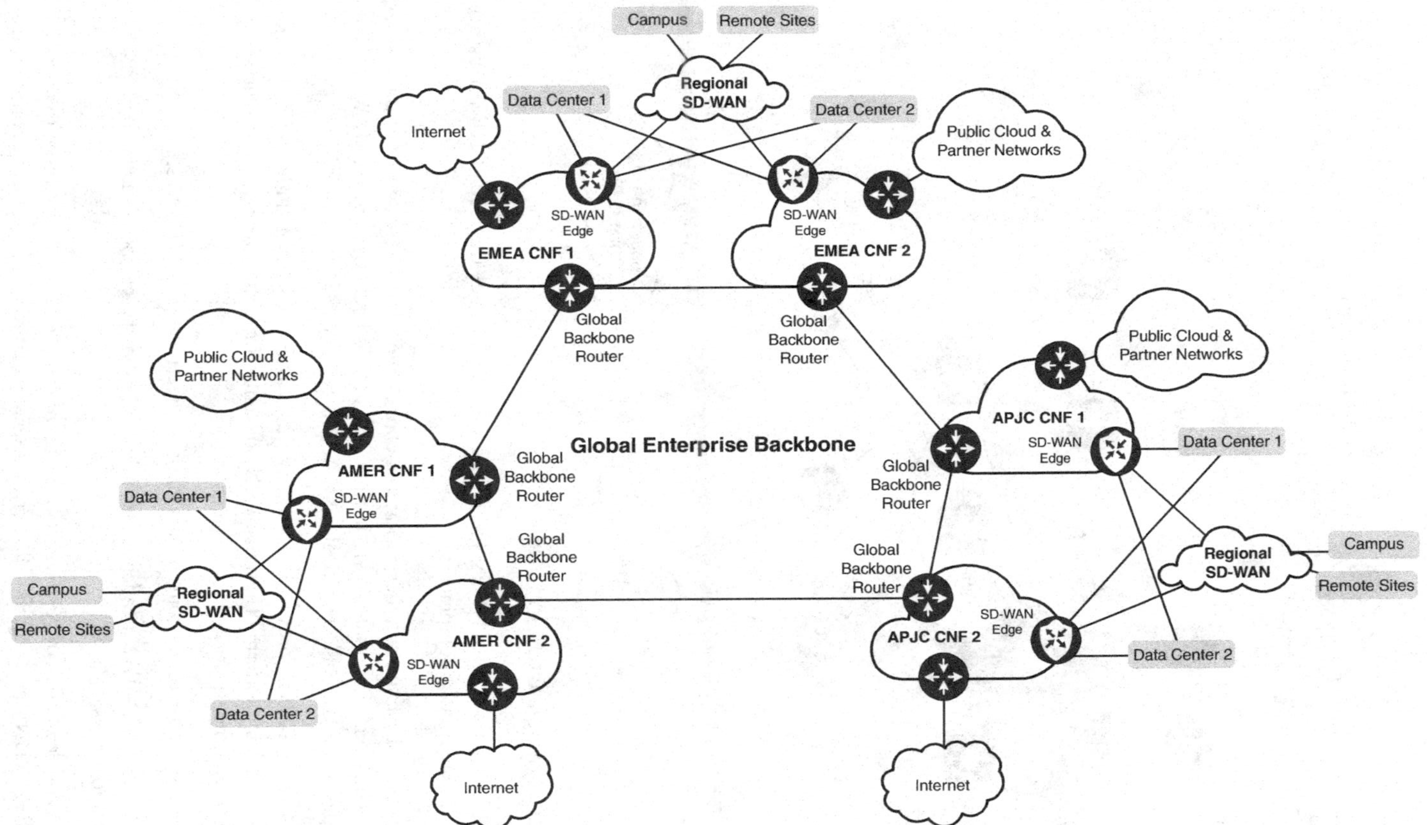

Figure 10-7 *Global WAN Architecture*

Figure 10-8 looks deeper into a single-CNF architecture.

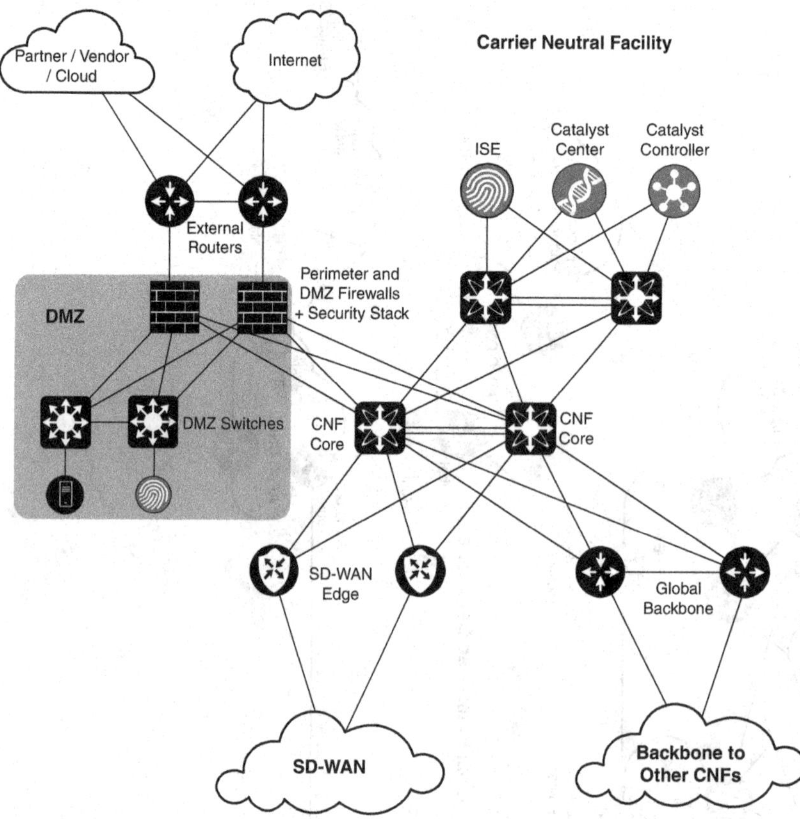

Figure 10-8 *Single-CNF Architecture*

Looking deeper at the CNF level in Figure 10-8, we can see that each CNF consists of the following set of equipment:

- A pair of Nexus switches acting as a core of the CNF. These switches will connect to different components within the CNF, such as backbone router, SD-WAN Edge, perimeter firewalls, and local CNF Access switches.
- A set of devices providing a security stack. These devices include DMZ switches, internal and external firewalls, VPN concentrator, secure web gateway, and ISE for guest authentication.
- A pair of backbone routers providing connectivity to other CNFs.
- A pair of SD-WAN headends providing hub-and-spoke connectivity to all the remote sites.
- A couple of pairs of Nexus access layer switches providing connectivity to internal ISE, DHCP, DNS, and other mission-critical servers that require low-latency connectivity.

- A pair of external routers that terminate all external links such as Internet, partner connectivity, and cloud connectivity.

This design is highly modular and replicable. The other five CNFs in the network are exactly identical and provide a similar level of connectivity. The way routing is configured between these CNFs, in the event that one CNF fails, others can take over the traffic immediately. There are some restrictions, such as the Internet sessions that rely on Network Address Translation (NAT); if that fails, the sessions have to be re-established. To limit that possibility, each CNF has dual high-capacity Internet connections with the organization's own public IP space. This provides Network Address Translation across the region, and traffic movement is seamless across the same CNF.

Automation Strategy

The deployed network is highly scalable, resilient, and flexible, but a good level of understanding is required to operate it efficiently. This is not a traditional flat network although there are network controllers that are responsible for deploying individual domains. Network operation is more involved than that. Especially day-2 operations. Every time a new VLAN or a VN needs to be created, many steps are involved—from configuring Cisco Catalyst Center, Catalyst SD-WAN Manager, ISE, to other non-controller managed devices. This particular use case provided us with a great opportunity to build a workflow-based framework that ran small scripts and application programming interface (API) calls to various controllers and deploy the desired intent.

The high-level block diagram in Figure 10-9 shows what the intent-based network deployment looks like. Here, individual technologies and solutions need to be either directly configured via CLI or via some form of a controller. For example, SD-Access uses Catalyst Center to configure all Catalyst switches and wireless infrastructure; Catalyst SD-WAN Manager configures all SD-WAN infrastructure, ISE, and traditional IOS-XE switches and routers; and Nexus switches need to be configured directly. Firepower firewalls can be configured via Firepower Management Console (FMC); similarly, Palo Alto firewalls are configured and managed by Panorama.

By utilizing some simple Ansible playbooks and Python scripts, we can create an intent-based workflow. This workflow determines simple operational tasks such as creating a VLAN or an access control list. These can be executed so that an order of operation can be followed and all relevant controllers can be configured via API calls. For the devices that are not managed via APIs, an automated script can be run to configure devices that are not managed by any form of controllers. This method drives standardization and operational efficiency, and most importantly, to achieve 99.999 percent, it reduces the human error element, ensuring all change controls execute without any impact to the network.

Security

For any network transformation, network security is paramount. It is implied that with any network transformation, security is a given consideration. However, when it comes to the network security of manufacturing plants, more than just the network access needs to be validated. With regards to security at a typical manufacturing facility, it has been divided into two parts: first the perimeter, IT DMZ, and OT DMZ; and second, NAC and microsegmentation.

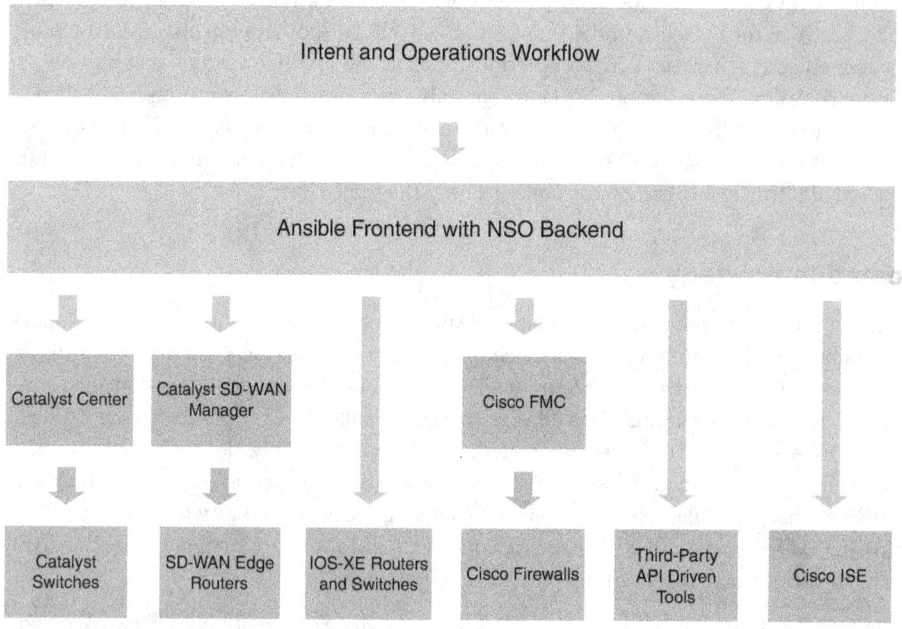

Figure 10-9 *Automation Block Diagram*

Perimeter, IT, and OT DMZ

Perimeter security prevents unauthorized access to the network from outside of the organization. This is determined by placing firewalls at the perimeter. For this organization, corporate users and endpoint traffic needing Internet access were backhauled to the regional CNF. This design considered a regionalized security stack to inspect the traffic and firewall as necessary. Any vendors and organization employees needing remote access to the organization's network use VPN termination to the nearest regional CNF. Their Internet traffic is also backhauled to the CNF and then uses a centralized security stack for inspection and enforcement. For guest Internet, the deployed solution did not need to inspect the guest traffic due to low volume and complete traffic isolation. Hence, all the guest Internet traffic was offloaded directly to the SD-WAN Edge routers using the direct Internet access feature. Figure 10-10 shows this high-level perimeter security architecture.

IT Internet DMZ is required to host certain applications and servers in the isolated space. These applications are to be determined and are inclusive of partner and IT security stack components. There are dedicated 1 RU high-performance switches that will provide DMZ connectivity. As shown in Figure 10-11, these switches will be connected to perimeter firewalls. These perimeter firewalls will have separate inside and outside interfaces separated by VLANs, which will have different security zones and connectivity requirements. Figure 10-11 shows this high-level IT DMZ architecture.

Similar to IT Internet DMZ, there will be an OT DMZ, which will support critical OT applications behind the firewall. This DMZ will provide controlled access to OT endpoints and their application servers. The overall architecture of this design will be similar to Internet DMZ with dedicated 1 RU high-performance DMZ switches providing 1G, 10G, 25G, and 40G/100G connectivity to the servers and firewalls. Similar to Internet DMZ, the inside and outside interfaces of the firewalls for the DMZ access will be separated by VLANs and put into different security zones or dedicated firewalls. The OT DMZ will be connected to OT firewalls located in the MDF room. Figure 10-12 shows the high-level architecture of the OT DMZ.

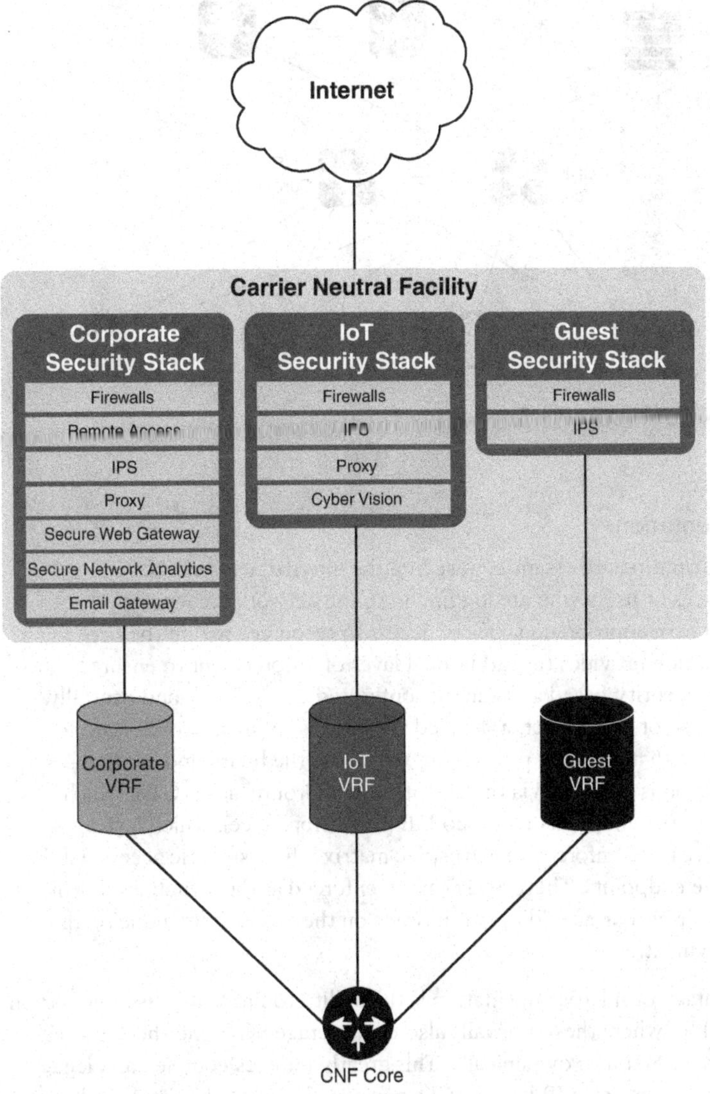

Figure 10-10 *Perimeter Security*

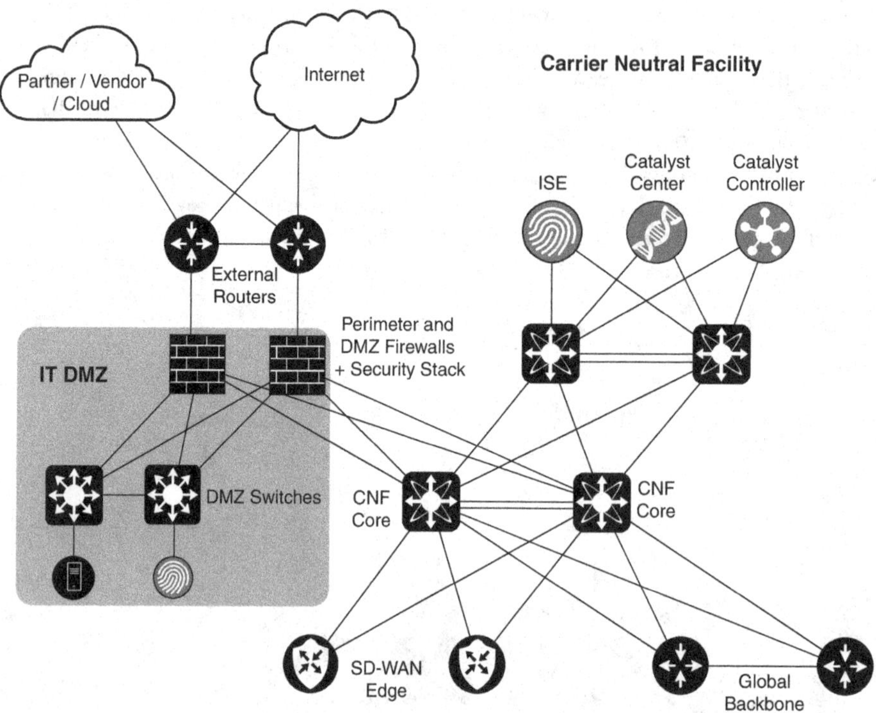

Figure 10-11 *IT DMZ*

NAC and Microsegmentation

NAC and microsegmentation are essential to secure the internal network. NAC ensures that the devices or users who are logging in to the network are legitimate authorized users and have appropriate types of access to resources within the network. Microsegmentation provides that additional layer of enforcement to ensure access to resources is identity based and can be configured dynamically and centrally. During the design phase of the project, a detailed security assessment would need to be conducted to ensure that the right policies are set across the board and are scalable. Microsegmentation is achieved via the use of Secure Group Tags (SGTs), which are assigned to each of the endpoints by Cisco ISE (NAC Appliance), which leverages TrustSec. These SGTs can be enforced in a TrustSec matrix where specific access will be granted to each of the endpoints. These SGTs can be enforced at the switch level, which takes away the need for procuring additional firewalls on the IT/OT side, reducing the overall cost of deployment.

Another major advantage of microsegmentation is the ability to integrate Cisco or certain firewalls with Cisco ISE, where these firewalls also can leverage SGTs and the TrustSec matrix to enforce inter-VN traffic dynamically. This greatly reduces complex and legacy methods of enforcing traffic using IP-based ACLs because dynamic identity-based SGACLs are much more scalable and can be enforced with centralized policy.

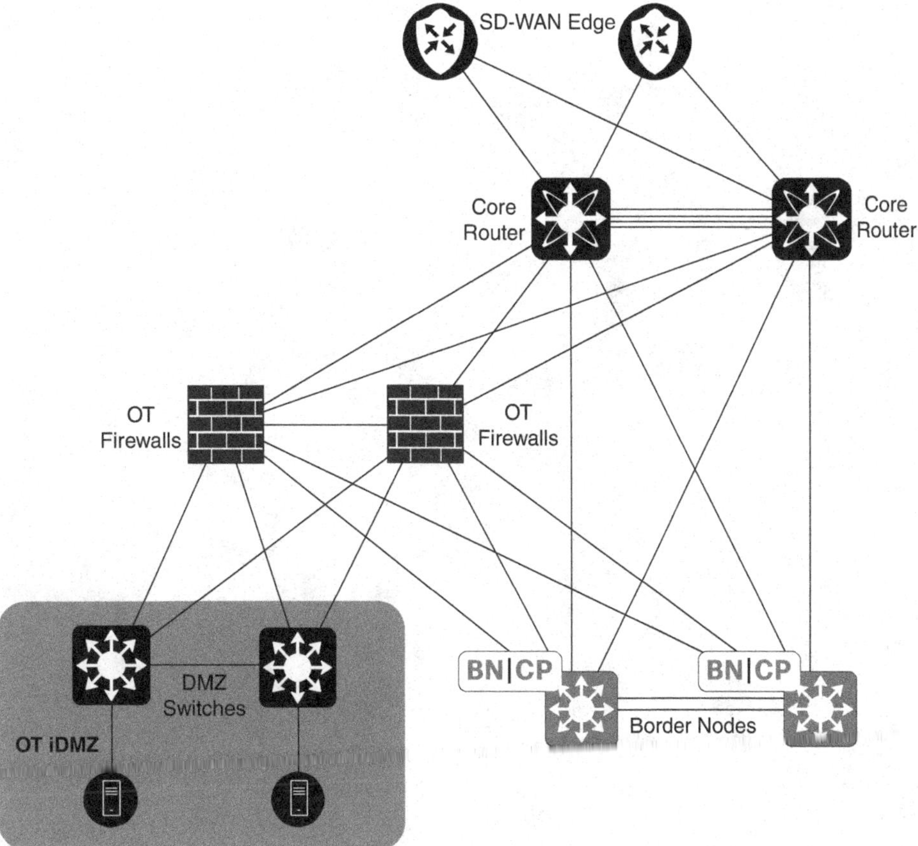

Figure 10-12 *OT iDMZ*

Summary

Looking at the architecture in this case study, it is highly evident that all the business and technical requirements were captured. All in all, this is a highly scalable, supportable, and sustainable network that can grow and expand as needed. The factory of the future is not just about OT space and how to make that more efficient, but also how to enable networks connecting the OT space more efficient. The model in this architecture enables IT as a Business, where a network team can cross-charge for support and services to manufacturing business units. This way, business units get their service-level agreements on problem resolution, and IT gets indirect revenue to make networks more resilient and grow as needed.

Chapter 11

Financial Use Case

In this chapter, we discuss the following:

- SDA in the campus environment
- Multi-tier SD-WAN topology in the WAN environment
- An enhanced security posture with support for end host quarantining

Use Case Overview

Within the financial sector, as with many verticals, numerous regulatory agencies force strict compliance policies. These policies may vary from state to state, and may vary largely from country to country. While a user at a site located in the United States should be able to make a phone call to another user in Switzerland, that traffic path may need additional security measures in place to protect the global financial institution. Imagine a vulnerability in a workstation in one location being able to spread throughout the entire global environment. This would be devastating for any company. So, security and the WAN design must account for the ability to isolate countries. But what about multiple locations within a country? How can the financial enterprise maintain banking operations while still ensuring the overall security? How does an enterprise allow guests at a location to use the wireless network while ensuring they do not have access to the corporate environment? Additionally, the enterprise wants the end-user experience to be the same regardless of how those users connect to the network or where.

In traditional enterprise networking, all of these goals were achieved by tightly managing the IP space and manually writing lengthy access control lists to allow or deny the appropriate traffic. In many cases, this might also require manually managed policy-based routing to ensure traffic traversed the security domain.

As the use case is discussed in this chapter, we address the following key points for the business:

- Segmentation must be introduced to isolate these groups: corporate users on corporate devices, corporate users on their own devices, physical security devices, guests, ATMs.
- IoT and physical security zones must be separated by vendor, and within a specific vendor, must create security zones to limit traffic flows.
- Corporate traffic within a particular country does not require inspection. All traffic ingressing/egressing a country requires inspection.
- Segmentation must be maintained between all campus locations.
- Any device may be quarantined based on posture. Any quarantined device must not be able to access any resource except for remediation services.
- Individual countries connect to regional data centers via regional service providers at a few chosen locations. Those in-country hub locations connect to other in-country campuses via different WAN SPs.
- While dual fault tolerance is not specifically required, the loss of an entire data center or the services at that data center is considered only a single fault.
- No single point of failure may take down the production system.
- Modularity is supported, providing support for multiple campus topologies.

This use case leverages SDA, SD-WAN, and security posture to meet the desired design.

Campus Design Modularity

A financial institution has various campus locations spread across the country, region, or globe. Depending on the location of the campus, there may be only a handful of users or multiple tall buildings full of employees, contractors, and additional endpoints. Additionally, the location may have a requirement for on-site dedicated services, connectivity to business-to-business clients, or dedicated trading floors. Also, a campus may have very few users; however, it serves as a backup location for primary users in the event the main location is unavailable.

Migrating to a new architecture in a global environment can be difficult. This is often the case in many businesses. Personnel at one location have different requirements than at another. It is important to create a standard that addresses all of the potential requirements and, more importantly, to strictly follow the standard after it is created.

The first main design decision was to utilize the SDA–SD-WAN two-box solution, putting the SDA border nodes at the core of the local campus network. This instantly allows the SDA and SD-WAN environments to be designed and deployed separately, as well as fuels the transition toward a standardized, modular design. The SD-WAN Edges may be interchanged based on throughput requirements without affecting the design of the SDA campus. Meanwhile, the SD-WAN Edges hand off the required service VPNs for the location to the core (the SDA border nodes) regardless of the size of the campus location or individual service requirements.

To maintain segmentation between the two environments, VLANs across a dot1Q trunk are used for macrosegmentation, as well as inline tagging in the CMD header for microsegmentation. In Figure 11-1, three different campus environments are shown. Notice that while the size of the campus changes, as well as the service requirements, the connectivity between the SDA and SD-WAN environments does not.

Now that the SDA border nodes are at the core of the local campus network, they also become the handoff point for all other services at the location. Again, the size of the campus does not affect the support for the other modules—B2B, local services, dedicated trading floors, and so on. Figure 11-2 illustrates how the various other modules may be connected to the core layer without changing the now-developing standard. Not all connections are shown for the sake of simplicity. The firewall connection remains an access layer link because it was configured prior to migration. The SDA border nodes serve as the core of the network following network design best practices for modular high-throughput switching.

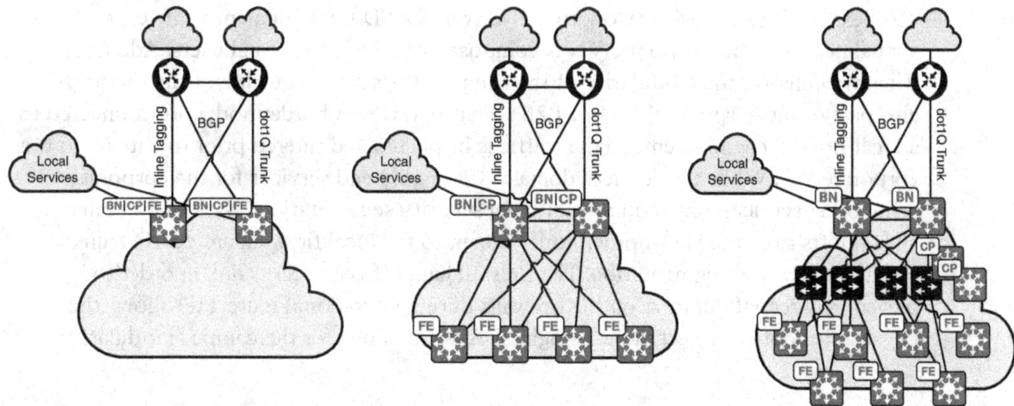

Figure 11-1 *SDA Campuses as a Module*

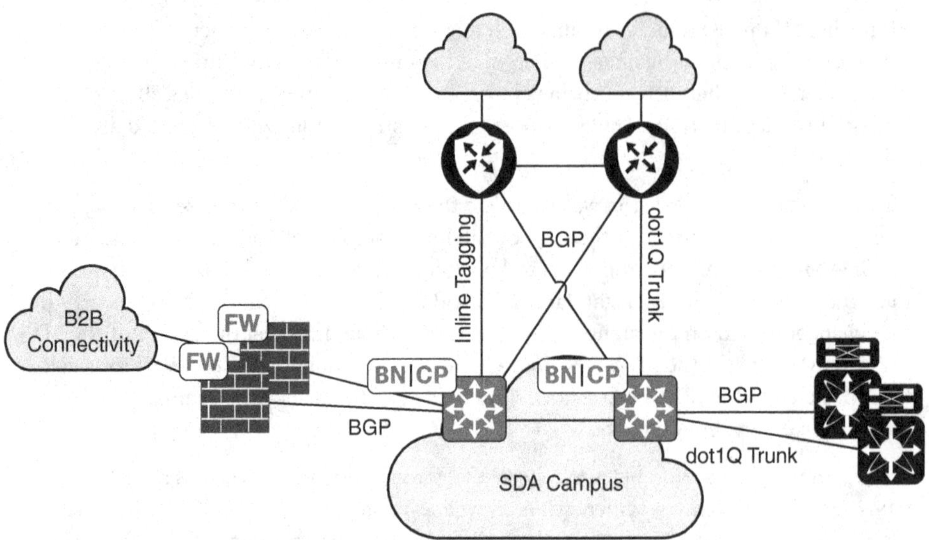

Figure 11-2 *SDA Campus with Modular Services*

Campus Macrosegmentation

Now that we've presented a high-level discussion of how the various modules will connect to each other, a discussion on the segmentation in the campus is needed. SDA itself requires a virtual network for the underlay, the Infra_VN. This is actually the global routing table on the SDA Catalyst switches; however, it is still a unique virtual network that must be included in the design. This VN will be used to handle the management traffic of the Catalyst fabric switches, the connectivity between SDA devices for VXLAN-encapsulated traffic, and CAPWAP traffic for the wireless environment.

The next obvious virtual network to consider in the SDA environment is the corporate virtual network. The corporate VN is composed of all of the normal users. Additionally, when we consider the modularity of the campus, the services outside of the fabric are also part of the corporate VN. In a B2B scenario, the SDA border nodes are connected to a local firewall environment, so the traffic is inspected and filtered prior to entry into the corporate VN. While the services domain is primarily end services for the corporate VN, some other services may require additional security segmentation. With that in mind, all handoffs from the SDA border node, except to the local firewall, are dot1Q trunks to maintain the macrosegmentation. The firewall handoff is an access link in order to prevent any reconfiguration on the firewalls during migration. Figure 11-3 shows the physical handoffs supported on a single SDA border node for the campus modularity.

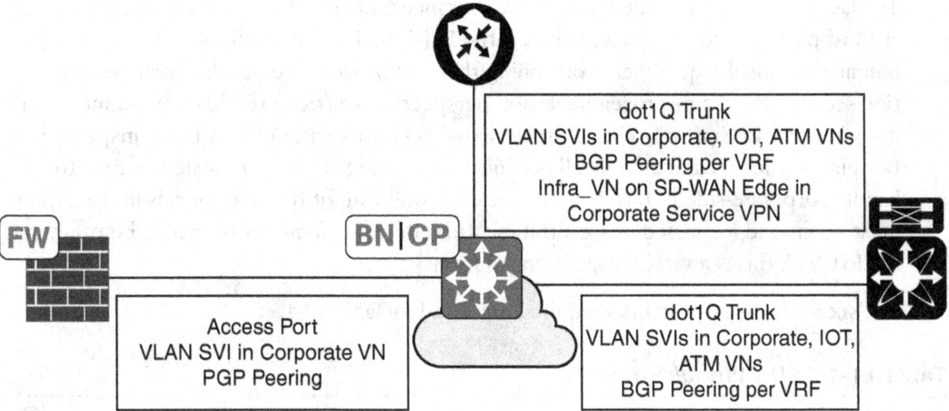

Figure 11-3 *One BN Physical Handoff*

Two VNs have been defined for the campus environment; however, the segmentation requirements are just starting to be met. Financial institutions tend to characterize four main locations in the network enclave: the data center, the campus, the branch, and the ATM locations. Realistically, it is not uncommon for two or more general locations to coexist at a single physical location. But how are they defined? The easiest to define is the ATM. It is a specialized location in the network that provides a kiosk to end clients. The data center is also easy to define because it provides a centralized collection of services for the corporate environment. The terms *campus* and *branch* seem to mean the same; however, for simplicity, accept that a branch is a location where money is exchanged with end clients in person, whereas a campus does not have that capability. It is possible for a branch to be in the bottom floor of a downtown building that is itself a campus, complete with an ATM outside; however, for the purposes of our modular campus, they will still be considered as separate logical environments.

At a high level, ATMs connect to the network through a local router and provide a kiosk to end clients to obtain or deposit currency or perform electronic transactions. All of this automated business must be maintained securely on the network. Additionally, this traffic should be segregated from other traffic on the network, to ensure even internal users are not able to interfere with these business operations. Therefore, the ATMs themselves will be a unique virtual network, the ATM VN.

In a large campus environment, it is not unusual to have guests and contractors onsite to interact with the daily business operations. These are not actual employees of the financial institution, but they all provide services or resources necessary to run the business. Therefore, it is not uncommon for the enterprise to provide wireless and potentially wired connectivity for these users. Also, corporate users may bring their own phones or other electronic devices that need some access on the network. Therefore, two additional virtual networks are created: Guest and BYOD. These two VNs will perform similarly: traffic is not to be trusted until it is inspected in a security domain in the network. However, the Guest VN will provide users only with Internet access while the BYOD VN can provide corporate users with access to limited corporate services as required.

The last virtual network addresses the requirements of our physical security, as well as third-party vendor equipment. This is the IoT VN. The IoT environment has some unique additional requirements on zoning that will be discussed in the microsegmentation section. From a macrosegmentation perspective, traffic in the IoT environment must not interact with traffic from the other virtual networks without first being inspected. Because any local campus firewall is connected to the SDA BNs as an access port to handle corporate-side B2B traffic, the local firewall cannot be used for this inspection. It must be instead inspected as a central location. Because some services may be offsite in the IoT VN, this is a viable inspection solution.

The six SDA virtual networks required are listed in Table 11-1.

Table 11-1 *SDA Virtual Networks*

Virtual Network	Description
Infra_VN	Cisco SDA Fabric Underlay
Corporate	Corporate-owned endpoints not specifically assigned to another VN
IoT	Third-party vendor equipment, physical security devices
ATM	ATM devices
Guest	Noncorporate users
BYOD	Personal devices used by corporate employees

Campus Microsegmentation

As part of the macrosegmentation solution, the capability to quarantine any user, service, or endpoint is required. Therefore, a unique Quarantine SGT is defined with a straightforward policy. Quarantined devices may send and receive data only to designated remediation services with a Remediation_Servers SGT. The quarantine requirement means that the ISE deployment will need to be able to issue Change of Authorization (CoA) for any endpoint, not unusual for ISE in an SDA deployment, but it will also require Adaptive Network Control (ANC). The ANC will be utilized without enabling Port Bounce. In this way, the endpoint will move to the Quarantine SGT, but DHCP will not have to be reperformed, leaving the device in the same IP pool in the same VN with the same IP address initially obtained (or statically configured). At this point, the primary security concern of quarantining hosts, endpoints, or users is achieved while allowing the device access to correct issues.

However, this quarantining scenario makes the assumption that ISE is the service performing all of the profiling and analysis. How can this be extended further so that other services issue a request to quarantine a host? This can be easily accomplished via integration with ISE using pxGrid. In Figure 11-4, a third-party server is monitoring the corporate environment. At some point in time, it is determined that the host be moved to quarantining. The reason could be software compliance, such as out-of-date software, recognized malware, or perhaps the user is doing something suspicious on the network. The third-party server sends a message via pxGrid to the ISE pxGrid Policy Service Node (PSN). Based on the authentication session information, an ISE PSN will send a CoA to the SDA fabric edge node with the endpoint attached. The SDA fabric edge node will now start sending the endpoints traffic with a source SGT of Quarantine. All rules related to the Quarantine SGT will be applied appropriately to isolate the end host. When the CoA is changed successfully, ISE will then use pxGrid to notify the third-party server of the successful change.

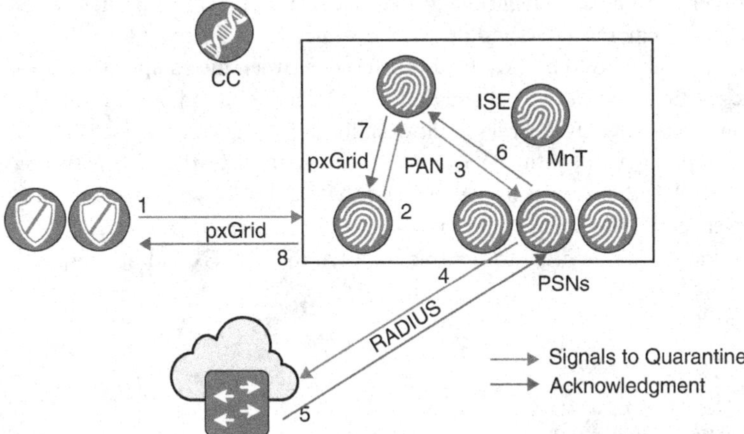

Figure 11-4 *ISE-FE Quarantining with a Separate Profiling Service*

Within the corporate VN, other microsegmentation is mainly a function of business requirements. At a minimum, we may want to consider such microsegmentation as Admins, Users, Servers, and Secure_Servers. This minimal segmentation would allow Admins more access, such as SSH, to entities on the network that normal Users may not require. There could be other use cases where certain services, such as Secure_Servers, require heightened security with fewer users allowed access. Perhaps only HR_Users should access HR_Servers via a proprietary protocol while the HR_Servers should still be manageable by Admins. These individual rulesets per use case can be easily worked out for that particular use case. This is not limited to the finance vertical.

Moving outside of the corporate virtual network, the Guest and BYOD VNs are easy to address. For these VNs, the Guest users are only allowed to access the Internet, and the BYOD users are able to access resources only after inspection. Therefore, each VN will have only one SGT—Guest or BYOD SGT respectively—and the traffic will be carried to a DMZ where Internet access is available for both, as well as increased security inspection for the BYOD users before being permitted access to the rest of the network.

The ATMs are located in their own ATM VN. They will need only a single ATM SGT for the environment. The centralized services the ATMs interact with are part of the corporate VN within the data center space, so traffic to or from ATMs to these services will be allowed while all other nonmanagement traffic will be denied.

We're left with the IoT VN that had the requirement around multiple vendor-specific zones. The easiest use case to visualize is that of the security camera. In Figure 11-5, a particular vendor has been used for their security cameras and DVRs. Depending on the campus size, the DVR may be at that particular location or at another larger location. The security cameras are IP based and connected to SDA fabric edge nodes. Realistically, an IP camera should be streaming its video feed to the vendor's DVR, which may be able to control the pan, tilt, and zoom of the camera. Other than basic network protocols, such as DHCP, the camera should not have any other flows. The vendor's DVR does not need to interact with the HVAC unit. It should be interacting only with its cameras and be accessible to the security admins. As mentioned, and as shown in Figure 11-5, these three entities—the security admin, the DVR, and the camera—may be in different locations. Therefore, the IoT VN will need to be extended somehow between the campus locations. In Figure 11-5, the traffic between two cameras in the IoT VN is blocked; however, traffic between the camera and the DVR server is allowed. Even if the DVR server exists at a separate location, the policy will continue to allow just this specific traffic flow without any updates to ACLs. The admin exists in the corporate VN and is allowed to access the DVR server; however, the traffic between the two is now forced across the centralized firewall and inspection devices in order to traverse between the IoT VN and the corporate VN.

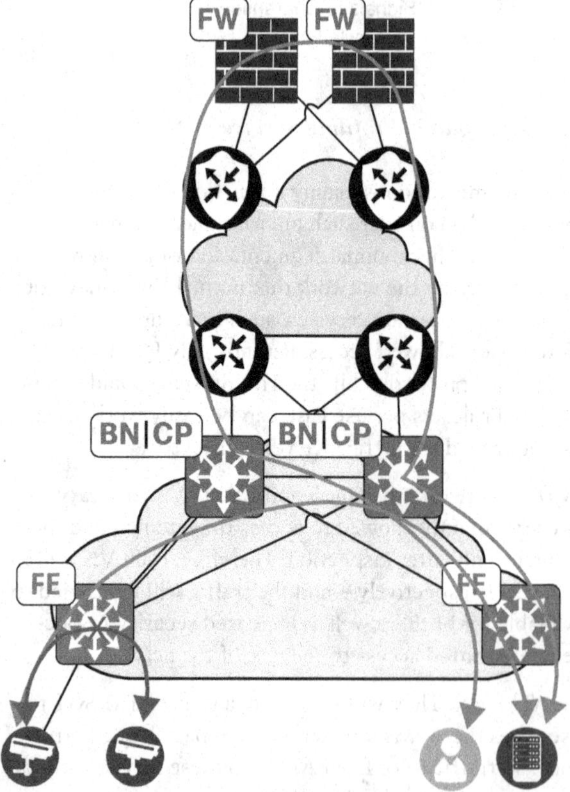

Figure 11-5 *IoT Camera Zones*

From a policy perspective, two SGTs will be required for this one scenario. The IP cameras will utilize a vendor-specific Zone-1 SGT, Vendor1Zone1 SGT, while the DVRs will have a second SGT, Vendor1Zone2 SGT. The rules for the Cisco TrustSec are straightforward. Vendor1Zone1 SGT is only able to send and receive traffic with Vendor1Zone2 SGTs. This means that no users, no equipment from other vendors, not even other cameras from the same vendor, are able to communicate with an individual security camera. It can only send and receive data with its DVR. Keep in mind that if the camera needs specific network services, those would have to be added to the permissions.

The rules for the DVR are also simple. The Vendor1Zone2 SGT can, of course, send and receive data with the Vendor1Zone1 SGT, but also with the Security Admins in the corporate VN. Because traffic between the IoT environment (the DVRs) and the corporate environment (the Security Admins) requires inspection, both virtual networks extend between campuses via the SD-WAN environment as separate service VPNs. Routing between the two VNs occurs at the data center via security inspection devices. By extending the IoT VN as a unique service VPN, the cameras at a small campus, Site 1, may be controlled and recorded by the DVRs at a larger campus, Site 2. Meanwhile, the Security Admin may be in some other region geographically in the corporate VN, while their traffic with the DVR traverses the data center security domain to interconnect the IoT and corporate virtual networks. Table 11-2 shows the allowed traffic patterns for the IoT VN. All other traffic is dropped in the IoT environment.

Table 11-2 *IoT SGT Allowed Traffic*

Source SGT	Allowed Destination SGT
Vendor1Zone1	Vendor1Zone2
Vendor1Zone2	Vendor1Zone1, Security_Admin
Security_Admin	Vendor1Zone2

The same multizone logic applies for other vendor equipment. Each new vendor in the IoT space gets two SGTs. The Zone 1 SGT is permitted traffic only with the vendor's Zone 2 SGT. The Zone 2 SGT devices are then allowed traffic only with the appropriate Admin SGT through the IoT-Corporate interchange in the data center security environment.

Extending Campus Segmentation

As briefly mentioned in the previous section, some segmentation must be maintained between different campuses. Therefore, we should address what virtual networks must be extended and how.

The corporate VN is the easiest to address. It is needed at all locations. Therefore, one SD-WAN service VPN will be created for the interconnectivity of campuses in the corporate space; however, in the requirements of the financial institution, traffic between countries should be inspected. With that in mind, then, a country-specific service VPN is created for the corporate VN in that country. This means that traffic between countries will be required to exit the SD-WAN environment in the data center from one country's service

VPN to be inspected prior to reentry in another country's service VPN. Figure 11-6 illustrates the interconnectivity in the data center between any two countries (A and B).

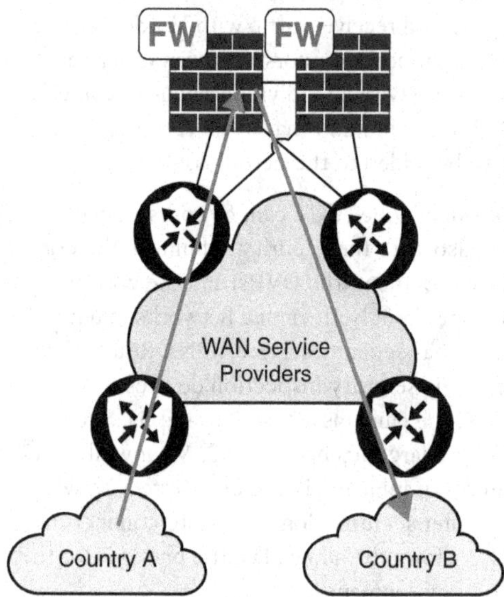

Figure 11-6 *SD-WAN Country DC Connectivity*

So, the SD-WAN country-specific service VPN for corporate is full mesh in the country that allows traffic directly between any two campuses in the same country, but SD-WAN forces the traffic through the DC inspection to reach another country. In the ATM VN, almost all traffic to or from the ATM will be destined or originated from centralized services in the data center; however, the potential exists in some countries for local in-country service requirements. To keep the SD-WAN centralized policy simplified, a country-specific ATM service VPN is created. In the discussion of the SD-WAN centralized policy, the significance of this decision will be visible. Just as with the corporate country-specific service VPN, the ATM country-specific service VPN will allow ATM traffic to local services if required and otherwise force all traffic through the data center security domain, while isolating the ATM traffic from all other traffic in the network.

For the same reasons discussed in the ATM country-specific service VPN, the IoT environment will have a country-specific service VPN. This extends the IoT VN between campuses in the same country, allowing for the application of the vendor Zone 1 and Zone 2 SGT policy. At this point, SD-WAN now requires three service VPNs for each country: one each for Corporate, IoT, and ATM. Each of these service VPNs will be full mesh inside its respective country. What about the remaining three SDA virtual networks in the country—Infra_VN, Guest, and BYOD?

The Infra_VN requires connectivity outside the campus for Catalyst Center, management, and so on. However, in this use case, continued macrosegmentation is not a requirement. Therefore, the Infra_VN will extend to the SD-WAN Edges, but on the SD-WAN Edge, the subinterface will be part of the country-specific corporate service VPN. An administrator on the location that requires management access to an SDA fabric edge device will have their traffic hairpin on the site's SD-WAN device without having to leave the actual location. The CTS policy configured in the corporate VN will permit or deny the traffic access appropriately.

For Guest, those devices require isolation and access to the Internet only. BYOD devices are the same as Guest except with the requirement of additional access after inspection. Therefore, SDA CP/BNs are provisioned inside the data center as a unique SDA site, and the location is set up as a Multi-Site Remote Border. The actual term for the location seems to change every few Catalyst Center/SDA releases, so it may also be known as other terms, including VN Anchoring. Figure 11-7 illustrates the traffic flow from one campus location to the DMZ environment in the data center via the Multi-Site Remote Border. While there is a local control plane/border node for the SDA Fabric Site, the device only serves as an underlay transit path toward the DC DMZ. The traffic from the campus fabric edge node is VXLAN encapsulated across the SD-WAN environment in the country-specific corporate service VPN to the Multi-Site Remote Border in the data center. Remember that the Infra_VN was connected to the country-specific corporate service VPN at the SD-WAN Edge at the campus location. While route summarization is allowed from the countries toward the data centers, the host RLOC routes of the Multi-Site Remote Borders must be advertised nonsummarized toward the remote country campuses. This is a requirement of the SDA fabric edge nodes to ensure the appropriate VXLAN encapsulation occurs.

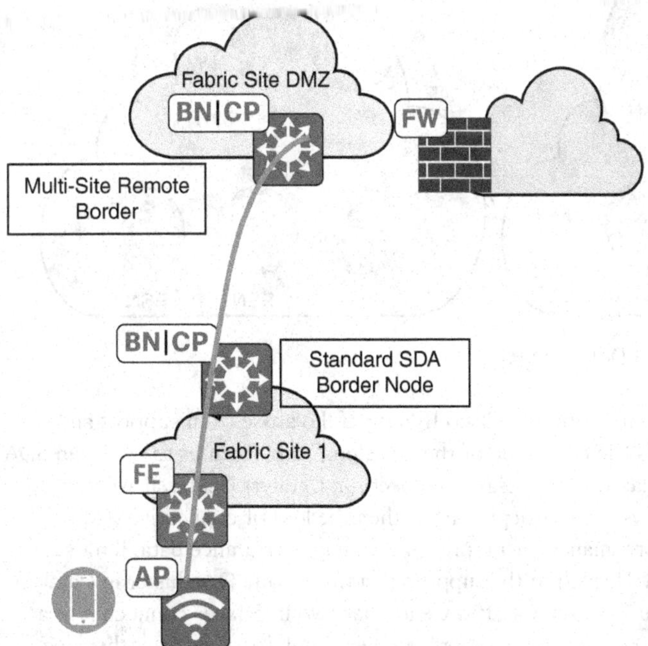

Figure 11-7 *DC Multi-Site Remote Border*

SDA Data Center Services

Before we discuss the SD-WAN policy requirements, an examination of the data center services for the IBN architecture is required. As mentioned in the requirements, no single failure may disrupt the functioning of the system. Additionally, many financial entities are highly cloud averse. Therefore, this section discusses the design and deployment of a fully redundant SDA management plane, as well as fully redundant SD-WAN management and control planes.

The SDA management plane consists of ISE and Catalyst Center. With ISE, redundancy is fairly easy to achieve via a multi-node ISE deployment. Two Policy Administration Nodes, or PANs, are deployed, one in each of two data centers in the region. Likewise, two Monitoring and Troubleshooting Nodes, or MnTs, are deployed, one in each data center. For the pxGrid support, one dedicated ISE PSN is used in each data center for pxGrid services. If SXP is required, then a pair of dedicated PSNs for SXP may also be deployed, one in each data center. One pair of SXP PSNs will support only 200 SXP peerings, and only four pairs of SXP PSNs are supported in a single ISE multi-node deployment. Therefore, consider using a pair of IOS-XE routers to scale the SXP peerings, if necessary. The PSNs are scaled based on endpoint requirements and deployed at multiple locations. Figure 11-8 illustrates the ISE deployment model in a region across the two data center locations.

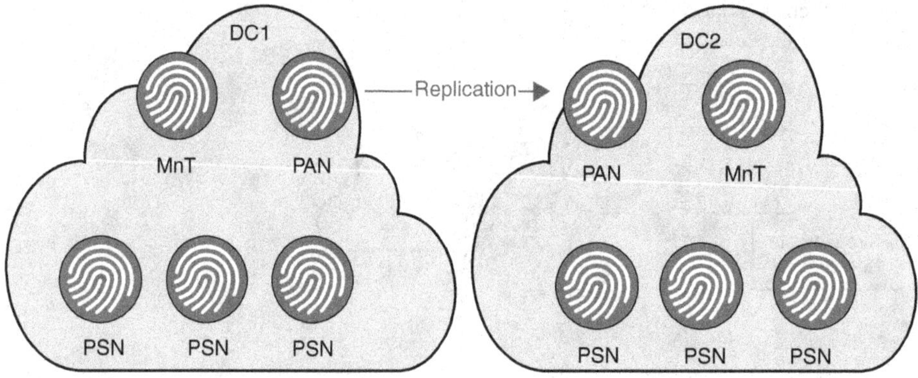

Figure 11-8 *ISE Multi-Node Deployment*

Many features and enhancements in the Cisco IBN portfolio arose from support and design requirements of this use case. One of the more profound features to evolve in SDA is the support of high availability and disaster recovery in Catalyst Center. If we were to deploy a single-node Catalyst Center deployment, then the loss of connectivity to the device would interrupt fabric management, prevent streaming assurance data, limit scaling capabilities, and so on. This led to the support of a three-node HA cluster in Catalyst Center. As shown in Figure 11-9, the Catalyst Center has two interfaces connected to a switch in the data center. One interface supports a Layer 2 link between the other two Catalyst Centers at the location, allowing for communication and replication between the devices. The other interface is the enterprise interface allowing for Layer 3 connectivity of the Catalyst Center to the remainder of the network. This interface supports a virtual IP address that represents to the network all three cluster members on the same subnet. The Catalyst Center supports two other interfaces to further isolate management traffic flows; however, they are unused here for this use case.

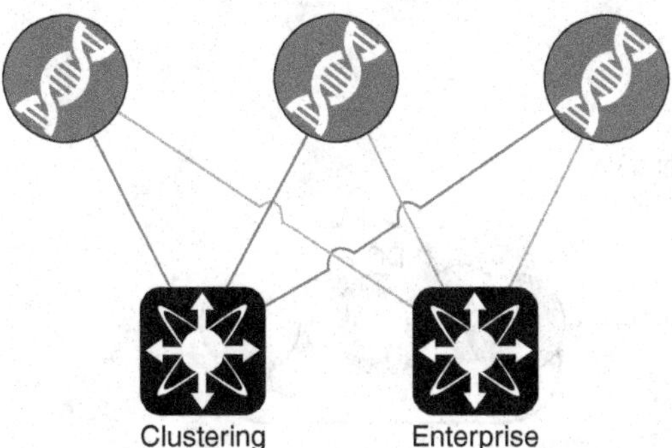

Figure 11-9 *HA Catalyst Center with Single Interface Links*

This deployment of Catalyst Center is more redundant than a single-node deployment; however, notice that a single switch may still disrupt the management plane traffic or the assurance data, for instance. This issue led to the development of redundant interfaces in the Catalyst Center chassis, as is normally seen in port channels. This development gives rise to the cabling shown in Figure 11-10.

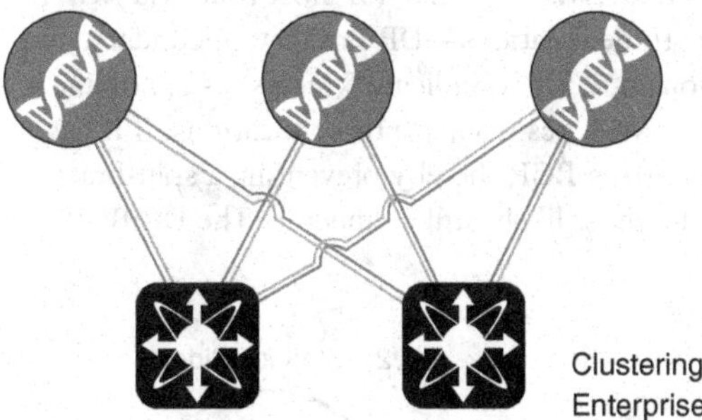

Figure 11-10 *HA Catalyst Center with Redundant Interfaces*

While the redundancy support is more robust, notice that all of the equipment still exists in a single data center. The requirement was that no single failure should take down the system. What if the single failure is the loss of a data center due to catastrophic reasons? To fulfill the requirements, Catalyst Center Disaster Recovery was introduced to allow for an identical Catalyst Center deployment in a separate location to receive incremental replication data of 15-minute intervals, as well as support to become the active location. For the system to be fully automated for recovery, a third node, the witness VM, is deployed at a third geographical location, as shown in Figure 11-11.

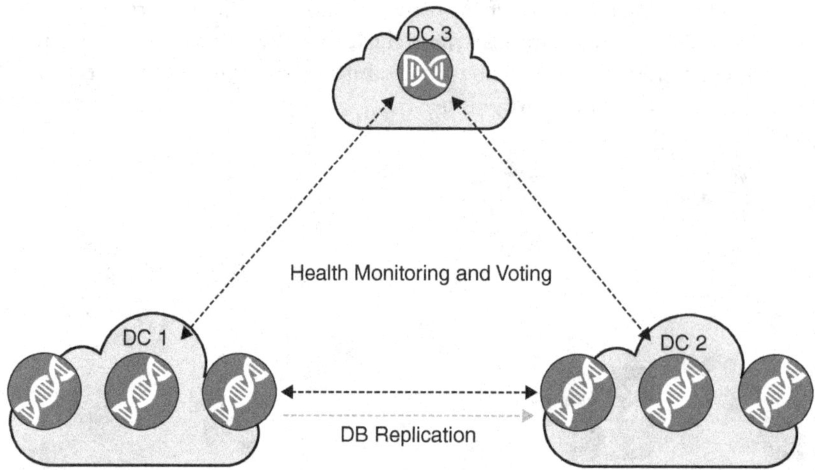

Figure 11-11 *Catalyst Center Disaster Recovery*

With an HA cluster and a single virtual IP in the subnet, it was easy for the network devices to interact with Catalyst Center. They sent the traffic to the HA VIP, and the data center routing brought the traffic to the data center and the Catalyst Center cluster. However, now a virtual IP address must be created to support the two different Catalyst Center clusters. Therefore, the HA VIP for each cluster is part of the local subnet, and another DR VIP that represents all of Catalyst Center DR deployment is created. Additionally, the active-side Catalyst Center advertises the DR VIP host route via BGP to the directly connected Layer 3 device. The three locations—DR Primary, Secondary, and Witness—communicate with other locations directly to indicate which sites are online. For a site to remain active, it must maintain two votes from the three locations. If it has its only own vote, it will withdraw the route from BGP, thereby preventing a split-brain scenario because the other two locations are most likely still connected. The DR BGP process is illustrated in Figure 11-12.

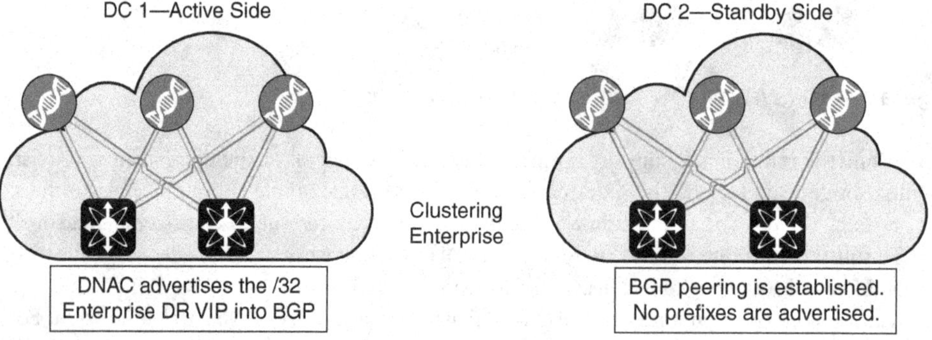

Figure 11-12 *Catalyst Center Disaster Recovery BGP*

SD-WAN Data Center Services

Just as with ISE and Catalyst Center, a fully redundant deployment on-premises for Catalyst SD-WAN Manager, Catalyst SD-WAN Validator, and Catalyst SD-WAN Controller is required across redundant data centers. For Catalyst SD-WAN Validator and Catalyst SD-WAN Controller, this requirement is accomplished easily—similar to the multi-node ISE deployment—by deploying in pairs divided across both data centers based on scaling requirements. Because all of these services are virtual machines, including the Catalyst SD-WAN Manager, the physical cabling redundancy is handled by the host server, in this case, a UCS chassis. Therefore, only a single interface for VPN 0 and another for VPN 512 are presented to the Catalyst SD-WAN Validator and Catalyst SD-WAN Controller. For Catalyst SD-WAN Manager, additional VPN 0 interfaces are presented for clustering.

The data center redundancy requirement is more difficult for the Catalyst SD-WAN Manager and led to the development of system-triggered disaster recovery and administrator-triggered disaster recovery. The two DR systems are deployed the exact same way, except the system-triggered disaster recovery supports an additional third site, following the Catalyst Center model, to prevent a split-brain scenario. At this time, support for the system-triggered disaster recovery has been discontinued from engineering.

In both systems, the active Catalyst SD-WAN Manager replicates database information to the standby Catalyst SD-WAN Manager deployment. Control connections are maintained from the active-side Catalyst SD-WAN Manager to all other devices. Remote devices do not have control connections to the secondary Catalyst SD-WAN Manager deployment. During switchover, the Catalyst SD-WAN Validator signals to all of the devices to move their Catalyst SD-WAN Manager control connections to the standby Catalyst SD-WAN Manager deployment. The control plane between the Catalyst SD-WAN Controllers and the SD-WAN Edges is not disrupted during the process. Figure 11-13 illustrates the OMP control connections between the different devices in a Catalyst SD-WAN Manager DR deployment.

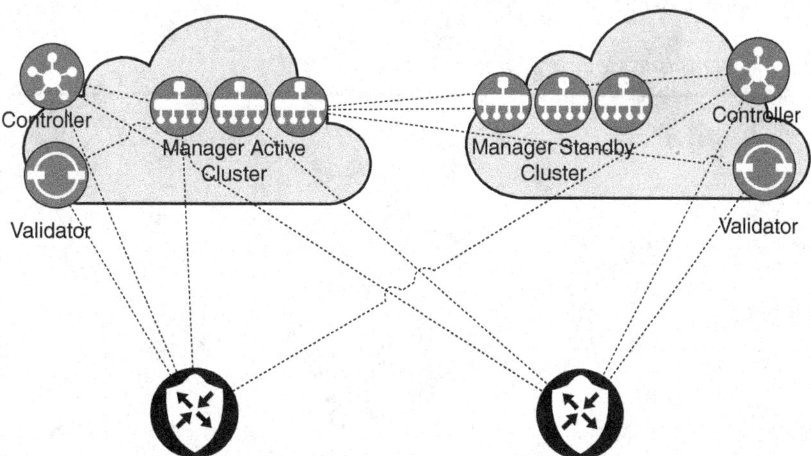

Figure 11-13 *DR Catalyst SD-WAN Manager Control Connections*

SD-WAN Centralized Policy

As discussed throughout this use case, this multinational environment has high security requirements, including segregation of countries. A particular region will have two or more data centers with headend SD-WAN Edges providing multiple countries with access to the shared services. Within an individual country, there may be requirements for a strict hub-and-spoke topology or full-mesh topology, depending on the service provider circuits.

Therefore, as shown in Figure 11-14, site IDs for SD-WAN are created based on a system that identifies the region and country to influence policy.

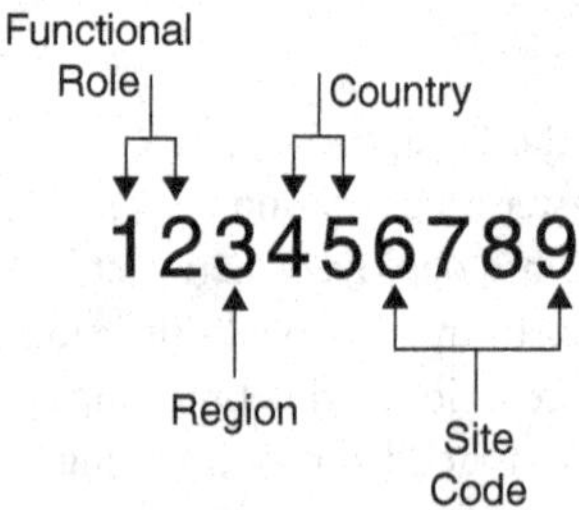

Figure 11-14 *Site IDs*

Because a country-specific VPN will be deployed only in the country or at the data center, per VPN control policy is not required. The three service VPNs per country will all use full-mesh or hub-and-spoke topology with the data centers based on a country policy utilizing site IDs. In the configuration shown in Example 11-1, four site lists are created: one for each data center, one that represents all data centers, and one for all of the sites in the country. For simplicity, only three-digit site IDs are used for illustration. Sequences 30 and 40 are required for the full-mesh topology in the country and are omitted for hub-and-spoke.

Example 11-1 *Site ID-Based Country Control Policy*

```
! Per-Country Control Policy
policy
 lists
  site-list SL-DCs
   site-id 100-199
  !
  site-list SL-DC1
   site-id 101
  !
  site-list SL-DC2
   site-id 102
  !
```

```
  site-list SL-CountryX
   site-id 500-599
  !
control-policy CP-TO-COUNTRYX
  sequence 10
   match route
    site-list SL-DCs
   !
   action accept
   !
  !
  sequence 20
   match tloc
    site-list SL-DCs
   !
   action accept
   !
  !
  ! Seq 30 and 40 for full-mesh; omitted for hub-spoke
  sequence 30
   match route
    site-list SL-CountryX
   !
   action accept
   !
  !
  sequence 40
   match tloc
    site-list SL-CountryX
   !
   action accept
   !
  !
  default-action reject
 !
!
apply-policy
 site-list SL-CountryX
  control-policy CP-TO-COUNTRYX out
!
```

The CP-TO-COUNTRYX control policy handles the hub-and-spoke and full-mesh requirements of individual countries, but the data centers have firewalls. How is symmetric routing maintained to ensure state on the firewalls? The country side does not have firewalls deployed, so maintaining state is not a requirement on this side. Therefore, the previous policy works for the country side.

The policy not only should maintain state but also should load-balance traffic across the data centers. The best way to write the policy for the data centers then is to use the VPNs. Recall that each country will have three dedicated service VPNs. Therefore, if Country X prefers DC1 while Country Y prefers DC2, and symmetric routing is maintained, both requirements for load balancing and symmetric routing are met.

In Example 11-2, each data center is configured with one inbound and one outbound control policy based on VPN membership. As a note, the OMP tag at the DC SD-WAN Edge is signaled to the service-side devices in BGP to maintain the route symmetry. Sequence 30 was created with a new site list that includes all of the remote locations to allow the TLOC entries in.

Example 11-2 *Headend Control Policy*

```
! Per-Country Control Policy
policy
 lists
  vpn-list VL-CountryX
   vpn 1-5
  vpn-list VL-CountryY
   vpn 6-10
  site-list SL-ALL-REMOTES
   site 200-999
 !
 control-policy CP-FROM-DC1
  sequence 10
   match route
    vpn-list VL-CountryX
   action accept
    set
     preference 100
  sequence 20
   match route
    vpn-list VL-CountryY
   action accept
    set
     preference 50
  default-action accept
 control-policy CP-FROM-DC2
  sequence 10
   match route
    vpn-list VL-CountryX
   action accept
    set
     preference 50
```

```
  sequence 20
   match route
    vpn-list VL-CountryY
   action accept
    set
     preference 100
  default-action accept
control-policy CP-TO-DC1
  sequence 10
   match route
    site-list SL-CountryX
   action accept
    set
     omp-tag 100
  sequence 20
   match route
    site-list SL-CountryY
   action accept
    set
     omp-tag 50
  sequence 30
   match tloc
    site-list SL-ALL-REMOTES
   action accept
  default-action reject
control-policy CP-TO-DC2
  sequence 10
   match route
    site-list SL-CountryX
   action accept
    set
     omp-tag 50
  sequence 20
   match route
    site-list SL-CountryY
   action accept
    set
     omp-tag 100
  sequence 30
   match tloc
    site-list SL-ALL-REMOTES
   action accept
  default-action reject
!
```

```
apply-policy
 site-list SL-DC1
  control-policy CP-TO-DC1 out
  control-policy CP-FROM-DC1 in
 site-list SL-DC2
  control-policy CP-TO-DC2 out
  control-policy CP-FROM-DC2 in
!
```

The logic of these policies can then be scaled out using the same format to support additional data center headend locations and remote countries. We should point out that using TO and FROM in the control plane policy naming helps to ensure proper application of the policy at the apply-policy site level.

Summary

This use case presented new engineering challenges with increased redundancy in the data centers and stretched the limits on scalability in the IBN portfolio. Breaking down all of the requirements and considering each individually led to a successful design that stressed standardization and modularity.

Chapter 12

Retail Use Case Using CNF, SD-WAN, and ACI

In this chapter, we discuss the following:

- Data center and Carrier Neutral Facility (CNF) architecture for retail
- SD-WAN architecture for retail
- Catalyst and Meraki campus/branch design for retail
- Hybrid cloud ACI integration for a retail e-commerce application

Use Case Overview

The retail enterprise used as a use case for this chapter has an expansive reach, with multiple stores serving communities nationwide, along with critical backstage facilities like the corporate HQ, regional division offices, district offices, distribution centers, and supply plants. A pivotal part of the infrastructure for this retail enterprise is the regional Carrier Neutral Facilities (CNFs), which consist of different infrastructure components. These components ensure connectivity to all retail and backstage locations using SD-WAN technology. Additionally, they offer connectivity for public/hybrid cloud services through cloud exchange colocation, manage the Internet edge, provide Data Center Fabric (ACI - Application Centric Infrastructure) for hosting hybrid cloud retail applications, and serve as a core backbone interconnecting all building blocks that constitute the retail infrastructure.

In this chapter, we address the following key points pertaining to the business and operational objectives of this infrastructure, which includes

- Streamlining the network by implementing enterprisewide standards and simplifying the WAN/access design across all retail and backstage locations
- Expediting the cloud strategy while minimizing costs and mitigating risks by utilizing the Carrier Neutral Facilities as the central hub for WAN connectivity, access to hybrid cloud services, and the Internet edge

- Implementing end-to-end macrosegmentation across the WAN/access, CNF, Data Center Fabric (ACI), Internet, and cloud edge
- Implementing end-to-end microsegmentation using automated and distributed policies
- Enabling Internet access through Secured Internet Gateways (SIGs) for all retail and backstage locations
- Integrating Azure Cloud Native Services with ACI in the Data Center Fabric

Overall Design

The holistic blueprint for the architecture of this retail enterprise use case includes various critical elements. It encompasses Carrier Neutral Facilities strategically positioned on both the eastern and western coasts of the United States, connected via a dedicated backbone. The utilization of CNFs across the east and west coasts offers significant advantages for nationwide businesses. Key benefits include geographical redundancy, minimized latency, and enhanced network resilience, allowing seamless traffic rerouting during regional disruptions. This configuration ensures extensive coverage for serving customers, partners, and suppliers nationwide, meeting the operational needs of a retail enterprise on a nationwide scale.

Figure 12-1 offers a comprehensive view of the various building blocks that constitute the overall enterprise architecture for this use case.

The Carrier Neutral Facilities employ Cisco ACI as a software-defined Data Center Fabric. In this setup, ACI seamlessly integrates with Microsoft Azure through the use of Cisco Cloud ACI (Cisco Cloud Network Controller, or CNC) and ACI Nexus Dashboard Orchestrator (NDO). This integration facilitates smooth interconnection, abstraction, and normalization, ensuring a uniform application of network and security policies for hybrid applications across both Azure and on-premises ACI environments.

Cisco SD-WAN plays a pivotal role in WAN overlay networking, establishing a transport-independent overlay across all retail and backstage locations. This allows the use of various transports in an active-active mode to extend WAN connectivity to the CNFs. The Secured Internet Gateways within the CNFs serve as secure gateways for Internet traffic, providing robust protection against a variety of cyber threats.

Additionally, Cisco Meraki switches and access points are deployed at retail stores and backstage locations. Using a cloud-based management architecture, these devices simplify deployment and management, providing centralized visibility and insights into both wired and wireless networks across all locations through a unified interface.

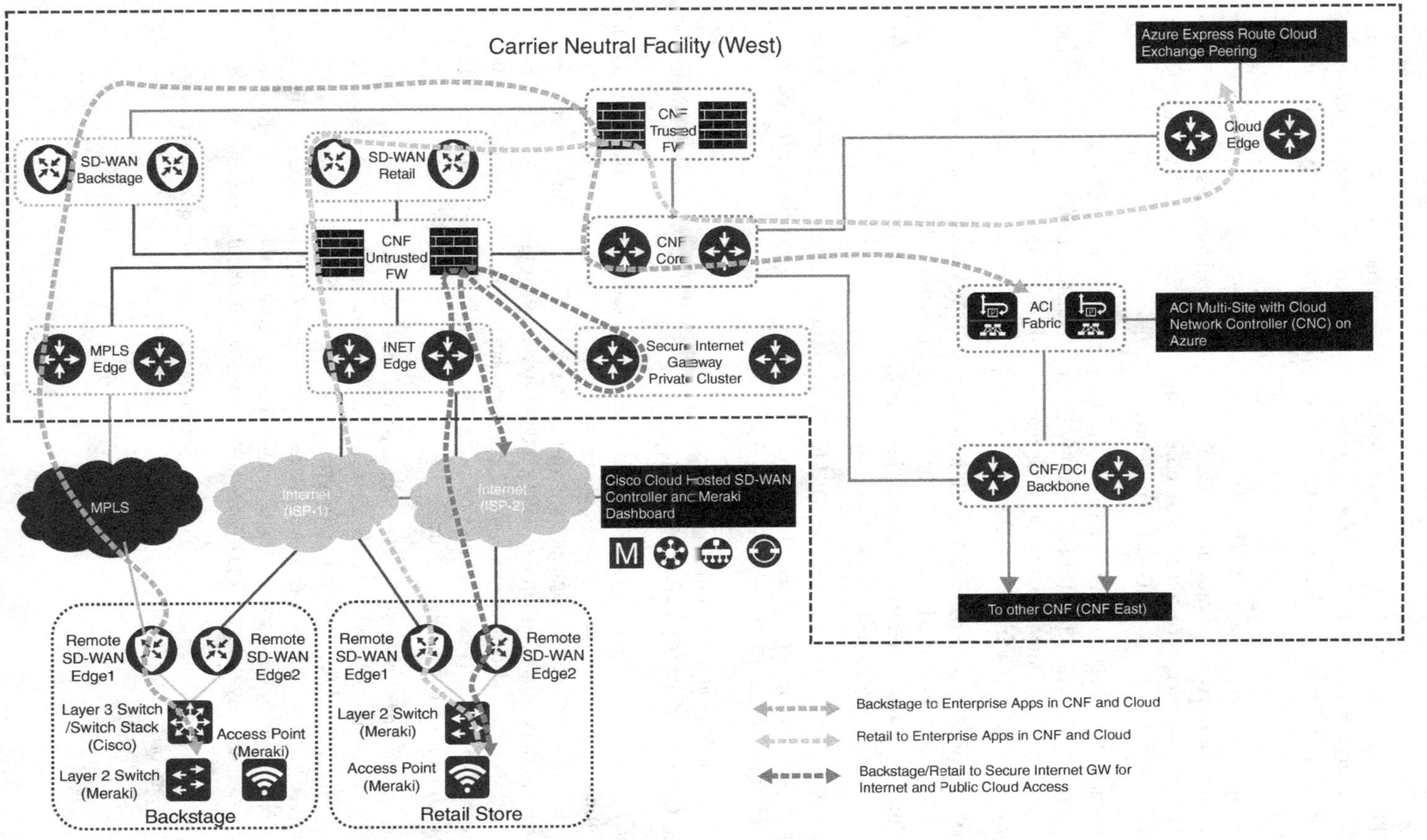

Figure 12-1 *Overall Enterprise Architecture*

The CNF infrastructure comprises additional essential components, including the MPLS Edge, facilitating the extension of MPLS WAN connectivity to the CNFs. The infrastructure also includes the Internet edge, interfacing with multiple Internet service providers (ISPs) to extend Internet connectivity to the CNFs and the SIGs housed within them.

The infrastructure features a CNF untrusted firewall as the first line of defense against untrusted traffic from private and public WANs. This firewall includes distinct zones for MPLS, the Internet, a trusted zone for core connectivity, and an SD-WAN zone linking the WAN transport to the SD-WAN headends.

Internally, dedicated SD-WAN headends exist for both retail and backstage sites, functioning as tunnel endpoints (TEPs) for SD-WAN-encapsulated traffic from remote sites. These headends facilitate connectivity for remote sites to the data center services hosted in the CNF and the public cloud (Azure).

The CNFs also house a trusted firewall, including an SD-WAN zone for fusion routing and policy enforcement for service-side traffic across multiple VPNs. This firewall includes a trusted zone for connectivity into the CNF core, backbone/DCI, and traffic bound for services in ACI and Azure cloud.

Finally, the setup incorporates CNF/DCI backbone routers, providing peer connectivity for L3Out peering from the ACI fabric and DCI connectivity to other CNFs located in different regions.

Data Center and CNF Design

Each component within the CNF, as depicted in Figure 12-2, utilizes eBGP as the routing protocol for route exchange. Correspondingly, each component is configured with a unique private ASN. Although all routes are exchanged using the default routing table, known as the global routing table (GRT), a dedicated intersite-network VRF, referred to as the ISN VRF, exists to enable control and data plane connectivity between ACI sites across CNFs and between ACI sites on-premises in the CNF and ACI sites on the public cloud, in this case, the Azure cloud.

Additionally, the service-side VPNs, which provide macrosegmentation across the SD-WAN, are incorporated into the default VRF (GRT) on the trusted firewall. This means the trusted firewall has two functions. It acts as the policy enforcer for traffic between SD-WAN VPNs (east-west) and traffic from the WAN to services in the ACI and Azure cloud (north-south). It also enables fusion routing, which allows for inter-VPN route exchange by uniting all SD-WAN VPN routes within the default routing table.

Figure 12-3 shows the routing policies between the various functional blocks within the CNF network.

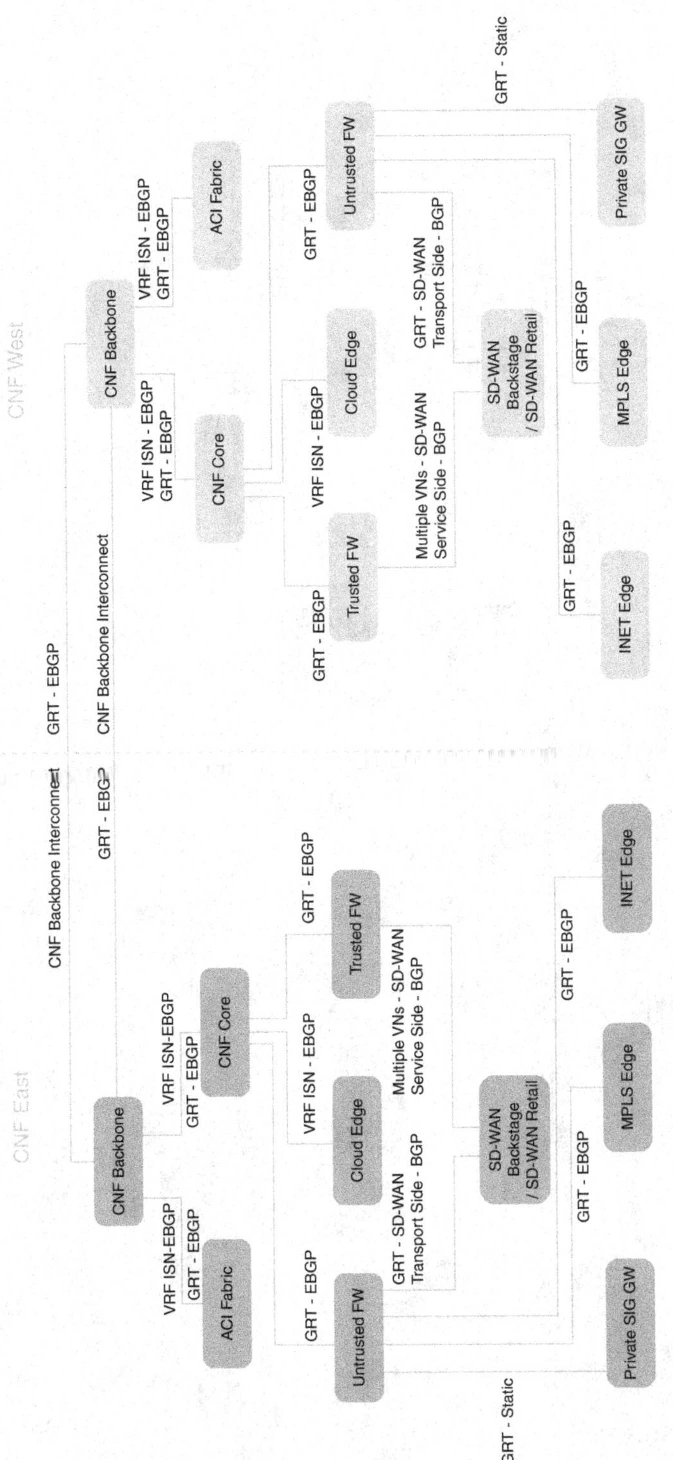

Figure 12-2 *Overall CNF Design*

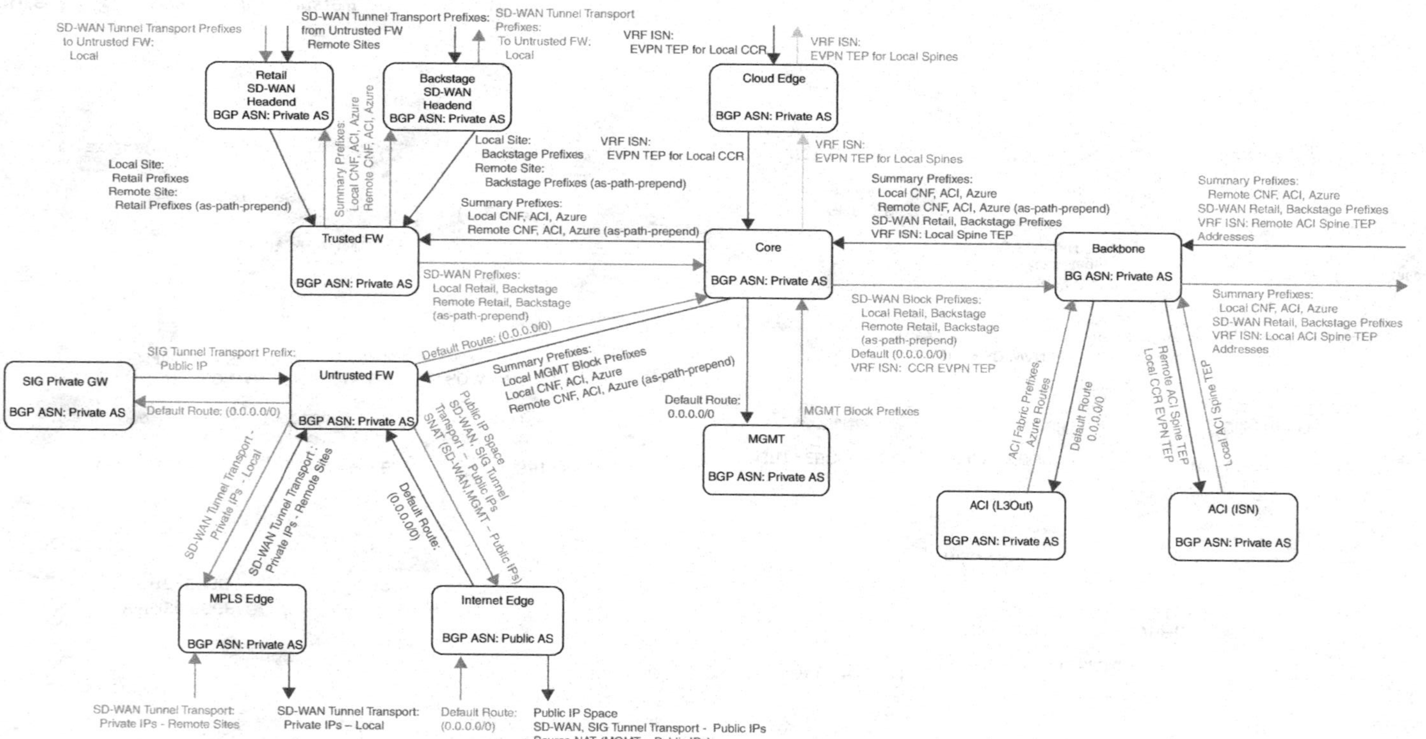

Figure 12-3 *CNF Routing Design and Policies*

Internet Edge

The Internet edge functional block includes two routers set up to exchange routing information with two distinct Internet service providers to ensure redundancy. These routers establish internal BGP (iBGP) peering between them and external BGP (eBGP) using the retail customer's public ASN, and they advertise the public IP address space designated for that specific CNF/DC. Additionally, these routers are set to perform source Network Address Translation (NAT) for internal infrastructure devices requiring outbound Internet communication in the SD-WAN block and management (MGMT) network block.

The routing policy implemented at the Internet edge functional block is as follows:

- Accept Public IP address space designated for the local CNF/DC and public IPs for SD-WAN, SIG tunnel transport, and subsequently advertise these public prefixes to the Internet.
- All traffic aimed for advertised public IP prefixes is received from the Internet.
- Accept default-route (0.0.0.0/0) from the ISP provider and advertise to the external untrusted firewalls.

MPLS Edge

The MPLS exchange block consists of two routers configured as headend provider edge (PE) routers. They exchange MPLS infrastructure prefixes for SD-WAN underlay reachability between the remote SD-WAN Edges and the CNF SD-WAN Edges (aka SD-WAN headends). In this scenario, the headend PEs establish iBGP peering between them and eBGP peering with the untrusted firewall (FW) cluster pair.

The routing policy implemented at the MPLS exchange block includes the following:

- Advertise SD-WAN tunnel transport prefixes for the local SD-WAN headend routers in the CNF.
- Receive SD-WAN tunnel transport prefixes for remote SD-WAN Edge routers at backstage locations.

Untrusted FWs

Untrusted firewalls, in CNF, refer to firewalls that manage traffic coming from untrusted networks or sources. These networks could be public networks like the Internet, or any external network like the unmanaged MPLS network that is not under the control of the organization. The term *untrusted* does not necessarily mean that the network or source is harmful or malicious, but it is a way to categorize and manage network traffic based on its origin. This firewall encompasses distinct zones for MPLS, the Internet, a trusted zone for core connectivity, and an SD-WAN zone linking the WAN transport to the SD-WAN headends.

The routing policy implemented at the untrusted firewall block includes the following:

From the CNF Core:

- Accept local MGMT block IP prefixes.
- Accept summary prefixes for all local CNF, ACI prefixes, and Azure CIDR prefixes.
- Accept summary prefixes for all remote CNF, ACI prefixes, and Azure CIDR prefixes with prepended BGP AS-Path.

To the CNF Core and SIGs:

- Advertise default-route (0.0.0.0/0) received from the Internet edge.

From the Internet Edge:

- Receive default-route (0.0.0.0/0).

To the Internet Edge:

- Originate/advertise public IP address space and public NAT pools designated for the local CNF/DC.
- Advertise public IPs for SD-WAN and SIG tunnel transport.

From the MPLS and Internet Edge:

- Receive SD-WAN tunnel transport prefixes for remote backstage and retail sites and advertise them to the SD-WAN headends.

To the MPLS and Internet Edge:

- Advertise SD-WAN tunnel transport prefixes for the local SD-WAN headend routers in the CNF.

SD-WAN Headends

SD-WAN headends in this infrastructure serve as the central or hub nodes, connecting all spokes (backstage locations and retail stores) in the network. All enterprise traffic from backstage locations and retail stores (except Internet traffic) is backhauled through the SD-WAN headends.

The routing policy implemented at the SD-WAN headends includes the following:

From SD-WAN Retail Stores and Backstage Locations:

- Accept retail stores IP prefixes.
- Accept backstage IP prefixes.

To SD-WAN Retail Stores and Backstage Locations:

- Advertise summary prefixes for all local CNF, ACI, and Azure prefixes using OMP network statements.
- Advertise summary prefixes for all remote CNF, ACI, and Azure prefixes using OMP network statements.

Note Network statements in OMP are used on all SD-WAN headends in all CNFs to advertise local and remote CNF, ACI, and Azure prefixes. Network statements for summary prefixes using a common configuration template on CNF headends ensure that the same set of summary prefixes are advertised to the remote backstage and retail stores from both CNFs and that there is no deviation.

From the Trusted FW:

- Accept summary prefixes for all local CNF, ACI, and Azure prefixes.
- Accept summary prefixes for all remote CNF, ACI, and Azure prefixes.

To the Trusted FW:

- Advertise local backstage and retail store prefixes.
- Advertise remote backstage and retail store prefixes with prepended BGP AS-Path.

Note In this case, the *remote* backstage and retail store prefixes are prefixes from remote sites that consider another CNF to be their primary hub site.

Trusted FWs

The trusted firewalls control the traffic between the trusted internal network and the SD-WAN. The trusted firewall encompasses an SD-WAN zone for fusion routing and policy enforcement for service-side traffic across multiple SD-WAN VPNs and a trusted zone for connectivity into the CNF core, backbone/DCI, and traffic bound for services in ACI and Azure cloud.

The routing policy implemented at the trusted FW includes the following:

From the CNF Core:

- Accept summary prefixes for all local CNF, ACI, and Azure prefixes.
- Accept summary prefixes for all remote CNF, ACI, and Azure prefixes with prepended BGP AS-Path.

To the CNF Core:

- Advertise local backstage and retail store prefixes.
- Advertise remote backstage and retail store prefixes with prepended BGP AS-Path.

> **Note** Again, the *remote* backstage and retail store prefixes are prefixes from remote sites that consider another CNF to be their primary hub site.

Core

As the name suggests, the Core functional block facilitates connectivity to every other functional block within the CNF. The following route policies are implemented on the Core:

From the Untrusted Firewalls:

- Accept the default-route (0.0.0.0/0).

To the Untrusted Firewalls:

- Advertise local MGMT block IP prefixes.
- Advertise summary prefixes for all local CNF, ACI prefixes, and Azure CIDR prefixes.
- Advertise summary prefixes for all remote CNF, ACI prefixes, and Azure CIDR prefixes with prepended BGP AS-Path.

From the Trusted Firewalls:

- Accept local backstage and retail store prefixes.
- Accept remote backstage and retail store prefixes with prepended BGP AS-Path.

To the Trusted Firewalls:

- Advertise summary prefixes for all local CNF, ACI prefixes, and Azure CIDR prefixes.
- Advertise summary prefixes for all remote CNF, ACI prefixes, and Azure CIDR prefixes with prepended BGP AS-Path.

From MGMT block:

- Accept MGMT block IP prefixes.

To MGMT block:

- Advertise default-route (0.0.0.0/0).

From CNF Backbone:

- Accept summary route(s) for local ACI L3Out learned IP prefixes.
- Accept summary route(s) for remote ACI L3Out learned IP prefixes.
- Accept summary route(s) for local CNF IP address spaces.
- Accept summary route(s) for remote CNF IP address spaces with prepended BGP AS-Path.
- Accept summary route(s) for local Azure CIDR prefixes.
- Accept summary route(s) for remote Azure CIDR prefixes with prepended BGP AS-Path.
- Accept retail stores IP prefixes from remote CNF.
- Accept backstage IP prefixes from remote CNF.

To CNF Backbone:

- Advertise MGMT block IP prefixes.
- Advertise local backstage and retail store prefixes.
- Advertise remote backstage and retail store prefixes with prepended BGP AS-Path.
- Advertise default-route (0.0.0.0/0) learned from the untrusted firewalls (Internet block).

From Cloud Edge:

- Accept EVPN TEP (tunnel endpoint) addresses for local Cisco Cloud Routers (CCRs) in VRF ISN.

To Cloud Edge:

- Advertise EVPN TEP (tunnel endpoint) addresses for the spines on the local ACI fabric in VRF ISN.

Cloud Edge

The cloud edge routers employ the CNFs Azure Express Route (ER) Cloud Exchange peering to establish EBGP peering with Microsoft Enterprise Edge Routers (MSEE). This EBGP peering, when combined with the EBGP peering between the cloud edge routers and the core routers in VRF ISN, creates underlay connectivity between the on-site ACI fabric in the CNF and the Cisco Cloud Routers in Azure Infra VN. The primary role of the underlay IP network is to ensure IP reachability necessary for the communication of the overlay control plane (BGP EVPN) and data plane (VXLAN) between the CNF on-site ACI location and Azure. The following route policies are implemented on the cloud edge:

From Core:

- Accept EVPN TEP (tunnel endpoint) addresses for the spines on the local ACI fabric in VRF ISN.

To Core:

- Advertise EVPN TEP (tunnel endpoint) addresses for local Cisco Cloud Routers (CCRs) in VRF ISN.

From Microsoft Edge Router (Express Route):

- Accept EVPN TEP (tunnel endpoint) addresses for local Cisco Cloud Routers (CCRs) in VRF ISN.

To Microsoft Edge Router (Express Route):

- Advertise EVPN TEP (tunnel endpoint) addresses for the spines on the local ACI fabric in VRF ISN.

MGMT

The management block provides Out of Band (OOB) management connectivity for ACI spine and leaf switches, APICs, Nexus Dashboard Orchestrator (NDO), and other infrastructure appliances and networking nodes in the CNF. The following is the proposed routing policy for this block.

From Core:

- Accept the default-route (0.0.0.0/0).

To Core:

- Advertise MGMT block IP prefixes.

CNF Backbone

The CNF Backbone encompasses a set of routers designed to establish DCI connectivity among CNFs. Additionally, these routers are linked to ACI border leafs to engage in BGP peering with L3Outs, facilitating route exchange between CNFs and the associated ACI fabric.

The backbone relies on the default routing instance (VRF GRT) to manage local and remote CNF, ACI, SD-WAN, and Azure prefixes. Furthermore, VRF ISN is utilized to ensure underlay reachability between ACI sites and connectivity both among ACI sites and with the Azure cloud. The ISN VRF serves as the platform for exchanging IP reachability information concerning multi-site tunnel endpoints. These TEPs are configured on spines within each on-premises ACI fabric, and in the case of the Azure cloud, they convey TEPs for Azure Cisco Cloud Routers.

The following route policies are implemented on the CNF Backbone:

From Remote CNFs, on the Default VRF (VRF GRT):

- Accept remote CNFs' IP address space (summarized).
- Accept remote ACI L3Out learned prefixes (summarized).
- Accept remote Azure CIDR prefixes (summarized).
- Accept retail store IP prefixes.
- Accept backstage IP prefixes.

From Remote CNFs, on VRF ISN:

- Accept remote ACI multi-site TEP prefixes.

To Remote CNFs, on the Default VRF (VRF GRT):

- Advertise local CNFs' IP address space (summarized).
- Advertise local ACI L3Out learned prefixes (summarized).
- Advertise local Azure CIDR prefixes (summarized).
- Advertise retail store IP prefixes learned from the local SD-WAN block.
- Advertise backstage IP prefixes learned from the local SD-WAN block.

To Remote CNFs/DCs, on VRF ISN:

- Advertise local ACI multi-site TEP prefixes.

From ACI Fabric, on Production L3Out:

- Accept IP prefixes belonging to the ACI fabric.
- Accept Azure CIDR prefixes.

To ACI Fabric, on Production L3Out:

- Advertise default-route (0.0.0.0/0) learned from Internet Edge block.

From ACI Fabric, on VRF ISN:

- Accept ACI multi-site TEP prefixes advertised by local ACI spine switches via eBGP and place them in VRF ISN.

To ACI Fabric, on VRF ISN:

- Advertise ACI multi-site TEP prefixes learned from remote backbone routers.
- Advertise Azure CCR TEP prefixes learned from the cloud edge block.

From Core:

- Accept local backstage and retail store prefixes.
- Accept remote backstage and retail store prefixes with prepended BGP AS-Path.
- Accept default-route (0.0.0.0/0) learned from the untrusted firewalls (Internet block).

To Core:

- Advertise summary route(s) for local ACI L3Out learned IP prefixes.
- Advertise summary route(s) for remote ACI L3Out learned IP prefixes.
- Advertise summary route(s) for local CNF IP address spaces.
- Advertise summary route(s) for remote CNFs IP address spaces with prepended BGP AS-Path.
- Advertise summary route(s) for local Azure CIDR prefixes.
- Advertise summary route(s) for remote Azure CIDR prefixes with prepended BGP AS-Path.
- Advertise retail stores IP prefixes from remote CNF.
- Advertise backstage IP prefixes from remote CNF.

From Core, on VRF ISN:

- Accept Azure CCR TEP prefixes learned from the cloud edge block.

To Core, on VRF ISN:

- Advertise ACI multi-site TEP prefixes advertised by local ACI spine switches.

ACI

The ACI fabric at each CNF is set up with two L3Outs (see Figure 12-4). The first is the production L3Out, utilized for external routing protocol peering and external route exchange from the production tenant VRF. This tenant/VRF encompasses BD subnets for internal production workloads, including on-premises web workloads; on-premises Kubernetes clusters for backend services; and on-premises shared services such as internal DNS, NTP, Active Directory, MS Exchange, Identity Store; and on-premises SQL databases. The second L3Out is the ISN L3Out, which facilitates TEP reachability to EVPN peers in other ACI fabrics across different CNFs. Additionally, it enables TEP reachability to Cisco Cloud Routers on the Azure cloud.

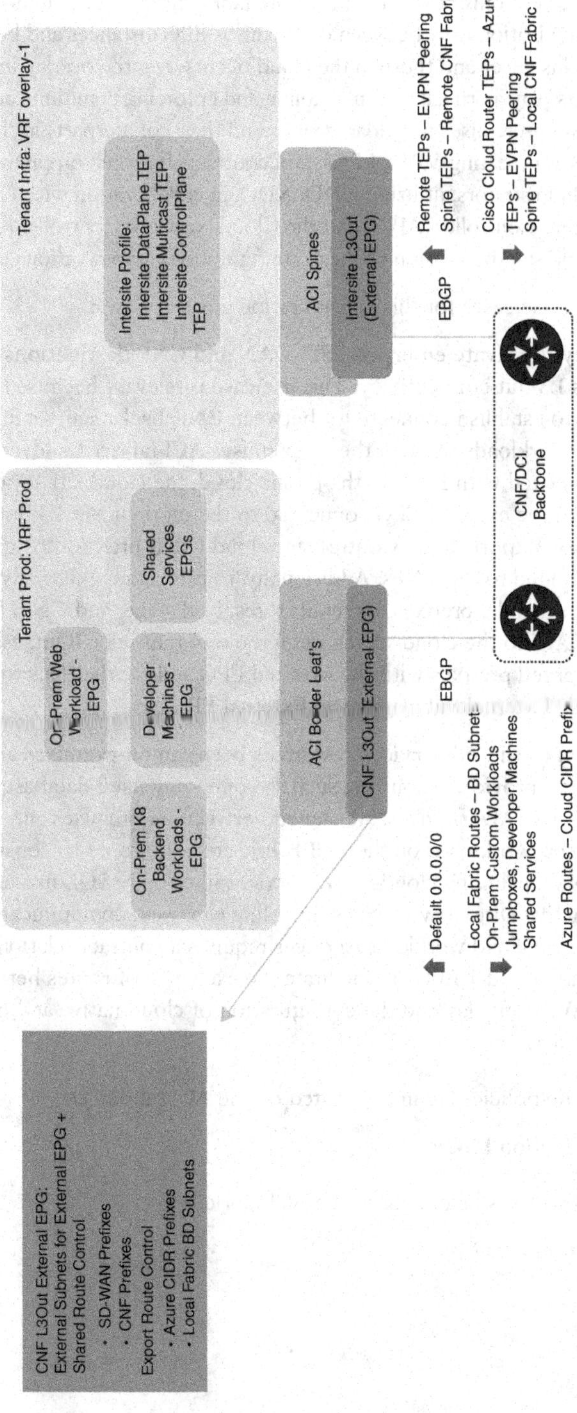

Figure 12-4 *ACI Logical Design*

In this specific deployment scenario, the VRF instance for the Production environment extends its presence not only across the multi-site fabric in the CNFs but also into Microsoft Azure. The communication flow between on-premises EPG instances and between on-premises EPG instances and those in the cloud occurs over the overlay intersite network. Contracts play a crucial role in enabling and enforcing communication and route exchange between on-premises workload groups and their counterparts in the Azure cloud. The responsibility for creating VRFs, EPGs, and contracts between on-premises and cloud EPGs lies with administrators, utilizing NDO. NDO, in collaboration with Cisco Application Policy Infrastructure Controller (APIC) and the Cloud Network Controller (CNC), manages the deployment and standardization of these configurations across various environments.

The two pertinent use cases for this configuration are as follows:

1. **Connectivity to private enterprise SD-WAN and CNF destinations using on-premises L3Out connectivity:** This use case is relevant because there is a requirement to establish connectivity between CNF, backstage, retail stores, and public cloud workloads through the on-premises ACI fabric. To advertise CIDR prefixes associated with EPGs in the public cloud, the cloud CIDR prefixes are configured within the external EPG connected to the on-premises L3Out. It's crucial to set the flag to "Export Route Control" for cloud CIDR prefixes to advertise those prefixes outbound to the CNFs. Additionally, to propagate externally learned prefixes (for example, prefixes for retail stores, backstage, and CNF) from the on-premises ACI to the cloud site through the on-premises L3Out, associate the externally learned prefixes with the external EPG and set the flags to "Shared Route Control" and "External Subnet for the External EPG."

2. **Consumption of shared-services resources between on-premises and cloud:** Shared-services provider resources, such as commonly used databases, DNS, and Active Directory (AD) services, are shared between on-premises and cloud applications and users. Workloads on the ACI Fabric are configured to consume services from the cloud, including cloud-native services like Azure SQL-managed instances and Azure Active Directory services. Enabling east-west communication between on-premises and cloud workloads/services requires a contract relationship between consumer and provider EPGs to facilitate the exchange of routes between the two sites using EVPN overlay and the configuration of cloud-native and on-premises security policies.

The following route policies are implemented on the ACI fabric:

To Core, on Production L3Out:

- Advertise IP prefixes belonging to the ACI fabric.
- Advertise Azure CIDR prefixes.

From Core, on Production L3Out:

- Accept default-route (0.0.0.0/0) learned from Internet edge block.

To Core, on VRF ISN:

- Advertise ACI multi-site TEP prefixes advertised by local ACI spine switches via eBGP and place them in VRF ISN.

From Core, on VRF ISN:

- Accept ACI multi-site TEP prefixes learned from remote backbone routers.
- Accept Azure CCR TEP prefixes learned from the cloud edge block.

SD-WAN Design

The SD-WAN is designed using a hub-and-spoke structure, utilizing MPLS and Internet transports as the IP underlay for connecting SD-WAN tunnel IP sources and destinations. Backstage sites are set up to use both MPLS and the Internet as the two underlay transports for SD-WAN, while retail stores rely on dual Internet connections from different providers for underlay connectivity. This underlay routing system, supported by MPLS and Internet providers, facilitates both control and data plane tunnels for overlay connectivity:

- Control plane tunnels use Datagram Transport Layer Security (DTLS) between SD-WAN Edge and SD-WAN controllers. This environment defaults to DTLS. For this specific use case, the SD-WAN controller deployment employs a Cisco CloudOps deployment model with dedicated controllers.
- Data plane tunnels use IPsec between SD-WAN Edge devices, opting for "IPsec" over "GRE" due to the encryption requirement in this environment.

Figure 12-5 provides an overview of the SD-WAN design.

SD-WAN Edges establish connectivity with controllers hosted on the Internet through all accessible transports. To enable SD-WAN Edges in forming DTLS tunnels with cloud controllers, traffic originates from the VPN 0 "transport" interface, a component of the underlay. In the case of SD-WAN Edges within CNF, these underlay interfaces are associated with the retail and backstage zones on the untrusted firewalls. These firewalls are specifically configured to permit outbound traffic from retail and backstage zones to the INET zone. Furthermore, they dynamically facilitate the return traffic from controllers on the INET zone back to the SD-WAN Edges transport linked to the retail and backstage zones.

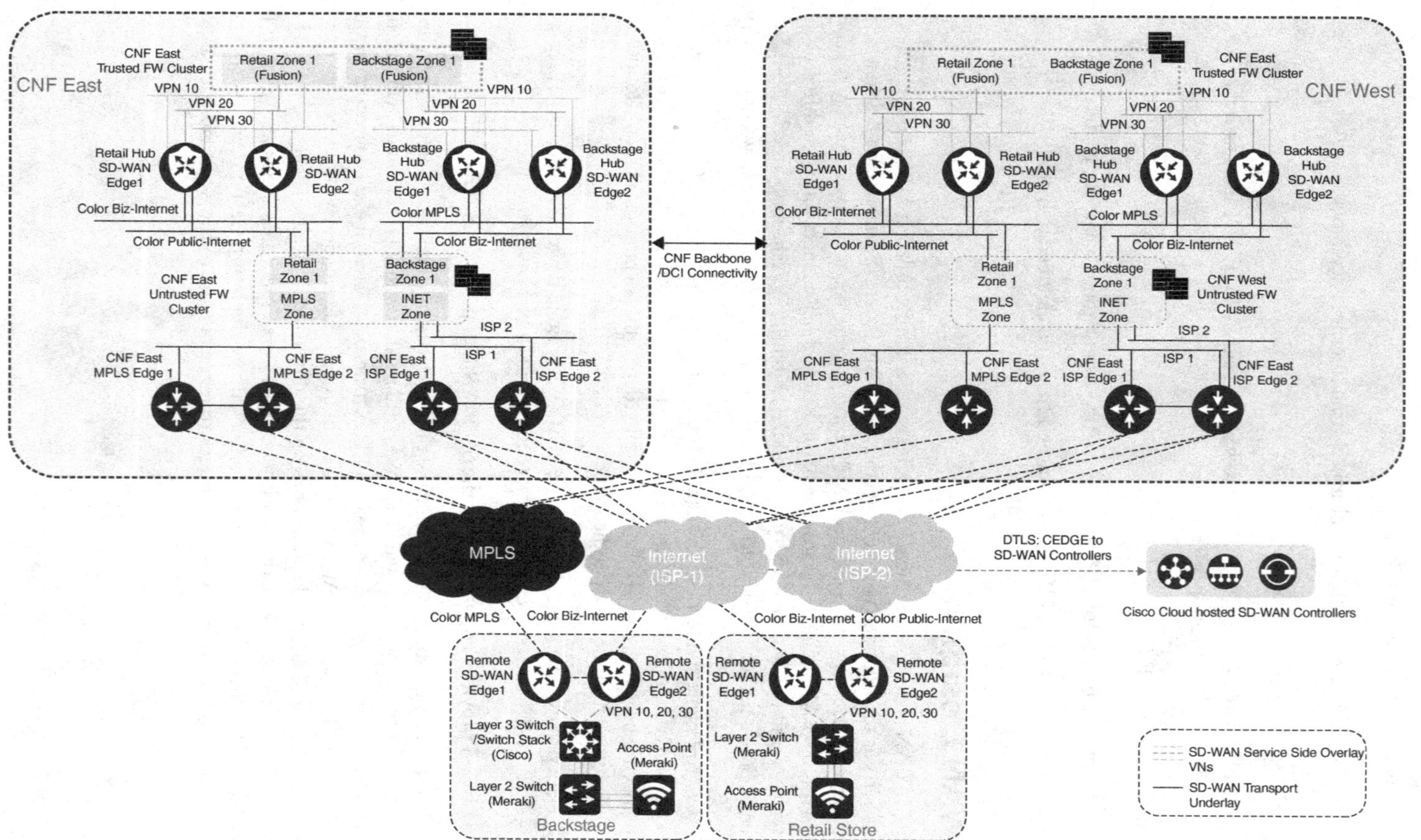

Figure 12-5 *SD-WAN Design Overview*

For retail store SD-WAN Edges, they establish connectivity to the controllers using the Internet transport, which terminates on their uplink interfaces. Similarly, in the case of backstage locations, connectivity to the controllers via the Internet transport directly traverses the ISP network. However, for backstage locations utilizing the MPLS transport, controller connectivity follows a northbound path to the CNF, traverses the MPLS zone on the untrusted firewalls, and then is permitted outbound to route through the INET zone toward the Internet.

Each SD-WAN Edge, whether in the CNF, retail store, or backstage sites, is equipped with two interfaces in VPN0, requiring the assignment of two distinct colors on each edge. In the CNF, for edge routers serving as headends for retail stores, VPN0 interfaces are designated with the colors "biz-Internet" and "public-Internet." For CNF backstage headends, the colors are "mpls" and "biz-Internet." In retail stores, uplinks in VPN0 to the first Internet provider receive the "biz-Internet" color, while the uplink to the second Internet provider is assigned the "public-Internet" color. Likewise, for backstage sites, the uplink to the MPLS transport in VPN0 is configured with the "mpls" color, and the uplink to the Internet transport is configured with the "biz-Internet" color.

In designing the SD-WAN solution, a notable challenge was achieving scalability and ensuring that traffic sourced in the same region as the CNF maintains affinity to local CNFs. Scalability concerns were mitigated by implementing scalable pods, while addressing the traffic affinity challenge involved defining centralized policies to control traffic flows between CNFs and remote locations, all while maintaining active-active redundancy.

A pod comprises devices designated as SD-WAN headends, each dedicated to serving specific remote sites. This implies that each pod includes pairs of SD-WAN Edge routers at each CNF, specifically assigned to a set (group) of remote sites. Different instances of pods are utilized for retail stores and backstage sites, uniquely identified by tunnel group identifiers (see Figure 12-6). These identifiers offer precise control over the tunnel establishment process. In this setup, a Transport Locator (TLOC—a unique identifier for a router's WAN interface serving as a tunnel endpoint) establishes tunnels exclusively with remote TLOCs sharing the same tunnel group. Consequently, all TLOCs configured for a pod, whether backstage or retail, have a dedicated tunnel group identifier. This configuration ensures that tunnels are established solely between TLOCs within the same pod or group. Additionally, with the restrict option enabled alongside the tunnel group option, TLOCs form an overlay tunnel exclusively with remote TLOCs possessing the same tunnel group ID and TLOC color.

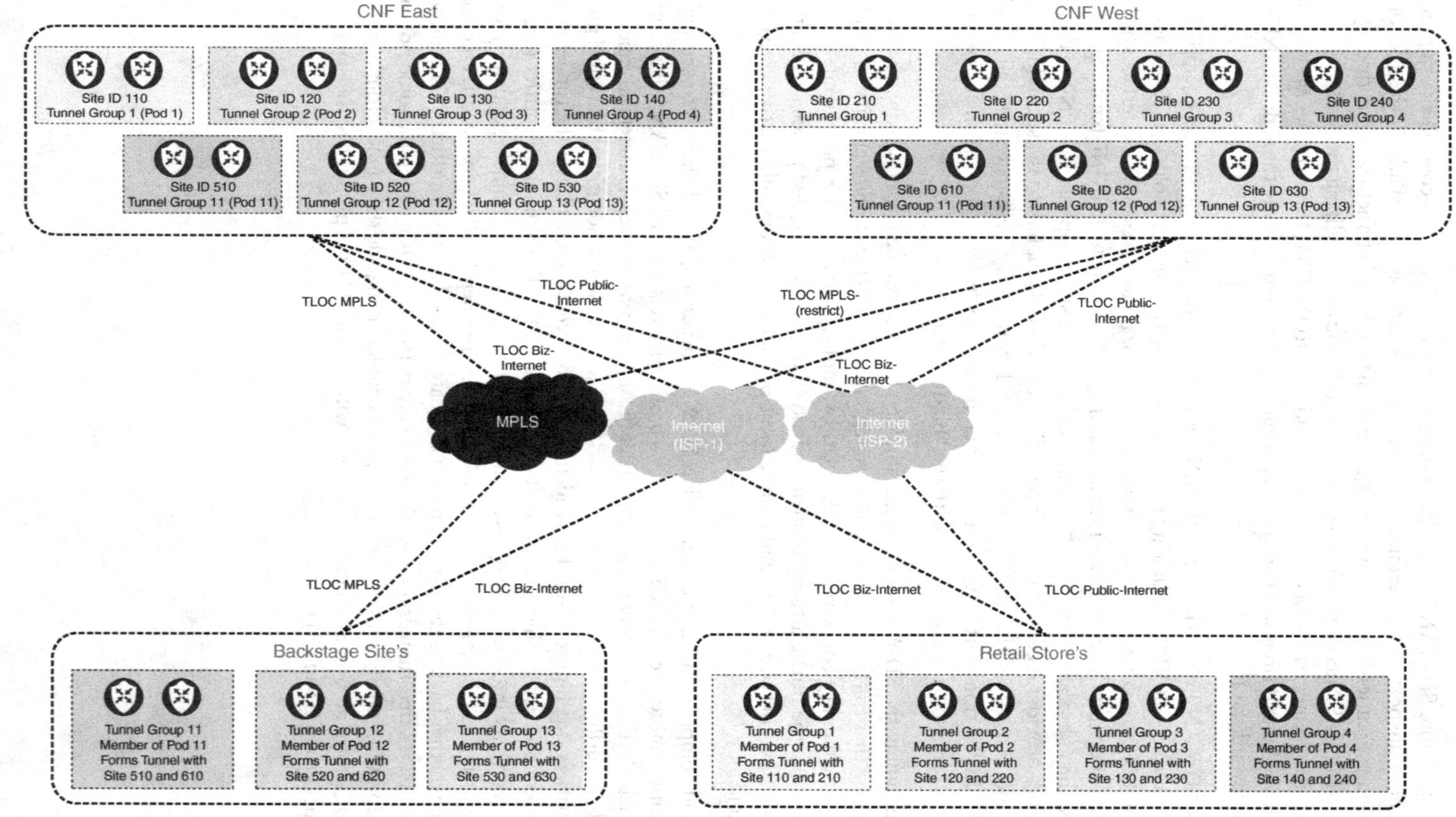

Figure 12-6 *SD-WAN Scalable Pod Architecture*

Table 12-1 offers a summary of the configuration parameters employed in achieving the scalable pod architecture. The table lists only one pod for each backstage and retail for brevity.

Table 12-1 *TLOC Tunnel Groups and Color*

Transport	Pod ID	TLOC Color	Option	TG-ID
Retail CNF	1	biz-Internet	no-restrict	1
	1	public-Internet	no-restrict	1
Retail Remote	1	biz-Internet	no-restrict	1
	1	public-Internet	no-restrict	1
Backstage CNF	11	mpls	restrict	11
	11	biz-Internet	restrict	11
Backstage Remote	11	mpls	restrict	11
	11	biz-Internet	restrict	11

In the context of this deployment, the estimated capacity for the pod was around 160 Gbps, with an allocation of 80 Gbps per CNF and 40 Gbps per SD-WAN Edge. However, the actual throughput is contingent on the interplay of hardware, software, features, and the specific uplink/downlink bandwidth utilized on the SD-WAN Edges. For this particular deployment, it was considered both secure and within well-tested scalable limits to designate 40 Gbps of throughput per SD-WAN Edge. Despite the fact that each SD-WAN Edge has the capability to handle more than 40 Gbps of traffic individually, the decision to opt for 40 Gbps was a precautionary measure. This choice ensures that if an entire CNF were to fail, a single SD-WAN Edge pair could proficiently manage the entirety of stores and backstage traffic for that specific pod.

It's also essential to note that approximately 40 percent of traffic from retail stores and backstage sites is anticipated to be directed to the Internet and rerouted to the SIGs hosted in the CNF. This consideration was factored in when calculating the expected throughput for each pod headend pair and determining the sizing for the SIGs. For instance, in a scenario with 900 retail stores having a bandwidth of 100 Mbps and 40 percent SIG bandwidth, the total expected throughput on the pod acting as the headend for these stores would be 54 Gbps. This calculation, derived from 900 * 100 Mbps * 0.6 (non-SIG BW), falls below the estimated limit of 80 Gbps per CNF.

Another critical consideration is the BFD scale per SD-WAN Edge on the headends. In this deployment, each SD-WAN Edge had the capability to support 8000 BFD tunnels. For example, in a hub-and-spoke topology comprising 900 remote sites per pod, two SD-WAN Edges per remote site, and each SD-WAN Edge equipped with two TLOC colors for uplink transport, the total number of tunnels/BFD sessions would be approximately 3600. This figure remains comfortably below the maximum supported limit of 8000 tunnels.

Advertising Routes to Remote Sites

Concerning the route advertisement to remote sites, it is imperative that CNF SD-WAN Edges advertise "non-SIG" prefixes consistently from the CNF SD-WAN Edge routers to the retail/backstage SD-WAN Edge routers. The prefixes being advertised are identical from both CNF1 and CNF2. This uniformity ensures that remote sites learn identical prefixes from both CNFs, and SD-WAN centralized control policies help maintain traffic affinity to local CNFs for destinations in the same region as the remote site. However, if one CNF advertises a unique prefix not advertised by the other CNF, the remote site will direct traffic to the CNF advertising the distinctive prefix. Hence, it is crucial that CNFs only advertise identical prefixes. The SD-WAN Edges utilize OMP network statements to specify the non-SIG subnets that are advertised to the remote sites. These OMP network statements are uniform across all CNF SD-WAN Edge routers in a given pod and are controlled by configuration templates that prohibit any deviation.

Figure 12-7 illustrates the functioning of routing advertisements from the CNF to remote sites. We employ centralized route policies (outbound control policy) from Catalyst SD-WAN Controller to remote sites, utilizing TLOC preferences to guide remote sites in favoring paths learned from either CNF-East or CNF-West. It is essential to note that while an inbound control policy influences Catalyst SD-WAN Controller RIB (Routing Information Base), impacting the entire overlay fabric, the outbound control policy influences specific routers matched by the applied site list. In this case, we employ two distinct outbound control policies: one with a higher TLOC preference for paths learned from CNF-East, utilizing the site list SPOKES-CNF-EAST, and another with a higher TLOC preference for paths learned from CNF-West, utilizing the site list SPOKES-CNF-WEST.

Receiving Routes from Remote Sites

Routes acquired from remote sites through Overlay Management Protocol (OMP) undergo redistribution into BGP at the CNFs. The issue lies in the default behavior where both CNFs redistribute the prefixes from remote sites into the CNF core with identical BGP AS-Path lengths, resulting in uniform BGP metrics. Consequently, the routing within the CNFs becomes unpredictable when directing outbound traffic to a remote site.

To circumvent this issue and introduce more predictability, configurations are implemented to ensure that traffic destined for the same region as the CNF adheres to local CNFs. In essence, policies and configurations are orchestrated to control the flow of traffic, directing outbound traffic from the CNFs to the remote sites to prefer the local CNF egress.

There are two key tasks to achieve this objective:

1. Routes are identified from remote sites that prefer CNF-East versus routes that prefer CNF-West. A centralized control policy is used to identify these routes based on the site-id of the SD-WAN remote sites and assign an OMP tag (1 for sites preferring CNF-East, 2 for sites preferring CNF-West).
2. The CNF SD-WAN Edges are configured with OMP-to-BGP redistribution configuration featuring a route map. This route map is used to match the OMP tag and apply AS-Path prepending to the routes into the CNF core/backbone based on the tag.

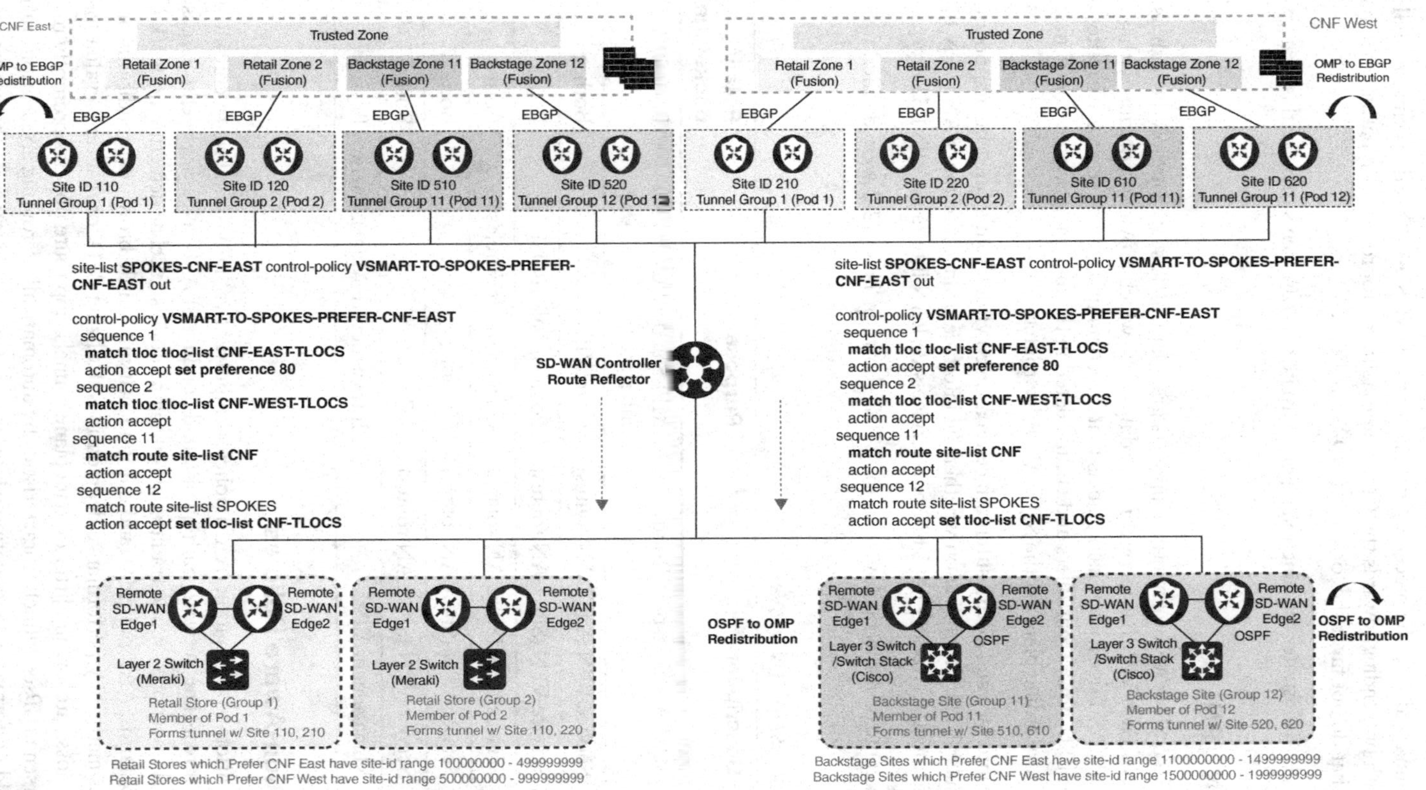

Figure 12-7 *Advertising Routes to Remote Sites*

In summary, due to the preceding two steps, the CNF SD-WAN Edges employ BGP AS-Path prepending towards the CNF core/backbone for routes originating from remote sites that do not favor the local CNF SD-WAN Edge.

Figure 12-8 illustrates the functioning of the route advertisements to make this strategy work.

SD-WAN VPN

The Cisco SD-WAN architecture supports granular traffic segmentation through use of VPNs. Each VPN has its own forwarding table, which provides isolation within the SD-WAN Edge router, using labels that are communicated as service attributes to the Catalyst SD-WAN Controllers and encapsulated in the incoming packets for identification in the forwarding plane on the SD-WAN Edge routers.

Every interface and dot1Q subinterface on a Cisco vEdge router must be mapped to a particular VPN, depending on whether the interface connects to the WAN (VPN 0), a management network (VPN 512), or a service-side LAN interface (VPN1-511).

In the context of this deployment, the VPNs shown in Table 12-2 were defined for specific purposes.

Table 12-2 *SD-WAN VPNs*

VPN Number	Description	Purpose	Retail/ Backstage/Both
0	SD-WAN Transport Routes	MPLS and WAN-Facing Interfaces	Both
1	Service-VPN (Site LAN routes)	Corp VPN	Both
10	Service-VPN (Site LAN routes)	Point of Sale (POS)	Retail
11	Service-VPN (Site LAN routes)	Guest Wired/Wireless	Both
12	Service-VPN (Site LAN routes)	Vendor	Both
13	Service-VPN (Site LAN routes)	IoT	Both
512	Management VPN	Infrastructure Management	Both

Application-Aware Policies

Application-aware routing (AAR) policies empower the SD-WAN fabric to continually monitor real-time network path quality and conduct SLA-driven assessments across optimal transports. While traditional routing protocols excel at detecting network blackout scenarios, AAR policies stand out in identifying subtle brownout conditions or soft failures marked by performance degradations. Utilizing BFD for real-time evaluation of packet loss, latency, and jitter on data plane tunnels, app route policies promptly respond to worsening IPsec tunnel characteristics by automatically rerouting application traffic to avoid performance degradation. Upon the network's recovery from the brownout, the AAR policy seamlessly restores the traffic to its original path.

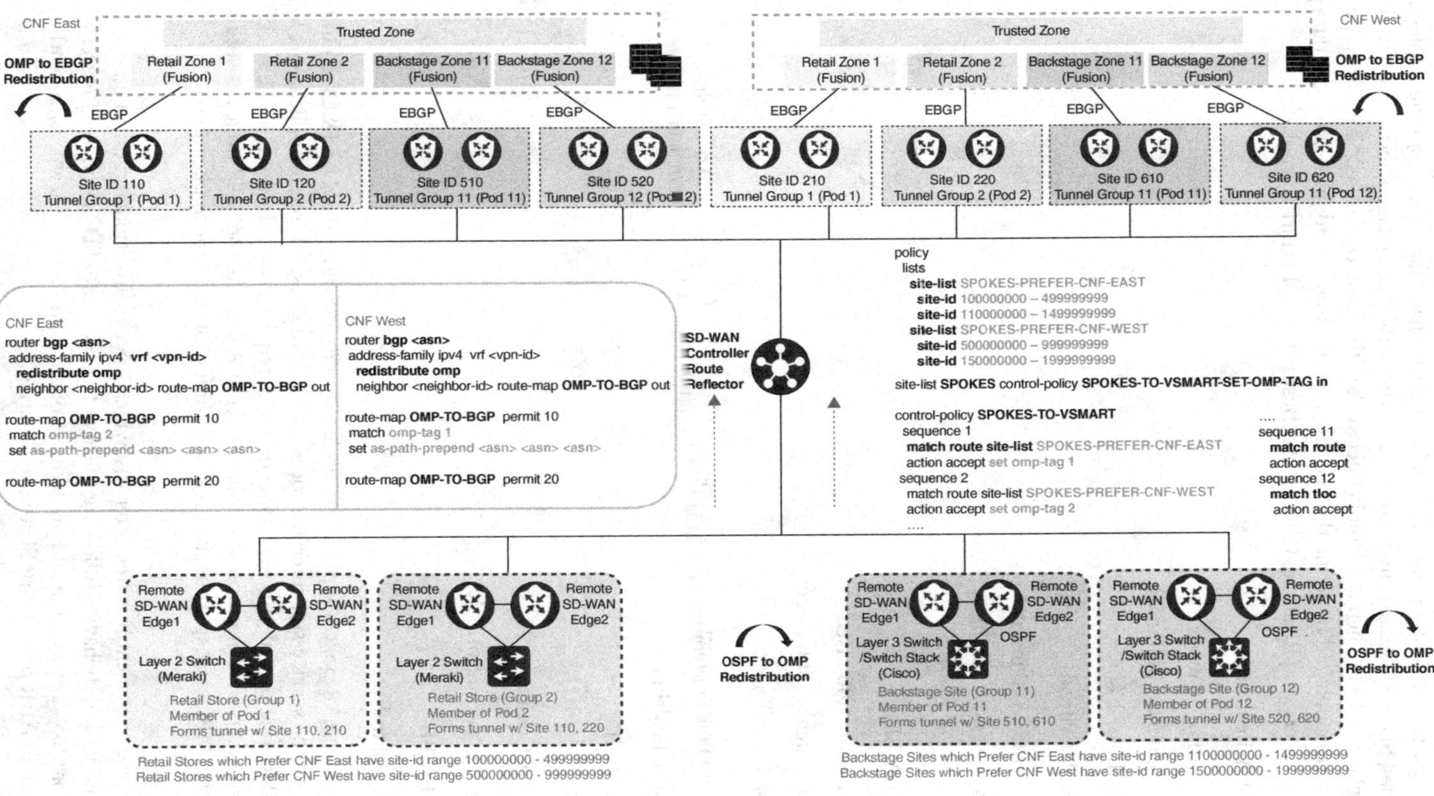

Figure 12-8 *Receiving Routes from Remote Sites*

In this particular deployment, AAR policies (centralized data policies) were implemented, allowing SD-WAN Edge routers to evaluate the performance characteristics of available data plane tunnels when determining network paths for applications. SLA-Class specifications were employed to define the maximum jitter, latency, and packet loss for data plane tunnels catering to Realtime, Critical, and Best Effort (BE) traffic types.

1. SLA-Realtime
   a. Jitter: 30 msec
   b. Latency: 300 msec
   c. Loss: 1%
2. SLA-Critical
   a. Jitter: 100 msec
   b. Latency: 300 msec
   c. Loss: 3%
3. SLA-BE
   a. Jitter: 500 msec
   b. Latency: 500 msec
   c. Loss: 3%

The following applications were mapped to each SLA-Class in the AAR policy:

1. SLA-Realtime
   a. VoIP
   b. Video
2. SLA-Critical
   a. POS (Point of Sale)
3. SLA-BE
   a. All traffic

Within the AAR policy, applications undergo categorization based on DSCP and/or IP prefix on the service-side interface for all SD-WAN Edges. For retail, applications follow ECMP routing over all transports meeting SLA requirements. However, in the backstage scenario, even when multiple transports meet SLA criteria, the AAR policy is set to prioritize MPLS transport as the preferred choice for real-time applications.

Note This deployment features enterprisewide QoS classification and queuing, extending end-to-end per-hop-behavior following the six-class model. In SD-WAN, local ingress policies for QoS classification and marking, as outlined in Table 12-3, are consistently applied before AAR policies for SLA-based routing.

Table 12-3 *Enterprisewide Classification and Marking*

Class	DSCP (match-any)	Bandwidth Percent
VoIP	EF	Priority Queue (25)
Realtime Interactive (Video)	CS4	20
Signaling, Critical-Apps (POS)	CS3, AF31	10
Management, Transactional Data	CS2, AF21	15
Bulk Data	CS1	5
Class-Default	CS0	25

Securing Internet Access with SIG

The Secure Internet Gateway (SIG) is a network security service positioned between users and the Internet, offering advanced network protection by scrutinizing web transactions across multiple security levels. In this deployment, SIG functions as the next hop to the Internet for all remote sites, including retail stores and backstage sites. SD-WAN Edges at the remote sites establish an IPsec tunnel to the SIG private gateways in the CNFs, utilizing active/standby tunnels based on the regional proximity of the CNF to the remote site.

Automated tunnels are employed to provision the data plane IPsec tunnels from the remote site to the primary (active) and secondary CNFs (standby). This entails a three-step process that includes:

1. Configuring API credentials supplied by the SIG provider.

```
# Remote SD-WAN Edge

secure-Internet-gateway
 <SIG credentials for API access>
```

2. Configuring data plane tunnels on the SD-WAN Edge for primary and secondary CNF and defining which tunnel is primary and which tunnel is backup.

```
# Remote SD-WAN Edge

interface Tunnel100101
 description Primary CNF Tunnel 1
 no shutdown
 ip unnumbered GigabitEthernet1
 ip mtu 1400
 tunnel source GigabitEthernet1
 tunnel destination dynamic
 tunnel mode ipsec ipv4
```

```
 tunnel protectional ipsec profile if-ipsec1-ipsec-profile
 tunnel vrf multiplexing

interface Tunnel100201
 description Secondary CNF Tunnel 1
 no shutdown
 ip unnumbered GigabitEthernet1
 ip mtu 1400
 tunnel source GigabitEthernet1
 tunnel destination dynamic
 tunnel mode ipsec ipv4
 tunnel protectional ipsec profile if-ipsec1-ipsec-profile
 tunnel vrf multiplexing

interface Tunnel100301
 description Primary CNF Tunnel 2
 no shutdown
 ip unnumbered GigabitEthernet2
 ip mtu 1400
 tunnel source GigabitEthernet2
 tunnel destination dynamic
 tunnel mode ipsec ipv4
 tunnel protectional ipsec profile if-ipsec1-ipsec-profile
 tunnel vrf multiplexing

interface Tunnel100401
 description Secondary CNF Tunnel 2
 no shutdown
 ip unnumbered GigabitEthernet2
 ip mtu 1400
 tunnel source GigabitEthernet2
 tunnel destination dynamic
 tunnel mode ipsec ipv4
 tunnel protectional ipsec profile if-ipsec1-ipsec-profile
 tunnel vrf multiplexing

SD-WAN
interface Tunnel100101
 tunnel-options tunnel-set secure-Internet-gateway-zscaler
tunnel-dc-preference primary-dc source-interface GigabitEthernet1
 exit
interface Tunnel100201
 tunnel-options tunnel-set secure-Internet-gateway-zscaler
tunnel-dc-preference  secondary-dc source-interface
GigabitEthernet1
```

```
 interface Tunnel100301
 tunnel-options tunnel-set secure-Internet-gateway-zscaler
tunnel-dc-preference primary-dc source-interface GigabitEthernet2
 exit
interface Tunnel100401
 tunnel-options tunnel-set secure-Internet-gateway-zscaler
tunnel-dc-preference  secondary-dc source-interface
GigabitEthernet2

SD-WAN
 service sig vrf global
  ha-pairs
   interface-pair Tunnel100101 active-interface-weight 20 Tunnel
100201 backup-interface-weight 20
   interface-pair Tunnel100301 active-interface-weight 80 Tunnel
100401 backup-interface-weight 80
```

3. Directing user traffic to SIG using centralized data policies (on Catalyst SD-WAN Controller). Note that although using a data policy is enough to steer the Internet-bound traffic to SIG GWs, a static route is needed to the backstage SD-WAN Edges at the remote sites to advertise the default route to the site-local L3 switches via OSPF.

```
#Cisco SD-WAN Controller

policy
 data-policy SPOKES
  vpn-list ALL-VPNs
   sequence 11
    match
     destination-ip 0.0.0.0/0
    !
    action accept
    sig

# Remote SD-WAN Edge
ip SD-WAN route vrf <vpn-id> 0.0.0.0/0 service sig
ip cef load-sharing algorithm src-only
```

Campus/Branch Design

Figure 12-9 provides an overview of the LAN design for both the retail stores and backstage sites.

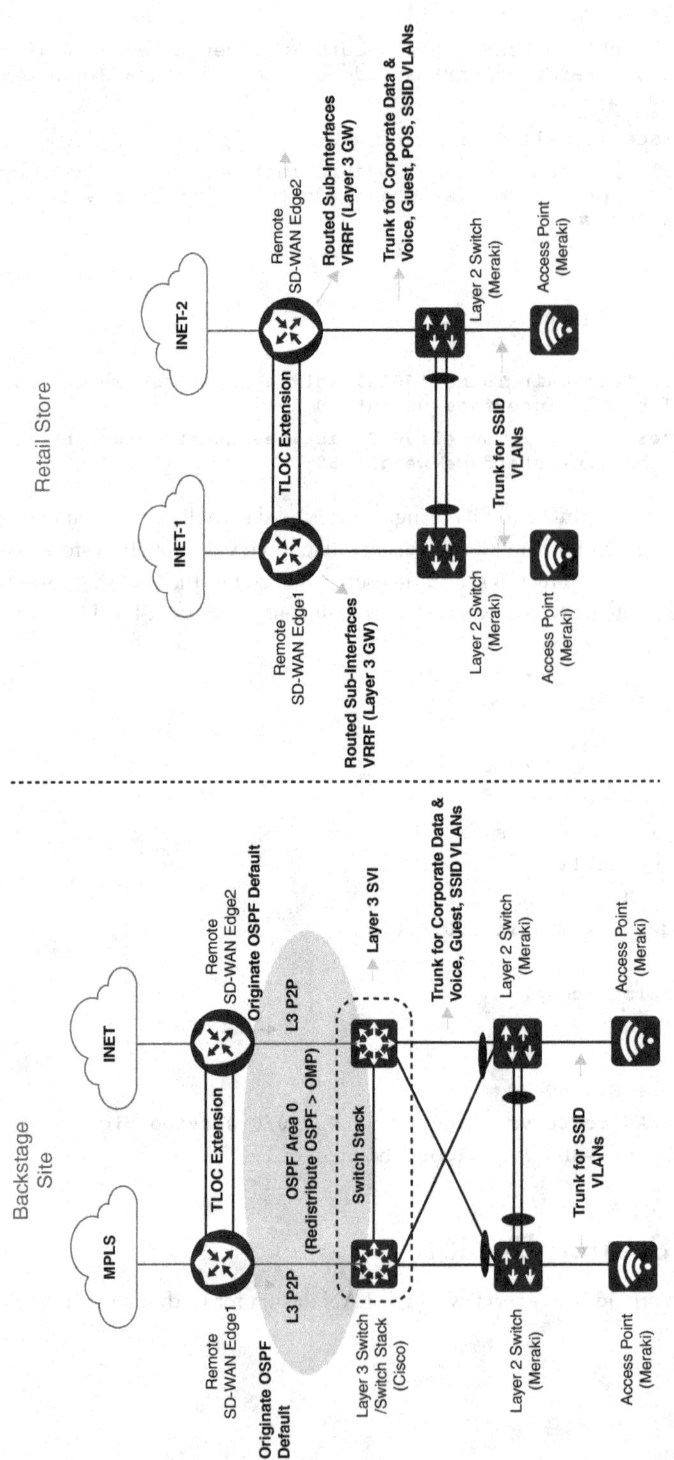

Figure 12-9 *LAN Design Overview*

Backstage Site

Backstage sites utilize a single MPLS and Internet transport. One SD-WAN Edge router connects to the MPLS connection, while the other is linked to the Internet transport. The MPLS-connected router is set up with a private tunnel color "mpls," while the Internet-connected one is configured with the public tunnel color "biz-Internet." Direct interconnect links between the two routers establish TLOC extensions for MPLS and the Internet, with each extension being unidirectional. Specifically, one link extends SD-WAN Edge-1 MPLS to SD-WAN Edge-2, and the other link extends SD-WAN Edge-2 Internet to SD-WAN Edge-1.

On the LAN side, the SD-WAN Edge routers interface with a Cisco Layer 3 (L3) switch. In the presence of two L3 switches, they are consolidated into a single switch stack. VLANs at the sites terminate on Switched Virtual Interfaces (SVIs) on the L3 switch, which handles inter-VLAN routing. The default gateway for each VLAN points to the SVI on this L3 switch. The L3 switch connects through multiple /30 routed subinterfaces, with each subinterface providing VRF-Lite routing for individual VRF/VPN to the SD-WAN Edge router. Each of these subinterfaces is configured with OSPF for route exchange of corresponding VPN routes with the SD-WAN Edge routers. For all VPNs, the L3 switch receives a default route from the SD-WAN Edge and advertises all local subnets to them. On the SD-WAN routers, different subnets for the site received in OSPF across different VPNs are redistributed into OMP.

Downstream from the L3 switch or switch stack are the Meraki access switches; user endpoints and other endpoints in the site terminate directly on the front panel ports of these Meraki L2 switches. Meraki access points also terminate on the same switches on a designated set of front panel ports trunked with wireless SSID VLANs. Each of these Meraki switches has port-channel trunk uplinks upstream to the L3 switch to trunk all wired and wireless VLANs. The VLAN list per site type is listed in Tables 12-4 through 12-7.

Table 12-4 *VLAN List—Division Segments*

VLAN Name	VPN
Corp Data	Corp VPN (VPN1)
VoIP	Corp VPN (VPN1)
Guest Wireless	Guest VPN (VPN11)
Management	Management VPN (VPN 512)
Vendor	Vendor VPN (VPN 12)
Building Services	IoT VPN (VPN 13)

Table 12-5 *VLAN List—Backstage Distribution Center*

VLAN Name	VPN
Corp WIFI	Corp VPN (VPN1)
Corp Data	Corp VPN (VPN1)
VoIP	Corp VPN (VPN1)
VoIP WIFI	Corp VPN (VPN1)
Guest Wireless	Guest VPN (VPN11)
Guest Wired	Guest VPN (VPN11)
Management	Management VPN (VPN 512)
Vendor	Vendor VPN (VPN 12)
Building Services	IoT VPN (VPN 13)
Dematic	IoT VPN (VPN 13)
Zebra	IoT VPN (VPN 13)

Table 12-6 *VLAN List—Backstage Plant*

VLAN Name	VPN
Corp WIFI	Corp VPN (VPN1)
Corp Data	Corp VPN (VPN1)
VoIP	Corp VPN (VPN1)
VoIP WIFI	Corp VPN (VPN1)
Guest Wireless	Guest VPN (VPN11)
Guest Wired	Guest VPN (VPN11)
Management	Management VPN (VPN 512)
Vendor	Vendor VPN (VPN 12)
Zebra	IoT VPN (VPN 13)

Table 12-7 *VLAN List—Backstage District Office*

VLAN Name	VPN
Corp WIFI	Corp VPN (VPN1)
Corp Data	Corp VPN (VPN1)
VoIP	Corp VPN (VPN1)
Management	Management VPN (VPN 512)

Retail Site

Retail sites employ dual Internet transport, with one SD-WAN Edge connecting to ISP1 and the other to ISP2. The router linked to ISP1 is set up with a public tunnel color "biz-Internet," and the other router is configured with a public tunnel color "public-Internet." Once again, direct-connection links between these routers establish TLOC extensions, enabling dual ISP connectivity from each SD-WAN Edge.

For LAN connectivity, user endpoints and other site endpoints terminate directly on the front panel ports of Meraki L2 switches. Meraki access points also terminate on the same switches, utilizing a specific set of front panel ports trunked with wireless SSID VLANs. In contrast to backstage sites, retail stores, considering their scale and size, do not incorporate L3 switches in the overall LAN design. Instead, the Meraki switches feature direct port-channel trunk uplinks upstream to the SD-WAN Edge routers, facilitating the trunking of all wired and wireless VLANs. All VLANs at the site terminate on subinterfaces on the LAN service-side-facing interface of each SD-WAN Edge router within their respective VRFs. The default gateway for each VLAN points to the virtual VRRP IP address configured on both SD-WAN Edge routers. The determination of which SD-WAN router is the Active or Standby for each VLAN is based on the requirements of each VLAN. No routing is configured toward the LAN, and different subnets are advertised into OMP on the SD-WAN Edge by redistributing connected subnets.

The VLAN list for the retail store is provided in Table 12-8.

Table 12-8 *VLAN List—Retail Stores*

VLAN Name	VPN
Corp WIFI	Corp VPN (VPN1)
Corp Data	Corp VPN (VPN1)
VoIP	Corp VPN (VPN1)
VoIP WIFI	Corp VPN (VPN1)
POS	POS VPN (VPN10)
Guest Wireless	Guest VPN (VPN11)
Management	Management VPN (VPN 512)
Vendor	Vendor VPN (VPN 12)
Utilities	IoT VPN (VPN 13)

Cisco TrustSec and Meraki Adaptive Policy

Security policies governing this retail deployment necessitated both macrosegmentation of traffic from remote sites to the CNF and microsegmentation for east-west traffic within and between sites. As previously mentioned, the design of the retail network ensures that communication between macrosegments (VRFs) from remote sites is facilitated by the trusted firewall in the CNF, thereby enforcing policy for all inter-VRF traffic through an L4-L7 firewall in the CNF.

However, traffic within a VRF—whether it's between VLANs within the same site or across remote sites within a pod—undergoes microsegmentation using Cisco TrustSec and Meraki adaptive policy. The choice of these technologies for configuring and enforcing microsegmentation in intra-VRF traffic stems from their operational simplicity compared to alternatives such as access lists or distributed firewalls at the remote sites.

Cisco TrustSec and, correspondingly, Meraki adaptive policies streamline the provisioning and administration of secure access to network services and applications by categorizing traffic based on the contextual identity of the endpoint rather than its IP address. Both Cisco TrustSec and Meraki adaptive policies leverage Security Group Tags (SGTs) at the point of network access. SGTs represent a policy group assigned to a network endpoint based on user, device, and location attributes. Endpoints can have SGTs assigned in various ways, such as static assignment to a switch port, static assignment per SSID, dynamic assignment via radius (wired and wireless dot1x), and static IP-to-SGT mapping. In this deployment, a combination of static and dynamic assignments was employed based on the capabilities supported by the endpoints.

The SGT serves as the endpoint's access entitlement, and all traffic originating from the endpoint carries the SGT information as inline traffic tags, providing the endpoint's group identity to the next-hop in the path. Similar to 802.1q trunking, inline tagging adds an ether-type called Cisco Metadata (CMD) before the IP header of the packet, with the SGT for the endpoint carried in the CMD header (see Figure 12-10). Inline tagging encapsulates every packet from a source, and the CMD encapsulation is preserved on a per-hop basis. Therefore, each hop must support preserving and propagating the CMD header through the network as policies are enforced at the destination hop (final hop). In this deployment, all devices at the remote site, including Meraki access switches, Meraki access points, Cisco L3 Switch Stack Core, and Cisco SD-WAN Edge routers, are capable of preserving and propagating the inline tags.

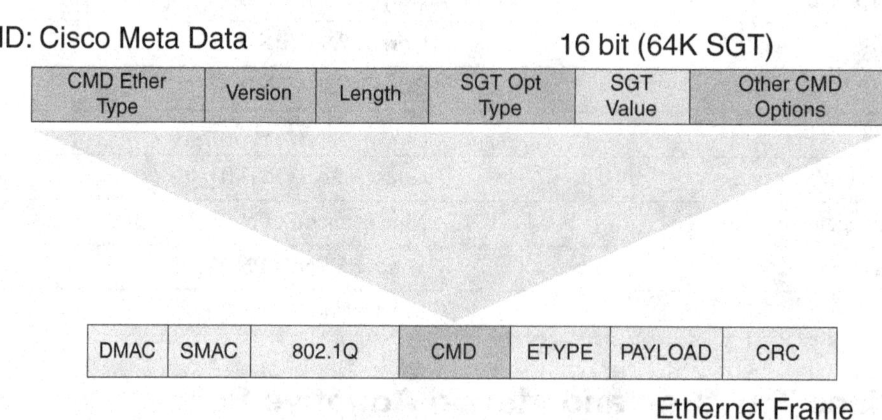

Figure 12-10 *CMD with SGT for Inline Tagging*

SGTs and the associated security policies (Allow All, Deny All, Custom ACL) for Meraki adaptive policies constitute organization-wide configurations established in the Meraki Dashboard; these policies are then propagated to all requisite Cisco Meraki devices.

In parallel, Cisco ISE operates as the policy administration point for defining SGTs, security group access control lists (SGACLs), and pushing them onto Cisco Catalyst devices. Because this deployment encompasses both Cisco Catalyst and Cisco Meraki devices, we leverage the inherent integration within ISE to synchronize Cisco ISE TrustSec policies, covering SGACLs and SGTs to the Meraki Dashboard (see Figure 12-11). This synchronization process transforms them into adaptive policy groups (SGTs) and custom ACLs (SGACLs) within the Meraki Dashboard, facilitated through the use of Meraki Dashboard APIs. This strategic approach streamlines the configuration of security groups and policies, with ISE acting as the centralized and only policy source for defining policies across both the Cisco TrustSec domain and the Meraki adaptive policy domain.

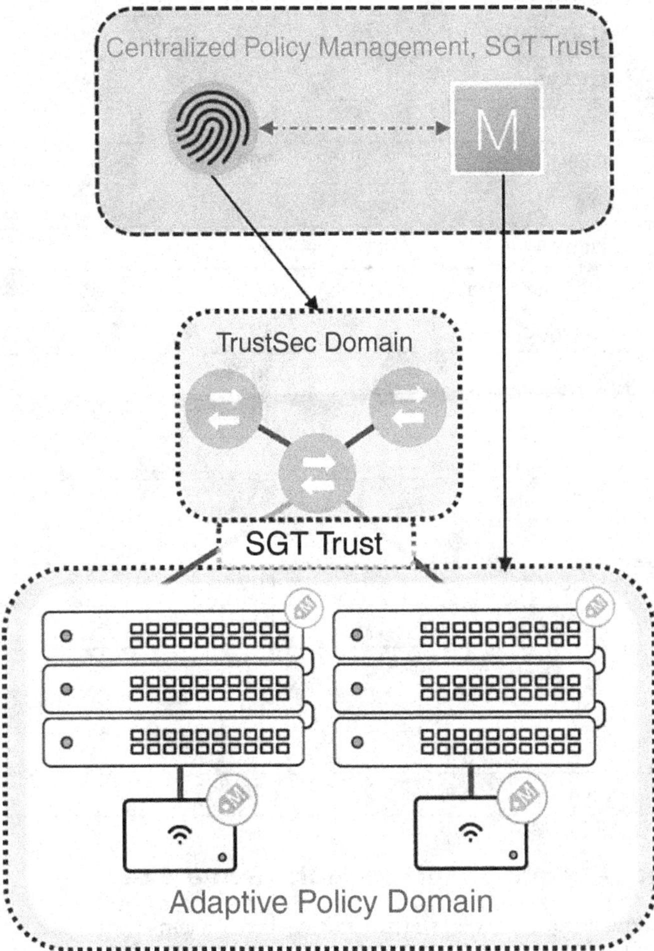

Figure 12-11 *IST Meraki SGT Trust*

Table 12-9 lists the security policy groups and their associated SGT values, along with a description of each group's function.

Table 12-9 *SGT Assignments*

SGT Group	SGT Name	SGT Value
Infrastructure SGTs		
	Unknown	0
	Peer-to-Peer	2
Corporate SGTs		
	Default	100
	Corp Data EPs	101
	Corp Static EPs	102
	Corp VoIP EPs	103
	Quarantine	104
Guest SGTs		
	Guest	200
IoT SGTs		
	Default	300
	Building Services	301
	Dematic	302
	Zebra	303
	Utilities	304
POS SGTs		
	POS	500
Vendor SGTs		
	Vendor-1	601
	Vendor-2	602
CNF		
	CNF	700
SIG		
	SIG	800

East-West Enforcement Between Endpoints in the Same Site

SGT assignment and enforcement for east-west traffic (traffic which remains within the LAN of the site) is achieved by the Meraki equipment in the case of both the backstage sites and the retail stores (see Figure 12-12). Meraki switches and APs are configured to tag endpoint traffic, propagate SGTs, and enforce policies. Polices are enforced within a VRF (microsegmentation) wherein wired and wireless users in the same SGT are allowed to communicate while wired and wireless users in different SGTs are denied by default, with specific use cases for to allow traffic using custom ACLs (SGACLs).

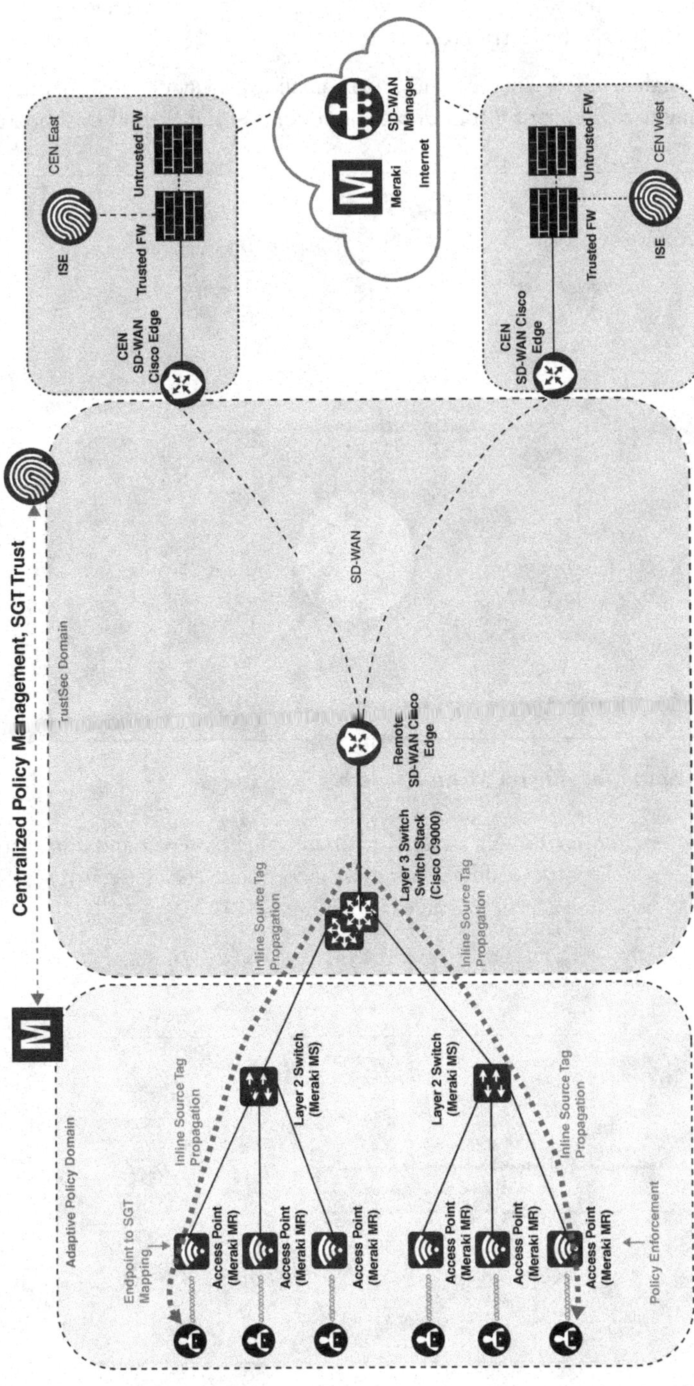

Figure 12-12 *East-West Enforcement Using Inline SGTs*

The tagging process on Meraki switches through the Meraki Dashboard includes two options: static tagging, where a switchport is directly assigned to a tag, or dynamic tagging, which uses radius attributes.

For static assignment (see Figure 12-13), you can allocate a switchport to a specific tag by navigating to **Switching > Monitor > Switch Ports** in the Meraki Dashboard.

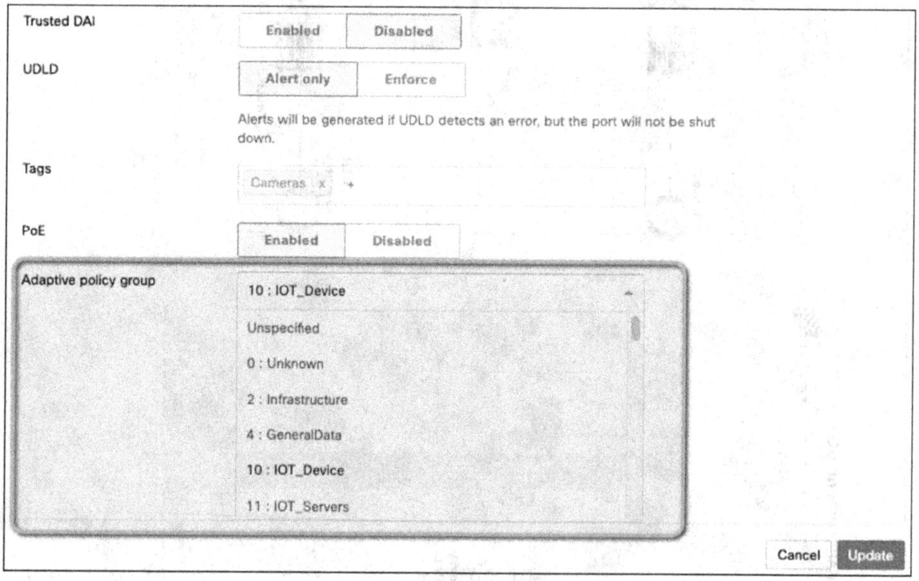

Figure 12-13 *Static Tagging on Meraki Switch*

For dynamic assignment through a radius attribute value (AV) pair and dot1x, to allocate an SGT value to a client, the radius server must incorporate the cts:security-group-tag AV pair in the radius access-accept message (see Figure 12-14):

```
cisco-av-pair:cts:security-group-tag={SGT value in HEX}-{revision
number}
```

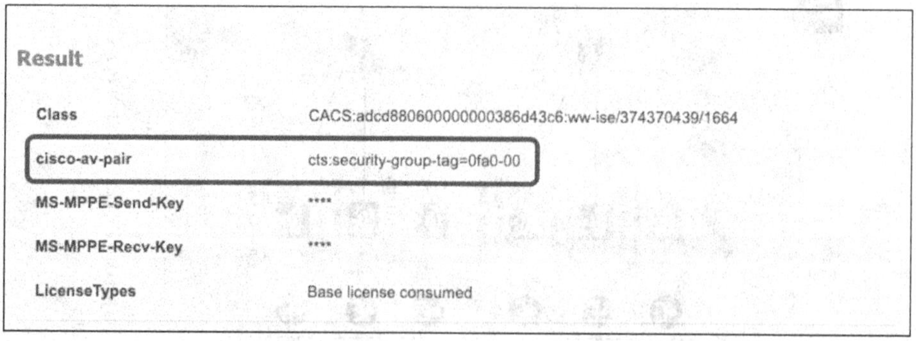

Figure 12-14 *Cisco AV-Pair Results*

Similarly for Meraki access points (APs), to apply a static tag to an SSID, you configure it under **Wireless > Access Control > Radius > Adaptive Policy Group** (see Figure 12-15).

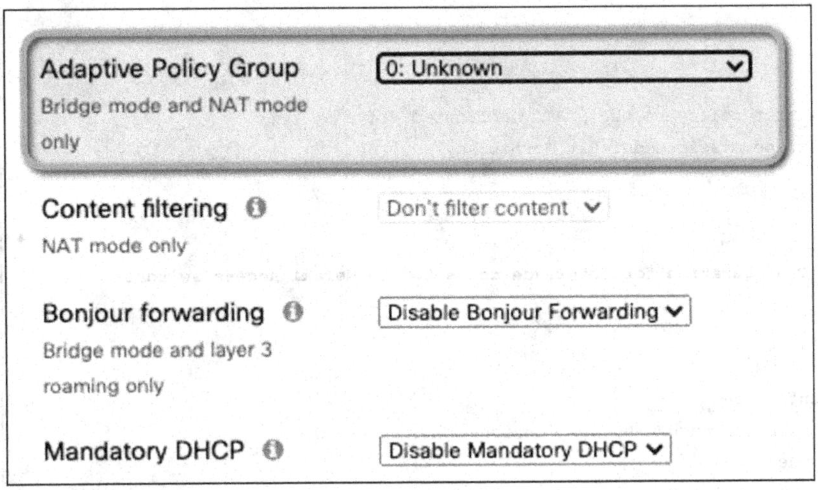

Adaptive Policy Group
Bridge mode and NAT mode only
0: Unknown

Content filtering
NAT mode only
Don't filter content

Bonjour forwarding
Bridge mode and layer 3 roaming only
Disable Bonjour Forwarding

Mandatory DHCP
Disable Mandatory DHCP

Figure 12-15 *SSID Tagging on Meraki AP*

In this scenario, all clients connected to the SSID receive the designated tag. However, if the SSID is set up to authenticate wireless clients through a radius server, the SGT obtained via the radius AV pair is applied.

The network for backstage sites has been standardized with Catalyst switching in the core of the network and Meraki switching in the access, so the Catalyst switches are required to support inline SGTs.

To enable SGT transit support on Catalyst switches, a minimal configuration is required, as shown in Example 12-1. Given that these Catalyst switches serve as aggregation switches without direct endpoint connectivity, there is no need for them to carry out any enforcement measures.

Example 12-1 *SGT Transit Configuration on Catalyst Switch*

```
# Global Configuration

configure terminal
!
#sets the system/infrastructure sgt
cts sgt 2

#enables SGT policy globally on the switch
cts role-based enforcement

#enables SGT policy on the specific VLANs
cts role-based enforcement vlan-list <vlan-list>
!
```

```
#creates a global default permit policy
ip access-list role-based Permit_Any
 permit ip
!

#sets the default policy to the SGACL configured above
cts role-based permissions default Permit_Any
!
exit

# Interface Configuration for interface connected to Meraki access switches

configure terminal
!
interface <interface>
description <link-connectivity-description>
switchport mode trunk
switchport trunk native vlan <native-vlan>
switchport trunk allowed vlan <vlan-list>

#Enables SGT encapsulation and will bounce the port
cts manual

#Sets the port to an infrastructure trusted port
 policy static sgt 2 trusted

#Disables enforcement on the port allowing for enforcement to happen downstream
no cts role-based enforcement
!
exit
```

With the configuration on the interface shown in Example 12-1, the following will occur:

- If a frame is received with an SGT assigned, the switch will honor that tag.
- If a frame is received with no encapsulation, it will be encapsulated and marked **0 - Unknown.**
- No policy enforcement will occur inbound on this port. This is desired to make sure that the policy is enforced where the destination endpoint is attached.

The Meraki uplink interface connected to the Catalyst switch is set up to permit CMD encapsulation. Additionally, it is configured with a standard infrastructure-to-infrastructure tag. The configuration for the Meraki uplink interface on the Meraki Dashboard is outlined in Figure 12-16:

- **Type: Trunk**—Required for SGT propagation to be configured.
- **Peer SGT capable: Enabled**—Turns on CMD encapsulation.

- **Adaptive Policy Group: 2: Infrastructure**—Enables a peer-to-peer tag of 2 (standard infrastructure-to-infrastructure tag). This is the best practice for all tag-based security deployments.

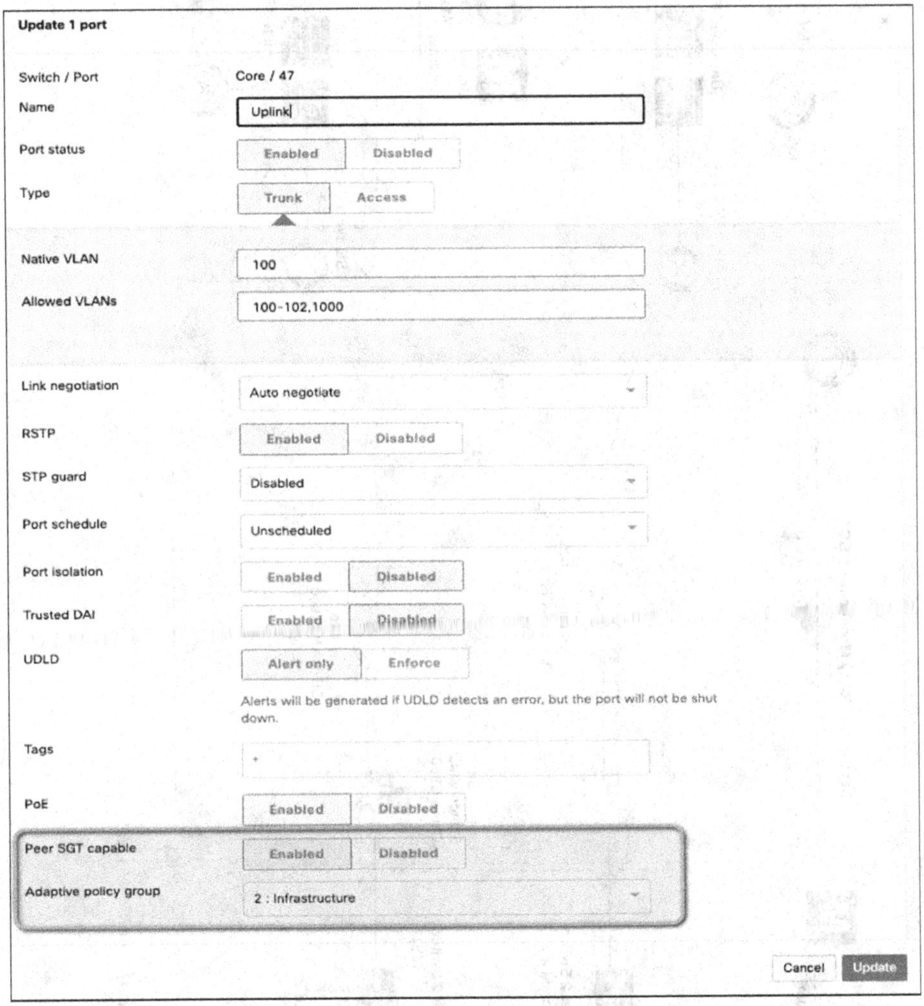

Figure 12-16 *Meraki Uplink Configuration for Peer SGT*

East-West Enforcement Between Endpoints in Different Sites

Communication between SD-WAN sites within a pod is facilitated through the SD-WAN fabric, routing traffic to the SD-WAN headend routers in the CNF. This is achieved by configuring spoke-to-spoke route advertisements with a TLOC next-hop set to the CNF headends. The SD-WAN routers support inline SGTs, ensuring the propagation of tags end-to-end between sites, with policy enforcement occurring on the destination Meraki device within each site (see Figure 12-17).

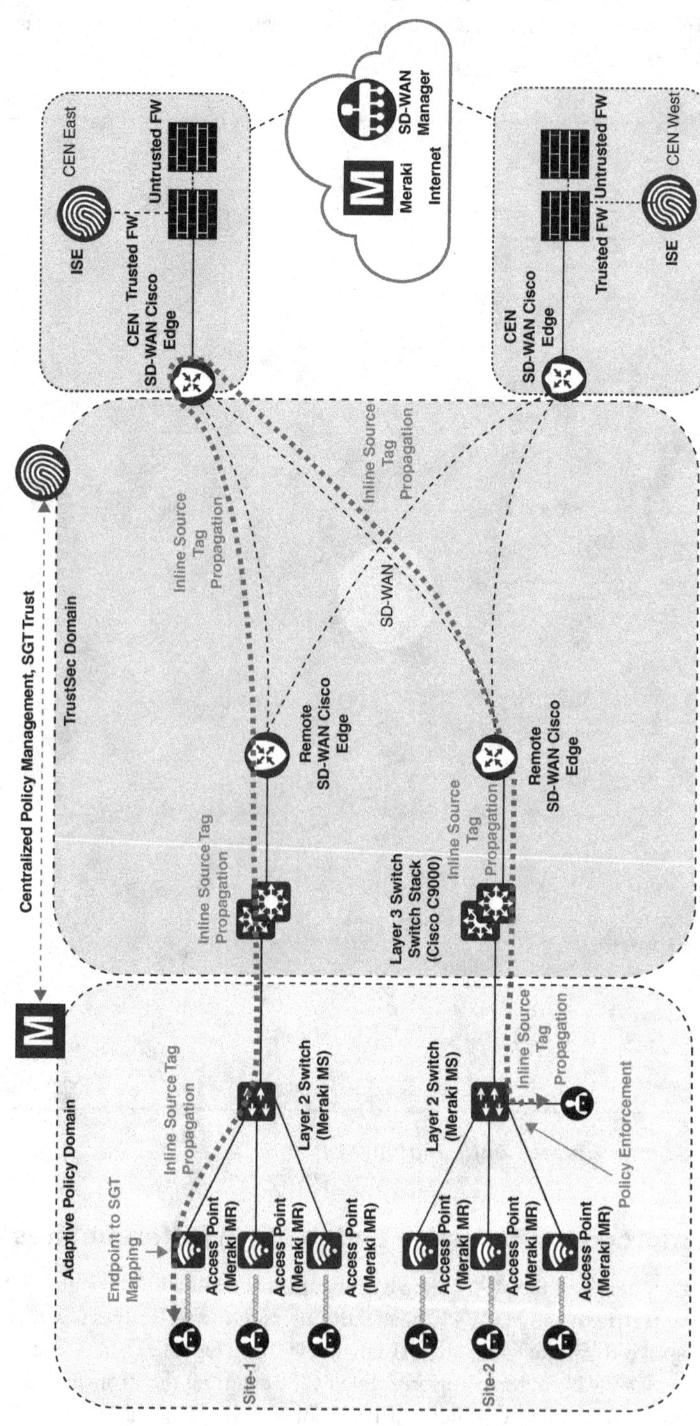

Figure 12-17 *East-West Enforcement Between Sites*

In the illustrated setup, both Site-1 and Site-2 are equipped with TrustSec-enabled Meraki switches/APs and Cisco Catalyst switches, interconnected with SD-WAN Edge devices. The Meraki switch or Meraki AP in Site-1 assigns SGT labels to traffic from endpoints, propagating SGT inline tags within the Ethernet CMD frame toward the Catalyst switch. The Catalyst switch, in turn, forwards the SGT inline tag to the SD-WAN Edge routers in Site-1. These SD-WAN Edge routers then de-encapsulate the CMD frame, extract the SGT, and propagate it over SD-WAN IPSec tunnels toward the CNF.

Figure 12-18 depicts the inclusion of SGT within an SD-WAN packet. Within the CNF, the SD-WAN Edge routers extract the SGT while performing an IP lookup for the destination in Site-2, reinforcing the SGT on the tunnel toward the SD-WAN Edges in Site-2. The SD-WAN Edge routers in Site-2 extract the SGT from SD-WAN, generate the Ethernet CMD frame, and replicate the received SGT. The Meraki switch in Site-2 inspects the received SGT, cross-referencing it against the destination SGT to determine whether the traffic should be allowed or denied.

Outer IP Header	UDP Header	IPSEC Header	MPLS Lable	VPN Label 16 bits	MDATA Header	SGT 16 bits	Inner Client IP Header	Original Payload	IPSEC Trailer

Figure 12-18 *SD-WAN–SGT Propagation*

SGT Mapping for DC Endpoints for North-South Flows and SIG Traffic

The enforcement of SGT policies operates bidirectionally, meaning that the destination device in any direction of a flow should not only be capable of tagging and propagating SGT but also enforcing allow or deny policies by cross-referencing the source SGT against the destination SGT.

Regarding traffic directed to the data center, despite the presence of an L4-L7 firewall for policy enforcement, it is imperative to tag all data center prefixes in the CNF under one SGT. This facilitates the adaptive policy process for all traffic inclusive of data center traffic because devices in both the SD-WAN domain and the Meraki domain at remote sites are configured to enforce TrustSec/adaptive policies. When all prefixes are consolidated from the CNF under a single SGT at the source (CNF headend SD-WAN Edge routers), any traffic destined from the CNF to remote sites is explicitly allowed under a policy checked on the Meraki destination devices. Similarly, traffic originating from remote sites (Meraki access) to the CNF is scrutinized on the CNF headend SD-WAN Edge, assigned a destination tag of CNF, and explicitly allowed. This ensures comprehensive inline tagging for all prefixes, preventing data center traffic from being untagged or in an unknown state within the TrustSec domain (see Figure 12-19).

Similarly, for SIG traffic, all traffic received on the SIG tunnels is configured with a SIG tag to enable tag propagation and enforcement of SIG flows across the SD-WAN and Meraki TrustSec domains.

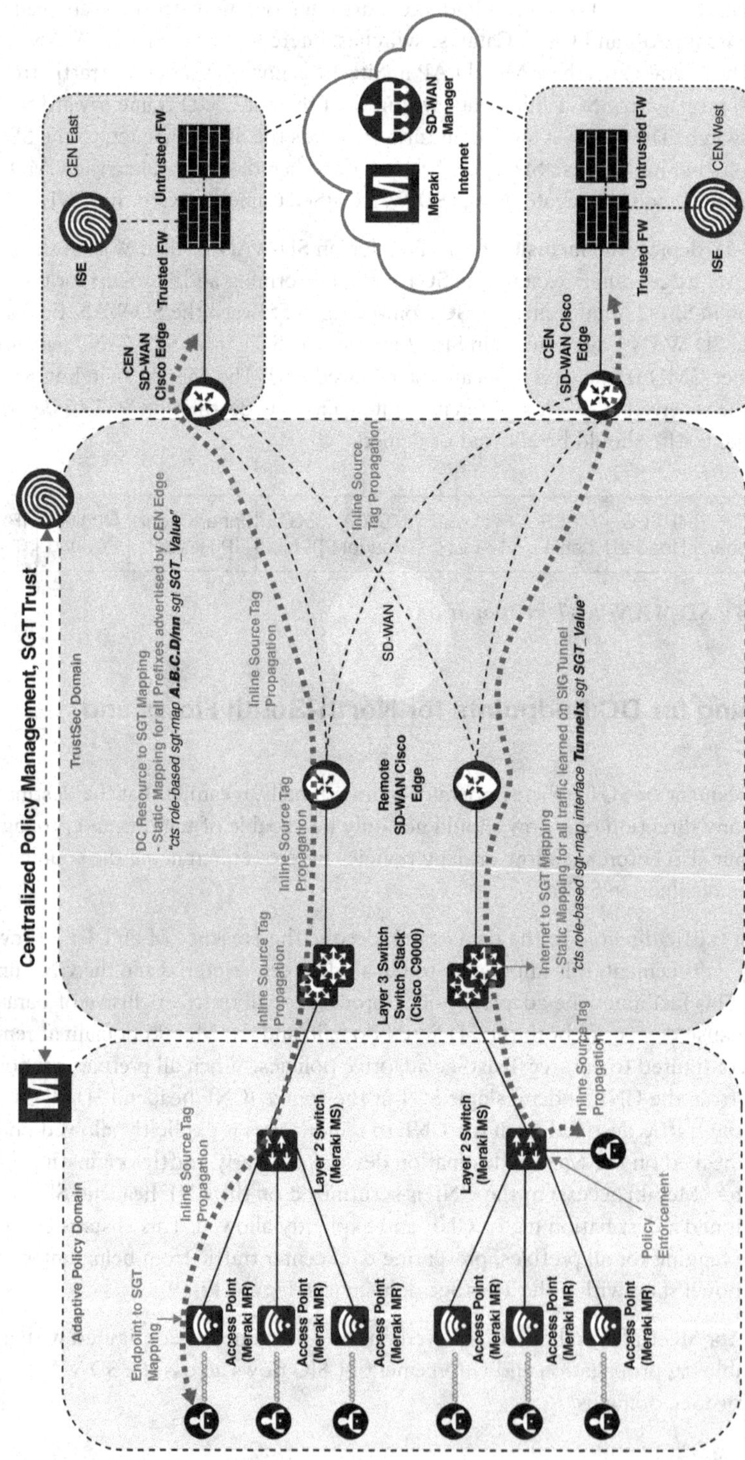

Figure 12-19 *SGT Mapping for DC Endpoints and SIG Traffic*

Hybrid Cloud Integration

In this specific deployment, a hybrid cloud integration is employed, connecting Azure and Cisco ACI. With workloads distributed across the ACI fabric in CNFs and Azure VNs, the ACI and hybrid cloud integration empowers this enterprise to uphold a unified security and network policy stance throughout their hybrid environment. The management of these policies as well as the overlay interconnectivity between the sites is centralized through the Cisco Nexus Dashboard Orchestrator (NDO) and Cisco Cloud Network Controller (CNC).

While the ACI fabric within the CNFs caters to internal components of the e-commerce application (on-premises web workloads, on-premises Kubernetes clusters for backend services), and on-premises shared services such as internal DNS, NTP, Active Directory, MS Exchange, Identity Store, and on-premises SQL databases, the deployment on Azure focuses on external components of the same microservices-based e-commerce application utilizing Azure Web App Service, Azure Kubernetes Service, and Azure Managed SQL Instance service with a multi-region deployment.

Key features of this solution for application development include the following:

- It is developed as microservices and deployed using Azure Kubernetes Service (AKS).
- The application is active in two regions, with load balancing facilitated by Azure Front Door.
- The application utilizes availability zones (AZs) for all considered services to maximize availability within a single Azure region, distributing components across physically separate data centers inside a region.
- The application utilizes a content delivery network for low-latency global access to static content.
- You can implement continuous integration and continuous deployment (CI/CD) with Infrastructure as Code using Azure DevOps. Use the same container images to deploy both to the public cloud and on-premises.

The outlined architecture in Figure 12-20 presents the framework for the e-commerce retail application, encompassing a web application frontend, backend services, a database, and additional functionalities.

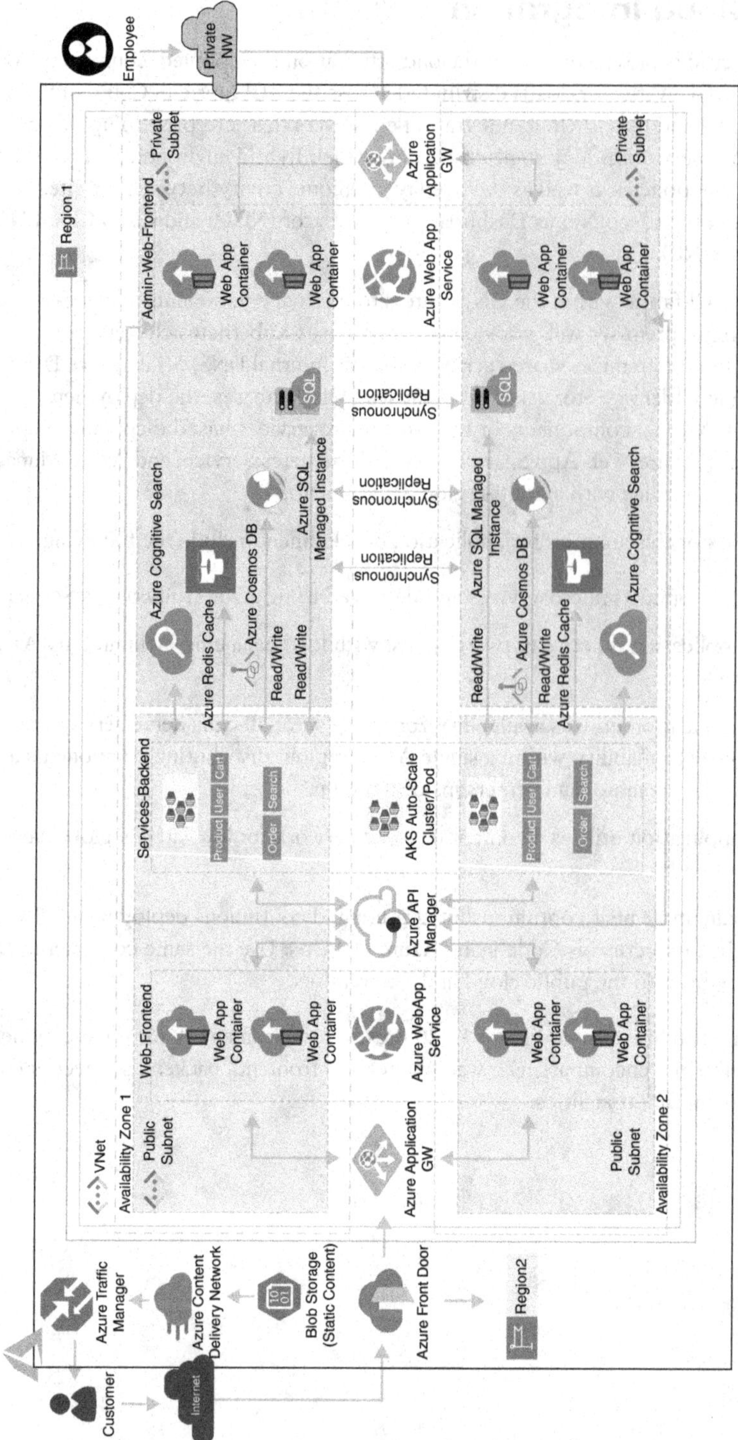

Figure 12-20 *Azure Architecture—Retail Ecommerce Application*

- **Web Application Frontend:**

  The frontend of the e-commerce application serves as the user interface for customers, facilitating interaction with the application. It is responsible for displaying product information, enabling users to add products to their cart, and initiating the checkout process.

  External access to the web application over the Internet is facilitated through Azure Front Door and Azure Application Gateway hosted in the public subnet. For internal (employee) access, the Azure Application Gateway alone is utilized. Azure Front Door aids in load balancing traffic across regions with global traffic routing capabilities. On the other hand, the Azure Application Gateway functions as a Layer 7 (HTTP/S) load balancer and web traffic manager. It employs URL path-based routing to distribute incoming traffic across availability zones and offloads encryption to enhance application performance. The Azure Application Gateway also incorporates the Web Application Firewall (WAF) to safeguard against common web-based attack vectors.

  The compute for the web frontend is hosted on Azure Web App service, offering fully managed hosting for web applications, including websites and web APIs. Utilizing Web App for Containers, developers have the capability to deploy and operate containerized web applications on either Linux or Windows. In this specific deployment, we employ Linux containers. This service provides a managed platform for deploying a single artifact containing an app and its dependencies. Containerized web apps on Azure App Service can scale as needed and utilize streamlined CI/CD workflows. The web app service frontend communicates with the backend through an API gateway.

- **API Gateway:**

  The API gateway serves as a single-entry point for all client requests to the backend services. It manages incoming requests, directs them to the appropriate backend service, and returns the corresponding response to the client.

  Embracing an API-first approach, the application gateway integrates with the API manager. The API manager is configured with separate base URLs for internal and external access. The application gateways, in turn, are configured with path-based routing rules to redirect URL requests from both internal and external users either to the API manager or to a backend pool for the web app service. Alternatively, it directs requests to a backend pool with no target (dead end—sink pool). This configuration safeguards the Internet-facing public endpoint of the API manager and provides flexibility to expose only selected APIs externally while keeping others internal.

- **Backend Services:**

  The backend of the e-commerce application encompasses various microservices, each dedicated to specific functionalities:

  - **Authentication Service:** Responsible for user authentication and authorization, the authentication service provides endpoints for user registration, login, and logout.
  - **Product Service:** Tasked with managing product information, the product service provides endpoints for retrieving product details, creating new products, and updating existing products.
  - **Cart Service:** The cart service manages user shopping carts, offering endpoints for adding products, updating quantities, and removing items.
  - **Order Service:** The order service oversees orders placed by users, providing endpoints for creating new orders, retrieving order history, and updating order statuses.

  A microservice represents a unit of code that is loosely coupled and can be independently deployed. These microservices commonly communicate through well-defined APIs and are identified through some form of service discovery. It is essential for this service to remain accessible even when workloads are in flux. The Kubernetes Service object offers a natural approach to model the needs of a microservices architecture. In this deployment, the Azure Kubernetes Service (AKS) offers a managed Kubernetes cluster specifically hosted in the Azure cloud for backend microservices.

- **Database and Data Management:**

  The database serves as the repository for all essential data within the e-commerce application, encompassing user details, product information, shopping cart contents, and order history. Its role extends to both storing and retrieving data, with a primary focus on ensuring data consistency and integrity.

  In the context of a microservices architecture, a fundamental principle is to prevent services from sharing data storage solutions. Each service should autonomously manage its unique dataset to mitigate hidden dependencies and inadvertent coupling arising from shared data schemas. This approach also allows each service to utilize the most suitable data store based on its specific requirements. In this deployment, the avoidance of local cluster storage aims to decouple data from individual nodes, opting instead for external services like Azure SQL Managed Instance Database and Azure Cosmos DB to handle persistent data for each service.

  Azure Cosmos DB, a fully managed, high-performance NoSQL database service, serves dual purposes as a session store for persistent session data, such as shopping cart details, and as the product database. Its schema-less nature offers considerable flexibility in seamlessly incorporating new product categories and attributes into the existing catalog.

The Azure SQL Managed Instance (MI) database hosts user and orders databases, providing a reliable, structured, and scalable solution that strongly supports data integrity, security, and the execution of complex queries.

In addition to the core database, supplementary services like Azure RedisCache and Azure Cognitive Search play crucial roles. Azure RedisCache serves as both a session store for volatile data and a caching layer for the product catalog, effectively reducing I/O and associated costs on CosmosDB. Furthermore, Azure Cognitive Service facilitates the loading of product catalog data into the Azure Cognitive Search Index, delivering rapid and highly scalable search functionality.

All the services mentioned boast multi-region and multi-zone capabilities, fortified with support for replication and disaster recovery.

Azure Service Deployment and Connectivity Considerations

It's crucial to note that while various services such as Azure Application Gateway, Azure API Manager, Azure Web App, Azure EKS, Azure SQL MI, Azure Cosmos DB, Azure Web App, Azure RedisCache, and Azure Cognitive Search are inherent Platform-as-a-Service (PaaS) offerings by Azure, only specific services among them can be deployed as dedicated instances within a virtual network (VNet). These can be directly accessed through either private or public connectivity to the VN. Conversely, there are services that cannot be deployed within a VN and are exclusively accessible through Azure private endpoints and/or Azure public service endpoints.

A private endpoint establishes a secure and private connection to an Azure service using Azure Private Link. It utilizes a private IP address from your virtual network, seamlessly integrating the service into the virtual network. On the other hand, service endpoints leverage public routable IP addresses, allowing the virtual network resources to use private IP addresses to connect to an Azure service public endpoint through the Azure backbone network. With service endpoints enabled when you access the resource from inside Azure, you still use the public IP, but the traffic never leaves Azure. It also allows you to lock down a resource so that it is accessible from only one or more of your Azure VNs. On the other hand, a private endpoint gives a resource a private IP in addition to a public IP. This means it's possible to access it from anywhere on your internal network, not just Azure VNs.

In this particular deployment, as illustrated in Figure 12-21, most service instances, including the application gateway, API manager, Web App service, and EKS, are deployed as dedicated instances within individual subnets within the same VN. Precise control over inbound and outbound network access for each subnet or service is maintained through network security groups. Services like Cosmos DB and Azure Cognitive Search, which cannot be deployed as dedicated instances within a VN, are accessed using private endpoints.

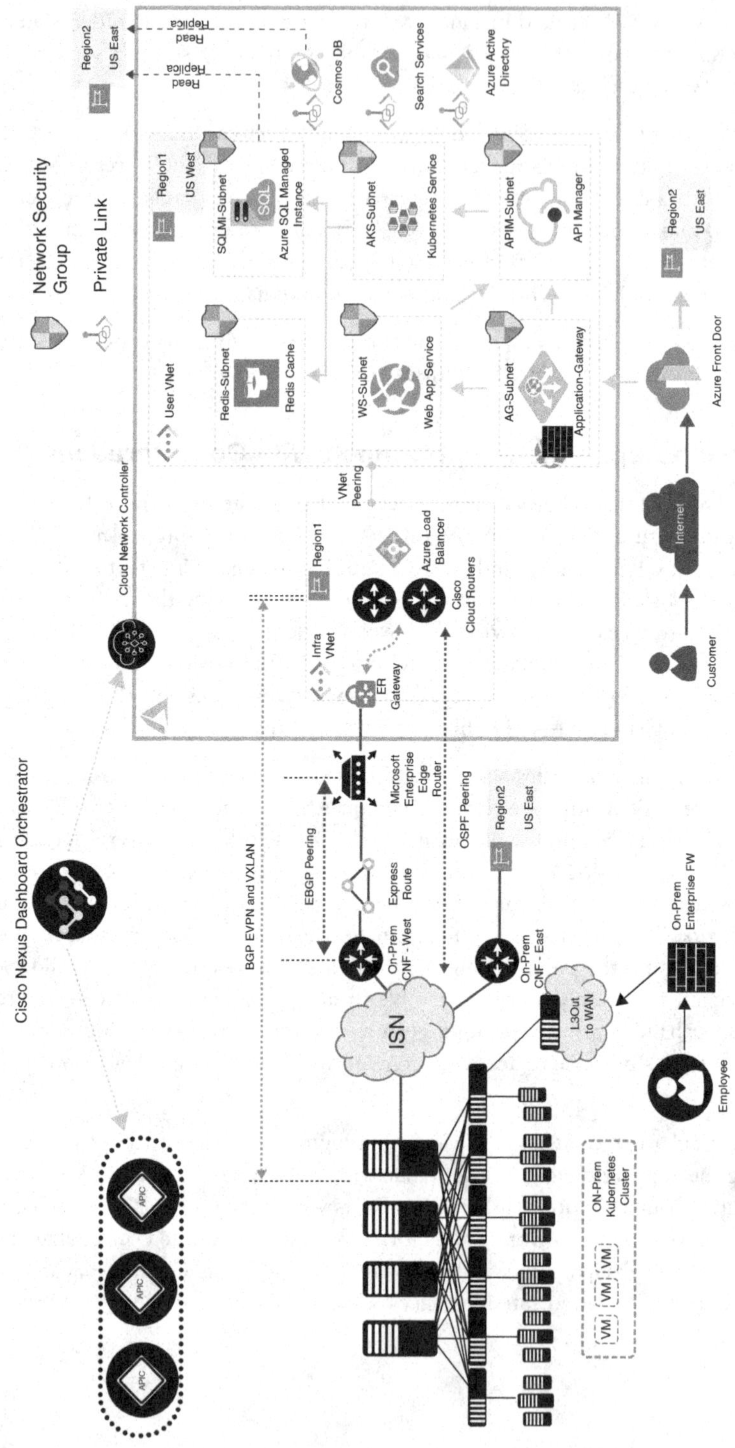

Figure 12-21 *Azure Service Deployment and Connectivity*

- **Internet Users Connectivity Management:**

  For external Internet users, connectivity is overseen through global resources like Azure Front Door, which acts as a universal entry point for all incoming HTTP(S) traffic from the Internet. Azure Front Door ensures load balancing between regions based on proximity and service availability. Additionally, Azure CDN is utilized to serve static images and content to Internet users. Traffic directed from Azure Front Door is channeled to application gateways, where the application gateway, equipped with URL path-based routing, strategically redirects API traffic to the API manager and web portal traffic to the Web App Service. The application gateway is enhanced with network security groups and a Web Application Firewall to regulate incoming requests. It further facilitates routing to targets with no services attached, often referred to as dead ends.

  At the API manager level, APIs are configured to accept calls using either the /internal pattern or the /external pattern. Serving as an API gateway, the API manager functions as a single entry point for all client requests to backend services. This encompasses direct API requests from external and internal users, as well as API requests from the web app service portals. The backend services are configured to access services within the same VN, such as the SQL MI database and Redis-Cache, or services outside the VN, such as Cosmos DB and Search services, using private links.

- **Internal Users Connectivity Routing:**

  Internal user connectivity is routed through the ACI overlay connectivity between the Cisco Cloud Routers and the ACI spines in the CNF. The overlay network leverages Azure Express Cloud Exchange connectivity, which includes redundant on-premises CNF routers, the Microsoft Enterprise Edge router, and the Express Route Gateway, forming the underlay. This setup ensures IP reachability from the spines to the Cisco Cloud Routers.

  Using BGP as the control plane, the overlay connectivity engages in the reciprocal exchange of cloud CIDRs with the on-premises network. A contract relationship between cloud EPGs and the on-premises ACI L3Out facilitates the exchange of cloud CIDR prefixes out the L3Out in the CNFs to the CNF core and backbone. Additionally, it enables the exchange of CNF and SD-WAN prefixes learned via the on-premises L3Out to the cloud. VXLAN serves as the mechanism for data transport between the spines and the Cisco Cloud Routers.

  Each CNF establishes a direct connectivity link to the corresponding Azure region. Specifically, CNF-East establishes a connection to Azure East, while CNF-West connects to Azure West. The CNF backbone network plays a crucial role in facilitating interconnectivity between Azure regions and remote sites.

Cloud Services (PaaS) Integration with ACI

Cisco ACI provides robust support for the seamless integration of Azure's cloud-native (PaaS) services. This integration is designed to streamline workload connectivity and automate security rule enforcement for these services using ACI. PaaS services supported by ACI can take two forms: they can either be cloud-native managed services deployed within a VN, created and managed through Cloud Network Controller and Nexus Dashboard Orchestrator, or they can be cloud-native services accessible to the managed VN through private and public services endpoints.

All cloud-native services are encapsulated within a cloud service endpoint group (EPG) for each service instance, as illustrated in Figure 12-22. Contract and/or service-graph relationships between these cloud service EPGs facilitate network communication and security policy (network security group policies) enforcement for communication between cloud EPGs as well as between the cloud EPGs and the external EPGs for internet and on-premise access.

Configuring a cloud-native service EPG, with either public or private connectivity, involves the following steps:

1. **Azure Service-Type Selection:** Choose the specific Azure service type, such as Azure-SQL, Azure-AKS, or Azure-APIGW.

2. **Deployment Type Choice:** Opt for PaaS (cloud-native), PaaS managed (cloud-native managed), or SaaS (third-party marketplace/service) as the deployment type.

3. **Access Type Selection:** Determine whether the access should be private or public.

4. **VRF (Virtual Routing and Forwarding) Selection:** Specify the Virtual Routing and Forwarding context.

5. **Private Link Label Assignment:** If the access type is private, assign the private link label to associate the service EPG with a private subnet.

6. **Service Endpoint Selector Choice:** Choose from options like Tag, Region, IP, Service Resource-Name, Cloud Resource ID (Azure's ID for the resource), or URL (alias or FQDN identifying the service).

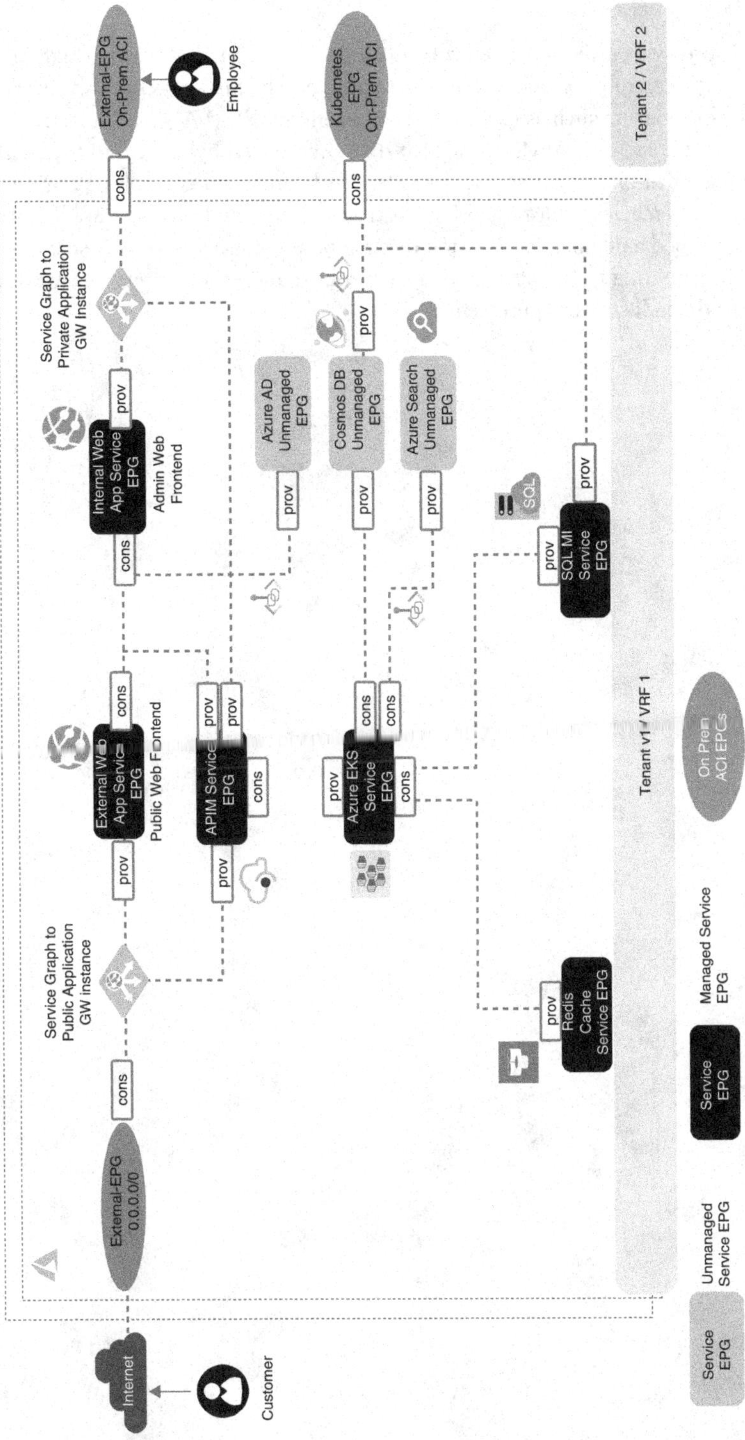

Figure 12-22 *Integration of Azure Cloud Native Services with Cisco ACI*

Summary

In this chapter, we delved into the evolving landscape of retail networks, highlighting the growing trend of adopting a cloud-first strategy. The infrastructure revolves around essential components such as Carrier Neutral Facilities, SD-WAN for WAN overlay, Meraki for user access, and Cisco ACI for data centers and hybrid cloud applications. This strategic combination empowers retailers with enhanced control, flexibility, and resilience in overseeing their network infrastructure, remote users, and applications. The chapter provided a detailed exploration of each building block and their seamless integration, contributing to the development of a robust and efficient retail network design tailored to the industry's requirements.

Chapter 13

Public Sector Use Case

In this chapter, we discuss the following:

- Managing the lifecycle of private applications using Application Centric Infrastructure (ACI)
- Understanding private WAN design, segmentation, and architecture using MPLS Segment Routing (MPLS-SR)
- Using private Infrastructure-as-a-Service (IaaS) platforms and their integration with ACI
- Automating the infrastructure using network-as-a-code concepts

Use Case Overview

This chapter delves into enterprise architecture within the public sector domain, encompassing components and technologies designed to uphold the mission-critical communication and data exchange needs of government organizations. Public sector networks encounter unique challenges due to the sensitivity of government data and the imperative to comply with specific regulations. Security, scalability, and reliability emerge as the primary considerations in the infrastructure of public sector networks.

The public sector network examined in this chapter serves as a mission-critical network spanning a major U.S. city, connecting 450 remote stations via MPLS Segment Routing (MPLS-SR). It incorporates three hub locations with data center (DC) and disaster recovery (DR) functions utilizing Application Centric Infrastructure (ACI) to support private applications, Internet connectivity, connections to external vendors, and cloud exchanges. Additionally, five core locations house campus offices and provide point-of-presence capacity for terminating sub-loop connectivity for MPLS rings originating from remote sites.

In this chapter, we delve into key aspects related to the business and operational objectives of this infrastructure, including

- Streamlining application deployment by enabling seamless transition of applications/services across different lifecycle phases (production, development, user-acceptance testing), while reducing complexity and enhancing simplicity.
- Implementing workload microsegmentation in data centers and enforcing L4-L7 policies for segments across remote sites, the wide area network (WAN), and the data center. This ensures authorized users have access to designated information through approved means, emphasizing data integrity.
- Ensuring high availability through redundant systems and a redundant architecture deployed enterprisewide.
- Enhancing operational efficiency through automation, leveraging capabilities to expedite deployment of new sites and new services, while actively managing risks via automated testing and validation.

Overall Design

The enterprise architecture in this public sector context involves several key components, including an extensive private wide area network (WAN) that utilizes MPLS and Interior Gateway Protocol (IGP) with segment routing capabilities. This network seamlessly connects remote locations to data centers, ensuring smooth connectivity across the entire enterprise. Additionally, private software-defined fabric-based data centers leverage Application Centric Infrastructure with two fabrics at each data center site. The core fabric is dedicated to hosting essential private applications, while the DMZ fabric is designed for public-facing workloads. The DMZ fabric also facilitates connectivity to the Internet, cloud exchanges, and other affiliated networks, encompassing vendor networks and those of other public sector agencies.

Furthermore, remote sites utilize Cisco Catalyst switches and Cisco Catalyst access points to provide both wired and wireless LAN connectivity for users and devices at each location. The LAN segments at each site extend onto the MPLS-SR WAN, enabling access to services deployed in the data center and supporting inter-site connectivity for services like VoIP. Wireless controllers are deployed in the data center, with all wireless traffic being tunneled or encapsulated back to the data centers, covering both corporate employee and guest access. Throughout the network, traffic between various building blocks or network segments is directed through policy enforcement points at different locations for L4-L7 inspection. Figure 13-1 offers a comprehensive view of the enterprise architecture encompassing data centers, the MPLS WAN core, and remote sites.

The MPLS-SR core network is composed of a core-ring/core-loop spanning three data center locations and five additional core sites. Furthermore, there are 60 sub-loops that connect back to the core-ring/core-loop, establishing connections with approximately 450 remote stations. The foundational physical connectivity for both the core and the sub-loops is facilitated through a privately managed optical transport network (OTN), incorporating Cisco Optical Controllers, Cisco OTN switching, Cisco transponders, and Cisco Reconfigurable Optical Add-Drop Multiplexers (ROADMS), details of which go beyond the scope of this chapter.

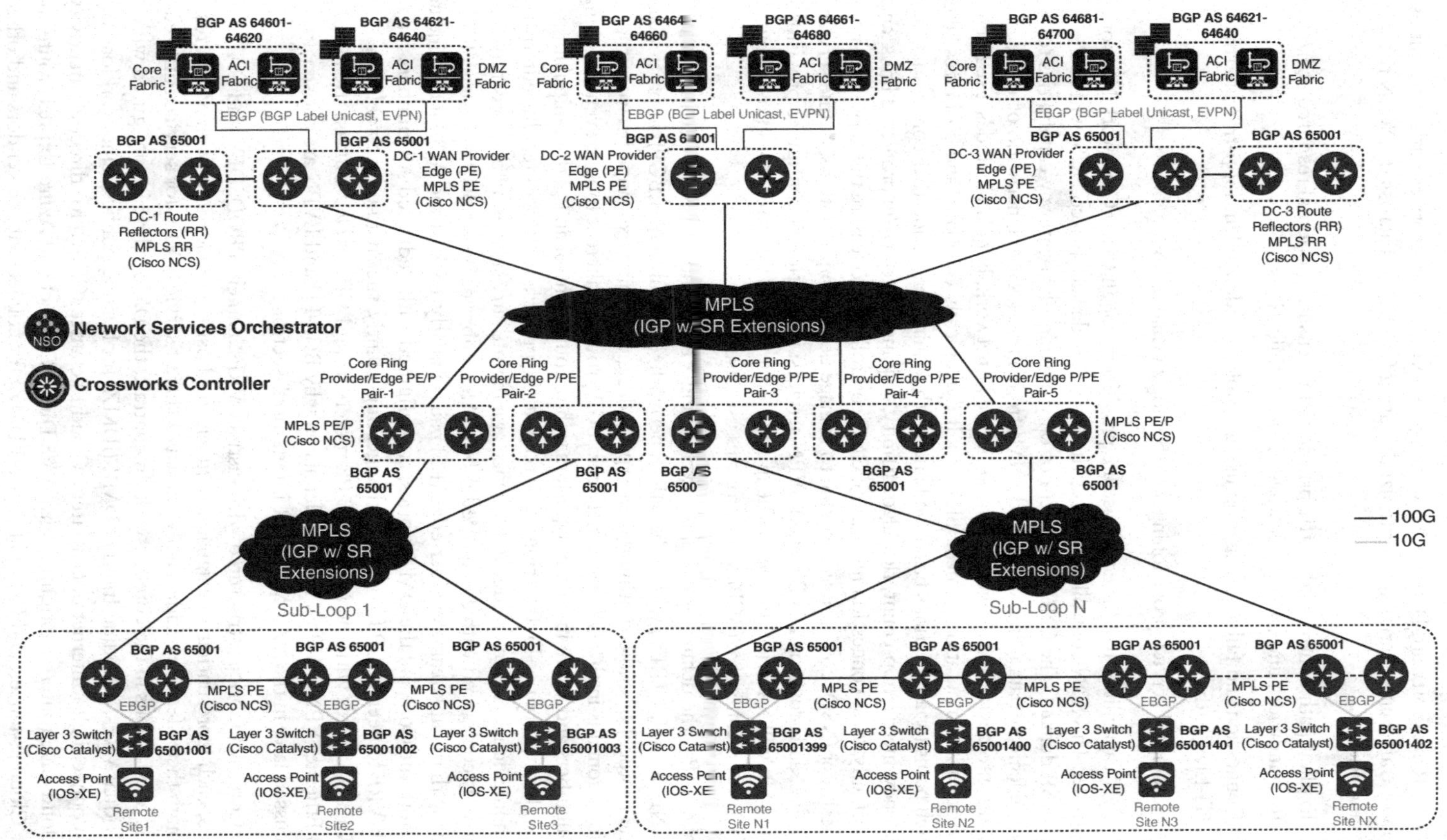

Figure 13-1 *Overall Enterprise Architecture*

MPLS-SR and Software-Defined Networking (SDN) equip enterprises with capabilities to support traffic engineering and optimized routing for all flows across the WAN network. This includes

- Explicit path control and traffic prioritization, ensuring optimal resource utilization for bandwidth and latency-sensitive critical applications
- Congestion and failure mitigation using topology-independent loop-free alternate (TI-LFA) paths
- Automated service provisioning and topology visualization

The SDN capabilities for this enterprise are provided through Cisco Crosswork Network Controller. This SDN controller manages the Cisco XR devices (Cisco NCS) within the MPLS-SR domain. The CNC controller not only provides data-gateway capabilities to ingest telemetry data using SNMP and gNMI from all nodes in the network, offering insights into device and service health across the IP network, but also includes a segment-routing path computation element (SR-PCE). It dynamically calculates and optimizes label switch paths for applications based on bandwidth requirements and other constraints such as latency, metric, hop-count, flex-algo, affinity, disjoint, protected/unprotected links, and importantly, local congestion mitigation. CNC controllers also feature the network services orchestrator (NSO) configuration engine to manage device configurations, define service packages, and provision L2VPN and L3VPN services; in addition, it configures provisioning for the SR-MPLS service transport. The illustration in Figure 13-2 presents an overview of the routing architecture (BGP) design for this use case.

While BGP is the default protocol for exchanging VPNv4 and EVPN service prefixes (ELINE, ELAN, ETREE) within the MPLS network, external BGP (EBGP), in particular, is the protocol of choice within the enterprise design for route exchange between the various domains in this enterprise network. BGP provides inherent loop prevention using AS-numbers and, more importantly, offers tighter route control and path manipulation through a plethora of BGP attributes, making it the preferred protocol for this enterprise. Each individual customer-edge (CE) device at a remote site, such as a Layer 3 catalyst switch, is configured with a dedicated 4-byte AS number to peer EBGP on a per-VRF basis with the upstream provider-edge (PE) pair. Similarly, each of the ACI fabrics, including both the Core and the DMZ fabrics, is configured with dedicated AS numbers for each VRF to peer EBGP for route exchange. Importantly, the ACI fabric establishes EBGP adjacencies with the MPLS DC PE routers using BGP Labeled Unicast (BGP-LU) and Ethernet VPN (EVPN). Further details on why BGP-LU and EVPN are chosen are discussed later in the "ACI MPLS-SR Integration" section.

The Core ACI fabric is structured with distinct VRFs, namely PROD, DEV, and UAT VRFs, each representing a designated segment for hosting applications as they progress through their lifecycle. Additionally, there is a shared-services VRF for services utilized by all applications in the core network. In contrast, the DMZ fabric is configured with individual VRFs, including Internet DMZ (IDMZ) for hosting public-facing workloads and connecting to Internet edge routers, Cloud Exchange (CEXC) for direct connectivity to cloud edge routers configured with AWS Direct Connect and Azure Express routes to Gov Cloud instances, and External DMZ (EDMZ) for connectivity to vendors and other government agency networks using external edge routers.

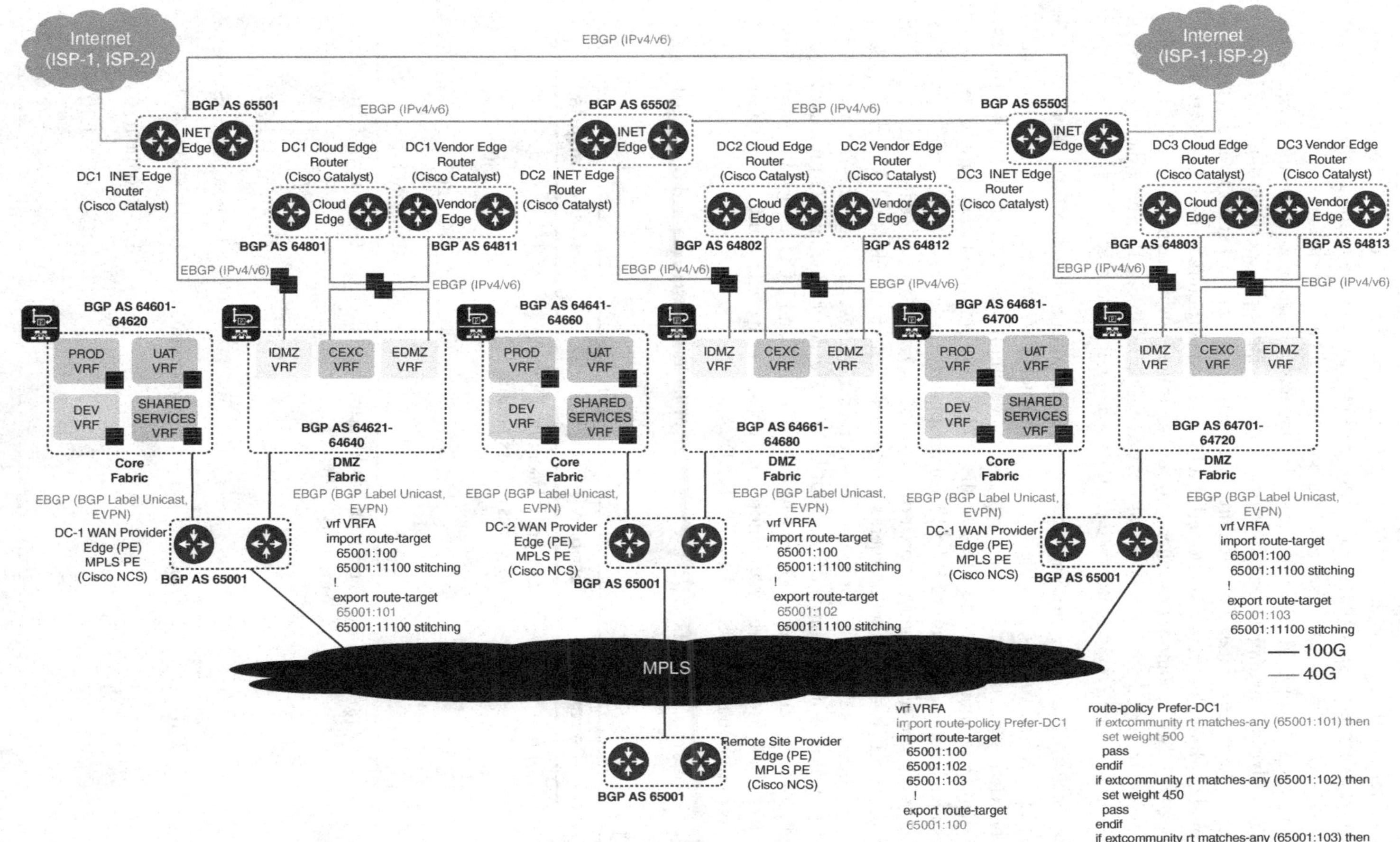

Figure 13-2 *Enterprise Routing Architecture Using BGP*

The Internet edge routers at DataCenter-1 (DC-1) and DataCenter-3 (DC-3) are multihomed to the same set of Internet service providers, also establishing a full-mesh EBGP network between themselves. This design ensures fallback routing and redundancy in the event of upstream failure and device or link failures. It guarantees continuous accessibility to citizens consuming mission-critical public-facing applications through the Internet, even in the face of catastrophic failure. Connectivity to vendor networks and cloud providers through external vendor edge and cloud edge routers utilizes BGP attributes along with BGP communities when exchanging routes with external peers. This is done to define preferred ingress and egress data center paths among the three data centers for vendors and cloud regions attached to more than one data center.

Routes learned through various data centers, when consumed in the VRFs on the MPLS DC-PE headend routers, are annotated with distinct route-targets for each VRF in each data center site. For common prefixes (such as default route or other data center routes) learned from multiple data centers on the MPLS core, individual route-targets for routes from each data center assist MPLS PEs at remote sites. They use these route-targets in a route policy to determine their preferred DC-PE for transit to both data center and external destinations—be it the Internet, a vendor network, or a cloud. In this scenario, PE routers at remote sites are configured with distinct BGP weights against each route-target for each VRF learned from individual DCs. All routes learned from DC-1 are assigned higher weights compared to routes learned from DC-2 and DC-3 across all remote sites. This configuration ensures that remote sites consistently prefer routes from DC-1 over other duplicate routes learned from other DCs.

In the context of this use case, the VPNs listed in Table 13-1 were defined on the MPLS Core.

Table 13-1 *MPLS-SR VPNs*

VRF Name	Description	Purpose	Route-Targets
VRFA	Enterprise	Enterprise User and Device Networks across remote sites	DC-1: 65001:101 DC-2: 65001:102 DC-3: 65001:103 Remote Sites: 65001:100
VRFB	Peripherals	Peripheral workstations, printers, Smart/IoT devices	DC-1: 65001:201 DC-2: 65001:202 DC-3: 65001:203 Remote Sites: 65001:200
VRFC	VOIP	Voice over IP communications	DC-1: 65001:301 DC-2: 65001:302 DC-3: 65001:303 Remote Sites: 65001:300

VRF Name	Description	Purpose	Route-Targets
VRFD	Quarantine	Quarantine	DC-1: 65001:401 DC-2: 65001:402 DC-3: 65001:403 Remote Sites: 65001:400
VRFE	Surveillance	Cameras, Surveillance Systems	DC-1: 65001:501 DC-2: 65001:502 DC-3: 65001:503 Remote Sites: 65001:500
VRFG	Management	In-Band Management	DC-1: 65001:601 DC-2: 65001:602 DC-3: 65001:603 Remote Sites: 65001:600

For the remote sites, the illustration in Figure 13-3 presents an overview of the LAN design. At each remote site, a dedicated pair of IOS XR NCS provider-edge (PE) devices facilitates WAN delineation between the MPLS-SR network and the LAN. These PE devices are configured to establish VPNV4 peering with the route-reflectors in the MP-BGP MPLS-SR domain. Additionally, they are configured for EBGP peering with the downstream Layer 3 catalyst switch (customer edge, or CE) on each Virtual Routing and Forwarding (VRF) instance. The EBGP peering serves to advertise the remote MPLS-SR-learned (best) prefixes down to the CE, and reciprocally, the CE advertises local routes toward the MPLS-SR domain.

The PE-CE link at each site is a Layer 3 point-to-point configuration with multiple subinterfaces, where each subinterface corresponds to a specific VRF for establishing EBGP peering. The Layer 3 catalyst switch (CE) is multi-homed to both PEs using the same Layer 3 point-to-point links and is configured with Equal-Cost Multipath (ECMP) to enable load-balancing across both uplinks to the PE devices for all flows directed toward the data center or other remote sites.

Furthermore, the Layer 3 switches (CE) function as the routed gateway for each specified VLAN, where each Switched Virtual Interface (SVI) associated with a VLAN is linked to an individual VRF. These VLANs are then trunked downstream to Layer 2 switches, connecting directly to user/device endpoints. In the case of wireless access, the downstream Layer 2 switches establish access connectivity to Cisco access points (APs). These APs are centrally managed through a wireless controller positioned in the data center ACI network, overseeing both enterprise and guest wireless access. All traffic originating from wireless points is tunneled through the MPLS-SR network, traveling upstream to the data center controllers before reaching termination points on routed gateways defined within the ACI fabric.

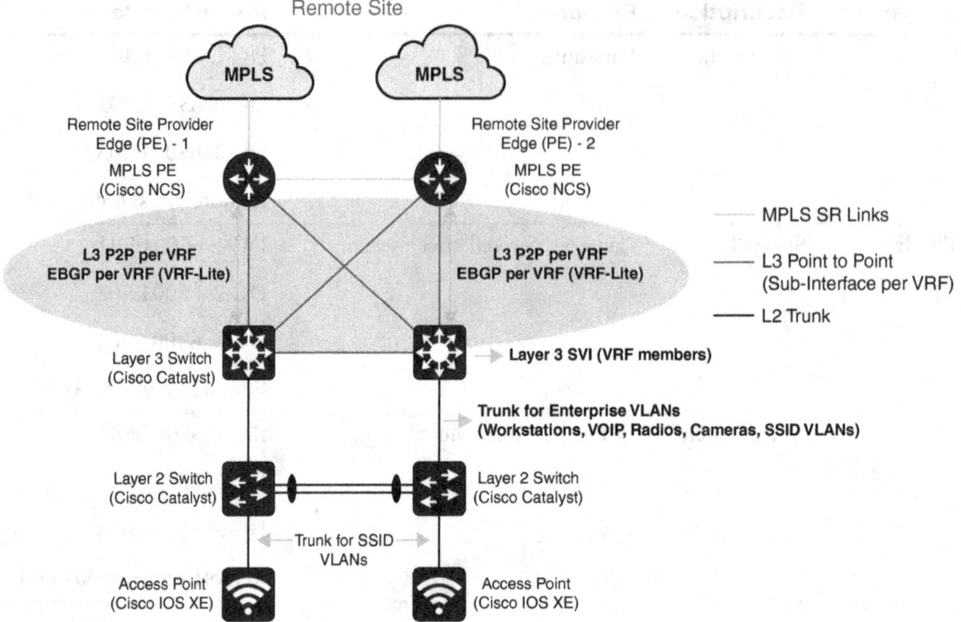

Figure 13-3 *Connectivity at Remote Sites*

ACI MPLS-SR Integration

The integration of MPLS-SR with ACI offers an automated and scalable data center (DC) handoff by employing a unified control-plane session (BGP EVPN) for all Virtual Routing and Forwarding instances. This approach, as opposed to utilizing a per-VRF interface and routing protocol, makes it the preferred solution for implementing multiple VRFs between the ACI DC and DC-PEs. Through this integration, a singular EVPN-based control-plane session is utilized to convey both DC and WAN prefixes, employing the EVPN address family. Additionally, MPLS labels for VRFs and the SR color community are carried within this session. Moreover, a single BGP label unicast (BGP-LU) session is employed for the exchange of underlay SR/MPLS labels. This integrated solution is highly suitable for this deployment, particularly considering the substantial number of VRFs implemented in both the WAN and the data centers.

Figure 13-4 illustrates the logical design for ACI and MPLS-SR integration on the Core ACI fabric. In this deployment, an SR-MPLS infrastructure L3Out is configured in the Infra Tenant on the ACI border leafs for the core fabric. This setup facilitates the establishment of underlay BGP-LU and overlay BGP-EVPN sessions with the DC-PEs in each data center. Tenant VRFs are defined and linked to the infra L3Out to import/learn MPLS-VPN WAN prefixes from the DC-PEs. Simultaneously, they export/advertise the DC prefixes to the MPLS-VPNs on the DC-PEs.

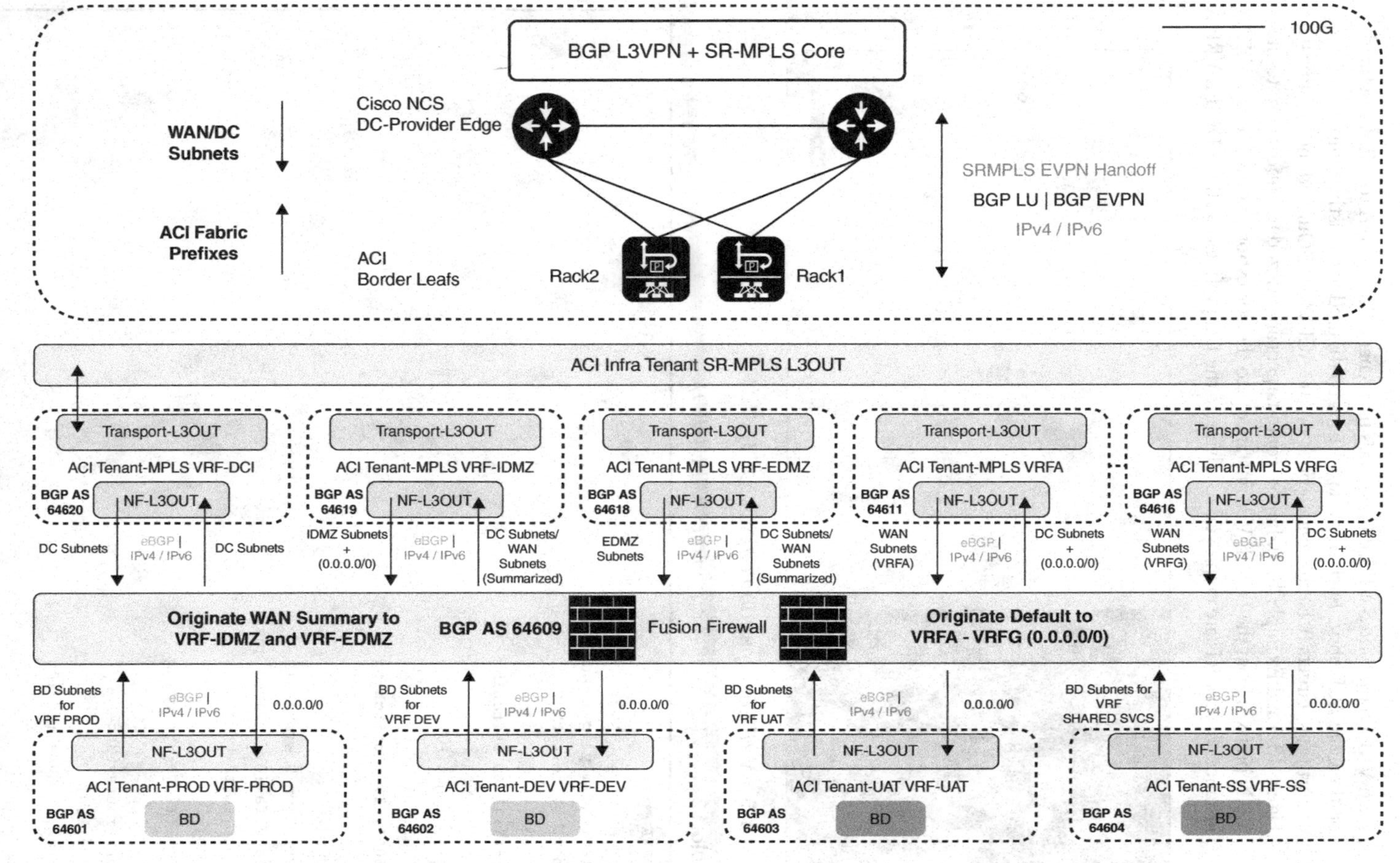

Figure 13-4 *Core-Fabric—MPLS-SR Integration*

Several key considerations for this deployment include

- Each VRF on the MPLS-VPN corresponds to a tenant VRF (VRFA to VRFG) defined on the Core ACI fabric. Each of these VRFs is configured with distinct import/export route-targets (RTs) that match both on the ACI VRF L3Out and the DC-PEs (see Figure 13-5 and Example 13-1). Import route-targets are utilized to import remote-site WAN prefixes from the DC-PE VRF instance into the corresponding ACI tenant VRF instance. Export RTs are employed to advertise the DC prefixes to all the DC-PE VRFs.

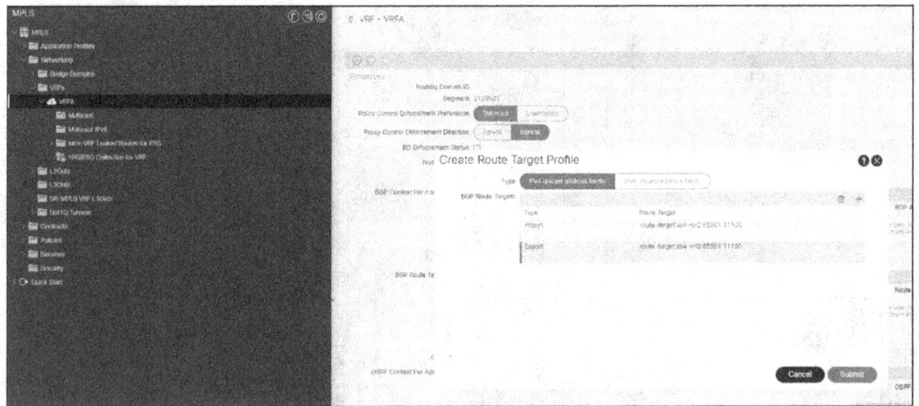

Figure 13-5 *VRF Configuration on ACI (DC1)*

Example 13-1 *VRF Configuration on DC-PE (DC1)*

```
vrf VRFA
 description Enterprise
 address-family ipv4 unicast
  import route-target
   65001:100
   65001:11100 stitching
  !
  export route-target
   65001:101
   65001:11100 stitching
  !
vrf VRFB
 description Peripherals
 address-family ipv4 unicast
  import route-target
   65001:200
   65001:11200 stitching
  !
 export route-target
   65001:201
   65001:11200 stitching
  !
```

```
vrf VRFC
 description VOIP
 address-family ipv4 unicast
  import route-target
   65001:300
   65001:11300 stitching
  !
  export route-target
   65001:301
   65001:11300 stitching
  !
vrf VRFD
 description Quarantine
 address-family ipv4 unicast
  import route-target
   65001:400
   65001:11400 stitching
  !
  export route-target
   65001:401
   65001:11400 stitching
  !
vrf VRFE
 description Surveilliance
 address-family ipv4 unicast
  import route-target
   65001:500
   65001:11500 stitching
  !
  export route-target
   65001:501
   65001:11500 stitching
  !
vrf VRFG
 description Management
 address-family ipv4 unicast
  import route-target
   65001:600
   65001:11600 stitching
  !
  export route-target
   65001:601
   65001:11600 stitching
  !
!
```

- Tenant VRFs connect to a fusion firewall, which consolidates routing across VRFs into one global routing table and enforces policies for inter-VRF traffic between remote sites. This design meets the business requirement for centralized L4-L7 firewall enforcement of all inter-VRF communication between remote sites. The fusion firewall originates a default route toward the remote sites in each VRF (VRFA to VRFG), ensuring that all inter-VRF traffic follows the default route through the MPLS WAN core to the fusion firewall before routing into the other VRF. Additionally, DC subnets from PROD, DEV, UAT, and Shared-Services VRFs are advertised downstream to the remote sites.
- Example 13-2 presents a configuration snippet detailing EVPN and BGP-LU peering between the DC-PE in DC1 and the Core ACI fabric. From the configuration, it is evident that only routes originating from BGP ASNs sourced in the DCs are permitted inbound on the DC-PEs from the ACI fabric. Additionally, routes learned from the core fabric in DC-1 are configured with higher local-preference to prioritize the default route and summary prefixes originated in DC-1 over those in DC-2 and DC-3.

Example 13-2 *EVPN and BGP-LU Configuration on DC-PE (DC1) for Core ACI Fabric*

```
as-path-set ORIGINATED-IN-DC1
  ios-regex '_64601$',
  ios-regex '_64602$',
  ios-regex '_64603$',
  ios-regex '_64604$',
  ios-regex '_64609$',
end-set
!
route-policy ALLOW-BGP-EVPN-CORE-ACI-IN
 if as-path in ORIGINATED-IN-DC1 then
  set local-preference 500
  pass
 else
  drop
 endif
end-policy
!
route-policy ALLOW-BGP-EVPN-CORE-ACI-OUT
 pass
end-policy
!
prefix-set ALLOW-BGP-LU-2-ACI-IN
  <ACI Loopback addresses>
end-set
!
```

```
prefix-set ALLOW-BGP-LU-2-ACI-OUT
  <Local DC-PE Loopback0 address>
end-set
!
route-policy ALLOW-BGP-LU-ACI-IN
 if destination in ALLOW-BGP-LU-2-ACI-IN then
   set community NO-ADVERTISE
   pass
 endif
end-policy
!
route-policy ALLOW-BGP-LU-ACI-OUT
 if destination in ALLOW-BGP-LU-2-ACI-OUT then
   pass
 endif
end-policy
!
router bgp 65001
neighbor-group ACI_BORDER_LEAF_BGP-LU
  address-family ipv4 labeled-unicast
   route-policy ALLOW-BGP-LU-ACI-IN in
   route-policy ALLOW-BGP-LU-ACI-OUT out
  !
 !
 neighbor-group ACI_CORE_FABRIC_BORDER_LEAF_BGP-EVPN
  ebgp-multihop 2
  update-source Loopback0
  address-family l2vpn evpn
   route-policy ALLOW-BGP-EVPN-CORE-ACI-IN in
   route-policy ALLOW-BGP-EVPN-CORE-ACI-OUT out
   import stitching-rt reoriginate
   advertise vpnv4 unicast re-originated stitching-rt
   advertise vpnv6 unicast re-originated stitching-rt
   next-hop-self
  !
 !
```

- Defaults originated on the fusion firewalls are also advertised to the DC workload VRFs (PROD, DEV, UAT, Shared-Services), ensuring that all inter-VRF east-west and north-south traffic originating locally from the DC workloads undergoes L4-L7 enforcement.

- Apart from the tenant VRFs used for WAN extension onto the ACI fabric, three distinct VRFs—VRF-INET, VRF-EDMZ, and VRF-DCI—are configured exclusively only on the DC-PEs (see Example 13-3). These VRFs facilitate route-exchange for core DC prefixes between data centers and for Internet, cloud, and external prefixes between the core and DMZ fabrics, locally and between data centers. Unique route-targets are configured for each of these VRFs on the DC-PEs and the ACI fabric, allowing the import/export of VRF routes within their respective VRFs between the ACI and MPLS WAN domains. WAN summary prefixes for remote sites are originated on the fusion firewall and advertised to the EDMZ and INET VRFs; this allows the EDMZ- and INET-sourced traffic to route back to the remote sites through the core fusion firewall. WAN summary prefixes originated in the DC-1 are preferred using higher local-preference over summary prefixes originated in DC-2 and DC-3.

Example 13-3 *VRF Configuration on DC-PE for INET, DCI, and EDMZ (DC1)*

```
vrf DCI
 description Enterprise
 address-family ipv4 unicast
  import route-target
   65001:997
   65001:11997 stitching
  !
  export route-target
   65001:997
   65001:11997 stitching
  !
vrf EDMZ
 description Peripherals
 address-family ipv4 unicast
  import route-target
   65001:998
   65001:11998 stitching
  !
  export route-target
   65001:998
   65001:11998 stitching
  !
vrf IDMZ
 description Peripherals
 address-family ipv4 unicast
  import route-target
   65001:999
   65001:11999 stitching
  !
  export route-target
   65001:999
   65001:11999 stitching
  !
 !
```

- The DCI VRF on ACI serves as an ingress/egress transit VRF for all east-west DC communication between workloads across the three data centers. The IDMZ VRF on ACI facilitates east-west transit routing to all Internet-bound destinations from DC and remote-site workloads, while the EDMZ VRF on ACI enables east-west transit routing to all external-bound destinations (vendor prefixes, cloud CIDRs) from DC and remote-site workloads.

Similar to the core fabric, the DMZ fabric (see Figure 13-6) is configured with an SR-MPLS infrastructure L3Out within the Infra Tenant on the ACI border leaves. This configuration enables the establishment of underlay BGP-LU and overlay BGP-EVPN sessions with the DC-PEs in each data center, mirroring the setup in the core fabric. Tenant VRFs dedicated to IDMZ and EDMZ are defined and associated with the infra L3Out. This association allows them to import/learn MPLS-VPN WAN prefixes from the DC-PEs while concurrently exporting/advertising IDMZ/EDMZ prefixes to the respective MPLS-VPNs on the DC-PEs.

The IDMZ and EDMZ VRFs on DC-PEs across the three data centers utilize BGP local-preference to prioritize DC-1-originated IDMZ/EDMZ routes over any duplicate prefixes learned from DC-2 and DC-3. This configuration (Example 13-4) ensures a consistent preference for IDMZ/EDMZ prefixes learned from DC-1 over other duplicates from DC-2 and DC-3.

Example 13-4 *EVPN and BGP-LU Configuration on DC-PE (DC1) for DMZ Fabric*

```
route-policy ALLOW-BGP-EVPN-DMZ-ACI-IN
 set local-preference 500
 pass
end-policy
!
route-policy ALLOW-BGP-EVPN-DMZ-ACI-OUT
 pass
end-policy
!
prefix-set ALLOW-BGP-LU-2-ACI-IN
  <ACI Loopback addresses>
end-set
!
prefix-set ALLOW-BGP-LU-2-ACI-OUT
  <Local DC-PE Loopback0 address>
end-set
!
route-policy ALLOW-BGP-LU-ACI-IN
 if destination in ALLOW-BGP-LU-2-ACI-IN then
   set community NO-ADVERTISE
   pass
 endif
end-policy
!
```

```
route-policy ALLOW-BGP-LU-ACI-OUT
 if destination in ALLOW-BGP-LU-2-ACI-OUT then
   pass
 endif
end-policy
!
router bgp 65001
neighbor-group ACI_BORDER_LEAF_BGP-LU
  address-family ipv4 labeled-unicast
   route-policy ALLOW-BGP-LU-ACI-IN in
   route-policy ALLOW-BGP-LU-ACI-OUT out
  !
 !
 neighbor-group ACI_DMZ_FABRIC_BORDER_LEAF_BGP-EVPN
  ebgp-multihop 2
  update-source Loopback0
  address-family l2vpn evpn
   route-policy ALLOW-BGP-EVPN-DMZ-ACI-IN in
   route-policy ALLOW-BGP-EVPN-DMZ-ACI-OUT out
   import stitching-rt reoriginate
   advertise vpnv4 unicast re-originated stitching-rt
   advertise vpnv6 unicast re-originated stitching-rt
   next-hop-self
  !
 !
```

Figures 13-7 through 13-9 showcase the SR-MPLS handoff label exchange:

1. ACI-BL advertises an aggregate label for VRF using the BGP EVPN address-family.
2. BGP-LU advertises an implicit null label because DC-PE and ACI-BL are directly connected.
3. A server leaf encapsulates the packet into the VXLAN header and forwards to the border leaf.
4. The border leaf de-encapsulates the VXLAN header and encapsulates a packet into SR-MPLS with an inner (aggregate) VRF label. Because BL and DC-PE are directly connected, an outer label won't be present in the packet due to an implicit null label advertisement from DC-PE.
5. DC-PE de-encapsulates the packet coming from BL and encapsulates it again based on the prefix/color for the destination.
6. DC-PE receives the SR/MPLS packet from the SP core.
7. DC-PE sends the SR-MPLS packet to BL with an inner (aggregate) VRF label. Because BL and DC-PE are directly connected, an outer label won't be present in the packet due to an implicit null label advertisement from ACI-BL.
8. BL de-encapsulates the SR-MPLS packet and encapsulates it to the VXLAN header in the ACI fabric.

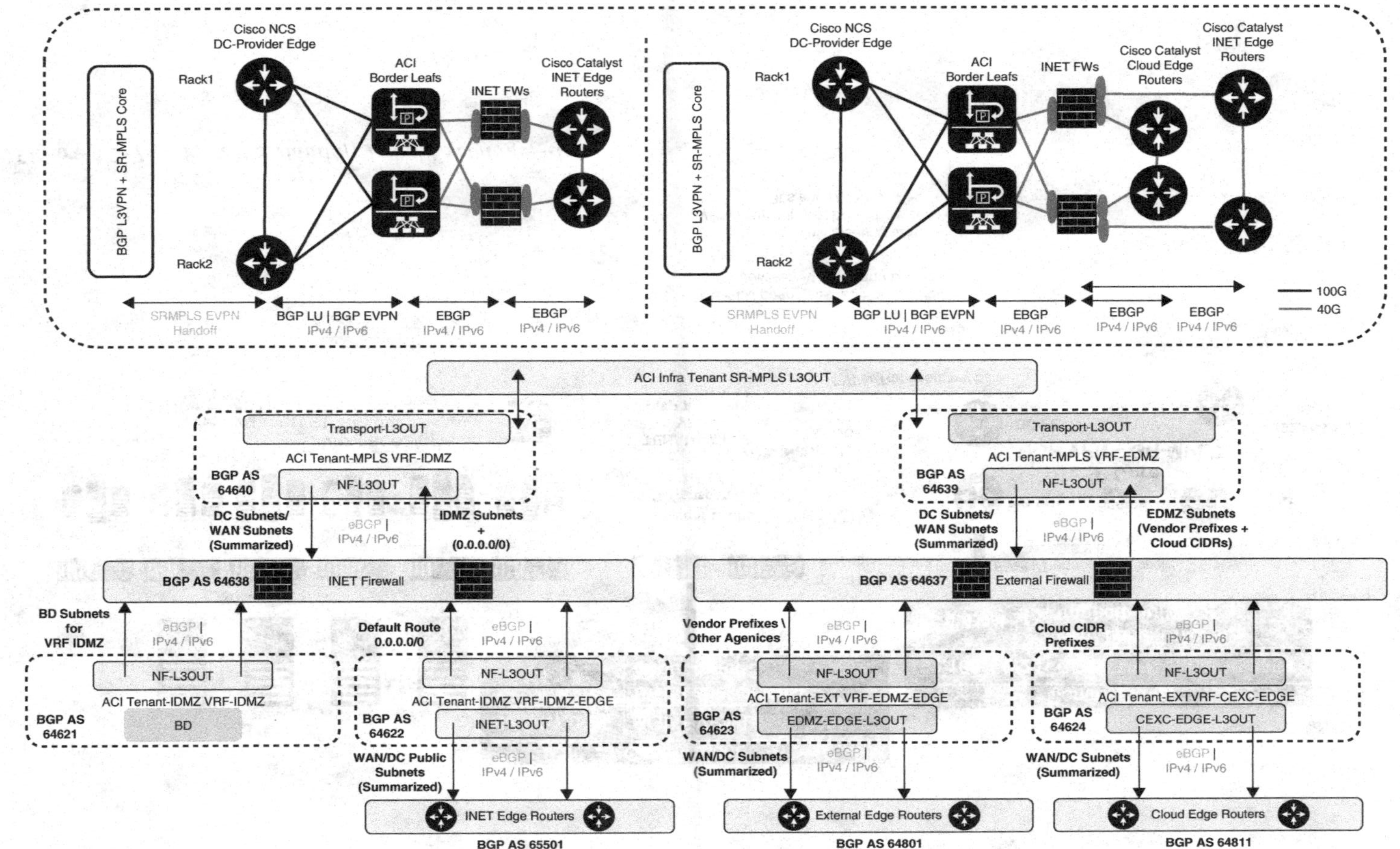

Figure 13-6 *DMZ-Fabric—MPLS-SR Integration*

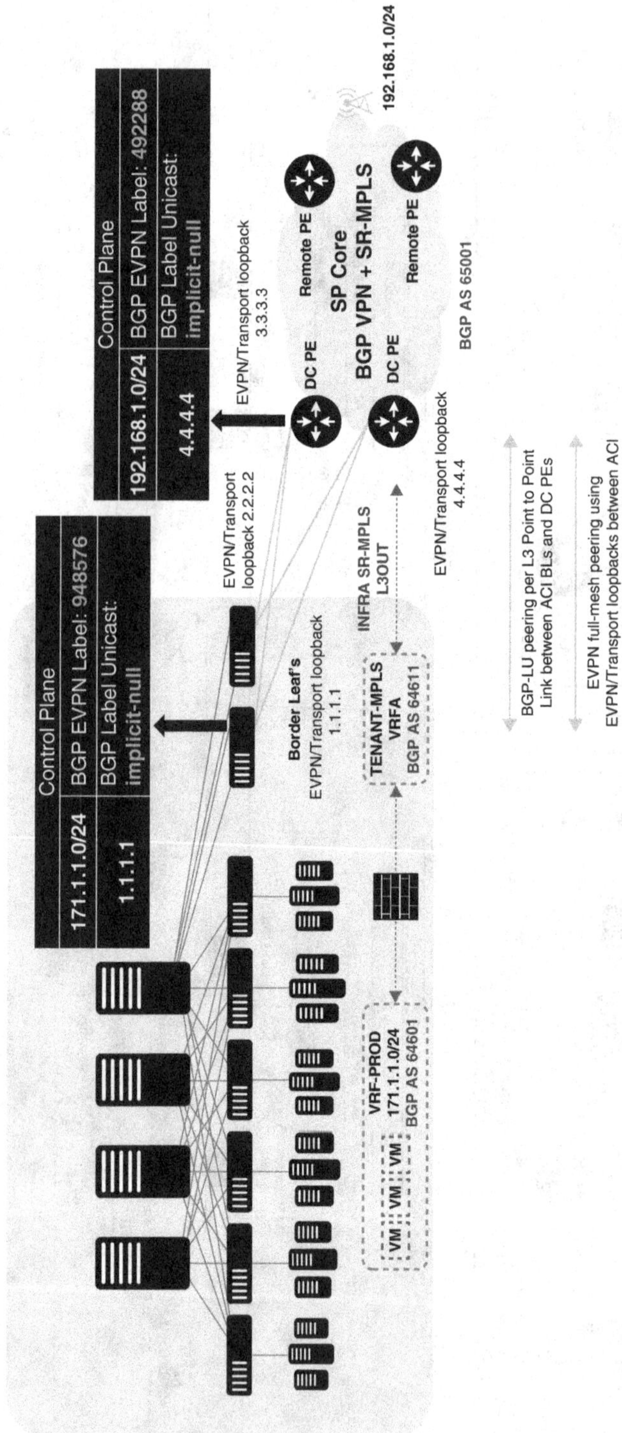

Figure 13-7 *SR-MPLS Handoff Label Exchange—1*

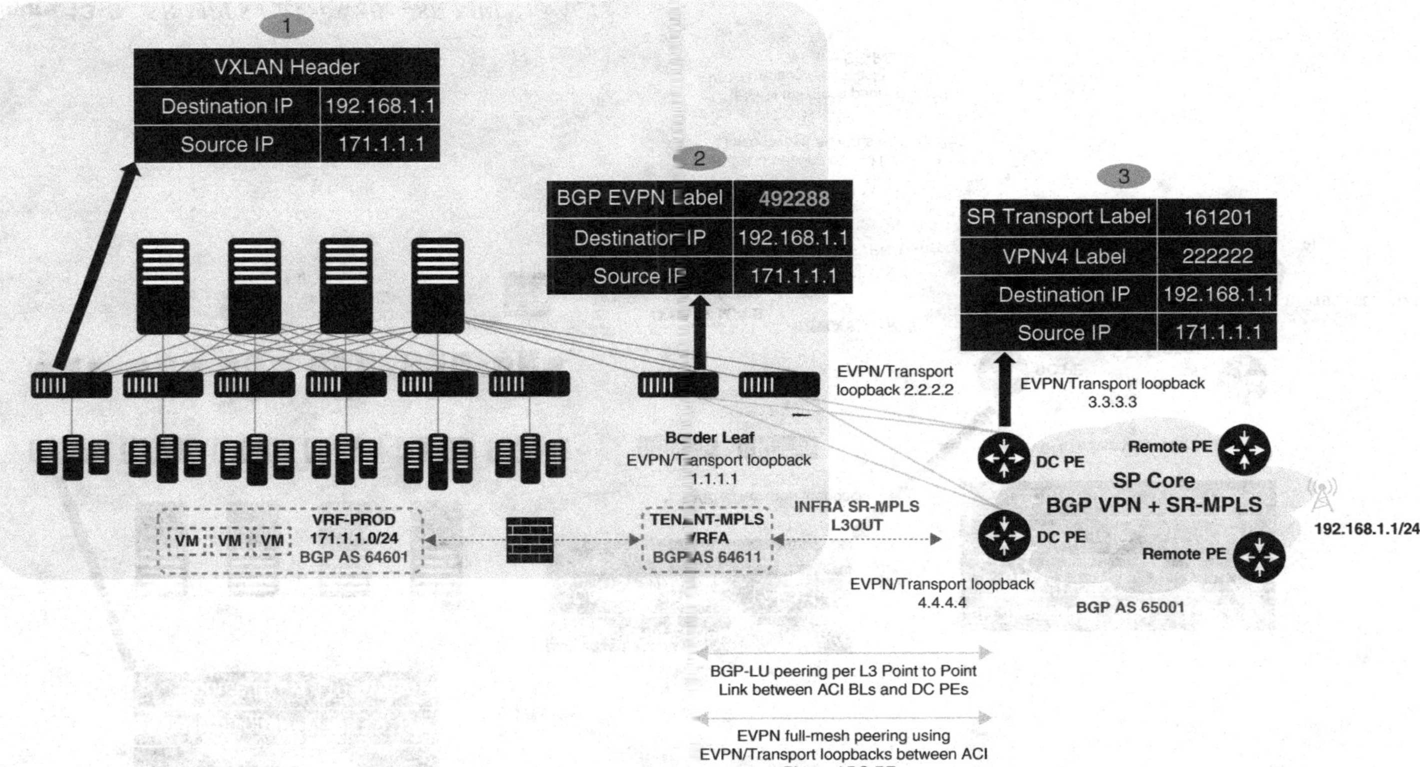

Figure 13-8 *SR-MPLS Packet Walk—ACI to SR-MPLS*

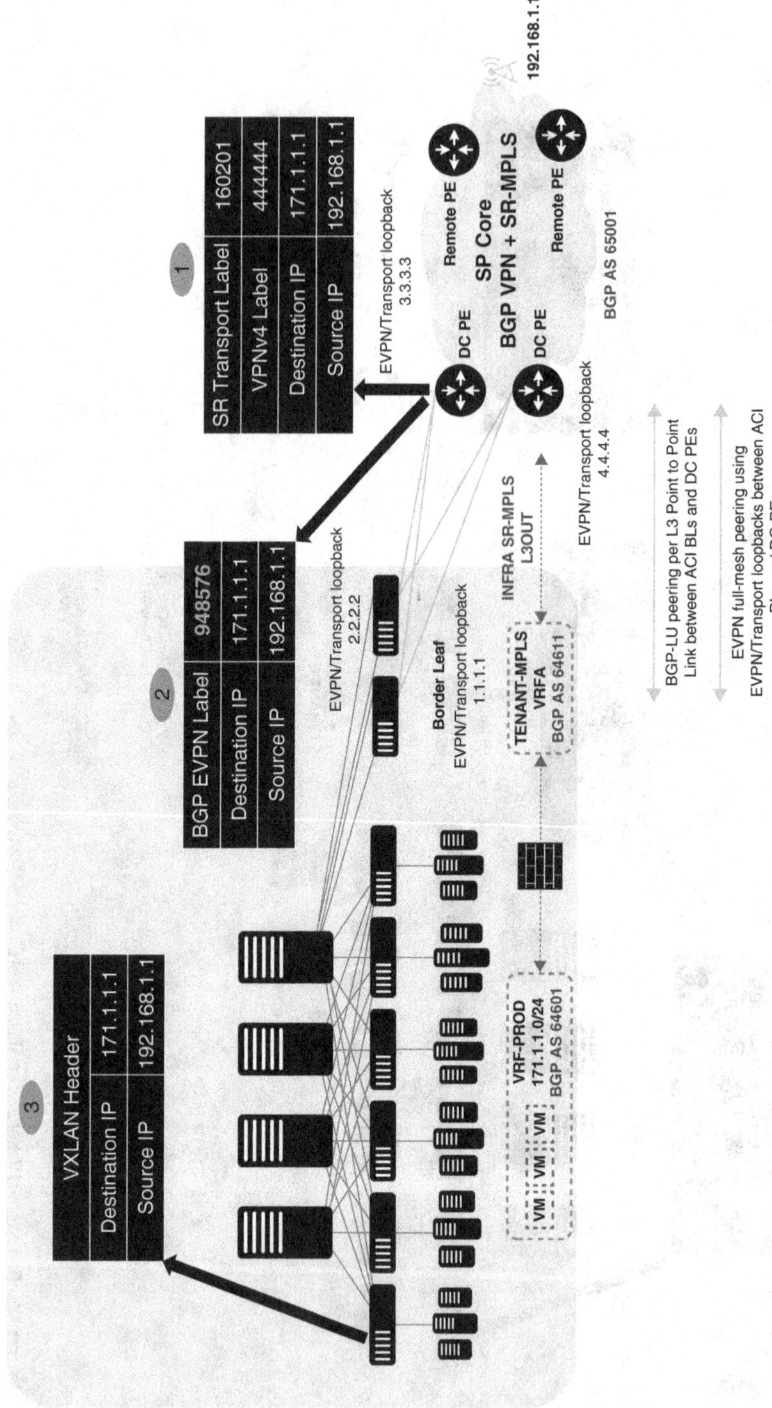

Figure 13-9 *SR-MPLS Packet Walk—SR-MPLS to ACI*

ACI Logical Design and VMM Integration

In this deployment, the tenant network incorporates distinct domains, including Production (PROD), Development (DEV), User Acceptance Testing (UAT), and Shared Services. Each of these tenant domains operates as a separate forwarding and management entity within the same infrastructure.

These tenants establish an organized infrastructure to support applications and services across their lifecycle stages. Notably, the DEV and UAT tenants replicate the configuration structure of the PROD tenant. This uniformity in tenant configuration enables the smooth transition of new applications or services hosted on the data center fabric as they move from development to testing and eventually into production.

As illustrated in Figures 13-10 and 13-11, each of these tenants initially deployed multiple bridge domains with a network-centric approach. In this design, one bridge domain (BD) corresponded to one endpoint group (EPG) and one VLAN (1BD = 1EPG = 1VLAN). Essentially, a network-centric design indicates that each Ethernet VLAN aligns with one broadcast domain and one security group in ACI. While this design was initially employed to simplify the transition from a legacy classical Ethernet domain to a fabric-based infrastructure, post-migrating all network segments onto ACI, the network transitioned to use endpoint security groups (ESGs) to fulfill granular microsegmentation and workload security requirements for each application on the fabric.

In ACI, for efficient management of endpoints and workloads with similar security requirements, they are grouped into entities like endpoint groups (EPGs), and communication is regulated through security policies (contracts). Although this approach works seamlessly and has proven effective, an EPG is inherently tied to a single bridge domain because EPGs concurrently define both networking and security policies. Initially, there were no options to define a security group that could span across multiple "bridge domain/broadcast domain" boundaries. ESGs enable the definition of security policies spanning multiple BDs, allowing the grouping and application of policies to any number of endpoints across various BDs under a given Virtual Routing and Forwarding (VRF) instance, all while maintaining the original forwarding behavior on those BDs. With ESGs, while forwarding still occurs at the BD/EPG level, security enforcement is elevated to the ESG level.

The ESG design for this deployment utilizes multiple security zones per application, where individual endpoints/workloads are mapped to an ESG via tag selectors across any subnet or VLAN on a given VRF instance. ESG tag selectors require Virtual Machine Manager (VMM) integration with read-write mode. In this case, a significant portion of the compute install-base utilizes VMware ESXi, and VMM integration with VMware vCenter is used to pull VM tags and VM names from the ESXi install-base. To use VM tags for ESG mapping, the VMM domain for this deployment is configured with **enable tag collection**, and **allow micro-segmentation** is also configured for all EPGs associated with the VMM domain. The **enable tag collection** knob retrieves VM tags and VM names from the VMM domain, and the **allow micro-segmentation** knob prevents the VMware Distributed Switch (VDS) from switching the traffic locally for traffic in the same port group but configures the VDS to use private VLANs (PVLANs) to proxy all the traffic to ACI leafs for policy enforcement.

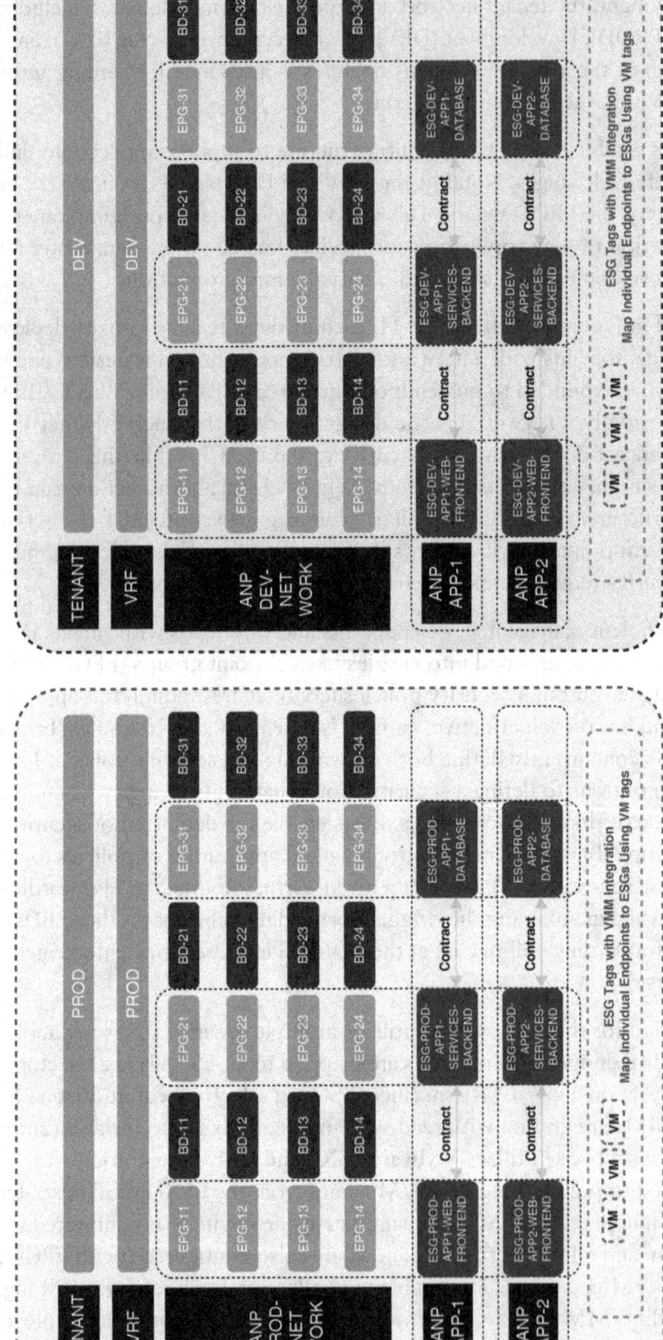

Figure 13-10 *ACI Core Fabric—Logical Tenant Model (PROD and DEV)*

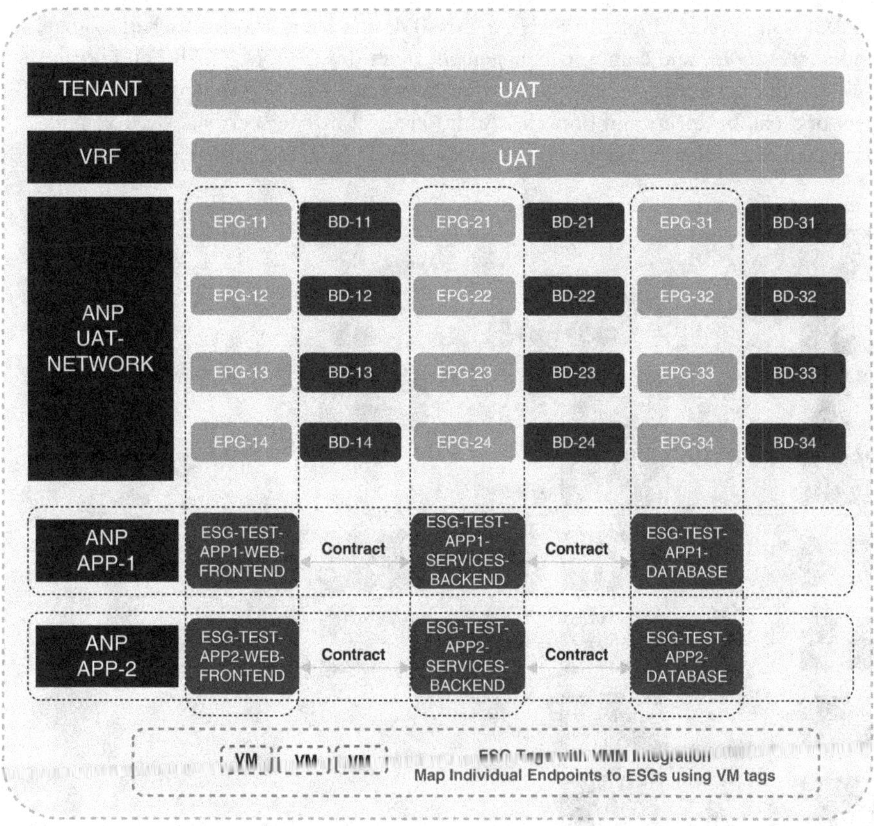

Figure 13-11 *ACI Core Fabric—Logical Tenant Model (UAT)*

An application profile is created for each application, and within the application profile, three distinct security groups (ESGs) are defined for granular segmentation: one for the web frontend, one for the service backend, and one for the database. Workloads for different applications are configured with distinct VM tags and VM names corresponding to their application tiers, and these tags/names are configured as key values in the ESG tag selectors to match the workloads to their corresponding ESGs defined on the ACI fabric. All communications between ESGs are governed using contracts, and in this case, granular policies for contract enforcement are discovered using Application Dependency Mapping (ADM) tools like Cisco Secure Workload.

In addition to the tenant dedicated to workloads and applications, this configuration incorporates a shared-services tenant (see Figure 13-12). This tenant serves as a centralized focal point for hosting common or shared services essential not only for other tenants within the fabric infrastructure but also for external domains and user groups. Within this deployment, the shared-services tenant is employed to accommodate shared services such as backup, replication, and IP storage (iSCSI, CIFS, NFS). Specifically, for iSCSI, ACI is utilized to emulate a SAN-A/SAN-B design for network-attached storage. It also houses storage and compute management functions (ALOM, CIMC) and creates a high-availability network for state connections between L4-L7 service appliances, including network load balancers and firewalls. Additionally, it manages critical services and functions encompassing Active Directory, DNS, DHCP, NTP, and global load balancers.

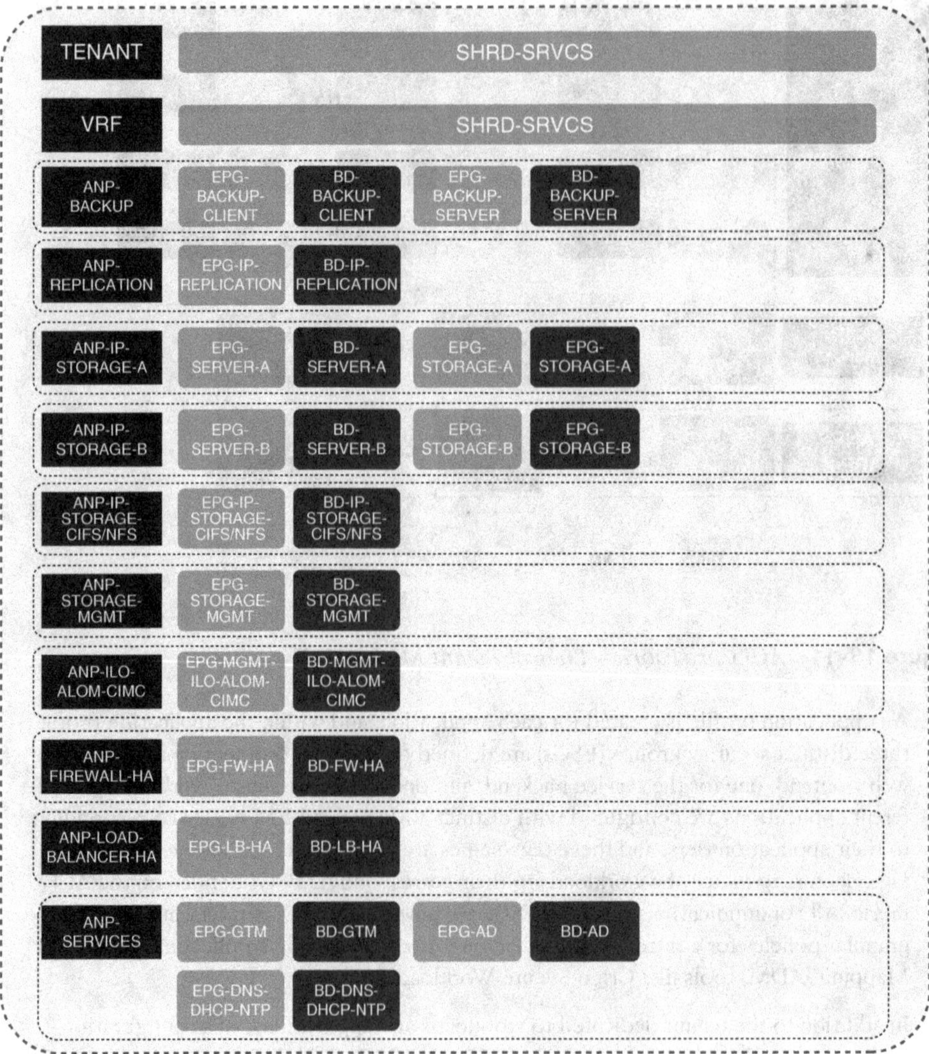

Figure 13-12 *ACI Core Fabric—Logical Tenant Model (Shared Services)*

VMM Integration

While ACI inherently automates policies, including network and security functions within its fabric—such as tenants, VRFs, BDs, EPGs, and ESGs—it also possesses the capability to integrate with Virtual Machine Managers (VMMs) external to the fabric. This integration allows the extension of the same policies to other domains. The communication of policies created in ACI and, subsequently, the automation of network and security functions in the virtual machine domain, as well as vice versa, are enabled through this integration.

ACI establishes a federation with the VMM, dynamically translating ACI policies and subsequently pushing them to the VMM. This process instantiates VLANs, port-groups, and virtual switches on the hypervisors on servers connected to ACI leaf switches. The federation, along with other control plane exchanges between the two domains, facilitates the automated end-to-end stitching of network and security functions across both domains. Moreover, it enables the dynamic attachment of compute workloads to their respective security groups (EPGs/ESGs) on ACI without requiring any manual intervention.

It's noteworthy that ACI provides administrators with the flexibility to create multiple VMM domains within the same ACI fabric. In this deployment, ACI integrates with three VMM domains: VMware, OpenStack, and the Kubernetes container domain.

Figure 13-13 illustrates the steps employed in this deployment to integrate with the vCenter-based VMware domain and UCS Manager (UCSM) for automating network functions across the stack, spanning from the leaf switch through the UCSM-managed fabric interconnects to the VMware vCenter managed Virtual Distributed Switch (VDS).

It's important to highlight that a simple adjustment in the assignment of port groups to VMs allows for the seamless progression of VMs from development tenants to a UAT tenant and subsequently to the production network. This smooth transition is facilitated by maintaining identical BD subnets across all three tenants and ensuring that these BD subnets remain private to the development and UAT tenants, with no external advertising. This configuration enables effortless pivoting of workloads from one domain to another up until production, where they can be advertised externally outside the production tenant.

In addition to the VMware domain, OpenStack plays a significant role in this deployment. OpenStack is an open-source cloud computing platform designed for both private and public clouds. Its modular architecture is built on various components and projects, each handling different aspects of cloud computing, including compute, storage, networks, and more.

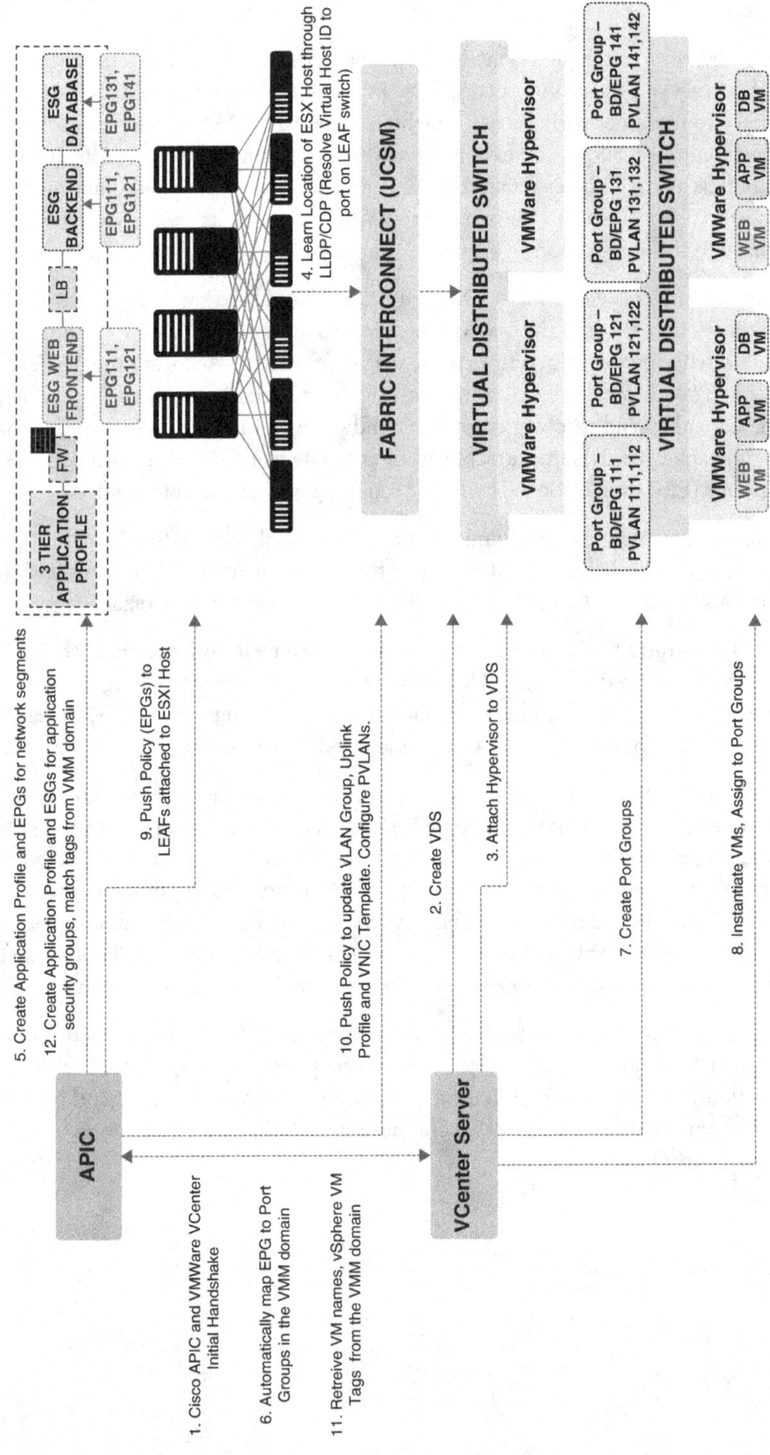

Figure 13-13 *ACI Core Fabric—VMM Integration (VMware)*

Key components of OpenStack include

- **Compute (Nova):** This component controls and manages virtual machines, supporting multiple hypervisors.
- **Storage (Glance, Swift, Cinder):** This component manages instance/VM image storage, cloud object storage, and persistent block storage.
- **Dashboard (Horizon):** This web application provides resource control with a self-service portal and API support.
- **Identity (Keystone):** This component supports centralized policies, tenant management, RBAC, and external identity integration (LDAP).
- **Networking (Neutron):** This component provides Layer 2 (L2) and Layer 3(L3) networking services, IP address management (IPAM), private/public NAT, plugins to external hardware, network services including DHCP, Load Balancer as a Service (LBaaS), and Firewall as a Service (FWaaS).
- **Orchestration (Heat):** This component offers a template-based orchestration engine for faster application deployment.

While in our deployment each of these projects or components runs as a service on dedicated servers (controllers) in a highly available mode, our focus in the context of this chapter is on Neutron, the project/component responsible for providing network connectivity to various OpenStack instances.

Neutron serves as the cloud networking controller within OpenStack, delivering Network as a Service (NaaS). It operates using a pluggable, API-driven solution, enabling the definition of L2/L3 connectivity, networking services (NAT, LB, FW, VPN services), and addressing across the OpenStack install base.

The core components of the OpenStack Neutron networking service include

- **Neutron Server:** This central component handles API requests, orchestrates communication, and implements the core Neutron API to interact with plugins.
- **Neutron Plugins (Mechanism Drivers):** This component is responsible for integrating Neutron with various networking technologies and services, offering a pluggable architecture.
- **Neutron Agents:** This component is responsible for specific networking tasks on compute or network nodes, interacting with the Neutron server. Examples include L2 agent, DHCP agent, and metadata agent.
- **Neutron Database:** This component stores network-related information such as topologies, subnets, and ports, interacting with the Neutron server.
- **Message Queue (Optional):** This component facilitates communication between Neutron components using a message queue service like RabbitMQ.

The reference implementation shown in Figure 13-14 illustrates Neutron's architecture, where a Layer 2 agent (Neutron L2 agent) runs on each Nova Compute node, a Layer 3 agent (Neutron L3 agent) operates on dedicated network/controller nodes, and the Neutron server (controller) nodes host other agents/plugins for network services like DHCP and NAT.

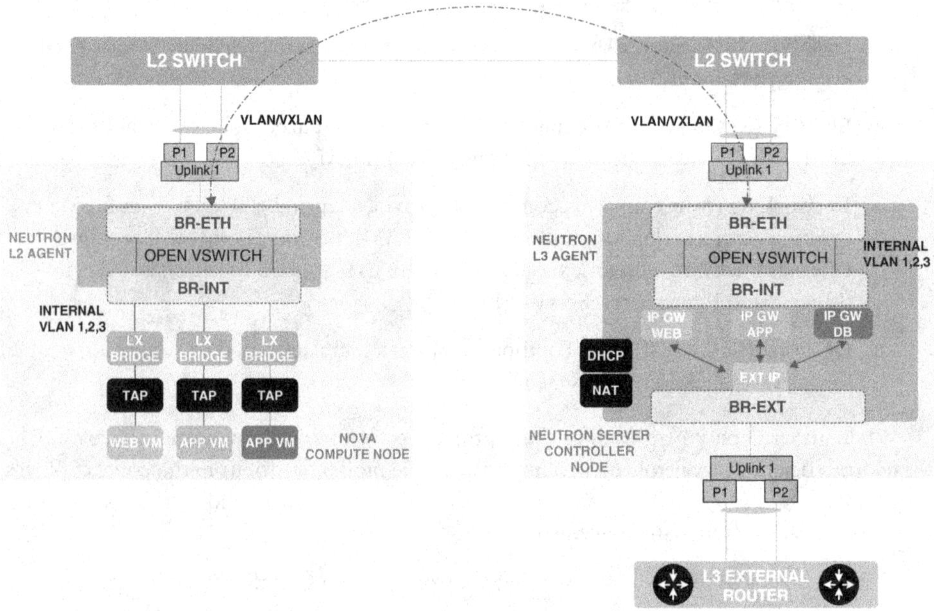

Figure 13-14 *Reference Implementation of Neutron Service*

While this setup offers a practical networking solution for OpenStack instances, it comes with certain challenges:

- Layer 2 and Layer 3 services are restricted to fundamental provisioning.
- In the case of overlay services like VXLAN, servers may lack hardware offload support for tunnel encapsulation/decapsulation.
- All communications between OpenStack instances and external routing domains must be routed through centralized Neutron servers with the L3 agent, potentially leading to bottlenecks and redundancy issues.
- Networking services such as NAT, DHCP, and VPN run centrally on Neutron servers, once again introducing concerns about bottlenecks and redundancy.

This deployment (see Figure 13-15) employs the Cisco ACI OpenStack plugin to overcome the challenges outlined earlier. The plugin, designed for Cisco ACI, utilizes the Cisco ACI fabric as the backend to establish networking for OpenStack instances. By enabling standard Neutron calls, the ACI OpenStack plugin empowers the creation of networking structures in Cisco ACI directly from OpenStack.

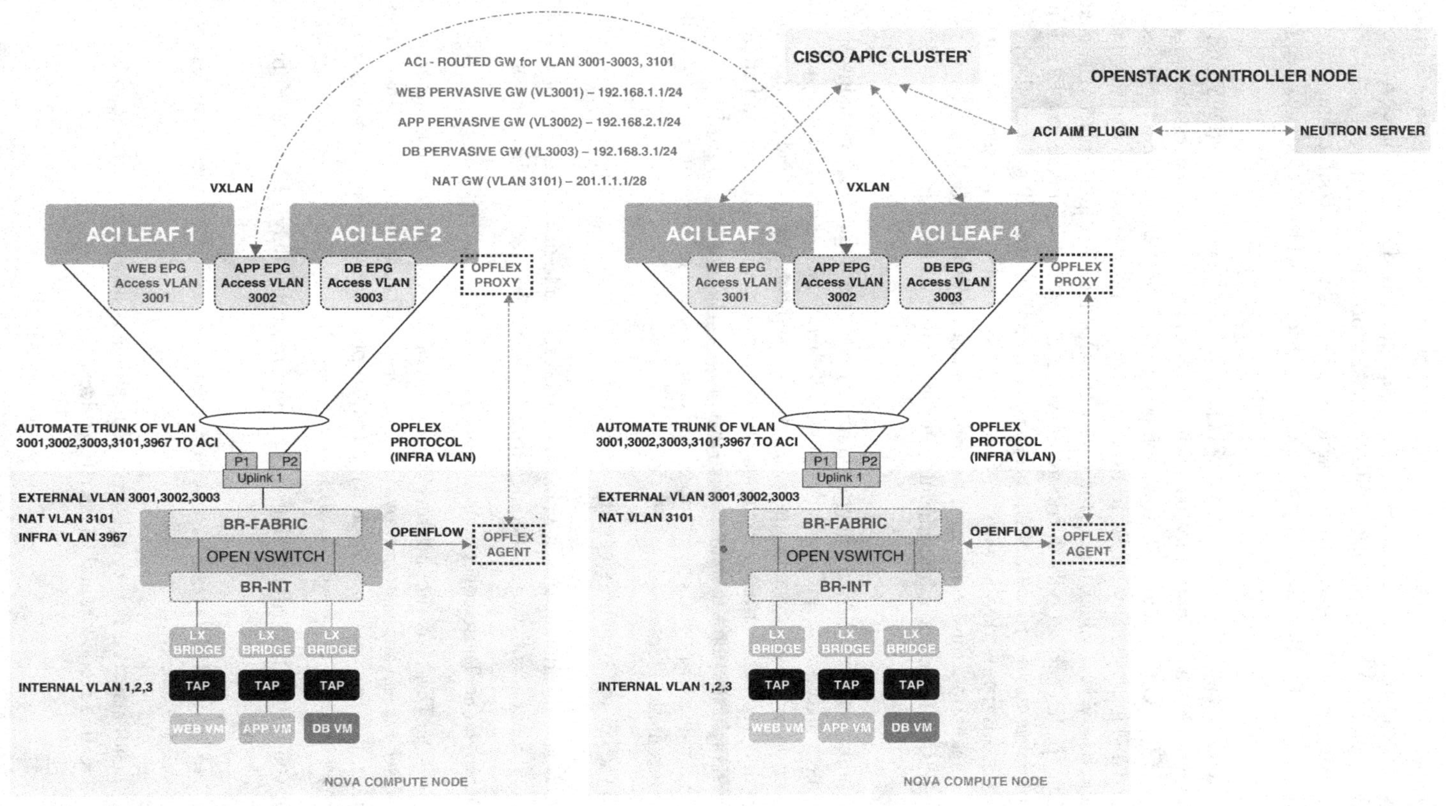

Figure 13-15 *OpenStack—ACI Integration*

The OpenStack Neutron controllers in this setup incorporate a Cisco ACI Integration Module (AIM) to ensure automatic enforcement of policy synchronization. Neutron calls for instantiating new OpenStack networks or services, based on OpenStack networking models, are received, and translated into Cisco AIM policies for ACI. ACI AIM is responsible for storing the translated APIC policies in a local database, configuring Cisco APIC through REST API calls, and maintaining configuration synchronization between the two domains.

In this deployment, Cisco APIC also takes charge of the Open vSwitch (OVS) and OVS rules on each Nova compute node using the OpFlex protocol. This necessitates the installation of Cisco OpFlex and OVS agents on every compute node, wherein these agents are managed and instructed by the APIC using the OpFlex Proxy functions on the upstream leaf switches. With OpFlex mode, the Cisco ACI OpenStack plugin replaces the Neutron node data path, enabling fully distributed Layer 2, Layer 3 anycast gateway, DHCP, metadata optimization, distributed NAT, and enforcement of floating IP policies. This effectively offloads the overlay networking functions from the OpenStack servers/controllers to ACI. In addition, this deployment option integrates a Virtual Machine Manager on Cisco APIC, offering the fabric administrator maximum visibility into the OpenStack cloud.

In addition to utilizing VMM integration for VMware and OpenStack domains, this deployment incorporates ACI integration with Kubernetes. Kubernetes, an open-source container orchestration system, automates the deployment, scaling, and management of containerized applications, leveraging Docker for container execution and adding advanced orchestration capabilities. A typical Kubernetes cluster architecture consists of one or more master nodes, one or more worker nodes, and a distributed key-value datastore (for example, etcd).

Within the cluster, key constructs include

- **Pod:** This scheduling unit in Kubernetes represents a logical collection of one or more containers that are scheduled together and share the same IP address.
- **Deployment:** These collections of pods provide the same service.
- **Services:** This construct informs other parts of the Kubernetes environment about the services an application provides. The Service IP address and port remain constant, allowing communication without disruption even as pods change. Service types include
  - ClusterIP: This is the default service type reachable only within the Kubernetes cluster.
  - NodePort: This type is exposed on a static port on each node's IP, accessible outside the cluster.
  - LoadBalancers: This type is exposed externally using an external load balancer, creating NodePort and ClusterIP services.

  - ExternalName: This type is used when services in different namespaces need access to services in other namespaces using DNS names.

- **Namespace:** This is the consolidated space where Pods, Deployments, Services, and so on, converge.

Kubernetes networking inherently presents complexities due to the distributed nature of containerized applications. Managing networking across multiple pods, nodes, and services becomes challenging with numerous containers and significant east-west communication. Addressing segmentation challenges such as securing the infrastructure, providing network isolation between namespaces, controlling external communication for exposed services, and managing internal access to external services and endpoints requires a specification for container workload networking. This specification is realized through Container Network Interface (CNI) plugins.

Figure 13-16 provides an illustration of the Kubernetes constructs mentioned earlier.

While various Container Network Interfaces are available, this deployment uses ACI CNI, which offers several key advantages, including

- **IP Address Management:** ACI CNI provides IP addresses and management capabilities for both pods and services within the Kubernetes cluster.
- **Distributed Routing and Switching:** Integrated VXLAN overlays are implemented fabricwide and on Open vSwitch (OVS), ensuring distributed routing and switching capabilities.
- **EPG-Level Segmentation with Annotations:** ACI CNI allows flexible segmentation at the EPG level, enabling the use of a single EPG for the entire cluster or mapping each deployment to an EPG, controlling inter-deployment service traffic through contracts. Alternatively, each namespace can be mapped to its own EPG, utilizing contracts for inter-namespace traffic. Annotations and labels further allow specification of communication rules among groups of pods and other network endpoints within a namespace.
- **Distributed Policy Enforcement:** Network policies from both Kubernetes and ACI contracts are enforced in the Linux kernel of every server node where the container runs. Contracts are also enforced on all leaf switches in the fabric when applicable. Both mechanisms can be used in conjunction for comprehensive policy enforcement.
- **Consolidated Visibility:** VMM integration provides consolidated visibility into Kubernetes networking.

Key components in this integration include

1. ACI-CNI Plugin:

   a. ACI Containers Controllers (ACC): Installed primarily on master nodes, ACC handles IPAM, source NAT, endpoint state, policy mapping (annotations), load balancing, and communicates with the APIC, pushing Kubernetes configurations and policies.

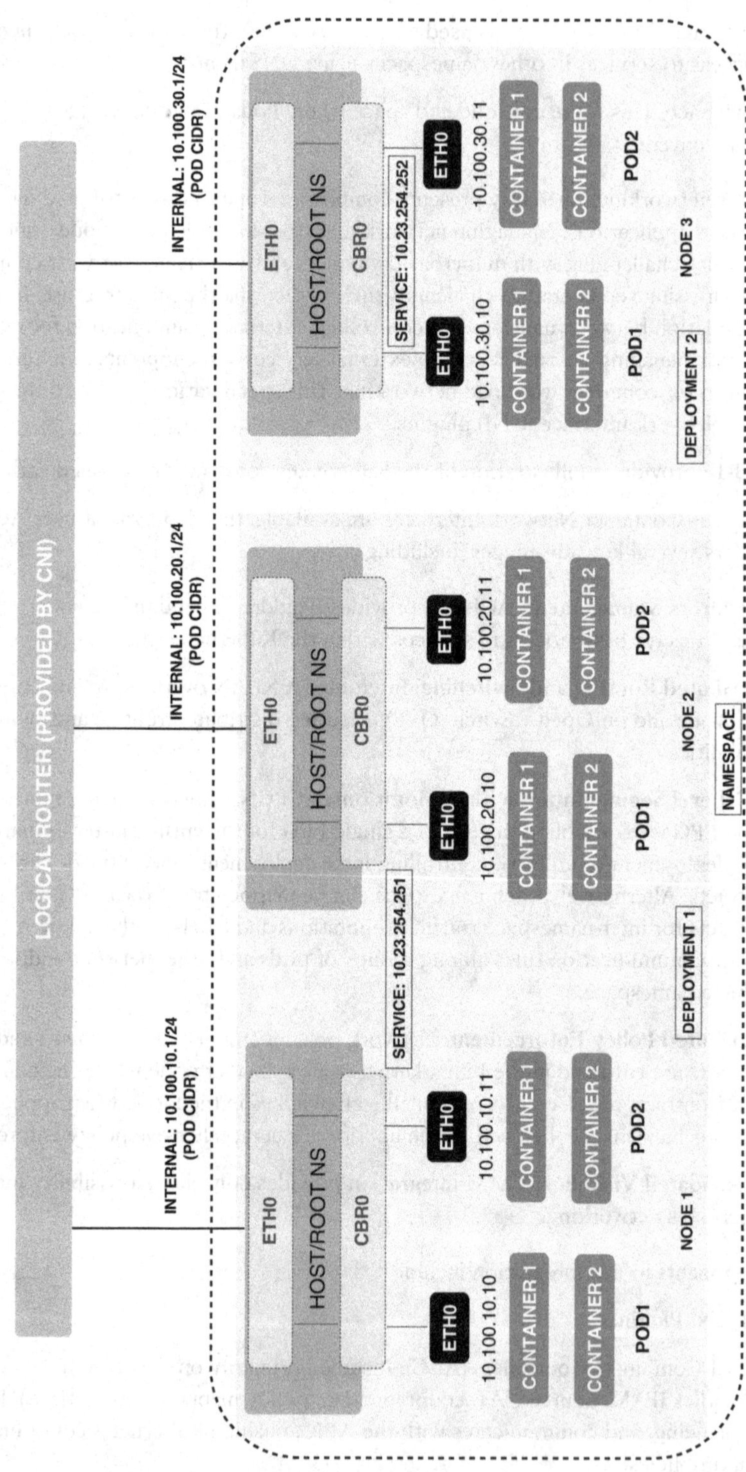

Figure 13-16 *Kubernetes Cluster*

b. ACI Containers Host: This DaemonSet has three containers running on every node. It includes a designated daemon for managing broadcast/multicast traffic; a designated daemon to manage pod IPAM and container interface configuration; and lastly a designated OpFlex-agent daemon for OVS configuration, security groups, and load-balancing services.

c. ACI Open vSwitch (OVS): Another DaemonSet running on every node, it is the OVS enforcing networking and security policies provisioned through the OpFlex agent.

2. OpFlex Protocol:

a. ACI-CNI utilizes the OpFlex protocol for communication between Kubernetes nodes and the ACI fabric, facilitating the exchange of information related to networking policies, endpoint groups, and other configurations.

Figure 13-17 illustrates the creation of various networks within the ACI integration, utilized by Kubernetes. Node-subnets are employed for SSH access and managing nodes, facilitating node-to-node API communication through VLAN 3900. Pod-subnets assign unique IP addresses to each deployed pod. Cluster-IP subnets are designated for "Cluster-IP" assignments in services. Node-service subnets play a role in ACI Service Graphs (SGs) for Policy-Based Redirection (PBR) concerning external services. Each node is assigned an IP, and external service traffic from outside the fabric is redirected and load-balanced to the assigned node IPs via VLAN 3950. The External Service subnet represents the externally exposed IP for a specific service. This IP is matched in the external EPG associated with L3Out and then aligned with an ACI Service Graph for Policy-Based Redirection to the previously mentioned node-service IPs. OpFlex communication utilizes Infra VLAN 3967.

Infrastructure Automation and Orchestration

Figure 13-18 showcases the tools and methods employed for automating the provisioning and configuration of infrastructure devices and services in this deployment. Infrastructure automation entails the utilization of control systems to automate the provisioning and configuration of infrastructure components. On the other hand, infrastructure orchestration involves employing a control system to coordinate and manage multiple automated tasks and processes, aiming to accomplish specific outcomes or workflows.

Some of the key elements in this architecture comprise

- **IT Service Management (ITSM):** This tool encompasses features such as incident management, change management, problem management, and a service catalog. It enables the enterprise to define and publish new services, fulfilling service requests through dynamic forms and integration with other systems. In this deployment, ServiceNow is used as an ITSM tool.

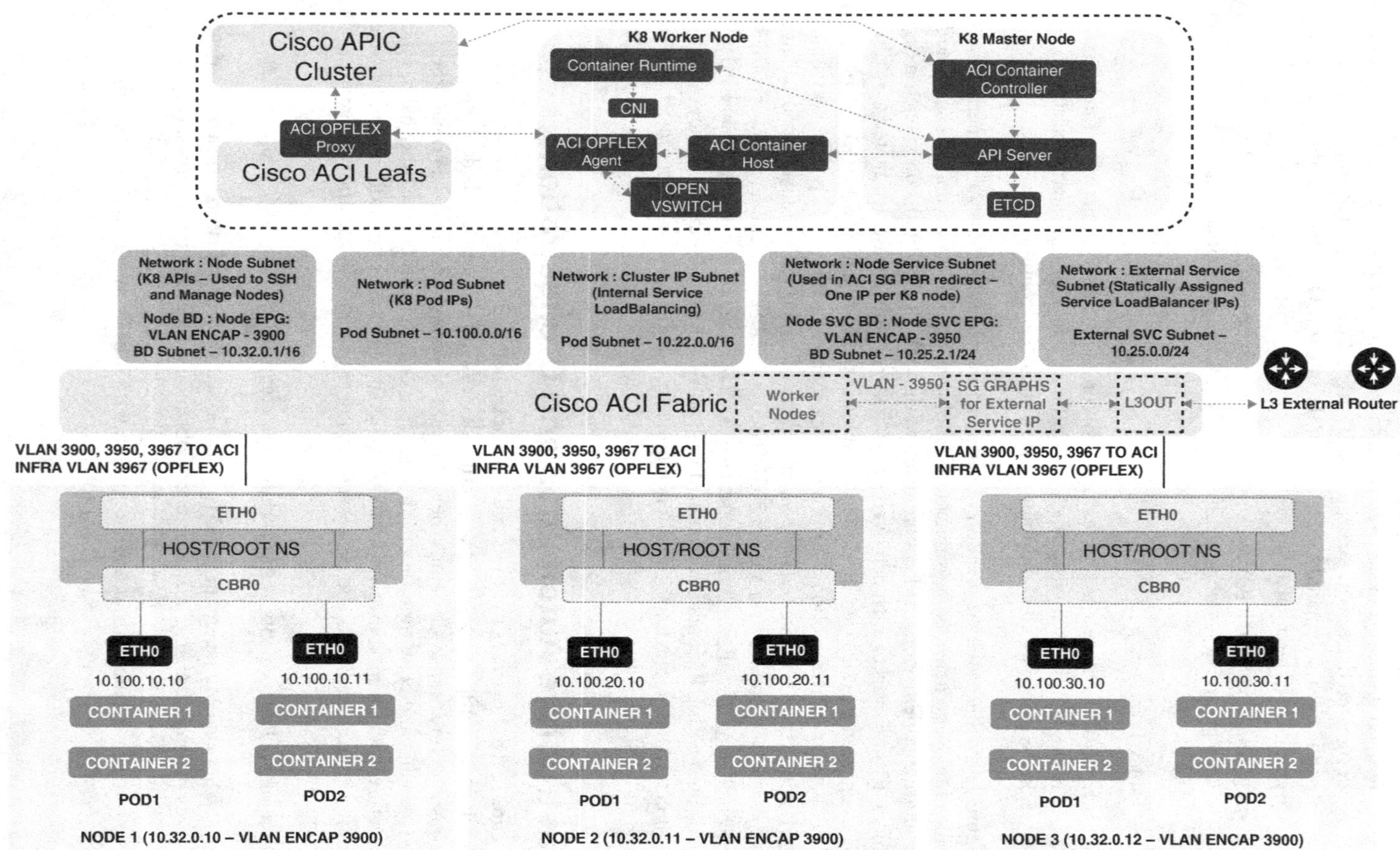

Figure 13-17 *Kubernetes Cluster with ACI Integration*

- **Infrastructure Workflow Engine:** This workflow engine encompasses workflow automation with minimal to zero code required for repetitive tasks. It offers a development canvas for creating workflows using both predefined and custom activities (atomic task units). The engine utilizes northbound Swagger-based APIs to receive instructions from systems like ITSM, employing southbound REST-based interfaces for communication with downstream devices and controllers. Additionally, it incorporates drivers (Python-based libraries) for sending notifications on workflow results and other alerts. In this deployment, Cisco CrossWorks Workflow Engine is utilized to define and automate repetitive tasks for the MPLS-SR domain.

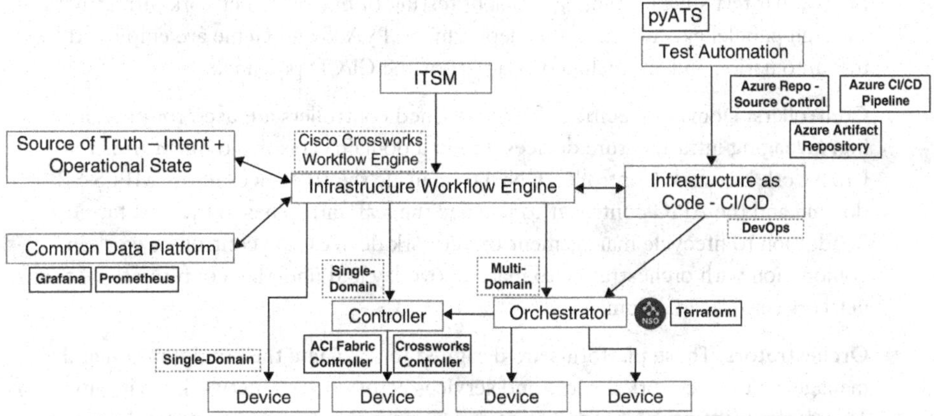

Figure 13-18 *Automation and Orchestration—Reference Design*

- **Source of Truth:** These authoritative sources track infrastructure inventory and manage resource allocation. Infoblox serves as the source of truth in this deployment, managing and tracking IP addresses, service identifiers, service names, and mapping of these services to devices and locations in the network.

- **Data Platform:** The data platform comprises tools that gather data from various points across the network to enhance insights and provide visibility into infrastructure status and performance. While the monitoring tool supports the visualization of data from multiple sources and includes alerting capabilities to notify infrastructure administrators when specific conditions and thresholds are met, the database tool is specialized in handling time-stamped data for the purpose of tracking and analyzing infrastructure metrics over time. In this deployment, Grafana is utilized for dashboarding, and Prometheus is employed as the time-stamped database, respectively.

- **Infrastructure as Code (IaC):** This involves applying CI/CD principles to network infrastructure, employing automation scripts and templates to define and govern network configuration in a code-like structure. The deployment makes use of Azure Repo for source code version control—that is, version control for network configurations as code. The Azure CI/CD pipeline takes charge of executing and validating changes, triggering whenever there's an incremental modification requested to the main branch of the code, indicating an incremental adjustment to the network configuration. Each CI/CD pipeline initiates the creation of a persistent workspace for executing the pipeline and utilizes a container image with all the necessary dependencies. The Azure Artifact Repository is employed to store binaries and outcomes linked to each execution (network change). These Azure tools work in tandem to manage state and automate gradual configuration changes for services within the ACI fabric and the MPLS-SR domain.

- **Test Automation:** This process involves the use of automated tools, scripts, and workflows to conduct network testing and validation. Utilizing configuration parsers and reusable libraries of test functions, it facilitates the creation and execution of modular test suites, enabling efficient testing of extensive network infrastructures through parallel execution. In this deployment, PyATS and Genie are employed for test automation and are included as a part of the CI/CD pipeline.
- **Controllers:** Domain-specific software-defined controllers are used for provisioning, managing infrastructure devices within a domain. This deployment uses the Crosswork Network Controller (CNC) to manage the IP devices in the MPLS-SR domain and the APIC controller to manage the leaf and spines in the ACI fabric. In addition to lifecycle management of network devices, the controllers work in conjunction with orchestrators to manage overlay and underlay configurations for network services in a domain.
- **Orchestrators:** These platforms are designed to automate the configuration and management of network devices and services across diverse network environments. This deployment uses NSO to define and manage the configurational and operational state of network devices and services in the MPLS-SR network using standards YANG-based data models. This deployment also uses orchestration capabilities of Terraform and its integration with the CI/CD pipeline to define and manage the configurational and operational state of network devices and services on the ACI fabric. Both NSO and Terraform integrate with the CI/CD pipelines for automated testing and configuration version control.

Figure 13-19 illustrates the execution of CI/CD workflows in this deployment. All network configurations are stored in a version control system (Azure Repo), which manages and monitors changes in the network. Incremental modifications to existing configurations are initially pushed to a feature branch. These feature branches act as secure spaces where network developers can safely work on their proposed configurations. A CI/CD pipeline is then executed in the feature branch to validate the incremental configuration change for syntax and semantic checks, all without affecting the master branch.

Upon successful validation of syntax and semantics in the feature branch, a pull request is initiated to merge the feature branch into another branch. This action triggers an additional CI/CD pipeline, deploying and validating the configuration change in a test environment before integrating the changes into the main codebase. After the configurations pass all comprehensive test sets successfully, network developers request the merging of their branch with the master configurations. This, in turn, triggers another CI/CD pipeline to undergo the approval process, deploy, and validate the change in the production environment.

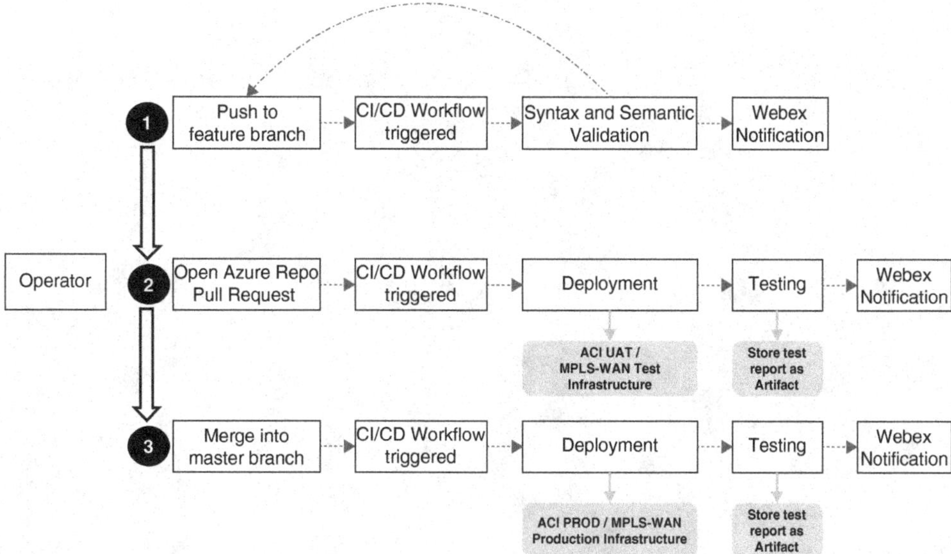

Figure 13-19 *CI/CD Workflow*

Summary

This chapter delved into the intricacies delved into the intricacies of designing and structuring network infrastructure in the contexts of government and public services. It thoroughly explored an enterprisewide design within a public sector deployment, covering best practices for tenant design and workload segmentation for private applications in ACI. The chapter highlighted the benefits of integrating ACI with distinct VMM domains and demonstrated how VMM automation can facilitate a seamless transition of applications across development, testing, and production environments. Additionally, it addressed the design considerations for private WAN, segmentation, and architecture using MPLS Segment Routing (MPLS-SR) and its integration with ACI. Furthermore, the chapter delved into the domain of infrastructure automation, emphasizing the role of Infrastructure as Code in streamlining processes.

Chapter 14

Transportation Use Case

In this chapter, we discuss the following:

- SD-Access in the campus environment
- Multi-tier SD-WAN topology in the WAN environment
- ACI segmentation in the data center

Use Case Overview

Transportation systems encompass numerous agencies and services.

As the use case is discussed in this chapter, the following key points for the business are addressed:

- Segmentation must be utilized in the data center to isolate applications.
- Segmentation must be extended across the WAN environment.
- Cellular support is provided for segmented transportation vehicles.
- Segmentation must be maintained between all campus locations.
- Dispatchers must be able to access only their agency-specific services.

This use case leverages ACI, SD-Access, and SD-WAN to meet the desired design.

Overall Design

In this environment, each agency and service must be maintained in isolated environments within the data center. Numerous data center fabric options are available; for this use case, ACI was chosen for its proven record in the data center for segmentation and scalability. Each agency will be isolated within its own ACI tenant, which will then provide agency-specific services and security. The segmentation will be extended to the remote locations and vehicles via an SD-WAN topology with cloud-hosted Catalyst SD-WAN Manager, Catalyst SD-WAN Validator, and Catalyst SD-WAN Controller. SD-Access is then used at campus locations, such as dispatch centers, to maintain the end-to-end segmentation and policy.

The new end-to-end multi-domain architecture will obviously not be turned up in one maintenance window, or even in just a few windows. The services that are currently shared in the data center must be accessible for all environments throughout all of the changes. Also, because various operational teams manage the different environments, each domain should be independent of the others while also accommodating the fact that different domains will deploy at different rates. As an example, in the data center, agency 1 may have already migrated to exist only in ACI, while agency 2 exists in both ACI and the legacy environments as a result of ongoing migration. Other agencies might still exist in the legacy environment. At the same time, remote locations and the WAN environment may be migrating at differing rates themselves.

Therefore, each domain—SD-Access, SD-WAN, and ACI—will be designed to be independent of each other. To facilitate all of the conceivable traffic patterns and to support the independent migration strategies and timelines, engineers must first consider the potential traffic flows in the data center. Figure 14-1 illustrates how a single data center is migrated initially to support a new DC aggregation layer.

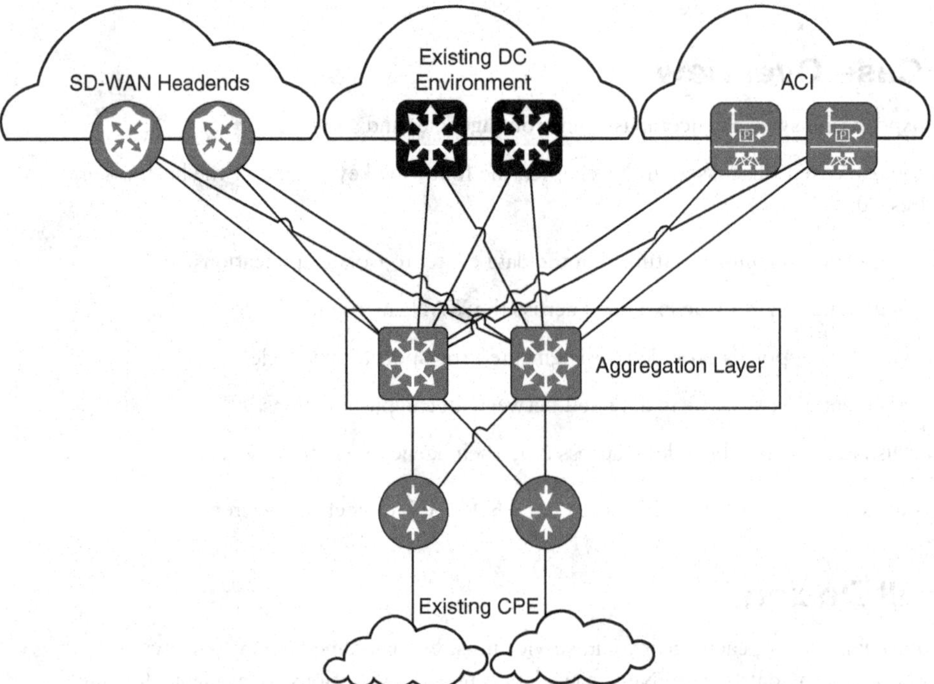

Figure 14-1 *Data Center Aggregation Layer*

In some organizations, a data center aggregation layer may already exist. This layer allows for all other domains in the data center to be considered as individual groupings or pods. The DC aggregation layer supports high-speed, high-bandwidth routing and switching between the other pods and allows for the ACI and SD-WAN environments in the data center to be deployed independently. The layer will now provide network access to the ACI environment via the ACI border leafs and the SD-WAN service-side environment, as well as all of the legacy data center environment.

The DC aggregation layer will address the requirements for modularity in the data center environment between ACI, SD-WAN, and the legacy environment; however, it will present some new challenges with remote site routing unless carefully considered. The routing is discussed later in this chapter. So far, the modularity pieces of the SD-WAN and SD-Access environments have not been discussed.

Similar to the earlier financial use case, the SD-Access and SD-WAN environments will utilize the two-box solution. This solution will allow for campus locations to deploy SD-Access regardless of whether SD-WAN is already provisioned at the site or not. Additionally, the WAN environment may be able to move faster by deploying SD-WAN Edge routers at each location with a standard template for non-SD-Access locations and another for SD-Access locations. Moving the campus environment to SD-Access, then, only requires attaching the SD-Access version template to the already-provisioned SD-WAN Edge with the appropriate new variable values.

The SD-Access campuses themselves also will be modular in design. Regardless of campus size, the SD-Access will be utilized as a single module that is then capable of direct connectivity to any other modules, including the WAN module, that may be necessary for the location.

Different teams of personnel support the different domains. There are also different requirements at each location, even within the same domain. Therefore, a strict standardized design must be created up front to accommodate all of the various agency requirements that are then followed throughout all of the deployments.

The ACI and SD-WAN environments must hand off to each other via the DC aggregation layer. Also, at each location that supports SD-Access, SD-Access and SD-WAN hand off directly to each other. Because segmentation of the agencies must be maintained after it is created, a standardized table of reserved dot1Q VLAN numbers is created for each agency tenant. For instance, tenant (agency) 1 may be given VLAN 3001. This VLAN is then utilized for all of the inter-domain handoffs for agency 1 throughout the entire environment. Making the SD-WAN service VPN the same value further simplifies the design and improves the operational efficiency. Including the same value as part of the tenant name in ACI and the VN name in SD-Access makes it easier for operations personnel to further identify the usage.

Data Center Design

Focusing on just the data center, this section examines the design and routing requirements and how they are addressed. The first concern is how to route traffic between legacy and new domains. In the beginning, all traffic will flow only in the global routing table. If the business already has some macrosegmentation through VRF-Lite, then this concern may already be addressed via some form of fusion routing; however, most likely, all traffic will reside only in the global routing table. As ACI and SD-WAN begin their individual migrations, at some point, some services will reside in the ACI environment, whereas others will reside in the legacy environment. At the same time, some remote locations will have been migrated to SD-WAN, while other locations will still be utilizing the original WAN topology.

During this phase of the deployment, which will exist to some extent until the final migrations are completed, traffic must be able to flow as optimally as possible between all environments. Figure 14-2 shows the interconnectivity between the various domains, SD-WAN, ACI, the legacy data center, and the legacy WAN, with the addition of the DC aggregation layer.

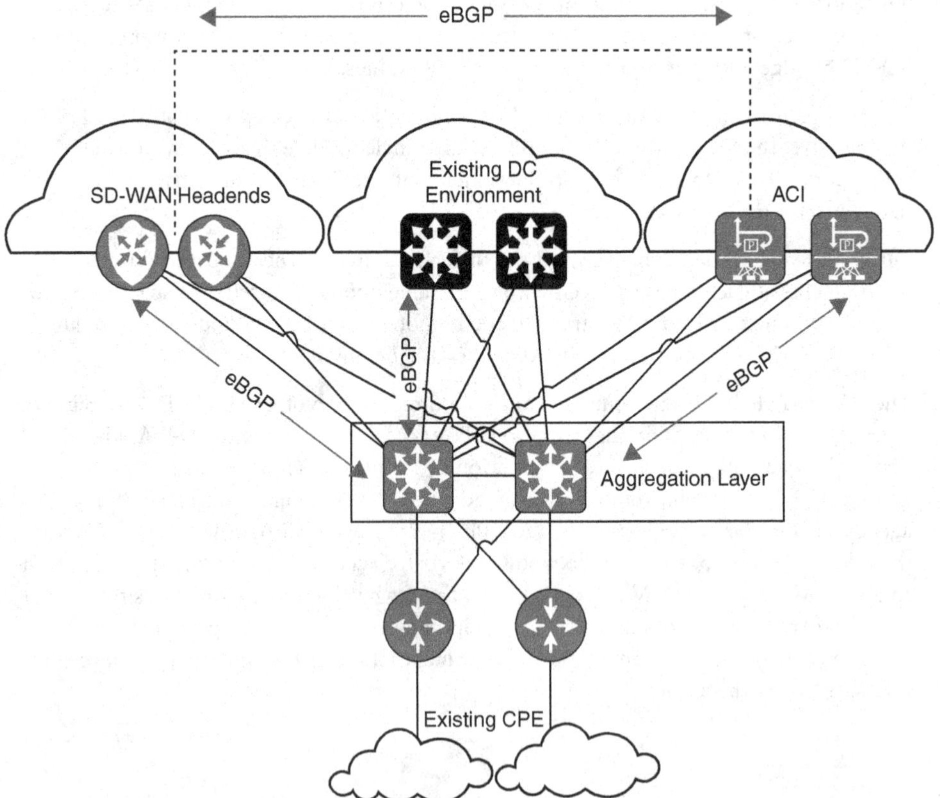

Figure 14-2 *Data Center Design*

The first important note is that only the global routing table exists on the DC aggregation layer. Consequently, the aggregation layer can perform fusion routing as needed between the legacy and IBN environments. Notice the use of dashed lines from the SD-WAN Edge headend devices and the ACI environment in the figure. As discussed, the DC aggregation layer uses only the global routing table. Therefore, to maintain segmentation, for any tenant/service VPN that exists in either ACI or SD-WAN, but not both, the ACI or SD-WAN environment will use the transport VLAN to peer with the DC aggregation layer. When both ACI and SD-WAN in the data center are configured to support a particular tenant, then the SD-WAN peering to the DC aggregation layer for that particular tenant is removed, if necessary. This allows for the service VPN and the ACI tenant to be directly stitched together and simplifies the routing configurations on the DC aggregation layer. Maintaining both BGP peerings (SD-WAN to aggregation layer and ACI to aggregation layer) creates unneeded additional complexity in the data center and WAN routing design.

From a routing perspective, as shown in Figure 14-3, each module in the data center will utilize its own ASN with eBGP peering between itself and the DC aggregation layer. Nonmigrated remote locations will exist in the global routing table and are sourced from the legacy WAN ASN. Nonmigrated services in the data center will be in the global routing table and are sourced from the legacy data center ASN. The ACI border leafs will source the networks for tenants that have begun migration to ACI. For remote locations that have migrated to SD-WAN, those remote location networks will appear to come from the headend SD-WAN Edges to the aggregation layer. For remote locations that have migrated to SD-WAN and have begun migration to ACI, the remote location will appear to arrive from the ACI border leafs, as well as the SD-WAN headends but with an additional as-path hop. This could potentially lead to some adverse routing scenarios if other BGP routing policies have been applied. Additionally, some security services within the ACI environment may be required to occur. For this reason, removing the "short-circuit" BGP peering from the SD-WAN Edge headends to the aggregation layer will drive traffic between the SD-WAN domain and the remaining domains through the ACI services environment for that tenant prior to traversing the aggregation layer.

From a high level, this routing topology is quite straightforward; however, the design has not yet addressed redundant data centers. Using eBGP prevents looping; however, it does not prevent suboptimal routing. Consider a prefix that originates from the legacy data center environment in DC1. For simplicity, imagine that the ACI environment is not yet operational. Figure 14-3 illustrates how the prefix is advertised to the data center aggregation layer. The data center aggregation layer advertises the prefix to both the SD-WAN environment and the legacy WAN environment. In SD-WAN at DC1, the prefix is advertised into OMP. Meanwhile, the prefix is advertised across the service provider environment to the secondary data center, DC2. The prefix is advertised to the data center aggregation layer at DC2 and then to the SD-WAN devices and legacy data center environment. At this point, the same prefix is advertised by the DC2 SD-WAN Edges into OMP. Without any policy considerations, the prefixes from the DC2 SD-WAN Edge are the same preference as the DC1 SD-WAN Edge advertisements. Even with a dedicated Data Center Interconnect (DCI) between the two data centers, this type of phenomenon will occur due to the redundancy aspects of the environment.

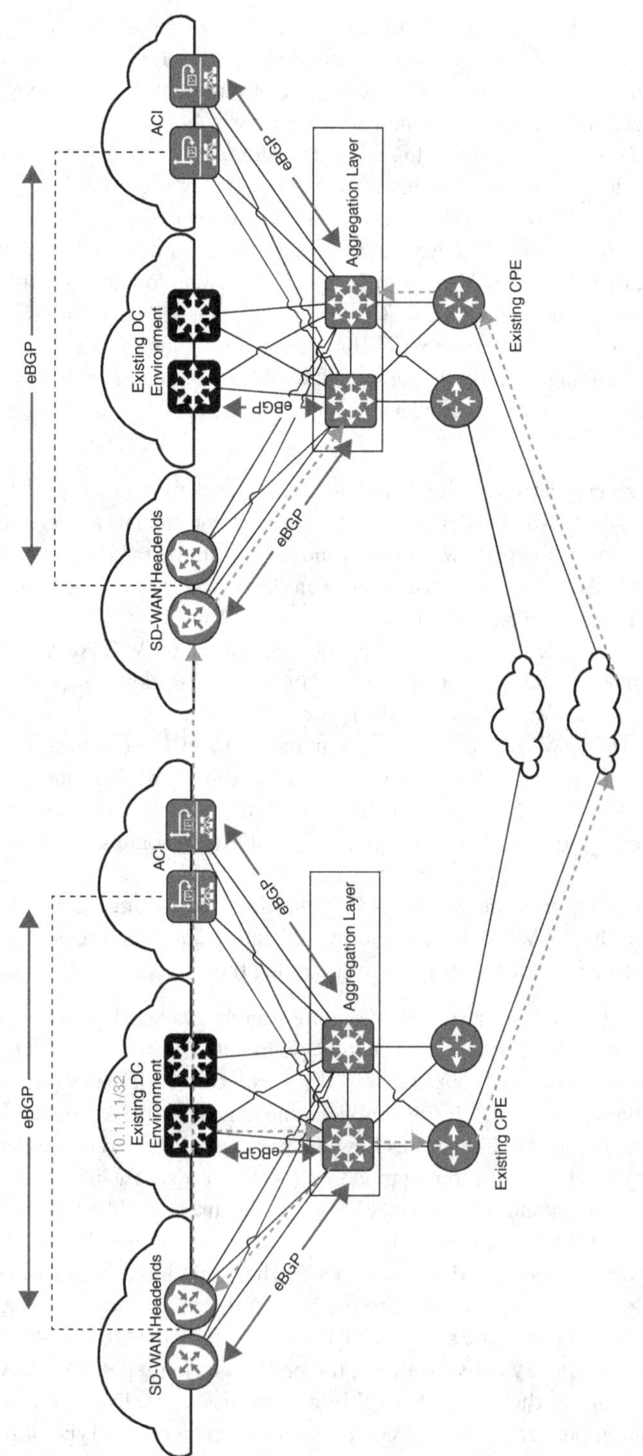

Figure 14-3 *Suboptimal DC Routing*

To prevent suboptimal routing while still maintaining the redundant backup paths, a policy must be created to ensure that traffic follows the more optimal pathway. In this scenario, it is recommended to standardize a set of community values that are added to the prefixes and propagated through the environment with the prefix advertisements. For instance, the community X is identified to signify that a prefix originated from the DC1 location. When that prefix arrives at a headend SD-WAN Edge, the SD-WAN Edge translates the BGP community to a specific OMP tag. For instance, at DC1, the DC1 community X is translated to OMP tag 100 while the DC2 community Y is translated to OMP tag 50. At first glance, we may want to use the BGP communities as part of the OMP policy configuration. However, this creates unneeded complexity in the OMP control policies. Using the OMP tags, the same control policy may be used inbound with DC1 and DC2 to translate the OMP tag to OMP preference values. The SD-WAN Edge could simply translate the BGP community to an OMP preference; however, setting the OMP tag allows the prefix to be identified inside the OMP environment later on, if desired.

Just as the service provider could inadvertently become a suboptimal transit path, the DCI and ACI environments could also potentially become suboptimal routing pathways. As such, liberal use of community marking on BGP prefixes is important to ensure proper optimal routing while providing backup routing pathways when needed. Therefore, any device that sources a prefix in BGP must mark the source location with a location-specific community. Doing so prevents such oddities as a point-to-point network that exists in DC1 from appearing to be preferred from DC2, for instance. If ACI is advertising a prefix that appears to exist in both data centers, then that prefix must be marked with the correct community that identifies it as preferred from DC1, DC2, or both, as desired. In this way, the policy created for the environment will continue to function normally, driving traffic between domains in the optimized and desired fashion.

After the community system is created, it scales easily beyond two data center environments and allows for support of more complicated policy in a straightforward fashion. For instance, suppose DC3 provides some services; however, it should never be a transit path for traffic between either DC1 or DC2 and the remote locations. Traffic between DC3 and the other two DCs should take the SD-WAN pathways. Therefore, prefixes with the DC1 or DC2 community are not advertised from the DC3 data center aggregation layer to the SD-WAN Edges, and, in OMP, only the prefixes with the DC3 community are advertised toward the DC1 and DC2 SD-WAN devices. Other scenarios, depending on the client, may be created; however, the use of the OMP tags for SD-WAN preference for egress and the BGP communities for location origination allows for effective policy management and control.

Campus Design

At the remote campuses, such as a dedicated dispatch center, the campus is designed from a modular perspective, allowing for the SD-Access environment to be scaled and managed separately, if required, from the other functional modules. SD-WAN Edge routers are used for the WAN connectivity across the service provider transports. By utilizing the SD-Access–SD-WAN two-box solution, the SD-Access border nodes are the core of the local campus network. This instantly allows the SD-Access and SD-WAN environments to be designed and deployed separately, as well as fuels the push toward a standardized, modular design. The SD-WAN Edges may be interchanged based on throughput requirements without affecting the design of the SD-Access campus. Meanwhile, the SD-WAN Edges hand off to the core (the SD-Access border nodes) regardless of the size of the campus location or individual service requirements.

In Figure 14-4, three different scale models for SD-Access are shown. In each scenario, the other functional blocks at the campus are connected to the two SD-Access border nodes that provide the traditional core layer connectivity. The difference in the three models is the number of tiers or levels in the topology required to support the number of endpoints at that particular campus location. The modular design allows for easily adding or removing functional blocks from a campus with time, as well as somewhat painless expansion in the SD-Access fabric itself, if required.

Based on the agencies that are utilizing a particular campus location, the local SD-WAN edge devices are provisioned with the appropriate service VPNs. As mentioned previously, a standardized mapping for VLAN–ACI Tenant–SD-Access Virtual Network–SD-WAN Service VPN will create a system for easily adding, removing, and managing the various architectural domains at each location, even by disparate teams within the organization.

Transportation-Specific Entities

The data centers and the various campuses, such as dispatch centers, are not the only locations in the overall network topology. Some agencies may provide support to buses and trains that will require additional network services. For these network locations, an SD-WAN Edge router is utilized to connect the network to the bus or train. Due to the prevalence of cellular coverage in the modern world, it is not uncommon to use a cellular transport with the SD-WAN router to provide an easy underlay transport.

Imagine a new smart bus running its route through a major city. The driver must be able to communicate with dispatchers within their own agency. Perhaps, there is a kiosk or other screen that presents route information to the riders. Additionally, there may be guest Wi-Fi services that allow users to check their accounts, and so on. All of these services may be easily accomplished, as shown in Figure 14-5, even as the bus is following its route through the city. Even the bus's exact GPS location is known as it is advertised in the system so that commuters waiting at various stops ahead know when the next bus will arrive.

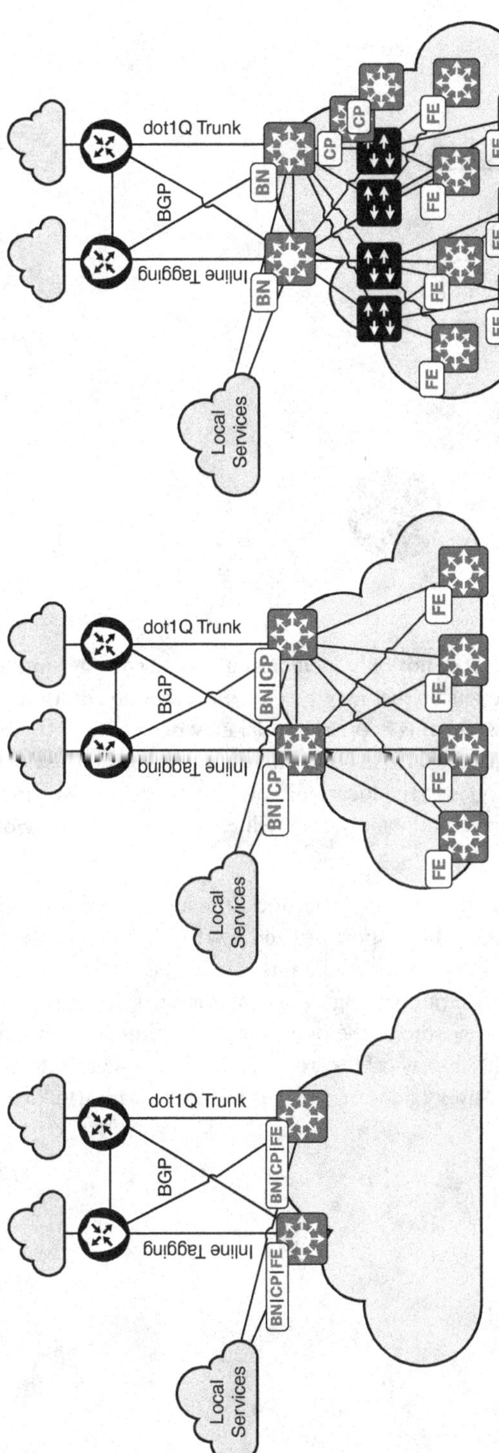

Figure 14-4 *SD-Access Campus Models*

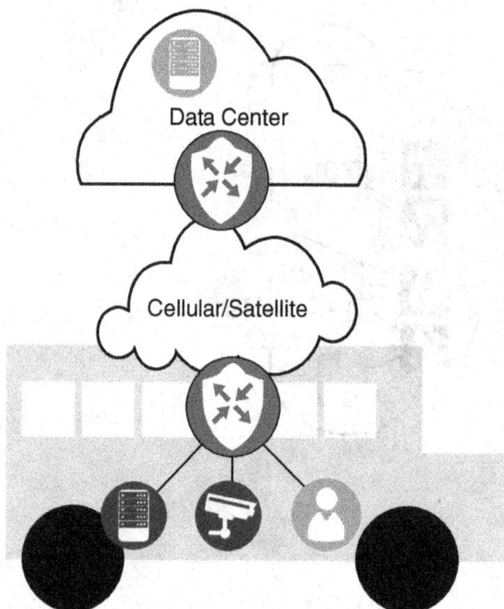

Figure 14-5 *Bus Network*

The transportation industry not only includes buses and subways in the city, but also larger trains, ships, and trucks that may be carrying cargo in addition to the travelers. In each of these scenarios, the bus network model may be extended to accommodate the larger scenario. The ship scenario is quite interesting. When a cruise ship is docked, it has access to physical lines at the location; however, after it is disconnected, the available transport bandwidth is limited mainly to satellite. How does the network accommodate these changes?

As Figure 14-6 shows, when the ship is in dock, the local wired network actually becomes a private, preferred transport utilized by the SD-WAN routers. Because the SD-WAN environment requires and maintains certain security features, such as IPsec traffic and allowlist device onboarding in the environment, if the wired connections are compromised, the exposure to the organization is mitigated. This also prevents any routing churn in the ship as cables are connected or disconnected because the SD-WAN environment simply adds or removes transports, allowing for a seamless user experience.

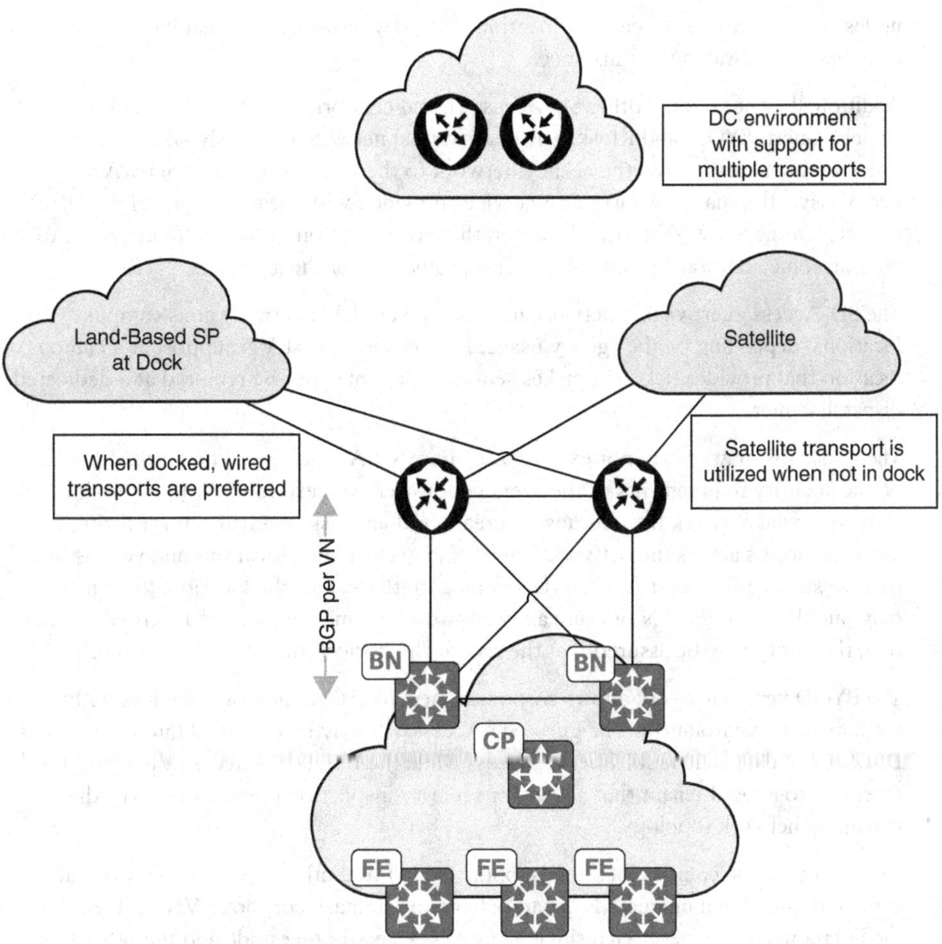

Figure 14-6 *Docked Ship Network*

Campus Macrosegmentation

In all of the domains—SD-Access, ACI, SD-WAN—some form of underlay network exists. SD-Access defines the global routing table used as the underlay as a virtual network, the Infra_VN. For the campuses, as well as the vessels that require SD-Access due to size (for example, trains and ships), the SD-Access Infra_VN will be used to handle the management traffic of the Catalyst fabric switches, the connectivity between SD-Access devices for VXLAN-encapsulated traffic, and CAPWAP traffic for the wireless environment.

For all of the vessels, there will be a corporate virtual network. On the vessel, this SD-Access VN supports all of the crew and devices for normal operational usage. At the various campus locations, the corporate VN not only encompasses the agency users and devices, but it also includes any devices that exist outside the Core/SD-Access border nodes that are part of the campus location. This may include additional local servers that exist behind firewalling, for instance.

Additionally, one to three other SD-Access virtual networks may be found on the vessels: Guest, BYOD, and Kiosk. The guest virtual network obviously allows the guest users remote access across the agency network to the Internet. From an SD-WAN perspective, this may be simple DIA services provided with local enterprise firewall services on the SD-WAN router; however, there is the option to backhaul the traffic to provide some additional means of security protection for the agency.

The SD-Access guest virtual network may also be available in the various campus locations, depending on the agency usage. For instance, guest VN support at a campus location that provides ticketing makes sense, while it may not be required at a dedicated dispatch center.

The kiosk VN may or may not exist as a separate SD-Access virtual network, depending on the security requirements of the agency; however, we describe how to maintain it in its own virtual network here because it greatly reduces risk of a bad actor utilizing the kiosk for access across the network. This VN may exist at all locations and vessels that provide support for guest services. Depending on the size of the location, there may be only one device in the VN or quite a few; however, by maintaining the macrosegmentation, the entity may be assured that the risk of the device(s) has been minimized.

The BYOD virtual network allows corporate users to utilize their own devices within the corporate environment. The guest SD-Access VN may be extended into a dedicated DMZ in the data centers for Internet access while the BYOD SD-Access VN could be extended to an ACI tenant that allows for security inspection prior to access to the remaining network topology.

Depending on the campus location, support for IoT and other physical infrastructure may be required in a unique VN separate from the primary corporate VN. In Figure 14-7, the interconnections between a single Core/SD-Access border node and the other blocks are shown.

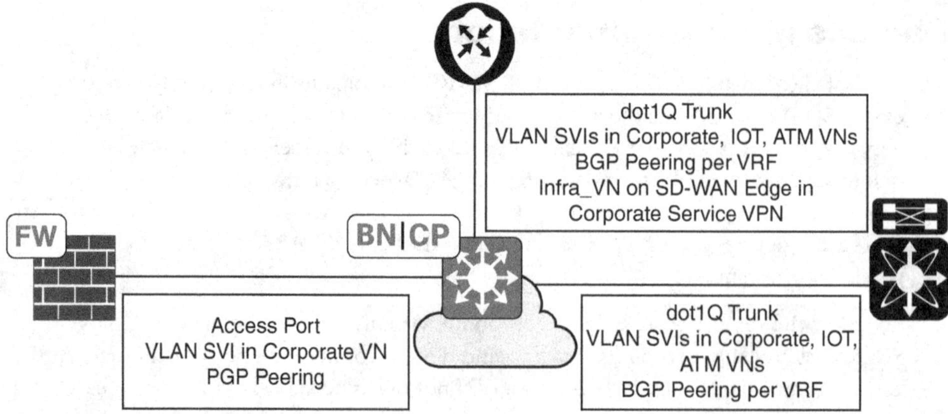

Figure 14-7 *One BN Physical Handoff*

The potential SD-Access virtual networks that may be found at a single location are listed in Table 14-1.

Table 14-1 *SD-Access Virtual Networks*

Virtual Network	Description
Infra_VN	Cisco SD-Access Fabric Underlay
Corporate	Corporate-owned endpoints not specifically assigned to another VN
IoT	Third-party vendor equipment, physical security devices
Kiosk	Kiosk devices, display monitors
Guest	Noncorporate users
BYOD	Personal devices used by corporate employees

DC and WAN Macrosegmentation

The intent is for the macrosegmentation to be continued throughout the WAN environment into the data center services via SD-WAN and ACI. This section discusses how the campus macrosegmentation is extended throughout the environment.

Regardless of remote location, whether it is a vessel, data center, dispatch center, or general campus facility, every location is connected via the WAN underlay by an SD-WAN Edge router. The service VPN membership provisioned on a particular SD-WAN Edge router will determine exactly what ACI services are available to a location.

Consider that the corporate VN on a bus may require different services from the corporate VN on a ship. For instance, the ACI tenant in the data centers providing the ship centralized services may be a different ACI tenant from the bus services. Therefore, even though the bus and the ship have an SD-Access corporate virtual network, the SD-WAN environment uses a different service VPN for each of those locations—one for ships and one for buses in this example. Even though the two locations have the same named SD-Access virtual network, they are completely isolated via the SD-WAN environment from each other, meaning that they must be stitched together in the data center via a shared ACI tenant or other fusion routing mechanism if access between them is required.

Continuing the example further, drivers between buses may need direct communication between each other for traffic updates. The SD-WAN Edge routers may be configured for dynamic tunnels in the corporate bus service VPN to allow for a direct tunnel that is located between the vessels when required and is later torn down to prevent unneeded overhead.

As described, even though the SD-Access locations may reuse the names of the virtual networks, the SD-WAN environment isolates different locations based on actual usage. You may notice that on the surface this seems to violate the standardized mapping requirement mentioned earlier; however, Table 14-2 demonstrates three mappings to make the point clear while illustrating that the mapping requirement is a hard requirement. The table compares a possible buildout for the SD-Access guest virtual network with the SD-Access corporate virtual network at two distinct entities.

Table 14-2 *Virtual Network Mappings*

	Guest	Corporate Bus	Corporate Ship
VLAN	3101	3001	3002
SD-Access VN	Guest	Corporate	Corporate
SD-WAN Service VPN	3101	3001	3002
ACI Tenant		Corporate Bus	Corporate Ship

The data center continues the macrosegmentation into the ACI environment. In these locations, the standardized VLANs from all of the possible SD-WAN service VPNs tie into the various ACI tenants following the established standard. As mentioned previously, the SD-WAN Edge routers peer directly to the ACI border leafs for those service VPNs that have already been migrated into ACI while the other service VPNs have the SD-WAN Edge router peering directly with the DC aggregation layer to support the legacy environment.

Microsegmentation

The macrosegmentation of the entire topology creates a large, segmented environment that may not require much additional work via microsegmentation. However, depending on the enterprise's use case, some microsegmentation may be required.

Consider the bus scenario. Here, microsegmentation may be overkill and create unneeded complexity. There may be only two corporate users on the bus—the driver and a conductor, for instance. That leaves corporate devices, guest users, and the kiosk devices. Therefore, the SD-Access microsegmentation rules for a bus would be a single SGT (CorporateBus) for the corporate environment VN that allows reachability between all CorporateBus devices or users on the bus. The bus personnel could have a second SGT separate from CorporateBus as CorporateUser if devices and users require different policies in general. For the guest VN, all users have the guest SD-Access VN, and guest-to-guest traffic is blocked. The kiosks are in their own VN with the kiosk SGT. Kiosks are only allowed to send and receive data from KioskServers that are located in the ACI environments.

So far, the SD-Access SGTs listed in Table 14-3 have been defined with minimal policy to accommodate the bus scenario.

Table 14-3 *SD-Access Bus SGTs*

SGT	Description
CorporateBus	Corporate devices on the bus
CorporateUser	Corporate bus users—driver, conductor
Kiosk	Kiosk device or display monitor
KioskServer	ACI kiosk servers
Guest	Noncorporate users and devices

The ship, train, and airline environments may be larger; however, their microsegmentation requirements may be matched with the bus environment or expanded as required. Here, the enterprise should take care to prevent overcomplicating the environment without real advantages.

In each of these environments and in the larger campus environment, the base SGTs used on the bus environment may be extended for additional microsegmentation usage. This would mostly be around the corporate VN, where there may be additional microsegmentation requirements for human resources personnel, services, and so on. These requirements will vary by entity.

The SD-Access SGT values are propagated between the various locations via the SD-WAN environment. Inside the data center, the translation between the SGTs in the SD-WAN environment and the EPGs in the ACI environment requires work with ISE as an intermediary. Configuring ISE to support the translation of SD-Access SGTs to an ACI EPG is possible; however, the translation results in the EPGs only available in one tenant. Depending on the ACI microsegmentation requirements, it may be more feasible to maintain a separate policy in the ACI environment that does not require the microsegmentation markings to be maintained between the ACI environment and the SD-Access–SD-WAN environment.

SD-Access Data Center Services

All of these architectures require data center services to be deployed and maintained. As is normally the case, the enterprise would not want a single failure to disrupt the functioning of the system. Obviously, transport vessels themselves may be self-contained in the event they lose connectivity to the WAN intermittently; however, the impact of those instances should be minimized. This section discusses the design and deployment of fully redundant management planes.

The SD-Access management plane consists of ISE and Catalyst Center. With ISE, redundancy is fairly easy to achieve via a multi-node ISE deployment. Two Policy Administration Nodes (PANs) are deployed, one in each of two data centers in the region. Likewise, two Monitoring and Troubleshooting Nodes (MnTs) are deployed, one in each data center. For the pxGrid support, one dedicated ISE PSN is used in each data center for pxGrid services. If SXP is required, then a pair of dedicated PSNs for SXP may also be deployed, one in each data center. One pair of SXP PSNs will support only 200 SXP peerings, and only four pairs of SXP PSNs are supported in a single ISE multi-node deployment. Therefore, consider using a pair of IOS-XE routers to scale the SXP peerings, if necessary. The PSNs are scaled based on endpoint requirements and deployed at multiple locations. Figure 14-8 illustrates the ISE deployment model in a region across the two data center locations.

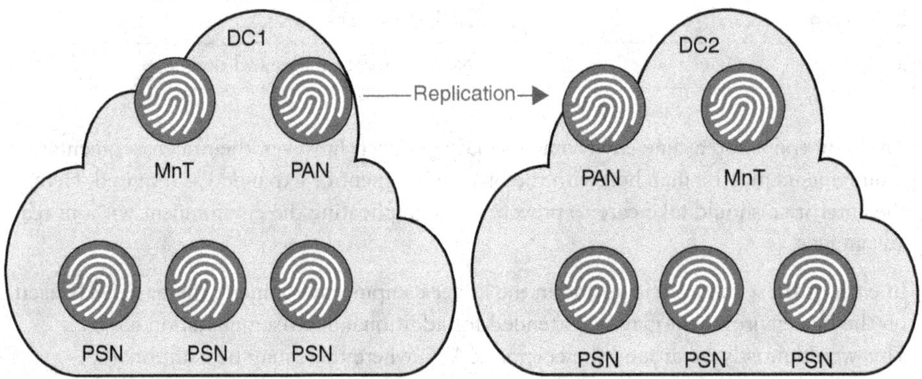

Figure 14-8 *ISE Multi-Node Deployment*

SD-Access supports high availability and disaster recovery in the Catalyst Center. If we were to deploy a single-node Catalyst Center deployment, then the loss of connectivity to the device would interrupt fabric management, prevent streaming assurance data, limit scaling capabilities, and so on. HA cluster support was developed to address some of these issues. As shown in Figure 14-9, the Catalyst Center has two interfaces connected to a switch in the data center. One interface supports a Layer 2 link between the other two Catalyst Centers at the location, allowing for communication and replication between the devices. The other interface is the enterprise interface, allowing for Layer 3 connectivity of the Catalyst Center to the remainder of the network. This interface supports a virtual IP address that represents to the network all three cluster members on the same subnet. The Catalyst Center supports two other interfaces to further isolate management traffic flows; however, they are unused here for this use case.

This deployment of Catalyst Center is more redundant than a single-node deployment; however, notice that a single switch may still disrupt the management plane traffic or the assurance data, for instance. This has led to the development of redundant interfaces in the Catalyst Center chassis, as is normally seen in port channels. This development gives rise to the cabling shown in Figure 14-10.

While the redundancy support is more robust, notice that all of the equipment still exists in a single data center. Some entities may have the requirement that no single failure should take down the system. What if the single failure is the loss of a data center due to catastrophic reasons? To fulfill the requirements, Catalyst Center disaster recovery is introduced to allow for an identical Catalyst Center deployment in a separate location to receive incremental replication data of 15-minute intervals and support to become the active location. For the system to be fully automated for recovery, a third node, the witness PC, is deployed at a third geographical location, as shown in Figure 14-11.

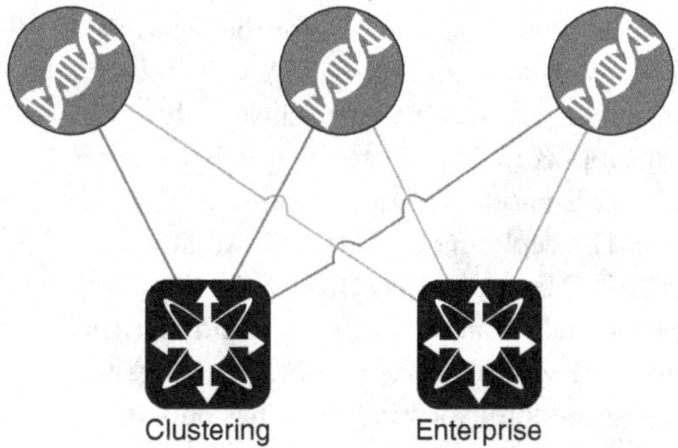

Figure 14-9 *HA Catalyst Center with Single Interface Links*

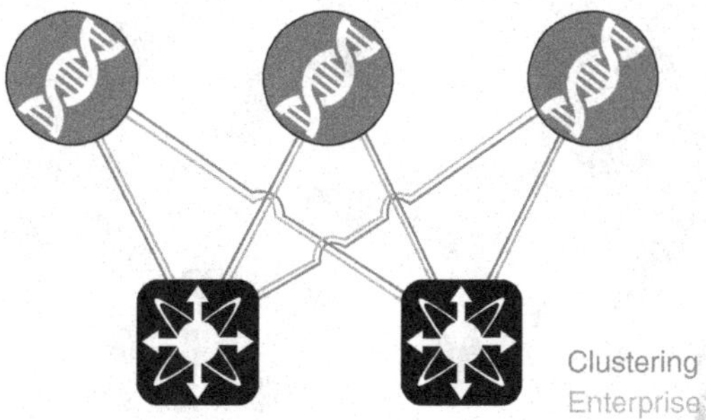

Figure 14-10 *HA Catalyst Center with Redundant Interfaces*

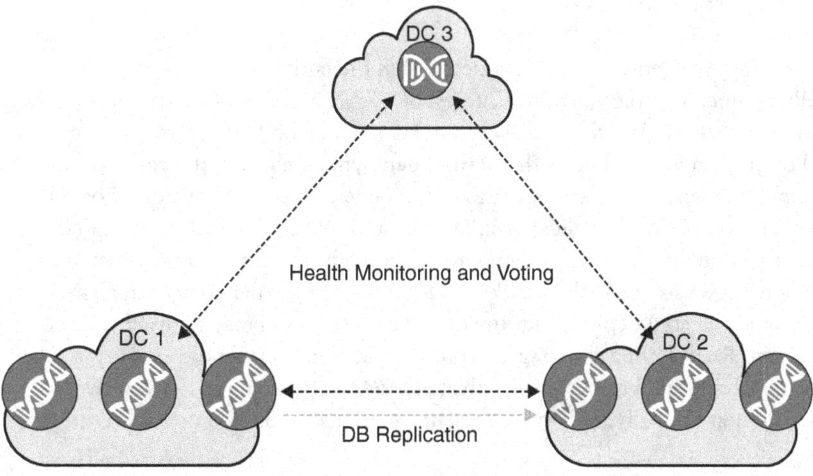

Figure 14-11 *Catalyst Center Disaster Recovery*

With an HA cluster and a single virtual IP in the subnet, it was easy for the network devices to interact with Catalyst Center. They sent the traffic to the HA VIP, and the data center routing brought the traffic to the DC and the Catalyst Center cluster. However, now a virtual IP address must be created to support the two different Catalyst Center clusters. Therefore, the HA VIP for each cluster is part of the local subnet, and another DR VIP that represents all of Catalyst Center DR deployment is created. Additionally, the active-side Catalyst Center advertises the DR VIP host route via BGP to the directly connected Layer 3 device. The three locations—DR Primary, Secondary, and Witness—communicate with each other directly to indicate which sites are online. For a site to remain active, it must maintain two votes from the three locations. If it has only its own vote, it will withdraw the route from BGP, thereby preventing a split-brain scenario because the other two locations are most likely still connected. The DR BGP process is illustrated in Figure 14-12.

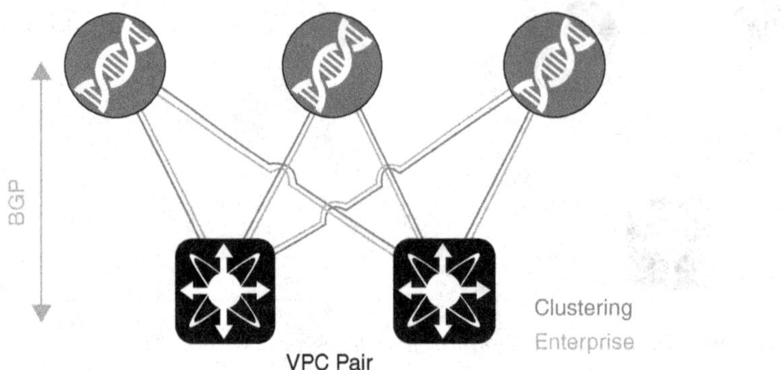

Figure 14-12 *Catalyst Center Disaster Recovery BGP*

While ISE and Catalyst Center are provisioned within the entity's data center environments, a fully redundant deployment of Catalyst SD-WAN Manager, Catalyst SD-WAN Validator, and Catalyst SD-WAN Controller in the cloud may be the preferred alternative instead of on-premises. While both are valid deployment models, the cloud option provides simplified management for operations personnel, especially via cloud-hosted options. For Catalyst SD-WAN Validator and Catalyst SD-WAN Controller, the cloud deployment and scaling easily address any redundancy options the enterprise may have. With a cloud-managed solution, the Catalyst SD-WAN Manager may be a single virtual machine or a clustered deployment. In either case, snapshots may be used to back up a deployment. Redeploying the snapshot provides fast recovery in the event of a catastrophic disaster. Even without the Catalyst SD-WAN Manager, the network would continue to function normally; only management functions would be impacted until the services are restored.

For cloud-managed environments, Catalyst SD-WAN Manager disaster recovery provides only limited improvement over the backup and snapshot approach. However, for on-premises deployments of SD-WAN services, the Catalyst SD-WAN Manager DR feature may be considered a viable option for both disaster recovery and planned maintenance activities.

SD-WAN Centralized Policy

In this use case, the topology may extend to numerous countries or regions within a country or city. It is expected that the deployment will have two or more data centers with headend SD-WAN Edges providing access to the centralized services. As mentioned previously in the discussion of intercommunication between buses, dynamic tunnels may be required between transportation vessels. Otherwise, their communication patterns are more hub-and-spoke with the data centers. However, the physical campus locations may require a more typical full-mesh topology. As shown in Figure 14-13, site IDs for SD-WAN are created based on a system that uses the location and agency identifiers to determine topology.

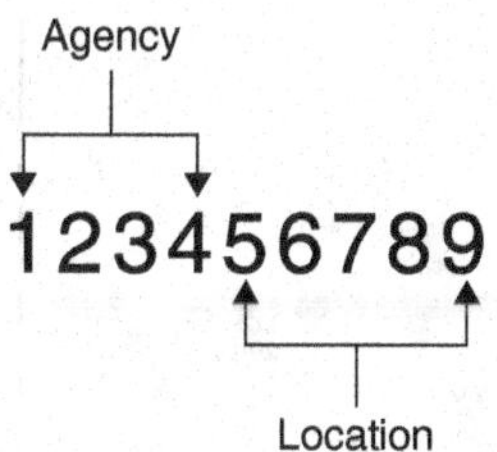

Figure 14-13 *Site IDs*

Because the control policy applied to a site depends on the site's location and role, and the service VPNs at that particular location type are standardized, only a very limited per VPN control policy may be required. Specifically, for the service VPN providing guest support, it is strictly hub-and-spoke with the data centers only at all locations. However, the service VPNs used for the corporate services at all of the facilities may be full-mesh (campuses) or hub-and-spoke topology with an optional dynamic tunnel component (buses, ships, and so on). Using dynamic tunnels between all remote sites as dictated by the traffic flows may simplify the application and management of the policy overall. The policy in Example 14-1 uses a simplified numbering system to illustrate how the dynamic policy and VPN topologies could be configured and deployed. The actions in sequences 30 and 40 are used to set the backup TLOCs for the other spoke OMP routes to the hub TLOCs. This example shows only the centralized policy required for the dynamic tunnels; other configurations are required to utilize the feature, such as enabling traffic engineering on the hubs themselves.

Example 14-1 *Site ID Dynamic Tunnel Control Policy*

```
! Dynamic Tunnel Control Policy
policy
 lists
  site-list SL-DCs
   site-id 1000-1099
  !
  site-list SL-BUSES
   site-id 2000-2199
  !
  tloc-list TL-HUBS
   tloc 10.0.0.1 color public-internet encap ipsec
   tloc 10.0.0.1 color biz-internet encap ipsec
 !
 control-policy CP-TO-BUSES
  sequence 10
   match route
    site-list SL-DCs
   !
   action accept
   !
  !
  sequence 20
   match tloc
    site-list SL-DCs
   !
   action accept
   !
  !
  sequence 30
   match route
    site-list SL-BUSES
   !
   action accept
    set
     tloc-action backup
     tloc-list TL-HUBS
   !
  !
  sequence 40
   match tloc
    site-list SL-BUSES
   !
```

```
    action accept
   !
   default-action reject
  !
 !
apply-policy
 site-list SL-BUSES
  control-policy CP-TO-BUSES out
 !
```

The CP-TO-BUSES control policy handles the hub-and-spoke requirement with dynamic tunnels between buses for the buses themselves. Similar control policies may be written for the remaining nonhub locations in the environment. The example provided would allow for dynamic tunnels for any service VPNs that exist at both sites. For the corporate VPN, this is the desired behavior; however, other service VPNs may not desire the direct site connectivity. Therefore, Example 14-2 extends the original policy with per VPN logic. Notice that only sequence 30 is changed; it now utilizes a VPN list and a TLOC list.

Example 14-2 *Dynamic Tunnel Control Policy with Per VPN Enhancement*

```
! Per-Country Control Policy
policy
 lists
  vpn-list VL-CORPORATE
   vpn 3100
  !
  site-list SL-DCs
   site-id 1000-1099
  !
  site-list SL-BUSES
   site-id 2000-2199
  !
  tloc-list TL-HUBS
   tloc 10.0.0.1 color public-internet encap ipsec
   tloc 10.0.0.1 color biz-internet encap ipsec
 !
 control-policy CP-TO-BUSES
  sequence 10
   match route
    site-list SL-DCs
   !
   action accept
   !
  !
```

```
  sequence 20
   match tloc
    site-list SL-DCs
   !
   action accept
   !
  !
  sequence 30
   match route
    site-list SL-BUSES
    vpn-list VL-CORPORATE
   !
   action accept
    set
     tloc-action backup
     tloc-list TL-HUBS
   !
  !
  sequence 40
   match tloc
    site-list SL-BUSES
   !
   action accept
  !
  default-action reject
 !
!
```

Without any requirements on symmetric routing, route preference configurations are minimized. However, it would be expected that the traffic destined to DC1 should be preferred to ingress at DC1 over DC2. Here, the communities in BGP may be used to influence the OMP route preference in SD-WAN. Alternatively, advertising DC-specific prefixes from its data center while advertising general summary routes from all data centers is another method to easily manage this preferred routing scenario.

Summary

This use case is difficult due to all the domains that must be managed and stitched together. However, taking the requirements of the whole system and addressing them based on the features and functionality in a given architecture help to limit the complexity. Standardization across the entire enterprise allows for simpler designs and deployment.

Index

A

D

E

G

H

I

J - K - L

M

N

O

P

Q

R

S

T

U

V

W

X - Y

Z